FOUNDATION PRESS

RACE LAW STORIES

Edited By

RACHEL F. MORAN
Robert D. & Leslie-Kay Raven Professor of Law
University of California, Berkeley School of Law

DEVON WAYNE CARBADO
Professor of Law
UCLA School of Law

FOUNDATION PRESS
75TH ANNIVERSARY

THOMSON

WEST

This publication was created to provide you with accurate and authoritative information concerning the subject matter covered; however, this publication was not necessarily prepared by persons licensed to practice law in a particular jurisdiction. The publisher is not engaged in rendering legal or other professional advice and this publication is not a substitute for the advice of an attorney. If you require legal or other expert advice, you should seek the services of a competent attorney or other professional.

Nothing contained herein is intended or written to be used for the purposes of 1) avoiding penalties imposed under the federal Internal Revenue Code, or 2) promoting, marketing or recommending to another party any transaction or matter addressed herein.

© 2008 By THOMSON REUTERS/FOUNDATION PRESS
　　　　395 Hudson Street
　　　　New York, NY 10014
　　　　Phone Toll Free 1–877–888–1330
　　　　Fax (212) 367–6799
　　　　foundation–press.com
Printed in the United States of America

ISBN 978–1–59941–001–2

 TEXT IS PRINTED ON 10% POST CONSUMER RECYCLED PAPER

For Asmara Tringali-Carbado
DWC

For my Parents
RFM

*

ACKNOWLEDGMENTS

I would like to thank the UCLA School of Law, the UCLA Academic Senate and the Fletcher Foundation for providing grants that supported the production of this volume. I also thank the Jamestown Project and Dean Michael Schill for encouraging me to pursue it. I would like to acknowledge the UCLA School of Law's Critical Race Studies Program, which provided an intellectual context in which I could productively work on *Race Law Stories*. I am deeply appreciative of the services of the UCLA Hugh & Hazel Darling Library at UCLA School of Law, and in particular the work of Linda Karr-O'Connor and Jenny Lentz, both of whom provided extraordinary research support. In terms of additional research support, I want to also acknowledge the talented and creative work of several research assistants without whose help we could not have completed *Race Law Stories*: Emily Wood, Jennifer Katz, Jacob Clark, and Andre Wellington. I would also like to thank several colleagues, who provided invaluable feedback on this project and in so doing helped to make it better: Kimberlé Crenshaw, Carole Goldberg, Laura Gómez, Cheryl Harris, Jerry López, Russell Robinson, Jerry Saul Sarabia, and Leti Volpp. I am especially thankful to each of the contributors for participating in this project and to Fordham Law School for hosting a conference organized around *Race Law Stories*; the conference provided the contributors with a wonderful opportunity to present and obtain feedback on early iterations of their chapters. I am incredibly grateful to Rachel Moran, my co-editor, for her vision and for her commitment to *Race Law Stories*. Without her extraordinary insight, hard work, depth of knowledge, and analytical sophistication, *Race Law Stories* would not have been possible. I am grateful as well to scholars who write in the area of race and the law, and in particular Critical Race Theorists, whose work created a scholarly field out of which *Race Law Stories* grows. Finally, I thank Paul Caron for conceiving of the Law Stories series and Foundation Press for including a book on race within it. Foundation Press's decision in this respect helps to create the very thing *Race Law Stories* was charged to reflect: a race law canon. John Bloomquist, Jim Coates, and Junior Torres played a crucial role in helping us to realize our vision, a vision that is grounded in a central idea within Critical Race Theory that narratives can broaden and deepen our understanding of law and legal institutions.

DWC

I would like to thank the University of California, Berkeley School of Law and the Berkeley campus for summer funding and sabbatical support that enabled me to do this research. I am also grateful to Fordham Law School, which invited me to become the Bacon-Kilkenny Distinguished Visiting Professor of Law during Fall 2005. This visit afforded me the opportunity to do in-depth work on my chapter and to present a version of it during a faculty workshop. In addition, Fordham sponsored a workshop that permitted all of the authors to think collectively about the project as well as a public conference that showcased the stories in the book. Dean William Treanor, Helen Herman, and Darin Neely played key roles in making the workshop and conference a reality. I also benefited from the chance to present earlier versions of my chapter at Emory University School of Law, Rutgers Law School, UCLA School of Law, and the University of Minnesota Law School. I received very able assistance from the Berkeley Law Library, particularly Alice Youmans, as well as from Sonia D. Cook and Jenny Lam, who worked with me in editing some of the chapters. I am deeply appreciative of the many pioneering attorneys and legal scholars who made it possible to imagine *Race Law Stories*. Of course, my co-editor Devon W. Carbado has made tremendous contributions in this regard—both through his earlier writings and through his remarkable creativity and insight in shaping and refining this volume. In addition, all of the contributors were generous with their time, their expertise, and their perspective. Their stories make a powerful statement about the promise of a race law canon. Foundation Press's commitment to a project on race law also is noteworthy. John Bloomquist, Jim Coates, and Junior Torres encouraged us to pursue an ambitious intellectual agenda, and I am honored by the confidence that they have shown in us. Finally, I want to acknowledge the tremendous insight of Paul Caron, who created this series because he believes that stories matter. I hope this volume, along with the others, proves him right.

RFM

RACE LAW STORIES

FOREWORD

The Unfinished Business of Race

Michael Omi* and Howard Winant**

Justice is not blind, and with respect to race, it most certainly is not colorblind. The law "makes race." It does so by narration: defining and inscribing the meaning of racial categories, assigning specific legal rights and privileges, establishing the parameters of individual and collective social identities, and directing the distribution of material resources. The legal construction of race and corresponding racialization of individuals and groups pose fundamental questions regarding one's position in the prevailing social order: Who is free? Who is a citizen? Who is white? They also raise questions regarding the policies and practices that police racial regimes: Who can immigrate? Who can marry whom? Who can vote? Who is in a protected class?

In the volume you have before you, editors Devon W. Carbado and Rachel F. Moran have assembled a stellar group of contributors to explore these questions. Their approach constitutes the beginnings of what they call a "race law canon." They use and extend the methods and theoretical insights of Critical Race Theory ("CRT"), an insurgent approach to racial studies that while deeply concerned with the law, transcends "mere" legal studies to examine the broader racial foundations and racial structures of U.S. society.[1] CRT exhumes the atrocities of our historical past and confronts their continuing curse; it articulates the ways in which race, gender, and class inequality converge and interpenetrate; and it focuses our attention on the problems of structural discrimination, unequal treatment, and the incomplete nature of democracy in our social order.

The cases presented here, famous, not-so-famous, and infamous, compellingly capture the "back story" behind race law. They highlight various forms of claims-making among litigants, offer insightful doctri-

---

* Professor of Sociology, University of California, Santa Barbara.
** Associate Professor of Ethnic Studies, University of California, Berkeley.

1. CRT has also been applied to racial theory and race law beyond the U.S., for example in Brazil and Europe. *See, e.g.*, Celina Romany, *Critical Race Theory in Global Context, in* Crossroads, Directions, and a New Critical Race Theory (Francisco Valdes, Jerome McCristal Culp, and Angela P. Harris, eds. 2002); Tanya Katerí Hernandez, *To Be Brown in Brazil: Education and Segregation Latin American Style*, 29 NYU Rev. L. & Soc. Change 683 (2004-2005).

nal analysis of legal opinions, and assess the broader impact of the issues of racial injustice that continue to reverberate in their wake. *Race Law Stories* helps us to discern the significance of these cases: the stories that constitute the volume illustrate how race is understood, how racism is challenged, and how race is reinscribed in ways that perpetuate forms of domination and oppression. While the cases presented here are stories of repression, injustice, and the denial of civil and human rights, they are also stories of self-assertion and self-activity, of insurgency and insistence in the quest for equality, justice, and freedom.

Taken as a whole, the stories narrate how race is constantly being reinterpreted: as natural fact, social fact, or mere illusion; as scientific truth or common sense; as pressing and immediate conflict or mere relic of a benighted past. Our own theory of racial formation was in part inspired by a similar story, a court case (*Jane Doe v. the State of Louisiana*[2]) that revealed the state's capacity to assign social identities — and hence social status and "life-chances" — by enforcing the irrational and seemingly arbitrary rules of racial classification.[3] In 1977, a forty-three-year old woman, Susie Guillory Phipps, who self-identified as white, was designated as black in her birth certificate in accordance with a 1970 Louisiana state law that deemed anyone with more than 1/32nd "Negro blood" to be black. She unsuccessfully sued the Louisiana Bureau of Vital Records to change her racial classification to "white." Her story illustrated the profound relationship of racial meanings to racial social structures (what we termed *racial projects*) and the ways race is continually being contested and re-formed through a process of racialization. "Representing" race, narrating it, telling stories about it (as Susie Guillory Phipps did in her lawsuit), is at the core of the racial formation process.

The legal cases presented in *Race Law Stories* are narratives of racialization, the construction of racial identity. Racialization shapes the very terms of individual and group existence and legal standing. Race law stories are not only bivariate: black/white; they are multivariate. In contrast to the prevailing black/white model of race in the United States, the stories and cases presented in this volume involve a number of distinct racialized groups who in specific historical moments find themselves contesting their subordinate social definition and location in the U.S. racial hierarchy. Are Native Americans a "political" as opposed to a "racial" group? Can Japanese be considered white? In what ways are Mexican Americans white and how does this affect the group's legal standing?

---

2. Doe v. State of Louisiana, 479 So. 2d 369 (La. Ct. App. 1985).

3. *See generally* Michael Omi and Howard Winant, *Racial Formation in the United States: From the 1960s to the 1990s* (2d. 1994).
......

One of the key themes that emerges from *Race Law Stories* is the ideology of colorblindness and its fundamentally contradictory character. On the one hand, colorblindness can be called upon as a rationale for forcibly dismantling the historical legacy of segregation and discrimination. On the other hand, it can be evoked to question the legitimacy of policies and practices, both state-based and private, designed to mitigate racial inequality. In addition, as several of the stories suggest, colorblindness and inequality often coexist, sometimes quite comfortably, sometimes not. Colorblindness and racism can be mutually sustaining.

The *Brown v. Board of Education* decision, the most significant race case of the twentieth century, is illustrative of these contradictions. *Brown's* legacy remains deeply contested and unresolved. What has been particularly difficult for the popular imagination to grasp is the idea, as articulated most notably after *Brown* by Justices Thurgood Marshall and Harry Blackmun, that we need to "notice race" in order to challenge the patterns of persistent racial inequality and to advance a more democratic and emancipatory social and political agenda. A common belief of contemporary colorblind racial ideology is that with the right tools, the right policies, the right "stories," we can "get beyond" race. A key lesson to be drawn from the race law canon being founded here is that such an optimistic perspective is not only a utopian but a potentially dangerous goal. "Getting beyond" race is a chimera, an idea that contains within it the specters of forced assimilation and the achievement of racial uniformity, if necessary by violent and repressive means.[4]

Our society was founded on racial difference and conflict. No master narrative, no magic formula, can undo this historical fact and the immense racialized social structure it has generated and sustained. Despite Justice Harlan's ambiguous and contradictory claims to the contrary, the U.S. Constitution itself remains a racial document.

Race matters are still unsettled and new challenges continually appear. The increased visibility and state recognition of multiracial identities create a new set of issues with respect to civil rights enforcement, among other things. In 1997, a proposal to add a separate multiracial category to the Census was rejected by the Office of Management and Budget's ("OMB") Interagency Committee for the Review of Racial and Ethnic Standards. Instead, the thirty-agency task force recommended that OMB Statistical Directive 15 be amended to permit individuals to "mark one or more" racial categories when identifying themselves on the Census or other government forms. This recommendation was adopted by the OMB, but the ability of individuals to check more than one racial

---

4. For more on this point, see Eric D. Weitz, *A Century of Genocide: Utopias of Race and Nation* (2003); Zygmunt Bauman, *Modernity and the Holocaust* (1991).

"box" has led to significant debate about data collection and presenta-
tion: sixty-three racial combinations are now possible (126 possibilities
when combined with the "ethnic" category of "Latino/Hispanic").[5] With
respect to civil rights monitoring and enforcement, an individual who is
of one "minority" race and white is now classified as belonging to the minority race. If one identifies with two or more minority races, the race
that a complainant alleges was the basis for discrimination becomes the
focus of scrutiny. All this opens up a Pandora's box regarding self-iden-
tity and social location. Individual and group identities, access to political rights such as citizenship, and "life-chances" are thrown into doubt
once more by state management of racial meanings and categories. The
overall legal consequences of assuming or assigning multiracial identities thus require further, indeed permanent, scrutiny and review.

Many of the cases in *Race Law Stories* highlight both the conver-
gences and contradictions between "race science" and commonsense or
popular understandings of race. In the current period, it has been widely assumed that biological notions of race and racial difference have
been thoroughly discredited and replaced with an understanding of race
as a social construction. But as Angela Onwuachi-Willig notes in the
conclusion of her chapter, "biological race is making a comeback." In the
field of pharmacogenomics, "ethnic designer drugs" are being researched
and developed that assume biological, genetic differences between the
races. NitroMed's drug BiDil, specifically marketed to blacks who suffer
from congestive heart failure, is a controversial example of using an individual's race as a handy proxy for ascertaining that individual's susceptibility to disease and responsiveness to drug treatment.[6]

One can tell a similar story with respect to DNA evidence in the
field of forensics, which has led to the exoneration of unjustly convicted
inmates. But, as Onwuachi-Willig notes, DNA evidence also has been
utilized as a high-tech tool for racial profiling by law enforcement agencies. The determination of a suspect's race, based on shaky predictors,
raises troubling questions regarding the deployment of genetic information in criminal investigations. While DNA ancestry tests have become
a popular way for individuals to trace their "roots," they also have been
employed to determine, among other things, membership in American
Indian tribes. Black Seminole Freemen sought DNA testing in order to
regain tribal benefits denied them when the Seminole Nation of Oklahoma changed its constitution in 2000 to exclude black members who

---

5. The issues of multiracial classification and their policy consequences are addressed in Joel Perlmann
and Mary C. Waters (eds.), *The New Race Question: How the Census Counts Multiracial Individuals*
(2002).

6. On the development of BiDil see Jonathan Kahn, *How a Drug Becomes "Ethnic": Law, Commerce,
and the Production of Racial Categories in Medicine,* 4 Yale J. Health Pol., L. & Ethics 1 (2004).

did not meet the tribe's blood-quantum requirements.[7] These conflicts and contradictions, and a host of others, suggest that the current reinscription of race as a biological category will provoke ongoing legal claims regarding the relationship of social identity, science, and structural inequality.

The impressive historical sweep and depth of analysis in *Race Law Stories* inspires us all to consider the dynamics of race and racism in the "post-civil rights" era. What has changed in the racial system of the United States since the rise and fall of the civil rights movement? What, if anything, remains of the "old" white supremacist racial regime? What was accomplished by all the blood, sweat, and tears expended in the cause of civil rights, perhaps the most significant social movement in the nation's history?

Today the meaning and effectivity of the race concept is in crisis. "[C]risis," Gramsci wrote, "consists precisely in the fact that the old is dying and the new cannot be born: in this interregnum, morbid phenomena of the most varied kind come to pass."[8] In this crisis, the "post-civil rights" ideology of colorblindness collides head-on with the intrinsic and ineluctable presence of racial rule and racial domination. We can see this collision in operation when we examine any of today's pressing racial issues, for example, racial profiling.[9] Indeed, many of the race law stories examined in this volume, though based in the historical past, remain sources of racial crisis in the twenty-first century. Discrimination in education, housing, or employment; the equal application of citizenship policy and immigration law; the recognition of voting rights; and indeed human rights are as endangered today as they were in an earlier time.

Perhaps what is most revealing in the stories presented in this volume is the courts' insistence on their prerogative to interpret the meaning of race and to determine what aspects of a litigant's identity, behavior, or appearance are race- (or gender-) based.[10] Courts remain free to invoke or ignore both scientific claims and assertions of common sense. The arbitrary character of the race law canon is in the end the greatest

---

7. Ziba Kashef, *Race for a Cure*, ColorLines 40 (September/October 2007).

8. Antonio Gramsci, *Selections from the Prison Notebooks* 276 (Hoare and Nowell-Smith eds. 1971).

9. In *(E)racing the Fourth Amendment*, 100 Mich. L. Rev. 946 (2002), Devon Carbado argues that racial profiling reveals the ways that racial rule continues to remain both coercive and despotic in a period often seen as "post-civil rights," i.e., *after* the enactment of reforms that supposedly assured racially-defined minorities of equal treatment by state agencies.

10. As Paulette Caldwell notes in this volume, court decisions that refuse to consider "the interactive and mutually-reinforcing impact of race and gender as well as their independent effects" reveal a simultaneous avowal and disavowal of the power to decide both what is "racial" and what is "gendered." The judicial system operates here with the same colorblind disengenousness that the 1896 Supreme Court showed in *Plessy*.

evidence for the centrality of narrative in civil rights law and indeed human rights law.

Race remains "unfinished business" and will continue to be so in an era when the contradiction between formal equality and structural inequality is normalized; and when two incompatible and competing "stories" — one colorblind, the other color-conscious — shape the unstable equilibrium that characterizes racial formation in the United States today. Because the meaning of race is still unsettled, its competing "stories" take shape in the form of claims-making by litigants in pursuit of racial equality and social justice. Uncertainty and contrariety are continually reproduced in the decisions that shape the race law canon: sometimes reaffirming old notions, sometimes seeking to establish new understandings of both race and rights. This unfinished business is the broader story that *Race Law Stories* presents and opens up for critical scrutiny.

FOUNDATION PRESS

RACE LAW STORIES

*

Introduction

Devon W. Carbado and Rachel F. Moran

The Story of Law and American Racial Consciousness—Building a Canon One Case at a Time

In Defense of a Race Law Canon

Do we need a race law canon? The answer is not obviously "yes." Some would say that the cases *Race Law Stories* engages do not constitute a distinct area of law because those cases are subsumed within the broader fields of civil rights and constitutional law. Inasmuch as Foundation Press has already published both a *Constitutional Law Stories* and a *Civil Rights Stories*, there is no need for *Race Law Stories*.[1] Others would agree that race law is an independent field of study, but they would disagree about how to understand the relationship between race and law.

Because of these disagreements, there is no race law canon as such. Few law schools offer courses that focus specifically on race except as occasional seminars. In fact, of the more than 190 accredited law schools in the United States, as of the publication of this volume, only UCLA School of Law offers a Critical Race Studies Program, which includes a formally organized race law curriculum.[2] These curricular realities mean that *Race Law Stories* can not simply be a collection of the stories behind leading cases on race law; this anthology must offer a vision of what a race law canon might look like. Although it is our hope that the vision *Race Law Stories* presents will push the discussion about race and law school curricula further along, we do not present *Race Law Stories* as a

---

[1] *Constitutional Law Stories* (Michael C. Dorf, ed. 2004); *Civil Rights Stories* (Risa Goluboff & Myriam E. Gilles, eds. 2007).

[2] American Bar Association, *Section of Legal Education & Admissions to the Bar, at* http://www.abanet.org/legaled/approvedlawschools/approved.html (last visited Jan. 14, 2008); Overview of the Critical Race Studies Program, UCLA Law, *at* http://www.law.ucla.edu/home/index.asp?page=2599 (last visited Jan. 14, 2008).

definitive, once-and-for-all representation of a race law canon. We view this anthology as a starting point.

Happily, we are not beginning with a blank slate. We have inherited a number of Critical Race Theory readers and a handful of casebooks on race and the law and civil rights.[3] But for these prior works, *Race Law Stories* would not have been possible. At the same time, when reviewing these readers and casebooks, we discovered that there is no consensus (with a few exceptions like *Brown v. Board of Education* and similarly iconic decisions) about which cases count as the canon of race law. In this sense, the absence of a stable race law canon has been reflected not only in the marginalization of race in law school curricula, but also in the very texts designed, at least in part, to instantiate a canon on race and the law.

The failure to consolidate a race law canon undoubtedly reflects a general ambivalence about the significance of race. In our national rhetoric, racial injustice often is treated as an aberration or an accident in an otherwise democratic system. Race is a scar on the body politic, a superficial wound that has healed or soon will. Race is something that happened, not something that is happening; it resides in the past and should not exist in the future. To the extent that race is recognized as a contemporary social dynamic—as something that is happening now—it is equated with skin color, a biological irrelevancy that has no bearing on our innermost selves, economic and political realities, educational opportunities, and overall social experience. These ideological commitments are not merely reflected in the law; they are constituted by law.

Consider, for example, how Justice Sandra Day O'Connor thinks about race in the context of voting rights. In determining the constitutionality of a redistricting plan in *Shaw v. Reno*,[4] a case Daniel P. Tokaji discusses in his contribution to this volume, O'Connor notes that part of what is worrisome about reapportionment plans is that they put in "one district individuals who belong to the same race, but who are otherwise widely separated by geographic and political boundaries, and who may

---

[3] *See. e.g.*, Charles F. Abernathy, *Civil Rights and Constitutional Litigation: Cases and Materials* (2006); Roy L. Brooks, et al., *Civil Rights Litigation: Cases and Perspectives* (2005); Dorothy A. Brown, *Critical Race Theory: Cases, Materials, Problems* (2d ed. 2007); Kimberlé Crenshaw, et al., *Critical Race Theory: The Key Writings That Formed the Movement* (paperback ed. 1996); Richard Delgado & Jean Stefancic, *Critical Race Theory: An Introduction* (2001); F. Michael Higginbotham, *Race Law: Cases, Commentary, and Questions* (2005); John C. Jeffries, Jr., et al., *Civil Rights Actions: Enforcing the Constitution* (2007); George Martinez, et al., *A Reader on Race, Civil Rights, and American Law: A Multiracial Approach* (2001); Juan Perea et al., *Race and Races* (2d ed. 2007); Adrienne Katherine Wing, *Critical Race Feminism: A Reader* (paperback ed. 2003).

[4] 509 U.S. 630 (1993).

have little in common with one another but the color of their skin."[5] For O'Connor, because race is reducible to skin color, race consciousness is not only suspect, it is potentially if not presumptively dangerous. It reproduces the racism of the past and undermines our commitment to colorblindness. This conception of race impedes our ability to imagine a race law canon. After all, what place is there for such a field if race is nothing more than skin color; if contemporary racism does not exist; if our Constitution is colorblind? Isn't civil rights law necessary only because past racial injustices must be rectified? And why expend efforts on building a race law canon when those injuries are largely behind us and the promise of a colorblind society lies ahead? Doesn't the focus on establishing a race law canon entrench and rigidify the very thing we aim to destabilize and eliminate: race?

Race Law Stories rejects these ideological assumptions. It demonstrates that American race law cases have never been colorblind. Indeed, if there is a single principle that unites race law cases across disparate doctrines and historical periods, it is that they are all race-conscious—which is to say, they all take race into account. This is not to suggest that they do so in precisely the same way and to precisely the same end. They do not. As Ian Haney López and Michael A. Olivas's contribution to *Race Law Stories* attests, the racial consciousness of *Brown v. Board of Education* is very different from that in *Hernandez v. Texas*, notwithstanding that both cases adjudicate the meaning of the Equal Protection Clause and that the Supreme Court decided them within two weeks of each other. Among other differences, *Brown* focuses on African Americans, while *Hernandez* addresses discrimination against Mexican Americans. Moreover, while *Brown's* antidiscrimination intervention is predicated upon the recognition of African Americans as a distinct non-white racial group, *Hernandez* does not stake out that position with respect to Mexican Americans. These significant differences should not obscure that both *Brown* and *Hernandez* are unequivocally race-conscious. Both draw upon and articulate ideas about racial categorization, racial meaning, and racial inequality. Both rely on and help to entrench the cognizability of race as an identity and a social practice. And both are unintelligible without reference to race.

These general observations about and features of race consciousness obtain across the cases in *Race Law Stories*. In this respect, one can understand the chapters that constitute this volume as a collective narrative about law and American racial consciousness, a collective narrative that *Race Law Stories* unfolds one case at a time. As will become clear, this collective narrative is decidedly multiracial, plays itself out across a number of doctrinal contexts, and reflects moments of both

---

[5] *Id.* at 647.

inequality and equality. Moreover, it is a narrative that is inextricably linked to the establishment of the United States as an independent nation-state and to the expression of American democracy in political and everyday life. As Robin Lenhardt's chapter reveals, sometimes this story is about love, as it was with Andrea Pérez (a Mexican–American woman) and Sylvester Davis, Jr. (an African–American man); in 1947, this interracial couple attempted to marry across the color line. Sometimes the story is quite literally about hair, as when Renee Rodgers sued American Airlines for promulgating a grooming policy that prohibited its public-contact employees from wearing fully braided hairstyles. As Paulette Caldwell notes in her chapter on the case, in ruling that the policy did not discriminate against black women, the court invoked the hairstyle that Bo Derek sported in the movie *10*. The court reasoned that because the no-braids policy would have affected Bo Derek (a white woman), it was not discriminatory against Renee Rodgers (a black woman).

Paradoxically, sometimes the story is that a race law case purports not to be about race at all, as in *Morton v. Mancari*, explored in Carole Goldberg's chapter. That decision sought to suppress race consciousness by describing Native American identity as political, not racial. Ironically, this approach was used to uphold an affirmative action program in the Bureau of Indian Affairs. And sometimes the racial story is about the very notion of American belonging, as illustrated by Erika Lee's chapter on birthright citizenship, a principle that the Supreme Court affirmed in *United States v. Wong Kim Ark*, and by Ronald Sullivan's chapter on *Prigg v. Pennsylvania*, a case in which the Court upheld the Fugitive Slave Act of 1793, thereby allowing the removal of free blacks from non-slaveholding states to slaveholding states.

As already should be apparent, the story of law and American racial consciousness is inscribed not only in the language in which the United States Supreme Court and lower courts speak—that is to say, case law. It is inscribed as well in the lives of real people in real historical moments pushing back against real racial injustices. This is the complexity we attempt to capture in *Race Law Stories*: an account of law and American racial consciousness that reflects the specific ways in which people from different racial groups have struggled to become—formally and substantively—a part of "We, the People." Our methodology for doing so includes storytelling, not the fictional variety but the sort of richly textured, highly contextual accounts that can be used to interrogate formal legal principles.[6]

---

[6] Critical Race Theory ("CRT") has been roundly criticized for employing storytelling as a method of legal analysis. *See* Daniel A. Farber & Suzanna Sherry, *Beyond All Reason: The Radical Assault on Truth in American Law* (1997); Daniel A. Farber & Suzanna Sherry, *Telling Stories out of School: An Essay on Legal Narratives*, 45 Stan. L. Rev. 807

Telling Stories Out of Law: The Structure and Organization of Race Law Stories

Central to our conception of *Race Law Stories* is an understanding of legal cases as narratives. Reggie Oh and Thomas Ross's chapter on *City of Richmond v. J.A. Croson* explicitly develops this theme. The thinking, in part, is this: Embedded within every legal case is a story—about winners and losers, about justice and injustice, and about heroes and villains. How this story is told is a function of who is doing the telling. One narrator's triumphal account is another's story of devastating defeat. The villain in one narrative is the hero in another. The line between justice and injustice unavoidably turns on perspective. All of this is to say, legal cases are never "just there." Like other narratives, they are always already the product of representational choices.[7]

Certainly, this is true of the narratives that constitute *Race Law Stories*. Some of the stories focus on the litigants; others on political figures; still others on lawyers; and others still on judges. Some of the narratives are celebratory; others are condemnatory. Some highlight the intricacies of race and gender; others reveal the intersection of race and immigration. Some focus on specific legal doctrines; others foreground broader structural dynamics, such as conquest and colonialism. Given these complexities, part of our challenge was to organize the chapters in an intelligible way. To meet this challenge, we divided the book into the following four sections: "Birth of a Nation: Formal Citizenship and Sovereignty"; "Separate and Unequal: Classification and Caste"; "Our Constitution is Colorblind: The Doctrine of Race Neutrality"; and "With All Deliberate Speed: Race–Conscious Remedies."

While each part of *Race Law Stories* has a certain thematic coherence, the authors within each section speak from different doctrinal, historical, and racial positions. We have studiously avoided compartmentalizing *Race Law Stories* into sections that focus on specific racial groups.[8] Instead, we adopt a multiracial and racially integrative approach

---

(1993). Many CRT scholars continue to defend the storytelling methodology. *See* Richard Delgado, *On Telling Stories in School: A Response to Farber & Sherry*, 46 Vand. L. Rev. 665 (1993); Richard Delgado, *Storytelling for Oppositionists and Others: A Plea for Narrative*, 87 Mich. L. Rev. 2411 (1988); Daria Roithmayr, *Guerillas in Our Midst: The Assault on Radicals in American Law*, 96 Mich. L. Rev. 1658, 1670–73 (1998). While we do not believe that storytelling is a necessary or the most crucial part of CRT, this approach has played an important role in establishing the genre.

[7] Reginald Oh, *Re-mapping Equal Protection Jurisprudence: A Legal Geography of Race and Affirmative Action*, 53 Am. U. L. Rev. 1305, 1314 (2004) (citing Hayden White, *The Content of the Form: Narrative Discourse and Historical Representation* 4–5 (1987)).

[8] *See* Devon W. Carbado, Race, Law and Citizenship: Black Civil Rights Responses to Japanese American Internment (manuscript on file with author) (exploring the problem of "racial compartmentalism").

throughout. All too often, race law scholars fail to realize that Jim Crow was not just an issue for blacks and whites. It directly affected and targeted other racial groups as well. A similar point can be made about immigration—specifically, that there is a tendency to think of immigration as a Latino/a or an Asian–American issue. In fact, immigration law and policy reach across racial groups.[9] And so does each section of *Race Law Stories*.

Birth of a Nation: Formal Citizenship and Sovereignty

Race has played an integral part in defining America's national identity. After the heady rhetoric of the Declaration of Independence sparked a successful revolution, the fledgling United States of America embarked on the hard work of nation-building. The drafters of the Constitution took a sober second look at the rhetoric of radical egalitarianism in the Declaration, and they blinked. The adoption of the Constitution in 1787 and its ratification one year later depended on a compromise, one that integrated slavery into the very fabric of American democracy. Nor was this the end of the role race would play in forging our country's identity. In short order, in 1790, Congress further entrenched slavery and adopted an immigration law that restricted naturalization to whites. In 1793, Congress passed the Fugitive Slave Act, which allowed slaveholders to turn to federal courts for assistance in recapturing runaways who had fled to free states. Eventually, Congress moved to adopt whites-only voting rules in every territory except Illinois.[10] These actions demonstrated that race was far from a superficial wound on the body politic; in fact, race played a constitutive role in defining that body politic.

For many, the United States Supreme Court's 1857 decision in *Dred Scott v. Sandford*[11] is the paradigmatic anti-canonical case that illustrates the courts at their worst in dealing with questions of race, citizenship, and sovereignty.[12] There, the Court nullified the Missouri Compromise of 1820, a federal law that struck a fragile balance between

---

[9] *See* Kevin R. Johnson, *Immigration, Civil Rights, and Coalitions for Social Justice*, 1 Hastings Race & Poverty L.J. 181 (2003); Devon W. Carbado, *Racial Naturalization*, 57 Am. Q. 633 (2005); Lolita Buckner Innis, *Tricky Magic: Blacks as Immigrants and the Paradox of Foreignness*, 49 DePaul L. Rev. 301 (1999).

[10] Philip A. Klinkner with Rogers Smith, *The Unsteady March: The Rise and Decline of Racial Equality in America* 28–29 (paperback ed. 1999).

[11] 60 U.S. (19 How.) 393 (1857).

[12] Christopher L. Eisgruber, *The Story of* Dred Scott: *Originalism's Forgotten Past, in Constitutional Law Stories, supra* note 1, at 151–52 (Michael C. Dorf ed. 2004). For another account of the *Dred Scott* case, see Xi Wang, *The* Dred Scott *Case* (1857), *in Race on Trial: Law and Justice in American History* 26 (Annette Gordon–Reed ed., 2002). *See generally* Mark Graber, Dred Scott *and the Problem of Constitutional Evil* (2006).

slave and free states. The Compromise permitted slavery to persist but prohibited its expansion to territories newly acquired through the Louisiana Purchase. The Court, in a splintered decision that spawned nine separate opinions, found that the Compromise violated a constitutional right to own slaves.[13]

In the process, the Court rejected Dred Scott's claim that though once a slave, he had become free by residing in territories where slavery was prohibited. The Justices found that Dred Scott, as "a Negro, whose ancestors were imported into this country, and sold as slaves ... could not become a member of the political community formed and brought into existence by the Constitution of the United States."[14] As a result, he was not entitled to the rights, privileges, and immunities that it guaranteed. As a black man, whether slave or free, Dred Scott existed beyond the boundaries of formal federal citizenship.

The Court's opinion made clear that the Constitution aspired to build a white nation. In reaching this conclusion, the Court hoped to end the relentless political struggle between pro- and anti-slavery factions as the nation expanded westward. Yet, instead of protecting the nation-building project by according constitutional protection to slaveholder rights, the *Dred Scott* decision pushed the country toward a profound political rupture, one that would ultimately lead to a bloody Civil War.[15]

The drama of *Dred Scott* has rightly earned a place in the anti-canon of race law, but the decision should not blind us to the manifold ways in which race has influenced the nation-building project. Indeed, almost ten years before Chief Justice Roger Taney decided *Dred Scott*, America ended its war with Mexico. Mexico had long been on America's expansionist agenda. As early as 1787, "Benjamin Franklin had identified Mexico ... as [a] target[] for further expansion."[16] It was not until the 1840s, however, that America's expansionist agenda, or Manifest Destiny, took hold. As Laura Gomez notes, "[f]or many, Manifest Destiny conjures up a moment of national triumph before the dark years of conflict over slavery that culminated in the Civil War."[17] Gomez rightly argues that this conception of Manifest Destiny obscures that it was "a cluster of ideas that relied on racism to justify a war of aggression against Mexico."[18]

---

[13] Eisgruber, *supra* note 12, at 157.

[14] 60 U.S. (19 How.) at 403 (opinion of Taney, C. J.).

[15] Eisgruber, *supra* note 12, at 174–78; Wang, *supra* note 12, at 42–43.

[16] Perea et al, *supra* note 3, at 258.

[17] Laura E. Gomez, *Manifest Destinies: The Making of the Mexican American Race* 3 (2007).

[18] *Id.*

President James Polk played a significant role in effectuating this war. In 1845, Polk succeeded in annexing Texas.[19] While the 1836 Treaty of Velasco had secured Texas's independence from Mexico, it was not yet part of the United States.[20] That incorporation would have to wait until March 1, 1845, when President-elect Polk succeeded in inspiring Congress to admit Texas to the Union.[21] Polk's post-inaugural efforts to purchase California from Mexico were not so successful.[22] He came to realize that the only other way he could possess this vast region was by war—and, more particularly, a war in which Mexico was the perceived aggressor.[23] Thus, in 1845, America's investment in and commitment to waging a war against Mexico was firmly in place. War itself would come the following year. In March of 1846, President Polk moved American troops into the disputed territory between the Nueces River and the Rio Grande, thus precipitating a conflict with Mexican troops.[24] "Mexico has . . . shed American blood upon American soil," Polk told the Congress on May 11, 1846.[25] This affront, he suggested, demanded a decisive response. He asked Congress for a declaration of war, which he shortly got.[26]

As historian Rodolfo Acuña has observed, "The poorly equipped and led Mexican army had little chance against the expansion-minded Anglos."[27] Within two years the war was over. The Treaty of Guadalupe Hidalgo, which remains under-studied in American law schools despite its crucial role in understanding the Mexican–American experience, made California and other parts of the Southwest part of the United States. At best, the treaty conferred formal citizenship on the Mexicans who remained in the newly acquired American territory after the war. These Mexicans found themselves on the other side of a border they did

---

[19] Polk had not yet been inaugurated on the first of March when Congress passed the Joint Resolution reflecting this commitment. Joint Resolution for Annexing Texas to the United States, H.R.J. Res. 8, 28th Cong. (1845). However, his position on the matter and his political efforts are reflected in his Presidential inaugural address, which he delivered four days later. *See* James K. Polk, Inaugural Address, Mar. 4, 1845.

[20] Treaties of Velasco, Rep. of Tex.-Mexico, May 14, 1836.

[21] *See* Joint Resolution for Annexing Texas to the United States, *supra* note 19.

[22] Gene M. Brack, *Mexican Opinion, American Racism, and the War of 1846*, 1 West. Hist. Q. 161, 161 (1970); The White House, *James K. Polk–Biography*, at http://www.white house.gov/history/presidents/jp11.html.

[23] The White House, *supra* note 22.

[24] James K. Polk, Message on War with Mexico, May 11, 1846.

[25] *Id.*

[26] *Id.*; The White House, *supra* note 22.

[27] Rodolfo Acuña, *Occupied America: A History of Chicanos* 13 (1988).

not cross. While conquest and expansionism had brought them into the United States, white supremacy kept them trapped inside the box of formal citizenship. Deemed racially inferior, they were considered unfit for the exercise of any real rights.

But even the extension of formal citizenship—or what one might think of as a kind of colonial naturalization—was highly contestable. Polk wanted the property (Mexico) without the people (Mexicans). Formal citizenship was the racial price he had to pay for his territorial ambitions. This political compromise meant that Mexicans themselves would have the citizenship rights that Chief Justice Taney could not imagine extending to blacks. At the same time, because Mexicans were not perceived to be of pure "Anglo–Saxon" racial stock but instead viewed as an impure and racially mixed group, they experienced the Jim Crow color line of separate and unequal before it was formally articulated as such in the South. As Laura Gomez observes, Mexican Americans became white by law but non-white by social practice.[28] This liminal status was a direct result of the ideology and practice of Manifest Destiny.

Nor were Mexicans the only non-white group whose "American" identity was forged at the interstices of conquest and expansionism. At the outset, the United States had to grapple with the problem of treaties that accorded Native American tribes semi-sovereign status.[29] The tribes were something of an anomaly in a nation that equated whiteness with fitness for citizenship and self-governance. The heavy hand of the law might require that the treaties be honored, but the heavier hand of the politics of nation-building relegated tribes to a position of inferiority as non-whites. The "peculiar" position that Native Americans found themselves in did not escape Chief Justice Taney in *Dred Scott*.[30] Indeed, he drew upon it to distinguish Native Americans from people of African descent. Taney reasoned that "although they [Native Americans] were uncivilized, they were yet a free and independent people, associated together in nations or tribes, and governed by their own laws."[31] According to Taney, America treated Native Americans as foreign governments, "as much so as if an ocean had separated the red man from the white."[32] This was not so, he maintained, with respect to Africans. In effect,

---

[28] Gomez, *supra* note 17, at 4.

[29] Judith Resnik, *Dependent Sovereigns: Tribes, States and the Federal Courts*, 56 U. Chi. L. Rev. 671 (1989).

[30] *Cf.* Kenneth Stampp, *The Peculiar Institution: Slavery in the Ante–Bellum South* (Vintage Books ed., 1989).

[31] *Dred Scott*, 60 U.S. (19 How.) at 403.

[32] *Id.* at 404.

"Taney extraterritorialize[d] Indians (people who were actually here) and intraterritorialize[d] blacks (people who had in fact been separated from white inhabitants by an ocean)."[33] He did this to suggest that whereas Native Americans were naturalizable, blacks were not. "While it has been found necessary, for their own sake as well as our own, to regard them as in a state of pupilage,"[34] Taney maintained, Native Americans as subjects of foreign governments could, unlike blacks, become American citizens.

The notion of Native Americans as at once sovereign, uncivilized, and "in a state of pupilage" permeates the case law on Native Americans, as Rennard Strickland's story of the *Cherokee Cases*[35] reveals. The Cherokee Nation was primarily concentrated in Georgia, a state that was becoming aggressively hostile to the Cherokee when the federal government did not completely remove all Native Americans from the state under the Georgia Compact of 1802. Georgia, a state in which slavery and hence presumptions of racial inferiority were deeply entrenched, increasingly extended its laws into Cherokee lands. The Cherokee Nation soon realized that the only way its members could regain their rights under treaties with the United States was through the United States Supreme Court. Strickland demonstrates how the status of Native Americans as both sovereign and inferior influenced the Court's resolution of the conflict. As his account shows, the racialization of the Cherokee people left them vulnerable to marginalization and exile. The tribe was eventually forcibly removed from its homeland, decimated, and divided by internal feuding.

Though often treated as an egregious departure from American law and values, *Dred Scott* in fact built on the tragic consequences of earlier decisions that denied blacks due process protections in the name of federal power. As Professor Ronald S. Sullivan Jr. explains in the story of *Prigg v. Pennsylvania*,[36] Justice Joseph Story upheld the Fugitive Slave Act in 1842, despite his personal reservations about slavery. *Prigg* was, in 1842, the first pronouncement on slavery by the Supreme Court. Margaret Morgan, the subject of the case, was a black woman whose parents, although never formally emancipated, lived in freedom on their owner's estate in Maryland, a slave-holding state. Morgan married an emancipated black man from Pennsylvania, with whom she raised six children. The couple initially lived in Maryland but eventually moved to

---

[33] Carbado, *supra* note 9, at 644.

[34] 60 U.S. (19 How.) at 403–404.

[35] Cherokee Nation v. Georgia, 30 U.S. (5 Pet.) 1 (1831); Worcester v. Georgia, 31 U.S. (6 Pet.) 515 (1832).

[36] 41 U.S. (16 Pet.) 539 (1842).

Pennsylvania, where they lived happily until Morgan and her children were seized, enslaved, and forcibly taken back to Maryland by the son-in-law of her parents' deceased owner. Justice Story believed that respect for federal power and the preservation of comity among slave and free states were essential to the nation-building project. As a result, he read the federal Fugitive Slave Act to provide that the federal government had the sole power to regulate the recapture of runaway slaves. The price for this display of unity was borne by blacks, who even when free could not fully protect themselves from being kidnapped and enslaved by a master who claimed them as his property. As Sullivan argues, this price was palatable because of pervasive beliefs in the racial inferiority of blacks, beliefs that Story undoubtedly shared, whatever his views on slavery.

While the notion of black inferiority lived on after the Civil War and the end of slavery, this ideology had to contend with the Reconstruction Amendments, which, among other things, conferred formal citizenship on blacks.[37] In particular, the Fourteenth Amendment expressly repudiated the logic of *Dred Scott* and earlier cases such as *Prigg*. But formal citizenship for blacks did not necessarily mean formal citizenship for other non-whites—even those who were born on American soil. Notwithstanding the Fourteenth Amendment's language that "All persons born or naturalized in the United States, and subject to the jurisdiction thereof, are citizens of the United States,"[38] there was a very real question about whether this language applied to the Chinese, who by the end of the nineteenth century were already perceived to be irreducibly foreign and thus incapable of being folded into the nation-state. As Erika Lee notes in the story of *United States v. Wong Kim Ark*,[39] the presumptively permanent foreign status of Chinese people was inscribed in a federal statute: the 1790 naturalization law that restricted naturalization to whites. Wong Kim Ark did not dispute his status as a non-white person ineligible to naturalize. The question was whether the Fourteenth Amendment naturalized him (in the same way that it had naturalized the recently emancipated slaves) as a function of his birth in the United States.

Understood in this way, Wong Kim Ark's case forced a contestation between a federal statute and a constitutional provision. The naturalization law equated an ascribed characteristic, race, with presumptive unfitness for citizenship. The Constitution equated another ascribed trait, place of birth, with presumptive fitness. As a person of Chinese descent born in the United States, Wong Kim Ark brought these conflict-

---

[37] U.S. Const., amends. XII, XIV, XV.

[38] U.S. Const., amend. XIV, § 1.

[39] 169 U.S. 649 (1898).

ing claims into sharp relief. Was he fit by birth or unfit by race? Ultimately, the Court held in 1898 that Wong was an American citizen, yet his race continued to make his citizenship suspect—a subject of speculation by immigration officers who required extensive documentation whenever he sought to reenter the United States after traveling abroad. While home might have been where Wong's heart was, home was never a place for his race. To put the point slightly differently, and to borrow from Gloria Anzaldua, after acquiring formal citizenship, Wong Kim Ark was "at home, a stranger."[40] He became "not quite, not American,"[41] "foreign in a domestic sense."

The phrase "foreign in a domestic sense" comes from *Downes v. Bidwell*,[42] the case Pedro A. Malavet discusses in his contribution to this volume. As the United States became a colonial empire at the very historical moment in which it was constituting itself as a post-slavery nation-state, race played a critical role in determining how newly acquired territory would be incorporated. This question of incorporation was never just about places; it was also always about people. Before the Civil War, Congress and the states had battled over the future of slavery on the assumption that all territories were on the path to statehood. Later, however, a model emerged in which some areas could remain perpetually dependent possessions with only limited sovereignty.[43] In the story of *Downes v. Bidwell*, Malavet shows how a 1901 case that was superficially about trade in fact turned on the perceived unfitness of the Puerto Rican people for self-governance. A shipment of oranges spawned a racially inflected meditation that helped to relegate the newly-acquired territory of Puerto Rico to the status of an insular possession—"foreign in a domestic sense"—rather than a site of self-determination. This structural arrangement rendered the residents of unincorporated territories like Puerto Rico second-class citizens, both inside and outside the borders of America's national identity. Meanwhile, on the mainland, a similar dynamic was at play. It, too, was producing second-class citizens—but through a formal system of racial classification and caste.

Separate and Unequal: Classification and Caste

Given how centrally race has figured in the construction of national identity, no one should be surprised that race also plays a central role in defining personal identity. Far from being a superficial matter of skin

---

[40] Carbado, *supra* note 9, at 639 (drawing on Gloria Anzaldua to advance a theory of racial naturalization).

[41] *Id.* at 639.

[42] 182 U.S. 244 (1901).

[43] Efren Rivera Ramos, *The Legal Construction of American Colonialism: The Insular Cases (1901–1922)*, 65 Rev. Jur. U.P.R. 225, 236–39 (1996).

color, race has often determined individuals' life chances. Even after the Civil War and the Reconstruction Amendments, Jim Crow segregation left blacks separate and unequal by law.[44] Two Supreme Court cases in particular facilitated the government's use of racial classifications to both police the color line and create a deeply subordinating caste system: *Pace v. Alabama*[45] and *Plessy v. Ferguson*.[46]

In *Pace*, the Court confronted a challenge to an antimiscegenation law that banned marriage between blacks and whites. The state of Alabama argued that the law did not violate the equality guarantees in the Fourteenth Amendment because members of each race faced equivalent penalties for crossing the color line. The Justices agreed, noting that the regulation of marriage was primarily a state concern and that the punishment was directed at the offense rather than a particular race.[47] The decision led to a proliferation of bans on intermarriage, and fourteen years later, the Court extended its "separate but equal" analysis to uphold segregation in public places in *Plessy*.[48]

In *Plessy*, a man who was "of mixed Caucasian and African descent in the proportion of seven-eighths Caucasian and one-eighth African blood"[49] unsuccessfully challenged his expulsion from a whites-only train car as a violation of the constitutional rights secured to blacks under the Reconstruction Amendments. Part of the Court's analysis employed the same racial logic as *Pace*. According to Justice Henry Billings Brown's majority opinion, Plessy failed to demonstrate an equal protection violation because the Louisiana law in question separated blacks from whites and whites from blacks. In other words, as a formal matter, the law treated blacks and whites the same, so there was no constitutional problem.

Plessy's counsel advanced a second argument for overturning the law: The lawyers questioned the propriety of a statute that delegated to

---

[44] *See generally* C. Vann Woodward, *The Strange Career of Jim Crow* (commemorative ed. 2002).

[45] 106 U.S. 583 (1882).

[46] 163 U.S. 537 (1896). For accounts of the *Plessy* case, see Cheryl I. Harris, *The Story of* Plessy v. Ferguson*: The Death and Resurrection of Racial Formalism, in Constitutional Law Stories, supra* note 1, at 181; Thomas J. Davis, *Race, Identity, and the Law:* Plessy v. Ferguson (1896), *in Race on Trial: Law and Justice in American History, supra* note 12, at 61.

[47] 106 U.S. at 585.

[48] Rachel F. Moran, *Interracial Intimacy: The Regulation of Race and Romance* 80–81 (2001).

[49] Petition for Writs of Prohibition and Certiorari at 1, Plessy v. Ferguson, 163 U.S. 537 (1896) (No. 15,248).

private railway companies the power to determine who was black and who was white. In arguing the case before the United States Supreme Court, attorney Albion Tourgée, a noted advocate for racial equality, argued that whiteness was a valuable form of property and that railway employees were able to deprive individuals of that property without due process of law.[50] He noted that extensive race-mixture meant that it was often difficult, if not impossible, to determine racial identity. In any event, he concluded: "Why not count everyone as white in whom is visible any trace of white blood? There is but one reason to wit, the domination of the white race."[51]

In part, the Court neatly sidestepped this novel question by concluding that the issue of racial identity was a question of state law and that at any rate Plessy had not formally challenged his classification in the earlier proceedings.[52] But the Court also partially engaged Plessy's whiteness as property argument, observing that "we are unable to see how this statute deprives him of, or in any way affects his right to" a property interest in whiteness.[53] The Court reasoned that "[i]f he be a white man and assigned to a colored coach, he may have his action for damages against the company for being deprived of this so called 'property.' Upon the other hand, if he be a colored man and be so assigned, he has been deprived of no property."[54] The Court was inviting Plessy to litigate his racial identity.

This invitation was not necessarily disingenuous. In fact, and as Angela Onwuachi–Willig's account of *Hudgins v. Wright*[55] demonstrates, the practice of litigating racial identity has a long pedigree in American law, dating back to slavery. How courts resolved these cases could mean the difference between freedom and bondage. While a court's determination that a litigant was black or African always resulted in bondage, whiteness was not the only identity upon which one could ground a claim to freedom. Indeed, in *Hudgins*, the possibility of freedom was predicated upon Native American, not white identity. Decided by the Supreme Court of Appeals of Virginia in 1806, *Hudgins* involved the legal battle of three women to prove that they were free citizens, not slaves. This determination rested on whether they were proved to have

---

[50] Cheryl I. Harris develops this claim in her article *Whiteness as Property*, 106 Harv. L. Rev. 1707 (1993).

[51] Brief for Plaintiff in Error at 11, Plessy v. Ferguson, 163 U.S. 537 (1896) (No. 15, 248).

[52] *Plessy*, 163 U.S. at 549.

[53] *Id.*

[54] *Id.*

[55] 11 Va. (1 Hen. & M.) 134 (1806).

descended from a free American Indian woman, as they claimed, or an enslaved black woman, as the alleged slaveholder claimed. At one time it had been legal to enslave American Indians, but when the government of Virginia began to find it lucrative to increase trade between whites and American Indians, their enslavement was prohibited. As enslavement of blacks was still perfectly legal, the ability to distinguish oneself as descending from American Indians was critical to many people's freedom.

Onwuachi–Willig's careful parsing of the court's opinion reveals the enormous role that hair and phenotype can play in determining an individual's race. Yet, the fact that the case was decided in the context of slavery raises a question about its relevance today. Do we read this case only for the historical exegesis it provides, or do we read it as well for its contemporary relevance? Asked more pointedly, do people continue to litigate their race? If so, how difficult are these cases to resolve—and what is at stake? To the extent that neither slavery nor Jim Crow legislation is a part of the contemporary legal landscape, one might think that the problems engendered by racial classification have disappeared. As Onwuachi–Willig shows, however, this is not the case; the dilemmas and difficulties of categorizing people racially persist today, bedeviling both antidiscrimination law and efforts on the part of the federal government to count individuals by race for purposes of the United States census. Were Homer Plessy alive today, there would be a real question not only about how to count him but about how he would count himself on the census.

Because of the centrality of *Plessy* as an anti-canonical case about African Americans, we sometimes ignore the significance of the case for other racial groups, particularly Asian Americans. Yet, *Plessy* profoundly affected the lives of people of Asian descent. Largely, it was with a simple citation to *Plessy* that the Supreme Court in *Gong Lum v. Rice* rejected Martha Gong Lum's claim that her exclusion from a whites-only high school violated equal protection.[56] Significantly, the relevant Mississippi constitutional provision did not specifically mention the "yellow race"—one of the preferred terms, along with "Oriental," for Asian Americans—but only "white and colored races." Martha Gong Lum thus had to decide on which side of the color line she belonged. In effect, her answer was neither; more particularly, she refused to identify herself as either white or colored.[57]

---

[56] 275 U.S. 78 (1927).

[57] Sora Han argues that Gong Lum's claim shifted the racial lens from a black/white paradigm to a black/non-black paradigm, further entrenching the notion of blackness as the identity categorization to avoid. See Sora Y. Han, *The Politics of Race in Asian American Jurisprudence*, 11 Asian Pac. Am. L.J. 1, 2–24 (2006).

Only a few years earlier Takao Ozawa had found himself in a similar racial predicament. This time, the legal regime was not a state constitutional provision but a federal statute. As noted earlier, in 1790, Congress had limited naturalization to free white persons. Congress amended this statute in the context of Reconstruction so that "aliens of African nativity and ... persons of African descent" also were eligible for naturalization.[58] Like Martha Gong Lum, Ozawa had to decide whether he could find a path to citizenship as a white person or one of African descent. How would Ozawa situate himself? In the story of *Ozawa v. United States*,[59] Devon W. Carbado answers that question: Ozawa argued that he was white. For the most part, he based his claim on his success in assimilating to an American way of life and on the lightness of his skin.

But as Carbado notes, Ozawa also advanced a more radical claim that reflected his skepticism about the utility of whiteness as a category. As Ozawa explained in his brief, "there is not an absolutely white person existing on this earth."[60] Like Plessy, Ozawa found that the Court was unreceptive to his efforts to complicate racial identity. His petition for naturalization was denied, and eventually, other Asian-origin groups would encounter similar barriers. Even when anthropologists considered some groups, like Asian Indians, to be Caucasian, the Justices relied on a widespread common belief that these groups were in fact non-white.[61] In doing so, the Court cemented their place on the wrong side of the color line.

Importantly, people of Asian descent were not the only group who asserted whiteness to acquire citizenship. "Middle Easterners" did so as well.[62] As John Tehranian notes, "[t]he results of these cases were mixed."[63] Courts sometimes considered Middle Easterners white, as in *Ex parte Mohriez*, where a federal district court invoked "the sciences of algebra and medicine, the population and the architecture of Spain and of Sicily, the very words of the English language," to conclude that a

---

[58] 8 U.S.C. § 359 (1875), *amended by* 8 U.S.C. § 1422 (1952).

[59] 260 U.S. 178 (1922).

[60] Supreme Court Brief, *in Consulate General of Japan, Documentary History of Law Cases Affecting Japanese in the United States, 1916–1924*, at 15 (1978 reprint) (1925).

[61] United States v. Thind, 261 U.S. 204 (1923).

[62] We put this term in quotes here to signal our recognition that it is from a Western gaze that people became Middle Easterners. We deploy it nonetheless—and throughout the remainder of the introduction without quotes—because it continues to be a cognizable racial category both ascriptively and self-definitionally. *See generally* John Tehranian, *Compulsory Whiteness: Towards a Middle Eastern Legal Scholarship*, 82 Ind. L.J. 1, 11 (2007).

[63] *Id.*

man of Arab descent was white.[64] However, most often, courts reached the opposite conclusion, as in *In re Ahmed Hassan*.[65] In that case, the court focused on skin color, religion, and assimilability to conclude that Ahmed Hassan was unnaturalizable.

> Apart from the dark skin of the Arabs, it is well known that they are a part of the Mohammedan world and that a wide gulf separates their culture from that of the predominately Christian peoples of Europe. It cannot be expected that as a class they would readily intermarry with our population and be assimilated into our civilization.[66]

Like Ozawa, Hassan found himself on the non-white/non-black side of the color line, a racial position from which even formal citizenship was unattainable.

The question of situating individuals along the color line does not always involve racial categorization—whether, for example, a person is yellow or white. Sometimes the question is whether a person or group belongs on the color line at all. This is precisely the issue in the story of *Morton v. Mancari*,[67] Carole Goldberg's contribution to this volume. She describes yet another dilemma of federal classification: how to deal with the identity of Native Americans. Tribes have been the subject of special legislation based on a history of conquest and treaties that accorded them semi-sovereign status. At the same time, and as Rennard Strickland's chapter reveals, Native Americans have been racialized, and their racial inferiority often has been used as a justification to divest them of their land and their rights. Today, the tendency to treat tribes as either racial or political has significant consequences. The Court has become increasingly unreceptive to programs like affirmative action that weigh race in allocating jobs or government contracts. So, if Native American tribes have a purely racial identity, programs directed at their needs are suspect. If, however, the tribes are political entities, the programs are simply part of a complex and ongoing negotiation about the tribes' relationship as dependent sovereigns of the federal government.

Goldberg's story brings this formal legal question to life, showing how serendipity played a role in framing this key case in Native American law. Carla Mancari was a non-Indian employee at a Bureau of Indian Affairs school, who challenged affirmative action policies that were designed to encourage the hiring and promotion of Indians. During the litigation, a lawyer advocating on behalf of these policies, by happen-

---

[64] 54 F. Supp. 941, 942 (D. Mass. 1944).

[65] 48 F. Supp. 843 (D. Mass. 1942).

[66] *Id.* at 845.

[67] 417 U.S. 535 (1974).

stance, had a conversation that led him to appreciate the distinction between Indian identity as racial or political. The result was a victory in the Supreme Court that preserved the Bureau of Indian Affairs policies, even as the justices rejected other affirmative action programs.

Mexican Americans experienced a similar victory in 1954 in *Hernandez v. Texas*.[68] As in *Morton v. Mancari*, the Supreme Court did not employ an explicitly racial analysis. Decided shortly before *Brown v. Board of Education*,[69] *Hernandez* addressed the systematic exclusion of Mexican Americans from grand juries in Texas. As Ian Haney López and Michael A. Olivas's chapter on the case notes, there were important differences between *Brown* and *Hernandez*. *Brown* was a highly controversial case targeting Jim Crow segregation and was very much in the public eye, while *Hernandez*, which invoked the same principles but for a different group, was virtually unknown and unrepresented in the media. Moreover, while *Brown* was backed by many prominent groups with substantial funding and support, the lawyers for Hernandez had to scrape together the funds even to afford the Supreme Court filing fee and the trip to Washington, D.C. Finally, *Brown* treated African Americans as a distinct racial group; *Hernandez* did not do so with respect to Mexican Americans.

Notwithstanding the foregoing differences, the *Hernandez* Court, like the *Brown* Court, found wrongful discrimination. *Hernandez*'s ruling in this respect made the opinion "the first civil rights decision of the Warren Court." In extending Fourteenth Amendment protection to Mexican Americans, the Court did not characterize them as a distinct, non-white group. Indeed, lawyers on both sides of the litigation argued that Mexican Americans were white. This agreement "precluded a racial analysis for what was otherwise evidently a racial case." According to Haney López and Olivas, one positive aspect of the Court's refusal to treat Mexican Americans as a distinct and non-white race was that it forced the Court to adopt an anti-subordination approach, one that focused on hierarchy and social stratification, and not simply on formal racial classifications. In this sense, *Hernandez* helped to make clear that caste is often accomplished by, but does not require, formal classifications. This insight has largely disappeared into a contemporary normative claim that our Constitution is colorblind. Contrary to the lessons of history, today's Court treats race neutrality as a complete cure for discrimination, despite clear evidence of ongoing racial inequality.

---

[68] 347 U.S. 475 (1954).

[69] 347 U.S. 483 (1954).

Our Constitution is Colorblind: The
Doctrine of Race Neutrality

No book on race law would be complete without a discussion of colorblindness, that is, the doctrine of race neutrality. Justice John Marshall Harlan's dissent in *Plessy* is most often cited for this principle. According to Harlan, "Our Constitution is color-blind, and neither knows nor tolerates classes among citizens."[70] Although this was an important and radical position for Justice Harlan to stake out, it did not bespeak a commitment to social equality across the color line. Two passages in Justice Harlan's dissent made this clear. In one passage, Harlan observed that "[t]he white race deems itself to be the dominant race in this country. And so it is, in prestige, in achievements, in education, in wealth, and in power. So, I doubt not, it will continue to be for all time, if it remains true to its great heritage."[71] After reading this passage, one has to remind oneself that Justice Harlan was arguing against, not for, racial segregation. In short, "[w]hile in Harlan's view the law should be employed neither to separate the races nor to create a dominant race, he [was] comfortable with a society within which there [was] . . . racial dominance."[72]

Further along in his dissent, and again ostensibly in the spirit of anti-racism, Justice Harlan invoked the specter of the Chinese to question the constitutionality of the "separate but equal" doctrine. Again, he relied on images of racial inferiority even as he questioned segregation by law. As he wrote, "There is a race so different from our own that we do not permit those belonging to it to become citizens of the United States. Persons belonging to it are, with few exceptions, absolutely excluded from our country. I allude to the Chinese race. But by the statute in question a Chinaman can ride in the same passenger coach with white citizens of the United States."[73] Here, Harlan's colorblind constitutionalism co-existed comfortably with the notion of the Chinese as being unfit for citizenship. In fact, Harlan's dissent traded on the unnaturalizability of the Chinese. Because Justice Harlan was arguing only against state-sanctioned racial segregation, these passages reinforcing images of racial inferiority remain obscure, and his vision of colorblindness has become politically and constitutionally ascendant.

---

[70] *Plessy*, 163 U.S. at 537, 539 (Harlan, J., dissenting).

[71] *Id.*

[72] Carbado, *supra* note 9, at 647.

[73] Plessy, 163 U.S., at 561 (Harlan, J., dissenting). For an extended critique of Justice Harlan's dissent, see Carbado, *supra* note 9, and Devon W. Carbado, *Race to the Bottom*, 49 UCLA L. Rev. 1283 (2002). Gabriel Chin was one of the first to note the racial problematics of Harlan's dissent. *See* Gabriel J. Chin, *The Plessy Myth: Justice Harlan and the Chinese Cases*, 82 Iowa L. Rev. 151 (1996).

Indeed, *Brown v. Board of Education*[74] is often celebrated as the realization of Harlan's vision. In part, this is because *Brown* overruled *Plessy*, but it is also because of the manner in which *Brown* did so. In *Brown*, Chief Justice Earl Warren, writing for a unanimous Court, struck down laws mandating racial segregation in the public schools. The Court rejected *Plessy*'s "separate but equal" doctrine by finding that "[s]eparate educational facilities are inherently unequal."[75] Regardless of whether tangible resources like facilities, books, and teacher qualifications in black and white schools could be equalized, segregation by law inflicted irreparable, intangible harms on schoolchildren that would "affect their hearts and minds in a way unlikely ever to be undone."[76] Some scholars have read this language to suggest that racial classifications per se are unconstitutional, and that the Constitution requires race neutrality. *Brown* did not expressly articulate this race-neutral principle, but that is one of the most common ways in which the case is interpreted.

Significantly, in delegitimizing the racial classification at issue in *Brown*, Chief Justice Warren had more to draw on than Harlan's dissent. Only ten years earlier, the Court had decided another racial classification case, *Korematsu v. United States*.[77] In *Korematsu*, the Court confronted the internment of Japanese and Japanese–American residents who allegedly posed a threat to national security.[78] Much like in *Brown*, there was no dispute about whether there was a racial classification. The question was whether that racial classification was constitutional. In answering that question, *Korematsu* declared that "all legal restrictions which curtail the civil rights of a single racial group" are

---

[74] 347 U.S. 483 (1954). The literature on *Brown* is vast. Among the many accounts are Richard Kluger, *Simple Justice* (1975); Charles Ogletree, *All Deliberate Speed: Reflections on the First Half–Century of* Brown v. Board of Education (2004); Leland Ware, *The Story of* Brown v. Board of Education: *The Long Road to Racial Equality*, in *Education Law Stories* 19 (Michael A. Olivas & Ronna Greff Schneider eds. 2008); Risa L. Goluboff, Brown v. Board of Education *and the Lost Promise of Civil Rights*, in *Civil Rights Stories*, *supra* note 1, at 25; Mark Tushnet, Brown v. Board of Education (1954), *in Race on Trial: Law and Justice in American History*, *supra* note 12, at 25.

[75] 347 U.S. at 484.

[76] *Id.* at 494.

[77] 323 U.S. 214 (1944). For accounts of the case, see Neil Gotanda, *The Story of Korematsu: The Japanese–American Cases*, in *Constitutional Law Stories*, *supra* note 1, at 249; Roger Daniels, Korematsu v. United States *Revisited*, in *Race on Trial: Law and Justice in American History*, *supra* note 12, at 139.

[78] This is not entirely accurate in the sense that the Court never actually addressed the internment of Japanese Americans as such. *See* Jerry Kang, *Denying Prejudice: Internment, Redress, and Denial*, 51 UCLA L. Rev. 933 (2004).

constitutionally suspect.[79] This heightened standard of review, or what we now refer to as strict scrutiny, did little to help people of Japanese descent. The Court upheld the internment practices, leaving open the question of how vigorous the Court would be in striking down invidious racial classifications.

Although many believe that *Korematsu* was the first case to apply strict scrutiny to a racial classification, *Hirabayashi v. United States*,[80] which was decided one year earlier, in fact deserves that distinction, as Jerry Kang's story of the case observes. Gordon Hirabayashi was born and raised in a small Christian farming cooperative south of Seattle, Washington. When, at age twenty-four, he was ordered to evacuate, he took a moral stand against the mandate, despite his mother's deep desire to keep the family together. Rather than comply, he turned himself in to the Federal Bureau of Investigation, "armed with a four-page statement explaining the constitutional and moral grounds for his civil disobedience." Because Hirabayashi admitted to violating curfew and exclusion orders, his trial was short and his conviction assured. The judge granted his request to serve a ninety-day sentence for each offense, a longer sentence than initially given. The appeal was certified to the Supreme Court, bypassing Ninth Circuit review, and the American Civil Liberties Union took over Hirabayashi's defense.

In deciding the case, the Court avoided the issue of Japanese internment entirely by "segmenting" the case; it focused only on the conviction for a curfew violation and not violation of the exclusion order. The question presented became: "During a time of national peril, was the military's adoption of a mere curfew lawful?" Phrasing the issue this way allowed the Court to avoid the issue of the constitutionality of the entire internment machinery. As Kang notes, the Supreme Court reproduced this avoidance strategy in *Korematsu*, focusing on evacuation rather than detention. Kang goes on to describe the Japanese–American redress movement of the 1970s and 1980s, which turned on evidence that the United States government manipulated findings of fact to overstate the danger of sabotage and espionage in the internment cases. Ultimately, activists succeeded in getting an apology from the executive branch and modest reparations from Congress. In addition, attorneys got the federal courts to vacate the convictions of defendants like Hirabayashi. Despite these belated efforts to set the record straight, Kang suggests that the internment cases are cause for concern, not celebration. In his view, these are mainly stories of judges who dodged their responsibility, rather than of the power of law to work itself pure.

---

[79] 323 U.S. at 216.

[80] 320 U.S. 81 (1943).

If the internment cases were an abject lesson in the limits of law as an instrument of racial justice during wartime, then *Perez v. Sharp*[81] shows how the post-war promise of equality could transform legal doctrine. In *Perez*, a black man and a Mexican–American woman, who was classified as white, challenged California's ban on interracial marriage. At the time of their challenge, the United States Supreme Court had upheld an Alabama antimiscegenation statute in *Pace*, and the decision was still good law. Moreover, *Brown v. Board of Education* had yet to be decided. In the following decade, when *Brown* (and a series of cases issued shortly thereafter) dismantled the doctrine of "separate but equal" in public life, none of the opinions reached interracial intimacy. Indeed, based on the thinking that "one bombshell at a time is enough,"[82] the Justices refused to hear cases challenging bans on interracial marriage. By 1967, however, the Court felt confident enough to issue another decision striking down the legacy of segregation. In *Loving v. Virginia*,[83] Chief Justice Warren wrote for a unanimous Court in holding that antimiscegenation laws violated equal protection because they were designed to promote white supremacy. With one exception, the Justices also found that the statutes infringed on due process by burdening a fundamental freedom: the right to marry.[84]

But none of this would help Andrea Perez and Sylvester Davis. Indeed, as R.A. Lenhardt's story of *Perez* makes clear, at the time of the litigation, California was one of thirty states with antimiscegenation laws. When Perez and Davis took their case to the courts, they were represented by a lawyer who decided, in contrast to most such challengers, to "strike a blow . . . at the very heart of California's laws." He argued that the law violated the couple's freedom of religion, hoping that the California Supreme Court would exercise its original jurisdiction to hear the case without its ever going through the normal trial process. While the court was in fact persuaded to take the case, religion did not figure in the analysis. For Justice Roger Traynor, the case involved "the right to marry . . . the person of one's choice." According to Lenhardt, this characterization enabled Traynor to elucidate a colorblind understanding of race—that it is biologically irrelevant. With *Perez* as a part of its jurisprudence, the California Supreme Court became the first and

---

[81] 198 P.2d 17 (Cal. 1948).

[82] Walter F. Murphy, *Elements of Judicial Strategy* 193 (1964).

[83] 388 U.S. 1 (1967). For an account of the *Loving* case, see Peter Wallenstein, *Interracial Marriage on Trial:* Loving v. Virginia (1967), *in Race on Trial: Law and Justice in American History, supra* note 12, at 177; Robert A. Pratt, *The Case of Mr. and Mrs. Loving: Reflections on the Fortieth Anniversary of* Loving v. Virginia, *in Family Law Stories* 7 (Carol Sanger ed. 2007).

[84] Moran, *supra* note 48, at 98.

only state high court since Reconstruction to invalidate an antimiscegen-ation law.[85]

An important part of Lenhardt's story of *Perez* is her suggestion that the case offers important lessons that go well beyond those in *Loving*. For one thing, Justice Roger Traynor's majority opinion in *Perez* was far more skeptical of the legitimacy of racial categories than was Chief Justice Warren's opinion in *Loving*. Traynor's doubts reflected a heightened awareness of the dangers of an ideology of racial inferiority, the very philosophy that Americans had confronted in the war against Nazism. By contrast, in 1967, racial classifications had become necessary to implement desegregation decrees, and Warren was simply willing to take them for granted.[86] For another, *Perez* has become a centrally important precedent in the contemporary same-sex marriage movement, because Justice Traynor spent considerable time addressing the right to marry. By contrast, Chief Justice Warren relegated this issue to a couple of paragraphs at the end of the *Loving* opinion. To preserve a unified Court, Warren had to downplay this holding as a way to mollify col-leagues who worried about recognizing rights not set forth explicitly in the Constitution. Traynor presumably had no hope of a unanimous decision in *Perez*, and so was free to develop an account of the unique role that intimate associations play in forming an individual's identity. Explicitly rejecting the "separate but equal" doctrine in the context of marriage, Traynor noted that "the essence of the right to marry is freedom to join in marriage with the person of one's choice."[87] The antimiscegenation law violated this right because a person's chosen partner could be "irreplaceable,"[88] yet irretrievably unavailable by rea-son of race. Traynor's opinion drew together themes of equality and freedom in ways that are missing in both *Brown* and *Loving*.

Even as *Brown* and *Loving* assumed iconic status, the two decisions revealed some unresolved tensions in the Court's canon of colorblind-ness. After *Brown*, the Court had insisted on desegregation plans that used race to eliminate past discrimination "root and branch"[89] in school districts. Busing became the most conspicuous and contentious example of judicial reliance on color-conscious remedies.[90] *Loving*, by contrast, at least in part, espoused a norm of colorblindness, but the Court did not

---

[85] *Id.* at 84.

[86] *Id.* at 98–99.

[87] 198 P.2d at 20–21.

[88] *Id.* at 25.

[89] Green v. County Sch. Bd., 391 U.S. 430, 437–38 (1968); Swann v. Charlotte–Mecklenburg Bd. of Educ., 402 U.S. 1, 15 (1971).

[90] Gary Orfield, *Must We Bus?: Segregated Schools and National Policy* (1978).

contemplate "a state-run interracial dating service."[91] On the contrary, the fundamental right to marry meant that government officials had to respect personal choices, even if high rates of same-race marriage persisted after *Loving*. As a result, *Loving* became "the first modern civil rights decision to treat colorblindness and segregation as compatible concepts."[92]

The juxtaposition of the two cases revealed a fundamental dilemma: How could the Court's formal commitment to colorblindness be reconciled with the ongoing need for race-conscious remedies? In the area of school desegregation, the Court eventually retreated from busing orders. As school desegregation litigation moved to the North and West, the Justices limited the scope of relief in urban school districts marked by segregation and poverty. The Court exempted nearby suburban districts, typically with affluent, white student bodies, from busing orders unless there was proof that these districts had intentionally promoted interdistrict segregation.[93] Such evidence was hard to come by, and so schools remained racially identifiable.[94] Even in the South, the federal courts increasingly found that school districts were unitary; that is, they had eliminated the vestiges of past discrimination.[95] When desegregation remedies drew to a close, schools often became resegregated.[96]

The Court's retreat was not limited to school desegregation. Affirmative action was highly controversial because color-conscious policies could be adopted in the absence of an official finding of past discrimination. These programs seemed to fly in the face of the principle of colorblindness because they were adopted voluntarily, rather than in response to sanctions for constitutional wrongdoing. In the story of *City of Richmond v. J.A. Croson Co.*,[97] Reginald Oh and Thomas Ross reveal a relatively early doctrinal moment in which the Court struggled to manage the conflict between colorblindness and affirmative action. The case began when J.A. Croson Company filed a lawsuit against the City of

---

[91] Moran, *supra* note 48, at 8.

[92] Rachel F. Moran, *Loving and the Legacy of Unintended Consequences*, 2007 Wisc. L. Rev. 239, 262 (2007).

[93] Milliken v. Bradley, 418 U.S. 717 (1974).

[94] Gary Orfield, *Turning Back to Segregation*, in *Dismantling Desegregation: The Quiet Reversal of* Brown v. Board of Education 10–13 (Gary Orfield & Susan E. Eaton eds., 1996).

[95] Freeman v. Pitts, 503 U.S. 467 (1992) (Atlanta, Georgia); *see also* Board of Education v. Dowell, 498 U.S. 237 (1991) (Oklahoma City, Oklahoma).

[96] Orfield, *supra* note 90, at 14–22; Gary Orfield, *The Growth of Segregation: African Americans, Latinos, and Unequal Education*, in *Dismantling Desegregation: The Quiet Reversal of* Brown v. Board of Education, *supra* note 94, at 53.

[97] 488 U.S. 469 (1989).

Richmond because Richmond denied Croson's bid for a plumbing contract. The city refused Croson's bid because it failed to comply with the Minority Business Utilization Plan (the "MBUP"), a city plan that required contractors to "subcontract at least 30% of the dollar amount of the contract to one or more Minority Business Enterprises." Croson claimed that the MBUP violated the Fourteenth Amendment's Equal Protection Clause.

This case sparked bitter division among the Justices. As Oh and Ross explain, the conflicting opinions in *Croson* relied on distinct narratives that depicted affirmative action either as "simple racial politics"[98] or a modest concession to the ongoing realities of societal racism. The majority of the Justices considered the program a product of the black city council's pork-barrel politics and applied a rigorous strict scrutiny test to invalidate the set-aside plan. The dissenting Justices saw the initiative as a benign remedy to overcome the legacy of unequal access in the construction industry and would have applied a less stringent, intermediate standard of review to uphold the program. Oh and Ross argue that in this polarizing debate, none of the Justices fully appreciated the structural obstacles to full inclusion for non-whites in metropolitan areas. This was true, they argue, even with respect to Justice Thurgood Marshall, one of the most liberal Justices ever to sit on the Court and at that time the only African American. Marshall's opinion was deeply contextual, particularly when compared to the more abstract narratives of the other Justices, but nonetheless remained situated within the boundaries of the city of Richmond. According to Ross and Oh, by expanding the geographical scope to include the suburbs outside of the city, the Court's narrative would have become more about the "continuing political and socioeconomic powerlessness of African Americans" as white flight from the city both created the city's black majority and caused the city's economy to decline abruptly. The commitment to colorblindness, they argue, made this complex racial narrative difficult to tell.

The hold of colorblindness on American law transcends equal protection doctrine. As Kevin R. Johnson's account of *Whren v. United States*[99] demonstrates, colorblindness is a powerful force in the Fourth Amendment context as well. In *Whren*, police officers stopped a car, purportedly for a traffic violation, conducted a search, and found narcotics. The defendants contended that the stop was a pretext and that they had been victims of racial profiling. That profiling allegedly violated the Fourteenth Amendment, but what the defendants wanted was relief under the Fourth Amendment, which forbids unreasonable searches and sei-

---

[98] *Id.* at 493–94, 510 (plurality opinion of O'Connor, J.).

[99] 517 U.S. 806 (1996).

zures. If the trial court concluded that the search or seizure was unreasonable, any evidence acquired as a result would be inadmissible. Whren argued that the narcotics seized during the search should not be allowed into evidence because the police officer's decision to perform the traffic stop was based on race. Without the incriminating drugs, Whren's conviction would be overturned.

As Johnson notes, consistent with the logic of colorblindness, the Supreme Court ignored the racial elements of the case, among them, the fact that at least one of the officers was white and that the defendant and his passenger were black. More profoundly, the Court, in a unanimous opinion, rejected the argument that a racial profiling claim of the sort Whren advanced could be the basis for invoking remedies under the Fourth Amendment. As a result, the most meaningful relief for illicit racial profiling was not available to defendants, even if they could surmount the evidentiary challenges of proving discrimination. Johnson persuasively argues that the Court's decision in *Whren* means that racial profiling must be addressed in the political rather than the judicial arena. In the meantime, officers have a license to make racial distinctions that are justified as part of the war on drugs. These distinctions, like other racialized aspects of the criminal justice process, seem not to run afoul of the notion that our Constitution is colorblind.[100] This reliance on racial distinctions, on the one hand, and the denial of race-conscious remedies, on the other, is a more general problem in American law.

With all Deliberate Speed: Race–Conscious Remedies

The roots of the dilemma over race-conscious remedies can be found in *Brown* itself. Despite the fact that the Court spoke with a single voice, the school desegregation mandate could not be implemented without the support of Congress and the executive branch. The following year, in *Brown II*, the Court found that school integration would proceed with "all deliberate speed."[101] As it turned out, there was far more deliberation than speed. For the next decade, the Court maintained a studied detachment in the face of Southern resistance. Only when Congress passed the Civil Rights Act of 1964, which endorsed a principle of non-discrimination on the basis of race, did the Court begin vigorous efforts to enforce the integrationist ideal set forth in *Brown*. At the same time, state governments and the federal government began to take "affirma-

---

[100] *See* Devon W. Carbado, *(E)racing the Fourth Amendment*, 100 Mich. L. Rev. 946 (2002) (exploring the various ways in which Fourth Amendment jurisprudence is racialized); *See also* Angela J. Davis, *Arbitrary Justice: The Power of the American Prosecutor* (2007); Paul Butler, *Much Respect: Toward a Hip–Hop Theory of Punishment*, 56 Stan. L. Rev. 983 (2004).

[101] 349 U.S. 294 (1955).

tive" steps to improve the educational and workplace opportunities of people of color. This is the context in which affirmative action was born, not in the courts but in the crucible of politics.

As the story of *Croson* demonstrates, the Supreme Court has had little difficulty in striking down affirmative action programs. Recall that in *Croson*, the Court applied strict scrutiny, the most stringent level of judicial review, to conclude that the city of Richmond's set-asides in government contracting were unconstitutional. While the case centered on the conduct of a city government, there was no doubt that the Court's approach applied to both state and municipal affirmative action programs. All would be subject to strict scrutiny. But what about affirmative action programs promulgated by the federal government? Should the same level of scrutiny apply to them? Later in *Adarand Constructors v. Pena*,[102] the Court answered that question in the affirmative, despite Congress's special role in implementing norms of equality under the Fourteenth Amendment. The Court insisted that colorblindness required that all race-based classifications, whether hostile or benign, at whatever level of government, be subject to strict scrutiny, a test that (at least after *Korematsu*) increasingly seemed to be "strict in theory and fatal in fact."[103]

Despite this commitment to colorblindness, the Justices upheld race-based admissions in *Regents of the University of California v. Bakke*.[104] There, Allan Bakke, an applicant to medical school, challenged the University of California at Davis's policy of setting aside seats in the entering class for underrepresented minority students. He alleged that this "reverse discrimination"[105] violated the Equal Protection Clause as well as the non-discrimination principle set forth in Title VI of the Civil Rights Act. Four Justices agreed with Bakke, concluding that any use of race triggered strict scrutiny and that Davis had not offered a compelling justification for its program.[106] Four other Justices sided with Davis, finding that a lower level of judicial review should apply to affirmative

---

[102] 515 U.S. 200 (1995).

[103] Gerald Gunther, *The Supreme Court, 1971 Term—Foreword: In Search of Evolving Doctrine on a Changing Court: A Model for Newer Equal Protection*, 86 Harv. L. Rev. 1, 8 (1972). *But see* Adam Winkler, *The Federal Government as a Constitutional Niche in Affirmative Action Cases*, 54 UCLA L. Rev. 1931 (2007) (suggesting that there is a meaningful survival rate for strict scrutiny cases).

[104] 438 U.S. 265 (1978).

[105] *See* Luke Charles Harris & Uma Narayan, *Affirmative Action and the Myth of Preferential Treatment: A Transformative Critique of the Terms of the Affirmative Action Debate*, 11 Harv. BlackLetter L.J. 1 (1994) (challenging the notion of reverse discrimination).

[106] 438 U.S. at 418 (opinion of Stevens, J.)

action because it was designed to rectify inequality; under this interme-diate test, the Davis plan passed muster.[107] With the Justices split four to four, Justice Lewis Powell cast the deciding vote. He concluded that affirmative action in higher education could be justified by a university's compelling interest in diversity. By diversity, he meant "an atmosphere of speculation, experiment, and creation"[108] that was generated by bring-ing together students with different backgrounds and perspectives. Di-versity included not just race but other characteristics that shaped a person's world view.[109] Powell therefore insisted on individualized review of applicants, with race treated as one factor among others. He cited the undergraduate admissions program at Harvard as one that could survive strict scrutiny. By contrast, Davis's set-aside program resembled a group-based quota, so Powell found it unconstitutional.[110]

For almost eighteen years, the question of affirmative action's constitutional status in college and university admissions seemed reason-ably settled. In 1996, however, the Fifth Circuit Court of Appeals in *Hopwood v. Texas*[111] posed a direct challenge to the regime that *Bakke* had established. The court of appeals ruled that the Supreme Court had never held that diversity was a compelling state interest; only Justice Powell's lone opinion articulated that position. *Hopwood* turned the affirmative action world upside down. Colleges and universities had thoroughly internalized the *Bakke* holding in revamping their admis-sions processes. What were they to do now?

In 2003, the Supreme Court weighed in. When Barbara Grutter was waitlisted and denied admission, she brought suit alleging unconstitu-tional reverse discrimination at the University of Michigan's law school. When the Court granted *certiorari* in the case, no one knew whether the decision would place affirmative action on surer constitutional footing or whether, instead, it would delegitimize the policy altogether. Ultimately, the Court upheld affirmative action that relied on holistic review of applicants in *Grutter v. Bollinger*.[112] In rejecting Grutter's claim, Justice O'Connor not only reaffirmed Powell's diversity rationale but also linked it to core democratic values. Because elite institutions like Michigan's law school were pathways to leadership, O'Connor found that access was

---

[107] *Id.* at 336–40 (opinion of Brennan, J).

[108] *Id.* at 312 (opinion of Powell, J.) (citing Sweezy v. N.H., 354 U.S. 234, 236 (1957)).

[109] For a conception of what we might mean by the expression "racial diversity," see Devon W. Carbado & Mitu Gulati, *What Exactly is Racial Diversity?*, 91 Cal. L. Rev. 1149 (2003).

[110] *Bakke*, 438 U.S. at 315–24 (opinion of Powell, J.).

[111] 78 F. 3d 932 (5th Cir. 1996).

[112] 539 U.S. 306 (2003).

important to preserve a sense that groups from all walks of life have a fair chance to participate in shaping our nation's destiny.[113] Moreover, she concluded that the law school had treated applicants as individuals with race weighed as but one factor in admission. In seeking a critical mass of underrepresented students, Michigan pursued an aspiration, not a quota.[114]

Rachel F. Moran's story of the case makes clear that O'Connor's majority opinion, while an important victory, is part of a jurisprudence of fragmentation that has seriously weakened the Court's authority in matters of civil rights and affirmative action. The Court's ruling was anything but a resolution of the controversy surrounding race-conscious policies. Indeed, after *Grutter*, the electorate in Michigan passed a referendum that banned consideration of race in public decisionmaking.[115] As a result, the law school could no longer use the affirmative action program it had fought so hard to defend.

That the Court could not have hoped to resolve the contestation over affirmative action was evident from the very nature of the *Grutter* litigation itself. For one thing, and as Moran notes, a record number of organizations and institutions filed amicus briefs in this case, including Fortune 500 corporations and a group of retired generals, who argued that affirmative action was necessary to promote the national security of the United States. For another, there was intense controversy about the terms upon which the case should be argued. The student-intervenors unsuccessfully sought to redefine the litigation as an epic struggle over racial subordination, rather than a referendum on *Bakke*. Once the case was heard by the Supreme Court, the student-intervenors were not even allowed to participate in oral argument. According to Moran, these controversies, combined with the deep divisions among the Justices, suggest that the future of affirmative action remains up for grabs. Moreover, and as Ward Connerly's state-by-state anti-affirmative action ballot initiative project suggests, the Supreme Court will never be the final voice on the matter. As in California and Michigan, people will speak with their votes.

At the very least, this is worrisome. Historically, voting has been both a racialized opportunity and a racialized practice in the United States. As such, it is a context in which minorities are vulnerable to what Lani Guinier refers to as the tyranny of the majority.[116] As Daniel

---

[113] *Id.* at 332.

[114] *Id.* at 334–39.

[115] Proposal 2 (Nov. 7, 2006) (codified at Mich. Const. art. I, § 26).

[116] *See generally* Lani Guinier, *Tyranny of the Majority* (1994).

P. Tokaji's story of *Shaw v. Reno*[117] indicates, race-conscious redistricting
was one response to this problem of systematic underrepresentation in
the political process. Tokaji provides an in-depth account of one of the
most important civil rights laws in our country's history, the Voting
Rights Act.[118] First enacted to redress a history of exclusion, this legislation has clearly promoted access to the ballot box and helped to diversify
representation on city councils, in state legislatures, and in Congress.

In *Shaw*, the plaintiffs challenged two majority-black districts in
North Carolina, created to satisfy the Act's requirements, as products of
racial gerrymandering. Tokaji makes clear that the case pitted the
Justice Department's interpretation of voting rights law as color-conscious by congressional design against the Supreme Court's interpretation of the Equal Protection Clause as colorblind in cases like *Croson*
and *Adarand*. Ultimately, the Court rejected bizarrely-shaped districts
that highlighted race as the primary factor in how boundaries were
drawn. However, the Justices did leave room for race to play a role,
because race and political behavior were closely correlated in North
Carolina. In short, the Court demanded that remedies under the Voting
Rights Act be narrowly tailored, but the Justices refused to find that the
Act's very invocation of race was unconstitutional. The Court recognized
that the Act had become intricately entwined with notions of democratic
legitimacy and fair play. As a result, the Justices were understandably
reluctant to undermine a law that had so dramatically altered the
concept of "We, the People." At the same time, the Court was clear that
concerns about colorblindness do not disappear in the voting rights
context. According to the Court, "[r]acial classifications of any sort pose
the risk of lasting harm to our society."[119] Thus we should strive to make
race irrelevant; we should strive to make it unnameable; we should
strive not to see it.

Yet, as Eric K. Yamamoto and Catherine Corpus Betts's story of
Rice v. Cayetano[120] reveals, sometimes the Court goes out of its way to
see race—even when a strong argument can be made that race simply is
not there. In *Rice*, a wealthy white rancher challenged the electoral
process used to select board members for the Office of Hawaiian Affairs

---

[117] 509 U.S. 630 (1993) (*Shaw I*), *on remand sub nom.* Shaw v. Hunt, 861 F. Supp. 408
(E.D.N.C. 1994), *rev'd*, 517 U.S. 899 (1996) (*Shaw II*), *on remand*, No. 92–202–CIV–5–BR
(E.D. N.C. Sept. 12, 1997) (approving plan and dismissing claim as moot). Later, a related
case challenged the redistricting under the Voting Rights Act yet again. Cromartie v. Hunt,
1998 U.S. Dist. LEXIS 7767 (E.D.N.C. 1998), *rev'd*, 526 U.S. 541 (1999), *remanded*, 133 F.
Supp. 2d 407 (E.D.N.C. 2000), *rev'd sub nom.* Easley v. Cromartie, 532 U.S. 234 (2001).

[118] Pub. L. No. 89–110, codified at 43 U.S.C. §§ 1973 et seq.

[119] 509 U.S. at 657.

[120] 528 U.S. 495 (2000).

("OHA"). The OHA was designed to be a "receptacle for reparations"[121] that would better the lives of indigenous Hawaiians. To facilitate self-determination, only individuals of Hawaiian ancestry were permitted to vote for board members. As a result, Rice's request for a ballot was denied and he filed suit, alleging that the voting restriction violated his civil rights.

Yamamoto and Betts contend that the Supreme Court wrongly rejected the OHA's electoral limit. In their view, the Justices failed to recognize the special history and claims of indigenous peoples. By ignoring the impact of colonization on native Hawaiians, the Court was able to use the rhetoric of colorblindness not to avoid race but to invoke it. Rather than viewing Native Hawaiians as an indigenous group and a once-sovereign nation whose government the United States illegally overthrew, the Court framed Native Hawaiians as a racial group. Thus, unlike both the district court and the Ninth Circuit Court of Appeals, the Supreme Court did not conceive of OHA as facilitating a relationship of trust between the Native Hawaiians and the United States. After explicitly inserting race into the case, the Court ruled that OHA's voting regime was reverse discrimination. Yamamoto and Betts close their chapter by suggesting that, in the end, *Rice* is a case both about collective memory and about the power to name and describe one's own reality. The Native Hawaiians became a race by law, not by self-definition.

The issue of race by self-definition is particularly salient for Middle Easterners, across religious identity. As noted earlier, in the context of seeking naturalization, people of Middle Eastern descent argued that they were white. Sometimes this argument carried the day; most often it did not. As a formal matter, inside and outside the domain of "science," Middle Easterners today are classified as Caucasian or white. The question is whether, in terms of self-definition, they should embrace or reject that classification. How one answers this question has important race-conscious remedial implications. Only in 1987 did the Supreme Court make clear that though Middle Easterners are classified as white, they still can sue for racial discrimination.[122] Implicit in the Court's reasoning was the notion that Middle Easterners could be racially vulnerable. Our national response to the terrorist attack of September 11, 2001 has confirmed this assumption.

As Leti Volpp observes, "September 11 facilitated the consolidation of a new category that groups together persons who appear 'Middle Eastern, Arab, or Muslim.' "[123] While one can query whether this identi-

---

[121] Haw. Rev. Stat. § 10-3 (1993).

[122] *See* Saint Francis College v. Al-Khazraji, 481 U.S. 604 (1987).

[123] Leti Volpp, *The Citizen and the Terrorist*, 49 UCLA L. Rev. 1575, 1575–76 (2002).

ty is new, its particular consolidation in the wake of September 11th has, as Muneer Ahmad notes, rendered people perceived to be Middle Eastern, Arab, or Muslim vulnerable to state and private violence.[124] How should Middle Easterners respond to this? Should they affirmatively assert a Middle Eastern racial identity? More than that, should they draw on the consolidation of this racial identity to seek race-conscious remedies such as affirmative action in the political and legal arenas? The answer is not obviously yes, and not only because of concerns of essentialism and the reification of identity categories, but also because people of Middle Eastern descent are differentially vulnerable to discrimination. Those who "look white" and work their identities[125] to obscure their Middle Eastern origins might experience "short-run freedom from discrimination."[126] Put another way, there is an incentive for Middle Easterners who have what John Tehranian refers to as "assimilatory choices"[127] to exercise them. Hair can function as one such option. For example, to some Americans, facial hair on a Middle Eastern man signifies a terrorist. As a result of the potential for this signification, Tehranian "do[es] not go to the airport without shaving first. It is covering, plain and simple, and a rational survival strategy. [He] prefer[s] the close shave to the close full-body-cavity search."[128]

In a completely different context, Renee Rodgers confronted this very problem. That is, like Tehranian, she had to decide whether to allow her hair to make her vulnerable to discrimination. As Paulette M. Caldwell's story of *Rogers v. American Airlines*[129] discusses, Rodgers worked for American Airlines and was reprimanded for wearing a braided hairstyle on the job in violation of her employer's grooming code. For the most part, under federal employment discrimination law, female plaintiffs of color have had to choose between defining their injuries as either racial discrimination or gender discrimination. Yet, Caldwell argues, the prohibition on braids discriminated against Rodgers as an African–American woman, who was uniquely burdened in ways that did not affect her black male or white female colleagues. She faced what Kimberlé Crenshaw refers to as intersectional discrimination, that is,

---

[124] Muneer Ahmad, *A Rage Shared By Law: Post–September 11 Racial Violence as Crimes of Passion*, 92 Cal. L. Rev. 1259 (2004).

[125] *See generally* Devon Carbado & Mitu Gulati, *Working Identity*, 85 Cornell L. Rev. 1259 (2000).

[126] Tehranian, *supra* note 62, at 18.

[127] *Id.* For a general discussion of different kinds of passing strategies, see Carbado & Gulati, *Working Identity*, *supra* note 125. See also Kenji Yoshiro, *Covering*, 111 Yale L.J. (2002) (employing the language of covering to describe the same phenomenon).

[128] Tehranian, *supra* note 62, at 20.

[129] 527 F. Supp. 229 (S.D.N.Y. 1981).

discrimination on the basis of more than one axis of difference.[130] To be fully protected by law, Rodgers did not want to be compartmentalized, fragmented into either a race or a gender identity. As Caldwell notes, the *Rogers* court enforced that fragmentation nonetheless, refusing to analyze the case in intersectional terms.

Although most intersectionality theorists have focused on employment discrimination claims like the one in *Rogers*, Caldwell shows that this approach is relevant to other areas of the law such as jury selection. Currently, the Constitution prevents prosecutors from striking jurors on the basis of race or gender.[131] Drawing on a controversial article in the *New Yorker*,[132] Caldwell argues that some prosecutors fear that African–American women will become irrational holdouts in criminal cases. To avoid a hung jury, these prosecutors strike black women in disproportionate numbers based on prejudice and stereotyping. Yet, their exclusion from juries will not be remedied so long as black men (who can stand in for race) and white women (who can stand in for gender) are selected as jurors. Caldwell contends that intersectionality should apply here as well to protect against the compound and complex interaction of race and gender bias. Thus far, to a considerable extent, courts continue to be intersectionally blind.

This is partially a reflection of concerns about the proverbial slippery slope. As one court put it, "[t]he prospect of the creation of new classes of protected minorities [like black women], governed only by the mathematical principles of permutation and combination, clearly raises the prospect of opening the hackneyed Pandora's box."[133] But there is a normative concern as well. Intersectionality forces courts to be mindful of more differences than those associated with ostensibly "just race" or "just gender" discrimination claims. The more courts focus on differences, the less race-neutral their jurisprudential approach. Understood in this way, intersectionality threatens the very possibility of colorblindness and exposes its inadequacy. This helps to explain why one court refers to it as a "super remedy"[134] that is outside the legitimate boundaries of both gender- and race-conscious remedies.

---

[130] Kimberlé Crenshaw, *Demarginalizing the Intersection of Race and Sex: A Black Feminist Critique of Antidiscrimination Doctrine, Feminist Theory and Antiracist Politics*, 1989 U. Chi. L. F. 139 (1989). *See also* Angela P. Harris, *Race and Essentialism in Feminist Legal Theory*, 42 Stan. L. Rev. 581 (1990).

[131] Batson v. Kentucky, 476 U.S. 79 (1986) (race); J.E.B. v. Alabama, 511 U.S. 127 (1994) (gender).

[132] Jeffrey Rosen, *One Angry Woman: Why Are Hung Juries on the Rise?*, New Yorker, Feb. 24/Mar. 3, 1997, at 54.

[133] Degraffenreid v. General Motors, 413 F.Supp. 142, 145 (E.D. Mo. 1976).

[134] *Id.* at 143.

Intersectionality claims are even more problematic for courts when they involve sexual orientation. Under Title VII, sexual orientation as such is not a protected identity category. What this means concretely is that employers may legally discriminate on that basis—at least under federal law. One implication is that employers can invoke what one might call the "sexual orientation defense" to a plaintiff's claim of discrimination, whether intersectional or not. To understand how this might work, imagine that an employee is a black lesbian. Her employer knows this and terminates her, not because she violated a grooming policy but because she did not get along with other employees and was not collegial. To the extent that the fired employee brings a discrimination suit based on race or gender or both, her employer can respond that it did indeed discriminate but that discrimination was based on sexual orientation, not race or gender or a combination of the two. This sexual orientation defense is perfectly consistent with Title VII's antidiscrimination mandate.[135] In this sense, gays and lesbians of color are disadvantaged not only because they can not include their sexual orientation in an intersectional claim of discrimination but also because their sexual identity can function as a defense to discrimination claims based on aspects of their identities—like race and gender—that are protected under the law.

Renee Rodgers may or may not have known this, but her case is a useful window not only on the specific problem of intersectionality, but the more general problem of colorblindness. Colorblindness was designed to undo the formal classification schemes that arose to enforce a racial caste system. This explains the concept's constitutional genesis in Justice Harlan's *Plessy* dissent. Yet, the simple elimination of these categories alone will not address all the ways in which race can be institutionally entrenched. American Airlines did not prohibit black women from wearing braids; it prohibited all women from wearing braids. But as Caldwell notes, this seeming neutrality was deeply gendered and raced. Bo Derek notwithstanding, the intelligibility of white women is not linked to the all-braided hairstyle that the grooming policy prohibited. *Rogers* thus helps to illuminate a lesson the *Plessy* dissent teaches and that we as a society continue to ignore: that colorblindness and inequality can comfortably co-exist. Race-conscious remedies are therefore necessary at times.

More generally, *Rogers* along with the other stories in this volume reveal the extent to which race is deeply embedded in the American body politic and has created a tremendous social wound. Judges and policy-

---

[135] *See, e.g.*, Anthony E. Varona & Jeffrey M. Monks, *En/gendering Equality: Seeking Relief Under Title VII Against Employment Discrimination Based on Sexual Orientation*, 7 Wm. & Mary J. Women & L. 67 (2000). This intersectional problem also marginalizes gays and lesbians in antiracist and gay rights discourses. See Devon W. Carbado, *Black Rights, Gay Rights, Civil Rights*, 47 UCLA L.Rev. 1467 (2000).

makers continue to articulate colorblindness as the cure. This makes little sense. Colorblindness emerged in response to the formal classification schemes that the federal and state governments promulgated to enforce a racial caste system. The simple elimination of these categories alone can not address the ways in which race has been entrenched in the very structure of our democracy. Racism is part of us. "Our sense of ourselves as Americans, of others as Americans, and of the nation is itself, is inextricably linked to racism."[136] Race-conscious remedies are modest means of both addressing this problem and promoting democratic legitimacy. This is one of the important lessons a race law canon can teach.

Conclusion

Our starting point for thinking about *Race Law Stories* was a set of themes around which we would organize the volume: sovereignty and formal citizenship; classification and caste; colorblindness and race neutrality; and race-conscious remedies. While these themes are not exhaustive of the ways in which one might map the race law terrain, our sense was that we could productively employ them to fashion a coherent, theoretically disciplined, and representative set of materials on race and the law.

Although we have separated the themes in the book, we recognize that they are deeply interconnected and cut across different time periods and doctrinal areas of law. *Morton v. Mancari*, for example, is at once a case about sovereignty and citizenship, classification and caste, colorblindness, and race-conscious remedies. Moreover, the theme of classification and caste is as relevant to the slave law jurisprudence of the eighteenth and nineteenth centuries as it is to the voting rights case law of the twentieth and twenty-first centuries. For this reason, we present our themes as heuristics or placeholders, not hard categorical boundaries.

Moreover, as discussed earlier, in elaborating these themes, we are careful to recognize the complexity created by America's multiracial population. We have chosen cases that include blacks, Latina/os, Asian Americans, Native Americans, and whites. Further, to demonstrate the extent to which race law reaches into every aspect of our lives, the stories cover a range of contexts, including, but not limited to, education, employment, housing, criminal law, voting rights, immigration, and family law. We also have chosen both "top down" cases—that is, cases brought by formal organizations (like the Japanese American Citizens League) or the government—and those that were "bottom up"—that is, cases in which very ordinary people initiated or drove the litigation.

---

[136] Carbado, *Racial Naturalization*, *supra* note 9, at 651.

This comprehensive, comparative approach has helped us to offer a preliminary version of a race law canon. This canon differs substantially from civil rights and constitutional law and deserves its own place in the curriculum. Moreover, this canon must move beyond those cases that have achieved iconic or ignominious status. Some lawsuits involving race clearly stand a better chance of being canonized or demonized than others. Chief among those that achieve fame or notoriety are conflicts that reach the United States Supreme Court, which in turn establishes a precedent that endures long enough to be highly influential. Perhaps not surprisingly, then, most of the cases discussed in this book track that trajectory. But the volume also includes hidden gems: state and lower federal court cases that failed to reach the Supreme Court. These cases set precedents that were compartmentalized or contained, or were promptly overturned or ignored after they were decided. We consider them valuable discoveries because even though they have not become prominent, they are enormously instructive in demonstrating the multiple and complex ways in which race and law intersect. We hope that this book will draw attention to these cases, which deserve greater attention than race law scholars have so far afforded them.

The ultimate test of this volume's success lies with you, our reader. Our purpose will be served if you agree that these cases offer a unique opportunity to rethink the assumptions that shape the role of race in public and private conversations about equality, liberty, and national identity. If these stories help you to reflect critically on what race and the law mean in America, this book will do justice to the individuals, whether lionized or little-known, who brought these issues to life by daring to question the conventional wisdom about America's commitment to its most fundamental democratic values.

1

Rennard Strickland

The Tribal Struggle for Indian Sovereignty: The Story of the *Cherokee Cases*

Introduction

Almost two centuries after the Supreme Court decisions in the popularly named *Cherokee Cases*[1], John Marshall's opinions remain the foundation of Native American law and policy. These decisions are not just controlling for the Cherokee but for the whole of the Indian community. *Worcester* is among the five most frequently cited cases from the pre-Civil War United States Supreme Court. Furthermore, both the Congress and the Executive Branch, particularly the Bureau of Indian Affairs, rely upon the *Cherokee Cases* doctrines of trust responsibility, domestic dependent nations, tribal sovereignty, limitations on state powers, and the supremacy and sanctity of treaties.[2]

The *Cherokee Cases* are significant not only because of the doctrines which they set forth but also because of the historic times in which they

---

[1] Cherokee Nation v. Georgia, 30 U.S. (5 Pet.) 1 (1831); Worcester v. Georgia, 31 U.S. (6 Pet.) 515 (1832). The two cases are most frequently considered together since they grow from the same historic events.

[2] The most relevant and thoughtful analysis of these cases, along with *Johnson v. M'Intosh*, 21 U.S. (8 Wheat.) 543 (1823), is found in Lindsay Robertson, *Conquest By Law* (2005); *see also* Joseph C. Burke, *The Cherokee Cases: A Study in Law, Politics, and Morality*, 21 Stan. L Rev. 500 (1969); Jill Norgren, *The Cherokee Cases: Two Landmark Federal Decisions in the Fight for Sovereignty* (2004); Mary Young, Indian Removal and the Attack on Tribal Autonomy: The Cherokee Cases, in *Indians of the Lower South: Past and Present* (John K. Mahan ed., Gulf Coast History and Humanities Conference, 1975); Rennard Strickland & William Strickland, *The Court and the Trail of Tears*, Y.B. of the Sup. Ct. Hist. Soc'y 20 (1979); William F. Swindler, *Politics as Law: The Cherokee Cases*, 3 Am. Indian L. Rev. 7 (1975).

were decided. The cases were heard during what has come to be known as "the formative era" of Native American policy. Prior to the conclusion of the War of 1812, there was always the prospect of a foreign sovereign who might make alliances with the Indian tribes in the colonies and then within the United States itself. After the Louisiana Purchase and the victory in this final war with England, the tribes were essentially left with only one white nation with whom to negotiate: the struggling new United States. Thus, when the Marshall court took up the *Cherokee Cases*, it was helping to create the framework in which the relationship between the Native American and the European Settler (or Invader, depending upon one's perspective) would be established and ultimately settled. It is this relationship, this framework, this division of duty and responsibility, which prevails to this day in American Indian policy.

In the 1830s, these Indian questions were crucial issues: still in doubt, essentially unresolved, and often not yet even considered by the courts or legislature. It was necessary to create the framework for a working governance between the Indian Nations, the United States, and the individual states and the territories. It was also uncertain as to how treaties were to be interpreted and what obligations federally negotiated treaties imposed upon the states that considered themselves sovereign. Furthermore, there were questions of the obligation of the federal government to see that treaties were, in fact, honored. At the heart of these issues were debates over the meaning of sovereignty and how land was to be used. This case, we must remember, was being acted out against the background of the question of slavery and the role of the broader union. The Cherokees' support after the Court's decisions was, for example, undermined by the question of nullification coming from South Carolina. The states, especially in the South, differed on the question of the power relationship between the central and state government. South Carolina advanced the "nullification doctrine" that proclaimed that states had the power to override or nullify the federal actions at all levels. Many thought of these Indian issues and Indian conflict with the states as a "rehearsal for abolition." Additionally, both the population and pressure to settle westward were growing, making the Indian question one that influenced not only the availability of land, but the power and economic development of the sections. Sectionalism was a crucial question of the age and was a term, often used to refer to the differences between the North and the South on issues of slavery. Furthermore, in an age of social and religious activism, the desire to reform, Christianize, and "civilize" Natives clashed with the desire to exploit the country's resources.

To the Cherokee people, these cases mean even more. Knowing the story of the *Cherokee Cases*—and the tribal as well as national response to them—is at the heart of knowing what it means to be Cherokee.

These cases are intimately tied to the question of Native survival and the challenge of facing an impossible tribal dilemma. Tragically, but inevitably, they lead to the "Trail of Tears," the forced march in which the Cherokee lost more than one quarter of the entire tribal membership.[3] To non-Indians, these cases are remembered primarily for the response they purportedly elicited from President Andrew Jackson: "Marshall has made his law, now let him enforce it."[4]

My father, like most Cherokee men of his generation, was a great storyteller. He was born in 1905, two years before the "shotgun wedding" joining the Indian Territory and the Oklahoma Territory to create the new state of Oklahoma.[5] As a young man, he had been ordained a Methodist minister, although he spent most of his adult life in business, much like his white trader ancestors who had married into the Cherokee Tribe at the beginning of the nineteenth century. My brother, sister and I spent much of our young lives in a 1940 Chevrolet traveling between Muskogee, where we lived, and the Cherokee Capitol at Tahlequah. He donated time (his and ours) plus trunk loads full of toys to the Methodist children's home and the Cookson Hills Indian Mission. This, of course, did not keep us from going to the Stomp Dances or the Keetoowah Fires. In the ecumenical ways of Cherokees of his generation, he was equally at home telling ancient stories of the coming of fire, the little people, and the biblical plagues of Job as he was of repeating the tribal version of the *Cherokee Cases* and the tragedy of the forced migration on the Trail of Tears.

Before I was a first-grader at Longfellow Elementary School in Muskogee, I had heard chapter and verse of the tragic failure of the American legal system to honor the Supreme Court's decisions in the *Cherokee Cases* and the price the Cherokee people paid for that failure. Indeed, the events leading up to and following these cases with their dramatic, sometimes melodramatic, events were among his favorite tales. Sixteen thousand Cherokees were driven from their ancient homeland at gunpoint, despite a Supreme Court decision in their favor. I knew as a small child what all Cherokees remember: that only twelve-thousand

---

[3] The classic study of the Trail of Tears and Indian removal remains Grant Foreman, *Indian Removal: The Emigration of the Five Civilized Tribes* (1932). *See also* Amy H. Sturgis, *The Trail of Tears and Indian Removal* (2007); *The Cherokee Removal: A Brief History with Documents* (Theda Perdue & Michael Green eds., 2d ed. 2005); *Cherokee Removal: Before and After* (William L. Anderson ed., 1991).

[4] Whether or not he actually did say this is one of the great unanswered—and probably unanswerable questions of the *Cherokee Cases*. For sources and arguments, see Anton–Herman Chroust, *Did President Jackson Actually Threaten the Supreme Court with Non-enforcement of Its Injunction Against the State of Georgia?*, 4 Am. J. Legal Hist. 77 (1960).

[5] For an account of the historic relationships between Indian Territory and Oklahoma Territory, see generally Rennard Strickland, *The Indians in Oklahoma* (1980).

reached the new land. More than four thousand—one quarter of all Cherokees—died in what American historians clinically describe as "Indian Removal."[6] Like many Indian peoples of their generation, education was important to both my Osage Mother and Cherokee Father. I think it was hardly accidental that when it came time for my brother and me to write our dissertations that we both turned to the historical events and the tribal stories we had first heard from our father in their Native versions.[7] The account that follows reflects those stories and is told from a tribal perspective.

Case Background—The Cherokee-Georgia Conflict

The story of the Cherokee is richly chronicled by both Native and non-Native historians.[8] However, the prehistoric origin of the Cherokee people is shrouded in mystery. In historic times, the Cherokee were the largest of the Indian tribes of the southern frontier of English America. By the eighteenth century, the Cherokee numbered over ten thousand and lived in sixty or more scattered villages. As many as one half of their numbers had died as a result of the smallpox epidemics and the failure of their priestly leaders' attempted cures. Through a series of treaties, the Cherokee's lands continued to dwindle until the 1820s, when the major body of the tribe was concentrated primarily in Georgia and secondarily in Tennessee.

Most of the Cherokee villages were situated along small streams throughout the Appalachian Mountains. Hunting and warfare were central to the life of the aboriginal Cherokee. The tribe had earlier embraced agriculture, with powerful women maintaining control over use of the crops in what was essentially a matriarchal society divided into seven clans. From initial contact with DeSoto in 1540 to the signing of their first treaty with the American nation at Hopewell in 1785, the tribe struggled to resist white advancement. The original Cherokee lands, now treaty guaranteed, sat in the middle of the State of Georgia, exempt by United States Indian policy from state law, regulation and

---

[6] For a scholarly analysis of tribal demographics, see Russell Thornton, *The Cherokees: A Population History* (1990).

[7] Rennard Strickland, *Fire and the Spirits: Cherokee Law From Clan to Court* (1975); William M. Strickland, *Indian Dilemma: The Rhetoric and Reality of Cherokee Removal*, (unpublished manuscript on file at the University of Oklahoma Law Library).

[8] The introductory source for location and interpretation of this mass of primary and secondary material is Raymond D. Fogelson, *The Cherokees: A Critical Bibliography* (1978). *See also* Rennard Strickland, *In Search of the Cherokee History: A Bibliographical Foreword to the Second Printing* of Morris L. Wardell, *A Political History of the Cherokee Nation* (2nd ed., 1977). Those seeking additional information or clarification of Cherokee historical issues are referred to Robert Conley's recent history entitled *The Cherokee Nation* (2006) and to Theda Perdue, *The Cherokee Nation and the Trail of Tears* (2007).

taxation. Georgia was a particularly vicious adversary, having enacted an early colonial regulation granting to her citizens the right to exterminate "Indians at war" without even a declaration of war. In the so-called "Georgia Compact" of 1803–1804, the United States government addressed Georgia's land demands by promising to remove all Indians from within her external boundaries "as soon as possible" in exchange for Georgia's surrender of her colonial charter claims to all land extending to the Pacific Ocean. By the late 1820s, Georgia was increasingly hostile about the failure of the United States to have expended any effort to fulfill the provisions of the Compact.[9]

A series of events toward the end of the 1820s brought the smoldering hostility between the Cherokee and their Georgia neighbors into full flame. These events included the discovery of gold on Cherokee treaty lands within the boundary of Georgia, the adoption of a Cherokee tribal constitution based on the laws of the United States,[10] the continued failure of the United States to fulfill the promises of the Georgia Compact, the election of Andrew Jackson as the first westerner to hold the presidency, the passage of Jackson's Indian Removal Act,[11] designed to move eastern tribes to new lands west of the Mississippi, and finally the unilateral extension of a series of Georgia laws over the tribal treaty lands of the Cherokee. These new Georgia laws declared the Cherokee lands to be "Cherokee County" within the State of Georgia, and designated this as "surplus" land to be opened to Georgia citizens for settlement by lottery. Indians were denied the right to appear in court under this legislation, and non-Indians living within this Cherokee area were required to obtain a permit from officials of the State of Georgia.[12]

Justice in a Peaceable Manner

As the Cherokee Nation contemplated the escalating conflict with the state of Georgia, tribal leader Elias Boudinot, the editor of the *Cherokee Phoenix*, wrote a commentary for this Indian-sponsored newspaper. Using a mixture of English and the Cherokee syllabary created by the mixed-blood artist George Guest (a.k.a. Sequoyah), the paper ad-

---

[9] For the standard statement of the state position, see Wilson Lumpkin, *The Removal of the Cherokee Indians from Georgia.* (2 vols., Dodd, Mead & Co., 1907).

[10] *See generally* Rennard Strickland, *supra* note 7.

[11] Indian Removal Act of 1830, ch. 148, 4 Stat. 411.

[12] For a critical analysis of the legal aspects of these events, see Rennard Strickland, *Genocide at Law: An Historic and Contemporary View of the Native American Experience,* 34 U. Kan. L. Rev. 714 (1986). The major scholarly interpretation of continuing influences on the jurisprudence of Indian law is Phillip P. Frickey, *Marshalling Past and Present: Colonialism, Constitutionalism, and Interpretation in Federal Indian Law,* 107 Harv. L. Rev. 381 (1993).

dressed a series of policy and treaty issues as well as reporting on life in the Nation. The pages of the *Phoenix* tell this story from the perspective of Cherokee tribal leaders.[13] The Cherokee Nation saw the United States Supreme Court as their best hope for a resolution to the growing dispute. Indeed, the confidence of the tribal leadership in the Supreme Court was high. The Court, an institution which a generation earlier had been described to them as "wise, beloved old men," seemed a natural and hospitable forum to which the tribe might turn. Traditional Cherokee government had often been described as a gerontocracy, a leadership of tribal elders. In fact, the Cherokee Constitution of 1827 had established a tribal Supreme Court, which had only recently moved into its own National Supreme Court Building at New Echota in the Nation.[14] Thomas Jefferson had earlier spoken to a Cherokee delegation in Washington about the regularity of law, and even earlier, George Washington had talked to Cherokee delegates about Magna Carta and the Rule of Law.[15]

As the tribe contemplated getting its cause heard before the Supreme Court, Boudinot penned the following editorial for the *Cherokee Phoenix*:

> The Cherokees are for justice and they are trying to obtain it in a peaceable manner by regular course of law. If the last and legitimate tribunal decides against them, as honest men the Cherokees will submit and "the agony will be over." Will Georgia be as honest and submit to her own [United States] courts? . . . We will merely say that if the highest judicial tribunal in the land will not sustain our rights and treaties we give up and quit our murmurings. . . .[16]

In their efforts to resist the Jacksonian Indian policy of tribal removal west of the Mississippi, the Cherokees toured and lectured along the Eastern seaboard seeking Congressional support, attempted direct negotiations with the President and the federal Indian bureaucracy, and even pushed for some sort of compromise with Georgia's state officials. All of this was to no avail; Congress passed the Removal Act. Georgia fully extended her laws over the Cherokee Nation by sending the State Guard into the treaty lands, and ultimately, the state exercised its

---

[13] See *Cherokee Phoenix* editorials and reports on the Supreme Court litigation in the following issues: July 17, 1830; July 31, 1830; October 1, 1830; April 9, 1831; January 21, 1832; May 12, 1832; May 19, 1832; September 8, 1832; September 22, 1832; October 27, 1832; March 2, 1834.

[14] The building has been restored, and those who wish to tour it may do so.

[15] Rennard Strickland, *supra* note 7, at 51, 237.

[16] Elias Boudinot, Editorial, *Cherokee Phoenix*, July 3, 1830.

jurisdiction to hang a Cherokee citizen, Corn Tassel, for murder in defiance of a federal court order. The Cherokee delegation in Washington was advised and ultimately persuaded by Daniel Webster, Ambrose Spenser and Theodore Frelinghuysen that their only remaining course of action was to hire eminent counsel to present their cause before the Supreme Court.[17]

The Cherokees hired William Wirt to represent them. Wirt was one of the most distinguished and well-known attorneys of the age. He had been the Attorney General of the United States before Jackson took office. Wirt enjoyed his newly established private practice and proclaimed that he was happy to be out of the political world. When first approached, he was reluctant to take the case, but he was ultimately persuaded to represent the Cherokee Nation by the injustices being suffered by the tribe and the influence of his old friend Daniel Webster. The Cherokee people held Wirt in such esteem that for generations young men were given his name. At the beginning of the twentieth century, a young Cherokee graduate of the Vanderbilt law school, William Wirt Hastings, became one of the first Native Americans to serve in the U.S. House of Representatives.[18]

Getting the Cherokees Before the Court

The Court to which Wirt and his Cherokee clients turned was not itself as venerable or established an institution as it would later become. It had been less than three decades since Justice Marshall's decision in *Marbury v. Madison*[19] suggested the powerful role this court would ultimately play in the American republic. And the Court would go from *Marbury* to *Dred Scott*[20] without once again declaring an act of the United States Congress unconstitutionally void. In the field of Indian law, the United States Supreme Court had by the end of the third decade of the nineteenth century decided only a few important cases such as *Johnson v. M'Intosh*.[21] This case, the first of the so-called Marshall

---

[17] There are hundreds of broadsides, pamphlets, speeches, resolutions and town hall meeting records that demonstrate the significance of the Indian removal in domestic life and politics in the 1820s and 1830s. *See* Andrew Denson, *Demanding the Cherokee Nation: Indian Autonomy and American Culture* (2004).

[18] John P. Kennedy, *Memoirs of the Life of William Wirt, Attorney General of the United States* (2 vols., Blanchard and Lea, 1856); Joseph Charles Burke, William Wirt: Attorney General and Constitutional Lawyer (1965) (Ph.D. Dissertation, Ind. Univ.); Joseph C. Robert, *The Honorable William Wirt: The Many–Sided Attorney General*, Y.B. of the Sup. Ct. Hist. Soc'y 51 (1976).

[19] 5 U.S. 137 (1803).

[20] Dred Scott v. Sandford, 60 U.S. 393 (1856).

[21] 21 U.S. 543 (1823).

trilogy, firmly established that in conflicts over the sale of tribal lands, individual citizens did not have purchase rights but instead those rights rested only with the federal government. Prior to this time, Indian policy had remained primarily a matter of treaty negotiation, congressional enactment, military maneuvering, and executive decision-making.[22]

While Wirt contemplated the question of how to get the Cherokee case before the Court, tribal lands were overrun by Georgians who stole horses and cattle, ejected Indians from their homes, and seized their property. Little could be done because Georgia law prohibited Indians from testifying in court proceedings. Finally, after declaring the historic Cherokee Nation to be Cherokee County, Georgia, the state began a lottery to distribute Indian lands to white citizens. At Georgia's request, President Jackson removed federal troops from Indian land and turned all law enforcement, including tribal criminal law, over to the state.[23]

The magnitude of the crisis is demonstrated by a little-discussed but extremely important Georgia murder trial. A Cherokee farmer known as Corn Tassell was accused of killing another Cherokee tribal citizen. Corn Tassell was arrested and tried by Georgia. He was convicted and sentenced to hang. He and all of his Cherokee witnesses were prohibited from giving testimony at his trial. The question was not one of his guilt but rather one of Georgia's authority to enforce her state criminal code within the Cherokee Nation for acts between two Cherokee tribal members. William Wirt saw the Corn Tassell case as his opportunity to get the Cherokee cause before the Supreme Court.[24]

On December 12, 1830, John Marshall sent a Writ of Error ordering the State of Georgia to appear before his court. In response to the court's Writ, Governor George Gilmer sent a message to the Georgia legislature. He proclaimed that "so far as concerns the exercise of the power which belongs to the Executive Department, orders from the Supreme Court ... will be disregarded." The legislature responded with a Resolution setting forth that "his Excellency, the governor, be ... and every other officer of this state, is hereby requested and enjoined to disregard any and every [Supreme Court] mandate." Georgia boldly defied the Writ of Error and hanged Corn Tassel on Christmas eve of 1830.[25]

The Cherokees, the Court and Wirt now faced a challenge to the Rule of Law. Wirt, writing about the preparation of the *Cherokee Nation*

---

[22] *See generally* Francis Paul Prucha, *American Indian Policy in the Formative Years: The Indian Trade and Intercourse Acts, 1790–1834* (Harvard Univ. Press, 1962).

[23] Lumpkin, *supra* note 9.

[24] Marion Starkey, *The Cherokee Nation* 150 (1946); Journal of the House of Representatives of the State of Georgia, 441 (1830).

[25] Starkey, *supra* note 24.

case, remembered that at this time he outlined a number of questions, the answers to which would become the ultimate basis for his arguments in the *Cherokee Cases*. "I took up the question of the right of Georgia to extend her laws over these people, read all the speeches in Congress pro and con on the subject, the opinion of the President ... and gave the whole case a thorough examination." Wirt's lengthy memorandum explored all the possible arguments and evidence. He reviewed all Cherokee treaties, all Indian court cases, the practices of European nations, the international law of civilized states, United States laws and statutes, and the Constitution itself. Wirt had fully developed reasoning and supporting data for his Cherokee case, although he had yet to figure out a way to get the Court to hear it.[26]

All the Law Is Naught

After having completed the extensive memorandum, which formed the basis for all of his subsequent arguments before the Supreme Court and would ultimately provide the backbone for the final opinion of the Court itself in *Worcester*, Wirt was in great frustration, deeply convinced of the right of the cause. He concluded that if the Cherokees could not get the case before the Court, all the law was for naught. Thus, his focus shifted from the law of the case to the question of getting the case heard. Wirt believed he had four choices: a case by consent between Georgia and the Cherokees, a suit by Cherokee Chief John Ross against an officer of Georgia in a lower court, a Writ of Error against a Georgia Court, or a direct appeal to the original jurisdiction of the Supreme Court.[27]

William Wirt wrote directly to Governor Gilmer, suggesting that the state join with the Cherokees in taking a case directly to the Supreme Court. In a long, bitter letter, Gilmer rejected this proposal. "Your suggestion," his reply began, "that it would be convenient and satisfactory, if yourself, the Indians, and the Governor would make up a law case to be submitted to the Supreme Court ... cannot but be considered exceedingly disrespectful to the Government of the State." Gilmer then concluded: "both the letter and spirit of the powers conferred by the Constitution upon the Supreme Court forbid its adjudging such a case."[28] In other words, Georgia rejected outright the Court's authority to intrude on the state's autonomy in managing affairs within its borders, even if some of those affairs related to a people with an independent claim to sovereignty under federal treaties.

[26] Kennedy, *supra* note 18, at 256; William Wirt, *Opinion on the Right of the State of Georgia to Extend Her Law Over the Cherokee Nation*, Cherokee Nation (John F. Wheeler, Printer, 1830); Burke, *supra* note 2.

[27] Wirt, *supra* note 26.

[28] *The Ga. Messenger* (Macon, Georgia) September 4, 1830.

Another way had to be found to get the case before the Court. The idea of a suit by Chief Ross in one of the lower courts in all likelihood was rejected because of the time-consuming nature of such an appeal. In addition, the case would have gone before Associate Justice William Johnson, sitting on circuit, whose opinion almost certainly would have been unfavorable, as it turned out to be in the case which Wirt ultimately brought before the Supreme Court.

More by a process of elimination than anything else, in *Cherokee Nation v. Georgia*, Wirt came to seek original jurisdiction before the Supreme Court for the Cherokees as a foreign state. He had grave doubts that the Supreme Court would accept original jurisdiction, doubts which ultimately would prove to be warranted. We know from surviving correspondence that in preparing his case, Wirt sought legal advice on the jurisdictional question from a number of prominent lawyers, including Ambrose Spenser, Daniel Webster, Horance Binney and James Kent. All of them agreed that the Cherokees had a right to original Supreme Court jurisdiction under the constitutional provisions providing for cases involving foreign states. Wirt would so argue.[29]

Wirt also sought the answer to another question in preparation for the case: What were the general views of the Justices regarding Indian tribes and Indian removal? The fact that it was a very different legal world in the 1830s is reflected in a letter Wirt wrote to Judge Carr, asking him to find out Chief Justice Marshall's stand:

> [T]ell [Marshall] as I wish you to do, that there is no case yet depending which involves a decision on them; but that, unless the opinions of the Supreme Court, as already pronounced, prevent it, there may be questions of a delicate and embarrassing nature to the Supreme Court, which may be prevented by a correct understanding of the full scope of the decisions heretofore pronounced. I would speak to him with the confidence of a friend. . . . and leave it to him to say, whether he would or would not be willing to come out with the expression of his opinion, so as to prevent embarrassment and mischief. I cannot discover that there would be any impropriety either in his saying whether the principles I have mentioned are involved in the former decisions; or, what he may at present, think of these questions.[30]

Justice Marshall did not render a legal opinion to Carr, but he did express his opinion on the broader Indian question. Marshall wrote to Carr that "I have followed the [Removal Act] debate in both houses of Congress with profound attention, and with deep interest, and have

---

[29] Burke, *supra* note 2, at 511.

[30] Kennedy, *supra* note 18, at 258.

wished sincerely, that both the Executive and Legislative departments had thought differently on the subject. Humanity must bewail the course which is pursued, whatever may be the decision of policy." This was particularly encouraging to Wirt, who "knew that the legal decisions of the Chief Justice usually followed his sympathies."[31]

Before the Court in Cherokee Nation

The Court began to hear the case of *Cherokee Nation v. Georgia* on March 5, 1831. Both William Wirt and John Sergeant argued the case on behalf of the Cherokee Nation. Arguments extended over a two-day period. A substantial number of newspaper accounts record and critique their presentations. During this era, court cases were major public attractions, considered entertainment. In fact, both the House and Senate adjourned on these days so that Congress could attend. Sergeant opened the arguments for the tribe and spent more than four-fifths of his time on the question of the original jurisdiction of the Court. His primary arguments were presented in a syllogistic form, as follows:

- The Cherokees are either a state or a foreign nation.

- The Cherokees are not a state.

- Therefore, they are a foreign nation.

Sergeant argued that "the constitution knows of but two descriptions of states—domestic or foreign." The two attorneys divided their presentations into the logical and emotional aspects of the case. Wirt cast his appeals as questions of humanity and justice, a strategy in direct contrast to Sergeant's unemotional approach.[32]

The emotional nature of the arguments and the significance of the occasion were reinforced by the Cherokee delegation seated in the gallery. As one newspaper noted, the Indians looked "intelligent and respectable." Indeed, their deportment added weight to Wirt's argument that the Cherokees were a foreign nation, a sovereign people, not a band of lawless savage Indians. The injustices against the Cherokees that Wirt talked about were brought home by one member of the Indian delegation who "shed tears copiously during Mr. Wirt's address." The other Cherokees who attended cried at almost every important argument supporting

---

[31] Burke, *supra* note 2, at 510.

[32] Excerpts and analysis of the arguments of Wirt and Sergeant are drawn from contemporary newspapers and journals as well as published speeches and opinions. See John Sergeant, *Select Speeches of John Sergeant of Pennsylvania* (1832); *The Case of the Cherokee Nation Against the State of Georgia, Argued and Determined at the Supreme Court of the United States, January Term, 1831.* (Richard Peters ed., 1831) [hereinafter Peters].

their position. The show of tears, observers noted, was moving as well as convenient, for it reinforced the plight of the Cherokees.[33]

In balanced argumentation, Sergeant and Wirt clearly presented the Cherokee case. Georgia, in defense, was equally clear. No counsel for the state appeared. The choice not to appear spoke loudly. The Supreme Court, the state believed, had no jurisdiction over Georgia's internal affairs and Georgia was not bound by any of the Court's decisions. The governor and legislature repeatedly expressed these views. Had Georgia appeared, it would have contradicted this position; the failure to appear supported it. Georgia lost little by not appearing. The Justices were bound to support their own independent interpretation of the Constitution; they would decide in Georgia's favor in any event, as long as they determined that the Court lacked original jurisdiction over the dispute.[34]

The Opinion and an Invitation

As William Wirt feared, the Supreme Court found against the Cherokee Nation. Of the seven Justices, four rejected the Cherokees' jurisdictional position (John Marshall, William Johnson, John McLean, and Henry Baldwin), two upheld the Cherokee position (Smith Thompson and Joseph Story), and one was absent (Gabriel Duvall). In a sense, the Cherokee decision might best be described as a two, two, two split, with Marshall and McLean deciding that the Court did not have original jurisdiction but that the Cherokees were entities with specific rights. Those rights and the definitions of tribal nations were the most significant aspects of the opinions and remain crucial in interpreting American Indian law. Baldwin and Johnson decided that the Cherokee were not a state and had very few, if any, rights. Story and Thompson, on the other hand, decided that the Cherokees were entitled to original jurisdiction as a foreign state with independent legal and political rights. In another, broader sense, the court split might also be seen as a four to two decision, affirming Indian rights but denying the tribe the right to present its case before the Court. Justice Story later recalled that the dissenting opinion was penned at the suggestion of Chief Justice Marshall himself.[35]

Three opinions were delivered in the courtroom on the day the decision was rendered. Marshall read first, speaking for the majority. This opinion, in which he found against the Cherokees on original jurisdiction, was far from discouraging. "Their argument," Marshall concluded, "as intended to prove the character of the Cherokees as a

---

[33] *Boston Patriot*, March 23, 1831.

[34] For a more detailed analysis of the Georgia strategy, see Lumpkin, *supra* note 9.

[35] James McClellan, *Joseph Story and the American Constitution* 299 n. 115 (1971).

state, as a distinct political society, separated from others, capable of managing its own affairs and governing itself, has, in the opinion of a majority of the judges, been completely successful." Marshall even encouraged the tribe to find another case: "The mere question of right might perhaps be decided by this Court in a case with proper parties." Justices Baldwin and Johnson cast their opinion as a defense of Georgia's claim to sovereignty over Indian land. Their opinion was, in effect, an apology for Georgia's actions. The strongly pro-Cherokee opinion of Thompson was inserted into the proceedings although he did not deliver it in court. His opinion mirrored the exact arguments of Wirt and Sergeant. Richard Peters, the court reporter, included his opinion in the official report of the Court, although written and submitted at a later date. Peters also printed a separate volume on the case including a pro-Cherokee legal memorandum written by James Kent, treaties with the Cherokees, the Georgia Indian law, and federal statutes, as well as all of the Justices' opinions.[36]

Wirt had always been concerned about the jurisdictional question. Shortly before the arguments, he had written his wife expressing these concerns: "I feel rather despondent about my poor Indians," he noted, "not that I have the slightest doubt of the justice of these claims on the United States, but that I fear the Supreme Court may differ with me as to the extent of their jurisdiction over the subject."[37] Now that the Court had confirmed his fear, he was in a difficult position. The Cherokees had what amounted to an open invitation from the Chief Justice, encouraging them to find another case, and even hinting at the possibility of a positive outcome "in a proper case with proper parties." Now the task was to find the proper party to bring the case.

Finding the Proper Party

The arrest and conviction of Samuel A. Worcester, an American Board of Foreign Missions translator and missionary, gave the Cherokee Nation the case it hoped would support and protect tribal rights.[38] There was no longer a question of jurisdiction. The case, which proved to be suitable, came about as a result of a Georgia statute passed on December 22, 1830. The law required all white people residing in the Indian Territory within Georgia's boundaries after February 1, 1831 to obtain a

---

[36] Peters, *supra* note 32.

[37] Letter from Samuel Worcester (February 10, 1831), cited in Burke, *supra* note 2, at 251.

[38] The major biography of Samuel Worcester, based primarily on journals, diaries and letters, is Althea Bass, *Cherokee Messenger* (1936). The papers (The Worcester/Robinson Archives), including his prison journals, are on file at the McFarlin Library of the University of Tulsa.

license and swear allegiance to the state. A group of missionaries, including Samuel A. Worcester, not only failed to secure a license but also published a statement supporting the Cherokees. They openly defied Georgia law. They were warned to leave the tribal territory but refused and were arrested in March 1831 by the Georgia State Guard. At first, they were released because they were found to be Postmaster employees of the federal government and thus entitled to reside without a state permit among the Indians. President Jackson then removed Worcester as Postmaster of New Echota, and sent a letter to Governor Gilmer declaring that the ministers were no longer federal officials. The missionaries were then rearrested, convicted, and sentenced on September 15, 1831 to four years of hard labor. They were offered pardons if they agreed to leave the Indian Territory or if they obtained a license from the State of Georgia. All the missionaries agreed, save Samuel Worcester and Elizur Butler.[39]

In Samuel Worcester, the Cherokees could have found neither a better plaintiff nor a more loyal spokesperson. He was as articulate as he was determined, and the press took to his cause, which came to symbolize the power of a giant state oppressing an individual standing on moral principle in defense of the wronged. Worcester's long letters from the Milledgeville jail were reprinted in *The Cherokee Phoenix* and received wider circulation in other papers and missionary circles as well. These accounts are all the more meaningful because they are simple, factual, and dispassionate reports of the border-ruffian brutality of arrest, transportation out of the Cherokee Nation, and imprisonment at Milledgeville. Northern audiences were inflamed by incidents involving these conscientious objectors whose only civil disobedience was their refusal to sign a Georgia state loyalty oath. Worcester reported in one of his letters of the harsh treatment of his codefendant and fellow missionary Elizur Butler.[40]

The press reprinted and embellished the many stories of the missionaries' suffering. One story which Worcester felt compelled to deny was that the Georgia authorities had forced them "to aid in the construction of the lottery wheels, by means of which the land and gold mines of the Cherokees are distributed." Worcester and Butler did, however, do woodwork during their imprisonment, making a wood chest and a set of geometric shapes which have survived as evidence of their Puritan determination to fight the boredom of their long days and nights in a Georgia jail with constructive activity.[41]

---

[39] A thoughtful history of Native American church work is found in William G. McLoughlin, *Cherokees and Missionaries, 1789–1839* (1984).

[40] Letter from Samuel Worcester, *supra* note 37.

[41] *See* Samuel A. Worcester, *New Echota Letters: Contributions of Samuel A. Worcester to the Cherokee Phoenix* (Jack Kilpatrick & Anna Greta Kilpatrick eds., 1968). The

Once Again, Before the Court in Worcester

The American Board of Foreign Ministers hired Sergeant and Wirt to represent the missionaries imprisoned by the State of Georgia. The attorneys obtained a Writ of Error from the Supreme Court on October 27, 1831. The Writ was received by Georgia's newly-elected governor, Wilson Lumpkin. He responded to the Georgia legislature with the same message: "I will disregard all unconstitutional requisitions, of whatever character or origin they may be."[42] The legislature responded "that the State of Georgia will not compromit [sic] her dignity as a sovereign state, or so far yield her rights as a member of the Confederacy as to appear in answer to, or in any way become a party to any proceedings before the Supreme Court having for their object a revival or interference with the decisions of the state courts in criminal matters."[43]

The arguments in *Worcester v. Georgia* began on February 20, 1832, with Wirt setting forth the jurisdictional basis of this suit between a state and a citizen of another state. The court raised no question of jurisdiction and moved directly to the merits of the case. Wirt and Sergeant appeared for the missionaries; no one appeared for Georgia. The arguments and supporting evidence were essentially the same as in the earlier *Cherokee Nation* case. They were primarily drawn from that first memorandum that Wirt had written about the tribal rights of Indian people. Sergeant and Wirt's principal argument, repeated often and with many sources of support, was simply: "That the statute of Georgia under which the plaintiffs in error were indicted and convicted, was unconstitutional and void." The actions of the Cherokees and their friends were legal in the face of laws that "violated the Constitution, laws, and treaties of the United States." Again, Sergeant presented the logical, reasoned approach and Wirt a more emotional one. Indeed, Wirt's concluding argument was so moving that Chief Justice Marshall shed tears, something he had not done since the *Dartmouth College*[44] case.[45]

Again, while Wirt and Sergeant spoke logically and eloquently, Georgia did not speak. This time, however, Justice Marshall and the Court ruled in favor of the missionaries and their Cherokee friends. In

woodworks are found at the Five Civilized Tribes Museum and the University of Tulsa McFarlin Library.

[42] Lumpkin, *supra* note 9.

[43] *The Removal of the Cherokee Indians From Georgia,* Course Materials, N. Y. Univ. Law Ctr., Section 45, Part 4, (John Reid ed., n.d.).

[44] Trustees of Dartmouth College v. Woodward, 17 U.S. 518 (1819).

[45] A contemporary report is found at *N.Y. Daily Advertiser*, February 27, 1832; Burke, *supra* note 18, at 261.

what has become the most crucial and frequently cited case in American Indian law, Marshall found that Georgia had no right to extend her laws over the Cherokee Nation. The Chief Justice concluded: "The judgment ... condemning Samuel A. Worcester to hard labour in the penitentiary of the state of Georgia, for four years, was pronounced by that [Georgia] court under colour of a law which is void, as being repugnant to the Constitution, treaties, and laws of the United States, and ought, therefore, to be reversed and annulled."[46] The court thus decided in favor of the missionaries, upholding the constitutional rights of the Cherokees. Marshall spoke for the five to one majority in what has been applauded as one of his "most courageous opinions." Marshall was rendering the decision he wished he could have delivered in *Cherokee Nation*. Justice McLean also delivered an opinion supporting the missionaries although he felt the Indian rights to be temporary and thought the best policy might be removal. Justice Johnson was absent, and quite likely would have dissented. Justice Baldwin did dissent.[47] Justice Johnson's dissent followed the Georgia position that the state had the right to control land within its borders and that Worcester was being legally restrained.

Marshall constructed the opinion primarily from the arguments of Wirt as outlined in the original memorandum and as submitted in materials to the court. The *Worcester* opinion is a long and complex review of the history of Indian policy and Indian-white relations from initial contact to the present. Marshall's historic words still govern much of contemporary Native American life and policy, especially in informing tribal-state relationships. As Marshall concludes:

> The Cherokee nation, then, is a distinct community, occupying its own territory, with boundaries accurately described, in which the laws of Georgia can have no force, and which the citizens of Georgia have no right to enter, but with the assent of the Cherokees themselves, or in conformity with treaties and with the acts of congress. The whole intercourse between the United States and this nation is, by our constitution and laws, vested in the government of the United States.[48]

---

[46] *Worcester*, 31 U.S. (6 Pet.), at 561–63.

[47] For a detailed review, see sources cited *supra* note 2.

[48] *Worcester*, 31 U.S. (6 Pet.), at 561. This is perhaps the most quoted language from *Worcester*, used to define the relationships between Indian tribes, the states and the federal government. For a broader view of the unfolding policy emerging from these cases and the historic struggle for tribal sovereignty, see Rennard Strickland, *The Eagle's Empire: Sovereignty, Survival and Self–Governance in Native Law and Constitutionalism, in Studying Native America: Problems and Prospects* 247 (Soc. Sci. Res. Council, Russell Thornton eds., 1998).

Marshall's Law, Jackson's Response, and the Indian Dilemma

The events following the Supreme Court decision in *Worcester* remain in the hearts and minds of all Cherokee people. It is these stories, climaxing in the Trail of Tears and a bloody and long-lasting tribal civil war, that I remember my father telling. Cherokees were rounded up from their homes and driven to stockades to await the military guards assigned to accompany them as they were removed from their historic homeland and sent under armed guard west of the Mississippi to the new Indian Territory. To this day, it is said that every Cherokee knows where his or her ancestral family stood in addressing the difficult questions growing from the failure to honor the Cherokee victory before the Supreme Court. For, in truth, the ultimate, pragmatic victory belonged to Georgia and to President Jackson. This is the case in which Jackson is purported to have issued his famous challenge to the judiciary—"Marshall has made his law, let him enforce it."[49] Marshall had the law; Jackson had the troops. In historical perspective, it is as if President Eisenhower had sent federal troops into Little Rock to support Governor Faubus *against* the Supreme Court decision in *Brown v. Board of Education.*[50]

Georgia, as expected, refused even to acknowledge the Supreme Court's decision and kept the missionaries in jail. Cries of "Force Georgia" were heard all over the North. Jackson once again was called upon to support the Court. He refused. In reality, Jackson could not have enforced the decision even if he had wanted to: the Court could not have issued a writ of habeas corpus until its 1833 term, and since "the Georgia court never put its refusal in writing, it is arguable that the Supreme Court could not have awarded execution" even in its next term. The Cherokees recognized Jackson's reluctance to honor the Supreme Court's *Worcester* decision. Cherokee leader John Ridge warned his countrymen:

> [T]he Chicken Snake General Jackson has time to crawl and hide in the luxuriant grass of his nefarious hypocrisy until his responsibility is fastened upon by an execution of the Supreme Court at their next session. Now before the explained laws are carried into effect, it will, I fear, first be necessary to cut down this Snake's head and throw it down in the dust.[51]

---

[49] See discussion, *supra* note 4, and accompanying text.

[50] 347 U.S. 483 (1954). For a review of the *Cherokee Cases* in the context of the modern Court, see Rennard Strickland & William M. Strickland, *A Tale of Two Marshalls: Reflections on Indian Law and Policy, The Cherokee Cases, and the Cruel Irony of Supreme Court Victories,* 47 Okla. L. Rev. 111 (1944).

[51] *Cherokee Cavaliers: Forty Years of Cherokee History as Told in the Correspondence of the Ridge–Watie Boudinot Family* 8 (Edward Everett Dale & Gaston Litton eds., 1939) [hereinafter *Cherokee Cavaliers*].

Meanwhile, Georgia refused to free the missionaries, who remained locked in their cells in the Milledgeville penitentiary. On March 13, 1832, the *Macon Advertiser* summarized the post-*Worcester* legal battle:

> They [the missionaries] have been placed where they deserved to be, in the State Prison, and not all the eloquence of a Wirt, or a Sergeant, nor the decision or power of the Supreme Court can take them from it unless the State chooses to give them up, which, at this time is very improbable.[52]

Worcester wrote to the American Board of Foreign Missions, asking their advice on the proper course of action. On Christmas Day of 1832, the Board met in Pemberton Square in Boston to decide its position. The letter from Worcester was read and the Court's decision reviewed. Each person present gave his opinion. The Board's ultimate conclusion was that "Worcester and Butler might now honorably seek a pardon," and that the Cherokees must be advised that there was no longer any hope of resistance to removal. Worcester and Butler had been informed that as soon as they petitioned Georgia, they would be released from prison. After hearing of the Christmas Day decision, the missionaries applied for pardons. Worcester and Butler wrote to Governor Lumpkin on January 8, 1833: "We have this day forwarded instructions to our counsel to forbear the intended motion, and to prosecute the case no farther." On January 15th, the prisoners headed home to their mission in the Cherokee Nation. For Worcester, as well as the Cherokees, the judicial process had proven useless in the protection of their rights.[53] In justifying the decision to seek pardons, Worcester and Butler described the futility of their efforts to challenge Georgia's law in a letter to the *Missionary Herald*.

> There was no longer any hope, by our perseverance of securing the rights of the Cherokees, or preserving the faith of our country. The Supreme Court had given a decision in our favor, which recognized the rights of the Cherokees; but it still rested with the Executive Government, whether those rights should be protected, and it had become certain that the Executive would not protect them.[54]

After the debacle following the fleeting formal victory in *Worcester*, Cherokee unity in fighting Georgia's usurpations ended, and two tribal political factions emerged. One argued that the tribe should remove immediately. The other continued to believe that the American people would follow the dictates of their highest court. In truth, the tribe faced

---

[52] *Macon Advertiser* (Macon, Georgia), March 13, 1832.

[53] *The Missionary Herald, reprinted in* Starkey, *supra* note 24, at 205.

[54] Letter from Samuel Worcester, *supra* note 37.

the classic Indian dilemma: the Indian could not win. If the tribe signed the removal treaty, they would surrender their homelands and the graves of their beloved ancestors; if the tribe refused to sign, they would be driven at bayonet point away from their homelands and the graves of their beloved ancestors. The choice was no choice.[55]

Jackson's election to a second term suggested that removal was inevitable. The faction led by Major John Ridge feared that delays by the Cherokees would bring a forced military exile. Ridge and his followers urged the tribe to sign a treaty of peaceable removal to avoid this agonizing hardship. The conflict over removal climaxed in 1835 when a group of Cherokees signed the Treaty of New Echota,[56] exchanging their lands in Georgia for lands in the Indian Territory. Their political opposition, including elected Chief John Ross, characterized signing the treaty as "treason" and threatened death under a tribal law authored by Major Ridge himself. The provision made the sale of lands a crime of "outlawry" and placed the signatory beyond the protection of the law and subject to execution. The federal government solemnly guaranteed the safety of those who endorsed the treaty, but as Major Ridge said, "When I signed the treaty, I knew I had signed my death warrant. I looked into my open grave."[57]

In fact, military exile was the ultimate result of defiance. In 1836 and 1837, the Treaty Party faction under Major Ridge moved peacefully to what is now known as Oklahoma. With that body of Cherokees came Samuel A. Worcester, his family and others in the mission community. The Ross party held out. After the Treaty of New Echota was ratified by only one vote, the remaining sixteen-thousand tribal members were driven over the Trail of Tears in 1838 and 1839. Four thousand of those members died in this forced removal. The contrast between Ross's ragged and starving new arrivals and their fellow tribesmen, already prosperously settled into the new nation, graphically exposed party differences and revived bitter hostilities. Thus, as the Cherokee Nation prepared for a constitutional convention in the summer of 1839, the

---

[55] See generally Thurman Wilkins, Cherokee Tragedy: The Story of the Ridge Family and the Decimation of a People (1970); Morris Wardell, A Political History of the Cherokee Nation, 1838–1907 (1938); Theda Perdue, The Conflict Within: The Cherokee Power Structure and Removal, 73 Ga. Hist. Q. 465 (Fall 1989).

[56] Treaty with the Cherokee, U.S.-Cherokee, Dec. 29, 1835, 7 Stat. 478.

[57] For a three-generational impact, see the discussion from the perspective of grandson John Rollin Ridge, who was the first Native American lawyer admitted to practice law in a state jurisdiction, in Rennard Strickland, Yellow Bird's Song: The Dilemma of an Indian Lawyer and Poet, in Tonto's Revenge: Reflections on Indian Culture and Policy 1–15 (Univ. of N.M. Press, 1997).

leadership of the Ridge Treaty Party was killed by a group of masked men from the Ross party.[58]

Like the thousands of their fellow tribesmen who perished along the trail, many of the leaders of the Treaty Party paid for their response to the dilemma with their lives. They were executed, or assassinated, depending upon your political perspective, pursuant to the outlawry provisions of tribal law. Major Ridge had himself been an executioner in an earlier incident when Doublehead, who had sold tribal lands, suffered a similar fate. But an even crueler irony made Samuel Worcester witness to the loss of his valued Cherokee assistant and translator Elias Boudinot. On the morning of June 22nd, Boudinot was working at Worcester's Park Hill Mission when some Cherokee assassins came for him. Worcester's description of Boudinot's murder provides a haunting climax to this story of the Cherokee cases and deeper insight into the universal Indian dilemma.[59]

> Mr. Boudinot was yet living at my house. On Saturday morning he went to his house which he was building a quarter mile distant. There some Cherokee men came up inquiring for medicine, and Mr. Boudinot set out with two of them to get it. He had walked but a few rods when his shriek was heard by his hired men, who ran to his help; but before they could come the deed was done. A stab in the back with a knife, and seven gashes in the head with a hatchet, did the bloody work.... The murderers ran a short distance in the woods, joined a company of armed men on horse back, and made their escape.... He had fallen victim to his honest ... zeal for the preservation of his people. In his own view, he risked his life to save his people from ruin, and he realized his fears.[60]

Conclusion

We began this story from the perspective of the Cherokee Nation, exploring tribal attitudes and responses. We observed that the shadow of the Cherokee cases and the subsequent death of one-quarter of the tribal population on the Trail of Tears still darkens modern Native life and helps define the Cherokee sense of self. Let us conclude with an observation from quite a different perspective. The great French social observer Alexis de Tocqueville traveled throughout the United States during much of the removal controversy and the subsequent military force.

---

[58] Strickland, *supra* note 57, at 1–15. Rollin Ridge describes the execution of his grandfather from his remembrances as a twelve-year old eyewitness.

[59] For a broader perspective on Elias Boudinot, see Elias Boudinot, *Cherokee Editor: The Writings of Elias Boudinot* (Theda Perdue ed., 1983), and Ralph H. Gabriel, *Elias Boudinot, Cherokee and His America* (1941).

[60] Letter from Samuel Worcester to D. Greene (June 26, 1839), reprinted in *Cherokee Cavaliers, supra* note 51, at 177–78.

Indeed, he personally observed a group of Choctaws being loaded onto a riverboat to be shipped to the Indian Territory. This philosopher, aware as he was of much of what we have reviewed in this chapter, coldly set forth the American attitude and the cases and policy behind it in his evaluation of the United States treatment of Native peoples—a policy deeply rooted and continued through the *Cherokee Cases*. In his perceptive analysis of these events, de Tocqueville concluded:

> The Spaniards pursued the Indians with bloodhounds, like wild beasts; they sacked the New World like a city taken by storm, with no discernment or compassion; but destruction must cease at last and frenzy has a limit.... The conduct of the Americans of the United States toward the aboriginals is characterized, on the other hand, by a singular attachment to the formalities of law. The Spaniards were unable to exterminate the Indian race by those unparalled atrocities which brand them with indelible shame ... but the Americans of the United States have accomplished this ... purpose with singular felicity, tranquility, legally, philanthropically, without shedding blood, and without violating a single great principle of morality in the eyes of the world. It is impossible to destroy men with more respect for the laws of humanity.[61]

We have seen through the *Cherokee Cases* the failure of American constitutionalism and the operation of what contemporary scholars have come to call "Conquest by Law" or "Genocide at Law."[62] A careful review of the stories of *Cherokee Nation v. Georgia* and *Worcester v. Georgia* provides ample proof of what the Cherokees' storytellers have maintained since that era: Law is a double-edged sword whose blade always seems ready to find and cut away at the soft spots of Indian Nationhood. And yet, the Cherokees and other Indians continue to play within the white man's law because, for many purposes, the courts are the only game in town.[63]

*

---

[61] Alexis de Tocqueville, *Democracy In America* (Harry Reeve trans., as rev. by Francis Bowen, 1945), 1, 350, 354–55.

[62] *See, e.g.*, Strickland, *supra* note 12.

[63] *See* Robertson, *supra* note 2; *see also* Strickland, *supra* note 12.

2

Ronald S. Sullivan Jr.

Classical Racialism, Justice Story, and Margaret Morgan's Journey from Freedom to Slavery: The Story of *Prigg v. Pennsylvania*

Introduction

Most readers will not recognize the name Margaret Morgan. She held no public office; she performed no grand public service; her name is not enshrined on any statues or memorials. No public encomia record her life's work for posterity. Instead, for the most part, Margaret Morgan led an ordinary life. After growing up on a Maryland farm with her mother and father, in her late teenage years she met and married a young man and moved away from the family home. In time, Morgan and her new husband relocated to Pennsylvania, bought a home, and raised several children together.[1] Indeed, Margaret Morgan might have been the type of person Ralph Waldo Emerson described as among the common lot—an ordinary citizen who is central to the well being of the American democratic experience.[2]

---

[1] Joseph Nogee, *The* Prigg *Case and Fugitive Slavery, 1842–1850: Part I*, 39 J. Negro Hist. 185 (1954).

[2] *See* Ralph Waldo Emerson, *The American Scholar, in The Essential Writings of Ralph Waldo Emerson* 43, 43–64 (Brooks Atkinson ed., 2002). *See also* Jane Addams, *Democracy and Social Ethics* 9 (2002).

However, Margaret Morgan's story is far from ordinary: It is the story of *Prigg v. Pennsylvania*[3]—the first, and one of the most important, Supreme Court pronouncements on slavery.[4] Notwithstanding her quotidian accoutrements, Margaret Morgan was, as a formal legal matter, a Negro woman with "no rights which the white man was bound to respect...."[5] Although she had lived most of her life in de facto freedom, married a "free Negro," and moved with him to the free state of Pennsylvania, Morgan and her offspring were nonetheless subject to the whimsy of brute kidnappers. And so it was in 1837 that a lawyer, Edward Prigg, directed the abduction of Morgan and her children—forcibly moving them from Pennsylvania to Maryland, a slave-holding state—and thus consigned them to a life of slavery.[6]

Justice Story's holding in *Prigg* was controversial to say the least. First announcing that states had no authority to regulate the practices of slave catchers within their borders,[7] he then articulated a broad, unqualified common law right to reclaim runaway slaves—a right that was not subject to any regulatory authority or any form of process. The *Prigg* holding effectively facilitated the wholesale removal of blacks (many of whom were legally emancipated) to slave-holding states with little, if any, meaningful protections.[8] As a result, abolitionists regarded this decision as rabidly pro-slavery.

Even more controversial than the decision itself was the fact that it was authored by Justice Joseph Story, long thought to be a strong anti-slavery advocate.[9] Over the years, scholars have attempted to reconcile Justice Story's presumed anti-slavery ideals with his decidedly pro-slavery opinion in *Prigg*. This debate has largely been framed in terms of a wrenching conflict between Justice Story's moral disapprobation of slavery and his fealty to the rule of law, his role as a Justice, and principles of federalism.[10] But this putative moral-formal conflict may be

---

[3] 41 U.S. (16 Pet.) 539 (1842).

[4] Along with *Prigg*, Dred Scott v. Sandford, 60 U.S. (19 How.) 393 (1856), and Ableman v. Booth, 62 U.S. (21 How.) 506 (1858) are commonly regarded as the three most important slavery cases decided by the Court. *See* Robert M. Cover, *Justice Accused* 166 (1975).

[5] *Dred Scott*, 60 U.S. (19 How.) at 407.

[6] Nogee, *supra* note 1, at 185, 190.

[7] *Prigg*, 41 U.S. (16 Pet.) at 622–26.

[8] Because *Prigg* construed the Fugitive Slave Act as precluding any process outside of its ministerial process, many lawfully emancipated blacks were captured and placed in slavery pursuant to the Act. *See* Nogee, *supra* note 1, at 195, 198.

[9] *Id.* at 194. *See also* R. Kent Newmyer, *Supreme Court Justice Joseph Story: Statesman of the Old Republic* 346–58 (1985). *But see*, Barbara Holden–Smith, *Lords of Lash, Loom, and Law: Justice Story, Slavery, and* Prigg v. Pennsylvania, 78 Cornell L. Rev. 1086, 1116 (arguing that Justice Story's anti-slavery reputation is "exaggerated").

[10] Cover, *supra* note 4, at 238–43.

insufficiently descriptive. The aim of this chapter is to examine the traditional narratives that purport to explain *Prigg* and to suggest a new theoretical lens through which to understand the holding.

Prigg is best understood in light of its broad socio-philosophical context. The decision was issued at the height of "classical racialism"[11]—an essentialist theory of race that originated in the late eighteenth century. Under this theory, "races" are conceived of as distinct types (rather than biological variations) manifesting specific, genetically-linked character traits. These traits, in turn, are used to rationalize the race-based anti-egalitarian distribution of societal burdens and benefits.[12] Classical racialism naturalized social differences: non-whites were inferior as a result of their genes. "It's in the blood," the argument ran. This "natural" condition was used to justify the wholesale political, economic, social, and, for some, physical subordination of non-whites.[13]

Contrary to the claim that Justice Story faced a profound moral-formal conflict in *Prigg*, like many educated elites of his time, he was actually morally ambivalent on the issue of slavery. This ambivalence was animated by the norms of classical racialism. Rather than wrestling with a strong conviction that slavery was unjust, Justice Story simply weighed strong nationalistic values against his morally ambivalent stance on the legal subordination of blacks.

Margaret Morgan: From Freedom to Slavery

Neither history nor Justice Story's *Prigg* opinion records much of Margaret Morgan's life story. This should come as no surprise if Justice Story viewed Morgan as the personification of a stereotype rather than a person worthy of individual moral consideration.[14] Notwithstanding the dearth of historical record, a picture of Morgan's life and experience can be cobbled together from various sources. We know, for example, that Morgan's parents were a married couple owned by slaveholder John Ashmore.[15] Although Ashmore never formally emancipated Morgan's parents, he allowed them to build a home and live in freedom on his

---

[11] I borrow the term "classical racialism" from philosopher Paul C. Taylor whose recent book on the philosophy of race gives a remarkably clear, non-tendentious, and thorough philosophical analysis of race. Paul C. Taylor, *Race: A Philosophical Introduction* 43–47 (2004).

[12] *Id*. at 43–48.

[13] *Id*.

[14] *Id*. at 34.

[15] Thomas C. Hambly, Argument of Mr. Hambly, of York (Pa.) in the Case of Edward Prigg (1842), *reprinted in* 1 *Fugitive Slaves and American Courts: The Pamphlet Literature* 128 (Paul Finkelman ed., 1988).

Maryland estate.[16] As a result, Morgan grew up with the species of freedom that emancipated blacks experienced in the early nineteenth century.

At this point, however, the historical record gets fuzzy. Sometime after Ashmore died in 1824, then-Margaret Ashmore married Jerry Morgan, an emancipated black man from Pennsylvania.[17] The couple initially lived in Maryland but moved to Lower Chanceford Township, York County, Pennsylvania in 1832.[18] The couple had six children, some of whom were born in Maryland, a slave-holding state, while others were born in Pennsylvania, a free state.[19] The Morgans lived in Pennsylvania without incident until 1837, when Edward Prigg, Jacob Forward, Stephen Lewis, Jr., and Nathan Bemis seized Margaret Morgan and her six children, thus beginning their journey from freedom to slavery.[20]

The seizure was based on a claim of ownership made by Nathan S. Bemis, who was married to Susanna Ashmore Bemis, John Ashmore's daughter.[21] Three years before Ashmore died, he sold his considerable real estate interests to Susanna for a nominal price,[22] and upon Ashmore's death, his remaining personalty, including slaves, passed to his wife.[23] Significantly, Ashmore's will indicated that he owned "two slave boys, Tommy, age 12, and James, age 11," but the will failed to mention

---

[16] Holden–Smith, *supra* note 9, at 1122. Ashmore, himself, regularly proclaimed that he had freed Morgan's parents. *See* Hambly, *supra* note 15, at 128.

[17] Holden–Smith, *supra* note 9, at 1122. *See also* Paul Finkelman, *Story Telling on the Supreme Court:* Prigg v. Pennsylvania *and Justice Joseph Story's Judicial Nationalism*, 1994 Sup. Ct. Rev. 247, 275.

[18] Finkelman, *supra* note 17, at 275.

[19] *Id.* It is not clear how many children Morgan had in Maryland and Pennsylvania. The historical evidence, however, allows us to make some inferences. The 1830 U.S. Census for Harford County, Maryland records that the Morgan family consisted of Jerry and Margaret, plus two "free black" children. *Id.* (quoting Manuscript Census for Harford County, Maryland, U.S. Census 394 (1830)). The constraints of biology suggest that it is unlikely (though technically possible) that Morgan had four children between 1830 and 1832. The special verdict of the Pennsylvania trial court, however, found that only one of Morgan's children was born in Pennsylvania. Prigg v. Pennsylvania, 41 U.S. (16 Pet.) 539, 609 (1842). While this finding is physiologically possible, other accounts suggesting that Morgan had more than one child in Pennsylvania seem more accurate. *See, e.g.*, Finkelman, *supra* note 17, at 274 (citing *Prigg* oral arguments in which Morgan's counsel stated that Morgan had "several" children born in Pennsylvania).

[20] *See* Finkelman, *supra* note 17, at 276.

[21] *Id.* at 275. (citing Deed of Conveyance from John Ashmore to Susanna Bemis, May 11, 1821 (on file with Harford County Historical Society)).

[22] Finkelman, *supra* note 17, at 275.

[23] *Id.*

either Morgan or her parents.[24] Morgan, accordingly, had at least three good defenses against Bemis's ownership claim. First, if Morgan was neither sold to Susanna Bemis, nor devised to Ashmore's wife, then the Ashmore family had no cognizable property interest in Morgan. Second, Morgan had a credible argument that Bemis did not have standing to initiate a removal proceeding against either her or her children. Even if the Morgans were fugitive slaves,[25] they were the property of Ashmore's widow, not Nathan and Susanna Bemis. Third, the fact that some of Morgan's children indisputably were born in Pennsylvania should have persuaded the court that those particular children were free and therefore not subject to seizure under the Fugitive Slave Act.[26] Justice Story, however, glossed over these facts, disregarded extant principles of antebellum federalism, and penned a far-reaching decision that granted an unqualified right of recaption to slave catchers.[27]

As for Margaret Morgan and her children, history does not provide a clear record of their fate. By one account, the Morgans were eventually taken to John Ashmore's widow and enslaved.[28] By another account, the family was sold to slave owners unrelated to the Ashmores.[29] Still other accounts simply lose track of the Morgans after the courts formally declared them slaves and they were transported to Maryland.[30] But whichever version is accurate, it is clear that Morgan and her children were suddenly thrust into a life of slavery. Indeed, it must have been nothing short of Kafkaesque for Margaret Morgan and her children to go to sleep one evening as free people, only to awaken the next morning as chattel.

The Fugitive Slave Act and Justice Story's Decision

The *Prigg* court resolved the issue of whether states had any authority to regulate the removal of alleged runaway slaves within their borders. According to Justice Story's reading of the Fugitive Slave Act,

---

[24] *Id.* (citing John Ashmore Inventory, No. 1672, Sept. 28, 1824 (on file with Harford County, Register of Wills)).

[25] *See infra* notes 79–82 and accompanying text for additional arguments that Morgan was free as a matter of law.

[26] Act of Feb. 12, 1793, ch. 7, 1 Stat. 302 (1793). I shall hereinafter refer to this Act as either the Fugitive Slave Act of 1793 or the Fugitive Slave Act. *See also infra* note 83 and accompanying text.

[27] Prigg v. Pennsylvania, 41 U.S. (16 Pet.) 539 (1842).

[28] Allen Johnson, *The Constitutionality of the Fugitive Slave Acts*, 31 Yale L.J. 161, 166 (1921).

[29] Holden–Smith, *supra* note 9, at 1123.

[30] *Id.*

the federal government alone had the power to regulate the recapture of runaways.[31] In this sense, the decision evinced a profoundly nationalistic jurisprudence that, in consequence, facilitated both the unencumbered reclamation of runaway slaves and the unfettered kidnapping of free blacks. A brief history of the runaway slave debate will explain why this is so.

Since at least 1629, the North and South had been at loggerheads over the interstate regulation of runaway slaves.[32] The Constitution, once ratified, did not provide much guidance. The so-called Fugitive Slave Clause (which never actually used the word "slave") simply declared that "No Person held to Service or Labour in one State" and who escapes to another state shall be "discharged from such Service or Labour, but shall be delivered up on Claim of the Party to whom such Service or Labour may be due."[33] The Clause did not define what constitutes a sufficient "claim" by setting forth the evidence minimally required to demonstrate that a person was "held to service" in a slave-holding state and the process by which such a person should be "delivered up."

In 1793 Congress passed the Fugitive Slave Act to answer these questions, but the Act proved to be nearly as deficient as the Clause.[34] For one thing, the Act was largely ministerial, requiring almost no process.[35] It merely required the person claiming ownership to request a "certificate of removal" by bringing the arrestee before a judicial officer.[36] If granted, the certificate authorized the transportation of the alleged runaway. The proceeding was summary in nature and required little more than proof that the person in custody was the one named in

---

[31] *Prigg*, 41 U.S. (16 Pet.) at 622.

[32] Holden–Smith, *supra* note 9, at 1116 & n.176 ("The earliest regulation is probably that found among the freedoms and exemptions granted by the West India Company in 1629 to the settlers of the colonies of New Netherlands.").

[33] U.S. Const. art. IV, § 2, cl. 3.

[34] Holden–Smith, *supra* note 9, at 1087. Interestingly, like *Prigg*, the Fugitive Slave Act grew out of a dispute between Pennsylvania and a bordering slave-holding state, Virginia, regarding an alleged runaway slave. Three slave catchers, acting under the authority of the Fugitive Slave Clause, were indicted in Pennsylvania for violating a 1788 Pennsylvania law that proscribed "selling and disposing" black people as slaves, but the governor of Virginia refused to extradite the slave catchers. Pennsylvania and Virginia referred their dispute to President George Washington, who, in turn, referred the matter to Congress. Congress resolved the matter by promulgating the Fugitive Slave Act of 1793. *See* Holden–Smith, *supra* note 9, at 1116–17; *see also Prigg*, 41 U.S. (16 Pet.) at 539, 566–67.

[35] Act of Feb. 12, 1793, ch. 7, 1 Stat. 302 (1793).

[36] *Id.* § 3.

the warrant.[37] Additionally, nothing in the Fugitive Slave Act explicitly authorized the judicial officer to adjudicate an alleged runaway's claim that the slave owner did not have the legal right of reclamation.[38] Although the Act nowhere prevented courts from assessing the merits of the ownership claim, judges generally limited their role to a perfunctory review of the sworn testimony of the claimant or his agent as sufficient proof of ownership.[39]

The deficiencies in the Act actually facilitated the kidnapping of free blacks. Often, slave traders would knowingly target free blacks and then submit forged affidavits to the court.[40] A slave catcher merely had to aver that a black person was a runaway, and a judicial officer, history demonstrates, nearly always issued a certificate of removal.[41] Significantly, once a certificate was issued, it "served as conclusive proof against any claim to freedom by the captured person."[42]

In order to stem the tide of slave catchers kidnapping free blacks and selling them into slavery, some Northern states enacted so-called personal liberty laws to provide procedural protections for blacks who claimed they were emancipated. Accordingly, Pennsylvania enacted "An Act to Prevent Kidnapping" in 1820.[43] This anti-kidnapping law, in pertinent part, limited the class of state judicial officers authorized to issue certificates of removal. Moreover, the law required slave catchers to obtain an arrest warrant from a judicial officer *before* seizing the alleged runaway. Following seizure the slave catcher was required to bring the alleged fugitive before the same judicial officer who issued the warrant in order to seek a certificate of removal.[44] The aim of this legislation was to decrease the incidence of collusion between low-level, state judicial officers and slave catchers intent on illegally selling free blacks into slavery. By restricting authority to issue certificates to federal judges and high-level state court judges, the law achieved its desired effect. However, the Pennsylvania law also had the unintended—

---

[37] *Id.*

[38] *Id.*

[39] Holden–Smith, *supra* note 9, at 1118–19.

[40] *Id.*

[41] Thomas D. Morris, *Free Men All: The Personal Liberty Laws of the North, 1780–1861*, at 33–34 (1974). *See also* Holden–Smith, *supra* note 9, at 1119. Some judges even conspired with slave catchers to remove free blacks and sell them into slavery. *Id.*

[42] Holden–Smith, *supra* note 9, at 1119.

[43] *See* Nogee, *supra* note 1, at 191.

[44] This was Pennsylvania's second attempt to curb the kidnapping of free blacks. As discussed *supra* note 34, Pennsylvania's first attempt resulted in the promulgation of the Fugitive Slave Act.

or, as many Southerners believed, intended—effect of obstructing the lawful removal of enslaved fugitives,[45] as there simply were not enough eligible judges to hear the volume of cases brought under the Fugitive Slave Act.[46]

Pennsylvania's neighboring slave states began to complain that its anti-kidnapping law was "tantamount to 'an act of emancipation itself.' "[47] In 1826, in response to such complaints, Pennsylvania amended its anti-kidnapping statute to broaden the category of judicial officers authorized to issue certificates of removal to include, for example, aldermen and justices of the peace.[48] Significantly, however, the revised version retained meaningful procedural protections for seized blacks and criminal penalties for those illegally removing blacks from Pennsylvania.[49] In particular, the statute required that the judicial officer permit an alleged runaway to challenge the putative slave holder's claim of ownership.[50] This minimal process was manifestly different from the summary proceeding provided for by the Fugitive Slave Act; it was this gap in procedural safeguards that gave rise to the dispute in *Prigg*.

The conflict between Pennsylvania and Maryland over the disposition of Margaret Morgan was emblematic of a larger conflict between the North and South over the capture of alleged runaway slaves. From the perspective of Northern states, personal liberty laws like the 1826 anti-kidnapping law at issue in *Prigg* were necessary to protect the liberty interests of the state's free black citizens. But from the South's perspective, these anti-kidnapping laws created unreasonable procedural obstacles for slave owners attempting to regain their lawful property. For Southerners, these obstructionist tactics were exemplified by a Vermont judge who, when asked what would constitute sufficient proof of fugitive status under the Fugitive Slave Act, replied: "a bill of sale from the Almighty God."[51] Such comments suggested that the North had embarked on a campaign to undo slavery despite its constitutionally protected status. For every example of kidnapping schemes in which free blacks were sold into slavery under the Fugitive Slave Act, the South

---

[45] Some Northern legislators clearly intended personal liberty laws to thwart lawful attempts to remove enslaved persons. Morris, *supra* note 41, at 33–34.

[46] Holden–Smith, *supra* note 9, at 1120.

[47] *Id.* (quoting Nogee, *supra* note 1, at 192).

[48] Act of Mar. 25, 1826, ch. L, § 9, 1826 Pa. Laws 150 (1826).

[49] *See id.* § 3 (describing the warrant application process required before seizing "slaves"); *id.* § 4 (outlining the requirements for a warrant*); id.* §§ 1, 2 (outlining applicable punishments).

[50] *Id.* § 7 (setting forth the right to delay hearing to prepare testimony and evidence).

[51] Nogee, *supra* note 1, at 190.

cited examples of Northern judges, like the one in Vermont, who effectively blocked their right of reclamation.[52] These tensions threatened to pull apart the infant nation; *Prigg*, therefore, was integral to preserving the stability of a teetering union.

The circumstances that gave rise to *Prigg* began to take shape once Edward Prigg petitioned York County, Pennsylvania justice of the peace Thomas Henderson to issue an arrest warrant for Margaret Morgan and her children. Per the 1826 statute, once Prigg executed the warrant, he brought the Morgans before Henderson to request a certificate of removal.[53] Henderson, for some reason not reflected in the court record, declined to issue the certificate.[54] Nonetheless, without the required certificate of removal and in violation of Pennsylvania law, Prigg transported the Morgans to Maryland and into a life of slavery.[55] Soon thereafter, a Pennsylvania grand jury indicted Prigg and his co-defendants for violating the anti-kidnapping law. Maryland, however, refused to extradite the men to Pennsylvania.[56] After an extensive, two-year negotiation between the two states, Pennsylvania passed a law that required only one of the kidnappers, Edward Prigg, to be tried by a Pennsylvania jury. Prigg did not have to appear in person, and the trial would proceed on the basis of a set of facts stipulated by the parties.[57] Under the agreement, Pennsylvania would not enforce any adverse judgments against Prigg until the matter was resolved by the appellate courts, up to and including the United States Supreme Court.[58]

In 1842, the Supreme Court's decision in *Prigg* did resolve the dispute between Pennsylvania and Maryland—and, more generally, the dispute between the North and South—respecting the recapture of alleged runaways. Writing for the majority, Justice Story held Pennsylvania's law invalid because it was preempted by the Fugitive Slave Act of 1793.[59] The federal law, Justice Story reasoned, proscribed *any* state from passing *any* law that could obstruct slave catchers from reclaiming fugitive slaves.[60] The only process provided for under the Fugitive Slave Act was a summary proceeding to determine whether the alleged runa-

---

[52] *Id*. at 185–92.

[53] Holden–Smith *supra* note 9, at 1122.

[54] *Id*.

[55] *See* Finkelman, *supra* note 17, at 276; *supra* text accompanying note 20.

[56] Holden–Smith, *supra* note 9, at 1123–24.

[57] Prigg v. Pennsylvania, 41 U.S. (16 Pet.) 539, 557–58 (1842).

[58] *Id*. at 609.

[59] *Id*. at 622–25.

[60] *Id*.

way was the same person described in the warrant.[61] Even more significant, Justice Story articulated a broad common law right of recaption
enjoyed by slave owners, which permitted them to engage in self-help—
even contrary to the requirements of the Fugitive Slave Act—in order to
reclaim runaway slaves.[62] As such, even if Prigg violated the Act by
failing to secure a certificate of removal, his actions were nonetheless
lawful based on this broadly construed right of recaption.[63] Justice
Story's opinion was remarkable in both its pro-slavery reach and its
effect on blacks, both free and fugitive. *Prigg* shattered any procedural
barriers to the removal of blacks from free states to slave states.

Critiques of Justice Story's Opinion

Scholars have uniformly denounced Justice Story's opinion on ethical, jurisprudential, and formal-legal grounds.[64] In doing so, these critiques have presumed that Justice Story was torn between his sense that
slavery was wrong and his belief that the law must be upheld. A few
commentators have questioned just how deep his anti-slavery commitments ran, in part because he so readily sacrificed them to the imperatives of the rule of law. Yet whatever the reasons for taking Justice Story
to task, none of the existing scholarship examines *Prigg* through the lens
of Enlightenment race-thinking, particularly the racial metaphysics that
philosopher Paul Taylor labels "classical racialism."[65] This failure to
place *Prigg* in the context of the prevailing racial ideology of the time
has resulted in critiques and explanations that are partial at best.

Most legal academic commentators criticize the *Prigg* opinion along
an *ethical* dimension. The most articulate of these critiques comes from
Professor Robert Cover's seminal work, *Justice Accused*,[66] in which he
claims that Justice Story and other nineteenth-century Northern judges
suffered from a moral-formal dilemma in attempting to resolve slave
cases. That is to say, these judges upheld pro-slavery legal rules, even
when such rules offended their personal moral sensibilities. During this
time, positivism replaced natural law as the proper foundation for
judicial decisionmaking. Where explicit sources of law existed, such as
constitutions or statutes, judges deemed themselves bound by such

---

[61] *Id.* at 617.

[62] *Id.* at 613.

[63] *Id.*

[64] *See* Ronald M. Dworkin, *The Law of the Slave-catchers*, Times Literary Supplement
1437 (Dec. 5, 1975); Holden–Smith, *supra* note 9, at 1134–47; Finkelman, *supra* note 17, at
255–73.

[65] Taylor, *supra* note 11, at 43–47.

[66] Cover, *supra* note 4, at 8.

sources, whether or not they agreed with them. Hence, the dilemma: Should judges be guided by their moral sensibilities or by their fealty to positive law? Under a positivist regime, the answer was clear: Even if slavery was antithetical to his personal morality or the natural law, a judge's duty was to follow the explicit sources of law. As Cover puts it, the "tradition of positivism meant the judge ought to be will-less."[67]

Another analysis of Justice Story's opinion advances a *jurispruden-tial* critique. Ronald Dworkin, for instance, argues that the moral-formal dilemma did not force judges to uphold slavery. For Dworkin, moral principles do not exist exclusively within the domain of natural law, but rather, can additionally be used to interpret positive law.[68] According to Dworkin, Justice Story made a jurisprudential mistake in deciding *Prigg*: He could have concluded that the Constitution contained deep-rooted values central to any competent understanding of the document.[69] Indi-vidual freedom certainly would qualify as a central constitutional value undermined by the institution of slavery. Moreover, Dworkin concludes, norms of procedural justice required more protection than the Fugitive Slave Act offered and were not antagonistic to state procedural safe-guards like those erected by the Pennsylvania law.[70]

Dworkin's jurisprudential account is not wholly in conflict with Cover's descriptive account of Story's dilemma. Dworkin explains how judges should have (or could have) conceived of their role in the face of pro-slavery legal rules, but he does not speak to how judges actually conceived of their roles. In fact, both Cover's and Dworkin's accounts spring from the same root. Underlying both accounts is the assumption that a strictly textual reading of the Fugitive Slave Act required (or, at least, credibly supported) the pro-slavery *Prigg* opinion. For Cover, this result derived from fealty to formal, neutral principles of legal interpre-tation. For Dworkin, Justice Story's opinion resulted from an impover-ished jurisprudence. For both, putting moral considerations to one side, the Fugitive Slave Act required that the Court overturn Edward Prigg's conviction.

---

[67] *Id.* at 29.

[68] Dworkin, *supra* note 64.

[69] *See* Akhil Reed Amar, *Intratextualism*, 112 Harv. L. Rev. 747, 768 (1999) (arguing that we may infer certain principles from "deep constitutional intuitions" that inhere in the Constitution).

[70] In his intellectual biography on Justice Story, R. Kent Newmyer proposes yet another jurisprudential critique of Justice Story's slave cases, claiming that Justice Story relied, to his detriment, on Enlightenment rationalism as sufficient to resolve moral conflict. In Newmyer's view, Justice Story did not suffer from a moral failing, but rather the pitfalls of too robust a rationalism. Newmyer, *supra* note 9, at 245–46.

Recently, some scholars have challenged both Cover's and Dworkin's explanations by introducing a *formal-legal* critique of the *Prigg* decision. This critique does not accept the claim that the positive law required Justice Story to endorse slavery.[71] Even assuming the limits of positivism, these scholars maintain that the opinion employed poor legal reasoning, selective use of the facts, and a thin analysis of history to support an excessively pro-slavery opinion. According to this view, Justice Story drafted an intentionally pro-slavery opinion owing to his nationalistic values and jurisprudence.[72] Significantly, some scholars even reject the common assumption that Justice Story held substantial anti-slavery allegiances. Justice Story believed strongly in property rights and expansive national power, the argument goes, but he did not hold the abolitionist values commonly ascribed to him.[73] These scholars instead believe that Justice Story used abolitionist rhetoric in order to advance his interests in maintaining Northern hegemony in the face of increasing Southern political power.[74] Formal-legal critiques of Justice Story's *Prigg* opinion fall into three categories, each of which I discuss in turn: (1) his misguided analysis of the common law right of recaption, (2) his dismissive treatment of the Morgans' claims to freedom, and (3) the opinion's unnecessarily wide-ranging scope.

Common Law Right of Recaption

Much of Justice Story's opinion is based on a suspect understanding of the Fugitive Slave Clause's centrality to discussions held during the Constitutional Convention. In order to support his broadly articulated common law right of recaption, Justice Story claimed that the Fugitive Slave Clause was a necessary compromise between the North and South—one that was fundamental to the birth of the nation. As a result, the right of recaption derived from the Constitution itself.[75]

Although the South sought to protect its interest in slavery during the constitutional debates leading to ratification, there is little evidence that anyone at the Constitutional Convention "considered the Fugitive Slave Clause to be a particularly important part of the constitutional bargain over slavery."[76] The Clause was discussed at the Convention only

---

[71] *See, e.g.*, Holden–Smith, *supra* note 9, at 1091 (arguing that Story's anti-slavery reputation is "seriously overblown"); Finkelman, *supra* note 17, at 255–73.

[72] Holden–Smith, *supra* note 9, at 1134–39.

[73] *Id.*

[74] *Id.* at 1147.

[75] Prigg v. Pennsylvania, 41 U.S. (16 Pet.) 539, 611 (1842). Interestingly, the concurring opinions all assumed this unsupported historical conception. *Id.* at 626–58.

[76] Finkelman, *supra* note 17, at 264.

once and was adopted without debate or objection.[77] Even more significantly, the Clause was never mentioned in the Federalist Papers. In
investing the Clause with such deep significance, Justice Story appears
to have conflated the robust and, at times, acrimonious debate surrounding the "three-fifths" clause with the adoption of the Fugitive Slave
Clause. The South certainly understood the Clause as a victory but did
not view it "as either a major component of the constitutional bargain or
as something that would lead to federal enforcement."[78] On this record,
Justice Story's conclusion that the Constitution mandates an unfettered
common law right to reclaim runaways is profoundly exaggerated.

The Morgans' Claims to Freedom

Perhaps most troubling about Justice Story's opinion is its refusal to
engage substantive questions regarding the Morgan family's claims that
they were properly emancipated. First, and most obviously, the Morgan
children born in Pennsylvania (a free state) had good arguments that
they were free and therefore not subject to reclamation. Though Morgan's lawyer, Thomas C. Hambly,[79] argued that "several" of the Morgan
children were born there,[80] Justice Story devoted a grand total of one
line to the children, simply asserting that only one child was born in
Pennsylvania. Justice Story never wrestled with the status of this child,
nor did he explain how the Court determined that no other child was
born in Pennsylvania. He might have concluded that emancipated status
derived from the status of the parent rather than from birth in a
particular state, but his opinion was silent on this issue.[81]

As to Morgan herself, Justice Story's opinion provided no avenue to
challenge the presumed status of a fugitive slave. According to Justice
Story, slave owners had an unqualified right of recaption that could not
be abridged by any state process whatsoever. But the opinion does not

---

[77] Holden–Smith, *supra* note 9, at 1129. Even on this occasion, the discussion was not
at all robust. Pierce Butler and Charles Pinckney, both of South Carolina, made a motion
to amend the Constitution, which was met with two minor objections. The following day,
Butler and Pinckney introduced the extant language for the Fugitive Slave Clause without
objection or discussion. *Id.*

[78] Finkelman, *supra* note 17, at 263. "None of the supporters ... at the Convention
intimated that the Fugitive Slave Clause was a fundamental part of the bargain. Rather,
they pointed to it as a plus for the South, but not as a major clause." *Id.*

[79] Thomas Hambly did not earn a noteworthy place in history, even though he argued
such an important case. The most significant nugget that history records on Hambly's life
is that he edited a newspaper called the *York Republican* as late as 1832. *See* http://www.
ydr.com/op-ed/ci_3404345.

[80] *See* Act of Mar. 1, 1780, 1780 Pa. Laws, § III.

[81] Finkelman, *supra* note 17, at 280 (noting that pre-*Prigg* case law established that a
child born in the Commonwealth was free).

mention—even once—the competing right of free states to protect free black citizens from kidnapping. If Justice Story was correct that the Fugitive Slave Clause provided for at most a ministerial summary process, then blacks identified as runaways had no recourse in their home state to argue that they had been properly emancipated. Indeed, some state decisional law supported such a claim.[82]

The Scope of Justice Story's Opinion

Finally, and by way of summary, Justice Story's opinion is notoriously overbroad. Were Justice Story the anti-slavery advocate he and others claimed to be, he could have drafted a much narrower opinion. Take, for instance, the common law right of recaption. In Justice Story's words, the Fugitive Slave Clause "manifestly contemplates the existence of a positive, unqualified right" of reclamation.[83] Justice Story reasoned that the right of recaption derived from the Constitution itself, and that even the minimal process prescribed by the personal liberty laws offended slave-owners' right of recaption. He could have declared the Pennsylvania personal liberty law unconstitutional without announcing a sweeping right of recaption that, in effect, removed any protection whatsoever for free blacks kidnapped into slavery. Such a broad and unsupported reading of the Fugitive Slave Clause, critics argue, does not comport with Justice Story's reputation as an anti-slavery jurist.

* * *

My aim here is to be somewhat agnostic in regard to the merits of these competing critiques, except to say that each raises concerns that deserve careful attention.[84] Justice Story refused to consider serious anti-slavery arguments, an omission that has vexed scholars for years. So, what motivated him to write *Prigg* in the way that he did? Cover's ethical theory seems insufficient in light of the substantial formal-legal critique, which questions the integrity of Justice Story's legal reasoning. For Cover's theory to be correct, there must have been a dilemma—a conflict between the judge's personal morality and the perceived requirements of the law. The formal-legal critique undermines the notion that Justice Story was formally constrained by existing law in drafting *Prigg* in the exceedingly pro-slavery vocabulary he employed. Cover's analysis assumes that Justice Story was an anti-slavery proponent, but the record is not so clear and there are compelling counter-narratives that explain

---

[82] *See, e.g.*, State v. Harden, 2 Spears (SC) 151 (1832). *But see* Walkup v. Pratt, 5 H. & J. 51, 56 (Md. 1820) (rejecting the argument that living as a free person could establish status as free person).

[83] Prigg v. Pennsylvania, 41 U.S. (16 Pet.) 539, 612 (1842).

[84] For a more detailed critique of Story's opinion, see Holden–Smith, *supra* note 9, at 1128–34, and Finkelman, *supra* note 17, at 255–73.

Justice Story's failure to condemn slavery and to deter the kidnapping of free blacks.[85] Dworkin's jurisprudential critique similarly fails to offer an adequate explanation of *Prigg*. Dworkin assumes, as does Cover, that Justice Story wrote an honest opinion consistent with his perception that he was bound by law to uphold slavery. Here again, the formal-legal critique suggests otherwise.

So, might the formal-legal critique offer the better explanation—that Justice Story's desire to fortify national power simply trumped his abolitionist leanings? This form of argument may offer a partial explanation: Justice Story was committed to nationalistic values above all others, including his abolitionist beliefs. Although this argument offers a plausible explanation, it does not speak to how an abstract collective value like nationalism can co-exist with a dehumanizing institution like slavery.[86] The existing literature merely makes the naked claim without telling us why.

None of these critiques provides a coherent theory that explains why Justice Story wrote *Prigg* in such fervently pro-slavery vocabulary. The focus on jurisprudence, constitutional values, and legal reasoning does not adequately account for his profound subordination of the dignitary harms associated with the kidnapping of free blacks and the slave trade in general. *Prigg*'s grant of absolute authority to slave catchers to seize blacks—free or enslaved—signified more than fealty to certain nationalist norms. The pro-slavery tenor of the decision starkly revealed what race meant to Justice Story. Accordingly, the better way to understand *Prigg* is to locate the opinion in the broader discourse of classical racialism, which treated the inferiority of blacks as natural and inevitable.

Classical Racialism and Justice Story

Justice Story reached his intellectual maturity in the early to mid-nineteenth century, an historical moment defined by classical racialism—a brand of racial metaphysics that can best be understood in both semantic and structural vocabularies. Semantically, classical racialism assigns non-physical meaning to bloodlines, so that blackness is equated with irrationality, incivility, incompetence, and, thus, inferiority. Structurally, classical racialism works to rationalize the unequal distribution of societal benefits and burdens by establishing the ideological foundation for comprehensive racial domination.[87] This form of race-thinking,

---

[85] *See infra* text accompanying notes 132–134.

[86] Significantly, one variant of the formal-legal critique makes the claim that Justice Story did not hold strong commitments to abolitionist values at all. Holden–Smith, *supra* note 9, at 1091–1116.

[87] Taylor, *supra* note 11, at 24–25.

which may sound commonplace to the modern reader, represented a paradigmatic shift in the etiology of race in Western culture.[88]

The Origins of Classical Racialism

The human population is made up of smaller populations that have distinctive physiological and cultural characteristics.[89] From time immemorial, people have recognized these physiological differences, including skin color, height, and body shape, but the concept of race is a relatively new phenomenon in human history.[90] Pre-modern people "lived in a world of multiple peoples, rather than a world of a few races."[91] They often saw the world in "we/they" terms—cultured-us versus barbaric-them, Christian-us versus heathen-them, or believer-us versus infidel-them, for example.[92] Some ancient cultures, to be sure, equated skin color with primitivism; that is, they understood color as a marker for traits deeper than history or socialization.[93] But, the pre-moderns did not think in terms of *heritable* character traits, largely because they were not yet availed of the requisite scientific resources. Different looking people were different (and consequently deemed superior or inferior) for a host of reasons, including their religion, culture, climate, and locality. As philosopher K. Anthony Appiah puts it, "the physical body was important not as a cause but as a *sign* of difference."[94] In other words, the idea of inferior character, intelligence, ratiocination, and so forth, passing through bloodlines is a modern creation—one that did not come into existence until the late eighteenth century.[95]

---

[88] As philosopher K. Anthony Appiah points out, "current ways of talking about race are the residue, the detritus, so to speak, of earlier ways of thinking about race; so that it turns out to be easiest to understand contemporary talk about 'race' as the pale reflection of a more full-blooded race discourse that flourished in the last century." K. Anthony Appiah & Amy Gutmann, *Color Conscious: The Political Morality of Race* 38 (1996).

[89] Taylor, *supra* note 11, at 20–21. Physical anthropologists have long since discarded the term "race" in favor of "populations" to describe forms of human variation. Race as a category proved to be far too imprecise and problematic a construction. *Id.*

[90] Prior to the fifteenth century, populations rarely interacted. Geography accounted for the generational replication of physiognomy and cultural practice. *Id.*

[91] *Id.* at 22.

[92] Aristotle, for example, theorized that male, aristocratic Greeks had superior reasoning abilities and, thus, were cultured as opposed to the barbaric non-Greek population. *See* Aristotle, *Politics* 63 (H. Rackham trans., 1944). The idea of "race" as we understand it today is nowhere to be found in Aristotle's thinking.

[93] By way of example, the Chinese understood "the darker skin of the residents of Africa and South Asia, as well as the 'ash-white' skin of Europeans, as a sign of inferior culture and debased humanity." Taylor, *supra* note 11, at 22.

[94] Appiah & Guttmann *supra* note 88, at 50.

[95] The idea that we have not always understood human variation in the vocabulary of race is fairly well established. *See* Georges–Louis Leclerc, *A Natural History, General and*

Early notions of race began to form in the late fifteenth century around a number of world events that conspired in significant ways. One such event was the culmination of the *Reconquista*, when Ferdinand and Isabella expelled the last Moorish rulers from the Iberian Peninsula. As the Spaniards began to interact with other cultures on the peninsula, they developed deep-seated suspicions that the Moors and Jews (even those who had converted to Christianity) were somehow different—more than just culturally.[96] Though initially no vocabulary existed to give voice to this suspicion, over time, the Spaniards began to appropriate a vocabulary used by Southern Europeans to describe breeds of animals. Indeed, when the first Spanish dictionary was published in 1611, the term "raza"—the etymological origin of the word "race"—was defined as pointing both to "breeds of horses and, derisively, to people of Moorish or Jewish ancestry."[97]

Thus, an important semantic shift began to emerge. Whereas before, inferior status was associated with a geographic region, religion, or culture, the vocabulary of race allowed for the correlation of character traits with groups of people who shared certain biogenetic traits. This new form of race-talk took hold in the Americas during the period of European colonialism ushered in by Christopher Columbus's "discovery" of the Americas. This was the first time in history in which "vastly different peoples and cultures came together ... with some of those peoples appropriating the land and labor of some of the others on an unprecedented scale."[98] The notion of inferior and superior *razas* provided ideological content for the "right" to take "unused" land from backward and uncivilized *razas*.

This era—let's call it early-modern racialism—reached its conceptual maturity in 1684 with Francois Bernier's famous essay, *A New Division of the Earth*, in which Bernier introduced his theory that there were four or five different species of humans.[99] Bernier rejected the then-dominant understanding of human classification based on geography[100] and replaced it with a classification system based on physiognomy—roughly, hair texture, nose and face shape, and, of course, skin color.

Particular, in Race and the Enlightenment 15–28 (Emmanuel Chukwudi Eze ed., 1997); George M. Fredrickson, *Racism* 99–108 (2002).

[96] Taylor, *supra* note 11, at 39–41.

[97] *Id.* at 41. In 1611, *Tesoro de la Lengua Castellano o Espanola* was first published containing the term *"raza." Id.*

[98] *Id.* at 41.

[99] Bernier wavered between four or five because he could not decide whether Native Americans were white or some other species. Taylor, *supra* note 11, at 41–42.

[100] *Id.*

Bernier's theory, however, was monogenic; it presumed—consistent with Christian theology—that differences among populations represented variations from an ideal human type—white European. The further a human species varied from the ideal, the more inferior the species.

The Era of Classical Racialism

The classical racialism era—the historical period in which Justice Story wrote *Prigg*—began to develop in the late eighteenth century. Three publications serve as illustrative marks of the era's formation: Immanuel Kant's *On the Different Races of Man*, Thomas Jefferson's *Notes on the State of Virginia*, and Samuel George Morton's *Crania Americana*.[101] During this era, the monogenic project of naturalizing human difference of the early-modern racialism period gave way to a polygenic project that catalogued humanity into several distinct types. No longer were different races a product of mere variation; different races were typologically distinct, carrying "the heritability of essential traits across generations."[102]

Immanuel Kant

Philosopher Immanuel Kant played a leading role in the transformation of racial ideology. In 1775, Kant published *On the Different Races of Man*[103]—one of the most influential essays on race at the time[104]—which

---

[101] I use the phrase "illustrative marks" because these texts do not represent the breadth of Enlightenment thinking on race; rather, I chose these essays because, to my thinking, they best typify the important semantic shifts in Enlightenment racial discourse.

[102] Taylor, *supra* note 11, at 44.

[103] Immanuel Kant, *On the Different Races of Man*, in This Is Race 16 (Earl W. Count ed., 1950).

[104] *See, e.g., This Is Race, supra* note 103, at 704 ("Immanuel Kant produced the most profound raciological thought of the eighteenth century."). Some modern scholars wrongly dismiss Kant's work on race as recreational, but Kant "devoted the largest period of his career to research in, and teaching of, anthropology and cultural geography." *Race and the Enlightenment, supra* note 95, at 2. For examples of the dismissal or ignorance of Kant's work on race see, Hannah Arendt, *Lectures on Kant's Political Philosophy* 7 (Ronald Beiner ed., 1982); Howard Caygill, *A Kant Dictionary* (1995) (which contains no entry for "race"). In fact, at the University of Königsberg, where Kant spent his entire career, he taught many more courses in anthropology or geography (seventy-two) than in logic (fifty-four), metaphysics (forty-nine), moral philosophy (twenty-eight), or theoretical physics (twenty). *Race and the Enlightenment, supra* note 95, at 2-3. Indeed, Kant "introduced anthropology as a branch of study to the German universities," and introduced "the study of geography ... to Könisberg University." Emmanuel Chukwudi Eze, *The Color of Reason, in Postcolonial African Philosophy* 104 (Emmanuel Chukwudi Eze ed., 1997). Kant also produced voluminous writings in this area: *Anthropology from a Pragmatic Point of View, Physische Geographie, Conjectural Beginning of Human History, Bestimmung des Begriffs einer Menschenrace,* and *Observations on the Feeling of the Beautiful and the Sublime. Id.* at 104. There are sufficient grounds to infer that Kant certainly took this part of his work

foreshadowed the semantic shift to the polygenic discourse of classical racialism. Drawing on the earlier work of Benier, Carl von Linné, George–Luis Leclerc, Comte de Buffon, and David Hume, Kant theorized that four distinct human types existed, each possessing a particular "natural disposition."[105]

Between Benier's publication in 1684 and Kant's *On the Different Races of Man*, Enlightenment thinkers began to publish thicker accounts of Benier's central monogenic thesis that four or five human species existed.[106] Significantly, the physiognomic differences among the races were explained by theoretical commitments to environmentalism—an explanatory framework that tied human differences, including cultural differences, to climate and geography.[107] So, for example, the form of argument ran: since regions of Africa are exceedingly hot, Africans are the darkest peoples, grow no beards, and have short curly hair.[108]

Kant, however, was not satisfied with what he deemed narrowly environmental or geographical accounts of race. He required a more transcendental and, to his mind, philosophical rendering. As such, Kant acknowledged these descriptive theories, but further theorized that races were caused by *anlagen*, or "natural dispositions."[109] According to Kant, climate played a role in phenotypic expression only if a *keime*, or germ—that which is "inherent in the nature of an organic body"—already existed within the person to react with his environment in particular sorts of ways.[110] This "foresight of Nature," Kant argued, provided peoples with "inner furnishings" to produce phenotypic varieties upon

---

seriously, and did not understand himself to be writing mere journalistic pieces or conducting popular lectures on race.

[105] Kant, *supra* note 103, at 19.

[106] *See supra* note 102 and accompanying text.

[107] In 1735, for instance, Carl von Linné published *The System of Nature*, which articulated a then-popular Enlightenment notion that Nature (or Providence) assigned a precise position in nature to all living things. Carl von Linné, *The System of Nature*, in *Race and the Enlightenment*, *supra* note 95, at 10–14. David Hume published two important essays, *Of the Populousness of Ancient Nations* and *Of National Character* in 1748 and 1754, respectively. David Hume, *Of the Populousness of Ancient Nations*, in *Race and the Enlightenment*, *supra* note 95, at 29–30; David Hume, *Of National Character*, in *Race and the Enlightenment*, *supra* note 95, at 30–33.

[108] Comte de Buffon, *A Natural History, General and Particular*, in *This Is Race*, *supra* note 103, at 10–13. One early account theorized that blackness resided in the "cellular membrane" between the skin and the scarf-skin and that a long gestation in "hot water" causes the blackness. *Id*. at 13.

[109] Kant, *supra* note 103, at 19.

[110] *Id*.

interaction with the environment.[111] So, Africans, for example, reacted with their environment in the way that they did because it was their *anlagen* to do so. This *anlagen*, Kant reasoned, was Nature's plan, as "[c]hance or common mechanical laws could not have merely developed appropriately at long periods in various ways."[112]

Kant's thinking represents an important semantic intervention in the Enlightenment racial discourse. Talk of so-called *anlagen* was one of the first vocabularies to naturalize extant notions of hierarchical status among different peoples. It provided a quasi-scientific account of the Great Chain of Being—the notion of a divinely inspired hierarchy of species—which was more congenial to Enlightenment rationalist sensibilities than religious or mystical accounts. This scientific credence provided an additional vocabulary to justify white superiority and black inferiority. Kant's racial cosmogony was, however, firmly monogenic; he believed that blacks and whites belonged to the same species of humans.[113] That Kant espoused a theory of common ancestry is important because monogenism does not accomplish the same ideological work as polygenism. It is easier to subjugate a different sort of animal than it is to subjugate a mere variety of human being. So, at the height of the classical racialism era, Europeans used polygenic vocabularies to rationalize wholesale domination of other races. Such subjugation could be justified as the natural, scientifically proved order of things.[114]

Thomas Jefferson

In analyzing how racial theories came to influence thinking in the United States, Thomas Jefferson is an important figure for three reasons. First, he was a central figure in the development of American democracy and the country's cultural understanding of itself. Second, Jefferson was a leading intellectual and, thus, represents the best thinking of his day in any number of areas, including the etiology of race. Finally, Jefferson's race-thinking is illustrative of the type of moral ambivalence toward the legal subordination of blacks that Justice Story probably felt.

---

[111] *Id.*

[112] *Id.* Kant argues that the environment may be able to alter a particular individual, but a specific *keime* is necessary to provide "generative force that would be capable of reproducing itself." *Id.* at 20.

[113] Without much argument, Kant writes, "Negroes and Whites are not different species of humans ... but they are different *races.*" *Id.* at 17 (emphasis in original).

[114] Kant's physical anthropological musings of black inferiority present an irony. Contemporary race theorists readily deploy familiar Kantian themes as a basis for a theory of rights with anti-racist implications. *See generally* Lewis R. Gordon, *Bad Faith and Antiblack Racism* (1995).

A good starting point to understand Jefferson's race theory is Query XIV of *Notes on the State of Virginia*.[115] There, Jefferson advanced a "suspicion" (albeit with "great diffidence") that blacks "are inferior to the whites in the endowments both of body and mind."[116] Jefferson was not sure whether blacks were a typologically distinct race or were made different owing to their enslavement,[117] but he was certain that blacks were inferior in their reasoning abilities, imaginative capacities, potential for character development, and aesthetic potential.[118] Jefferson's suspicion, notably, used the vocabulary of early-modern racialism—races are *varieties* of humanity—and gestured toward classical racialism—races are *naturally* different.

Jefferson was convinced that blacks were not only intellectually inferior, but were also morally and aesthetically inferior. Indeed, Jefferson's *Notes* focused a good deal of attention on the aesthetic dimension of black inferiority. Jefferson made an interesting semantic move when he queried: "The circumstance of superior beauty is thought worthy of attention in the propagation of our horses, dogs, and other domestic animals; why not in that of man?"[119] By conflating his aesthetic critique with the budding science of breeding, he provided additional building blocks for the shift to a polygenic discourse. That is, he injected the language of biology[120] into an existing racial discourse that included intellectual, moral, and aesthetic claims marked by color. This semantic shift, in turn, strengthened ideological beliefs that inferior species of men deserved their subordinate status.

---

[115] Thomas Jefferson, *Notes on the State of Virginia* (William Peden ed., Univ. of N.C. Press 1955) (1781).

[116] *Id*. at 143.

[117] *Id*. ("I advance it therefore as a suspicion only, that the blacks, whether originally a distinct race, or made distinct by time and circumstances, are inferior to the whites in the endowments of body and mind.").

[118] Jefferson wrote, "Comparing them by their faculties of memory, reason, and imagination, it appears to me, that in memory they are equal to the whites; in reason much inferior, as I think one could scarcely be found capable of tracing and comprehending the investigations of Euclid; and that in imagination they are dull, tasteless, and anomalous." *Id*. at 139. Of Phyllis Wheatly, widely regarded as the first black poet, Jefferson remarked, "Religion indeed produced [her]; but it could not produce a poet. The compositions published under her name are below the dignity of criticism." *Id*. at 140.

[119] Jefferson, *supra* note 115, at 138.

[120] In the vocabulary of the time, "biology" was referred to as "natural history." The term "biology" was popularized in 1802 in a treatise by Gottfried Treviranus and Jean-Baptiste de Lamarck. Appiah & Gutmann, *supra* note 88, at 49 n.23 (citing William Coleman, *Biology in the Nineteenth Century: Problems of Form, Function and Transformation* 1 (1971)).

However, even though Jefferson held a firm belief that blacks were inferior to whites, he was nonetheless a proponent of emancipation.[121] Indeed, in adopting the Declaration of Independence, the Continental Congress deleted pro-emancipation language from Jefferson's original draft.[122] So, how can Jefferson's firm emancipative sentiments be squared with his equally strong conviction that blacks are subordinate? (We may also ask, as a related question, how he could harmonize his status as a slave owner with his advocacy of emancipation.) For Jefferson, racial differences made it impolitic for the races to live together under the same government,[123] and his solution was to deport blacks to "such a place as the circumstances of the time should render the most proper."[124] Yet, this pragmatic solution to a political problem did not speak to how he could be, simultaneously, both an abolitionist and a firm believer in black inferiority.

My suspicion—advanced without much diffidence—is that Jefferson did, in fact, hold both positions, but that his belief in black inferiority (and his attendant "suspicion" that such inferiority was heritable) was more deeply held than any egalitarian racial sentiments. The mistake that many scholars make is to presume (on fairly thin supporting evidence) that Jefferson's abolitionist leanings stood in relative equipoise with his other normative commitments. In fact, Jefferson's suspicion that blacks were inferior—either genetically or environmentally—rendered him ambivalent about their enslaved status, in much the same way that I argue Justice Story was ambivalent about the suffering of alleged fugitive slaves.

Samuel George Morton

Offering putatively scientific proof that blacks were typologically different than whites—a difference that explained blacks' natural inferiority in intellect and character development—Samuel George Morton is central to understanding Justice Story's decision in *Prigg*. Kant's musings in 1775 and Jefferson's suspicions in 1787 matured into recogniz-

---

[121] Appiah & Gutmann, *supra* note 88, at 42 (quoting Thomas Jefferson, *Autobiography, in Thomas Jefferson, Writings* 1, 18 (Merrill D. Peterson ed., 1984)) ("Nothing is more certain in the book of fate than that these people are to be free.").

[122] *Id.* at 43 (The "Christian king of Great Britain ... violat[ed] the most sacred rights of life and liberty in the persons of a distant people who never offended him, captivating & carrying them into slavery in another hemisphere, or to incur miserable death in their transportation thither.").

[123] Jefferson followed his now-famous quote, "Nothing is more certainly written in the book of fate than that these people are to be free," with, "Nor is it less certain that the two races, equally free cannot live under the same government." Appiah & Gutmann, *supra* note 88, at 42.

[124] Jefferson, *supra* note 115, at 138.

ably scientific theorization in 1839 with Morton's publication of *Crania Americana*.[125] Morton's research was widely believed to have established that: (1) Environment did not contribute to the formation of races; (2) Races were typologically different and not derivative of a common stock; and (3) Demonstrable differences in cranial capacities among the races proved differences in intelligence.[126] It is this last claim that received the most attention. Morton's cranial research, which gained popular acceptance as a dispositive ranking of human types, provided the rationale for the government's management of racial populations. Morton's work also had a profound effect on U.S. foreign and immigration policy, and led—quite directly—to the eugenics movement, which featured the notorious race-thinking of the Nazi movement.

Justice Joseph Story

By the mid to late 1800s, putatively scientific systems for distinguishing and ranking human types were firmly ensconced in the cultural ideology of the United States. As a result, the semantic shift to a full-blown polygenic discourse and attendant schemes for managing racial spaces were in place by the time Justice Story wrote his opinion in *Prigg*.[127] In arguing that Justice Story was impacted by this ideology, however, I must reconcile my claim with the popular view that he, like Jefferson, was an abolitionist.

Justice Story's reputation among scholars as a faithful abolitionist[128] derives primarily from two sources: a Grand Jury charge he delivered in 1819 and his opinion in *United States v. The La Jeune Eugenie*.[129] Justice Story's Grand Jury Instruction, delivered in Massachusetts and Rhode Island in 1819 and, once again, in Maine in 1820,[130] offered a heart-

---

[125] Samuel George Morton, *Crania Americana* (1839).

[126] *See, e.g.*, Dr. Prichard, Book Review, 10 J. Royal Geographical Soc'y London 552, 561 (1841).

[127] *See* Taylor, *supra* note 11, at 39–43.

[128] *See, e.g.*, Cover, *supra* note 4, at 119, 240; David P. Currie, *The Constitution in the Supreme Court: The First Hundred Years, 1789–1888*, at 245 (1985); Newmyer, *supra* note 9, at 377; Christopher L. M. Eisgruber, Comment, *Justice Story, Slavery, and the Natural Law Foundations of American Constitutionalism*, 55 U. Chi. L. Rev. 273, 279 (1988).

[129] 26 F. Cas. 832 (C.C.D. Mass. 1822) (No. 15,551). Professor Barbara Holden–Smith argues that biographers of Justice Story overwhelmingly rely on the 1819 Grand Jury instruction and *La Jeune Eugenie*, and that only two biographers, R. Kent Newmyer and Robert Cover, even mention other decisions to support his anti-slavery reputation. Cover, for example, mentions *United States v. Amistad*, 40 U.S. (15 Pet.) 518 (1841), as additional evidence, but "recognizes the limited nature of that victory for kidnapped Africans." Holden–Smith, *supra* note 9, at 1099 n.80.

[130] Holden–Smith, *supra* note 9, at 1100 n.81. That Justice Story's anti-slavery reputation is based on so sparse a record is quite remarkable, particularly in light of the breadth and strength of such claims in the literature. *See supra* note 9 and accompanying text.

wrenching account of what the newly enslaved African population experienced during the trans-Atlantic journey to America.[131] Three years
later, in 1822, Justice Story lamented the evils of the slave trade in *La
Jeune Eugenie*, describing it as "a traffic conceived in atrocious and
unfeeling cruelty; and sustained and sealed with blood."[132]

Despite this stirring rhetoric, Justice Story may not have been
motivated by abolitionist sentiments. The formal-legal critics provide a
compelling counter-narrative that casts Justice Story's anti-slavery vocabulary in a different light. At bottom, Justice Story may have used
powerful anti-slavery rhetoric to advance not a moral principle, but a
political goal—opposition to the Missouri compromise, an agreement
between pro- and anti-slavery factions of the Congress, which regulated
slavery in the western territories. Historical evidence, including Justice
Story's personal correspondence, suggests that around 1819 he became
engaged in the national debate over the annexation of Missouri:

> In opposing the Missouri Compromise, he indicated more than once
> that for him the question of the expansion of slavery was rooted in
> the conflict between New England and the South for hegemony over
> the national government. For him this was a contest of nationalism
> against confederation, a struggle for union over dis-union. For
> example, writing to Professor Edward Everett in 1820, Story com-
> plained that the South had gotten its way on the Missouri question
> by using the tactic "divide and conquer" against New England. He
> warned that the various political factions of New England must put
> their differences behind them and present a united front against the
> South.[133]

Justice Story's anti-expansionist sentiments, however, certainly do
not foreclose an anti-slavery sentiment. He could both favor New England's political supremacy and be repulsed by the institution of slavery.
So, why credit the formal-legal critique, which questions Justice Story's
abolitionist commitments? Sometimes silence speaks volumes. What is
striking about Justice Story's slavery jurisprudence is that he employed
anti-slavery rhetoric only in temporal proximity to an annexation conflict; he did not make similar moral claims in any other slavery cases.
Writing the remainder of his slavery opinions using a legalistic, unemotional vocabulary, Justice Story marshaled doctrine and relied on cold

---

[131] *See* 1 *Life and Letters of Joseph Story* 341–42 (William Wetmore Story ed., 1851).

[132] United States v. The La Jeune Eugenie, 26 F. Cas. 832, 851 (C.C.D. Mass. 1822)
(No. 15,551).

[133] Holden–Smith, *supra* note 9, at 1094. Justice Story objected to the annexation of
Texas, as well, "suppl[ying] the anti-expansionist forces with the constitutional arguments
against annexation." *Id.* at 1093. According to formal-legal critics, Justice Story's rhetoric
in both instances was a mere pretext to preserve New England's hegemony. *Id.* at 1093–94.

statutory analysis to arrive at results that were technically sound, even if they were morally questionable.[134]

In light of Justice Story's selective use of anti-slavery rhetoric, there is credible support for the claim that his words were born more out of political expediency than moral principle. His ability to subordinate principle to expediency reflects the racial metaphysics of classical racialism, which rationalized not just slavery, but other forms of oppression as well, including European adventurism in Africa, U.S. incursions in Hawai'i and the Philippines, and a robust eugenics movement. As in *Prigg*, these pernicious forms of exclusion often led to violent consequences.

The vocabulary of classical racialism—the result of a range of intellectual currents coming together over three centuries—justified the comprehensive racist domination of non-whites at an unprecedented level and to an unprecedented degree. Indeed, popular deployment of this vocabulary foreclosed the ability to attain any form of human solidarity, "the imaginative ability to see strange people as fellow sufferers."[135] Blacks became "other"—a typologically inferior sort of species—enabling whites to discount the suffering that slavery entailed.

Justice Story's ambivalence about slavery involved more than merely holding inconsistent views about blacks;[136] it may be described as a particular moral psychology that permitted him to dehumanize blacks. Once blacks were stripped of their fundamental human dignity, classical racialism provided the rationale for Justice Story to uphold slavery while at the same time invoking founding ideals without any sense of inherent contradiction. Justice Story's ambivalence allowed him to debase and devalue an entire race of people without sacrificing his claim to being a good, decent, God-fearing person.

Justice Story's ambivalence, like that of other nineteenth-century thinkers, required what philosopher Charles Mills calls an "epistemology

---

[134] *See id.* at 1104–16 (analyzing Story's other slavery opinions and finding that they are "narrow in their reasoning and devoid of any mention of the immorality of the trade").

[135] Richard Rorty, *Contingency, Irony, and Solidarity*, at xvi (1989).

[136] In the psychological literature, "attitude ambivalence" refers to an individual's simultaneously having both positive and negative opinions on the same object. *See, e.g.*, Michael Riketta, *Discriminative Validation of Numerical Indices of Attitude Ambivalence*, 5 Current Res. Soc. Psychol. 65 (2000). Attitude ambivalence has been linked to racial attitudes. One study found that having attitude ambivalence toward members of another race (e.g., having feelings of both aversion and friendly concern) predicted polarized cross-racial evaluations. R. Glen Hass et al., *Cross-Racial Appraisal as Related to Attitude Ambivalence and Cognitive Complexity*, 17 Personality & Soc. Psychol. Bull. 83, 89–91 (1991). The vast literature on attitude ambivalence can provide insights into the mindset of nineteenth-century jurists, even though these modern psychological tools did not exist at the time.

of ignorance," which rationalizes grossly unequal distributions of burdens and benefits.[137] According to Mills, this epistemology of ignorance is the foundation of what he terms the "Racial Contract," a theoretical framework for understanding racial domination as a distinct subject of moral and political philosophy, much like ideas of aristocracy, liberalism, socialism, and welfare capitalism.[138] The structure of racial domination, he argues, "is *itself* a political system, a particular power structure of formal or informal rule, socioeconomic privilege, and norms for the differential distribution of material wealth and opportunities, benefits and burdens, rights and duties."[139]

Significantly, Mills defines the Racial Contract along three dimensions—the descriptive, the normative, and the epistemological. As Mills explains, the Racial Contract is a "set of formal or informal agreements or meta-agreements" that categorize a "subset of humans as 'nonwhite' and of a different and inferior moral status, subpersons, so that they have a subordinate civil standing in the white or white-ruled polities."[140] As a result, "the moral and juridical rules normally regulating the behavior of whites in their dealings with one another either do not apply at all in dealings with nonwhites or apply only in a qualified form . . ., but in any case the general purpose of the Contract is always the differential privileging of the whites as a group with respect to the nonwhites as a group, the exploitation of their bodies, land, and resources, and the denial of equal socioeconomic opportunities to them."[141] This Contract explains "how society was created or crucially transformed, how the individuals in that society were reconstituted, how the state was established, and how a particular moral code . . . [was] brought into existence."[142]

For Mills, the Racial Contract is grounded in a "*preexisting* objectivist morality (theological or secular) . . . [that] constrains the terms of the political contract."[143] This "color-coded morality" in turn "restricts the possession of . . . natural freedom and equality to *white* men."[144] So, the Racial Contract, Mills argues, "requires its own peculiar moral and empirical epistemology, its norms and procedures for determining what

---

[137] Charles W. Mills, *The Racial Contract* 18 (1997).

[138] *Id.* at 1.

[139] *Id.* at 3.

[140] *Id.* at 11.

[141] *Id.*

[142] *Id.* at 10.

[143] *Id.* at 14.

[144] *Id.* at 16.

counts as moral and factual knowledge of the world."[145] White supremacy and black inferiority become background "facts" from which inferences are drawn. These purportedly factual claims require people to *misinterpret* the world in a way "validated by white epistemic authority. . . ."[146] As Mills notes, the Racial Contract "prescribes for its signatories an inverted epistemology, an epistemology of ignorance, a particular pattern of localized and global cognitive dysfunctions (which are psychologically and socially functional), producing the ironic outcome that whites will in general be unable to understand the world they themselves have made."[147] In short, the very notion of "whiteness"—developed over hundreds of years and associated with profound social, political, and economic consequences—depends on "structured blindness" to conquer, enslave, and dominate non-white peoples.[148]

This notion of a "Racial Contract" with its particular moral code or moral psychology begin to explain Justice Story's ambivalence toward slavery in *Prigg*. The vocabulary of classical racialism provided the foundation—the "facts"—that allowed institutions like slavery to exist in America despite a burgeoning democratic polity committed to freedom and equality. Classical racialism took black inferiority as a given. This vocabulary of inferiority permeated the late eighteenth- and nineteenth-century understandings of race. As I have said elsewhere, "our use of language conditions our understanding of ourselves. Language can . . . open up or shut down possibilities of being, doing, and understanding. . . . The languages we inherit, the ones we create, and the ones we discard all tell us something important about who we are and what our possibilities are."[149] Justice Story was defined by and helped to define the racial vocabulary of his day.

For Justice Story and his contemporaries, the vocabulary of classical racialism had both interpretive and expressive implications.[150] As an interpretive matter, this vocabulary allowed the public to understand the world in racialist terms that reduced human variety to crude stereotypes.[151] Hence, blacks as uncivilized, immoral, and incorrigibly ignorant

---

[145] *Id.* at 17.

[146] *Id.* at 18.

[147] *Id.* (emphasis in original).

[148] *See id.* at 19.

[149] Ronald S. Sullivan Jr., *Multiple Ironies:* Brown *at 50*, 47 How. L.J. 29, 50 (2003). *See also* Martin Heidegger, *Letter on Humanism, in Basic Writings* 217, 217 (David Farrell Krell ed., 1993); Taylor, *supra* note 11, at 4 (Language "is the medium of human culture and cognition.").

[150] *See* Taylor, *supra* note 11, at 4–7.

[151] *See id.*

became the popular lens through which an entire people was understood. As an expressive matter, classical racialism signified "the conditions under which certain inhabitants of what became the United States were considered subhuman, and hence fit to be treated as property, while others were considered an archaic model of humanity ..., and hence fit to be uprooted and pushed aside by the advance of civilization."[152] The interpretive and expressive aspects of classical racialism together effected not only the most intimate of interpersonal relationships, but also "the grandest of geopolitical policy choices."[153] As for Justice Story, the vocabulary of classical racialism permitted him to see the world counterfactually, to conceive of blacks as biologically inferior, and to give insufficient concern to their claims to freedom.

This vocabulary, animated by the epistemology of ignorance, treated the non-white population as inevitably inferior, both morally and intellectually, and permitted slavery and freedom, independence and colonialism, egalitarianism and domination to co-exist in relative harmony. Justice Story's opinion in *Prigg* reflects the foundations of classical racialism laid by Thomas Jefferson approximately sixty years earlier. Classical racialism offers a way to reconcile Jefferson the slave holder with Jefferson the freedom fighter and to square Jefferson's writings on the equality of all men with his "suspicions" of black inferiority.[154] For both Story and Jefferson, political debates about the treatment of non-white populations took the form of contemporary arguments on, say, the treatment of animals, not arguments about persons with equally valued moral claims to humane treatment.

Classical racialism did not irredeemably infect the thinking of every late eighteenth- and early nineteenth-century American. Some, but not all, abolitionist counter-narratives were in tension with accounts of blacks as less than fully human. Hence, Jefferson had "suspicions" rather than "knowledge" of black inferiority, and Justice Story experienced moral ambiguity rather moral certainty about slavery's correctness. The influence of classical racialism is absent in the many critiques of the decision in *Prigg*. That Justice Story was morally ambivalent about the effects of slavery is consistent both with the preponderant Enlightenment racial discourse and his conspicuous silence on the slavery issue outside of the national annexation debates. Justice Story's dilemma grew out of a racial discourse that could not imagine blacks as equal, regardless of whether they were free.

---

[152] *Id.* at 6.

[153] *Id.* at 7.

[154] Jefferson's masculinist formulations are, quite obviously, problematic on grounds of gender equality. Although I limit my project here to race and the law, this does not diminish the legitimacy of gender critiques that could be lodged.

Conclusion

In the end, *Prigg* is a tale of two stories. Not only does *Prigg* tell the story of Margaret Morgan's journey from freedom to slavery, but it also tells a story about one of our most respected Supreme Court justices. For centuries now, race has insinuated itself into almost all of our human relationships. In Justice Story's era, race was conceptualized in the most rigidly essentialist vocabularies, and his ambivalence toward the slavery question derived from the racial vocabulary of his day, which relegated blacks to a sub-human, typologically distinct category. That Margaret Morgan and her children's fate were lost somewhere in the interstices of history epitomizes this lack of regard for or interest in the sufferings of the black community. At a minimum, Margaret Morgan's story reminds us that the law, like every other human institution, is informed, to varying degrees, by the social ethos. Classical racialism not only affected economic and immigration policy, but it framed the very background assumptions that allowed an institution as heinous as slavery to receive continued sanction under law. Subordination and stratification became the price of a shared national identity—a cruel truth that was framed not as a choice but as an inescapable reality.

*

3

Erika Lee

Birthright Citizenship, Immigration, and the U.S. Constitution: The Story of *United States v. Wong Kim Ark*

Introduction

The principle of birthright citizenship is one with which most Americans are familiar: If a person is born in the United States, that individual is recognized as a citizen, regardless of color or race. The Fourteenth Amendment, which declares that "[a]ll persons born or naturalized in the United States, and subject to the jurisdiction thereof, are citizens of the United States and of the State wherein they reside," provides the constitutional foundation for this principle.[1]

But the notion of birthright citizenship has not always been un-controversial. Indeed, the issue was litigated in an 1898 Supreme Court case involving Wong Kim Ark, a Chinese American restaurant cook and native of San Francisco, who, on August 31, 1894, returned to California after a visit to China.[2] To the surprise of this twenty-four-year-old, he

---

[1] U.S. Const. amend. XIV, § 1.

[2] The details and quotations from Wong Kim Ark's Supreme Court case are drawn from *United States* v. *Wong Kim Ark*, 169 U.S. 649 (1898). The information about Wong Kim Ark's life in the United States, employment, migration between China and the United States, and negotiations with U.S. immigration officials are taken from his immigration file housed at the National Archives Pacific Branch in San Bruno, California: File 12017/42223; Box 458; Return Certificate Application Case Files of Chinese Departing, 1913–1944; Records of the Immigration and Naturalization Service (San Francisco), Record Group 85; National Archives and Records Administration—Pacific Region (San Bruno, CA) [hereinafter cited as Wong Kim Ark Return Case File, San Francisco, NA–P]. The details of Wong Kim Ark's legal case at the federal district court can be found in the federal district court

was denied re-admission into the United States by immigration officials of the U.S. Customs Service.[3] U.S. Collector of Customs John H. Wise claimed that Wong—though born in the United States—was not a U.S. citizen because his parents were Chinese persons ineligible for citizenship. According to Wise, Wong was excludable as a laborer "of the Mongolian race" under the Chinese Exclusion Act of 1882, which prohibited the immigration of Chinese laborers, restricted entry to Chinese belonging to a few "exempt" classes (merchants, students, teachers, travelers, and diplomats), and barred all Chinese immigrants from naturalized citizenship.[4] A self-described "zealous opponent of Chinese immigration," Collector Wise was attempting to apply the exclusion laws as broadly as possible, including to Chinese Americans such as Wong.[5] Wise ordered that Wong be returned to China.

Wong and his lawyers challenged the decision with a writ of habeas corpus, claiming his right to be re-admitted into the United States based on his status as a U.S. citizen under the Fourteenth Amendment. The question for the court was: how does the United States determine citizenship? By jus soli (by soil) or by jus sanguinis (by blood)? The U.S. District Court for the Northern District of California ruled for Wong, but the U.S. District Attorney appealed the decision and the case was argued before the United States Supreme Court in March 1897. With a majority opinion by Justice Horace Gray, the Supreme Court ruled in Wong's

---

records, also housed at the National Archives Pacific Branch: Wong Kim Ark; Folder 11198; Box 594; Admiralty Case Files, 1851–1934, Northern District of California (San Francisco); Records of the District Courts of the United States, Record Group 21; National Archives and Records Administration—Pacific Region (San Bruno, CA) [hereinafter cited as Wong Kim Ark Admiralty Case File, San Francisco, NA–P].

[3] Prior to the passage of the Chinese Exclusion Act in 1882, there was neither a trained force of government officials and interpreters nor the bureaucratic machinery with which to enforce federal immigration laws. With the passage of the Act in 1882, the United States Customs Service, a department with no previous experience enforcing immigration laws, was called upon to enforce the exclusion laws. The Customs Service maintained jurisdiction over Chinese immigration cases for the first eighteen years of the exclusion era. In 1900, Congress transferred the administration of the exclusion laws to the Commissioner-General of Immigration (under the auspices of the U.S. Department of Treasury), but the everyday enforcement of the law still remained with the immigration officials in the Customs Service. Finally, in 1903, all Chinese immigration matters were placed under the control of the Bureau of Immigration and its parent department, the newly created Department of Commerce and Labor. *See generally* Carl E. Prince & Mollie Keller, *The U.S. Customs Service: A Bicentennial History* 173 (1989); Darrell Hevenor Smith & H. Guy Herring, *The Bureau of Immigration: Its History, Activities and Organization* 7, 9–10 (1924); The Sundry Civil Act, ch. 791, 31 Stat. 588, 611 (1900); Department of Commerce and Labor (Nelson) Act, ch. 552, § 4, 32 Stat. 825 (1903).

[4] Chinese Exclusion Act, ch. 126, 22 Stat. 58 (1882) (repealed 1943).

[5] Erika Lee, *At America's Gates: Chinese Immigration During the Exclusion Era, 1882–1943* at 52 (2003).

favor, declaring that Wong Kim Ark was indeed a U.S. citizen under the Fourteenth Amendment and could not be excluded from the country. The Court's ruling firmly secured the constitutional status of birthright citizenship.

This chapter tells the story of this largely overlooked Supreme Court case by discussing its origins and explaining its importance. As will become clear, the importance of *United States v. Wong Kim Ark* is directly linked to the divisive debate over race, immigration, and citizenship in late nineteenth-century America. As a matter of formal law, *Wong Kim Ark* settled this debate and made legal history by sustaining birthright citizenship for all persons born in the United States, regardless of race. As a matter of substantive citizenship, the debate about race and belonging in America raged on. For this reason, the aftermath of *Wong Kim Ark* is as important as the case itself. Indeed, the ways in which the principle of birthright citizenship was applied to and used by Chinese Americans, as well as the contemporary resonance of the case, help us to understand the impact of law on everyday people, hierarchies within American citizenship, current debates about immigration, and how history and memory are both forgotten and remembered. Part of the aim of this chapter is to remember the life history of Wong Kim Ark himself.[6] Buried in that history is a story about how American identity is negotiated both inside and outside the boundaries of formal citizenship.

Wong Kim Ark, the Chinese Exclusion Laws, and the Debate over U.S. Citizenship

Wong Kim Ark was born in San Francisco in 1873. His parents, Wong Si Ping and Wee Lee, were long-term California residents, and at the time of Wong's birth they lived in San Francisco's Chinatown. Wong Si Ping was a merchant who helped manage the Quong Sing and Company on Sacramento Street. Awash in anti-Chinese sentiment, 1870s San Francisco was hostile to Chinese. White workers, California politicians, and others rallied behind Denis Kearney, the leader of the anti-Chinese Workingmen's Party and readily answered his call that "the Chinese must go!"[7] Discriminatory state and local laws sought to exclude Chinese from certain occupations and neighborhoods. Stereotypes depicting Chinese as a dangerous racial menace proliferated in popular culture.[8] In 1876, H. N. Clement, a San Francisco lawyer, stood before a special California state senate committee and declared a crisis: "*The*

---

[6] Traditionally, Chinese names begin with the surname, as in Wong, and this is how Wong Kim Ark will be referred to in this article.

[7] On Denis Kearney, see Alexander Saxton, *The Indispensable Enemy: Labor and the Anti–Chinese Movement in California* 113–137 (1975).

[8] Robert G. Lee, *Orientals: Asian Americans in Popular Culture* at 15–82 (1999).

Chinese are upon us. How can we get rid of them? *The Chinese are coming.* How can we stop them?" he asked.[9] By 1882, the U.S. Congress heeded the call of Californians and other Westerners to protect them from the so-called "Chinese invasion" by passing the Chinese Exclusion Act. Chinese laborers became the first group excluded from the country on the basis of their race and class. As a result of the new law, Chinese immigration dropped drastically, and the numbers of Chinese returning to China increased. In 1890, S. J. Ruddell, the Chief Immigrant Inspector in San Francisco remarked that the number of stores in Chinatown were "decreasing every day." Should the trend continue, he predicted, the Chinese community might "completely disappear."[10]

Wong Kim Ark's family joined the exodus out of California. In 1890, all three family members sailed for China. His parents remained in China for the rest of their lives, but Wong Kim Ark returned to San Francisco several months later. Like the more than 300,000 Chinese admitted into the United States either as first-time immigrants or returning residents and citizens during the exclusion era, Wong Kim Ark found that employment opportunities were better in America than they were in China. Even during the exclusion era, Chinese referred to the United States as *Gum Saan* or "Gold Mountain." Moreover, for Wong, the United States was his home, and on his first return trip in 1890, Wong was recognized as a native-born citizen and quickly re-admitted into the country. He eventually joined an uncle and moved to the California Sierra Mountains where he became a restaurant cook.[11]

By the time Wong made a second trip to China in 1895, the United States was quickly moving towards greater immigration restriction, eventually affecting American-born Chinese like him. Zealous immigration officials and supporters of Chinese exclusion successfully campaigned to broaden the scope of the laws. In 1892, the Geary Act renewed the exclusion of laborers for another ten years and required all Chinese residents to register with the federal government for a certificate of residence (a precursor to the contemporary "green card"). In 1902, the exclusion of Chinese was extended to the newly-acquired American territories of Hawai'i and the Philippines. In 1904, the law was renewed without any time limit and remained in effect until its repeal in

---

[9] Special Comm. on Chinese Immigration, Cal. State Senate, *Chinese Immigration; Its Social, Moral, and Political Effect: Report to the California State Senate of Its Special Committee on Chinese Immigration* 275 (1878) (emphasis added).

[10] Lee, *supra* note 5, at 43–44; H.R. Select Comm. of Immigration and Naturalization, *Investigation of Chinese Immigration,* H.R. Doc. No. 51–4048, at 270–71 (1890).

[11] Wong Kim Ark Return Case File, San Francisco, NA–P.

1943.[12] As Wong's case makes clear, the exclusion laws were designed to regulate immigrants, but the government's enforcement procedures extended to all Chinese, including those citizens who were born in the United States and traveled abroad.

The Chinese exclusion laws are one lens through which *United States v. Wong Kim Ark* must be understood. From a broader standpoint, Wong Kim Ark's case also reflected the contested nature of American citizenship during the late nineteenth century and the role of Chinese immigration in redefining what it meant to be an American. The scope of naturalization in the United States was first codified in 1790 with the Naturalization Act passed that year. Both inclusive and exclusive, the law required just two years of residence in the United States before aliens could apply for citizenship. However, only "free white persons" were eligible for naturalization.[13] American citizenship was further redefined during the debate over slavery and during the Civil War and Reconstruction eras. Although the path was tortuous, citizenship slowly became more inclusive during those years. Following the Civil War, Congress passed a series of amendments and citizenship-related acts in order to grant citizenship and voting rights to the newly-freed African American slaves. The 1866 Civil Rights Act, passed over President Andrew Johnson's veto, guaranteed the principle of equality before the law, regardless of race. The Fourteenth Amendment to the Constitution, which was ratified in 1868, went even further to specify that "all persons born or naturalized in the United States ... are citizens of the United States."[14] In 1870, a new Naturalization Act extended the right of naturalization to "aliens of African nativity, and to persons of African descent."[15]

At the same time that U.S. citizenship and naturalization were being extended to Africans and African Americans, the question arose concerning whether or not Chinese immigrants—quickly recognized as the nation's latest racial "problem"—would be granted the right of naturalized citizenship as well. The U.S. government's answer was a resounding "no." In 1875, Representative Horace Page of California

---

[12] Geary (Chinese Exclusion) Act, ch. 60, 27 Stat. 25 (1892) (repealed 1943); Hawaiian Annexation Resolution, J. Res. 55 § 1, 30 Stat. 750, 751 (1898) (section on Chinese exclusion repealed 1943); Hawaiian Organic Act, § 101, ch. 339, 31 Stat. 141, 161 (1900) (section on Chinese exclusion repealed 1943); Chinese Exclusion Act, Pub. L. No. 57–90, 32 Stat. 176 (1902) (repealed 1943); Appropriations Deficiencies Act, Pub. L. No. 58–189, 33 Stat. 428 (1904) (repealed 1943).

[13] Naturalization Act, ch. 3, 1 Stat. 103 (1790) (repealed 1795). In 1795, the two-year residency requirement was changed to five. Naturalization Act, ch. 20, 1 Stat. 414 (1795).

[14] U.S. Const. amend. XIV, § 1.

[15] Naturalization Laws, ch. 254, 16 Stat. 254 (1870).

argued to Congress that the Chinese were "a class of people wholly unworthy to be entrusted with the right of American citizenship." Citizenship among the Chinese, he continued, would be used only "for corrupt purposes by corrupt individuals."[16] Other politicians claimed that unlike "Aryan or European races," the Chinese lacked "sufficient brain capacity . . . to furnish motive power for self-government," having "no comprehension of any form of government but despotism."[17] In 1877, a congressional committee investigating Chinese immigration concluded that the Chinese were "[a]n indigestible mass in the community, distinct in language, pagan in religion, inferior in mental and moral qualities, and all peculiarities. . . ."[18] Prohibiting them from citizenship was not only desirable, the committee concluded, it was also a "necessary measure" for the good of the public.[19]

The Chinese Exclusion Act of 1882 legitimized this belief by barring all Chinese immigrants from naturalized citizenship, but the question of birthright citizenship for Chinese born in the United States remained open. The first court case to rule on the question of birthright citizenship involved Look Tin Sing, a fourteen-year-old boy born in Mendocino, California, who attempted to reenter the United States in 1884 after studying in China. Because natives were not explicitly listed as an exempt class in the original Exclusion Act, and because Look Tin Sing had no documentation proving his membership in another exempt class, he was denied entry by immigration officials in San Francisco. Look appealed, and the Circuit Court for the District of California reversed the decision and ruled in his favor. Declaring that the Fourteenth Amendment provided that "all persons born or naturalized in the United States" were citizens, the court ruled that Look Tin Sing was indeed a citizen and that the Exclusion Act did not apply to him.[20] Following the *Look Tin Sing* ruling, the courts continued to recognize birthright citizenship for Chinese.[21]

But the ruling also had unintended consequences that would eventually jeopardize the right of American-born Chinese to reenter the country. As the exclusion laws and their enforcement grew increasingly restrictive during the 1890s, more and more Chinese attempted to enter

---

[16] H.R. Res. 4546, 43d Cong. (1875).

[17] *Report of the Joint Special Committee to Investigate Chinese Immigration*, S. Rep. No. 689, 44th Cong., 2d Sess. 3 (1877).

[18] *Id.*

[19] *Id.* at vii.

[20] *In re* Look Tin Sing, 21 F. 905, 910 (C.C.D. Cal. 1884).

[21] Lucy E. Salyer, *Laws Harsh as Tigers: Chinese Immigrants and the Shaping of Modern Immigration Law* 81 (1995).

the country by using illegal immigration strategies, including false claims of birth in the United States.[22] Exclusionists responded by launching a new campaign to challenge the extension of birthright citizenship to Chinese, hoping to close what they saw as an egregious loophole in the exclusion laws. This anti-Chinese faction argued that the principle of jus sanguinis, that is, blood or descent, should take precedence over jus soli, place of birth. Because federal laws prohibited Chinese immigrants from naturalizing, this faction believed that exclusion from citizenship should descend to their American-born children. This principle, exclusionists argued, was especially relevant for the Chinese, who were incapable of assimilation as a race. In 1884, lawyer George D. Collins argued in the *American Law Review* that children of Chinese "born upon American soil are Chinese from their very birth in all respects, just as much so as though they had been born and reared in China." They had inherited the deficient characteristics that made their parents so objectionable to Americans and were "utterly unfit [and] wholly incompetent, to exercise the important privileges of an American citizen." Collins would later assist the U.S. District Attorney in his case against Wong Kim Ark in the federal district court.[23]

The Federal District Court Case

Wong Kim Ark's return trip to California in 1895 took place right in the middle of this debate over birthright citizenship and its application to Chinese Americans. In November of 1894, Wong prepared for his short journey to China to visit his parents. Like all other American-born Chinese during the exclusion era, Wong realized that his status as a U.S. citizen was precarious. It was widely known that immigration officials could and did deny entry to those claiming birth in the United States. In order to facilitate their reentry into the country, American-born Chinese needed to adhere carefully to government regulations. This included the requirement that Chinese provide two non-Chinese (that is, white) witnesses to corroborate their claims to native birth.[24] Prior to his departure to China, Wong Kim Ark filled out the requisite paperwork

---

[22] Lee, *supra* note 5, at 189–220.

[23] George D. Collins, Note, *Are Persons Born Within the United States Ipso Facto Citizens Thereof?*, 18 Am. L. Rev. 831, 834 (1884); Salyer, *supra* note 21, at 99. On Collins' involvement in the *Wong Kim Ark* case, see Brief on Behalf of the United States by George D. Collins (Nov. 19, 1895), In re Wong Kim Ark, 71 F. 382, 384 (N.D. Cal. 1896).

[24] Beginning in 1892, the Department of Treasury instructed immigration officials that Chinese claiming citizenship had to prove their claim by evidence other than Chinese testimony, which standing alone was deemed to be unreliable. Lee, *supra* note 5, at 106; Senate Committee on Immigration, U.S. Congress, Alleged Illegal Entry into the United States of Chinese Persons, S. Doc. No. 55–120, at 9 (1897); U.S. Dep't of Treasury, Annual Report of the Commissioner–General of Immigration 76–77 (1902).

with immigration officials in San Francisco. He submitted a notarized affidavit with his photograph as a form of identification. The affidavit noted that Wong was a "citizen of the United States, born in the City and County of San Francisco." It spelled out Wong's intention to return to the United States and his entitlement (as a citizen) to do so. It also included the signed statements of three white witnesses, Wm. Fisher, F. Benna, and L. Selenger, who personally appeared before Notary Public Robert M. Edwards and testified that they knew Wong Kim Ark and that he had been born in San Francisco, California.[25] Eleven months later, Wong arrived back in San Francisco and was subjected to a routine interrogation. Answering in fluent English, he told the immigration official that he was twenty-four years old, that he had been to China once before and had been readmitted into the United States, that all of his family was in China, that he worked as a cook, and that "white men in San Francisco" could verify his birth in the United States. "You are sure you were born here?" the official asked. "Yes," answered Wong.[26]

Despite these answers, Collector John Wise denied Wong reentry and placed him in the custody of the U.S. marshal. Wong was detained aboard the steamship *Coptic*, on which he had sailed from China. Wong's detention lasted over four months. After 1910, Chinese detainees were housed in the barracks of the immigration station on Angel Island in the San Francisco Bay, but at the time that Wong Kim Ark returned to San Francisco, there was no government-run immigration detention or processing center. When the *Coptic* left San Francisco, Wong was transferred to another steamship, the *Gaelic*, and then onto the *Peking*.[27] Although little is known about the treatment of detainees like Wong on board the steamships, later accounts indicate that conditions for Chinese during the exclusion era in general were quite abysmal: crowded, dirty, and disease-infested. Moreover, Chinese, including those like Wong Kim Ark claiming to be citizens, were treated little better than criminals. Chinese often referred to the detention centers as "iron cages," or "Chinese jails." Once on Angel Island, Chinese chose to refer to the immigration station as "Devil Island" in order to better characterize their poor and unjust treatment.[28] While detained on the steamship, Wong was most likely given poor-quality food and a place to sleep, but

---

[25] Notarized Affidavit of Wm. Fisher, F. Benna, and L. Selenger (Nov. 5, 1894) (on file with Wong Kim Ark Return Case Files, San Francisco, NA–P).

[26] Interrogation of Wong Kim Ark on board the *Coptic* (Aug. 31, 1895) (on file with Wong Kim Ark Return Case Files, San Francisco, NA–P).

[27] In the Matter of the Application of Wong Kim Ark, for a Writ of Habeas Corpus, at 2 (Oct. 2, 1895) (on file with Wong Kim Ark Admiralty Case File, San Francisco, NA–P).

[28] *See* Marlon K. Hom, *Songs of Gold Mountain: Cantonese Rhymes from San Francisco Chinatown* 78 (1987).

very little freedom to do anything else during the four long months until his case was decided.

Like many other Chinese during the exclusion era, Wong Kim Ark challenged his exclusion from the United States. The significance of the case was immediately apparent when Thomas Riordan, a prominent San Francisco attorney who often represented the Chinese Consulate as well as the Chinese Six Companies, the umbrella organization for the large kinship and mutual benefit associations serving the Chinese in America, signed on to represent Wong. Long a defender of the Chinese, Riordan had argued a number of landmark cases that challenged racially discriminatory treatment under local, state, and federal laws. For instance, he represented Chae Chan Ping before the Supreme Court in a case that unsuccessfully challenged the constitutionality of the Scott Act of 1888.[29] That act prohibited any returning Chinese laborer from entering the country, even those who had been granted return certificates.[30] Riordan also coordinated the legal team that argued *Fong Yue Ting v. United States* before the Supreme Court in 1893. This case contested, also unsuccessfully, the constitutionality of the 1892 Geary Act, which had extended the exclusion of Chinese laborers for another ten years and required all Chinese in the United States to register with the U.S. government.[31]

Upon taking charge of Wong Kim Ark's defense, Riordan filed a writ of habeas corpus in the federal district court alleging that Wong was being "unlawfully confined and restrained of his liberty on board the steamship *Coptic*." The writ also claimed that Wong, as a native-born citizen, had a right to reenter the country, for he had been "born within the dominion, power, protection and obedience of the United States," and that he had "always subjected himself to the jurisdiction and dominion of the United States, and had been taxed, recognized and treated as a citizen of the United States."[32] Riordan also specifically pointed out that under the Fourteenth Amendment to the U.S. Constitu-

---

[29] Chae Chan Ping v. United States (*The Chinese Exclusion Case*), 130 U.S. 581 (1889).

[30] Laborers who had a lawful wife, child, or parent in the United States, or had property or debts due him worth at least $1,000 could be re-admitted. Act of Oct. 1, 1888, ch. 1064, 25 Stat. 504.

[31] Fong Yue Ting v. United States, 149 U.S. 698, 713 (1893); Salyer, *supra* note 21, at 47–58. For Riordan's involvement in challenging California state laws that discriminated against the Chinese, see Charles J. McClain, *In Search of Equality: The Chinese Struggle Against Discrimination in Nineteenth–Century America* 93, 102, 104, 107–09 (1994). For Riordan's involvement in *Chae Chan Ping* and the Scott Act, see *id.* at 194, 196, and for Riordan's role in *Fong Yue Ting* and the Geary Act, see *id.* at 204, 207, 209.

[32] Petition for Writ of Habeas Corpus, Amended (Nov. 11, 1895) at 3, In re Wong Kim Ark, 71 F. 382 (N.D. Cal. 1896) (No. 11198) (on file with Wong Kim Ark Admiralty Case File, San Francisco, NA–P).

tion, the laws excluding Chinese laborers were "inapplicable to a person born in the United States, and subject to its jurisdictions."[33]

U.S. District Attorney Henry S. Foote argued the case on behalf of the federal government. In his opinion, the question at hand was whether or not native-born Chinese could be considered citizens if their parents were not, and could never become, naturalized citizens. Foote argued that "birth alone does not constitute right to citizenship in the United States."[34] His primary contention was that the words "subject to the jurisdiction thereof" in the Fourteenth Amendment referred to the political jurisdiction of the United States.[35] In other words, Wong Kim Ark, though born within the territorial jurisdiction of the United States, was not subject to the political jurisdiction of the country because his parents remained Chinese subjects, allegedly loyal to the Chinese empire and not to the United States. "A child born in California, of Chinese parents, is, at the moment of birth, subject to a foreign power," he explained.[36] Similarly, lawyer George D. Collins' brief on behalf of the U.S. government sharply criticized the Fourteenth Amendment and its "disastrous consequences" of forcing the country to accept as native-born citizens "the rag tag and bob tail of humanity, who happen to be deposited on our soil by the accident of birth." According to Collins, Wong Kim Ark squarely fit into this category of unacceptable, "accidental" citizens whose "education and political affiliations" remained "entirely alien" to those of the United States.[37] Both Foote and Collins argued that since both of Wong Kim Ark's parents were "subjects of the Emperor of China," Wong himself inherited this nationality and was also a "Chinese person and a subject of the Emperor of China." A child born in the United States may "nominally be a citizen," but raised by alien Chinese parents, the district attorney reasoned, the child remained "an alien loyal to the country of his father and indifferent to the country of

---

[33] Petitioners Points and Authorities (Nov. 19, 1895) at 2, In re Wong Kim Ark, 71 F. 382 (N.D. Cal. 1896) (No. 11198) (on file with Wong Kim Ark Admiralty Case File, San Francisco, NA–P).

[34] Brief on Behalf of the United States by Henry S. Foote (Nov. 13, 1895) at 5, 7, In re Wong Kim Ark, 71 F. 382 (N.D. Cal. 1896) (No. 11198) (on file with Wong Kim Ark Admiralty Case File, San Francisco, NA–P).

[35] *Id.* at 1–2.

[36] *Id.* at 5.

[37] Brief on Behalf of the United States by George D. Collins (Nov. 13, 1895) at 4, In re Wong Kim Ark, 71 F. 382 (N.D. Cal. 1896) (No. 11198) (on file with Wong Kim Ark Admiralty Case File, San Francisco, NA–P).

this birth."[38] Conflating "Chineseness" with "alienness" and implying that being "Chinese" and being "American" were incompatible, the U.S. District Attorney declared that Wong could not possibly be considered an American citizen, for he had "been at all times, by reason of his race, language, color, and dress, a Chinese person."[39]

The District Attorney also warned that allowing Chinese persons such as Wong Kim Ark to be recognized as citizens would be extremely dangerous. Echoing the anti-Chinese movement, the brief asked, "Is it possible that any Court in the United States will deliberately force upon us as natural born citizens, persons who must necessarily be a constant menace to the welfare of our Country? ... We submit that such things cannot be without imperilling [sic] the very existence of our Country."[40] The district attorney's final contention was that since birthright U.S. citizenship should not apply to Wong Kim Ark, he should be excluded from the country as a Chinese laborer barred under the Chinese exclusion laws.[41]

Judge William Morrow of the federal circuit court of Northern California expressed sympathy for the government's position. A former California representative to Congress between 1885 and 1891, Morrow was "loyal" to anti-Chinese activists and had been "at the forefront of the campaign to make the Chinese restriction acts more severe."[42] Morrow demonstrated his support by explaining that "[t]he doctrine of the law of nations, that the child follows the nationality of the parents, and that citizenship does not depend upon mere accidental place of birth, is undoubtedly more logical, reasonable, and satisfactory...."[43] But, as historian Lucy Salyer has explained, Judge Morrow and his colleagues were "captives of law."[44] He did not allow his own agreement with the

---

[38] Points and Authorities of U.S. District Attorney, on Argument (Nov. 13, 1895) at 1–2; and Brief on Behalf of the United States by George D. Collins, *supra* note 37, at 5.

[39] Points and Authorities of U.S. District Attorney, *supra* note 37, at 2.

[40] Brief on Behalf of the United States by George D. Collins, *supra* note 37, at 6.

[41] Brief on Behalf of the United States at 6, *Wong Kim Ark*, 71 F. 382 (No. 11198), Points and Authorities of U.S. District Attorney at 6 (Nov. 19, 1895) (on file with Wong Kim Ark Admiralty Case File, San Francisco, NA–P).

[42] Salyer, *supra* note 21, at 33.

[43] *Wong Kim Ark*, 71 F. at 392.

[44] Salyer, *supra* note 21, at 69.

government's case to overturn the judicial precedent upholding birth-right citizenship for Chinese in earlier cases, especially *Look Tin Sing* decided in 1883. Referring to *Look Tin Sing*, Morrow wrote that "[t]he similarity of the essential facts between that case and the one at bar is obvious...."[45] From this vantage point, the political status and rights of Wong Kim Ark were clear. The Fourteenth Amendment, Morrow argued, was "sufficiently broad to cover the case of the petitioner. He is a person born in the United States."[46] Having found that Wong had not forfeited his right to return to the United States, Morrow ruled that his detention was illegal. "He should be discharged, and it is so ordered," he concluded.[47]

The Supreme Court Case

The government appealed the circuit court's ruling and the case proceeded on to the Supreme Court. Justice Horace Gray wrote the majority opinion, which was joined by six other Justices. Rejecting the government's distinction between political and territorial jurisdiction as a basis for conferring citizenship, Gray reiterated the lower court's finding that common law doctrine held that a person became a citizen by virtue of jus soli, his birth in the United States, rather than his blood line. "The right of citizenship [in the United States] never descends in the legal sense, either by the common law, or under the common naturalization acts. It is incident to birth in the country, or it is given personally by statute."[48] Even in the case at hand, although Wong Kim Ark's parents were "subjects of the Emperor of China," he became at birth a citizen of the United States. In his opinion, Justice Gray also noted two important issues. After studying the congressional debates over the Fourteenth Amendment, Gray argued that Congress had been fully aware that the amendment would apply to children born in the United States of Chinese parents.[49] Moreover, if the Court were to rule that the amendment excluded from citizenship the American-born children of subjects of other countries, the government would in effect be denying citizenship to "thousands of persons of English, Scotch, Irish, German, or other European parentage, who have always been considered and treated as citizens of the United States."[50] With this majority opinion, *Wong Kim Ark v. United States* affirmed that regardless of race,

---

[45] *Wong Kim Ark*, 71 F. at 387.

[46] *Id.*

[47] *Id.* at 392.

[48] *Wong Kim Ark*, 169 U.S. at 666.

[49] *Id.* at 698–99, 682.

[50] *Id.* at 694.

all persons born in the United States were, in fact, native-born citizens of the United States and entitled to all of the rights that citizenship offered.

Chief Justice Melville W. Fuller, joined by Justice John M. Harlan, authored the dissent, which expressed sympathy for the government's position, arguing that being "subject to the jurisdiction of the United States" should not be the sole ground for granting citizenship. The individual also must be "completely subject to [the] political jurisdiction" of the United States, owing "direct and immediate allegiance" to the country.[51] The issue at hand, the dissenters continued, was whether "permanent allegiance" to a nation was "imposed at birth without regard to circumstances."[52] The dissent thought not. A "mere change of domicil" to the United States by an "accident of birth" did not translate into a change of political allegiance.[53] The fact that Wong Kim Ark was of Chinese descent was perhaps the most important factor in this case. Drawing upon contemporary accounts of the Chinese as an unassimilable race, Justice Fuller described China as an "ancient empire, with its history of thousands of years, and its unbroken continuity in belief, traditions, and government."[54] Coming from such a culture, Fuller suggested, the Chinese could not be expected to embrace American customs or political beliefs.

In support of his position, Fuller pointed to previous court decisions that had upheld the constitutionality of the Chinese exclusion laws. In *Fong Yue Ting v. United States*, for example, the Court had affirmed that the Chinese were still "a distinct race ..., remaining strangers in the land, residing apart by themselves, tenaciously adhering to the customs and usages of their own country, unfamiliar with our institutions, and apparently incapable of assimilating with our people."[55] Moreover, Justice Fuller continued, the treaty between China and the United States signed in 1868 expressly disallowed Chinese from becoming naturalized citizens, and existing U.S. naturalization laws did the same. Justice Fuller argued passionately that "the children of Chinese born in this country do not, ipso facto, become citizens of the United States unless the Fourteenth Amendment overrides both treaty and statute."[56] Given such evidence, the dissent concluded that "[i]t is not to be admitted that the children of persons so situated become citizens by the accident of birth."[57]

---

[51] *Id.* at 724 (Fuller, J., dissenting).

[52] *Wong Kim Ark*, 169 U.S. at 722–23 (Fuller, J., dissenting).

[53] *Id.* at 723, 731.

[54] *Id.* at 725–26, 731.

[55] *Id.* at 731 (quoting Fong Yue Ting v. United States, 149 U.S. 698, 717 (1893)).

[56] *Wong Kim Ark*, 169 U.S. at 731–732 (Fuller, J., dissenting).

[57] *Id.* at 731.

As a matter of formal law, Justice Fuller's argument did not carry the day. However, as a matter of substantive citizenship, the argument continued to shape how people of Chinese ancestry experienced their American identity—as unequal citizens.

"Unequal Citizenship"—The Aftermath

Wong Kim Ark was enormously significant in establishing the constitutional status of birthright citizenship, but its immediate impact on Chinese Americans was more convoluted. Legal scholar Hyung–Chan Kim writes that it "opened ajar the hitherto closed door for Chinese-born in the U.S. to make entry into the community called the United States." This was an important victory for Chinese–American constitutional rights, but Kim points out that the case "did not have a major impact on the Chinese community in America as there were not many second-generation Chinese."[58] Similarly, Brook Thomas argues that "as important as [*Wong Kim Ark*] was and remains for a more inclusive vision of American citizenship, it was and is limited." The ruling provided a "formal definition of who can be a natural born citizen," but, as Thomas explains, it did not provide "a vision of the type of civic life that a citizen will be born into.... Whether a country has a *jus soli* or *jus sanguinis* determination of citizenship has little or no effect on how citizens interact with one another or the relation between citizens and the political body that governs them."[59]

A closer look at the status of Chinese Americans, including Wong Kim Ark himself, after the Supreme Court victory further supports these characterizations. On the one hand, the case protected the right of Chinese born in the United States to reenter the country in spite of the Chinese exclusion laws. Citizens such as Wong Kim Ark should have been able to return to the country without harassment. However, the protection granted to citizens by the case also opened the door to widespread illegal immigration. From 1894 to 1940, 97,143 Chinese claiming to be native-born citizens were readmitted into the country. They made up 48% of the total number of Chinese admitted. A large majority of these cases were likely fraudulent.[60] Given the U.S. government's reluctance to grant birthright citizenship to Chinese born in the United States in the first place and its suspicion that a great number of

---

[58] *Asian Americans and the Supreme Court* 26–27 (Hyung–chan Kim ed., 1992).

[59] Brook Thomas, *China Men*, United States v. Wong Kim Ark, *and the Question of Citizenship*, 50 Am. Q. 689, 701–02 (1998).

[60] Lee, *supra* note 5, at 189–220.

Chinese immigrants were posing as U.S. citizens in order to enter the country, *Wong Kim Ark* did not materially change the conditions under which American-born citizens were processed by immigration officials. Nor did the case result in Chinese Americans' complete inclusion into the American family. In an example of the hierarchical nature of U.S. citizenship, Chinese Americans were instead treated as second-class citizens, or "alien citizens."[61] In this way, Chinese Americans shared a similar fate as African Americans who were disfranchised and denied their civil rights under Jim Crow laws.

Wong Kim Ark had ruled that Chinese born in the United States were U.S. citizens and exempt from the exclusion laws, but the court did not define *how* citizenship or native birth could be proven. U.S. immigration inspectors established their own means of measuring citizenship status and "Americanness." In processing returning citizens, officials acted on racialized assumptions that the applicants were either fraudulent or inferior citizens. Chinese claiming citizenship after *Wong Kim Ark* still had to undergo the lengthy investigations and interrogations to which aliens were subjected in order to prove their nativity and their right to reenter the country. This process included the requirement that Chinese provide white witnesses to verify their claims of native birth.[62] In this way, relationships with white persons became a direct means of measuring "Americanness." Some Chinese could readily produce white witnesses to come to their defense, but it was a particularly large obstacle for the vast majority who remained segregated within Chinese communities. As one immigration official who disagreed with this ruling incredulously asked his superiors, "Who else [but the Chinese relatives of the applicant] would be likely to have the knowledge required as a witness in a case of native birth, if not those closely related to the party born?"[63] Over the years, producing white witnesses grew increasingly difficult. In 1910, the Chinese American organization known as the Native Sons of the Golden State (later renamed the Chinese American Citizens Alliance) complained to the U.S. Secretary of Labor that wit-

---

[61] Mae M. Ngai suggests that native-born Asian Americans and Mexican Americans have held formal U.S. citizenship, but have nonetheless remained "alien in the eyes of the nation." *See* Mae M. Ngai, *Impossible Subjects: Illegal Aliens and the Making of Modern America* 8 (2004).

[62] Because Chinese families often gave birth to their children at home, many Chinese American citizens did not have birth certificates. After the 1906 earthquake and fire in San Francisco destroyed all birth records in the city, such records were nearly impossible to find. Coincidentally, the destruction of birth records also provided an enormous opportunity for those with fraudulent claims to native birth. Lee, *supra* note 5, at 106.

[63] Collector of Customs to the Secretary of the Treasury (Mar. 30, 1899) (on file at File 53108/9–B, Subject Correspondence, Records of the Immigration and Naturalization Service, RG 85, National Archives [hereinafter I.N.S. Subject Correspondence, NA]).

nesses were "departing from the country, dying, or removing to parts unknown."[64]

Returning U.S. citizens of Chinese descent were also subjected to additional tests and procedures designed to prove their nativity and to measure their knowledge about the United States, and hence their "Americanness." Citizens were judged according to how well they could speak English, how much they conformed to American customs and dress, and how well they could identify local landmarks and recite basic facts about U.S. history. Immigrant inspectors, for example, clearly noted that Wong Kim Ark could speak English "fluently" when Wong returned from his first trip to China in July, 1890.[65] Moreover, it was not uncommon for immigration officials to note favorably that an applicant claiming citizenship dressed in American-style clothing. In recommending that applicant Moy Goon be landed in 1905, for example, immigrant inspector Alfred W. Parker noted that Moy was "an extraordinarily bright, intelligent Chinaman, dresse[d] in American clothes, and speak[ing] good English. By appearances and conduct, I should say that his claim to American birth is quite reasonable." Another reported that Moy used the American name "Charlie" and was "thoroughly Americanized" and "highly respected."[66] At times, citizen applicants were tested on their knowledge of the geography, history, and commonplace features of San Francisco's Chinatown or their claimed hometowns. Applicants were asked to give exact addresses and directions to local landmarks, including which modes of public transportation were available in those areas. In the eyes of immigration officials and exclusionists, such measures were necessary to ferret out any cases in which Chinese aliens were falsely claiming U.S. citizenship in order to enter the country. Although some of these tests certainly did help immigration officials expose fraudulent cases, they often required Chinese American citizens to meet high, and often absurd, standards.

Even if they succeeded in being readmitted into the United States, Chinese American citizens found that their citizenship offered little protection from government harassment, especially during immigration service raids, arrests, and deportation efforts of illegal immigrants. Invariably, Chinese American citizens were caught up in the dragnets. In

---

[64] S. G. Carpenter to Secretary of Commerce and Labor (Sept. 23, 1910) (on file at File 52961/24–b, Box 170, I.N.S. Subject Correspondence, NA).

[65] July 16, 1890 Interview at 2, (on file at File 12017/42223, Chinese Arrival Files, San Francisco, Records of the Immigration and Naturalization Service, RG 85, National Archives, Pacific Region, San Bruno, California [hereinafter Chinese Arrival Files, San Francisco, NA–P]).

[66] Report from Immigrant Inspector (Oct. 5, 1905) (on file at File 10079/6, Chinese Arrival Files, San Francisco, NA–P).

1910, the Native Sons of California issued a formal complaint to the Secretary of Commerce and Labor. Among their many grievances, the group charged that Chinese Americans suffered from constant harassment by immigration officials both when traveling abroad and when residing in the United States. The Chinese American citizen was "liable to arrest at any time and place by zealous immigration officials upon the charge of being unlawfully in the country.... He moves from place to place at his peril," the letter stated.[67] During the 1920s, Chinese immigrants and Chinese American citizens alike charged the immigration service with subjecting the Chinese in America to a "reign of terror." The Chinese American Citizens Alliance complained to Representative Julius Kahn of California that "our unoffending people are being treated with little more respect than animals and every guaranty [sic] of the Constitution against unlawful searches is being defied in this ruthless campaign just launched against our people."[68]

The precarious status of Chinese American citizens had longstanding, even generational, consequences. The shadow of exclusion left native-born Chinese Americans susceptible to the insecurity and alienation felt by all Chinese in America. The suspicion and harsh treatment that Chinese Americans endured caused many to re-evaluate their status as Americans as well as their place in the United States. Wong Kim Ark, for example, continued to work in the United States, but never made it his permanent home. He married and had four sons in China, preferring to see them periodically rather than bring them to the United States. He lived with his youngest son, Wong Yook Jim, for only three years during his entire lifetime, spread out over several years. Eventually, Wong Kim Ark retired to China at the age of sixty-two and never returned to the United States. He died in China shortly after World War II.[69]

Ironically, while Wong Kim Ark's legal efforts and Supreme Court victory are considered landmark cases in constitutional and civil rights history, he reaped little benefit in the course of his everyday life. His immigration records now housed at the National Archives regional branch in San Bruno, California reveal that he made three additional

---

[67] S. G. Carpenter to Secretary of Commerce and Labor (Sept. 23, 1910) (on file at File 52961/24–B, I.N.S. Subject Correspondence, NA). For more on the Native Sons of California and the Chinese American Citizens Alliance, see Sue Fawn Chung, *Fighting for Their American Rights: A History of the Chinese American Citizens Alliance, in Claiming America: Constructing Chinese American Identities During the Exclusion Era* 95 (K. Scott Wong & Sucheng Chan eds., 1998).

[68] Letter from Native Sons of California to Julius Kahn, Representative, U.S. House of Representatives (Oct. 24, 1923) (on file at File 55383/30, I.N.S. Subject Correspondence, NA).

[69] Bill Wong, *Yellow Pearls: Wong Kim Ark's Legacy*, AsianWeek (San Francisco, CA), Apr. 30–May 6, 1998, at 6 (hereinafter "*Wong Kim Ark's Legacy*").

trips to China: once in 1905, again in 1913, and a last trip in 1931. Each time, Wong laboriously filled out the routine paperwork, had his attorneys make sure everything was in order, and submitted himself to the same interrogations by immigration officials who questioned his right to return to the land of his birth. In what must have felt like an enormous insult, in 1931, Wong Kim Ark filled out a form titled "Application of *Alleged* American Citizen of the Chinese Race for Preinvestigation of Status." The form was required of all Chinese claiming citizenship by birth in the United States, but one would have thought that Wong Kim Ark, of all people, would have been exempt from these bureaucratic hurdles and institutionalized suspicion. There is no mention of his Supreme Court case in any of the records.[70]

Long after Wong's Supreme Court victory, Chinese immigrants and Chinese Americans, including Wong's own son, Wong Yook Jim, still had to endure the same types of humiliating treatment that Wong himself had challenged. When Wong Yook Jim applied for admission into the country in 1926, he was subjected to the very kind of institutionalized suspicion and questioning his father had faced in 1895. Although over thirty years had passed, little had changed. Chinese of all classes and backgrounds were still presumed to be excludable first, admissible second. Yook Jim's stay at the Angel Island immigration station was a relatively short two weeks, but the resentment and bitterness that he felt on behalf of all Chinese at the immigration station remained vivid for decades afterwards.[71] The experiences of Wong Kim Ark and other citizens are appropriate examples of the high personal costs that exclusion exacted from Chinese Americans in the first half of the twentieth century. Born in the United States, they were nevertheless lumped together with other Asians as "Orientals" or foreigners, and the codification and legitimization of anti-Asian racism in American immigration laws exacerbated their unequal status as citizens and cast a shadow on the entire community.[72]

Wong Kim Ark's Legacy

Over the course of American history, the divisive effects of immigration politics, racism, and xenophobia have affected many minority

---

[70] *See* In re Wong Kim Ark, Native Departing, #12017/1686 (Oct. 16, 1913) (on file with Wong Kim Ark Return Case File, San Francisco, NA–P); Application of Alleged American Citizen of the Chinese Race for Preinvestigation of Status (July 14, 1931) (on file with Wong Kim Ark Return Case File, San Francisco, NA–P) (emphasis added).

[71] Bill Wong, *Yellow Pearls: Native-born American*, AsianWeek (San Francisco, CA), Apr. 2–8, 1998, at 6 (hereinafter, *Native-born American*); Wong, *supra* note 69; Bill Wong, *Yellow Pearls: Claiming a Birthright*, AsianWeek (San Francisco, CA), May 21–27, 1998, at 6.

[72] Qingchao Wu, *Chinatowns: A Study of Symbiosis and Assimilation* 288 (1928).

groups. In the 1930s, local, state, and national officials launched aggressive deportation and repatriation programs targeting Mexicans and Mexican Americans throughout the Southwest. One recent estimate places the number of people of Mexican origin who were returned to Mexico, including American-born children, at one million.[73] During World War II, 120,000 Japanese Americans, two-thirds of whom were second-generation citizens born in the United States, were incarcerated in remote camps and forced to take loyalty oaths. In 1994, Californians attacked the Mexican immigration "problem" with Proposition 187, which barred California state agencies from providing benefits to illegal aliens. The anti-immigrant mood and government crackdown on "illegal immigration" that followed Proposition 187 placed the entire Mexican–American community at risk, and the treatment of Mexican Americans as perpetual "foreigners" is reminiscent of the Chinese exclusion era.[74] In 1995, 1997, 1999, 2003, 2005, and 2007, Congress has considered bills that would "deny citizenship at birth to children born in the United States of parents who are not citizens or permanent resident aliens," including children of undocumented immigrants and legal immigrants lacking permanent resident status, such as refugees.[75]

Contemporary legal scholars argue that the Supreme Court "misread" the Citizenship Clause in the Fourteenth Amendment in the Wong Kim Ark case in ignoring a distinction between citizenship based on "basic territorial jurisdiction" versus citizenship based on "complete jurisdiction," which would encompass a person's allegiance to a nation.[76]

---

[73] Francisco E. Balderrama & Raymond Rodriguez, *Decade of Betrayal: Mexican Repatriation in the 1930s* 122 (1st ed. 1995).

[74] Kevin R. Johnson, *Race Matters: Immigration Law and Policy Scholarship, Law in the Ivory Tower, and the Legal Indifference of the Race Critique*, 2000 U.Ill. L.Rev. 525, 525–57.

[75] These bills have been known as the Citizenship Reform Acts. The Citizenship Reform Act of 1995, H.R. 1363, 104th Cong. (1995) resulted in joint hearings held by the Subcommittee on Immigration and Claims and by the Subcommittee on the Constitution. The Citizenship Reform Act of 1997, H.R. 7, 105th Cong. (1997) was discussed in subcommittee hearings, but no vote was taken. The Citizenship Reform Acts of 1999, H.R. 73, 106th Cong. (1999), and 2003, H.R. 1567, 108th Cong. (2003) were referred to House subcommittees. The 2005 bill, which was not approved, was introduced by Representative Nathan Deal, a Republican from Georgia, as part of the House of Representatives immigration bill that aimed to end illegal immigration with tougher enforcement at the border and other measures. Citizenship Reform Act of 2005, H.R. 698, 109th Cong. The approved House legislation was the Border Protection, Antiterrorism, and Illegal Immigration Control Act of 2005, H.R. 4437, 109th Cong. (referred to the U.S. Senate Jan. 27, 2006). *See* Stephen Dinan, *GOP Mulls Ending Birthright Citizenship*, Wash. Times, Nov. 4, 2005, at A1. As of this writing, the Citizenship Reform Act of 2007, H.R. 133, 110th Cong. (2007) was referred to House committee.

[76] The legal scholar referring to the Supreme Court's misreading of the Wong Kim Ark case is John C. Eastman. Michael Sandler, *Toward a More Perfect Definition of "Citizen,"*

Others, such as Peter H. Schuck and Rogers M. Smith, suggest that to grant birthright citizenship to children of illegal immigrants or temporary visitor aliens born in the United States amounts to "citizenship without consent." Instead, they suggest that the Citizenship Clause of the Fourteenth Amendment be reinterpreted in order to make "birthright citizenship for the children of illegal and temporary visitor aliens a matter of congressional choice rather than of constitutional prescription."[77] Citizenship, they continue, should be based on "mutual consent—the consent of the national community as well as that of the putative individual member."[78] It is unclear whether or not the constitutional status of birthright citizenship will be brought before the Supreme Court any time soon. But, it is certain that the legacy of Wong Kim Ark's case will figure prominently in any legal decision.

For Chinese and other Asian Americans, Wong Kim Ark's legacy remains particularly significant. The Chinese exclusion laws were repealed in 1943 as part of a wartime measure to demonstrate goodwill to China, a U.S. ally in World War II.[79] But the long shadow of exclusion extended well into the late twentieth century in the form of large-scale historical amnesia. Chinese Americans sought to bury their painful pasts, and mainstream narratives of American history and American legal history ignored Chinese and other Asian Americans.[80] As a result, little was known about Wong Kim Ark and his case until recently. Knowledge of the case was not even passed on in Wong Kim Ark's own family. In 1998, Wong's only remaining child, Wong Yook Jim, admitted

---

64 Cong. Q. Wkly. 388, Feb. 13, 2006, at 388, *available at* http://www.cq.com/public/citizen ship.html.

[77] Peter H. Schuck & Rogers M. Smith, *Citizenship Without Consent: Illegal Aliens in the American Polity* 5 (1985).

[78] *Id.* at 6.

[79] Chinese Exclusion Repeal Act, Pub. L. No. 78–199, 57 Stat. 600 (1943). On the origins of the repeal and the changing status of Chinese during World War Two more generally, see K. Scott Wong, Americans First: Chinese Americans and the Second World War at 72–124 (Cambridge: Harvard University Press, 2005).

[80] The case was studied quite a bit while it was coming before the Supreme Court, but since then, it has not been the subject of extensive scholarly inquiry, and very little is known about Wong Kim Ark or the trial itself. See Henry C. Ide, *Citizenship by Birth—Another View*, 30 Am. L. Rev. 241, 241–52 (1896); Marshall B. Woodworth, *Citizenship of the United States Under the Fourteenth Amendment*, 30 Am. L. Rev. 535, 535–55 (1896); Marshall B. Woodworth, *Who Are Citizens of the United States?* Wong Kim Ark Case—Interpretation of Citizenship Clause of Fourteenth Amendment, 32 Am. L. Rev. 554, 554–61 (1898); Note, *Citizenship of Children of Alien Parents*, 12 Harv. L. Rev. 55, 55–56 (1898). On the absence of scholarly inquiry into Chinese immigration and American legal history, see Richard P. Cole & Gabriel J. Chin, *Emerging from the Margins of Historical Consciousness: Chinese Immigrants and the History of American Law*, 17 Law & Hist. Rev. 325, 325–64 (1999).

that he had known about the case for many years, but never shared the information with his own children or grandchildren. "I didn't know it was important. I didn't pay much attention," he explained.[81]

In recent years, however, *Wong Kim Ark v. United States* has begun to be recognized for its landmark status. In 1998, on the hundredth anniversary of the Supreme Court ruling, legal scholars, historians, and activists in San Francisco commemorated Wong's victory and emphasized its continuing relevance to a number of important public policy and legal issues, including immigration policy, public services for children of undocumented and illegal immigrants, bilingual education, affirmative action, and welfare reform.[82] John Trasviña, a former U.S. Justice Department official and Western States Regional Director of the U.S. Civil Rights Commission, explained the broad significance of *Wong Kim Ark*: "Everyone born in the U.S. benefits from this.... We no longer have to look at one's parents' immigration status. As long as you're native-born, you're a U.S. citizen."[83] Trasviña also suggested that the struggle for civil rights was far from over. Remembering Wong Kim Ark's struggle, he later remarked,

> is a way of recognizing that issues we face today have been around for one hundred years or more. We have made progress. But every time we make progress, we face other challenges, so it is important to remember people like Wong Kim Ark and what they did for minority Americans.[84]

Legal scholar Phil Tajitsu Nash even recently suggested to an audience of college students that Wong Kim Ark should be recognized as an "Asian American Malcolm X."[85] Whether or not Wong Kim Ark will be canonized to such a degree by a new generation of Americans remains to be seen. But in the realm of American legal history, Wong Kim Ark and his Supreme Court victory already mark some important truths about the impact that everyday people can have on the law as well as the ongoing relevance of race, immigration, and citizenship in defining what it means to be an "American."

*

---

[81] *Wong Kim Ark's Legacy, supra* note 69.

[82] *Native-born American, supra* note 71.

[83] Emil Amok, *Native Sons and Daughters*, Filipino Express, Apr. 5, 1998, at 11.

[84] *Native-born American, supra* note 71.

[85] Phil Tajitsu Nash, *Where are the Asian American Malcolm X's? Looking for Leaders in Asian America*, AsianWeek (San Francisco, CA), Mar. 2–8, 1996, at 7.

4

Pedro A. Malavet

"The Constitution Follows the Flag ... but Doesn't Quite Catch Up with It"[1]: The Story of *Downes v. Bidwell*

Introduction

The May 27, 1901 ruling of the United States Supreme Court in *Downes v. Bidwell*,[2] particularly Justice Edward Douglass White's opinion,[3] is today the most important of the Insular Cases. With the U.S. Armed Forces facing insurgency in the Philippines and political wrangling in Cuba and Puerto Rico following the Spanish American War, the policy motivations for the result in this case were straightforward. The United States was becoming a world power, which, at the turn of the twentieth century, meant becoming an imperial nation capable of holding colonies on which to establish military bases all over the world.[4]

---

[1] This is the quoted response of then Secretary of War Elihu Root when—after hearing a reading of the five opinions of the Supreme Court in the *Downes* case—confused reporters asked how the Justices had replied to the question "Does the constitution follow the flag?" *See* George Shiras III, *Justice George Shiras, Jr. of Pittsburgh* 191 (Winfield Shiras ed., 1953) (citing 1 Arthur Wallace Dunn, *From Harrison to Harding* 256–57 (1922)).

[2] 182 U.S. 244 (1901).

[3] *Id.* at 287–344 (White, J., concurring).

[4] *See generally* Warren Zimmermann, *First Great Triumph: How Five Americans Made Their Country a World Power* 8 (2002) ("John Hay, Captain Alfred T. Mahan, Elihu Root, Henry Cabot Lodge, and Theodore Roosevelt can fairly be called the fathers of modern American imperialism and the men who set the United States on the road to becoming a great power.").

Downes effectively provides constitutional authorization for this process by interpreting Article IV, Section 3, Clause 2 of the Constitution, the Territorial Clause, to give Congress almost unfettered authority to deal with territorial possessions.

The Territorial Clause provides:

The Congress shall have Power to dispose of and make all needful Rules and Regulations respecting the Territory or other Property belonging to the United States; and nothing in this Constitution shall be so construed as to Prejudice any claims of the United States, or of any particular state.[5]

Initially, this clause was applied to most of the thirty-seven territories that became states after the original thirteen colonies.[6] For example, Alaska and Hawai'i were at one time regulated by legislation passed by Congress, but that legislation was repealed or became obsolete after statehood.[7] Today, the clause applies to Puerto Rico, the Virgin Islands, Guam, the Northern Marianas, American Samoa, the Federated States of Micronesia, the Marshall Islands, and Palau.[8] Statutes passed under the authority of the Territorial Clause refer to these areas not as "territories," but rather as "possessions," "insular possessions," or "insular areas."[9] Pursuant to these statutes, the United States controls

---

[5] U.S. Const. art. IV, § 3, cl. 2.

[6] Texas, which, from the American perspective, seceded from Mexico and became a state after being an "independent Republic," is a possible exception. For a succinct distinction between the continental territories and the island territories, see Arnold H. Leibowitz, *Defining Status: A Comprehensive Analysis of United States Territorial Relations* 4–16 (1989).

[7] As to Alaska, see 48 U.S.C. §§ 21–488f (2003). Alaska was officially admitted to statehood on January 6, 1959. *See* Proclamation No. 3269, 24 Fed. Reg. 81 (Jan. 6, 1959); Act of July 7, 1958, Pub. L. No. 85–508, 72 Stat. 339. As to Hawai'i, see 48 U.S.C. §§ 611–21 (2003). Hawai'i was admitted by law as of March 18, 1959. *See* Act of Mar. 18, 1959, Pub. L. No. 86–3, 73 Stat. 4 (1959). Section 2 of this law provided for the new state to include

all the islands, together with their appurtenant reefs and territorial waters, included in the Territory of Hawai'i on the date of enactment of this Act, except the atoll known as Palmyra Island, together with its appurtenant reefs and territorial waters, but said State shall not be deemed to include the Midway Islands, Johnston Island, Sand Island (offshore from Johnston Island), or Kingman Reef, together with their appurtenant reefs and territorial waters.

Id.

[8] Leibowitz, *supra* note 6, at 3.

[9] *See generally* 48 U.S.C. §§ 731, et seq. (2003) (title named "Territories and Insular Possessions"). The Department of the Interior's Office of Insular Affairs currently defines the term "insular area" as follows:

A jurisdiction that is neither a part of one of the several States nor a Federal district. This is the current generic term to refer to any commonwealth, freely associated state,

or has a legal relationship with these eight populated island territories and controls several unpopulated islands.[10] The populated territories collectively have well over four million residents,[11] and among this group, the Samoans, as well as the residents of the three so-called Free Associated States—Micronesia, the Marshall Islands, and Palau—are not citizens of the United States.[12]

Some may consider a 1901 case to be ancient history, but *Downes* and its progeny still govern all of these regions.[13] This chapter will

possession or territory or Territory and from July 18, 1947, until October 1, 1994, the Trust Territory of the Pacific Islands. Unmodified, it may refer not only to a jurisdiction which is under United States sovereignty but also to one which is not, *i.e.*, a freely associated state or, 1947–94, the Trust Territory of the Pacific Islands or one of the districts of the Trust Territory of the Pacific Islands.

Office of Insular Affairs, Dep't of the Interior, Definitions of Insular Area Political Organizations, *at* http://www.doi.gov/oia/Islandpages/political_types.htm (last visited Aug. 27, 2006).

[10] In its "Island Fact Sheet," the Department of the Interior's Office of Insular Affairs identifies the unpopulated island territories of the United States under two designated categories: "United States Territories under the Jurisdiction of OIA," which includes Wake Atoll and certain areas of the Palmyra Atoll, and "U.S. Territories under the Jurisdiction of the U.S. Fish and Wildlife Service," which includes Baker Island, Howland Island, Jarvis Island, Johnston Atoll, Kingman Reef, Navassa Island, and most of Palmyra Atoll, often referred to together as the Guano Islands. Office of Insular Affairs, Dep't of the Interior, The Islands, *at* http://www.doi.gov/oia/Firstpginfo/islandfactsheet.htm (last visited February 4, 2007); *see generally* Leibowitz, *supra* note 6, at 3 (a listing of the current U.S. territorial possessions). On the Guano Islands, see Guano Islands Act of 1856, ch. 164, § 1, 11 Stat. 119 (codified at 48 U.S.C. § 1411 (2003)) ("Whenever any citizen of the United States discovers a deposit of guano on any island, rock, or key, not within the lawful jurisdiction of any other government, and not occupied by the citizens of any other government, and takes peaceable possession thereof, and occupies the same, such island, rock, or key may, at the discretion of the President, be considered as appertaining to the United States.")

[11] The Puerto Rican population of close to four million, as discussed below in note 15 and accompanying text, far exceeds the populations of other island territories, which the 2000 Census found were as follows: American Samoa, 57,291; Guam, 154,805; the U.S. Virgin Islands, 108,612; and the Commonwealth of the Northern Mariana Islands, 62,221. U.S. Census Bureau, United States Census 2000, The Island Areas, *at* http://www.census.gov/population/www/cen2000/islandareas.html (last visited Aug. 27, 2006).

[12] Leibowitz, *supra* note 6, at 449–51 (expressing some doubt about the matter, but noting that American Samoans are treated as "non-citizen nationals" of the United States). The three so-called Free Associated States (the Republic of the Marshall Islands, the Federated States of Micronesia, and Palau) are members of the United Nations with their own citizenship, independent from the United States. The Federated States of Micronesia and the Marshall Islands were admitted on September 17, 1991, and Palau was admitted on December 15, 1994. *See, e.g.*, Press Release, U.N. Dep't of Pub. Info., United Nations Member States, U.N. Doc. ORG/1469 (July 3, 2006), *available at* http://www.un.org/News/Press/docs/2006/org1469.doc.htm; *see generally* Leibowitz, *supra* note 6, at 639–703 (detailing the legal relationship between these three island and the United States).

[13] *See, e.g.*, Torres v. Puerto Rico, 442 U.S. 465 (1979); *see also* Margaret Leech, *In the*

explore the Insular Cases as a way to understand the role of race in articulating the relationship between American territorial expansion and American citizenship—between American empire and American democracy. The chapter begins by historicizing the *Downes* opinion. My aim here is threefold: (1) to provide a brief description of the effects of Spanish colonial rule on Puerto Rico; (2) to set forth the circumstances leading up to the Spanish American War; and (3) to illustrate how the outcome of that war helped to shape America's identity as a colonial power. Next, the chapter tells the story behind the *Downes* opinion itself, showing how the law reflected an uneasy balance between declaring the island to be both a U.S. possession, and one with a separate, not entirely "American" population. As this story and its aftermath will reveal, *Downes* and other early cases made clear that Puerto Rico did not enjoy the same status as states when it came to matters of commerce and trade. Because Congress exercised plenary power over the insular possessions, it could impose tariffs and taxes similar to those levied on foreign countries. A later generation of Insular Cases used Puerto Rico's separate and subordinate status to relegate its residents to second-class citizenship. Yet another generation of decisions make clear that the doctrine first set forth in *Downes* and elaborated in these later opinions remains good law today. The resiliency of decisions that signaled the rise of the United States as an imperial power is then explained by turning to the normative ideas about race, citizenship, and empire that lay behind the Insular Cases.

Social, Historical, and Legal Context: Our Islands and Their People[14]

The *Downes* case arose because Puerto Rico, a Spanish colony for over 400 years, had just been acquired by the United States as part of the spoils of war. Shortly before the war, Puerto Rico had enjoyed newfound autonomy under Spanish rule, and its residents expected that the American takeover would eventually lead to statehood or independence. As *Downes* and its progeny would make clear, however, U.S. officials devised a new model for insular possessions, one of territorial acquisition but only partial political incorporation.

Puerto Rico in 1901: Self–Government and Spanish Citizenship that Did Not Last Long

Puerto Rico is a group of islands bordered by the Atlantic Ocean and Caribbean Sea, the main island of which is the home to all but a few

---

Days of McKinley (reprint ed., Am. Political Biography Press 1999).

[14] José de Olivares, *Our Islands and Their People as Seen with Camera and Pencil* (William S. Bryan Wheeler ed., 1899) is a large two-volume coffee-table book set, which was sold door-to-door after the war, purportedly describing the new island territories.

thousand of the inhabitants. Puerto Rico is the most populous of the current island territories of the United States, with estimates in 2006 placing the number of residents at 3,927,188; perhaps not surprisingly, then, Puerto Rico figures prominently in most of the Insular Cases.[15] Because U.S. citizens have not moved to Puerto Rico in substantial numbers, Puerto Rico remains a culturally Latina/o island, even after more than one hundred years of U.S. occupation.[16] Additionally, a number of Puerto Ricans have migrated to the mainland. The 2000 Census found 3,406,178 persons in the fifty states and the District of Columbia who identified themselves as "Hispanic or Latino," specifically "Puerto Rican," making Puerto Ricans one of the largest Latina/o groups in the United States.[17]

For about five centuries before Christopher Columbus claimed the territory for Spain in 1493, Taino and Carib natives lived on the Puerto Rican islands. But the Spanish colonial period lasted for a little more than four centuries, during which period the people we now refer to as Puerto Ricans were—through racial, legal, political, and cultural processes—created.[18] On the eve of the Spanish American War in 1898, Puerto Rico and Cuba were the last outposts of Spain in the Americas. Mexico (the viceroyalty of New Spain) and Central America (the captaincy of Guatemala) became independent in 1821 in the aftermath of the Napoleonic invasion of Spain. Three years later, the Battle of Ayacucho in the Andes marked the end of the wars of independence in South America.[19]

---

[15] According to the 2000 Census, Puerto Rico's population was 3,808,610. U.S. Census Bureau, United States Census 2000, Census 2000 Data for Puerto Rico, at http://www.cen sus.gov/census2000/states/pr.html (last visited Aug. 27, 2006). The Central Intelligence Agency estimated that as of July 2006, Puerto Rico's population had risen to 3,927,188. CIA, The World Factbook, Puerto Rico, at https://www.cia.gov/cia/publications/factbook/geos/rq.html (last visited Aug. 27, 2006).

[16] According to the 2000 U.S. Census 98.8% of Puerto Rican citizens describe themselves as "Hispanic or Latino" and 95.1% as "Puerto Rican." U.S. Census Bureau, Profile of the General Demographic Characteristics: 2000, Geographic Area: Puerto Rico, at http://factfinder.census.gov/servlet/QTTable?_bm=y & -geo_id=04000US72 & -qr_name=DEC_2000_SF1_U_DP1 & -ds_name=DEC_2000_SF1_U (last visited Aug. 27, 2006).

[17] U.S. Census Bureau, Hispanic or Latino by Type: 2000, at http://factfinder.census. gov/serv let/QT Table?_bm=y & -qr_name=DEC_2000_SF1_U_QTP9 & -geo_id=01000US & -ds_name=DEC_2000_SF1_U & -redoLog=false (last visited Aug. 27, 2006).

[18] See generally Pedro A. Malavet, America's Colony: The Political and Cultural Conflict Between the United States and Puerto Rico 49–116 (2004) (chapters detailing Puerto Rico's culture from political and sociological perspectives).

[19] The Spanish empire in the Americas was almost totally lost between 1821 and 1824, though Cuba and Puerto Rico were still under Spanish control. See José Terrero, Historia de España 456–58 (Juan Regla ed., 1972).

In a process that had started with the revolution of September 1868 in Spain and continued with the new constitution of 1876,[20] the Spanish crown began to reconsider the legal regime governing the islands of Cuba and Puerto Rico. Article 89 of the Constitution of the Spanish Monarchy of 1876 gave the government the power to issue special legislation for the governance of the *"provincias de ultramar"* (the overseas provinces). Clause 2 gave Cuba and Puerto Rico the right to be represented in the Cortes—the Spanish legislative body—once special laws to that effect were enacted. Over the next few years, Spain granted Cuba and Puerto Rico increasing levels of home rule. Due to political turmoil in Spain, however, this constitutional authorization was not implemented in earnest until 1897.[21] On November 25, 1897, Spain enacted the Charter of Autonomy for Puerto Rico. The charter granted self-government by an elected lower chamber of the legislature, a partially elected and partially appointed upper legislative chamber, and an appointed high executive, known as the governor-general.[22] As part of the autonomy process, Spanish citizenship was formally granted to the native-born inhabitants of Cuba and Puerto Rico that same month.[23] A separate decree extended the civil rights guarantees of the 1876 Spanish constitution to Puerto Rico.[24] These reforms were designed to calm civil unrest on the island. For example, in the late 1890s, Luis Muñoz–Rivera, the leader of Puerto Rico's principal political group, the Autonomist Party, rejected plans for a military attack against the Spanish proposed by Puerto Rican pro-independence forces in exile in New York.[25]

The Charter of Autonomy set the stage for the final Spanish election in Puerto Rico. On March 27, 1898, 121,573 voters went to the polls. On

---

[20] See *Constituciones y Códigos Políticos Españoles 1801–1978*, 145 (Julio Montero–Díaz ed., 1998).

[21] *Puerto Rico: Leyes Fundamentales* 9–114 (Alfonso L. García–Martínez ed., 1989) [hereinafter *Leyes Fundamentales*].

[22] See Tit. I, art. 2, of the Charter of Autonomy, in "Historical Documents," *in* 1 *Puerto Rico Laws Annotated* 16 (Lexis Publishing Puerto Rico, 1999). In order to avoid confusion with the numbering of the laws themselves, I use *P.R. Laws Ann.*, vol. 1, p. xx when citing specific pages in this important historical volume of the *Puerto Rico Laws Annotated*, which transcribes in English many fundamental laws and historical documents that are essential to the discussion in this chapter. However, when citing Puerto Rican laws generally, I provide the legal citation for the statutes by using the abbreviation *P.R. Laws Ann.* followed by the appropriate title and section.

[23] Article 1 of the Decree of 9 November 1897 gave Spanish citizenship, on an equal footing with residents of the Peninsula, to the Spanish subjects in the Antilles. *See Leyes Fundamentales*, *supra* note 21, at 93.

[24] See José Trías Monge, 1 *Historia Constitucional de Puerto Rico* 128 (1980) [hereinafter *Historia Constitucional*].

[25] Olga Jiménez de Wagenheim, *Puerto Rico: An Interpretative History from Pre-Columbian Times to 1900* at 198–99 (1998).

July 17, 1898, the new local government was installed.[26] Puerto Rico's Autonomist and Liberal Parties welcomed the charter and elected the country's first homegrown government just weeks before the start of the Spanish American War.[27] But the Charter of Autonomy still proved unacceptable to the more stridently pro-independence Puerto Ricans in New York, some of whom encouraged the United States to invade. After Autonomist leaders in Puerto Rico rejected the call for revolution against Spain, officers of the Puerto Rico Section, a pro-independence group originally founded by exiles in 1892 as the Borinquen Club, met with Senator Henry Cabot Lodge in 1898 to ask the "United States government for help in evicting Spain from Puerto Rico."[28] The pro-independence *puertorriqueñas/os* in New York even provided interpreters and scouts for the U.S. Army. To be sure, many believed that the United States would quickly give Puerto Rico independence after the invasion, as would happen in Cuba. What pro-independence forces clearly underestimated in both Puerto Rico and Cuba was how disruptive America's imperial dreams would be for these islands. The concerns expressed by some Puerto Rican leaders were largely ignored. For example, Ramón Emeterio Betances worried that "if Puerto Ricans don't act fast after the Americans invade, the island will be an American colony forever."[29]

And indeed, in July 1898, the *americanos* invaded, and the Autonomist experiment ended before Puerto Rico had a real chance, however limited, to rule itself. Nevertheless, native political thinking and organizing had developed greatly during the nineteenth century, and when Americans arrived in Puerto Rico, they found sophisticated politicians and parties ready to support, challenge, and oppose the new sovereign.

Between September 1898 and April 12, 1900—following the quick American victory in the war—Puerto Rico was under military rule, supervised by the War Department.[30] During this period, the *"partidas,"*

---

[26] See Fernando Bayrón Toro, *Elecciones y Partidos Politicos de Puerto Rico* 129–39 (4th ed. 1989).

[27] It was an imperfect form of home rule, as the Spaniards retained the authority to appoint certain members of the upper chamber of the legislature and to set the eligibility requirements, which ensured that only the economically powerful classes would be allowed to run for office. The law required that candidates for office have "an annual income of four thousand pesos." Tit. III, art. 5 & 6 of the charter, *P.R. Laws Ann.*, vol. 1, pp. 2–3. *See* Pedro Malavet–Vega, *Historia de la Canción Popular en Puerto Rico: 1493–1898* at 293, 351, 448–49, 505–08 (1992) (explaining the income situation in Puerto Rico at the time). On the monetary units in Spanish times, see Fernando Picó, *Historia General de Puerto Rico* 9 (1986).

[28] Jiménez de Wagenheim, *supra* note 25, at 198–199.

[29] *See id.* at 200.

[30] *See generally* Raúl Serrano Geyls, 1 *Derecho Constitucional de Estados Unidos y Puerto Rico* 439–42 (1986) (describing the legal aspects of this early period of military rule);

well-organized mobs, fought in the mountains of Puerto Rico. This guerrilla class-warfare began with the poor attacking the Spaniards but quickly extended to attacks on wealthy *criollas/os* (creoles).[31] The targets were mostly white *mallorquines* (Majorcans) and *corsos* (Corsicans) who owned coffee plantations and, thus, controlled what was then the most powerful part of the island economy. These were the same immigrants who arrived after Spain opened Puerto Rico and Cuba to those fleeing the wars of independence in the Spanish Americas. At the expense of the Puerto Rican poor, the U.S. military restored "order" and earned the gratitude and allegiance of some of the Puerto Rican elites.[32]

Soon after the change in sovereignty, the former Pure and Orthodox Party became the pro-statehood Partido Republicano Puertorriqueño (Puerto Rican Republican Party). The party's goal was "the definitive and sincere annexation of Puerto Rico to the United States. Declaration of organized territory for Puerto Rico, as a prelude thereafter to become a State of the Federal Union."[33] Party leaders favored accelerating the Americanization project (the process of educating the Puerto Ricans in English to become "Americans"), which hopefully would lead to statehood. Accordingly, in the party's original political manifesto, leaders supported English as the language of instruction "in order to put the country ['*el país*' [sic], referring to Puerto Rico] in conditions more favorable soon to become a new State of the Federation."[34]

Luis Muñoz–Rivera continued to lead the Autonomist/Liberal Party, which also was undergoing a transformation after the invasion and

---

Carmen Ramos de Santiago, *El Gobierno de Puerto Rico* 55–60 (1986) (discussing how the military governed the island in the early years following the war); *see also* Raymond Carr, *Puerto Rico: A Colonial Experiment* 32–33 (1984) (discussing military rule immediately following the war). For an interesting description of the period, see Leibowitz, *supra* note 6, at 140–41.

[31] Creoles are persons of Spanish descent born in the colonies. *See generally* Fernando Picó, *1898: La Guerra después de la Guerra* 201–207 (1987) (concluding that the partidas were not a response to the United States invasion, but rather a rejection of the economic and social order that prevailed during Spanish times). *See also* Ángel Rivero Méndez, *Crónica de la Guerra Hispanoamericana en Puerto Rico* 465–72 (1973) (describing the partidas as the acts of thiefs, and how they were put down by the U.S. military and the new Insular Police).

[32] Picó, *supra*, note 31, at 195–196 (concluding that the U.S. military had "rehabilitated the wealthy [mostly non-creole] landowners as arbiters of the rural [economic and social] order," after noting that both poor and wealthy *criollos* continued to challenge military rule).

[33] *Manifiesto de los Dirigentes de la Agrupación de los Puros Ortodoxos Dirigido al País Invitando a la Formación del Partido Republicano Puertorriqueño, April 19, 1899, in* 1–1 *Puerto Rico: Cien Años de Lucha Política* 259–62 (Reece B. Bothwell–González ed., 1979) (translation by the author) [hereinafter *Lucha Política*].

[34] *Id.* at 261.

became the Partido Federal Puertorriqueño (Puerto Rican Federal Party) in October 1899. Perhaps surprisingly, the party's first official platform supported the immediate grant of territorial status to Puerto Rico and eventual statehood.[35] But it also favored the absolute autonomy of the island's municipal governments to handle what the party called *asuntos locales* (local matters), especially education.[36] This put leaders in direct conflict with the U.S. administrators and with the Puerto Rican Republican Party. On October 26, 1900, an editorial in *La Democracia*, the newspaper published by the Federal Party and edited by Muñoz–Rivera, criticized U.S. administrators as well as the Republican Party and its political thugs.[37] The editorial ended with a call for withdrawal from the first election. Consequently, in 1900 the Federal Party boycotted the election.

In the November 1900 election, of 123,140 registered voters in Puerto Rico, 58,367 voted for Republicans, and 148 voted for Federals. Republican candidates were elected to all thirty-five positions in the newly created House of Delegates, and the sole Puerto Rican delegate to the U.S. Congress, called the resident commissioner, also was a Republican. The Federal Party did not wholly withdraw from the 1902 elections, and its candidates were elected from two Puerto Rican districts. But the Puerto Rican Republican Party's candidate was again elected resident commissioner, and the majority of the delegates to the local legislative body were Republicans.[38]

The turn of the twentieth century was characterized by *turbas republicanas* (Republican mobs or riots). The former Autonomists and supporters of the Federal Party were attacked by violent gangs associated with the Republican cause. These planned, non-spontaneous acts of violence were generally tolerated, and sometimes supported, by the U.S. authorities. In some of the more serious attacks, for example, one that

---

[35] *Programa del Partido Federal, 1 de Octobre de 1899, in* 1-1 *Lucha Política, supra* note 33, at 271–72. In February 1904, the Federal Party dissolved itself and was reconstituted as the Partido Unión de Puerto Rico (Union Party of Puerto Rico). The party again included among its principal leaders Luis Muñoz–Rivera, the Autonomist Party founder, but it also now included Rosendo Matienzo–Cintrón, a prominent independence leader, as well as another important independence supporter, José de Diego. Again displaying the colonial political pragmatism that recognized strength in numbers, the party also included statehood supporters. Its name was specifically chosen to describe the intent to unify the party members' diverse political views regarding status. The official minutes of the convention can be found in 1-1 *Lucha Política, supra* note 33, at 282–85.

[36] *See Programa del Partido Federal, supra* note 35, parr. 6, p. 271, and parr. 11, p. 272.

[37] *El Retraimiento, La Democracia,* Oct. 26, 1900, *reprinted in* 1-1 *Lucha Política, supra* note 33, at 273–74.

[38] Bayrón Toro, *supra* note 26, at 115–16, 120–21.

took place on September 13, 1900, the *turbas* ransacked the offices of the Federal Party's newspaper, *El Diario de Puerto Rico*, destroying the printing equipment. The next day, the *turbas* shot at Muñoz–Rivera's home, but the authorities actually charged him and other Federal Party members with crimes. Although Muñoz–Rivera and the other defendants were acquitted of all charges on December 22, 1900, the atmosphere of fear and intimidation led many liberal politicians to flee Puerto Rico. Muñoz–Rivera left for New York early in 1901 with his wife and infant son, Luis Muñoz–Marín, and did not return to Puerto Rico until January 26, 1904.[39]

The United States in 1901: In the Afterglow of the Spanish American War

For the United States, the Spanish American War and the *Downes* ruling brought to an end the age of Northwest Ordinances and Jacksonian manifest destiny,[40] which had culminated in statehood, as the prevailing theory of territorial expansion of the United States, in favor of a new colonial paradigm. In the aftermath of the war and the U.S. takeover of Puerto Rico, the Philippines, Guam, and Cuba, the United States Supreme Court gave constitutional approval to the acquisition and control of island territories for the sake of legal, political, and military control, rather than for national territorial expansion, accompanied by "immigration and settlement" by persons of acceptable American stock who were already citizens of the United States.[41] Theodore Roosevelt called this "Americanism"; Henry Cabot Lodge labeled it the "large policy"; but it was imperialism, which the principal architect of America's naval doctrine at the time, Alfred T. Mahan, labeled as such and defined as "the extension of national authority over alien communities.... This broader

---

[39] *See, e.g.*, Bolívar Pagán, 1 *Historia de los Partidos Políticos Puertorriqueños, 1898–1956* at 74–75 (1972). Eventually, Luis Muñoz–Marín would become the first Puerto Rican-elected governor of the island.

[40] By this I mean the phrase as it was first used by Democrats aligned with President Andrew Jackson, who favored the incorporation of the Oregon territories, Texas and the spoils of the Mexican–American War into the United States, eventually as states of the union. More generally, it was used to justify expansion of the United States, again through statehood, from the Atlantic to the Pacific. I am not using it in the sense that mostly-Republican "expansionists" of the late 1890s and early twentieth century used it, since I prefer the clarity and distinguishability of the imperialism discourse, especially as it occurred around the elections of 1896, 1900, and 1904. *See generally* Julius W. Pratt, *Expansionists of 1898: The Acquisition of Hawai'i and the Spanish Islands* 1–33 (1936) (contrasting territorial expansion of the early nineteenth-century United States, mostly associated with Democrats, with the late nineteenth-century overseas expansionism advocated mostly by the Republicans). *See also* Zimmermann, *supra* note 4, at 13 (noting that most politicians who favored the concept avoided the term "imperialism" and barely tolerated "expansionism").

[41] *See* Balzac v. Porto Rico, 258 U.S. 298 (1922).

definition implies that a country does not have to own the territory of an
alien community in order to exercise imperial authority over it."[42]

Behind the political debate over territorial expansion was a professional debate over military doctrine. Prevailing doctrine deemed naval
power the most important way to project military and political authority
abroad. A show of force was seen as essential to being a strong player in
international political and economic affairs, and to ensuring the security
of the United States. No one influenced this thinking more than Alfred
T. Mahan, a graduate of the U.S. Naval Academy at Annapolis and a
commissioned naval officer. He became president of the Naval War
College, reportedly much to the chagrin of Annapolis and Navy authorities, in 1886. It was there that he became a naval history scholar and
developed a new vision of American naval doctrine.[43] This doctrine was
driven by the need to project American power abroad. It required a large
navy, with large capital ships, a canal in Panama, and the ability to
maintain naval coaling stations throughout the world, especially in the
Atlantic and Pacific Oceans. Mahan was a good scholar and a prolific
writer, and his books and magazine articles became highly influential in
political circles in Washington.[44] Two of his particularly important fans
were Massachusetts Senator Henry Cabot Lodge and future President
Theodore Roosevelt.[45]

Racism, supported by the pseudo-science of Social Darwinism, also
justified the takeover of lands belonging to "inferior races."[46] Rubin
Francis Weston explained:

Those who advocated overseas expansion faced this dilemma: What
kind of relationship would the new peoples have to the body politic?
Was it to be the relationship of the Reconstruction period, an

---

[42] Zimmermann, *supra* note 4, at 13.

[43] *See id.* at 85–122 (referring to Mahan as a "pen-and-ink sailor").

[44] See, e.g., Alfred T. Mahan, *Some Neglected Aspects of War* (1907), *reprinted in
Unilateral Force in International Relations* pp. 20 et seq. (1972). Mahan's best-known work
was *The Influence of Sea Power Upon History, 1660–1783*, published in 1890. This book,
along with another important volume of his, *The Interest of America in Sea Power, Present
and Future*, is available in electronic form at http://www.riapress.com/riapress/author.
lasso?goto=23 & -session=StoreSession:A443E9A0143122F717NPkODE8FAB (last visited
Aug. 27, 2006).

[45] Mahan and Roosevelt met at a critical time. In 1887, Mahan invited Roosevelt to
lecture at the War College on the subject of the War of 1812, which Roosevelt had studied
while a student at Harvard. Zimmermann, *supra* note 4, at 92.

[46] *See generally* Reginald Horsman, *Race and Manifest Destiny: The Origins of American Racial Anglo–Saxonism* 208–13 (1981) *in Race and Races: Cases and Resources for a
Diverse America* 254–58 (Juan F. Perea et al. eds., 2000) [hereinafter *"Race and Races"*]
(excerpt describing the role of anti-Mexican Anglo white racism in the Mexican–American
War).

attempt at political equality for dissimilar races, or was it to be the Southern "counterrevolutionary" point of view which denied the basic American constitutional rights to people of color? The actions of the federal government during the imperial period and the relation of the Negro to a status of second-class citizenship indicated that the Southern point of view would prevail. The racism which caused the relegation of the Negro to a status of inferiority was to be applied to the overseas possessions of the United States.[47]

Indeed, an important effect of the Spanish American War was to unite white southerners and northerners against a common enemy. In particular, the War served as a military reconciliation between white officers of the former Confederate armed forces and the professional military establishment. On Memorial Day in 1905, Senator Foraker, for whom Puerto Rico's Organic Act of 1900 was named, delivered an address in which he said:

> The Spanish–American War was attended with many good results, but one of the best was the impetus it gave to the restoration of cordial relations and the spirit of union and Americanism throughout the country. It gave the young men of the South an opportunity to put on the blue and show their loyalty and devotion to the flag, and to win, as they did, a heroic share of the glory and greatness that were added to the Republic; while their representatives in public life distinguished themselves by the conspicuous and patriotic character of their utterances and services. What has followed is but the natural result, and every survivor of the Union Army should be profoundly thankful that his life has been spared to see such a complete vindication of all that for which he contended.[48]

The War targeted the last Spanish island colonies in the Caribbean and Pacific. In President William McKinley's instructions to the U.S. delegation that negotiated the Treaty of Paris, he ordered that only one full territory be demanded from the Spanish: Puerto Rico.[49] Although the

---

[47] Rubin Francis Weston, *Racism in U.S. Imperialism: The Influence of Racial Assumptions on American Foreign Policy, 1893–1946*, at 15 (1972). Cornel West described the normative paradigm of "American" liberalism that produced these injustices. *See* Cornel West, *The Role of Law in Progressive Politics*, in *The Politics of Law: A Progressive Critique* 709 (David Kairys ed., 3d ed. 1998).

[48] Address of Senator Foraker at Arlington National Cemetery, Memorial Day, May 30, 1905, *available at* http://www.arlingtoncemetery.net/foraker-1905.htm.

[49] *Instructions of the President to the United States Peace Commissioners*, September 16, 1898, *in* U.S. Dep't of State, *Papers Related to the Treaty with Spain*, S. Doc. No. 56-148 at 3–4 (1901). These papers were initially secret, but on February 5, 1901, the Senate lifted the "injunction of secrecy" and ordered the publication of 3000 volumes. *Id.* at 1. I specify "full" territory because the U.S. did demand the cession of individual islands in the Ladrones and Philippine archipelagos, Guam and Luzón, respectively. *Id.* at 4, 7.

islands were important to the United States for military and economic reasons, their principal attraction was their strategic location when the Spanish American War broke out. Indeed, the acquisition of Puerto Rico was contemplated from the very conception of the new "American empire" by two of its principal architects:

> Assistant Secretary of the Navy Theodore Roosevelt, in a personal letter to Senator Henry Cabot Lodge, wrote: ". . . do not make peace until we get Porto Rico." Lodge replied: "Porto Rico *is not forgotten and we mean to have it*. Unless I am utterly . . . mistaken, the administration is now fully committed to the large policy that we both desire."[50]

After a failed ultimatum to Spain to pacify Cuba or leave,[51] the conflict began on April 25, 1898. Congress then declared war, retroactive to April 21, 1898, the date on which the U.S. warship *Nashville* had captured the Spanish ship *Buenaventura*.[52] Although the campaign cannot be described as long or especially bloody, young men on both sides died and those who lived did so in fear. In the Puerto Rico campaign, seventeen Spanish soldiers were killed, eighty-eight wounded, and 324 taken prisoner. Only three U.S. soldiers were killed, and forty were wounded, mostly by Puerto Rican irregular troops.[53] The Spanish forces in Puerto Rico did not put up much of a fight; the guns of San Juan had not been fired in hostility since they repelled the British invasion in 1797, and they had not been upgraded since then. The United States quickly captured the island. U.S. forces took Ponce, the largest city in the south, on July 28th, without firing a shot. At that time Major General Nelson Miles issued a proclamation announcing:

> To the inhabitants of Porto Rico: In the prosecution of the war against the Kingdom of Spain by the people of the United States, in the cause of liberty, justice, and humanity, its military forces have come to occupy the Island of Porto Rico [*sic*]. . . . They bring you the fostering arm of a nation of free people, whose greatest power is in its justice and humanity to all those living within its folds.
>
> The chief object of the American military forces will be to overthrow the armed authority of Spain and to give to the people of

---

[50] *The Puerto Ricans: A Documentary History* 89 (Kal Wagenheim & Olga Jiménez–de Wagenheim eds., 1996) (emphasis added).

[51] President William McKinley signed the resolution on April 20. On April 21, the U.S. ambassador to Spain delivered an ultimatum to the Spanish government, giving it until noon on April 23, 1898, to pacify Cuba or leave. *See* Rivero Méndez, *supra* note 31, at 18–24.

[52] *Id.*

[53] *Id.* at 28; Héctor Andrés Negroni, *Historia Militar de Puerto Rico* 340 (1992).

your beautiful island the largest measure of liberty consistent with this military occupation.... [We have] come to bring protection, not only to yourselves but to your property, to promote your prosperity and bestow upon you the immunities and blessings of liberal institutions of our government.[54]

By August 12, 1898, the United States had ended its military operations in Puerto Rico, and on September 14, 1898, most of the remaining Spanish troops left the island. October 18th was the final day for the official surrender of San Juan to the U.S. troops, and the last few Spanish soldiers sailed aboard the warship *Montevideo* on October 23rd.[55] The Treaty of Paris, signed on December 10, 1898, approved by the U.S. Senate, and ratified by the President in 1899, officially ended the Spanish American War, with the island of Puerto Rico as the United States' prize.[56]

The national election of November 1900 was won by "Imperialist" McKinley over "anti-Imperialist" William Jennings Bryan. Between the time of McKinley's reelection and his assassination at the end of 1901, he finished the takeover of the island territories, including, though somewhat reluctantly, the Philippines.[57] In the fall of 1900, the President and his administration had a strong interest in the Supreme Court cases that would define the President's authority over the newly conquered territories.

Mr. Bidwell and the 576 Boxes of Oranges from Mayagüez

Downes v. Bidwell is the principal storyline of the nine Insular Cases of the 1900 term.[58] The term "Insular Cases" was widely used in

---

[54] Carr, *supra* note 30, at 31.

[55] *The Puerto Ricans, supra* note 50, at 102–03.

[56] The official title is the Treaty of Peace between the United States of America and the Kingdom of Spain. *See P.R. Laws Ann.*, vol. 1, 16; *see also Race and Races, supra* note 46, at 327. Article II of the treaty reads: "Spain cedes to the United States the island of Porto Rico [sic] and other islands now under Spanish sovereignty in the West Indies, and the island of Guam in the Marianas or Ladrones." *Id.* at 327. The editors of the Puerto Rican legal collection changed the references to "Porto Rico" included in the original English to "Puerto Rico." *See P.R. Laws Ann.*, vol. 1, p. 17.

[57] Zimmermann, *supra* note 4, at 316 (discussing McKinley as a reluctant imperialist, especially about the Philippines); *see also id.* at 393 (noting that "Bryan made 'imperialism' the primary issue of his campaign"); *see also id.* at 401–02 ("[O]n September 6, 1901, President McKinley was shot ... at the mammoth Pan–American Exposition in Buffalo ... and he died on September 14 [1901].").

[58] Downes v. Bidwell, 182 U.S. at 244; De Lima v. Bidwell, 182 U.S. 1 (1901); Goetze v. United States, 182 U.S. 221 (1901); Crossman v. United States (*Hawaiian Case*), 182 U.S. 221; Dooley v. United States (*Dooley I*), 182 U.S. 222 (1901); Armstrong v. United States, 182 U.S. 243 (1901); Huus v. New York & Porto Rico S.S. Co., 182 U.S. 392 (1901); Dooley

the media and the legal literature to describe this litigation.[59] The Supreme Court itself designated these lawsuits as the "Insular Tariff Cases," as indicated in its statement of the case in *De Lima v. Bidwell*.[60] The use of the word "insular" rather than "territory" distinguished the new possessions from the territories existing prior to the Spanish American War, which were destined for eventual statehood. Accordingly, the United States Supreme Court used "Insular Cases" as a reference to the lawsuits resolved in 1901 involving the territorial possessions acquired after the Spanish American War, and beginning with *Hawai'i v. Mankichi*.[61] As used in this context, "insular" simply means "relating to, or constituting an island."[62]

Most of the cases involved the collection of taxes and tariffs on Puerto Rican agricultural products brought to the United States, but the disputes necessarily raised questions regarding the meaning of citizenship and how the U.S. Constitution would be applied to the new island territories. Taxes, crops, and citizenship were important themes in Puerto Rico in 1901. The island was still reeling, not so much from the Spanish American War as from the storm islanders called "San Ciriaco" (Saint Cyril), which hit Puerto Rico in August 1899, causing death as well as property and crop destruction.[63] A popular *seis*, the music of Puerto Rican farm laborers, blamed American racism and taxes for the Puerto Ricans' post-war and post-storm suffering. After bemoaning the loss of the coffee crop, the song attributed the troubles to U.S. imperialism rather than a natural disaster:

> I am, man, convinced/that the bad situation / does not depend on the cyclone / as many have believed. / The blame of the yanqui has been / that he hates us very, very much / and if what I hear is true, /

---

v. United States (*Dooley II*), 183 U.S. 151 (1901); Fourteen Diamond Rings v. United States (*The Diamond Rings*), 183 U.S. 176 (1901).

[59] *See, e.g.*, Charles E. Littlefield, *The Insular Cases, Address Before the American Bar Association* (Aug. 22, 1901), *in* 15 Harv. L. Rev. 169 (1901).

[60] 182 U.S. 1, 2 (1901).

[61] 190 U.S. 197 (1903). The Supreme Court has used the phrase "insular cases" in twenty-three of its published opinions, starting with *Mankichi*, and has referred more generally to the cases or the possessions twenty-eight times. Lexis Search conducted June 26, 2006. The most recent reference is *United States v. Lara*, 541 U.S. 193 (2004) (regarding tribal authority to prosecute crimes). The Court also makes passing reference to "insular possessions" in regard to the habeas corpus statute in Rasul v. Bush, 542 U.S. 466, 475 (2004) (case arising out of detentions in Guantánamo).

[62] *Webster's Ninth New Collegiate Dictionary* 628 (rev. ed. 1990).

[63] Pedro Malavet–Vega, *De las Bandas al Trio Borinquen: 1900–1927*, at 36–37 (2002).

when they collect the tax/how dangerous this is! / we are really bad off, *Perucho!*[64]

The song went on to indict the "absorbent [yanqui] race" for "not being able to take" the Puerto Ricans.

The Insular Cases were so important in their day that the filing of the cases was widely reported,[65] and oral arguments occurred over a period of ten days, with the resulting opinions occupying hundreds of pages over two volumes of the U.S. Reports. Soon after the cases were decided, the 56th Congress ordered a reprinting of the parties' written briefs and transcription of the oral arguments into a volume, which the Supreme Court Reports note—with some sense of awe—"amounted to 1075 pages."[66] Though May 27, 1901 was to be the last day of the term, the reading of the opinions in the Insular Cases took about five hours, forcing the court to reconvene the next day.[67] Due to the importance of the cases, "[t]he small courtroom was crowded to repletion throughout the day, prominent government officials and many attorneys being present, and the proceedings were followed from start to finish with keen interest."[68] Both the Washington Post and the New York Times ran front-page articles reporting on the decisions, noting that the room was full of government dignitaries, including Secretary of War Elihu Root.[69]

Elihu Root was a successful New York corporate lawyer with no military experience when he was selected for the position of Secretary of War by President McKinley. In choosing Root, President McKinley was "not looking for any one who kn[ew] anything about war or for any one who kn[ew] anything about the army; he [needed] a lawyer to direct the government of these Spanish islands."[70] The Insular Possessions were

---

[64] *See id.* at 37, 115 n.13 (noting that the song was published in the "labor newspaper El Pan del Pobre (the Poor Man's Bread), on 25 August 1901"). The song's original Spanish lyrics are: "Estoy, chico, convencido/ que la mala situación/ no depende del ciclón/ como muchos han creído./ La culpa del yanqui ha sido/ que nos odia mucho, mucho/ y si es cierto lo que escucho,/ cuando cobren el impuesto,/ ¡qué peligroso está esto!/ ¡qué mal estamos Perucho!" *Id.* (translation by the author).

[65] *See, e.g., Held Over By Supreme Court; Cases Involving Question Whether Porto Rico and Philippines Are Part of United States Postponed,* N.Y. Times, Nov. 13, 1900, at 8.

[66] *De Lima,* 182 U.S. at 3; H.R. Con. Res. 72, 56th Cong. (1901); *The Insular Cases: Comprising the Records, Briefs, and Arguments of Counsel in the Insular Cases of the October Term, 1900, in the Supreme Court of the United States, Including the Appendixes Thereto* (1901) [hereinafter *Insular Cases*].

[67] *Court Decides Insular Cases,* N.Y. Times, May 28, 1901, at 1.

[68] *Id.*

[69] *The Status of Our Insular Possessions,* Wash. Post, May 28, 1901, at 1; *Court Decides Insular Cases, supra* note 67.

[70] Leech, *supra* note 13, at 379; *see also* Zimmermann, *supra* note 4, at 147–48 (recounting the same story).

regulated through the War Department from 1898 until 1934, when that responsibility was shifted to the Department of the Interior.[71] As Secretary of War, Root therefore was an important figure in the Insular Cases and an interested and quite knowledgeable listener as the opinions were read.[72]

In the first opinion to be read, *De Lima*, the Court ruled that for the purpose of imposing import tariffs in the United States, Puerto Rico was not a foreign country but rather a U.S. territory.[73] Specifically, Justice Henry Billings Brown—speaking for himself, Chief Justice Melville Weston Fuller, and Justices John Marshall Harlan, David Josiah Brewer, and Rufus Wheeler Peckham—stated that "by the ratification of the treaty of Paris the island became territory of the United States, *although not an organized territory in the technical sense of the word.*"[74] Therefore, sugar from Puerto Rico was not "imported merchandise" under the general tariff laws of the United States[75] because the tariffs in those laws applied only to imports from foreign countries and George R. Bidwell, the collector of taxes at the port of New York, lacked the authority to levy tariffs on Puerto Rican products under the law. Accordingly, "the duties [on sugar imported from Puerto Rico] were illegally exacted, and . . . the plaintiffs [were] entitled to recover them back."[76]

But, anticipating his future concurrence in *Downes*, Justice Joseph McKenna—speaking for himself and Justices Edward Douglass White and George Shiras, Jr.—indicated in dissent that the status of Puerto

---

[71] *See* José Trías Monge, *Puerto Rico: The Trials of the Oldest Colony in the World* 58 (1997). This text incorrectly gives 1933 as the date, which is probably a typographical error, because the author's more detailed collection, and his original source, indicates 1934; *see also* Trías Monge, 2 *Historia Constitucional de Puerto Rico* 206-214 (1981) (discussing the transfer of authority to the Department of the Interior).

[72] *See* Philip C. Jessup, *Elihu Root* 348 (1938) (providing an interesting analysis of the correspondence and discussion between Root, then Secretary of State John Hay, and President McKinley on the subject of the territories, concluding that "Root did not trust Congress to do an efficient job in mapping out a form of colonial government [for the insular possessions]"). Shortly before his assassination, McKinley expressed his intention to create a bureau in the Department of State to deal with the insular possessions. On September, 14, 1901, Root wrote Hay to express his support for the "Bureau of Insular Affairs" at the Department of State, because supervision of the insular governments "can go where it belongs under civil control in the nearest approach we can make to a Department of Colonial Affairs." *Id.* at 349-50.

[73] De Lima v. Bidwell, 182 U.S. at 174 (narrowly construing the question presented in the case as "whether territory acquired by the United States by cession from a foreign power remains a 'foreign country' within the meaning of the tariff laws").

[74] *Id.* at 196 (emphasis added).

[75] *Id.* at 175.

[76] *Id.* at 200.

Rico represented "a relation to the United States between that of being a
foreign country absolutely and of being domestic territory absolutely."[77]
Where the majority had seen only two categories, foreign countries and
domestic territories, the dissenters saw three: "foreign countries," such
as Spain, "domestic territory[, such] as New York," and "[b]etween
these extremes ... other relations, ... Porto Rico occup[ying] one of
them."[78] The majority had noted the distinction between U.S. territories
that are "organized" and those that are "not organized," but, as their
votes in *Downes* would make clear, four of the five members of that
majority (Fuller, Harlan, Brewer, and Peckham) did not intend that
distinction to have constitutional significance either in setting the limits
of federal authority over the insular possessions or in extending civil
rights to their residents.

In fact, *De Lima* was immediately eclipsed by the reading of the
Downes decision. *Downes* is the most important of the Insular Cases,
because it interprets the Foraker Act of April 12, 1900,[79] which turned
Puerto Rico into an "organized" territory—one that is subject to a
congressional organic statute. The Act—named after the Republican
Senator from Ohio, Joseph Benson Foraker—authorized a U.S.-appoint-
ed civilian government to be established on the island, and provided for
its chief executive, the governor, to be named by the President of the
United States.[80] Additionally, the President appointed the members of
the cabinet, known as the Executive Council, who also acted as the upper
legislative house. The lower house of thirty-five delegates was elected by
the people of Puerto Rico. The Act further provided that the Chief
Justice and associate Justices of the island's supreme court would be
appointed by the President of the United States. In addition, the Act
created the Federal District Court for Puerto Rico.[81] This regime lasted
until 1917, when it was replaced by the Jones Act.[82]

---

[77] *Id.* at 220 (McKenna, J., dissenting).

[78] *Id.* at 200–01.

[79] The facts in *De Lima* occurred in fall 1899, before passage of the Foraker Act.

[80] *See* Foraker Act, ch. 191, 31 Stat. 77 (1900) (codified as amended in scattered
sections of 48 U.S.C.). The Act is also transcribed in vol. 1 of the *Laws of Puerto Rico
Annotated*, under the heading "Historical Documents." *See P.R. Laws Ann.*, vol. 1, pp. 24–
48. *See also* Foraker Act § 17, *in P.R. Laws Ann.*, vol. 1, 36–37.

[81] *See generally* Foraker Act §§ 18–27, 33–34. Section 27 provides that the Executive
Council shall be one of the two houses of the legislative assembly. This appointed body
arguably has been the most important element in the process of "Americanizing" Puerto
Rico. *See* Pedro A. Cabán, *Constructing a Colonial People: Puerto Rico and the United
States, 1898–1932*, at 122–26 (1999).

[82] *See* Jones Act of 1917, ch. 145, 39 Stat. 951, 953.

During discussion of the Foraker Bill, the U.S. Senate changed the references to "Puerto Rico" contained in the original draft to "Porto Rico," which was used in the final proposal and was only changed by law in 1932.[83] Beyond the misspelling of Puerto Rico's name, the Senate made a more significant change: It removed from the draft of the bill any reference to extending the United States Constitution to the territory of Puerto Rico. This set up the legal question that would be resolved in *Downes*: Does the Constitution *automatically* apply in a U.S. territory? The Senators' decision was explained thusly:

> The change was made because of the opinion expressed by the members of the committee that our Constitution is not suited to the Puerto Rican people. The opinion was also quite general that the extension of the Constitution was not necessary. Some of the Senators [sic] expressed the opinion that the natives of the island were not yet prepared for jury trials.[84]

What started out as a bill to extend civil rights and government to Puerto Rico, and to include the island in the free trade internal to the United States, became a much simpler organic act to enable civilian government for the island. Republican protectionists scuttled the free trade provisions and substituted a tax.[85] Therefore, the Foraker Act imposed a tax of "fifteen per centum of the duties which are required to be levied, collected, and paid upon like articles of merchandise imported from foreign countries" on Puerto Rican imports into the United States.[86] On November 20, 1900, Bidwell, the same collector of customs at the port of New York involved in *De Lima*, demanded $659.35 in taxes, a not insubstantial sum for that day:

> upon thirty-three (33) boxes of oranges … from the port of San Juan … and … upon 543 boxes of oranges, [also] the product of the island of Porto Rico, consigned to these plaintiffs ["Samuel B. Downes, doing business under the firm name of S.B. Downes &

---

[83] *See Government of Puerto Rico; Senate Committee on the Island Discusses the Foraker Bill and Makes Changes*, N.Y. Times, Jan. 28, 1900, at 4. *See also* Act of May 17, 1932, ch. 190, 47 Stat. 158 (codified at 48 U.S.C. § 731a (1999)) ("That from and after the passage of this resolution [May 17, 1932] the island designated 'Porto Rico' in the Act entitled 'An Act to provide a civil government for Porto Rico, and for other purposes,' approved March 2, 1917, as amended, shall be known and designated as 'Puerto Rico.' All laws, regulations, and public documents and records of the United States in which such island is designated or referred to under the name of 'Porto Rico' shall be held to refer to such island under and by the name of 'Puerto Rico.' ").

[84] *Government of Puerto Rico, supra* note 83, at 4.

[85] Leech, *supra* note 13, at 487–89 (detailing the development of the bill in Congress).

[86] Foraker Act § 3. This was a change from the originally proposed bill, reportedly as a result of protests from and lobbying by sugar producers and citrus farmers. *See* Leech, *supra* note 13, at 488.

Company,"] at the port of New York and brought thither from the port of Mayaguez in the said island of Porto Rico during the month of November, 1900, by the steamer Ponce.[87]

The plaintiffs paid under protest, got their oranges and, represented by the New York City law firm Coudert Brothers,[88] filed their suit that same day! The complaint, which was personally verified under oath by Samuel B. Downes, alleged a case "arising under" the Constitution, specifically:

> the said oranges were not liable to duty, the same not having been imported from any foreign country within the meaning of any valid statute or executive order of the United States, but were merchandise which must, under and by virtue of the provisions of the Constitution of the United States in that regard, be admitted to free entry in any port of the United States.[89]

Procedurally, this case arose during the period of the Evarts Act of 1891, during which the circuit courts lost their appellate jurisdiction to the newly-created courts of appeals, but retained their original trial jurisdiction.[90] Additionally, this was not long after the lower federal courts were first granted original jurisdiction over federal question complaints by the Judiciary Act of 1875,[91] and the case predates the 1938 enactment of the Federal Rules of Civil Procedure. Therefore, rather than filing a motion to dismiss under Rule 12 of the current Federal Rules of Civil Procedure, the United States Attorney for the Southern District of New York, Henry L. Burnett, filed a demurrer arguing "[t]hat the complaint does not state facts sufficient to constitute a cause of action."[92] On November 30, 1900, Circuit Judge Henry Lacombe heard

---

[87] Transcript of Record, Downes v. Bidwell, 182 U.S. 244 (1901) (No. 507), *reprinted in Insular Cases, supra* note 66, at 724.

[88] Paul Fuller was a partner at Coudert Brothers, which represented the private litigants in the most important Insular Cases, along with Frederic R. Coudert, Jr. Fuller was born in 1856, orphaned of mother and abandoned by his father. He was raised by Charles Coudert and became a prominent attorney in the New York Bar. He helped to found Fordham Law School and was its dean. *See* Metropolitan Corporate Counsel, *The Paul Fuller Memorial Children's Service Program: Coudert Brothers LLP Globalizes Pro Bono, at* http://www.metrocorpcounsel.com /current.php?artType=view & artMonth=August & artYear=2004 & EntryNo=1474 (last visited Aug. 27, 2006).

[89] *Insular Cases, supra* note 66, at 724.

[90] *See* Erwin Chemerinsky, *Federal Jurisdiction* 22–23 (1989) (citing Act of Mar. 3, 1891, ch. 517, 26 Stat. 826). According to Chemerinsky, "In 1911, the circuit courts were eliminated and their original trial jurisdiction transferred to the district courts." *Id.* at 23 (citing Act of Mar. 3, 1911, ch. 231, 36 Stat. 1087).

[91] Act of Mar. 3, 1875, ch. 137, 18 Stat. 470. *See generally* Chemerinsky, *supra* note 90, at 222.

[92] *Insular Cases, supra* note 66, at 725.

oral arguments and ruled in favor of the defendant, ordering the complaint dismissed and awarding costs to the defendant.[93] The next day, judgment was entered dismissing the action and taxing costs in the amount of sixteen dollars and thirty cents.[94] Downes filed a writ of error and notice of appeal with the circuit court on December 5, 1900. Judge Lacombe officially allowed the matter to proceed, and John A. Shields, clerk of the court, certified a nineteen-page record for appeal on December 7, 1900, with costs paid by canceling a "ten-cent U.S. internal revenue stamp."[95] The case was filed with the U.S. Supreme Court on December 11, 1900 and assigned case number 507.[96]

Justice Brown announced the Court's decision to uphold the lower court ruling, but he wrote only for himself. The other Justices filed separate opinions to explain their reasons for upholding the tax. Justice Brown concluded:

> that the Island of Porto Rico is a territory appurtenant and belonging to the United States, but not a part of the United States within the revenue clauses of the Constitution; [and] that the Foraker act is constitutional, so far as it imposes [discriminatory] duties upon imports from such island [to the United States].[97]

Justice White's concurring opinion, joined by Justices Shiras and McKenna, the same three who had subscribed to McKenna's dissent in *De Lima*, had the most votes. Articulating what would eventually become the accepted doctrine, Justice White found that Puerto Rico, and by analogy Guam and the Philippines, was an organized, but *unincorporated*, territory of the United States—that is, part of the United States under the Territorial Clause,[98] but subject to absolute congressional legislative authority under that provision and the Necessary and Proper Clause of the U.S. Constitution.[99]

---

[93] Order, Downes v. Bidwell, 182 U.S. 244 (1901) (No. 507), *reprinted in Insular Cases, supra* note 66, at 725.

[94] Judgment, *Downes*, 182 U.S. 244 (No. 507), *reprinted in Insular Cases, supra* note 66, at 726.

[95] Writ of Error, *Downes*, 182 U.S. 244 (No. 507), *reprinted in Insular Cases, supra* note 66, at 721; Clerk's Memo with Judge's Authorization, *Downes*, 182 U.S. 244 (No. 507), *reprinted in Insular Cases, supra* note 66, at 721–722; Certification of the Record, *Downes*, 182 U.S. 244 (No. 507), *reprinted in Insular Cases, supra* note 66, at 722. The system of canceling stamps to pay court filing fees is still used in the local courts in Puerto Rico.

[96] *Insular Cases, supra* note 66, at 729.

[97] *Downes v. Bidwell*, 182 U.S. at 287. The Foraker Act required "the payment of '15 per centum of the duties which are required to be levied, collected, and paid upon like articles of merchandise imported from foreign countries.' " *Id.* at 247–48.

[98] U.S. Const. art. IV, § 3, cl. 2.

[99] U.S. Const. art. I, § 8, cl. 18.

Justice Gray, the final vote for the bare majority, issued a separate concurrence.[100] In it, he sought to limit the impact of the majority's position by characterizing Puerto Rico's status as temporary: "If Congress is not ready to construct a complete government for the conquered territory, it may establish a temporary government, which is not subject to all the restrictions of the Constitution."[101] Justice White's opinion also included an important caveat suggesting that territorial status could not last forever:

> Conceding, then, for the purpose of the argument, it to be true that it would be a violation of duty under the Constitution for the legislative department, in the exercise of its discretion, to accept a cession of and permanently hold territory which is not intended to be incorporated, *the presumption necessarily must be* that that department, which within its lawful sphere is but the expression of the political conscience of the people of the United States, will be faithful to *its duty under the Constitution, and therefore, when the unfitness of particular territory for incorporation is demonstrated, the occupation will terminate.* I cannot conceive how it can be held that pledges made to an alien people can be treated as more sacred than is that great pledge given by every member of every department of the government of the United States to support and defend the Constitution.[102]

Despite these reassurances, neither opinion sought to set a time limit on the Foraker Act's provisions, and to this day, Puerto Rico remains an unincorporated territory of the United States, albeit with an increasingly powerful locally elected government.

Despite its division, the majority rejected the argument that, in matters of taxation, Congress could not treat the U.S. territory of Puerto Rico differently than a state; thus, Puerto Rican exports to the U.S. mainland were subject to duties not imposed on products of the states, and import tariffs on oranges, sugar, or any other Puerto Rican product were legitimately imposed by Congress.[103] Most importantly, the *Downes* majority gave Congress almost unfettered discretion to do with Puerto Rico what it wanted.

---

[100] Downes v. Bidwell, 182 U.S. at 344–47 (Gray, J., concurring).

[101] *Id.* at 346. This position was eventually adopted by a majority of the Court in *Balzac*, 258 U.S. 298, 305 (expressly adopting White's opinion as controlling).

[102] *Id.* at 343–44 (White, J., concurring) (emphasis added).

[103] In other words, the equal taxation provision of the Constitution did not benefit Puerto Rico. *See* U.S. Const. art. I, § 8, cl. 1 ("The Congress shall have Power To lay and collect Taxes, Duties, Imposts and Excises, to pay the Debts and provide for the Common Defence and general Welfare of the United States; but all Duties, Imposts and Excises shall be uniform throughout the United States.").

The four dissenting Justices—Chief Justice Fuller and Justices Harlan, Brewer, and Peckham—joined a single dissenting opinion authored by Chief Justice Fuller.[104] The dissent called for constitutional values to prevail over the desire for empire that turned Puerto Rico into a separate and subordinate possession:

> [The Founders] may not, indeed, have deliberately considered a triumphal progress of the nation, as such, around the earth, but as [Chief Justice John] Marshall wrote: "It is not enough to say that this particular case was not in the mind of the convention when the article was framed, nor of the American people when it was adopted. It is necessary to go further, and to say that, had this particular case been suggested, the language would have been so varied as to exclude it, or it would have been made a special exception."
>
> This cannot be said, and on the contrary, in order to the successful extension of our institutions, the reasonable presumption is that the limitations on the exertion of arbitrary power would have been made more rigorous.[105]

Justice Harlan issued a separate dissent, which has come to be held in high regard.[106] In his opinion, he found the sui generis distinction between "incorporated" and "unincorporated" territories less than compelling:

> I am constrained to say that this idea of "incorporation" has some occult meaning which my mind does not apprehend. It is enveloped in some mystery which I am unable to unravel. In my opinion, Porto Rico became, at least after the ratification of the treaty with Spain, a part of and subject to the jurisdiction of the United States in respect of all its territory and people, and Congress could not thereafter impose any duty, impost, or excise with respect to that island and its inhabitants, which departed from the rule of uniformity established by the Constitution.[107]

In short, the dissenters did not believe that the insular possessions should be relegated to an uncertain status between independence and statehood based on special exceptions or the manipulation of vague legal terms.

Downes established that, in matters of taxation, Congress could treat the U.S. territory of Puerto Rico differently than a state; thus, Puerto Rican exports to the U.S. mainland were subject to duties not

---

[104] Downes v. Bidwell, 182 U.S. at 347–75 (Fuller, C.J., dissenting).

[105] *Id.* at 374–75.

[106] *Id.* at 375–91 (Harlan, J., dissenting).

[107] *Id.* at 391.

imposed on products in interstate commerce.[108] More importantly, the *Downes* majority gave Congress almost unfettered discretion to do with Puerto Rico what it wanted. For those who believed that territorial expansion based on an imperialist and colonial model was sound national policy, the obvious contradictions between Justice Brown's positions in *De Lima* and *Downes* were intellectually indefensible. As a result, Justice White's concurring opinion became the preferred theory for the pro-empire view. This was not lost on the New York Times, which editorialized soon after the cases that:

> The *De Lima* case was a stumbling block for Justice Brown. By asserting in that case the principle that cession and possession made Porto Rico a part of the territory of the United States he invalidated much of the reasoning by which he reached, in the *Downes* case, the conclusion that for purposes of tariff legislation the island is not territory of the United States within the prohibition which the Constitution lays upon Congress respecting uniform taxes. In making this assertion we are supported by the high authority of Horace Gray and by the clearly reasoned opinion of Justice White, speaking for himself and Justices Shiras and McKenna, concurring in the view that the Porto Rican tariff is not repugnant to the Constitution, but reaching that conclusion by a process of reasoning and interpretation solidly based upon the historical practice and judicial sanctions of a century of territorial increase. It would have been better for the reputation of the Supreme Court had the task of writing its opinion in the controlling case of *Downes* been committed to Justice White.[109]

Some of the most prominent legal thinkers of the time took positions on the matter, most notably in early issues of the Harvard Law Review and the Yale Law Journal. Indeed, the early volumes of those two journals are full of articles debating the legal status of the new island territories. For example, Harvard Law School Dean Christopher Langdell supported unfettered congressional authority,[110] as did Simeon E. Baldwin.[111] Recognizing that U.S. administrators were in effective

---

[108] See *supra* note 103.

[109] Editorial, *The Court and the Opinions*, N.Y. Times, May 29, 1901, at 8. The *New York Times* editorial also noted another strength in Justice White's opinion: it overruled *Dred Scott v. Sandford*. *Id.*

[110] C. C. Langdell, *The Status of Our New Territories*, 12 Harv. L. Rev. 365, 379–392 (1899) (detailing how, in the author's view, most provisions limiting congressional authority to legislate did not apply to the new territories).

[111] *See, e.g.*, Simeon E. Baldwin, *The People of the United States*, 8 Yale L.J. 159, 159 & 167 (1899) (arguing that the phrase "the People of the United States" in the preamble of the Constitution limited the applicability of the Constitution to citizens of the states); *see*

control of the conquered territories, Baldwin addressed executive powers, and, referring specifically to the power of the presidency, he wrote: "all honest men, not blinded by party passion, felt that the President held great constitutional functions, which made him, in his sphere, little short of the dictator of the Republic."[112] More generally, this legal scholarship interpreted the Territorial Clause along three very different lines: (1) It conferred absolute congressional power, totally unfettered by other constitutional constraints; (2) It granted almost completely unfettered congressional authority, which was limited by fundamental constitutional guarantees; and (3) It implied the "Constitution Follows the Flag," meaning that all constitutional guarantees and constraints on congressional power applied in the territories.[113]

Downes effectively established different types of "domestic territories," but now in concurrence rather than in dissent as in *De Lima*. White's distinction between incorporated and unincorporated territories was important, because at that time the United States already had other territories, most of which were then believed to be on their way to statehood, including Arizona, New Mexico, Oklahoma, Alaska, and Hawai'i. The status of these territories made arguments about absolute congressional authority unacceptable to scholars such as Abbott Lawrence Lowell.[114] Lowell objected that "[t]he narrower view of the Constitution, that which limits its provisions to the area of the States [might] allow[] Congress to confiscate property in the District of Columbia or in a Territory without compensation, or ... to pass a bill of attainder against a resident of Washington or of Arizona, and order him hung without trial."[115]

Although the *Downes* decision triggered some controversy among legal scholars, its admittedly fragmented holdings would come to be a shared constitutional vision that today enjoys almost unanimous support among the Justices, no matter their political stripes. There is currently little doubt that the Constitution does not follow the flag and that Congress has broad discretion to govern insular possessions that are

---

also Simeon E. Baldwin, *The Constitutional Questions Incident to the Acquisition and Government by the United States of Island Territory*, 12 Harv. L. Rev. 393 (1899) (upon approval of the Treaty of Paris by the U.S. Senate, authority to govern the territories would be transferred from the executive to the legislative branch).

[112] Simeon E. Baldwin, *Absolute Power, an American Institution*, 7 Yale L.J. 1, 19 (1897).

[113] *See* Trías Monge, 1 *Historia Constitucional*, *supra* note 24, at 238 (providing a succinct analysis of the legal literature of the time).

[114] Abbott Lawrence Lowell, *The Status of Our New Possessions—A Third View*, 13 Harv. L. Rev. 155 (1899).

[115] *Id.* at 156–57.

permanently in limbo, moving neither toward statehood nor independence. *Downes* came to achieve this authoritative status through a series of later decisions, all of which are treated as part of the Insular Cases.

The Aftermath of Downes

In evaluating the aftermath of *Downes*, some authors take a broad view, identifying the Insular Cases as a complex series of decisions that helped create the "American Empire."[116] One might also situate the cases even more generally within the law of conquest or the "right of discovery."[117] My aim is to examine these cases as constitutional moments in which the Supreme Court both legitimized and helped to effectuate a second age of American territorial expansion at the turn of the twentieth century.

Most students of American law know *Dred Scott v. Sandford*[118] for its shameful definition of African slaves as non-citizens and chattel property rather than individuals entitled to constitutional rights. But *Scott v. Sandford* was also a Territorial Clause case in which the majority stated:

> The power to expand the territory of the United States by the admission of new States is plainly given; and in the construction of this power by all the departments of the Government, it has been held to authorize the acquisition of territory, not fit for admission at the time, but to be admitted as soon as its population and situation would entitle it to admission. *It is acquired to become a State, and not to be held as a colony and governed by Congress with absolute authority.*[119]

Scott v. Sandford represents the first age of American territorial expansion, characterized by conquest of the native inhabitants followed by colonization by the growing U.S. immigrant population.

The nine Insular Cases of the October 1900 term ushered us into a second age of expansion that did not involve territorial incorporation into the nation through statehood, but rather the holding of colonies subject to almost absolute congressional authority. After the nine cases decided in the October 1900 term, the Court addressed a series of "intermediate cases," resolved between 1903 and 1922, in which first the

---

[116] *See, e.g.*, Guadalupe T. Luna, *On the Complexities of Race: The Treaty of Guadalupe Hidalgo and* Dred Scott v. Sandford, 53 U. Miami L. Rev. 691, 708–711 (1999) (noting that *Scott v. Sandford* gave constitutional authority for constructs of citizens and noncitizens within U.S. territorial control).

[117] *See, e.g.*, Johnson v. M'Intosh, 21 U.S. (8 Wheat.) 543 (1823).

[118] 60 U.S. (19 How.) 393 (1856).

[119] *Id.* at 447 (emphasis added).

Fuller Court, then the White Court in 1910, and finally the Taft Court in 1921, tried to agree on a single constitutional doctrine in their application of the Territorial Clause. These cases demonstrated that the unincorporated status of a territory could lead to second-class citizenship for its residents.

These intermediate cases start with *Hawai'i v. Mankichi* in 1903, in which the court ruled that Hawaiian territorial law, not the Seventh Amendment, governed the defendant's right to a criminal jury trial. Justices White and McKenna concurred, stating that Congress had not expressly incorporated Hawai'i; therefore, full constitutional protections such as the right to jury trial did not apply.[120] *Mankichi* was soon followed by *Gonzáles v. Williams*, a unanimous ruling written by Chief Justice Fuller in favor of a Puerto Rican woman seeking entry into New York City after the Immigration Commissioner had declared her a foreigner and excluded her from the city.[121] The court held that Puerto Ricans, while not U.S. citizens, are nonetheless subjects or "nationals" of this country, and therefore not foreigners for purposes of the immigration laws. Later in 1904, the Court issued *Kepner v. United States*,[122] *Binns v. United States*,[123] and, more importantly, *Dorr v. United States*, in which a majority reaffirmed the incorporation doctrine first articulated by Justice White in *Downes*, and found that the Philippines constituted an unincorporated territory.[124]

In 1905, a case involving territorial Alaska, *Rassmussen v. United States*, reiterated the result of the 1901 decisions and continued to solidify a prevailing view from among the many articulated by the Justices in the earlier opinions.[125] Writing for the majority, Justice White ruled that Alaska, unlike Puerto Rico, was an incorporated territory of the United States, with full constitutional protections for its residents. Other cases that applied White's incorporation doctrine in this period were *Dowdell v. United States*[126] in 1911, and *Porto Rico v. Rosaly*[127] in 1913. In *Rosaly*, then-Chief Justice White wrote for a unanimous court

---

[120] Hawai'i v. Mankichi, 190 U.S. 197, 218–21 (1903) (White, J., concurring).

[121] Gonzales v. Williams, 192 U.S. 1 (1904).

[122] 195 U.S. 100 (1904).

[123] 194 U.S. 486 (1904) (involving taxation in Alaska).

[124] Dorr v. United States, 195 U.S. 138 (1904).

[125] Rassmussen v. United States, 197 U.S. 516 (1905).

[126] 221 U.S. 325 (1911) (holding that *Dorr* disposes of the matter and that the Philippine Supreme Court properly affirmed defendants' convictions after requiring trial court to supplement record on appeal).

[127] 227 U.S. 270 (1913).

that Puerto Rico was a "completely organized Territory [of,] although not . . . incorporated into the United States."[128]

The Foraker Act—the Organic Act for Puerto Rico interpreted in *Downes*—was replaced by the Jones Act of 1917, making changes to the local government and, most significantly, giving Puerto Ricans U.S. citizenship.[129] In 1922, *Balzac v. Porto Rico*[130] applied the Jones Act and, in the process, turned Justice White's concurrence in *Downes* into normative constitutional doctrine, and still quite applicable precedent. The court unanimously affirmed *Downes*, citing Justice White's opinion and the incorporation doctrine as controlling, which helped to clarify the constitutional relationship between Puerto Rico and the United States.[131] On the specific facts of the case, *Balzac* ruled that even after the grant of U.S. citizenship to the residents of Puerto Rico, not all U.S. constitutional protections applied to the territory:[132] fundamental rights, generally those guaranteed by the Due Process Clause, would automatically apply to U.S. citizens living in the unincorporated territories, but personal freedoms, such as the rights to trial by jury and uniform taxation, would not.[133] This decision is often considered the last of the Insular Cases because subsequent opinions have simply reinforced the doctrinal approaches adopted in *Downes* and *Balzac*.

The Supreme Court came close to overruling these two decisions in the 1957 case of *Reid v. Covert*,[134] but could muster only a plurality. The

---

[128] *Id.* at 274 (quoting New York *ex rel.* Kopel v. Bingham, 211 U.S. 468, 476 (1909)) (ruling that the Puerto Rican government enjoyed sovereign immunity). *See* Rebecca S. Shoemaker, *The White Court: Justices, Rulings, and Legacy* 3 (2004); Walter F. Pratt, Jr., *The Supreme Court Under Edward Douglass White, 1910–1921* at 88 (1999).

[129] See Jones Act of 1917, § 5, *P.R. Laws Ann.* vol. 1, pp. 72–73, (conferring U.S. citizenship on all "citizens of Porto Rico [*sic*]"; it adopted the definition of Puerto Rican citizenship included in § 7 of the Foraker Act). This new law, however, left some confusion about Puerto Rican citizenship that required judicial resolution. *See* Jones Act of 1917, § 13, *P.R. Laws Ann.* vol. 1, p. 83; § 43, *P.R. Laws Ann.* vol. 1, p. 120. *See also* Ediberto Román, *The Alien–Citizen Paradox and Other Consequences of U.S. Colonialism*, 26 Fla. St. U. L. Rev. 1 (1998) (a detailed study of the legal issues related to the grant of U.S. citizenships to the Puerto Ricans); Puig Jimenez v. Glover, 255 F.2d 54 (1st Cir. 1958) (plaintiff born in Puerto Rico in 1922 who resided on the island for fourteen years, but whose return from a visit to Spain was delayed from 1936 to July 1941 because of the Spanish civil war, was a U.S. citizen pursuant to the Jones Act, because she established her residence in Puerto Rico prior to the trip to Spain and her absence was involuntary).

[130] 258 U.S. 298 (1922).

[131] *Id.* at 305 (stating that "the opinion of Mr. Justice White of the majority, in *Downes v. Bidwell*, has become the settled law of the court").

[132] *Id.*

[133] *Id.* at 312–13.

[134] 354 U.S. 1 (1957).

case involved two civilian women, both U.S. citizens, tried by military tribunals for killing their husbands, members of the U.S. armed forces, on American military bases in England and Japan. The Court held that depriving the women of their right to a jury trial in a civilian court violated their constitutional rights, ruling that the Constitution protects citizens when they are outside of the United States. Specifically criticizing *Balzac* and *Downes*, Justice Hugo Black, joined by Chief Justice Earl Warren and Justices William Douglas and William Brennan, wrote:

> This Court and other federal courts have held or asserted that various constitutional limitations apply to the Government when it acts outside the continental United States. While it has been suggested that only those constitutional rights which are "fundamental" protect Americans abroad, we can find no warrant, in logic or otherwise, for picking and choosing among the remarkable collection of "Thou shalt nots" which were explicitly fastened on all departments and agencies of the Federal Government by the Constitution and its Amendments. Moreover, in view of our heritage and the history of the adoption of the Constitution and the Bill of Rights, it seems peculiarly anomalous to say that trial before a civilian judge and by an independent jury picked from the common citizenry is not a fundamental right.[135]

But concurring in the result only, Justices Felix Frankfurter and John Marshall Harlan II[136] distinguished the Insular Cases, believing them to be good law. In his opinion, Justice Frankfurter put it this way:

> The results in the cases that arose by reason of the acquisition of exotic "Territory" do not control the present cases, for the territorial cases rest specifically on Art. IV, § 3, which is a grant of power to Congress to deal with "Territory" and other Government property. Of course the power sought to be exercised in Great Britain and Japan does not relate to "Territory."[137]

That Puerto Rico is still one of the "exotic territories" was confirmed in 1978 in *Califano v. Torres*,[138] when the Supreme Court reiterated the Insular Cases' holding that Puerto Rico is an unincorporated territory of the United States. While living in the states, Cesar Gautier Torres, Carmelo Bracero Colón, and a third party identified by the Court only as "Vega," had received Supplemental Security Income through a

---

[135] *Id.* at 8–9 (footnotes omitted).

[136] Justice Harlan was the grandson of Justice John Marshall Harlan who had eloquently dissented in *Downes. See* David Shultz, *Encyclopedia of the Supreme Court* 196–97 (2005).

[137] *Reid*, 354 U.S. at 53 (Frankfurter, J., concurring).

[138] 435 U.S. 1 (1978) (per curiam).

federal Social Security Administration program for "qualified aged, blind, and disabled persons."[139] When they moved to Puerto Rico, however, their benefits were canceled. The Supreme Court let this discrimination stand, explaining:

> [t]he exclusion of Puerto Rico in the amended program is apparent in the definitional section.... [T]he Act ... states that no individual is eligible for benefits during any month in which he or she is outside the United States. The Act defines "the United States" as "the 50 States and the District of Columbia."[140]

The Justices then concluded that "we deal here with a constitutional attack upon a law providing for governmental payments of monetary benefits." Such a statute "is entitled to a strong presumption of constitutionality." As the Court explained, "So long as [the statute's] judgments are rational, and not invidious, the legislature's efforts to tackle the problems of the poor and the needy are not subject to a constitutional straitjacket."[141]

The "rational basis" for Congress's action in this case was later described by the Court in *Harris v. Rosario*: "In [*Califano*], we concluded that a similar statutory classification was rationally grounded on three factors: Puerto Rican residents do not contribute to the federal treasury; the cost of treating Puerto Rico as a State under the statute would be high; and greater benefits could disrupt the Puerto Rican economy."[142] In ruling that the lower level of reimbursement provided to Puerto Rico under the Aid to Families with Dependent Children program did not violate the Fifth Amendment's Equal Protection Clause, *Harris* exposed Puerto Rico's continued unincorporated territorial status. Justice Thurgood Marshall noted in his dissent that three of his contemporaries on the Court had expressed opposition to *Downes* and its denial of constitutional protections to U.S. citizens, but they did not join him here. Marshall concluded that *Harris* ultimately illustrated how the

---

[139] *Id.* at 2.

[140] *Id.* (citations omitted).

[141] *Id.* at 5 (citations omitted) (quoting Mathews v. de Castro, 429 U.S. 181, 185 (1976); Jefferson v. Hackney, 406 U.S. 535, 546 (1972)). *See* Malavet, *supra* note 18, at 155–58 (describing the Puerto Rican economy generally, specifically identifying the Puerto Ricans as the poorest American citizens).

[142] Harris v. Rosario, 446 U.S. 651, 652 (1980). Although Puerto Ricans do not pay federal income taxes, they do pay Social Security and other federal taxes, and additionally, it is difficult to conceive how $300 million for children's welfare would negatively disrupt the Puerto Rican economy. *See* Malavet, *supra* note 18, at 155–58 (discussing Puerto Rico's economy).

Insular Cases had become entrenched constitutional doctrine that accorded some Americans second-class citizenship.[143]

As of the writing of this chapter, the most recent reference to the Insular Cases can be found in Justice Clarence Thomas's concurring opinion in *United States v. Lara*[144] in 2004. There, citing *Reid*, he wrote: "The 'Insular Cases,' which include the Hawai'i and Puerto Rico examples ... involved Territories of the United States, over which Congress has plenary power to govern and regulate."[145] As long as the Insular Cases remain good law, Congress, in the exercise of its authority under the Territorial Clause, may unilaterally change the statutory relationship between the United States and its territories. Moreover, one Congress cannot bind another, which makes statutory language purporting to limit future legislative enactments unconstitutional.[146]

Attempts to create formal Puerto Rican citizenship have been legally and politically rebuffed. For example, in 1997, socialist Juan Mari–Bras renounced his U.S. citizenship, hoping to retain only Puerto Rican citizenship as his legal citizenship, and the Supreme Court of Puerto Rico held that Puerto Rican citizenship was independent of U.S. citizenship because of certain provisions of Puerto Rican law.[147] On the day *before* that opinion was issued, however, the Puerto Rican law alluded to in the opinion was amended to require both U.S. citizenship and Puerto Rico residency in order to become a citizen of the island, making the matter of law addressed in the opinion moot.[148] As a result, Puerto Ricans are limited to the legal citizenship of the United States but they are not entitled to the full enjoyment of the rights usually associated with that citizenship.

---

[143] *Harris*, 446 U.S. at 653–54 (Marshall, J., dissenting).

[144] *Lara*, 541 U.S. at 214 (Thomas, J., concurring).

[145] *Id.* at 225.

[146] *See* I.N.S. v. Chadha, 462 U.S. 919 (1983); *see also* Bowsher v. Synar, 478 U.S. 714, 733–34 (1986) (finding that the provisions of the 1985 balanced budget act, the Gramm–Rudman–Hollings Act, requiring specific executive action to reduce the deficit violated constitutional separation of powers).

[147] Ramírez de Ferrer v. Mari Brás, 144 P.R. Dec. 141 (1997). Plaintiff Miriam Ramírez–de Ferrer is a pro-statehood activist who was a Puerto Rican senator. Juan Mari–Brás is the founder of the Movimiento Pro Independencia and the Socialist Party of Puerto Rico.

[148] *P.R. Laws. Ann.* tit. 1, § 7 (1997), *amended by* Law 132 of Nov. 17, 1997, § 1; *see also* Pedro Malavet Vega, *Derechos y Libertades Constitucionales en Puerto Rico* 589 n.1454 (2003) (discussing the controversy that arose as a result of the rather curious timing of the amendment to the statute).

Downes' *Legacy: Citizenship of a Second Class*

The most enduring effect of *Downes* is its definition of a diminished level of citizenship for territorial subjects of the United States.[149] Section 1 of the Fourteenth Amendment reads, in part: "All persons born or naturalized in the United States, and subject to the jurisdiction thereof, are citizens of the United States and of the State wherein they reside."[150] To the extent that this provision creates formal universal U.S. citizenship, it is belied by the reality of that citizenship, which is often constructed on the basis of fault lines defined by essentialized notions of race. The territorial peoples are just one example of this citizenship construct, and one can easily include American Indians,[151] African Americans,[152] Asian Americans, and Mexican Americans[153] among the victims.[154]

The citizenship status of Puerto Ricans was left unclear at the end of the Spanish American War, when Article IX of the Treaty of Paris provided:

> Spanish subjects, *natives of the Peninsula*, residing in the territory over which Spain by the present treaty relinquishes or cedes her sovereignty, may remain in such territory or may remove therefrom, retaining in either event all their rights of property, including the right to sell or dispose of such property or of its proceeds; and they shall also have the right to carry on their industry, commerce and professions, being subject in respect thereof to such laws as are applicable to other foreigners.
>
> The civil rights and political status of the native inhabitants of the territories hereby ceded to the United States shall be determined by the Congress.[155]

---

[149] Until Puerto Ricans were granted U.S. citizenship in 1917, they were, in the words of a Democratic U.S. senator, "without a country." Still, under international law, Puerto Rican citizenship is not recognized. *See* Carr, *supra* note 30, at 36.

[150] U.S. Const. amend. XIV, § 1. The section continues as follows: "No State shall make or enforce any law which shall abridge the privileges or immunities of citizens of the United States; nor shall any State deprive any person of life, liberty, or property, without due process of law; nor deny to any person within its jurisdiction the equal protection of the laws."

[151] *See, e.g.*, Johnson v. M'Intosh, 21 U.S. (8 Wheat.) 543 (1823).

[152] *See, e.g.*, Dred Scott v. Sandford, 60 U.S. (19 How.) 393 (1856).

[153] As detailed by Guadalupe Luna, Mexicans were dispossessed of their land despite their formal U.S. citizenship and their legal rights. Guadalupe T. Luna, *Chicana/Chicano Land Tenure in the Agrarian Domain: On the Edge of a "Naked Knife,"* 4 Mich. J. of Race & L. 39 (1998); *see also Race and Races, supra* note 46, at 262.

[154] To this limited study, we might add the mistreatment of Native Hawaiians. *See* Eric K. Yamamoto, Carrie Ann Y. Shirota & Jayna Kanani Kim, *Indigenous Peoples' Human Rights in U.S. Courts, in Moral Imperialism: A Critical Anthology* 300 (Berta Esperanza Hernández–Truyol ed., 2002).

[155] Treaty of Paris, U.S.–Spain, art. IX, Dec. 10, 1898, T.S. No. 343, *reprinted in P.R. Laws Ann.*, vol. 1, 20 (emphasis added).

Although the *peninsulares* (natives of the Iberian Peninsula) were given the option to retain their Spanish citizenship, the native-born Puerto Ricans were not. They lost the Spanish citizenship they had been granted in late 1897. Yet again, the island's native inhabitants became subjects, but not citizens, of a colonial power. Despite the language of the treaty, until Congress acted on the matter, the legal citizenship of Puerto Rico's non-Spanish inhabitants was defined by the U.S. courts, initially and enduringly, in *Downes*. *Downes* effectively defined the legal rights of the inhabitants of the territories of the United States, as well as the power of the federal executive and legislative branches to regulate the land and its people.

Two decades later, in *Balzac v. Porto Rico*,[156] the Supreme Court, in adopting the incorporated/unincorporated territories categories created by White, constitutionally constructed the U.S. citizenship of Puerto Ricans as second class as long as they remained in the territory of Puerto Rico. The Court distinguished between the rights of U.S. citizens living in Puerto Rico and those of U.S. citizens living in "the United States proper." As long as Puerto Ricans chose to remain on the island, they would enjoy the formal status but not the full rights of American citizenship. *Balzac* thus distinguished between Puerto Ricans as individual U.S. citizens and Puerto Ricans as collective inhabitants of Puerto Rico. As individuals, they were free "to enjoy all political and other rights" granted to U.S. citizens *if* they "move[d] into the United States proper," but as long as they remained on the island, they could not fully enjoy the rights of U.S. citizenship.[157] The Court explained the motivation behind this construction of Puerto Rican second-class citizenship in nativistic terms when it distinguished the island from Alaska:

> Alaska was a very different case from that of Porto Rico. It was an enormous territory, very sparsely settled and offering opportunity for immigration and settlement *by American citizens*. It was on the American Continent and within easy reach of the then United States. It involved none of the difficulties which incorporation of the Philippines and Porto Rico presents.[158]

This statement clearly assumes that Puerto Rican U.S. citizens are not the "American citizens" who could resettle an "American" state. While recognizing the impossibility of creating an Anglo–Saxon majority in Puerto Rico, the Court also constructed Puerto Ricans as "others." Because Puerto Ricans are so "other," the incorporation of the territory into the United States could not be inferred; it had to be clearly

---

[156] 258 U.S. 298 (1922).

[157] *Id.* at 311.

[158] *Id.* at 309 (emphasis added).

expressed by Congress.[159] To this day, Congress has not expressed itself on the matter of incorporation and full extension of constitutional guarantees to Puerto Rico.

Conclusion: Forgotten Cases and Invisible Citizens

The Fuller Court is often remembered in law schools for invalidating the first national income tax[160] and declaring a state law prohibiting more than sixty hours in a work-week unconstitutional,[161] but its most famous case is *Plessy v. Ferguson.*[162] With the exception of Justice McKenna, who was appointed in January of 1898,[163] all the members of the *Downes* Court were members of the Court that decided the notorious *Plessy* in 1896—a decision in which Justice Brewer did not participate and Justice Harlan dissented.[164] But while the "separate but equal" standard of *Plessy* was relegated to the historical trash bin by *Brown v. Board of Education,*[165] the *Downes* decision is still good law. By relieving

---

[159] Again, the Supreme Court is rather clear in *Balzac*:

The jury system needs citizens trained to the exercise of the responsibilities of jurors . . . Congress has thought that a people like the Filipinos or the Porto Ricans, trained to a complete judicial system which knows no juries, living in compact and ancient communities, with definitely formed customs and political conceptions, should be permitted themselves to determine how far they wish to adopt this institution of Anglo–Saxon origin, and when.

Id. at 310.

[160] Pollock v. Farmers' Loan & Trust Co., 158 U.S. 601 (1895), *superseded by* U.S. Const. amend XVI.

[161] Lochner v. New York, 198 U.S. 45 (1905) (invalidating a New York penal statute forbidding employers from requiring workers to exceed sixty hours in a work week).

[162] 163 U.S. 537 (1896) (7–1 decision).

[163] *See* 3 *The Justices of the Supreme Court of the United States: Their Lives and Major Opinions* 861 (Leon Friedman & Fred L. Israel eds., 1997) [hereinafter *Justices of the Supreme Court*].

[164] J. Gordon Hylton explains why Justice Brewer did not participate in the decision:

The final line of the United States Supreme Court opinion in the landmark case of *Plessy v. Ferguson* states, "Mr. Justice Brewer did not hear the argument or participate in the decision of this case." Because of the untimely death of his daughter, the 58–year old Justice had been forced to leave Washington, D.C. for his home in Leavenworth, Kansas, on April 13, 1896, the day *Plessy* was argued before the Court. Without Brewer, the Court voted 7 to 1 to uphold Louisiana's "separate but equal" public accommodations law. Only Justice John Marshall Harlan, a former slaveholder from Kentucky, agreed that the challenged "Jim Crow" statute violated the Fourteenth Amendment's guarantee of equal protection of the laws.

J. Gordon Hylton, *The Judge Who Abstained in* Plessy v. Ferguson: *Justice David Brewer and the Problem of Race*, 61 Miss. L.J. 315, 315–16 (1991) (footnotes omitted).

[165] 347 U.S. 483 (1954).

Congress and the President of most constitutional limitations on the exercise of their discretion, the Supreme Court in *Downes* intended to allow the government some flexibility in dealing with new territorial possessions. But that flexibility has now become a permanent system for the regulation of an island empire, rather than a transitional process as it was for Cuba and even the Philippines.

The late Chief Justice William H. Rehnquist, in his book *The Supreme Court*,[166] discussed why President Theodore Roosevelt had demanded to know how Oliver Wendell Holmes would vote on the Insular Cases before nominating him to replace the retiring Horace Gray on the Supreme Court. In a letter to Holmes' sponsor, Senator Henry Cabot Lodge, Roosevelt wrote:

> The majority of the present Court who have, although without satisfactory unanimity, upheld the policies of President McKinley and the Republican party in Congress, have rendered a great service to mankind and to this nation. The minority—a minority so large as to lack but one vote of being a majority—have stood for such reactionary folly as would have hampered well-nigh hopelessly this people in doing efficient and honorable work for the national welfare, and for the welfare of the islands themselves, in Porto Rico and the Philippines. No doubt they have possessed excellent motives and without doubt they are men of excellent personal character; but this no more excuses them than the same conditions excused the various upright and honorable men who took part in the wicked folly of secession in 1860 and 1861.
>
> Now I should like to know that Judge Holmes was in entire sympathy with our views [on the Insular Cases].[167]

Rehnquist then concluded that "Holmes was duly appointed an associate justice [effective December 8, 1902[168]], and largely fulfilled Roosevelt's expectations of him with respect to the so-called Insular Cases, which were a great issue at that time, although they are scarcely a footnote in a text on constitutional law today."[169]

The late Chief Justice is, of course, correct that *Downes* and the Insular Cases are treated as a legal footnote. But they should not be. As President Roosevelt's litmus test for appointment of one of the best-

---

[166] William H. Rehnquist, *The Supreme Court* 215–17 (new ed. 2001).

[167] *Id.* at 216.

[168] 3 *Justices of the Supreme Court*, *supra* note 163, at 878.

[169] Rehnquist, *supra* note 166, at 217. Justice Holmes acquiesced in the continued imposition of the White doctrine in the *Insular Cases*, but did not expressly embrace it. Accordingly, he concurred in the result in *Balzac*, but without a written opinion. 258 U.S. 298, 314 (1922).

remembered Justices in history indicates, these decisions were critical to the determination of the kind of country that the United States was to become. Moreover, *Downes* is living constitutional doctrine daily affecting the lives of millions of Puerto Ricans who are relegated to second-class citizenship and leaving a United States territory in a permanent state of constitutional uncertainty about its future. The Insular Cases are indeed the enduring legacy of the Fuller Court and an essential part of the legal development of our nation. *Downes v. Bidwell* constitutionally defines the nation that we are. If we study it seriously, rather than relegating it to legal obscurity, we might become the nation that we wish to be.

5

Angela Onwuachi–Willig

Multiracialism and the Social Construction of Race: The Story of *Hudgins v. Wrights*

Introduction

In the case of *Hudgins v. Wrights*,[1] the Supreme Court of Appeals of Virginia[2] delivered an important lesson on the non-genetic nature of race—the manner in which race is socially determined by both physical and non-physical proxies. *Hudgins* involved the legal battle of three women—a grandmother, a mother, and a granddaughter—who struggled to prove that they were free citizens, not slaves, by offering evidence to refute a white slaveowner's claim that they descended from an enslaved black woman instead of a free American Indian woman.[3]

The social context in which the *Hudgins* decision was issued is critical to understanding its impact and enduring lessons. Beginning in the late seventeenth century, disputes about the racial background of individual persons in Virginia became significant. Due to a rapidly growing system of bondage that presumptively marked all blacks as slaves, persons who could "earn" the racial label of white or American Indian in Virginia worked hard to capture one of those labels because

---

[1] 11 Va. (1 Hen. & M.) 134 (Va. 1806).

[2] The Supreme Court of Appeals of Virginia, which served as a model for the United States Supreme Court, was created in 1779 as one of four superior courts in Virginia. Though initially judges never rendered written opinions, the Virginia Constitution was amended in 1851 to require judges to state, in writing, the reasons for their rulings. The name of the court was changed to its current title, the Supreme Court of Virginia, by the Virginia Constitution of 1970. *See* The Supreme Court of Virginia, History, http://www. courts.state.va/scov/cover.htm (last visited Feb. 4, 2007).

[3] *Hudgins*, 11 Va. (1 Hen. & M.) at 136–38.

such racial identities essentially placed them outside of a life of slavery and on the side of either freedom or indentured servitude. Thus, for Jacky, Maria, and Epsabar Wright, who, like others after them, were seeking to prove their freedom by disclaiming blackness, the determination of their racial identity was transformative in that it would signify either their independence or their enslavement.

Hudgins v. Wrights demonstrates the impact of a growing multiracial population on Virginia's racial classification laws in a society that required segregation to preserve slavery. Specifically, this story analyzes how *Hudgins* helped to establish a system of racial definitions that entrenched a black class of enslaved labor within the tobacco economy. The chapter begins with the emergence of the slave system in Virginia and details how definitions of race shifted with the growth of a mixed-race population that threatened the stability of segregation and slave labor. This account also illustrates how the small numbers of American Indians and their propensity to escape intensified the need to isolate blacks, who generally could be identified by the most commonly used proxy for race—skin color—in a system of long, hard enslavement. Thereafter, the chapter tells the story of *Hudgins v. Wrights* from trial through appeal, culminating in a finding that the Wrights were free women because they descended from an American Indian on their maternal side. As the litigation makes clear, the three women's fate was determined not just by their appearance, which complicated the task of categorizing them because of their mixed racial heritage, but also by their families' reputation and conduct within their communities. Finally, the chapter ends with a discussion of the contemporary significance of the *Hudgins* decision, highlighting an enduring societal belief in pure biological classifications of race even in the face of a growing multiracial population and a continued practice of identifying race based on both physical appearance and community perceptions.

Slavery and Freedom in Virginia

Hudgins was decided in 1806, a time when the determination of a person's race as black in Virginia was life-altering in a way that could establish bondage or freedom, and, in some cases, life or death. The burden of blackness in Virginia was not always so heavy. Although the first group of blacks arrived in Virginia in 1619,[4] the enslavement of blacks was not officially sanctioned by law until 1661.[5] Before then,

---

[4] Robert S. Cope, *Carry Me Back: Slavery and Servitude in Seventeenth Century Virginia* 5–6, 11 (1973).

[5] *Id.* at 11; *see also* Betty Wood, *Slavery in Colonial America 1619–1776*, at 8 (2005) (noting that blacks had not immediately been enslaved by the English and that "their legal status remained somewhat ambiguous until the late seventeenth century"); Adele Hast, *The Legal Status of the Negro in Virginia 1705–1765*, 54 J. Negro Hist. 217, 218 (1969)

although some blacks were unofficially enslaved by whites, it was not unusual to find blacks who toiled in Virginia's tobacco fields alongside whites as indentured servants.[6]

Changing mores and economic imperatives laid the foundation for the 1661 slave law. As a moral matter, many white Virginians viewed enslavement as an acceptable practice to inflict on blacks, whom they believed to be inferior heathens.[7] When the law was passed, the black population in the colony had grown to approximately 950 residents, making blacks three to four percent of the state's population—a fairly large increase from the small population of only twenty-three blacks in 1625.[8] In the eyes of many white Virginians, blacks had become a readily available and plentiful pool of labor. More importantly, as a social and financial matter, white Virginians viewed slavery as economically rational and necessary. To their minds, white indentured servants were too costly in an agricultural economy because of social customs that required payment for their work with wages and future land grants. American Indians were too impractical due to their susceptibility to disease and their familiarity with the land, which made it easy for them to escape from their masters.[9] Indeed, in 1661—the same year in which the enslavement of blacks officially became legal—the Virginia Assembly passed a statute that prohibited the sale of American Indians as slaves and permitted American Indians to be used only as indentured servants for no "longer time than English of the like ages should serve by act of assembly."[10]

Under this system of legalized slavery, blackness became a life-changing status in the state of Virginia. Although a few blacks in Virginia were born free or were able to purchase freedom for themselves

---

("The first Negroes brought into Virginia in 1619 were probably considered similar to indentured white servants."). *But see Hudgins*, 11 Va. (1 Hen. & M.) at 137 ("From the first settlement of the colony of *Virginia* to the year 1778, . . . all *negroes, Moors,* and *mulattoes,* except *Turks* and *Moors* in amity with *Great Britain,* brought into this country by sea, or by land, were SLAVES."). Two other states had legally sanctioned slavery before Virginia—Massachusetts in 1641 and Connecticut in 1650. *See* Cope, *supra* note 4, at 11.

[6] *See* Cope, *supra* note 4, at 11.

[7] *See id.* at 9 ("Since the English commonly associated the color black with sin, it was all too easy to arrive at the conclusion that God had decreed perpetual bondage as part of Africans' punishment."); Hast, *supra* note 5, at 219 ("In its early years in Virginia, slavery was justified as permissible with heathen people.").

[8] *See* Wood, *supra* note 5, at 8.

[9] *Id.* at 9–10.

[10] Laws of Virginia, Mar. 1661, 14th Charles II, at 143 ("*And be it further enacted* that what Englishman trader, or other shall bring in any Indians as servants and shall assigne them over to any other, shall not sell them for slaves nor for any longer time than English of the like ages serve by act of assembly.").

or their family members,[11] the vast majority were relegated to a life of harsh, forced slave labor within the state's tobacco economy. In most instances, slaveowners provided their slaves with only minimal amounts of food, clothing, and shelter.[12] For example, slaves generally lived in sparsely furnished log cabins of about twelve by fourteen feet with mud filling the spaces between the logs.[13] Additionally, slaveowners often failed to give their slaves any shoes to wear and provided no more than two sets of clothing per year: one set to wear in the summer and the other to wear in the winter.[14] The food provided to slaves was sparse, too, often consisting of a standard weekly provision of corn and, at times, a piece of pork.[15] Socially, slaves faced the routine loss of loved ones because slave families easily could be separated by the sale of one or more relatives.[16]

The atrocities of slavery in Virginia were visited not only on mono-racial blacks but also on people of mixed racial heritage—black and white or black and American Indian. Being of "partial white blood" did not change one's status from black slave or servant to free person. Confronted with an increasing population of mixed-race children—primarily born as a result of the brutal sexual assault and rape of black women by white slaveowners[17]—the Virginia Assembly in 1662 passed an

---

[11] Anthony S. Parent, Jr., *Foul Means: The Formation of a Slave Society in Virginia, 1660–1740*, at 107 (2003) (noting that some blacks "even became freeholders and slave-holders").

[12] *See* Wood, *supra* note 5, at 46–47; *see also* Damian Alan Pargas, *Work and Slave Family Life in Antebellum Northern Virginia*, 31 J. Fam. Hist. 335, 344–46 (2006) (describing conditions of slavery during eighteenth century Virginia).

[13] *See* Kenneth Morgan, *Slavery and Servitude in North America, 1607–1800*, at 81 (2000); Wood, *supra* note 5, at 46–47.

[14] *See* Wood, *supra* note 5, at 46.

[15] *See id.*

[16] *See id.* at 43 ("[S]lave families had absolutely no guarantee that their[] [marriages] would be a lifetime relationship. . . . [I]t was a relationship that could be destroyed at any time and for any reason. In their legal capacity as property, enslaved people could be sold, given away in wills or as gifts, and even gambled away."); Angela Onwuachi–Willig, *The Return of the Ring: Welfare Reform's Marriage Cure as the Revival of Post–Bellum Control*, 93 Cal. L. Rev. 1647, 1656 (2005) ("In fact, because slave families were so frequently ripped apart by the slave market, slave couples often recited vows such as 'until death or distance do us part.' " (quoting Leon F. Litwack, *Been in the Storm so Long: The Aftermath of Slavery* 240 (1979))); Andrew T. Fede, *Gender in the Law of Slavery in the Antebellum United States*, 18 Cardozo L. Rev. 411, 416 (1996) (" 'The separation of slave families was possibly the most inhumane aspect of chattel slavery.' " (quoting Andrew Fede, *People Without Rights* 221 (1992))).

[17] *See* Rachel F. Moran, *Interracial Intimacy: The Regulation of Race and Romance* 24, 27–28 (2001); *see also* Mitchell F. Crusto, *Blackness as Property: Sex, Race, Status, and*

act declaring that mixed-race children inherited the status of their mothers.[18] Under this act, the mixed-race child of a black slave mother became the property of the mother's owner.[19] For the first time, Virginia categorized individuals of multiracial ancestry by placing the vast majority of them on the side of blackness and thus slavery. In 1691, the Assembly declared that even the small population of mixed-race children of white mothers would become indentured servants until age thirty, thereby cementing the non-whiteness of multiracial people.[20]

Being born free or buying one's freedom did not necessarily save individuals with black ancestry, whether multiracial or not, from the horrors of slavery. A free black could be made a slave if, at any given moment, he or she could not produce documents that established a claim to freedom.[21] Some free blacks were relegated to bondage despite their proof of freedom. Additionally, they suffered some of the same hardships that their enslaved counterparts endured. Free blacks were frequently

---

Wealth, 1 Stan. J. C.R. & C.L. 51, 67, 81–82 (2005) (enslaved blacks "were legally classified and treated as 'property' under their master's control" and "were expected to 'breed' enslaved children, adding to their master's wealth"); Eugene D. Genovese, *Roll, Jordan, Roll: The World the Slaves Made* 415 (1976) (noting the way in which black women were raped and sexually assaulted during slavery); Randall Kennedy, *Interracial Intimacies: Sex, Marriage, Identity, and Adoption* 42–46 (2003) (describing the sexual assault of black women by their slavemasters); Kate Manning, *Crossing the Color Line*, L.A. Times, Mar. 30, 2003, at R3; Robert P. McNamara, Maria Tempenis, & Beth Walton, *Crossing the Line: Interracial Couples in the South* 24 (1999) (describing black women's vulnerability to rape during the antebellum period); *accord* Nancy F. Cott, *Public Vows: A History of Marriage and the Nation* 58–59 (2000) (describing the role that sexual violations against slave women played in the abolitionist movement and abolitionist literature).

[18] Cope, *supra* note 4, at 11; Hast, *supra* note 5, at 220.

[19] *See* Wood, *supra* note 5, at 44 (noting that because of this law, "every slave child represented a potentially lucrative capital asset as well as a potentially valuable worker").

[20] *See* Trina Jones, *Shades of Brown: The Law of Skin Color*, 49 Duke L.J. 1487, 1503–04 (2000); *cf.* Moran, *supra* note 17, at 21 ("As slavery hardened the lines between whites and blacks, the racial tax on mulattoes increased. Their curtailed privileges clearly identified them as nonwhite. . . ."). White women who gave birth to mixed-race children were either heavily fined or sentenced to indentured servitude for five years. *Id.*; Marie-Amélie George, *The Modern Mulatto: A Comparative Analysis of the Social and Legal Positions of Mulattoes in the Antebellum South and the Intersex in Contemporary America*, 15 Colum. J. Gender & L. 665, 674 (2006); Carter G. Woodson, *The Beginnings of Miscegenation of the Whites and Blacks*, in *Interracialism: Black–White Intermarriage in American History, Literature, and Law* 42, 47 (Werner Sollors ed., 2000); *see also* Hast, *supra* note 5, at 222 ("The most severe punishment was given any white woman having a child by a Negro or mulatto father. . . ."). The drafters of the Act, however, knew that a white woman would rarely submit herself to the social ostracization and punishment that would come with bearing the children of a black man. *See* George, *supra*, at 674 (discussing various other reasons for regulating white women's sexuality).

[21] Cope, *supra* note 4, at 34.

separated from loved ones who were sold to owners in other regions, and
even worse, free blacks sometimes had to purchase their family members
and keep them as slaves.[22] Finally, free blacks held few of the privileges
enjoyed by free white citizens, having no right to testify against whites
in court, own firearms, attend school, or roam freely in their surround-
ings.[23]

Given the cruelty of slavery and the ease with which free blacks'
freedom and limited rights could be stripped away,[24] no white person in
Virginia—including indentured servants—desired the usual fate of any
blacks—free or enslaved.[25] Similarly, although American Indians were
not enslaved as systematically as blacks were,[26] no white person was
envious of the position of tribal members.[27] Like blacks, American
Indians were forced into hard labor as captives of war beginning in the
second half of the seventeenth century—though their labor was primari-

---

[22] *See id.* at 32. Free blacks' practice of keeping family members and friends enslaved
began as a way for free blacks to procure the freedom of their loved ones. Before 1806,
purchases of enslaved family members were generally followed by immediate manumis-
sions. After passage of an 1806 Virginia law requiring manumitted blacks to leave the state
within twelve months, free blacks "continued to purchase their relatives but held them as
slaves, refusing to decree their banishment by executing a deed or will of manumission."
Samll Goldsmyth et al., *Colored Freemen as Slave Owners in Virginia*, 1 J. Negro Hist. 233,
239–41 (1916). In 1712, after one Virginian planter freed sixteen of his slaves, the Virginia
General Assembly was asked to enact legislation to prohibit manumission. Such a law was
passed in 1723, officially forbidding "the freeing of any slave, on any pretense, 'except for
some meritorious service,' as judged by the governor and Council." Hast, *supra* note 5, at
220–21; *see also* Ellen D. Katz, *African–American Freedom in Antebellum Cumberland
County, Virginia*, 70 Chi.-Kent L. Rev. 927, 942 (1995) (citing "revealing a conspiracy" as
one example of meritorious service).

[23] Paul Finkelman, *The Centrality of the Peculiar Institution in American Legal
Development*, 68 Chi.-Kent L. Rev. 1009, 1014–15 (1993).

[24] Cope, *supra* note 4, at 34.

[25] *Id.* at 40 ("The most congenial companion of the free Negro aside from his own class
was the Negro slave. The free Negro seldom regarded slavery as a social class status
inferior to his own position during the seventeenth century in Virginia."); George, *supra*
note 20, at 676–77 ("Over the course of the seventeenth and eighteenth centuries, free
mulattoes and blacks were forged into the same legal category, one that was prohibited
from exercising many of the fundamental rights of citizenship, including the right to vote,
hold office, possess firearms, convene meetings, and be protected from unlawful searches
and seizure." (footnote omitted)); *accord* Finkelman, *supra* note 23, at 1014 ("Free blacks
in the South were better off than enslaved blacks, but they remained second class members
of society."); Hast, *supra* note 5, at 235 ("In many important areas of civil rights and
citizenship, free Negroes were classified with slaves.").

[26] Cope, *supra* note 4, at 42 ("At no time in Virginia's history, however, was there any
great number of Indians held either in temporary or permanent bondage.").

[27] *See id.* at 41 ("In the overall view of colonial society, nevertheless, the Indian was
regarded as inferior to the White, but somewhat higher than the Negro.").

ly as indentured servants.[28] Prior to Bacon's Rebellion in 1676, it was illegal for whites to enslave American Indians, but American Indians could still be held in indentured servitude.[29] In this sense, until 1676, the laws of Virginia worked to maintain a racial hierarchy of enslavement and labor—with whites as free persons, American Indians as hard laborers, and blacks as slaves. In fact, from 1670 to 1676, legislation racialized the two classes of forced labor by categorizing them as either black slaves or American Indian servants. Specifically, a 1670 colonial enactment provided that non-Christians who were imported into Virginia by shipping (usually Africans) would be slaves for life, while those non-Christian children who came by land (usually American Indians) would be servants until age thirty, and those non-Christian adults who came by land (again, usually American Indians) would be servants for twelve years.[30]

This racially coded system of hard labor disappeared briefly between 1679 and 1691 when the colony of Virginia allowed white slaveowners to hold American Indians in bondage along with blacks. In 1676 and 1679, the Virginia Assembly formally legalized the enslavement of American Indians who were captured during war.[31] In 1682, all restrictions on the enslavement of American Indians and blacks in Virginia were removed, legitimating the sale and trade of both blacks and American Indians.[32]

With fewer restrictions on slavery, the slave trade grew in prominence in Virginia, and the black population there increased from 23 in 1625, to 300 in 1655, and to 20,000 in 1702.[33] At the same time that black slavery was expanding exponentially, the Virginia Assembly was working to increase trade between whites and native American Indians by fostering mutual goodwill. Consequently, in 1691, the same year that the Assembly determined that mixed-race children of white mothers

---

[28] Much of the resistance to the enslavement of American Indians before the mid-century was due to fears that, in retaliation, American Indians would enslave whites who were captured during wars. *See id.* at 45.

[29] *Id.* at 45–46 ("In March, 1662, the Assembly passed a law stating that no Indian accepted in the colony as a servant should be sold as a slave or held for a longer period than English servants of like age or condition of servitude."). *But see id.* at 45 (noting that slavery of American Indians was practiced by colonists during this time despite its illegality).

[30] Cope, *supra* note 4, at 12; Laws of Virginia, Oct. 1670, 22d Charles II, at 283.

[31] Parent, *supra* note 11, at 114; Cope, *supra* note 4, at 14, 46; *see also Hudgins v. Wrights*, 11 Va. (1 Hen. & M.) 134, 138 (Va. 1806); *see, e.g.*, Laws of Virginia, June 1676, Bacon's Laws, at 346; Laws of Virginia, Feb. 1676–77, 29th Charles II, at 404.

[32] Parent, *supra* note 11, at 114; Cope, *supra* note 4, at 14, 46; *see* Laws of Virginia, Nov. 1682, 34th Charles II, at 491; *see also Hudgins*, 11 Va. (1 Hen. & M.) at 139.

[33] Cope, *supra* note 4, at 23–26.

were no longer born free, Virginia prohibited the enslavement of American Indians who were brought to or arrived in the colony after 1691.

In essence, by 1691, and certainly by 1705,[34] the Virginia legislature had cemented the lines of difference among white, black, and American Indian by enacting a statute to allow free trade with American Indians, thereby making it illegal for an American Indian to be born or brought into slavery after that critical year.[35] Under the statute, a declaration that one's maternal ancestor was an American Indian who was either born or arrived in Virginia after 1691 became critical to the freedom of those who had white or native-looking appearances and were alleged to be slaves descended from black women. As the stakes associated with racial identity took on profound significance, disputes over the classification of individuals with an ambiguous appearance or ancestry made their way into the courts. These battles over the color line and who was slave or free bring us directly to the story of *Hudgins v. Wrights*.

A Struggle for Freedom by Disclaiming Blackness

At issue in *Hudgins* were the rights of a mother, a daughter, and a granddaughter who had sued for their freedom from Holder Hudgins, a white slaveowner in Virginia. While Jacky, Maria, and Epsabar Wright[36] maintained that they were descended from a free American Indian woman and were therefore free themselves, Hudgins claimed that they were descended from a black female slave and were therefore his slaves. Specifically, Hudgins proclaimed "that they [were] descended from a negro woman by an *Indian*."[37] The power of race in Virginia's slave economy was so great that it influenced every aspect of the legal proceedings, even the evidentiary rules that governed the case. The courts struggled to determine who should bear the burden of proof when individuals had a phenotypically ambiguous appearance that left them in the perilous space between bondage and freedom.

The Trial: A Surprising Victory and a Referendum on Slavery

At trial, the parties presented evidence of ancestry, appearance, and reputation before Chancellor George Wythe of the Richmond District

---

[34] *See infra* notes 46, 51, and 69–70 and accompanying text.

[35] *See* Laws of Virginia, Apr. 1691, 3d William & Mary, Act IX, at 69; Laws of Virginia, Oct. 1705, 4th Anne, Ch. L2, at 468.

[36] Peter Wallenstein, Indian Foremothers: Race, Sex, Slavery, and Freedom in Early Virginia, *reprinted in The Devil's Lane: Sex and Race in the Early South* 65 (Catherine Clinton & Michele Gillespie, eds. 1997); Jason A. Gillmer, *Suing for Freedom: Interracial Sex, Slave Law, and Racial Identity in the Post–Revolutionary and Antebellum South*, 82 N.C. L. Rev. 535, 601 (2004).

[37] *Hudgins*, 11 Va. (1 Hen. & M.) at 134.

Court of Chancery. The Wrights offered proof that their genealogy could be traced back to Butterwood Nan, an American Indian woman. Additionally, they drew on the testimony of various witnesses, one of whom swore that he had seen Butterwood Nan and that she was "an old Indian," and another of whom described Butterwood Nan's daughter, Hannah, as a woman with long, black hair and "the right *Indian* copper colour."[38] A third witness, Robert Temple—in fact, a witness of Hudgins'—testified that Butterwood Nan's father was known to be an Indian; Temple was silent, however, about her mother.[39] The witnesses also explained the basis for their inferences, all declaring that they often had seen American Indians.[40]

At the trial's end, Chancellor Wythe denied Hudgins' claim and declared each of the three women to be free on two grounds: (1) The women did not look black, but instead had the appearance of a person of white and American Indian ancestry; and (2) Slavery violated Virginia's Declaration of Rights and thus was illegal in the state.[41] Because of his opposition to slavery, Chancellor Wythe found "that whenever one person claims to hold another in slavery, the *onus probandi* lies on the claimant."[42] This presumption against bondage placed the burden of proof squarely on Hudgins, regardless of the Wrights' appearance, and the ambiguities surrounding their identity made it impossible for him to prevail.

The Arguments on Appeal: Debating the Basis for Determining Racial Identity

On appeal, the parties once more staked out their positions on the three women's racial identity. Hudgins, through his attorney Edmund Randolph,[43] made two different arguments. First, Randolph contended that the women had not sufficiently proven their genealogy to warrant a presumption that they were free. Randolph insisted that Chancellor Wythe had been improperly influenced by the plaintiffs' white appearance because "the whole of the testimony proved [the three women] to

---

[38] *Id.*

[39] *Id.* at 134, 142 (noting with suspicion that the appellant witness's "memory seem[ed] only to serve him so far as the interest of the appellant required").

[40] *Id.* at 133–34 ("[A]ll those witnesses deposed [stated] that they had often seen *Indians*.")

[41] *See* Finkelman, *supra* note 23, at 1020 (citing *Hudgins*, 11 Va. (1 Hen. & M.) at 141). Interestingly, Chancellor Wythe had previously freed his own slaves. *See* Paul Finkelman, *The Dragon St. George Could Not Slay: Tucker's Plan to End Slavery*, 47 Wm. & Mary L. Rev. 1213, 1218 (2006).

[42] *Hudgins*, 11 Va. (1 Hen. & M.) at 134.

[43] John J. Reardon, *Edmund Randolph: A Biography* 353 (1975).

have been descended from a slave." Their physical appearance was not an appropriate basis for decision, for "[w]hether they are *white* or not, cannot appear to this Court *from the record*."[44] Alternatively, Randolph argued that even if the women were found to have descended from an American Indian woman, the women still should be identified as slaves since such "female ancestor was brought into this country between the years 1679 and 1705, and under the laws then in force, might have been a slave."[45] Rejecting 1691 as the year when Virginia first prohibited the enslavement of American Indians, Randolph maintained that no such rule was in effect until 1705. He argued that "[i]n all the cases decided by this Court on the present question, the act of 1705 has been considered as restricting the right of making slaves of *Indians:* and those cases are authority with me."[46]

In response, the three women again declared their freedom as originating from a native American Indian in the maternal line. Suing *in forma pauperis*,[47] the women, through attorney George K. Taylor, stressed the most commonly used proxies for race—skin color and outward appearance—to establish their claim to freedom.[48] Importantly, Taylor asked, "What more than strong characteristic features would be required, to prove a person *white*?"[49] Then, turning to the evidence, Taylor highlighted those parts that, he said, "clearly proved the appellees to have descended from *Indian stock*."[50] He focused particularly on the testimony regarding the appearance of Butterwood Nan's daughter, Hannah. After noting that American Indians were legally free persons in Virginia, except between 1679 and 1691—or at the latest 1705—Taylor offered proof that the women descended from Indians brought into Virginia after 1705, making it "incumbent on the appellant to prove that they [were] slaves; the appellees [were] not bound to prove the contrary."[51]

In his final reply, Randolph shot back at Taylor for again invoking what he saw as an inappropriate reliance on outward appearance, proclaiming that "[t]he circumstance of the appellees' being *white*, has

---

[44] *Hudgins*, 11 Va. (1 Hen. & M.) at 134–35.

[45] *Id.* at 135.

[46] *Id.*

[47] *Id.* at 134.

[48] *Id.* at 135 (declaring to the court, "This is not a common case of mere *blacks* suing for their freedom; but of persons perfectly *white*.").

[49] *Id.*

[50] *Id.*

[51] *Id.*

been mentioned, more to excite the feelings of the Court as *men*, than to address them as *Judges*."[52] Randolph then went on to argue that the burden of proof in the case lay with the women because the "original *Indian* stock from which [they] descended, was derived from the *paternal* line."[53] Consequently, he maintained, the three women, and not Hudgins, had the burden of proving that they descended from a free American Indian woman. According to Randolph, Chancellor Wythe incorrectly placed the burden on Hudgins because "the maternal line must be established before the *onus probandi* is thrown on the other side."[54]

The Author of the Hudgins Opinion: A Study in Contradictions

The author of the Virginia high court's decision in *Hudgins* was none other than Judge St. George Tucker, who, in 1796, had publicly proposed an end to slavery in the state of Virginia.[55] Tucker, a former law professor at William and Mary, had argued in his dissertation for the eventual abolition of slavery in Virginia, noting that human bondage is "perfectly irreconcilable.... to the principles of a democracy, which form the foundation of our government."[56] Specifically, Tucker advocated a gradual process of abolition over 105 years.[57] Rather than an immediate end to slavery, Tucker pushed for this slower approach because of his concerns about unavoidable economic losses to slavemasters, the potential for damage to Virginia's economy,[58] and the risk of allowing freed blacks to become "a numerous, starving, and enraged banditti, upon the innocent descendants of their former oppressors."[59]

Having learned about the progressive abolition of slavery from revered and educated men in the North—such as Zephaniah Swift, a

---

[52] *Id.* at 136.

[53] *Id.*

[54] *Id.*

[55] *See* Finkelman, *supra* note 23, at 1020 (citing St. George Tucker, *A Dissertation on Slavery: With a Proposal for the Gradual Abolition of It, in the State of Virginia* (1796)).

[56] *See* Katz, *supra* note 22, at 928 & n.4 (quoting St. George Tucker, *A Dissertation on Slavery: With a Proposal for the Gradual Abolition of It, in the State of Virginia* 48 (reprinted 1861) (1796)).

[57] Finkelman, *supra* note 41, at 1229, 1235 (citing St. George Tucker, *A Dissertation on Slavery: With a Proposal for the Gradual Abolition of It, in the State of Virginia* 101 n.22 (Negro Univ. Press 1970) (1796)) (but noting that, contrary to Tucker's estimates, the process would actually take more than 120 years).

[58] Finkelman, *supra* note 41, at 1229 ("Without labor, the land of the Virginia elite would be worthless and useless.").

[59] *Id.* at 1229, 1235 (quoting Tucker, *supra* note 57, at 88).

Federalist congressman and opponent of slavery[60]—Tucker proposed the emancipation of slaves in stages. The first stage would occur through the freedom of all female children of current female slaves; these children, as a means of compensating slaveowners, would then be required to serve as indentured servants until age twenty-eight.[61] After this period of servitude, the women would receive "twenty dollars in money, two suits of clothes, suited to the season, a hat, a pair of shoes, and two blankets."[62] The male children of current female slaves, on the other hand, would become slaves for life.[63] Eventually, however, both the male and the female children of the female descendant would be born free, subject thereafter to twenty years of indentured servitude.[64]

Although Tucker wanted slavery to end gradually in Virginia, he also wanted all free blacks to leave his beloved state immediately. Were freed blacks to remain in Virginia, Tucker believed, they would become " 'idle, profligate, and miserable,' " and would potentially " 'become hordes of vagabonds, robbers, and murderers.' "[65] He recommended severe restrictions on emancipated blacks to push them out of Virginia (and ultimately America).[66] Tucker proposed curtailing their rights, including many political rights—such as voting, holding office, serving in the army, owning weapons, serving on a jury, and being a witness in court.[67] More importantly, Tucker proposed that free blacks be excluded from an important means of livelihood in Virginia—the purchase and transfer of land:

> Let no Negroe [sic] or mulattoe [sic] be capable of taking, holding, or exercising, any ... freehold, franchise or privilege, or any estate in lands or tenements, other than a lease not exceeding twenty-one years.... Nor be an executor or administrator; nor capable of making any will or testament; nor maintain any real action; nor be a

---

[60] *Id.* at 1223–24.

[61] *Id.* at 1229, 1235 (citing Tucker, *supra* note 57, at 89).

[62] *See* Katz, *supra* note 22, at 928 n.6 (quoting Tucker, *supra* note 56, at 48).

[63] Finkelman, *supra* note 41, at 1229, 1235 (citing Tucker, *supra* note 57, at 89).

[64] Katz, *supra* note 22, at 928 n.6 (quoting Tucker, *supra* note 56, at 48).

[65] Finkelman, *supra* note 41, at 1233 (quoting Tucker, *supra* note 57, at 77, 84).

[66] *See* Katz, *supra* note 22, at 928–29 nn.5, 7–8; *see also* Phillip Hamilton, *Revolutionary Principles and Family Loyalties: Slavery's Transformation in the St. George Tucker Household of Early National Virginia*, 55 Wm. & Mary Q. 531, 536 (1998).

[67] Finkelman, *supra* note 41, at 1238 (quoting Tucker, *supra* note 57, at 88, 101 n.22); Hamilton, *supra* note 66, at 536 ("Tucker confessed that he chose to 'accommodate' racism in order to 'avoid as many obstacles as possible to the completion of so desirable a work, as the abolition of slavery.' ").

trustee of lands or tenements himself, nor any other person to be a trustee to him or to his use.[68]

These conflicting principles about slavery and the rights of blacks would shape Judge Tucker's approach to *Hudgins*. He had, after all, authored his dissertation on the gradual abolition of slavery only ten years earlier.

The Decision: Multiracialism and the Contingencies of Identity

Writing for the Supreme Court of Appeals of Virginia in *Hudgins*, Judge Tucker affirmed the trial court's decision to identify the Wrights as free women on the basis of their ancestral heritage—as women descended from native American Indians on their maternal side. Before declaring the court's ultimate conclusion, Judge Tucker established that 1691, not 1705, was the date after which American Indians could no longer be brought into slavery in the state of Virginia:

> By the adjudication of the General Court, in the case of *Hannah and others* against *Davis*, April term, 1777, all American Indians brought into this country since the year 1705, and their descendants in the maternal line, are *free*. Similar judgments have been rendered in this court. But I carry the period further back, ... to the 16th day of *April*, 1691, the commencement of a session of the General Assembly at which an act passed, entitled "*An Act for a free trade with Indians*," ... the enacting clause of which, I have reason to believe, is in the very words of the act of 1705, upon which this Court have pronounced judgment in the cases referred to.[69]

From this interpretation of Virginia's statutes, Judge Tucker declared that American Indians were prima facie presumed to be free. So long as there was evidence to show maternal American Indian ancestry, the claiming slaveholder had to show that this ancestor was brought to Virginia after 1679 (the point at which the enslavement of American Indians had become legal in the state) and before 1691 (the point at which an act made all American Indians arriving thereafter free).[70]

Unlike Chancellor Wythe, Judge Tucker allocated the burden of proof depending on the physical appearance of the parties. Where white persons or American Indians, or their descendants in the maternal line—meaning those who physically appeared to belong to one of those groups—were alleged to be slaves, the burden as to their status rested with the party who claimed ownership.[71] On the other hand, if the

---

[68] *See* Katz, *supra* note 22, at 928 n.8 (quoting Tucker, *supra* note 56, at 91–92) (alterations in original).

[69] Hudgins v. Wrights, 11 Va. (1 Hen. & M.) 134, 137–38 (Va. 1806) (footnote omitted).

[70] *Id.* at 138–39.

[71] *Id.* at 139 ("If one *evidently white*, be notwithstanding claimed as a slave, the proof lies on the party claiming to make the other his slave." (emphasis added)); *see also* Mark V.

plaintiffs were black (or physically appeared to be black), the burden of proof rested with the individuals who sought their freedom. As stated by Judge Spencer Roane in a separate concurrence:

> *In the case of a person visibly appearing to be a negro*, the presumption is, in this country, that he is a slave, and it is incumbent on him to make out his right to freedom: but in the case of a person visibly appearing to be a white man, or an *Indian,* the presumption is that he is free, and it is necessary for his adversary to shew [sic] that he is a slave.[72]

In *Hudgins*, because of the white-looking appearance of the granddaughter, and the gradual shades of difference in color of the mother and the grandmother,[73] the court declared that the women, as American Indians, were presumptively free.[74] The burden then fell on Hudgins, the purported owner, to prove that the three women were in fact descended from either a black female slave or from an American Indian female slave who had been brought into Virginia between the years of 1679 and 1691.

In reviewing the trial court's decision, Judge Tucker held that there was sufficient evidence to substantiate the trial court's determination that the family of women descended from an American Indian through the maternal line. That evidence included testimony from Mary Wilkinson and Robert Temple that revealed that "the plaintiffs [were] in the maternal line descended from *Butterwood Nan*, an old *Indian* woman" who was approximately sixty years old in 1755; testimony from Robert Temple that Butterwood Nan's father was an American Indian; and testimony from several witnesses that Hannah, the daughter of Butterwood Nan, "had long black hair . . . and [was] generally called an *Indian* among the neighbours. . . ."[75]

Judge Tucker also relied, however, on his observations of the laws as connected "with the natural history of the human species."[76] One view of this history included the reputation of the women among their neigh-

---

Tushnet, *The American Law of Slavery 1810–1860,* at 157 (1981) (discussing the differing burdens of proof based on physical appearance); George, *supra* note 20, at 677–78 (same).

[72] *Hudgins*, 11 Va. (1 Hen. & M.) at 141 (Roane, J., concurring) (first emphasis added).

[73] *Id.* at 134.

[74] *Id.* at 139 (majority opinion) ("[A]ll *American Indians* are prima facie FREE: and . . . where the fact of their nativity and descent, in a *maternal* line, is satisfactorily established, the burthen of proof thereafter lies upon the party claiming to hold them as slaves. To effect which, according to my opinion, he must prove the progenitrix of the party claiming to be free, to have been brought into *Virginia*, and made a slave between the passage of the act of 1679, and its repeal in 1691.").

[75] *Id.* at 137.

[76] *Id.* at 139.

bors, all of whom testified that the women's maternal ancestors were American Indians.[77] Thus, in many ways, the question in *Hudgins* was, did the white community regard and accept these women as American Indian rather than black?[78] The witnesses repeatedly gave a positive response to this question. Judge Tucker further elaborated on his understanding of natural history, which allowed a judge the ability and the right to decide if a challenged individual was white, American Indian, or black "from his own view."[79] After all, the physical features of blacks and American Indians were so distinct that they could not be confused with one another any more easily than "the glossy, jetty cloathing [sic] of an *American* bear [could be confused with] the wool of black sheep...."[80] Specifically, Judge Tucker noted that persons of African descent had been stamped with three distinct characteristics that would not and could not readily disappear: dark skin, a flat nose, and woolly hair—the strongest "ingredient in the African constitution"—which

> predominates uniformly where the party is in equal degree descended from parents of different complexions, whether white or *Indians*; giving to the jet black lank hair of the *Indian* a degree of flexure, which never fails to betray that the party distinguished by it, cannot trace his lineage purely from the race of native *Americans*.[81]

---

[77] *Id.* at 142 (Roane, J., concurring) ("This general reputation and opinion of the neighbourhood is certainly entitled to *some* credit: it goes to repel the idea that the given female ancestor of *Hannah* was a *lawful* slave; it goes to confirm the other strong testimony as to *Hannah's* appearance as an *Indian*. It is not to be believed but that *some* of the neighbours would have sworn to that concerning which they *all* agreed in opinion....").

[78] *See* Ariela J. Gross, *Litigating Whiteness: Trials of Racial Determination in the Nineteenth Century South*, 108 Yale L.J. 109, 118–21 (1998) (detailing how determinations of race by juries during the nineteenth century often turned on witness testimony regarding hair color, hair texture, facial features, and social performances); *see also* Daniel J. Sharfstein, Essay, *The Secret History of Race in the United States*, 112 Yale L.J. 1473, 1479–80 (2003) (discussing how "scholars have shown how scientific notions of race such as genealogy or physical appearance have never been the courts' sole or even preferred type of evidence for determining race").

[79] Hudgins, 11 Va. (1 Hen. & M.) at 140 (majority opinion). Although disagreeing with the Judge on other points, Judge Spencer Roane agreed with Judge Tucker that "[t]he distinguishing characteristics of the different species of the human race are so visibly marked, *that those species may be readily discriminated from each other by mere inspection only.*" *Id.* at 141 (Roane, J., concurring) (emphasis added). Professor Adrienne Davis has termed "this physical component scopic in that it relies on the inspecting and scrutinizing gaze of a (white) individual in order to discern and assign racial identity." Adrienne D. Davis, Essay, *Identity Notes Part One: Playing in the Light*, 45 Am. U. L. Rev. 695, 705 (1996).

[80] *Hudgins*, 11 Va. (1 Hen. & M.) at 140.

[81] *Id.* at 139.

All of these observations of law commingled with natural history eventually led Judge Tucker and his colleagues to reach the conclusion that Hannah could not possibly have had long, black hair, been of copper complexion, or been reputed to be an American Indian in her community unless "her mother had ... an equal, or perhaps a larger portion of *Indian* blood in her veins."[82] Thus, Hannah was presumptively free.

In a separate concurrence, Judge Roane made clear that he did not agree that descent from the maternal or paternal line could be determined from a judge's view. However, he did agree that Hudgins had failed to meet his burden of proof by failing to show that the three women descended from either a black female slave or a rightfully held American Indian female slave.[83] Like Judge Tucker, Judge Roane was especially persuaded by the evidence regarding the appearance of Hannah. He found that "[n]o testimony can be more complete and conclusive than that which exists in this cause to shew [sic] that *Hannah* had every appearance of an *Indian*."[84] Judge Roane argued that if *"Hannah's* grandmother ... were a *negro*, it [would have been] impossible that *Hannah* should have had that entire appearance of an Indian which is proved by the witnesses."[85] In essence, as Professor Ian Haney López has indicated, "[a]fter unknown lives lost in slavery, Judge Tucker freed three generations of women because Hannah's hair was long and straight."[86]

Notably, however, Judge Tucker—who, despite owning slaves,[87] taught his law students that slavery was a moral wrong—failed to give any weight to his own intellectual and political views on slavery[88] in the

---

[82] *Id.* at 137; *see also id.* at 143 (Roane, J., concurring) (stating that "[t]he mother and grandmother of *Hannah* must therefore be taken to have been *Indians*").

[83] *Id.* at 141–42.

[84] *Id.* at 142. Judge Roane also seemed to be influenced by the appearance of the three women themselves, noting in his opinion: "In the present case it is not and cannot be denied that the appellees have entirely the *appearance* of white people...." *Id.* at 141.

[85] *Id.* at 142.

[86] Ian F. Haney López, *The Social Construction of Race: Some Observations on Illusion, Fabrication, and Choice*, 29 Harv. C.R.-C.L. L. Rev. 1, 2 (1994).

[87] Finkelman, *supra* note 41, at 1216–18 (describing Tucker as a man conflicted about slavery and noting that Tucker owned more than 100 slaves and negotiated the purchase and sale of human beings as part of his work as an attorney); Hamilton, *supra* note 66, at 531 ("St. George Tucker ... faced conflicting loyalties: he wished to eliminate slavery to fulfill the Revolution's ideological promise, but he also wanted to safeguard his family's property to preserve its wealth, power, and prestige.").

[88] Finkelman, *supra* note 41, at 1222–23. Tucker declared in his dissertation: "Slavery not only violates the Laws of Nature, and of civil Society, it also wounds the best Forms of

Hudgins opinion. He rejected his former teacher Chancellor Wythe's decision at the trial level to grant the Wrights freedom on the grounds that slavery was illegal in Virginia. Judge Tucker asserted that Virginia's Declaration of Rights did not outlaw slavery because it did not apply to those who were not free. He declared:

> I do not concur with the Chancellor in his reasoning on the opera-
> tion of the first clause of the Bill of Rights, which was notoriously
> framed with a cautious eye to this subject, and was meant to
> embrace the case of free citizens, or aliens only; and not by a side
> wind to overturn the rights of property, and give freedom to those
> very people whom we have been compelled from imperious circum-
> stances to retain, generally, in the same state of bondage that they
> were in at the revolution, in which they had no *concern, agency* or
> *interest*.[89]

After the *Hudgins* decision, a panel of judges delivered a decree of the Supreme Court of Appeals of Virginia, ordering the permanent status of blacks as slaves.[90] Thus, although the three women would be free, the enslavement of blacks would endure for more than half a century longer—until the issuance of the Emancipation Proclamation in 1863.[91] In the end, at the same time that "*Hudgins* may have secured freedom for Virginia's tiny and dwindling population of Indians, ... it simultaneously tightened the chains of bondage on the Commonwealth's huge black population."[92] Indeed, in 1812, Judge Tucker further tight-ened the chains by preventing his stepson, Charles Carter, from taking action to emancipate his own slaves.[93]

Government: in a Democracy, where all Men are equal, Slavery is contrary to the Spirit of the Constitution." *Id.* at 1222 (quoting Tucker, *supra* note 57, at 1).

[89] *Hudgins*, 11 Va. (1 Hen. & M.) at 141.

[90] *Id.* at 144 (Lyons, P.J., concurring) ("This Court, not approving of the Chancellor's principles and reasoning in his decree made in this cause, except so far as the same relates to white persons and native *American Indians,* but entirely disapproving thereof, so far as the same relates to native *Africans* and their descendants, who have been and are now held as slaves by the citizens of this state, and discovering no other error in the said decree, affirms the same.").

[91] The Proclamation did not translate into true freedom for many slaves until long after the Civil War's end when the federal government forced plantation owners to acknowledge the freedom of blacks. *See* Litwack, *supra* note 16, at 173, 181–83.

[92] Finkelman, *supra* note 41, at 1214. By 1756, fifty years before the *Hudgins* decision, 120,156 of 173,316 Virginia residents were black. *See* Hast, *supra* note 5, at 218.

[93] Finkelman, *supra* note 41, at 1242.

Larger Lessons about the Challenges of Multiracialism

The primary lesson of *Hudgins v. Wrights* is one often repeated by scholars: Race is not biologically defined but is instead socially construct-ed.[94] As Professor Ian Haney López has highlighted, "[t]here are no genetic characteristics possessed by all Blacks but not by non-Blacks; similarly, there is no gene or cluster of genes common to all Whites but not to non-Whites."[95] Likewise, Professor Adrienne Davis has described ways in which space and place may alter a person's identity in the view of the surrounding community members, detailing how she is perceived as black in some places, but non-black in others.[96]

Years earlier, William D. Zabel unknowingly demonstrated the social construction theory of race in his paper *Interracial Marriage and the Law*, in which he discussed states' varying standards for determining which multiracial individuals were black for purposes of enforcing antimiscegenation statutes. Zabel clarified that, in the face of a growing mixed-race population, determinations of individuals' blackness varied from state to state, not based purely on scientific distinctions, but rather on local customs of acceptable racial mixtures. He asked:

> Who is a Negro under [these] laws? There is no uniform definition, so it is difficult to know. The different definitions create racial chameleons. One can be Negro in Georgia because he had a one-half Negro great-grandmother, and by crossing the border into Florida, become a white because Florida makes him a Negro only if he had a full Negro great-grandmother. The most common definition uses an unscientific percentage-of-blood test usually classifying a Negro as "any person of one-eighth or more Negro blood." If a blood test is to be used and one-eighth Negro blood, whatever that means, makes you Negro, why does not one-eighth of white blood make you white?[97]

---

[94] *See* Davis, *supra* note 79, at 696–719 (specifically exploring the construction of whiteness); Angela P. Harris, *Foreword: The Jurisprudence of Reconstruction*, 82 Cal. L. Rev. 741, 774 (1994) (" '[R]ace' is neither a natural fact simply there in 'reality,' nor a wrong idea, eradicable by an act of will."); Michael Omi & Howard Winant, *Racial Formation in the United States: From the 1960s to the 1990s*, at 55–60 (2d ed. 1994) (analyzing race as an evolving set of social meanings that are formed and transformed under a constantly shifting society); Angela Onwuachi–Willig, *Undercover Other*, 94 Cal. L. Rev. 874, 883–84 (2006) (noting that "[s]ociety imposes identities on people").

[95] Haney López, *supra* note 86, at 11.

[96] *See* Davis, *supra* note 79, at 697–701.

[97] William D. Zabel, *Interracial Marriage and the Law*, in *Interracialism: Black White Intermarriage in American History, Literature, and Law*, at 54, 57 (Werner Sollors ed., 2000). Even white citizens during the eighteenth and nineteenth centuries, including slaveholders, understood the non-biological nature of race, as demonstrated by newspaper advertisements searching for runaway slaves. *See* Sharfstein, *supra* note 78, at 1476

As Zabel's account of multiracialism suggests, the Wrights, as women of mixed ancestry, challenged the very assumption that races are entirely separate as a biological matter. Through their court case, they delivered an important lesson about racial fluidity. After all, their race was not determined by any unique gene, known to exist only in American Indian women. Rather, it was influenced by commonly held social beliefs among the judges about how American Indian women looked and behaved. For the Wrights, their fate as either free American Indian women or legally-defined black slaves depended not just upon the fairness of their skin or the straightness of their hair but the exercise of their non-black identity and their recognition as non-black by neighboring whites.

Indeed, the performance of a non-black identity was critical to determinations of race during a period in which people resided in relatively small communities, from which courts could enlist testimony about the different parties' reputations and ancestries. Although urbanization, industrialization, and immigration complicated this means of classifying persons according to race, conduct remained important to these racial trials for centuries. For example, Professor Ariela Gross has extensively detailed how the performance of whiteness—the way in which a person exercised the privileges of white citizenship and was accepted by other whites in the community—"positively" affected a court's determination of his or her status as white or black during nineteenth-century trials.[98] In her account, Gross demonstrated that a person's behavior and reputation figured almost as much as appearance in decisions about racial status in these trials.

Concerns about racial ambiguity and the dilemmas of classification in a segregated society persisted into the twentieth century. During this period, racial passing was becoming more prevalent, and racial classifica-

---

(noting that whites in the post-Reconstruction South "had a basic awareness that racial identity was something that could be disputed and creatively argued, at least in the courtroom"). For example, on January 6, 1836, slaveowner Anderson Bowles published an advertisement in the *Richmond Whig* searching for a slave who had run away, describing the young man as a "negro" with "straight hair," who was "nearly white" such that "a stranger" would suppose there was "no African blood in him." William Goodell, *Slavery and Anti-Slavery: A History of the Great Struggle in Both Hemispheres* 265 (1852). Similarly, on April 22, 1837, in his advertisement in the *Newbern Spectator*, Edwin Peck offered 100 dollars for the return of a slave named Sam, described as having "light sandy hair, blue eyes, [a] ruddy complexion," and being "so white as very easily to pass for a white man." *Id.*

[98] Gross, *supra* note 78, at 156–57; *see also* Sharfstein, *supra* note 78, at 1479–80 ("In part, the color line was established, in the words of the South Carolina Supreme Court, by 'evidence of reputation as to parentage; and such evidence as was offered in the present case, of the person's having been received in society, and exercised the privileges of a white man.'" (quoting State v. Davis, 18 S.C. L. (2 Bail.) 558, 560 (1832))).

tions were becoming increasingly contingent upon and subject to individual manipulation. This fact concerned many white citizens, who feared racial fraud by intruding blacks.[99] Nevertheless, white citizens, on some level, were willing to acknowledge the lack of precision in biological determinations of race and maintained flexibility on standards of challenged whiteness because of one major driving force: the fear that they, or any other persons with the physical appearance of whiteness, could also fall prey to a determination of non-whiteness.[100] A quote from a railway conductor in the 1920s clearly reveals the ways in which many white Americans understood the fluidity of the color line. When the railway conductor was asked whether he had "any difficulty about classifying people who are very near the [color] line," he responded, "I give the passenger the benefit of the doubt."[101]

At the same time, however, underlying the legal determination of the Wrights as American Indian, instead of black, was an enduring belief in biological race. For many white Virginians, including Judge Tucker, there were "ingredients in the African constitution"[102] that could not readily disappear. These genetic ingredients made Judge Tucker confident that whites could ascertain race by physical appearance.

The fact is that, although whites understood the way in which multiracialism made phenotype ambiguous and subverted the reliability of community reputation, they deeply desired the determinism of biological race.[103] The 1896 decision of the U.S. Supreme Court in *Plessy v. Ferguson*[104] is a good example of the undying faith by whites in genetic-based racial distinctions. There, the Court upheld a Louisiana statute requiring separate railway cars for whites and blacks in the face of

---

[99] Moran, *supra* note 17, at 44–45 (detailing how some "light-skinned mulattoes" "[c]apitaliz[ed] on the influx of immigrants from southern Europe" to "pass themselves off as dark-skinned ethnics from the Mediterranean"); *see also* Kennedy, *supra* note 17, at 298 ("The most thoroughgoing effort in American history to prevent and punish passing began in Virginia in the 1920s. . . .").

[100] *See* Davis, *supra* note 79, at 706–07 (noting that one judge's main focus in *Hudgins* seemed "to be the safeguarding of whites from accidentally falling into the perils of slavery").

[101] Sharfstein, *supra* note 78, at 1500 (quoting Charles W. Chesnutt, *Remarks of Charles Waddell Chesnutt, of Cleveland, in Accepting the Spingarn Medal at Los Angeles* (July 3, 1928), *in Charles W. Chesnutt: Essays and Speeches* 510, 514 (Joseph R. McElrath, Jr. et al. eds., 1999)).

[102] *See supra* notes 79–81 and accompanying text.

[103] Haney López, *supra* note 86, at 6 (defining biological race as the view "that there exist natural, physical divisions among humans that are hereditary, reflected in morphology, and roughly but correctly captured by terns like Black, White, and Asian (or Negroid, Caucasoid, and Mongoloid)").

[104] 163 U.S. 537 (1896).

Homer Plessy's challenge to his categorization as black. Plessy was seven-eighths white and one–eighth black, and in his case, "the mixture of colored blood was not discernible."[105] As a result, he alleged that his segregation on an all-black car was arbitrary and improper. The Supreme Court noted that determinations of racial status as black or white varied from state to state and that it could "become a question of importance whether, under the laws of Louisiana, [Plessy] belongs to the white or colored race." At the same time, the Court reinforced the notion of race as biological and fixed by declaring that "[l]egislation is powerless to eradicate racial instincts, or to abolish distinctions based upon physical differences...."[106]

During the early 1900s, this idea of race as biologically fixed would become further entrenched by numerous states' adoption of the one-drop rule,[107] which provided that any person with one drop of black blood is black.[108] Again, as Judge Tucker hinted in his opinion in *Hudgins*, the belief was, and still is, that whiteness is so pure and blackness is so degrading that "ingredients in the African constitution" would "never fail[] to betray ... the party distinguished by it."[109] Under the one-drop rule, no amount of whiteness, no matter how great, could save an individual of black ancestry from what was viewed as the pollution of blackness, no matter how small.[110] Noted African–American author Lang-

---

[105] *Id.* at 541.

[106] *Id.* at 551–52.

[107] For example, the Census Bureau adopted the rule in 1920, stating:

> The term "white" as used in the census report refers to persons understood to be pure-blooded whites. A person of mixed blood is classified according to the nonwhite racial strain.... [t]hus a person of mixed white ... and Negro ... is classified as ... a Negro ... regardless of the amount of white blood.

Christine B. Hickman, *The Devil and the One Drop Rule: Racial Categories, African Americans, and the U.S. Census*, 95 Mich. L. Rev. 1161, 1187 (1997) (quoting 3 Bureau of the Census, U.S. Dep't of Commerce, Fourteenth Census of the United States: 1920, at 10 (1923)).

[108] Neil Gotanda, *A Critique of "Our Constitution Is Color-Blind,"* 44 Stan. L. Rev. 1, 26 (1991) ("The metaphor is one of purity and contamination: White is unblemished and pure, so one drop of ancestral Black blood renders one Black. Black ancestry is a contaminant that overwhelms white ancestry.")

[109] *See supra* note 79–81 and accompanying text.

[110] *See* Nadine Ehlers, *Hidden in Plain Sight: Defying Juridical Racialization in Rhinelander v. Rhinelander*, 4 Comm. & Critical/Cultural Stud. 313, 316 (2004) (explaining that " 'mixing' was imagined as that which polluted 'pure whiteness' because it introduced foreign non-white 'blood,' a fluid of 'racial essence' that was represented as a pathogen that both contaminated and degenerated the 'integrity of whiteness' "); Robert Westley, *First Time Encounters: "Passing" Revisited and Demystification as a Critical Practice*, 18 Yale

ston Hughes once proclaimed, "[H]ere in the United States, the word 'Negro' is used to mean anyone who has any Negro blood at all in his veins."[111]

In the end, whites still held fast to the idea of race as highly visible and easily recognizable, especially for blacks. This belief persisted despite a seemingly contradictory acceptance of race as defined by factors other than skin color, including conduct. No case demonstrates this point more strongly than *Rhinelander v. Rhinelander*,[112] a 1920s New York lawsuit in which Leonard Kip Rhinelander, a wealthy white socialite, filed for the annulment of his marriage to Alice Beatrice Jones, a woman of racially ambiguous heritage, on the ground that Alice had misrepresented her race. According to Leonard, Alice committed fraud by failing to inform him that she possessed colored blood.[113] To everyone's surprise, Alice chose not to litigate her whiteness, but instead admitted that she was of colored descent and argued that Leonard was aware of her race before the marriage. In support of her claim, she said that Leonard knew of her colored background because he had seen her naked body during premarital sexual relations. Playing upon the notion of race as easily recognizable, Alice's attorney offered as evidence Alice's bare skin.[114] Presumably, he agreed with Judge Roane in *Hudgins* that "[t]he distinguishing characteristics of the different species of the human race are so visibly marked, *that those species may be readily discriminated from each other by mere inspection only.*"[115]

L. & Pol'y Rev. 297, 311 (2000) ("Being white was a matter of blood, just as being Black was the pollution of blood.").

[111] Langston Hughes, *The Big Sea: An Autobiography* 11 (1940).

[112] The Association of the Bar of the City of New York, New York Supreme Court: Appellate Division—Second Department, Leonard Kip Rhinelander *against* Alice Jones Rhinelander, Case on Appeal, at 889 (Nov. 26, 1924–Dec. 5, 1925); Rhinelander v. Rhinelander, 157 N.E. 838 (N.Y. Ct. App. 1927); Rhinelander v. Rhinelander, 219 N.Y.S. 548 (S. Ct. App. Div. 1927); *see also* Angela Onwuachi–Willig, *A Beautiful Lie: Exploring* Rhinelander v. Rhinelander *as a Formative Lesson on Race, Marriage, Identity, and Family*, 95 Cal. L. Rev. 2393 (2007).

[113] *See* Jamie L. Wacks, *Reading Race, Rhetoric, and the Female Body in the* Rhinelander *Case, in Interracialism: Black White Intermarriage in American History, Literature, and Law* 162, 163 (Werner Sollors ed. 2000).

[114] *See* Earl Lewis & Heidi Ardizzone, *Love on Trial: An American Scandal in Black and White* 159–60 (2001) ("Alice's lawyers resorted to the comforting belief that race was easy to determine and differentiate. Alice, they repeated, was clearly black, for anyone with reasonable intelligence to see."); Wacks, *supra* note 113, at 164 ("Later that same day, over the objection of Leonard's attorney, Alice's attorney requested that Alice take her clothes off to allow the all-white, all-male, all-married jury and Leonard to inspect her skin color.").

[115] Hudgins v. Wrights, 11 Va. (1 Hen. & M.) 134, 141 (Va. 1806) (Roane, J., concurring) (emphasis added).

Ultimately, the jury returned a verdict for Alice, denying Leonard's request for an annulment. No doubt each juror wanted to believe, as Judge Tucker did in *Hudgins*, that he could tell the race of a person "from his own view."[116] This belief was comforting because it reinforced a racial hierarchy and hence whites' ability to preserve their favored position. Otherwise, as author Jamie Wacks notes, "The notion that a lower-class woman like Alice Jones ... could trespass into the world of a wealthy white man like Leonard Rhinelander questioned the boundaries between white and black ... [and] suggested the vulnerability of alleged white dominance."[117] Although many whites realized that race was not genetically decipherable, they also gravitated to a notion of fixed biological difference—they desired to believe that they would know race "when they saw it."

Today, the widespread societal belief in pure biological classifications of race persists, even as the multiracial population in this country continues to grow. Despite changes in the 2000 Census that allow individuals to mark more than one racial category in identifying themselves, many multiracial individuals are still not entirely "free to forge a unique identity, regardless of what strangers expect or how other family members define[] themselves."[118] As Professor Rachel Moran has indicated, "Even when individuals with mixed black and white ancestry try to disregard racial boundaries, the overwhelming reality of segregation reinstates them."[119] This reality remains especially true for blacks, who continue to be segregated by neighborhood and marriage in ways that other racial and ethnic groups are not.[120]

In sum, despite a plethora of literature on the social construction of race, a longing for biological race lingers. In fact, business is booming for companies, like DNA Print Genomics, that claim to be able to determine a person's ancestral heritage. Throughout the country, increasing numbers of college applicants are trying to uncover their ethnic ancestries through genetic testing in order to assert a minority identity and gain an "advantage" in the college admissions game.[121] Indeed, many teenagers

---

[116] *See supra* note 79 and accompanying text.

[117] *See* Wacks, *supra* note 113, at 166.

[118] Moran, *supra* note 17, at 160.

[119] Moran, *supra* note 17, at 175.

[120] *See* Rachel F. Moran, *The Mixed Promise of Multiculturalism*, 17 Harv. BlackLetter L.J. 47, 47–55 (2001).

[121] *See* Amy Harmon, *Seeking Ancestry, and Privilege, in DNA Ties Uncovered by Tests*, N.Y. Times, Apr. 12, 2006, at A1 (noting that "[p]rospective employees with white skin are using the tests to apply as minority candidates"); *see also* Angela Onwuachi–Willig, *The*

who grew up with a socially and phenotypically white identity are being tested so that they can claim a "biological race" on application forms that does not match their personal experience.[122] After exercising all the privileges of white citizens,[123] these students are staking a claim not to their genetic race, but to the preferential treatment that they view as coming with that genetics (without the social disadvantages).

For example, Matt and Andrew Moldawer, twins who knew that both of their birth parents were "white" and grew up in an adoptive white family, engaged in genetic testing, through which they learned that they were 9% Native American and 11% North African. They then used that information to garner a better financial aid package for college.[124] Likewise, the sister of Ashley Klett, whom DNA tests showed to be 2% East Asian and 98% European, checked the "Asian" box on her college application, an act she believes helped her earn a scholarship.[125]

This newly popular view of genetic race has done far more than simply satisfy personal curiosity or conveniently alter college applications and scholarships. As Professor Lisa Ikemoto has highlighted, "race is back on the biomedical research agenda ... [,] emerging as a legitimized explanation for medical and social issues."[126] For scholars like Ikemoto and Dorothy Roberts, a law professor who specializes in reproductive rights, this fascination with genetic race raises fears of a return to eugenics, which was used in the past to support laws—such as compulsory sterilization—that deeply discriminated against racial minorities.[127] In fact, both Ikemoto and Roberts decry the harm that could result from the ethnic-or race-based packaging of prescription drugs.[128]

Admission of Legacy Blacks, 60 Vand. L. Rev. 102, 182–85 (2007) (discussing the racial fraud of college applicants based on genetic testing).

[122] As Lester Monts, senior vice provost for student affairs at the University of Michigan, asserted, "If someone appears to be white and then finds out they are not, they haven't experienced the kinds of things that affirmative action is supposed to remedy." *Id.*

[123] In 1831, the South Carolina Supreme Court even described social experience as important evidence for determining racial identity. *See* Sharfstein, *supra* note 78, at 1479–80 (quoting State v. Davis, 18 S.C.L. (2 Bail.) 558, 560 (1832)).

[124] *Id.*

[125] *Id.*

[126] Lisa C. Ikemoto, *Race to Health: Racialized Discourses in a Transhuman World*, 9 DePaul J. Health Care L. 1101, 1101 (2005).

[127] *See id.* at 1102; Dorothy E. Roberts, *Legal Constraints on the Use of Race in Biomedical Research: Toward a Social Justice Framework*, 34 J.L. Med. & Ethics 526, 526–28 (2006).

[128] *See* Ikemoto, *supra* note 126, at 1124 ("Attempts to market products to particular racial groups—e.g. BiDil—may legitimize biological race."); Roberts, *supra* note 127, at

For example, BiDil has been advertised as treating heart failure specifically in African Americans.[129]

Similarly, critics have attacked the return to the notion of biological race in criminal law enforcement. Increasingly, DNA tests are being used, both in the United States and in the United Kingdom, to assist police in determining what a crime suspect looks like.[130] Despite repeated expressions of concern about how poorly DNA predicts physical appearance and about how such testing could lead to "genetic racial profiling, or promote the idea that certain races are more inclined than others to commit crimes," several law enforcement agencies are praising these new efforts, claiming that such testing has enabled them to solve violent crimes.[131] In fact, recently, the London police requested DNA samples from officers of Afro–Caribbean descent to compare them with evidence from nine unsolved rapes, declaring that such information put them " 'on the right track' in their investigation."[132]

Reliance on the idea of genetically based race has polluted various areas of the law, resulting in a kind of schizophrenic analysis of issues of discrimination. On the one hand, at least a minority of courts recognize (with undesirable consequences) the social construction of identity in their determinations of when to apply the Indian Child Welfare Act to a child removed from his home for adoption. The Act does not apply to a child whose American Indian parent has failed to develop any significant social, cultural, or political relationship with the Indian community.[133] This relationship can be established by showing that the parent has privately described herself as an Indian, observed tribal customs, voted in tribal elections, or maintained social contacts with other tribal members.[134] In applying the Act, courts at least acknowledge, despite their

---

528–29 (proposing "that the legal regulation of race in biomedical research should aim to promote social justice. . . . [which] holds that race is a socially constructed category without scientific basis that continues to produce health inequities, that these inequities require race-conscious legal remedies, and that biomedical research should be subject to legal regulation that promotes racial justice").

[129] See BiDil–Prescription Drug for African Americans with Heart Disease, http://www.bidil.com/.

[130] See Richard Willing, *DNA Tests Offer Clues to Suspect's Race*, USA Today, Aug. 16, 2005, *available at* http://www.usatoday.com/news/nation/2005–08–16–dna_x.htm.

[131] *Id.*

[132] *Id.*

[133] See Solangel Maldonado, *The Story of the* Holyfield *Twins:* Mississippi Band of Choctaw Indians v. Holyfield, *in Family Law Stories* (Carol Sanger ed., 2007).

[134] *In re* Santos Y., 112 Cal. Rptr. 2d 692 (Cal. Ct. App. 2001); *In re* Bridget R., 49 Cal. Rptr. 2d 507, 527 (Cal. Ct. App. 1996), *cert. denied*, Cindy R. v. James R., 519 U.S. 1060 (1997); *In re* Adoption of Crews, 825 P.2d 305 (Wash. 1992); *see also* Hampton v. J.A.L.,

questionable practice of determining native authenticity, the ways in
which performance—the exercising of community privileges and culture—can determine race in our racially polarized society. On the other
hand, as Professor Mario Barnes and I have noted, some courts simultaneously have rejected the social construction of race in Title VII employment discrimination cases. Judges have refused to recognize proxies for
race (such as names and accent) and have ignored the role of race and
racism in the prohibition of certain hair styles and clothing in workplace
grooming codes.[135] In these decisions, courts treat race as a biological fact
and overlook the ways in which it is defined through social practice.[136]

Conclusion

In the context of our post-slavery and post–civil rights world, the
case of *Hudgins v. Wrights* may seem like a distant memory of the past.
In truth, however, its lessons are growing each day. *Hudgins* provides an
excellent example of the way in which those in power have worked to
define and control race in order to maintain systems of racial oppression
and hierarchy. As we saw in *Hudgins*, the very burdens of proof for
different parties depended upon their racial appearance and thus stations in life, with those who looked black bearing the burden of proving
their freedom and those who looked white or American Indian possessing
a presumption of freedom.

Today, biological race is making a comeback. But, as *Hudgins*
demonstrates all too well, race is defined not by biology, but by proxies,
both physical and social—performance and authenticity. The law must
adapt to these understandings if we as a society are ever to achieve
complete equality. For example, although the census has formally recognized mixed-race identity, multiracial persons with a black appearance
have almost no practical claim to the non-black parts of their racial
identity. As Ward Connerly proclaimed about his own multiracial identity, people laugh "if he tries to identify himself as Irish based on the fact
that he is 37.5 percent Irish, 25 percent French, 25 percent black, and
12.5 percent Choctaw."[137] The fact is that the one-drop rule remains a
powerful force in identifying those who look black in the United States.

---

658 So.2d 331, 336 (La. Ct. App. 1995) (applying the existing Indian family test where a
child's mother was 11/16th Indian, was an enrolled tribal member, and had lived on a
reservation until she was nine years old, but had not maintained significant tribal ties
since then).

[135] *See* Angela Onwuachi–Willig & Mario L. Barnes, *By Any Other Name?: On Being
"Regarded as" Black, and Why Title VII Should Apply Even If Lakisha and Jamal Are
White*, 2005 Wisc. L. Rev. 1283.

[136] *See* Jones, *supra* note 20, at 1497 ("With racism, it is the social meaning afforded
one's race that determines one's status.").

[137] Moran, *supra* note 17, at 175; *see also* Amos N. Jones, *Black Like Obama: What the
Junior Illinois Senator's Appearance on the National Scene Reveals about Race in America*,

At the same time, *Hudgins* exposes the problems and challenges that multiracialism poses for racial classifications and order. The Wrights were able to capitalize on a situation in which phenotype was an unreliable guide to racial identity. In their lawsuit, the Wrights relied not just on their racially ambiguous appearance but also on their and their ancestors' performances within their communities to prove their non-blackness and thus gain their freedom. At the same time that *Hudgins* revealed an intense need to enforce the color line in a segregated system of slavery, the case also revealed the permeability of racial lines. Although the imperatives of policing racial boundaries through the one-drop rule continue to confine the racial options for those who are phenotypically black, multiracialism holds out more promise for multiracial individuals of non-black descent—or at least of indiscernible black descent—such as Japanese–Americans, American Indians, and white Latinos. These groups cannot only claim their mixed origins on the census but also may enjoy recognition as white or multiracial in their everyday lives. As Professor Rachel Moran has explained, to some extent, for these groups, the challenge has become one of maintaining a distinct racial or ethnic identity in the face of pressures to assimilate to a white identity.[138] *Hudgins* presages some of the difficulties of forging a identity that is neither black nor white in a society that still remains committed to these racial distinctions. Yet, the case also demonstrates that multiracialism can subvert the color line. As the multiracial population in the United States continues to grow, it is certain to challenge, through its very existence, the notion of race as biological and rigid, steadily destabilizing the assumptions that construct and preserve racial hierarchy.

*

---

and Where We Should Go From Here, 31 T. Marshall L. Rev. 79, 85 (2005) (asserting the same about Barack Obama's ability to claim a white identity).

[138] Moran, *supra* note 17, at 167–69.

6

Devon W. Carbado

Yellow by Law: The Story of *Ozawa v. United States*

Introduction

Over the past decade, scholars have paid increasing attention to Japanese–American constitutional history.[1] For the most part, this literature focuses on the government's decision during World War II to intern people of Japanese ancestry. This body of work is designed to demonstrate the extent to which, and precisely how, the Supreme Court acquiesced in various aspects of internment—curfew, evacuation, and detention—and to reveal the continuities between that acquiescence and current legal doctrine and social practices.[2]

Paying attention to the internment, and to the Supreme Court's role in legitimizing what the government euphemistically referred to as "relocation centers," makes sense.[3] Contained in the constitutional history of internment are important lessons about the racial work national security arguments can perform and about the role of race in constituting American national identity.[4] More narrowly, an engagement with the

---

[1] *See* Margaret Chon et al., *Race, Rights, and Reparation: Law of the Japanese American Internment* (Eric K. Yamamoto ed., 2001); Ian Haney López, *White By Law: The Legal Construction of Race* (2006); John Tehranian, *Performing Whiteness: Naturalization Litigation and the Construction of Racial Identity in America*, 109 Yale L.J. 817 (2000).

[2] *See* Dean Masaru Hashimoto, *The Legacy of* Korematsu v. United States: *A Dangerous Narrative Retold*, 4 Asian Pac. Am. L.J. 72 (1996); Jerry Kang, *Denying Prejudice: Internment, Redress, and Denial*, 51 UCLA L. Rev. 933 (2004); Eric L. Muller, *The Japanese American Cases—A Bigger Disaster Than We Realized*, 49 How. L.J. 417 (2006).

[3] Korematsu v. United States, 323 U.S. 214 (1944).

[4] *See* Aya Gruber, *Raising the Red Flag: The Continued Relevance of Japanese Internment in the Post-*Hamdi *World*, 54 U. Kan. L. Rev. 307 (2006); Jerry Kang, *Watching the Watchers: Enemy Combatants in the Internment's Shadow*, 68 Law & Contemp. Probs. 255 (2005); Eric L. Muller, *Inference or Impact? Racial Profiling and the Internment's True*

Supreme Court's jurisprudence on internment helps to reveal the relationship between the legal construction of race in judicial opinions and the existential realities of race in the social world.[5] Indeed, the experiences of people of Japanese ancestry in what Justice Owen Roberts referred to as "concentration camp[s]"[6] were, at least in part, the juridical effect of the legal construction of Japanese Americans as both foreign (regardless of their citizenship status) and unassimilable (regardless of their cultural practices). Put another way, in the context of Japanese–American internment, people of Japanese ancestry became in life what the Supreme Court in effect rendered them in law—irreducibly foreign.

But one has to be careful not to overstate the foregoing claim. For the trope of the Japanese as perpetual foreigners predates internment.[7] It has an earlier social, cultural, and doctrinal history. My aim in this chapter is to explore another historical moment in which that trope figured in constitutional discourse: 1922. In that year, Takao Ozawa attempted to persuade the Supreme Court that he was eligible for naturalization, and more particularly, that he was "white."[8]

Ozawa's argument was the direct result of a racialized immigration system. The Naturalization Act of 1790 restricted eligibility for citizenship to "any alien, being a free white person."[9] In the context of Reconstruction, and in part as a response to the antebellum holding in *Dred Scott* that blacks could not be citizens,[10] this act was amended to render "aliens of African nativity and ... persons of African descent" eligible for naturalization.[11] Though there was some concern that this

---

Legacy, 1 Ohio St. J. Crim. L. 103 (2003); Leti Volpp, *The Citizen and the Terrorist*, 49 UCLA L. Rev. 1575 (2002).

[5] *See* Devon W. Carbado, *(E)racing the Fourth Amendment*, 100 Mich. L. Rev. 946 (2000) (exploring this idea with respect to Fourth Amendment law).

[6] *Korematsu*, 323 U.S. at 226 (Roberts, J., dissenting).

[7] For good histories of Japanese experiences in the United States, see *East Across the Pacific: Historical and Sociological Studies of Japanese Immigration and Assimilation* (Hilary Conroy & T. Scott Miyakawa eds., 1972); David J. O'Brien & Stephen S. Fugita, *The Japanese American Experience* (1991); Paul R. Spickard, *Japanese Americans: The Formation and Transformations of an Ethnic Group* (1996).

[8] Ozawa v. United States, 260 U.S. 178 (1922).

[9] Naturalization Act of 1790, ch. 3, 1 Stat. 103.

[10] Scott v. Sandford, 60 U.S. 393, 404 (1856) ("We think [African Americans] are not ... and were not intended to be included, under the word 'citizen' in the Constitution, and can therefore claim none of the rights and privileges which that instrument provides for and secures to citizens of the United States.").

[11] 8 U.S.C. § 359 (1875), *amended by* 8 U.S.C. § 1422 (1952).

change might facilitate black emigration from the Caribbean to the United States, few people thought the numbers would be substantial. In this respect, the recognition of "aliens of African nativity and persons of African descent" as eligible for citizenship was a symbolic gesture. The racial parameters of the revised naturalization act remained in place for more than half a century. It was not until 1952, two years before *Brown v. Board of Education*,[12] that Congress passed the McCarran–Walter Act, which eliminated race as a basis for naturalization.[13]

In the meantime, Ozawa, and other people of Japanese descent, had to navigate this racialized legal landscape. Like other Asian litigants seeking to naturalize, Ozawa did not challenge race-based naturalization laws as inconsistent with the United States Constitution. Instead, drawing on both biological, social and performative conceptions of race, Ozawa argued that he was white. Neither the district court nor the Supreme Court agreed. Both insisted that Ozawa was yellow by law. The basis for that conclusion and its implications for law's role in constructing race are key questions that this chapter takes up.

More broadly, the chapter articulates a civil rights history of *Ozawa v. United States*. Notwithstanding that *Ozawa* is one of a few cases in which the rights of people of Japanese descent are squarely before the Supreme Court, not a single law review article sets forth the case's legal, political, and social context. Consequently, we know very little about how Ozawa got to the United States, how his case got to the Supreme Court, and how he shaped the timing and substance of the litigation. Nor do we know how the lawsuit figured in, helped to constitute, and was itself constituted by the civil rights consciousness of the Japanese–American community. Even less appreciated are the geo-political concerns that shaped how the U.S. and Japanese governments responded to the case as it journeyed through the courts and eventually received media attention.

This chapter fills these gaps and sheds new light on the district court and Supreme Court opinions. A full telling of *Ozawa*'s story demonstrates how both courts drew on popular and scientific sources of racial knowledge to conclude that people of Japanese descent were neither white nor Caucasian. More importantly, the chapter shows that these opinions helped to make Ozawa yellow. The inability of Japanese people to become citizens—their unnaturalizability—was not a *natural* fact but a *legally produced* reality. To put the point slightly differently, Takao Ozawa was not born yellow. He became yellow—at least in part by law.

---

12 347 U.S. 483 (1954).

13 McCarran–Walter Act, 8 U.S.C. § 1422 (1952).

The chapter begins with a brief history of people of Japanese ancestry in the United States from the late nineteenth century to the Supreme Court's decision in *Ozawa v. United States*. As will become clear, that history intersects with and is shaped by Chinese immigration. Indeed, to a significant extent, anti-Chinese nativism was re-articulated and redeployed against the Japanese. The latter became the new "yellow peril"—a construct that signified both the unwillingness and the incapacity to assimilate. The fear of the Japanese as foreign and unfit prompted exclusionary legislation and media hysteria in California. Presumably, these developments shaped how Ozawa experienced his years in San Francisco and might have pushed him to migrate to Hawai'i in 1906, the place from which he would litigate his right to naturalize.

The chapter then turns to the district court litigation. After Ozawa's petition for naturalization was denied, what motivated him to file suit? By 1916, at least six district courts had weighed in on the question of whether people of Japanese ancestry were eligible for naturalization, and each answered that question in the negative. Upon what basis did Ozawa conclude that he could contest the dominant racial idea—namely, that people of Japanese ancestry were not white? At least part of the answer can be found in Ozawa's brief, which Ozawa authored himself. Surprisingly, scholars have paid little attention to this document. Yet, it is the clearest expression of Ozawa's voice—of how he conceived of his relationship to America, of how he understood the naturalization statutes, and of how he thought about the relationship between race and Japanese identity, on the one hand, and the categories white, black and yellow, on the other. Despite Ozawa's efforts, the district court judge roundly rejected his petition for naturalization.

Ozawa's story could have ended here. After all, the conclusion that Ozawa was not white was unequivocal. Nevertheless, Ozawa determined to push on, appealing his case to the Ninth Circuit Court of Appeals. The next section of the chapter looks at how Ozawa's case drew the attention of immigrant leaders who were looking for a test case. As lawyers for the Japanese community took over Ozawa's representation, the arguments were shaped to build on pre-existing civil right initiatives to secure the right to naturalize.

The story then turns directly to the Supreme Court's opinion to explore how it confronted the question of Ozawa's racial identity. Ozawa had asked the Court to focus on his character and to discard outmoded and inaccurate biological definitions of race. Instead, the Court focused on two key and seemingly disconnected sources of guidance in interpreting racial classifications: science and common knowledge. The chapter explores the interdependency of these concepts in establishing and enforcing the racial parameters of the naturalization laws. The chapter concludes by explaining why the *Ozawa* litigation history is important to contemporary discussions of race. The short answer is this: In addition to exposing the rhetorical strategies the Supreme Court employed to constitutionalize the notion of the Japanese as permanently and irreducibly foreign, *Ozawa* reveals the role that law plays in constructing race—its categories, social meanings and existential realities.

Pushed and Pulled to America?

Ozawa v. United States is a story about immigration that fits into but also departs from the larger story of Japanese people being "pushed" and "pulled" to America. A significant pull factor for Japanese immigration to the United States in the late 1860s was the labor shortage created by increasing hostility among white Californians toward Chinese immigrants. This hostility culminated in the 1882 Exclusion Act, which prohibited Chinese immigration and naturalization.[14] A significant push factor was the economic, political, and legal restructuring of Japan—that is, its emerging "modernization." In the 1880s, as a part of this restructuring, Japan reversed its non-emigration policy and geo-political isolationism. Moreover, the Japanese government promulgated laws designed to remove feudal lords from their lands; as a result, a large percentage of Japanese agricultural laborers were forced off plots that they had tended for years.[15]

Displaced Japanese farmers migrated first to the sugar cane plantations of Hawai'i, with some moving to California to work in the citrus groves and vegetable fields.[16] Their numbers were relatively small at first, but by the time Takao Ozawa landed in San Francisco in 1894, close to 10, 000 Japanese émigrés were living in the continental United States.

Born in the Kanagawa Prefecture on June 15, 1875, Ozawa was nineteen years old when he arrived in California. What the precise push and pull factors were for him, we do not know. What we do know is that he graduated from Berkeley High School in Berkeley, California and

---

[14] This is somewhat of "an oversimplification" in the sense that Chinese laborers were still very much present during the first wave of Japanese immigration. Indeed, "[t]he earliest Japanese Labor gangs were in direct competition with the remaining Chinese, and had to resort to wage cutting to get employment." Roger Daniels, *The Politics of Prejudice: The Anti–Japanese Movement in California, and the Struggle for Japanese Exclusion* 8 (1966). The Chinese Exclusion act was renewed for another ten years in 1892 and extended indefinitely in 1904. *Labor Immigration Under Capitalism: Asian Workers in the United States Before World War II* 74 (Lucie Cheng & Edna Bonacich eds., 1984).

[15] Keith Aoki, *No Right to Own?: The Early Twentieth–Century "Alien Land Laws"* as a Prelude to Internment, 40 B.C. L. Rev. 37, 45 (1998).

[16] See Bill Ong Hing, *Making and Remaking Asian America Through Immigration Policy 1850–1990* at 27 (1993).

subsequently attended the University of California at Berkeley for three years before settling in what was then the territory of Hawai'i in 1906.

It is hard to know how much anti-Japanese sentiment Ozawa experienced in San Francisco. After all, booming agribusiness enterprises initially welcomed the Japanese labor force. Moreover, at the turn of the century, the Japanese were perceived to be less culturally and socially threatening than the Chinese. The claim that the Chinese were unassimilable was based in part on the fact that they lived in overcrowded and segregated "Chinatowns," that the community was largely male, and that the Chinese seemed to conceive of themselves as temporary visitors rather than permanent residents of America.

By and large, Americans did not perceive the first wave of Japanese immigrants in this way. Commenting on the public reaction to early Japanese émigrés, Roger Daniels observes that "[a] typical newspaper editorial pointed out that 'the objections raised against the Chinese ... cannot be alleged against the Japanese ... They have brought their wives, children and ... new industries among us.' "[17] Like Ozawa, many in the Issei (first-generation) community evidenced a genuine interest in building a permanent life in America, an interest that manifested itself in a variety of assimilationist practices that Ozawa himself would invoke to describe his relationship to American values, norms, and institutions.

Of course, America's acceptance of the Japanese was short-lived. Indeed, within the first decade of the twentieth century, people of Japanese decent would replace the Chinese as the new "yellow peril," a construct that "inscribe[d] on Japanese immigrants an image of disloyalty and allegiance to a threatening foreign military power."[18] But, in the meantime, there was no broad-based racialized movement against the early Issei arrivals.

A second reason to query whether Ozawa experienced significant racial hostility in San Francisco relates to the fact that he was not an agricultural laborer. Farm work became a significant (though certainly not the only) site for white and Japanese racial conflicts. In 1902, Oxnard business owners formed a labor contracting company whose "purpose was to undercut the independent Japanese labor contractors while at the same time lowering labor costs."[19] One year later, 500 Japanese and Mexican laborers organized the Japanese–Mexican Labor Association ("JMLA") and led 1200 workers on strike to demand that independent labor contractors be allowed to negotiate directly with

---

[17] Daniels, *supra* note 14, at 3.

[18] Aoki, *supra* note 15, at 47.

[19] Ronald Takaki, *Strangers from a Different Shore: A History of Asian Americans* 198 (1989).

producers. The successful strike was supported by the Los Angeles County Council of Labor which explicitly called for organization of the entire labor force, including the Japanese.

Organized labor at the national level responded differently to the JMLA, largely because of the presence of Japanese laborers. The Mexican president of JMLA, J. M. Lizarras, petitioned the American Federation of Labor ("AFL") to charter his organization, but AFL president Samuel Gompers agreed only on the condition that Japanese (and Chinese) laborers be excluded from membership. Although the Mexican wing of the JMLA stood by Japanese workers, the organization could not survive without the charter. More importantly, though, Gompers and the AFL called for the amendment of the 1882 Chinese Exclusion Act to include Japanese. The AFL's official publication, *American Federationist*, explained the exclusionary policies as follows: "White workers, including ignorant ones and the newcomers from southern and eastern Europe, possessed qualities enabling them to join and contribute to the labor movement. They could be taught the fundamentals of unionism and would stand shoulder to shoulder with faithful workers.... 'Unable to be assimilated,' the Japanese could not become 'union men.' "[20]

Because Ozawa was not a laborer, he would not have had firsthand experience with these labor battles. To what extent he was otherwise familiar with them is difficult to know. However, it is hard to imagine that when Ozawa departed for Hawai'i in 1906, he was unaware of the extent to which San Francisco had become openly hostile to the Japanese. In 1905, several events crystallized a growing anti-Japanese sentiment. Japan's defeat of Russia created a sense of geo-political anxiety within the United States, an anxiety that California newspapers reflected by focusing on the still-emerging Japanese community in the state. The *San Francisco Chronicle* carried headlines that read: "THE JAPANESE INVASION, THE PROBLEM OF THE HOUR," "JAPANESE A MENACE TO AMERICAN WOMEN," and "BROWN MEN AN EVIL IN THE PUBLIC SCHOOLS."[21] *The Examiner*, William Hearst's rival paper, ran stories framed with similar headlines.[22] In addition, the California legislature unanimously passed a resolution requesting that the federal government restrict Japanese immigration, a measure heavily covered in the press.[23] The Union Labor Party was enormously successful in local and county elections. In fact, "labor controlled the entire government of San Francisco, and it was the labor unions who most

---

[20] *Id.* at 200.

[21] Bill Hosokawa, *Nisei: The Quiet Americans* 82–83 (1969).

[22] Daniels, *supra* note 14, at 25.

[23] Hosokawa, *supra* note 21, at 82.

strongly opposed the influx of Japanese into California."[24] Representatives from different unions formed the Asiatic Exclusion League, which committed itself to anti-Japanese political organizing.[25] By the time Ozawa left California in 1906, and particularly after the earthquake in April, people of Japanese descent had become increasingly vulnerable to public assaults at the hands of white San Franciscans.[26] This growing violence got the attention of President Theodore Roosevelt, who deployed a federal investigator to the scene. The investigator found that the assaults were all too frequent to be explicable on grounds other than race.[27]

If Ozawa did not notice the "[t]he anti-Japanese thunderclouds"[28] forming in California, he would have been thoroughly unprepared for the impending racial storm: the San Francisco school board's proposal to segregate the fewer than 100 Japanese students it served.[29] The controversy centered on an order the San Francisco School Board issued on October 11, 1906, directing school principals to send Japanese children to "the Oriental school," a school to which Chinese students already had been assigned.[30] The school board's plan created a national and international crisis and was widely covered in the press. Prior to 1906, the federal government largely ignored political efforts on the part of public figures in California, including Governor Henry Gage, to get Congress to pass legislation prohibiting Japanese immigration. The school board's segregation initiative got President Roosevelt's attention; he promptly sent Victor Metcalf, Secretary of Commerce and Labor, to investigate. After failing to persuade the school board to rescind the segregation order, Metcalf "reported to President Roosevelt that it was hopeless to look for modification or repeal of the resolution."[31]

Nor was it clear that the courts would declare the resolution unconstitutional. Arguments that it violated an 1895 "most favored nation" treaty with Japan were less than compelling. For one thing, "the Treaty of 1895 did not contain a 'most favored nation' clause concerning

[24] Frank F. Chuman, *The Bamboo People: The Law and Japanese–Americans* 26 (1976).

[25] Daniels, *supra* note 14, at 27–28.

[26] Chuman, *supra* note 24, at 23.

[27] Daniels, *supra* note 14, at 33.

[28] Chuman, *supra* note 24, at 17.

[29] Nora M. Walsh, *The History of Chinese and Japanese Exclusion 1882–1924* at 31 (1947).

[30] Takaki, *supra* note 19, at 201.

[31] Chuman, *supra* note 24, at 25.

education."[32] For another, even if such a clause were interpreted to be implicitly a part of the treaty, it did not follow that the school board had acted unconstitutionally. Under *Plessy v. Ferguson*, which endorsed "separate but equal" services and facilities, racial segregation was not inconsistent with the notion of equal rights under the law.[33] In other words, the mere fact that the Japanese were being forced to attend an "Oriental" school did not, without more, mean that they were being denied equal protection.

President Roosevelt was experiencing tremendous pressure from the Japanese government, pressure he knew he could not afford to ignore. Nor could he ignore the anti-Japanese pressure from the West Coast. Feeling squeezed from all sides, Roosevelt initially "recommended to Congress that 'an act be passed specifically providing for the naturalization of the Japanese who come here intending to become American citizens.' "[34] Predictably, his recommendation engendered feelings of good will in Japan and widespread condemnation on the West Coast— and, in particular, on the San Francisco school board. The California papers, moreover, "w[ere] almost unanimous in opposing the President's views."[35]

California's swift and overwhelmingly negative response to President Roosevelt's intervention forced him to rethink his approach to racial politics on the West Coast. Specifically, Roosevelt came to realize that California's public officials had to play an active role in managing what had become a national and international crisis. To that end, he invited the then-Mayor of San Francisco, Eugene Schmitz, and members of the school board to Washington to explore a variety of proposals he could present to Japan. The seeds of the "Gentleman's Agreement" were planted in that meeting and grew in a series of subsequent negotiations between the President and Japan.

Under the Agreement, President Roosevelt promised not to support legislation restricting immigration from Japan and the Japanese government in turn agreed to restrict emigration of Japanese citizens to the United States. Roosevelt was, however, authorized to curtail Japanese immigration to the United States from Canada, Mexico, or Hawai'i. The Japanese government was satisfied with this arrangement, as were the political leaders in California. Indeed, when Congress passed the 1907 immigration bill (which included a provision authorizing the President to

---

[32] *Id.*

[33] 163 U.S. 537 (1896).

[34] Jiuiji G. Kasai, *The Relationship Between Japan and the United States*, Annals Am. Acad. Pol. & Soc. Sci., July 1914, at 260, 262.

[35] Chuman, *supra* note 24, at 28.

forbid secondary immigration to the United States), Mayor Schmitz commented "that the administration now shares, and that it will share, our way of looking at the problem and that the result we desire—the cessation of the immigration of Japanese laborers, skilled or unskilled, to this country, will be speedily achieved."[36] The school board rescinded its segregation order. The coda to all of this: On March 14, 1907, President Roosevelt issued an Executive Order specifically prohibiting Japanese immigration from Canada, Hawai'i, and Mexico.[37] Californians could tell themselves that they had effectuated Japanese exclusion. Japan could tell itself that it had prevented both the segregation of Japanese children and the passage of legislation barring immigration into the United States *from Japan*. A national and international crisis had been averted—for the moment.

By the time the dust from the San Francisco school board affair had settled, Ozawa was in Honolulu. Whether the foregoing events pushed him there is difficult to say. Still, it is hard to imagine that Ozawa was oblivious to the growing anti-Japanese movement in San Francisco. By the end of 1905, the racial campaign against the Japanese had become something more than "the tail to the anti-Chinese kite."[38] White exclusionists had raised the anti-Japanese kite well off the ground, if not fully aloft.

Nor do we know the extent to which Ozawa's experiences as an undergraduate at Berkeley shaped his decision to leave the Bay Area. Ozawa likely was one of a few Japanese students at Berkeley during this time.[39] Interestingly, the Hearst family, whose newspapers were stoking

---

[36] Takaki, *supra* note 19, at 203.

[37] Kazuo Ito, *Issei; A History of Japanese Immigrants in North America* 908 (Shinichiro Nakamura & Jean S. Gerard trans., Seattle: Japanese Community Service, 1973).

[38] Daniels, *supra* note 14, at 21 (commenting that "[i]n 1900 the anti-Japanese campaign . . . was mainly a tail to the anti-Chinese kite").

[39] Berkeley did not start systematically collecting racial demographic data pertaining to its student body until the early 1970s. Email from David Radwin, Principal Analyst, Office of Student Research, U.C. Berkeley, to Emily J. Wood, Research Assistant, UCLA School of Law Library (July 20, 2007) (on file with author). There seems to be a similar paucity of information about the racial composition of Berkeley High at the time. An online exhibit in the UC Digital History Archive of the Bancroft Library entitled The University of California at the Turn of the Century 1899–1900, makes no mention of the racial breakdown of the student body or faculty, and provides little insight into what life might have been like for minority students in general and Japanese students in particular. *The University of California at the Turn of the Century 1899–1900*, UC History Digital Archive (1999–2005), *available at* http://sunsite.berkeley.edu/uchistory/archives_exhibits/online_exhibits/1899/index.html. The exhibit does feature a number of photographs of students and faculty. The subjects of these photographs all appear to be of European–Caucasian racial derivation. In any case, there is not any discernible person of color depicted in the exhibit.

anti-Japanese sentiment in California, was heavily involved in the rapid development of the Berkeley campus.[40] What impact that had on campus culture, we do not know. What we do know is that Ozawa did not graduate from Berkeley but rather left after completing only three years. However, this was not entirely unusual; graduation rates at the beginning of the early twentieth century were only approximately 50%.[41]

Then, too, Ozawa might not have been pushed from San Francisco but rather pulled to Hawai'i because he believed that it was more racially tolerant than the mainland.[42] This does not mean that the Islands were free of racial prejudice.[43] Instead, the "wholesome influence" of native Hawaiians positively shaped (at least to some extent) how different racial groups interacted with one another.[44] When the Chinese first arrived, for example, they were not met with the kind of "treatment experienced by their fellow nationals in California."[45] Furthermore, since modern Hawai'i always had a multi-ethnic, multi-racial population, and interracial marriages were not uncommon,[46] individual minority groups were never subjected to the kind of attacks faced by the Chinese and then the Japanese in California.[47] Ozawa could have decided that Hawai'i was a better site than California to pursue his dream of becoming a naturalized citizen.

Whatever Ozawa's reasons for leaving the mainland, his departure occurred at the very moment when thousands of Japanese had begun to migrate in precisely the opposite direction—namely, from the Islands to the mainland. In 1898, after Hawai'i became an American territory subject to the United States Constitution, Japanese people who labored under an abusive contract system were suddenly liberated.[48] Experiencing themselves as free to work where they wished, many chose to pursue opportunities on the mainland. Employment agents from a number of

---

[40] Id.

[41] Id.

[42] William C. Smith, *Minority Groups in Hawai'i*, 223 Annals Am. Acad. Pol. & Soc. Sci. 36, 40 (1942) ("Visitors to Hawai'i characteristically comment on the friendly relations existing among the several ethnic groups.").

[43] Id.

[44] Id. at 40–41.

[45] Id. at 41.

[46] Id. at 42.

[47] Id.

[48] The contract system of labor was inconsistent with the United States Constitution, which had a regulatory effect on the newly acquired territory.

West Coast industries aggressively sought out these workers.[49] In fact, their recruitment efforts helped to produce a labor shortage on the Islands; the Hawaiian legislature responded by charging the recruiters an annual fee.[50]

Ozawa's arrival in Hawai'i did little to ameliorate this labor shortage. Ozawa worked as a sales clerk, not an agricultural worker. He took a job with one of the Big Five sugar companies in Honolulu, the Theo H. Davies Company.[51] Ozawa would work there for twenty-three years. It was his first and only job in Hawai'i.[52] Although the majority of Issei were farmers, it is not remarkable that Ozawa would end up with a job in sales. As successive generations of plantation workers acculturated in Hawai'i, the newest arrivals began as laborers, but then moved into other sectors of the economy. By the time Ozawa arrived in Hawai'i, the first generation of Issei already were beginning to leave farm work. Presumably, his educational background enabled him to ride this emerging wave of professional opportunities for people of Japanese ancestry.[53] As a result of these changes, by 1920 Japanese people were well-represented in the retail trades[54] as well as in service-oriented industries like auto garages[55] and building and carpentry.[56]

In the end, the short of Ozawa's experience in Hawai'i is that it was both typical and atypical of other Issei in Hawai'i. It was typical in that he went there to work within the sugar industry, but atypical in that the work he went there to do involved sales and not labor. It was typical in that his story involves living in both Hawai'i and California, but atypical in that he moved from the latter to the former and not the other way around. It was typical in that his children did not get anything out of Japanese schools, but atypical in that the reason was that he never sent

---

[49] Yukiko Kimura, *Issei: Japanese Immigrants in Hawaii* 14 (1988).

[50] *Id.* at 140 (Even the Japanese Consul General in Hawai'i attempted to forestall the Hawai'i-to-Mainland migration).

[51] Theo H. Davies & Co., *Wikipedia: The Free Encyclopedia* (2006), *available at* http://en.wikipedia.org/wiki/Theo_H._Davies_ & _ Co.

[52] Tomi Knaefler, *Battles and Brave Men to Remember Proudly*, Honolulu Star–Bull., Sept. 14, 1963 (on file with author).

[53] I am not suggesting that the Japanese who worked in professional or semi-professional settings experienced no discrimination. *See* Smith, *supra* note 42, at 43 (observing that "after gaining entry to certain professions people of Japanese descent encounter barriers, some of them very subtle, to be sure, while their Caucasian classmates, protected by vested rights, move unopposed into the preferred positions").

[54] *Id.* at 294.

[55] *Id.* at 295.

[56] *Id.* at 299.

them. It was typical that he was a practicing Christian, but atypical that he did not seem to attach much significance to the embrace of his Japanese heritage as an assimilatory motivation. In this sense, Ozawa's story intersects with but does not neatly trace the histories of others in his demographic.

The District Court Litigation: Yellow is Yellow

White Like Me: Ozawa's Brief

By the time Ozawa died in 1936 he had made Hawai'i his home. It was in Hawai'i that he met and married his wife, Masako; it was in Hawai'i that he raised his four daughters and only son, who would die while serving in the military during World War II;[57] and it was in Hawai'i that he began his litigation journey to the Supreme Court, a journey paved in part by a brief Ozawa himself authored.

---

[57] Knaefler, *supra* note 52.

Surprisingly, scholars have paid very little attention to Ozawa's brief.[58] Most have focused almost entirely on a single paragraph of the thirty-page document. As best I can tell, no one has fully explicated, interrogated, or theoretically situated Ozawa's arguments. Perhaps this is because Ozawa's brief was filed at the district court level and was not, therefore, a part of the Supreme Court litigation. Perhaps the explanation is that, in terms of organization, the brief is a mess. The argument headings Ozawa employs do very little to discipline the claims sandwiched between them. Perhaps the answer is not about organization but about substance—that is, the extent to which Ozawa's arguments are sometimes contradictory and other times little more than rhetorical gestures. Perhaps it is the simple fact that Ozawa authored the brief himself that accounts for its marginalization. Because Ozawa was not a lawyer, scholars (and particularly legal scholars) might have been disinclined to take his legal analysis too seriously.

Yet there is much to mine in Ozawa's brief. Notwithstanding problems of organization and argumentation, there is a logic and thematic coherence to at least some of his analysis. As I hope to demonstrate, a careful reading of Ozawa's brief reveals two sets of interrelated claims. The first set focuses on the extent to which Ozawa had successfully assimilated into mainstream American society. The second addresses the role of race in determining who can be an American.

"A True American"

According to Ozawa, "[i]n name, I am not an American, but at heart I am a true American."[59] His narrative strategy was to describe cultural and associational practices that explicitly delineated his attachment to America and his detachment from Japan. This part of the story is decidedly not about Japanese people as a racial group. It is about Ozawa, and more specifically, his relationship to American culture, values and institutions. One might query, then, whether Ozawa's self-representation here reflects a kind of racial exceptionalism, namely, that Ozawa was framing himself as an exception to the general rule that people of Japanese ancestry are unassimilable. But that would be putting the point too strongly. For as will become clear, elsewhere in his brief, Ozawa expressly contested the idea that Japanese people lacked the willingness and the capacity to assimilate. In this respect, it is more accurate to say that, in describing his social and familial life, Ozawa simply wanted to highlight his American credentials to shore up his *particular* claim to American citizenship, not to differentiate himself from or disidentify with other Japanese.

---

[58] *Naturalization of a Japanese Subject, In re* Ozawa, No. 274 (D. Haw. 1916) [hereinafter Brief].

[59] Brief, *supra* note 58, at 4.

Ozawa begins his American story by pointing out his loyalty and commitment to the nation. Unlike "General Benedict Arnold [who] was an American but at heart ... a traitor," Ozawa conceived of himself as a patriot, a "true American."[60] This dichotomy between "the traitor" and "the true American" would become particularly salient in the context of political and juridical discourses legitimizing the internment of Japanese people during World War II. But, by the end of the first decade of the twentieth century, the dichotomy already had meaningful social traction, marking the Japanese as suspect in terms of American patriotism. Ozawa's invocation of Benedict Arnold challenged this suspect identity. His aim was not only to advance a claim that he had been and would continue to be loyal and patriotic to America, but also to make explicit that he considered it a part of his civic duty to give back to America, "to do something good to the United States before I bid farewell to this world."[61]

For Ozawa, the proof of his "true American" identity was in the pudding of his assimilation—and, correlatively, his dis-assimilation from Japanese institutions and cultural practices. Ozawa made much of his proficiency in English. Indeed, one of his arguments that he was ultra qualified to be an American citizen was explicitly based on his fluency in English. Ozawa reasoned that "Section 8 [of the naturalization law] declares that no aliens shall hereafter be naturalized or admitted as a citizen of the United States who can not speak the English language; provided that the requirement of this section shall not apply to any alien who had, prior to the passage of this act, declared his intentions to become a citizen of the United States."[62] Because Ozawa had declared such an intention, the English language competency for naturalization did not apply to him. Thus, he perceived himself to be "more qualified [to be a citizen] than required by law."[63]

In addition to his language skills, Ozawa stressed that he had educated himself in "American schools for nearly eleven years ... [and] resided ... continuously within the United States for over twenty eight years."[64] During all of this time, he did not attend "any Japanese churches or schools."[65] Nor did Ozawa affiliate with any official Japanese institution. In fact, while the Japanese Consulate required all Japanese subjects to register with its office, Ozawa refused to do so. "I did not

---

[60] *Id.*

[61] *Id.*

[62] *Id.* at 3.

[63] *Id.*

[64] *Id.*

[65] *Id.* at 4.

report my name, my marriage, or the names of my children to the Japanese Consulate in Honolulu."[66] However, "[t]hese matters were reported to the American government,"[67] a fact that, to Ozawa, was an important signification of his broader efforts to integrate himself formally within American society.

Even—and perhaps especially—Ozawa's family life was structured around American cultural practices and social norms. To begin with, "I chose as my wife, one educated in American schools ... instead of one educated in Japan."[68] This is particularly significant in that between 1907 and 1923, "14276 picture brides came to Hawai'i."[69] In this sense, Ozawa's invocation of his wife's education was evidence not only of *her* American socialization but of *his* non-participation in a cultural practice that was common among the Japanese in Hawai'i—picture bride weddings.

Ozawa also stressed that, for the most part, he and his wife both "us[ed] the American (English) language at home."[70] As result, Ozawa's children were unable to "speak the Japanese language."[71] And they did not, as Ozawa's daughter Edith Takeya explains, "have any Oriental friends. My neighbors were all Caucasians."[72] Ozawa's children were thoroughly disconnected not only from the Japanese language but from Japanese cultural institutions and peers.

This was not the way many Issei socialized their second-generation Nisei children. Consider, for example, Japanese language schools. By World War I, Japanese language schools were so prevalent in Hawai'i that anti-Japanese agitators invoked them as evidence that the Japanese were both unassimiliable and disloyal.[73] As it turns out, "the language schools were generally unsuccessful in making their Nisei students fluent in Japanese."[74] Disinterested in the subject matter because of a cultural separation from Japan, "Nisei were more interested in English school than language school, and attended the latter only because their

---

[66] *Id.*

[67] *Id.*

[68] *Id.*

[69] Kimura, *supra* note 49, at 142–43.

[70] Brief, *supra* note 58, at 4.

[71] *Id.*

[72] *Race: The Power of an Illusion, available at* http://www.racematters.org/racethepow erofanillusion.htm.

[73] Kimura, *supra* note 49, at 41 (quoting *Pacific Commercial Advertiser* editor Edwin P. Irwin in 1920).

[74] *Id.* at 46.

parents wanted them to.''[75] Ozawa harbored no such desires for his children; he raised them in an English-only environment.

And he raised them as Christians, sending them "to an American Church and American School in place of a Japanese one.''[76] His religious choices reflected broader trends in the Japanese community. Most Issei were Buddhists.[77] In fact, many of the early Japanese language schools on Hawai'i were Buddhist institutions.[78] However, attendance at Buddhist religious services was sparse. One religious leader of the era suggested that this was "not [because of a] lack of believers of Hongwanji Sect ... It was due to self-humiliation because the immigrants were sensitive to the fact that they came to a Christian country. And earlier even Consul General [Taro] Ando and his consulate staff became Christian. Christians seemed to enjoy priority in everything. It appeared that only stupid people came to Hongwanji.''[79] Although subsequent efforts on the part of Buddhist religious leaders served to inspire renewed interest in the overt and active practice of Buddhism, this self-loathing anti-Buddhist sentiment echoed the larger theme of Americanization in Hawai'i at the time: to replace old cultural values with new ones.

Notwithstanding Ozawa's deep interest in assimilation, his complete disassociation from and disidentification with Japanese institutions is somewhat curious. At least some Japanese organizations were explicitly committed to westernization. Consider, for example, the Japanese Association of America ("JAA").[80] Formed in 1908, the JAA was a bureaucratic agency that helped to ensure that Japanese immigration to the United States met the requirements of the "Gentlemen's Agreement." As a major voice in the Japanese community, the organization sought to

---

[75] *Id.* at 47.

[76] *Id.*

[77] *Id. at* 153.

[78] Doremus Scudder, *Hawai'i's Experience with the Japanese*, 93 Annals Am. Acad. Pol. & Soc. Sci. 110, 113 (1921).

[79] Kimura, *supra* note 49, at 154 (quoting Honolulu Bishop Imamura).

[80] Leaders in the Japanese community founded the Japanese Deliberative Council of America in San Francisco in 1900. Its official purpose was to "expand the rights of Imperial subjects in America and to maintain the Japanese national image." Yuji Ichioka, *Japanese Associations and the Japanese Government: A Special Relationship, 1909–1926*, 46 Pac. Hist. Rev. 413 (1977). In an effort to expand its coverage of Japanese communities the Council held meetings in 1905 with various representatives of Japanese communities across the nation. The result was the United Japanese Deliberative Council of America in 1906, which again had San Francisco as its headquarters. The organization was soon, however, plagued by financial problems and internal strife and this led the Consul General Chozo Koike to urge community leaders to form the Japanese Association of America in 1908. *Id.*

mold the ideal immigrant through a moral improvement campaign for the Issei. This campaign was very much a westernization project, which had as its aim the abrogation of putatively "traditional" culture for a more modern aesthetic. This included the JAA's recommendation that Japanese women in America wear Western female clothing as opposed to *kimonos* and *obis*.[81] In addition, the JAA sponsored the creation of a textbook which outlined the "gendered expectations" of Issei women and which was distributed to picture brides in Tokyo before they came to the United States.[82]

The JAA also embarked upon an anti-gambling campaign in 1912. The ostensible aim of the campaign was to curb the financial dispossession as well as the general moral degeneration of those Japanese who participated in the kind of gambling offered by the Chinese. The deeper reason for the campaign can be found in the urge to decrease the numbers of Japanese falling into the "trap of Sinification"—that is to say, those who became yellow by association with the Chinese. The basis for moral reform and modernization was connected to the Japanese government's desire to prove to the West that the Japanese nation had the will and the capacity to modernize.

Ozawa's overall investment in assimilation is not surprising. The Japanese government itself advocated assimilation with the help of Christian and Buddhist leaders alike.[83] Both communities invoked "historic allusions" to justify this Americanization project: Japanese citizens should engage in culturally assimilatory American practices as a function of their loyalty to Japan. The agenda was to be carried out by Japanese subjects, who would be made to bear the burden of proving their modernity. It is decidedly less than clear whether Ozawa would have experienced the JAA's goal of "proving modernity" as a burden. Ozawa conceived of himself as a picture of modernity—and he willingly placed himself in that frame in the hope that others would see him that way as well. Yet, Ozawa likely would not have considered it *his duty as a Japanese subject* to present himself as modern. Having that sense of duty would be tantamount to acquiescing in a nation-building project for (as opposed to dis-assimilating oneself from) Japan.

In hypothesizing Ozawa's relationship to modernity, I do not mean to suggest that modernization and assimilation are precisely the same thing. They are not. However, with respect to people of Japanese descent, historically both modernity and assimilation have been part of

---

[81] Eiichiru Azuma, *Between Two Empires: Race, History and Transnationalism in Japanese America* 50 (2005).

[82] *Id.* at 53.

[83] *Id.* at 111–12.

the same discursive field, or what Edward Said refers to as Oriental-ism—a set of discourses that position the West and the East as opposi-tional dualities. More particularly, Orientalism represents the West as modern, enlightened, and democratic and the East as archaic, primitive, and despotic.[84] The notion that the Japanese were unassimilable explicit-ly traded on this East/West polarity. Only the subjects of modernity (that is to say, Western subjects) could assimilate; and Western subjects were by definition not Oriental. Understood in this way, both Ozawa and the JAA were contesting Orientalism. The JAA's contestation sounded in arguments about modernity. Ozawa's sounded in the language of assimi-lation.

In fact, as the late Yuji Ichioka observed, Ozawa was "a paragon of an assimilated Japanese immigrant."[85] Seemingly, he had a sincere investment in and commitment to American socialization. It is hard to read the account Ozawa provides and not conclude that, in terms of his everyday life, he was already an American—a modern Western subject. Certainly, Ozawa thought that he had been "living like an American."[86] His deep hope was that the law would finally catch up with and formally legitimize that reality.

And it was just that—a hope, not a demand. Or so Ozawa wanted the court to believe. The language of civil rights was nowhere to be found in his brief. His arguments were a gentle request of the nation-state. He was "humbly asking for admission and recognition as a citizen."[87] and nothing more. He employed the assimilationist facts of his life, which he maintained were "absolutely true,"[88] in order to do so.

Race: Character, Contrast, and Color

In addition to contending that he had a "strong attachment to the United States,"[89] Ozawa presented arguments that more directly en-gaged race. Read together, the argument headings in his brief advanced the following three claims: (1) The 1790 naturalization act was not a racial classification but rather a screening device for character; (2) The Japanese were white because they were neither black nor Chinese; and

---

[84] Edward Said, *Orientalism* (1978). *See also* Volpp, *supra* note 4 (drawing on Said to explain the treatment of "persons who appear Middle Eastern, Arab or Muslim" in the aftermath of 9/11).

[85] Yuji Ichioka, *The Early Japanese Immigrant Quest for Citizenship: The Background of the 1922 Ozawa Case*, 4 Amerasia J. 1, 10 (1977).

[86] Brief, *supra* note 58, at 23.

[87] *Id.* at 5.

[88] *Id.* at 4.

[89] *Id.*

(3) While race and racial categories did not really exist, the Japanese were white based on the color of their skin. I discuss each argument in turn.

White on the Inside: Race as Character

Ozawa explicitly argued that the 1790 naturalization statute did not rely on a racial classification scheme. The term "free white person" was "used simply to distinguish black people from others."[90] For Ozawa, slavery was a normative racial baseline; the naturalization statute did no more than reflect this baseline and did not establish new racial classifications.

According to Ozawa, the existence of slavery did not call into question the racial bona fides of our Founding Fathers. However, a racial reading of the naturalization statute would do so by attributing racism to them. Ozawa sought to avoid that attribution, which he believed would impose a dignitary harm not only on "the great founders of this great Union,"[91] but on the nation-state itself. Ozawa argued that, in offering a race-neutral interpretation of the naturalization statute, he was "[f]rom the bottom of my heart ... defend[ing] the honor of this great Republic."[92]

That defense required Ozawa to engage another founding father of sorts, Johann Friedrich Blumenbach, who played an enormously important role in establishing the field of physical anthropology. In his third edition of *On the Natural Variety of Mankind*, Blumenbach set forth five categories of mankind—Mongolian, American, Malayan, African and Caucasian.[93] Of these groups, the Caucasian, "[i]n general," he declared to be the "most handsome and becoming."[94] Prior to his work, neither "race" nor "Caucasian" circulated in popular venues, though by the mid-nineteenth century, both would be thoroughly normalized. Under Blumenbach's classification system, the Japanese were Mongolian, not white. Ozawa understood this. He knew as well that, by the time he filed suit, the conceptualization of the Japanese as Mongolian had been instantiated in several lower court opinions. He could not, therefore, proceed with an argument for Japanese naturalization without directly challenging Blumenbach.

---

[90] *Id.* at 14.

[91] *Id.* at 18.

[92] *Id.*

[93] Johann Friedrich Blumenbach, *On the Natural Variety of* Mankind (3d. ed., 1795) *in* Johann Friedrich Blumenbach, *The Anthropological Treatises of Johann Friedrich Blumenbach* 264 (Thomas Bendyshe ed. & trans., 1865).

[94] *Id.* at 265.

His challenge to Blumenbach was threefold. First, Ozawa argued that Blumenbach's approach was an "abandoned scientific theory."[95] Second, according to Ozawa, Blumenbach's theory of racial "classification was ... not generally known or current in the United States in 1790."[96] Thus, there was little reason to believe that the Congress relied upon Blumenbach racial regime in passing the naturalization law. Third, Ozawa maintained that Blumenbach (among other physical anthropologists), "without going out from Europe tried to classify the people living in different climates."[97] His work was therefore substantively and methodologically flawed and should have currency in neither law nor social policy. From Ozawa's perspective, then, it would be a mistake to invoke Blumenbach to support the claim that the term "free white person" in the naturalization statute was intended to operate as a racial classification.

Ozawa's analysis did not end there. To further support the idea that the term "free white person" was non-racial, Ozawa compared that term to another: "any white person." He explicated the difference between these two terms by invoking, of all things, white eggs:

> Whenever we speak of white eggs, we mean the eggs having white shells. Hence the term "white" does not indicate any quality of eggs. It only designates the color of eggs. On the other hand, when we speak of "fresh white eggs" we mean newly laid eggs. A white eggs [sic] may or may not be fresh. But a fresh white egg must always be fresh, that is, of good quality.... Similarly, in the expression, "White Persons," the word "white" designates the color of the person, but not quality.[98]

The gist of Ozawa's argument was that the "true intent" of Congress in employing the term "free white person" was to make the content of a person's character—one's worthiness, not one's race—relevant for the purposes of naturalization. He argued that the term "free white person" was not synonymous with the racial category "Caucasian." Quoting Madison, Ozawa maintained that the fundamental criterion for naturalization was whether a person was " 'worthy of mankind.' "[99] According to Ozawa, the claim that only people of European descent are "worthy of mankind" was both under- and overinclusive:

---

[95] Brief, *supra* note 58, at 19.

[96] *Id.*

[97] *Id.* at 18.

[98] *Id.* at 6–7.

[99] *Id.* at 20.

General Benedict Arnold was of European descent of a good family, but he became a traitor. Hence he was a person not wanted. On the other hand, Booker Washington was a poor black slave and was of African descent; but he had done a great deal of good to the United States, by uplifting the standard of his race.... Hence he was the person wanted by our founders.[100]

What distinguished these two cases, Ozawa reasoned, was not race but character.

It should not be surprising that Ozawa turned to Booker T. Washington to make an argument about character. One can only surmise the degree to which Ozawa was familiar with Washington's political life and social philosophy. However, given Ozawa's self-presentation as industrious, hard working, and committed to American values, it made perfect sense for him to invoke Booker T. Washington to make an argument about race and character. On several occasions, Washington publicly spoke out against the mistreatment of Japanese people. For example, in his address to the Fourth American Peace Conference, he expressed puzzlement at the fact that Americans would "humiliate" and "degrade" people of Japanese descent for practicing "our methods of industry and civilization."[101] The mistreatment of the Japanese, he argued, was "unworthy of our civilization."[102] In other contexts, Washington praised the Japanese and suggested that blacks could learn from the way in which these newcomers had made the most of opportunities in America. "The Japanese race," Washington noted, "is a convincing example of the respect which the world gives to a race that can put brains and commercial activity into the development of the resources of a country."[103]

That Washington would conceive of the Japanese in this way did not go without saying. There was a real concern within the black community that Japanese workers would replace black labor. For some blacks this generated feelings of "scorn."[104] But for Washington, the threat of

---

[100] *Id.* at 20–21.

[101] Booker T. Washington, *Address at the Fourth American Peace Conference* (May 1, 1913), *in* 12 Booker T. Washington, *The Booker T. Washington Papers* 146, at 146 (Louis R. Harlan & Raymond W. Smock eds., 1982).

[102] Washington, *supra* note 101, at 176.

[103] Booker T. Washington, *Putting the Most Into Life* 33 (1906).

[104] Arnold Shankman, *Ambivalent Friends: Afro–American Views of the Immigrant* 38 (1982). This is not to say that blacks as a whole were against Japanese immigration. It might be fairer to say that they were somewhat ambivalent. Blacks were concerned about black economic opportunities (which engendered a certain level of resentment about Japanese immigration) and about the racialization of immigration policy to delimit Chinese and Japanese immigration (which engendered a certain level of sympathy). *See generally*

immigrant labor—white and non-white—recommitted him to the idea of racial uplift: "hard work, acquisition of manual skills, establishment of small businesses and farms, and frugality; in short by pulling oneself up by the bootstraps."[105] For Washington, the success of immigrants in the face of economic hardship portended the success of African Americans. In an address to the Negro Business League in Chicago in 1912, Washington observed that "[i]f the Italians and Greeks can come into this country strangers to our language and civilization and within a few years gain wealth and independence by trading in fruits, the Negro could do the same."[106]

Significantly, Ozawa's discussion of Washington was not the only way in which blackness figured into his argument that the fundamental test for naturalization was character, not race. Blackness was also a part of a more specific claim about statutory interpretation. At the center of this claim was a question about the word "free": Why did "free" remain a part of the term "free white person" when the naturalization statute was amended after the Civil War to make people of African descent eligible for naturalization? If "free" was intended to function solely as a racial restraint on naturalization, there was no point in reproducing the term in the post-slavery amendment. For Ozawa, the explanation was obvious: The fact that "Congress did not strike out the term 'Free' from the law ... prove[s] that it was not used to exclude only *slave black or white*,"[107] but rather, the term "free" was used to exclude people with bad character.

Ozawa advanced a similar argument with respect to the Chinese. According to Ozawa, Congress did not intend to prevent Chinese naturalization under the 1790 naturalization statute. Instead, almost 100 years later, Congress had to pass the Exclusion Act, a *"special law prohibiting particular nationalities from naturalization."*[108] This Act would not have been necessary if the 1790 law already foreclosed the Chinese from becoming citizens. The passage of the Chinese Exclusion Act, like the term "free" in the amended naturalization statute, suggested to Ozawa that the chief purpose of the naturalization regime was not to draw racial lines but to screen out undesirables.

David J. Hellwig, *Afro-American Reactions to the Japanese and the Anti-Japanese Movement, 1906–1924*, 38 Phylon 93 (1977).

[105] David J. Hellwig, *Building a Black Nation: The Role of Immigrants in the Thought and Rhetoric of Booker T. Washington*, 31 Miss. Q. 538, 548 (1978) (characterizing Washington's racial ideology).

[106] *Id.* at 540.

[107] Brief, *supra* note 58, at 7.

[108] *Id.*

Needless to say, Ozawa did not conceive of himself as an undesirable. On the contrary, he maintained that he was precisely the kind of person that America should desire. "I neither drink liquor of any kind, nor smoke, nor play cards, nor gamble nor associate with any improper persons. My honesty and industriousness are well known among my Japanese and American acquaintances and friends."[109] From Ozawa's perspective, his "good character" and respectable living rendered him a "free white" person within the meaning of the naturalization statute.

This analysis also extended to people of Japanese descent more generally. They were free white people as well.[110] Indeed, according to Ozawa, "the only argument against the fitness of the Japanese for naturalization is their non-assimilability," an argument Ozawa considered "preposterous."[111] After all, the Japanese "have the greatest capacity for adaptation," so much so in fact that "[i]n art and literature, the criticism of the Japanese today is of abandonment of their ideas, and too easy adaptation of western methods."[112] Americans could not have it both ways, Ozawa implicitly suggested. That is, they could not, on the one hand, assert that the Japanese were "imitators" of culture, and, on the other, claim that they were "not capable of adapting ... to our civilization."[113]

Ozawa drew on empirical evidence to demonstrate the extent of Japanese assimilation. He argued that Japanese people had a low crime rate (their "convictions are chiefly, like the Chinese, for gambling"[114]), they ran productive and successful businesses,[115] and they did not degrade labor by working for lower wages than whites.[116] Moreover, Japanese people "have high ideals of honor, of duty, of patriotism, of family life."[117] For Ozawa, the foregoing constituted irrefutable evidence that the Japanese were assimilable.

Still, Ozawa was careful not to argue that the Japanese had fully assimilated. Not only would such an argument have been difficult to sustain as a factual matter, but from Ozawa's perspective, there were at

---

[109] *Id.* at 4.

[110] *Id.* at 15.

[111] *Id.* at 27.

[112] *Id.*

[113] *Id.*

[114] *Id.* at 28.

[115] *Id.*

[116] *Id.* at 27–28.

[117] *Id.* at 27.

least two good reasons why one should not expect complete assimilation. The first reason related to racism, as illustrated by state antimiscegenation laws directed at the Japanese. Some people had argued that the extent of same-race marriages within the Japanese community was evidence that Japanese people had no interest in assimilating. According to one commentator:

> There can be no effective assimilation of Japanese without intermarriage.... The laws of some states forbid such marriages, but even where such marriages are permitted and even encouraged, the Japanese themselves will not take advantage thereof. That is best demonstrated in Hawai'i where there is a great commingling of races; but the Japanese, comprising nearly half of the entire population of the Territory, and steadily increasing in number, maintain a wonderful degree of racial purity.[118]

Ozawa was aware of the currency of these claims and responded by invoking discrimination. His basic contention was that racial discrimination caused a certain degree of racial insularity.

The relationship between discrimination and insularity could cut two ways. Ozawa saw racism as mitigating the significance of Japanese insularity. Twenty years later, however, the Supreme Court justified procedures for internment during World War II by citing racial isolation. Even if this isolation was in part due to discrimination, the Court saw it as a factor that the government could legitimately invoke to raise concerns about loyalty: To the extent that the Japanese had been mistreated in law and society, it would be rational for them to be disloyal.[119] Perhaps Ozawa anticipated this line of argument. For while he employed racism to explain the extent of intraracial marriages within the Japanese community, he also wanted to be clear that, notwithstanding racism, Japanese people "do intermarry with whites, and the almost uniform testimony is that they have happy families and vigorous progeny, *preeminently American.*"[120] Still, his broader point was that the existence of racial discrimination made some degree of non-assimilation inevitable.

Ozawa offered a second reason why the Japanese might not assimilate completely, namely, the fact that at least some cultural practices, "particularly ... [with respect to] the women, are superior to our own."[121] Ozawa was not convinced that America's interests were served

---

[118] V.S. McClatchy, *Japanese in the Melting Pot: Can They Assimilate and Make Good Citizens?* 93 Annals Am. Acad. Pol. & Soc. Sci. 29 (1921).

[119] *See* Hirabayashi v. United States, 320 U.S. 81, 96–97 (1943).

[120] Brief, *supra* note 58, at 27 (emphasis added).

[121] *Id.*

by requiring Japanese people to give up these "superior" cultural attributes. Importantly, in employing the language of superiority, Ozawa was not suggesting that the Japanese were infallible: "Of course, they have race prejudice."[122] But so does America: "How about our treatment of the black man in the south, or the Oriental in the west?"[123] Moreover, the Jews were prejudiced as well, Ozawa argued, and to a greater extent than the Japanese. Japanese racial prejudices "are nothing compared with that of the Jew," Ozawa insisted, and "we gladly welcome and protect [the Jews] even in foreign lands." What was more, Jews "sit[] in the halls of Congress, in our highest courts, amongst our executives, in the marts of trade."[124] For Ozawa, it proved too much to invoke prejudice within the Japanese community as a basis for denying naturalization to people of Japanese descent. One's eligibility for naturalization should not turn simply on "[r]ace prejudice [which] will always exist,"[125] but on overall character and worthiness.

White by Contrast: The Japanese Are White Because They Are Neither Black Nor Chinese

Ozawa understood that in order to persuade a court that the Japanese were eligible for naturalization, he had to articulate a theory of whiteness. Assuming that "free" in the expression "free white person" went to character, a fundamental question remained: What was the signification of the word "white"? At first blush, Ozawa's answer appeared simple: The term "white" referred to people who were not black. Because the Japanese were not black, they necessarily were white. Ozawa supported this argument by referring to various state constitutions containing language which defined whiteness as the absence of a certain quantum of "African blood." Those provisions "sufficiently prove that the term 'White person' were [sic] used to include all persons other than black people."[126]

However, Ozawa understood that the rules of racial categorization were more complicated than that. Consider, for example, the Chinese. Were they black? If the answer was no, did their non-black identity, like the non-black identity of the Japanese, render them white? This would have been a difficult argument for Ozawa to make, not only because of the passage of the 1882 Chinese Exclusion Act, but also because of a California case with which Ozawa was presumably familiar and which the Supreme Court would subsequently cite in adjudicating Ozawa's

---

[122] *Id.*

[123] *Id.*

[124] *Id.*

[125] *Id.* at 28.

[126] *Id.* at 15.

case: *People v. Hall*.[127] In that case, George W. Hall, a white man, was accused of murdering Ling Sing, a Chinese man. After a four-day trial, the jury found Hall guilty of murder and sentenced him to be hanged. Hall appealed his conviction, arguing that the trial court committed error when it permitted a Chinese witness to testify against him. A state law provided, in relevant part, that "No Black, or Mulatto person, or Indian, shall be allowed to give evidence in favor of, or against a white man."[128] The government argued that, because the Chinese were not explicitly mentioned in the statute and because the Chinese were neither black nor mulatto nor Indian, the trial court properly admitted the testimony of the Chinese witness.

Writing for the California Supreme Court, Justice Hugh Murray disagreed. He found that (at least for the purposes of "our Constitutions and laws") the Chinese were black because they were not white. Underwriting Justice Murray's approach was the idea that the term "black" is both a specific identity (referring to the "American Negro") and a generic identity (referring to people who are not white). "The word 'Black' may include all Negros, but the term 'Negro' does not include all Black persons."[129] More generally, "we understand [the term 'Black'] to mean the opposite of 'White,' and that it should be taken as contradistinguished from all White persons."[130] Under this analysis, the Chinese were black.

Importantly, this argument about Chinese blackness was different from claims about the "negroization of the Chinese"—that is, arguments that, in terms of moral worthiness, intellectual capacity, and social behavior, people of Chinese descent were like people of African descent.[131] While images of the "Negroid Chinese" circulated in California newspapers in the mid- to late nineteenth century, the California Supreme Court did not explicitly trade on them. Its argument that the Chinese are black was not based on a comparative racial analysis, but on a generic understanding of blackness.

The court's generic approach to racial categorization did not stop at the borders of blackness; it extended to the category "Indian" as well. It, too, was "to be regarded as [a] generic term[]."[132] In this respect, the

---

[127] 4 Cal. 399 (1854).

[128] *Id.* at 399.

[129] *Id.* at 403.

[130] *Id.*

[131] Dan Caldwell, *The Negroization of the Chinese Stereotype in California*, 53 S. Cal. Q. 123 (1971).

[132] 4 Cal. at 402. The court advanced two additional arguments that the Chinese were Indian. According to the Court, when Christopher "Columbus first landed upon the shores

Chinese were not only black, they were also Indian. The court reasoned that its "generic" approach to racial categorization was necessary to avoid "the most anomalous consequences . . . The European white man who comes here would not be shielded from the testimony of the degraded and demoralized caste, while the Negro, fresh from the Coast of Africa, or the Indian of Patagonia, the Kanaka, South Sea Islander, or New Hollander, would be admitted, upon their arrival, to testify against white citizens in our courts of law."[133] For the California Supreme Court, there was "no doubt" that the Chinese were not white.[134]

Nor was the non-white racial identity of the Chinese in doubt to the Congress that passed the Exclusion Act. Ozawa understood this. Thus, he knew that he could not sustain a claim that the Chinese were white because they were not black. He had to modify his theory of whiteness accordingly. And so he did. His argument that people who are not black are white contained an important proviso: the Chinese. This proviso was rooted in a more general principle, the thrust of which went something like the following: To the extent that the government expressly indicated in case law or a statute that a particular non-black identity was not white, members of that group lacked the racial standing to claim white identity. Ozawa explained that this principle described the racial bind of the Chinese: "in 1882, Congress made a *special* law against the Chinese."[135] Ozawa referred to the Chinese Exclusion Act as a "special law" in part because he perceived it as a departure from the general rule that people who are not black are white.[136] But for the passage of this "special law," the Chinese could credibly claim whiteness. In fact, drawing on a

---

of this continent, in his attempt to discover a western passage to the Indies, he imagined that he had accomplished the object of his expedition, and that the Island of San Salvador was one of those Islands of the Chinese Sea, lying near the extremity of India. . . . Acting upon this hypothesis, and also perhaps from the similarity of features and physical conformation, he gave to the Islanders the name of Indians, which appellation was universally adopted, and extended to the aboriginals of the New World, as well as Asia." *Id.* at 400. "From that time, down to a very recent period the American Indians and the Mongolian, or Asiatic, were regarded as the same type of human species." *Id.* According to Justice Murray, the Chinese were Indian for another reason—both the Chinese and Native Americans were Mongolians. He based this claim both on the "similarity of the skull and pelvis" and on the overall physical appearance "of the two races." *Id.* at 401.

[133] *Id.* at 402.

[134] "There can be no doubt that as to the intention of the Legislature, and that if it had ever been anticipated that this class of people were not embraced in the prohibition, then such specific words would have been employed as would have put the matter beyond any possible controversy." *Id.* at 405.

[135] Brief, *supra* note 58, at 7 (emphasis added).

[136] Ozawa also focused on the Chinese Exclusion Act to make an argument that the term "Free White Person" in the naturalization statute was not intended to exclude any race from naturalization. *Id.*

1911 edition of Century Dictionary, Ozawa noted that the Chinese were within one of the four categories of the white race—"Chinese—Yellowish White."[137] However, the passage of the Exclusion Act superseded this categorization.

The Japanese were differently situated. Unlike the Chinese, there was "not a law against any Japanese [barring them] from naturalization."[138] Ozawa explicitly argued that "until any special law be made against Japanese as it was made against the Chinese, all good Japanese who are faithful to the United States ought to be admitted under the existing law."[139] At the core of this analysis was the notion that to be black or Chinese was to be non-white. Accordingly, the Japanese were white not only because they were not black; they were also white (and hence eligible for citizenship) because they were not Chinese.

White on the Outside: "Yellowish White" and the "Transparent Pink Tint" (But There Are No Real White Persons As Such)

Ozawa expressly argued that, in terms of color, the Japanese are at least as white as the Chinese—"Yellowish White"—which, as mentioned above, was one of the recognized categories of whiteness along with "Armenian—Pale White," "German—Florid or Rose," and "Italian—Brownish White."[140] But many Japanese were whiter than the "Yellowish white" baseline. For example, "[t]hose who live in central and northern part of Japan are much whiter than some of so-called white person [sic] in Hawai'i."[141]

Ozawa's argument that the Japanese were phenotypically white occupied even more rhetorical space in his brief to the Supreme Court. There, he observed that "[i]n general, the Japanese are lighter than other Asiatics, not rarely showing the transparent pink tint which whites assume as their own privilege."[142] Furthermore, "[l]adies of distinction who seldom go out without being covered are perfectly white."[143] Ozawa enlisted the foregoing descriptions of the Japanese body to suggest that the category "white" could not and should not be limited to people of European descent.

---

[137] Id. at 15.

[138] Id.

[139] Id. at 16.

[140] Id. at 15.

[141] Id. at 17.

[142] Supreme Court Brief, in Consulate General of Japan, Documentary History of Law Cases Affecting Japanese in the United States, 1916–1924, at 43 (1978 prtg., 1925).

[143] Id. at 45.

At the same time, Ozawa argued that "there is not an absolutely white person existing on this earth."[144] This argument was both a descriptive and a theoretical claim. The descriptive claim was that, in a literal sense, there were no white (or yellow) people. Indeed, Ozawa suggested that because no one "existing on this earth" is literally white, "all so-called white persons must be, in fact, are more or less colored persons."[145]

Ozawa went on to point out that a person's color was a function of geography. Ozawa first considered people in Hawai'i, his new home. They "are becoming either darker or more brown than they were when they came here."[146] He then turned to the Jews. According to Ozawa, their physical embodiment was also determined by geography. "[T]he bulk of the Jews who have lived for centuries in Asia present predominently [sic] an Asian physical type. And European Jews are mostly of the anthropological type met with among European race."[147] For Ozawa, this proved not only that the Jews were not a race, but also that neither white people nor yellow people existed as such.[148]

At this point, Ozawa already had moved from a descriptive to a theoretical argument—that racial categories "are not stable." Drawing on the work of an academic, he argued that "[r]ace in the present state of thing [sic] is an abstract conception, a notion of continuity in discontinuity, of unity in diversity. It is the rehabitation of a real but directly inattainable thing."[149] For Ozawa, the fact that race was both unattainable and indeterminate rendered it an impractical basis for naturalization. The Japanese, he argued, "are composed of many races.... Among Japanese we will find many Europeans naturalized or born."[150] Race-based naturalization laws could not manage these and other identity complexities.

One cannot help but wonder whether Ozawa had read Dean John Wigmore's 1894 *American Law Review* article on "American Naturalization and the Japanese."[151] Wigmore's point of departure was an argu-

---

[144] *Id.* at 15.

[145] *Id.*.

[146] *Id.* at 16.

[147] *Id.*

[148] *Id.*

[149] *Id.* at 15.

[150] *Id.* at 17.

[151] John Wigmore, *American Naturalization and the Japanese*, 28 Am L. Rev. 818 (1894).

ment that, for the most part, Americans were not resistant to Japanese naturalization:

> We may assume that no American is disposed to refuse to admit members of the Japanese nation to citizenship with us. That we should deliberately propose to rank as inferior to ourselves and unworthy of incorporation in our political society the members of a people to whom we and the whole civilized world have in the past quarter of a century become indebted for so much, implies an attitude of inflated conceit and ignorant prejudice of which there are no indications.[152]

While Ozawa did not expressly advance this particular claim, his arguments about the Chinese, about whiteness as a non-black identity, about the role of color in racial determinations, about the unmanageability of the category "white," and about the cultural contributions of the Japanese track several arguments that Wigmore advanced in his article. This is not to say that Ozawa's brief merely reproduced Wigmore's article. It assuredly did not. In fact, Ozawa's analysis departed from Wigmore's in two significant respects. First, Ozawa did not racially differentiate the Chinese from the Japanese. Wigmore spent considerable time doing exactly that. Indeed, one of his central claims was that "the Japanese nation has racially nothing to do with the Chinese."[153] Second, whereas Wigmore drew on modern anthropology to argue that "the term 'white' may properly be applied to the ethnical composition of the Japanese race,"[154] Ozawa's brief was suspicious if not critical of (even though to some extent it relied upon) racial designations based on science.

Of course, we can not know for sure whether Ozawa in fact read Wigmore's article. Yet it would be surprising if in the many hours he spent in the Supreme Court Library in the Judiciary Building researching American naturalization laws he did not encounter this work.[155] At any rate, whatever the sources of Ozawa's arguments, they faced an uncertain reception in the federal courts. Ozawa's first hurdle was district court judge Charles Clemons.

Judge Clemons's Naturalization Quiz: Who Cannot be Naturalized?

Although we know very little about Judge Clemons, what we do know is that he was no stranger to the issue of naturalization. Indeed, the very year he issued his opinion, he published "What An Applicant

---

[152] *Id.*

[153] *Id.* at 824.

[154] *Id.* at 827.

[155] Kimura, *supra* note 49, at 53.

For Naturalization Should Know About Our Government: A Quiz on the Constitution of the United States, with a Few Questions on American History" in a pamphlet circulated by the Citizenship Education Committee of the Young Men's Christian Association of Honolulu.[156] Clemons's quiz contained questions that bore specifically on the naturalization process. The most relevant for our purposes was one that asked: "Who cannot be naturalized?" Expressed in eight subparts, the answer included:

> (5) The Chinese
>
> (6) Those not included within the following classes: (a) "White Persons," (b) "aliens of African nativity and persons of African descent," or (c) "persons not citizens who owe permanent allegiance to the United States and (are) residents of any State or organized territory of the United States." The class (c) has been held to include Filipinos and Porto [sic] Ricans and people of our other insular possessions.[157]

What did these answers portend for Japanese generally and Ozawa specifically? Neither subpart 5 nor subpart 6 specifically mentioned the Japanese. Would Judge Clemons rule that, with respect to naturalization, the Japanese and the Chinese had the same racial standing because they were members of the same racial group? Alternatively, would he conclude that the Japanese were white? Or would Judge Clemons simply focus on the particularities of Ozawa's case—the extent to which Ozawa had internalized and practiced American cultural values and social norms—to grant Ozawa's petition for naturalization, without reaching the larger question of the appropriate categorization of the Japanese? The answer lies within his district court opinion.

The District Court Opinion: The Legal Product of Yellow

After briefly reciting the facts of the case and particularly highlighting the extent and nature of Ozawa's assimilation, Judge Clemons framed the central question as whether the term "free white person" in the naturalization statute extended to people of Japanese descent. Relying on precedent and a number of racial treatises, Judge Clemons concluded that the Japanese were yellow, not white. Importantly, while Clemons spent little time on the questions of character that dominated

---

[156] Charles F. Clemons, *What an Applicant for Naturalization Should Know About Our Government: A Quiz on the Constitution of the United States, with a few Questions on American History* (1916). The pamphlet set forth questions on and answers to both American history and basic features of America's constitutional democracy: "Who discovered America, and when?" "What is the birthday of the American nation?" "How is the right to vote protected?" "How is freedom secured from class distinctions such as prevail in Europe, for instance?" "In what ways may a bill become a law?" "What is the Supreme Law of the Land?" *Id.* at 3–5, 7, 9.

[157] *Id.* at 12.

Ozawa's brief, he made clear that his interpretation of the term "white" did not carry with it notions of superiority or inferiority. "Intelligent men, of course, agree with Dr. [William Elliott Griffis, a social scientist who had studied the Japanese] that the words 'Mongolian' and 'Oriental,' as mere epithets, can bear no sense of unworthiness or inferiority in the case of the Japanese people."[158] Furthermore, Clemons reasoned, worthiness as such was not the test for naturalization, as Ozawa had argued at length,[159] because Congress always understood "free" to be "the opposite of 'slave,' " not an expression of character.[160] For Clemons, both "free" and "white" were racialized terms. This was the way courts had construed them and Congress had at least implicitly "acquiesced in and adopted the interpretation that the courts had put upon its work."[161]

Judge Clemons's conclusion that race not character was the test for naturalization did not answer the question of whether Ozawa was naturalizable. Was Ozawa of the right—which is to say, white—race? To answer this question, Clemons had to engage Ozawa's claim that he was white because he was not Chinese and because no federal statute had formally racially classified the Japanese as non-white.

Judge Clemons's rejection of this claim was twofold. First, he argued that yellow or Oriental was a broad category to which both the Chinese and the Japanese belonged. Put another way, yellow transcended the boundaries of Chinese identity. Second, he repudiated the reasoning of *In re Halladjian*.[162] In that case, Judge [Francis Cabot] Lowell had to decide whether Armenians were white. Lowell answered the question in the affirmative. He argued that the statutory meaning of the term "white" was broad, referring not exclusively to the "European" or "white" race, but covering as well "substantially all the people of Asia."[163] He reached this conclusion in part by reasoning that "the word 'white' had been used in colonial practice, in the federal statutes, and in the publications of the government to designate persons not otherwise classified."[164] Because Armenians were not otherwise classified, they were, under Lowell's formulation, white.

---

158 *In re* Ozawa, No. 274 (D. Haw. 1916) *reprinted in* Appendix of Brief for the United States at 53, Ozawa v. United States, 260 U.S. 178 (1922) (No. 1) [hereinafter *District Court Opinion*] (emphasis added).

159 *Id.* at 40.

160 *Id.* at 55.

161 *Id.*

162 174 F. 834 (D. Mass. 1909).

163 *Id.*

164 *Id.* at 843. Recall that Ozawa made precisely the same claim. *See* Brief, *supra* note 58, at 7.

Judge Clemons was not persuaded by Lowell's analysis, which seemed to affirm Ozawa's argument that the Japanese were white. Clemons found that Judge Lowell placed too much reliance on the use of the words "white" and "black" in early census materials when those "classes" were virtually the only ones present in the colonies with the exception of natives.[165] Judge Clemons then went on to note that even Judge Lowell admitted that "when the Oriental population, as represented first by the Chinese, came to be appreciable" in the late 1800s, "the word 'white' ceased to be used as a catchall to designate those people."[166]

According to Judge Clemons, other cases supported the finding that the statutory meaning of white was more limited than Ozawa maintained. Consider, for example, the Supreme Court's 1884 decision, *Elk v. Wilkins*.[167] There, the Court held that Indians were ineligible to naturalize because they were not white.[168] Clemons further noted that in *Dred Scott*, Justice Roger Taney suggested that " 'Congress might ... have authorized the naturalization of Indians, because they were aliens and foreigners.' "[169] Rhetorically, Judge Clemons asked: "If Indians were excepted [from naturalization], then why not also races of the Orient, who though since found to be more adaptable to our manners and customs, were in earlier days regarded as strange peoples, of manners and customs incompatible with ours."[170]

Clemons then proceeded through a number of precedents and legal treatises that narrowly construed the statutory meaning of "white." First, Clemons cited Chancellor Kent's Commentaries: " 'The act of Congress confines the description of aliens capable of naturalization to 'free white persons.' ... Perhaps there might be difficulties ... as to the [classification of] ... the yellow or tawny races of the Asiatics, and it may well be doubted whether any of them are 'white persons' within the purview of the law.' "[171] Next, Clemons turned to dictum from *People v. Hall*: "the word 'white' has a distinct signification, which ex vitermini

---

[165] *District Court Opinion, supra* note 158, at 41 (emphasis added).

[166] *Id.* at 41.

[167] 112 U.S. 94 (1884).

[168] *Id.* at 104 ("Since the ratification of the Fourteenth Amendment, Congress has passed several acts for naturalizing Indians of certain tribes, which would have been superfluous if they were, or might become, without any action of the government, citizens of the United States.").

[169] *District Court Opinion, supra* note 158, at 42 (quoting Scott v. Sandford, 60 U.S. 393, 420 (1856)).

[170] *Id.*

[171] *Id.* at 43 (emphasis added).

excludes black, yellow, and all other colors."[172] Under the racial logic of *Hall*, the Japanese were yellow and, therefore, could not be white.

Clemons got the most mileage out of a long citation from the very first naturalization case, *In re Ah Yup*, where Circuit Judge Lorenzo Sawyer relied on a number of racial treatises to support the proposition that notwithstanding the literal vagueness of white person "those words ... have undoubtedly acquired a well-settled meaning in common popular speech, and ... are constantly used in the sense so acquired in the literature of the country, as well as in common parlance ... [to mean] a person of the Caucasian race."[173] Judge Sawyer's *Ah Yup* opinion concluded that Congress evidently did not intend to include in the term "white person" anyone other than individuals of the Caucasian race; moreover, Sawyer found "much in the proceedings of Congress to show that it was universally understood in that body ... that [white] excluded Mongolian."[174] To substantiate the claim that people of Japanese descent were excluded from the category "white," Sawyer relied on various racial taxonomies of the time.[175] In no ethnological division, Sawyer argued, was the "Mongolian" included in the term "white."[176] Judge Sawyer's analysis persuaded Judge Clemons that the Japanese like the Chinese were ineligible for naturalization.

Still, Judge Clemons understood that he had to respond directly to the claim Ozawa advanced about the significance of the Chinese Exclusion Act. Recall that Ozawa maintained that the Act's passage argued in favor of—not against—granting naturalization to the Japanese. His thinking was twofold: (1) that had Congress intended to prohibit Japanese naturalization, it would have done so expressly and (2) that Congress passed the Exclusion Act precisely because the naturalization act itself did not prevent Chinese naturalization.

Judge Clemons disagreed with both claims. First, Clemons emphasized the fact that *Ah Yup*, a case in which the court was clear that people of Chinese descent were ineligible for naturalization, was decided several years *before* the passage of the Exclusion Act. Thus, even without the Exclusion Act, the judiciary already had indicated that the Chinese were not free white persons. Second, according to Judge Clemons, the promulgation of racial classifications (such as the Exclusion Act) that specifically identified the Chinese was due to their growth in the population and not to the fact that, prior to those classifications, Chinese

---

[172] *Id.* at 44 (quoting People v. Hall, 4 Cal. 399, 403, 404 (1854)).

[173] *Id.* (quoting *In re* Ah Yup, 1 F.Cas. 223 (D. Cal. 1878)).

[174] *In re* Ah Yup, 1 F.Cas. 223, 224 (D. Cal. 1878).

[175] *Id.* at 223–24.

[176] *Id.* at 224.

people were considered white. The implication of this reasoning for the Japanese was clear: The absence of legislation that explicitly mentioned people of Japanese descent did not mean that the Japanese were white, but rather that they were not yet sufficiently numerous to justify separate racial attention.

Judge Clemons further supported his narrow interpretation of "white" by turning to a number of cases that specifically focused on the Japanese. In *In re Saito*, for example, Circuit Judge LeBaron Colt ruled expressly on the eligibility of the Japanese for citizenship.[177] According to Colt, the legislative history of the naturalization statute showed that "Congress refused to eliminate the word 'white' from the statute for the reason that it would extend the privilege of naturalization to the Mongolian race, and that when, through inadvertence, this word was left out of the statute it was again restored for the very purpose of such exclusion."[178] At least three other cases were in accord.[179] Against this backdrop, Judge Clemons argued that "no reported case is known in which a person of the Japanese race has been naturalized, in which the court has rendered a written opinion to justify its ruling."[180] For Judge Clemons, the fact that about fifty people had previously "been naturalized by State and Federal Courts" was insufficient to overcome these precedents.[181]

Clemons could have stopped there. He went on, however, to reject Ozawa's claim that the Japanese were as white as some European groups, so that the concept of whiteness was itself ambiguous and unreliable. The district court distinguished cases in which courts reasoned that the naturalization statute should be construed in light of recent developments rather than solely from the perspective of the framers' original intent.[182] As Clemons explained, "the decisions just referred to were dealing with border-line cases of races closely related to

---

[177] 62 F. 126 (D. Mass. 1894).

[178] *Id.* at 127.

[179] *In re* Buntaro Kumagai, 163 F. 922, 924 (W.D. Wash. 1908) (reserving the privilege of naturalization for "those of that race which is predominant in this country"); *In re* Knight, 171 F. 299 (D. N.Y. 1909) (denying naturalization to a person of both Japanese and Chinese ancestry based on the argument that neither Japanese nor Chinese were eligible for naturalization); and Bessho v. United States, 178 F. 245 (4th Cir. 1910) (expressly holding that the Japanese are ineligible for citizenship).

[180] *District Court Opinion, supra* note 158, at 48.

[181] *Id.* at 43.

[182] *See, e.g.*, Dow v. United States, 226 F. 145 (4th Cir. 1915); *In re* Mudarri, 176 F. 465 (D. Mass. 1910); and *In re* Sakharan Ganesh Pandit (cited in *District Court Opinion, supra* note 158, at 48).

what may be loosely called the 'European.' "[183] He reasoned that none of those cases involved people of Japanese descent. Why? The answer Clemons provided was that the ethnological divisions classifying the Japanese as "Mongolian or yellow race" guided both the 1875 legislature which adopted the revised statutes as well as the courts that interpreted it.

Clemons then proceeded to discuss a number of other ethnological and anthropological authorities to support his racial theory. His analysis began with Blumenbach and, more particularly, with Ozawa's challenge to his taxonomy: "Even if, as the petitioner contends, Blumenbach's classification is unscientific ... nevertheless, it has not yet been super- seded so far as to assimilate the Japanese with what for many years ... and especially before 1875, has been generally regarded as the 'white' race."[184] Next, Clemons looked to Tylor's "Anthropology" (1881) and the Encyclopedia Brittanica (11th ed., 1910) for the classification of the Japanese as Mongolian.[185] To make clear that the Japanese need not be "pure" Mongolian to be non-white, Clemons cited Captain F. Brinkley's "A History of the Japanese People" in which Brinkley noted that while there was "an element of white, Caucasian or Iranian, blood" in the Japanese, the Japanese were "essentially of the same race" as the Chinese and the Koreans.[186]

Presumably to bolster his argument that the Japanese were not white, Judge Clemons invoked the work of a "Japanese educator," Okabura Yoshisaburo, who published "The Life and Thought of Japan" in 1913.[187] Importantly, as cited by Clemons, Yoshisaburo's work itself reflected a nationalist, racist ideology of Japanese superiority by describ- ing the early Chinese and Korean immigrants to Japan as "swarms" that "lost their own identity" in an effort to assimilate to a presumptive- ly superior Japanese culture and people.[188] Although Yoshisaburo de- scribed "two distinct racial face types among the present Japanese," he cautioned readers to "remember[] ... that both these types are Mon- gol."[189] According to Judge Clemons, "[w]hether these [Okabura's] views

---

[183] *District Court Opinion, supra* note 158, at 48–49.

[184] *Id.* at 49.

[185] *Id.*

[186] *Id.* at 50 (quoting F. Brinkley, *A History of the Japanese People from the Earliest Times to the End of the Meiji Era* (1915)).

[187] *District Court Opinion, supra* note 158, at 50.

[188] *Id.* (quoting Okabura Yoshisaburo, *The Life and Thought of Japan* (1913)).

[189] *Id.* at 51 (quoting Yoshisaburo, *supra* note 188).

just quoted are wholly accurate or not, I do not undertake to say. They are at all events in line with the statements of scientific works."[190]

Finally, Clemons turned to Dr. Griffis's work on "The Japanese Nation in Evolution." Clemons began by observing the length to which Griffis went "to demonstrate ... that 'the Japanese people are not Mongolian.' "[191] However, Judge Clemons concluded that despite Griffis's belief that the "basic stock of the Japanese is Aino" ("a white race"), his findings ultimately support the proposition that the Japanese are not "white."[192] According to Clemons, Griffis had acknowledged the presence of "the Mongolian element" in people of Japanese descent. Further, Griffis described the Aino people (and thus presumably the "presence" of Aino "blood" in the "Japanese stock") as having been "crowded out."[193]

At this point, Judge Clemons was one analytical move away from delivering his holding. But, before doing so, he distinguished "the Magyars of Hungary and ... the very dark Portuguese, who are both freely admitted to citizenship, in spite of the fact that the former are Mongolic in origin and that the latter are in a strict sense of the word not 'white.' "[194] In the course of this discussion, Clemons cited *In re Mudarri*,[195] another opinion by Judge Lowell whose *Halladjian* decision the district court had roundly criticized. For Judge Lowell as for Ozawa, the entire system of racial classification came close to foundering on an absurdity: "Hardly anyone classifies any human race as white ... classification by ethnological race is almost or quite impossible."[196]

Judge Clemons, however, viewed Lowell's *Mudarri* opinion skeptically. Relying again on the *Encyclopedia Britannica* and *Webster's Dictionary*, Clemons argued: "Centuries before our first legislation on naturalization, the Magyars had 'become physically assimilated to the western peoples.' "[197] Then somewhat summarily, Judge Clemons found that the Magyars "have long been 'one of the dominant people of Hungary' ... and they, with the Portuguese ... are within the meaning of 'white,' as

---

[190] *District Court Opinion, supra* note 158, at 51.

[191] *Id.* (quoting William Elliot Griffis, *The Japanese Nation in Evolution: Steps in the Progress of Great People* (1907)).

[192] *District Court Opinion, supra* note 158, at 52.

[193] *Id.*

[194] *Id.* at 53.

[195] 176 F. 465 (D. Mass. 1910).

[196] *Id.* at 467.

[197] *District Court Opinion, supra* note 158, at 54.

commonly understood."[198] And that was that. Notwithstanding some non-white pedigree, the Magyars were white because they had "physically assimilated to the western peoples."[199] The Japanese had not performed that "physical assimilation," which, presumably, was to be distinguished from the cultural assimilation Ozawa described in his brief. In a seemingly conciliatory gesture, Judge Clemons was willing to concede that there might be some uncertainty as to the meaning of the word "white." But the remedy for that "lies, of course, with the legislative body."[200]

Judge Clemons was now ready to conclude. He ended, rather abruptly, this way: "the court finds that the petitioner is not qualified under Revised Statutes, section 2169, and must therefore deny his petition; and it is so ordered, in spite of the finding hereby made that he has fully established the allegations of his petition, and, except as to the requirements of section 2169, is in every way eminently qualified under the statutes to become an American citizen."[201] Conspicuously absent from this conclusion were the terms white and yellow. It was, however, precisely because Ozawa was the latter and not the former that he was outside of the racial borders of American citizenship.

Postscript: *Judge Clemons's Final Words*

Judge Clemons's opinion was not his last word on the matter. Subsequent to deciding the case, he wrote to the United States attorney of Hawai'i indicating that "[i]n my opinion in the Ozawa case, I might have added to the citation of Kent's Commentaries for the meaning of the word 'white', as understood early in the last century, the following from Francis Lieber's 'Legal and Political hermeneutics.' "[202] According to Lieber "everyone knows [white] is used to indicate the decendants [sic] of the Caucasian race, whose blood has remained unmixed with that of Negroes, Indians or that of any other colored race. The provision cannot be invalidated by the objection that no really white people exist."[203] It was Judge Clemons's view that "Doctor Lieber's international eminence as a jurist gives great weight to this as an authority in support of my decision."[204]

---

[198] *Id.*

[199] *Id.*

[200] *Id.* at 55.

[201] *Id.* at 55–6.

[202] Letter from Charles F. Clemons, United States District Court Judge, to S.C. Hunber, United States Attorney for Hawai'i (Aug. 31, 1917) (on file with author).

[203] *Id.*

[204] *Id.*

None of this is to say that Judge Clemons was unsympathetic to Ozawa's case. "It is indeed a pity," Clemons was reported to have said, "that a man so eminently qualified, morally and intellectually, may not become one of us. I cannot speak too highly of the briefs he has prepared. They evidence more originality, more thoughtfulness than many of the briefs of members of the bar."[205] There is reason to believe that Judge Clemons was not being disingenuous. In an op-ed "inspired by the Ozawa case" entitled "Race Lines and Colorlines," Clemons argued that "it is absurd ... that a man must be either 'white' or 'of African nativity' ... in order to become a naturalized citizen. And it is absurd, because there is really no such thing as a 'white' person."[206]

For Clemons, the legal predicament Ozawa found himself in was at least in part a function of the fact that the Japanese were misunderstood. In this sense, "[i]t is a good thing for this Territory to have one of her own native people, or at least one of largely Hawaiian blood, as delegate to Congress, in order to educate the people of the mainland States to the fact that the native Hawaiians are not like the aborigines of Africa or the wild men of some of the Pacific isles."[207] Quite apart from this misunderstanding was the unmanageability of the naturalization regime. Because, according to Clemons, America was "so mixed racially ... the statutory rule of eligibility to citizenship by naturalization [was] unworkable."[208] This was not a problem that Judges could fix, however. "The remedy for this anomaly lies with Congress."[209] And there was no good reason why Congress should "delay[] the radical cure of this international ill. How hypocritical so much prating about the 'international mind,' while retaining so much prejudice against mere radical 'color' as such!"[210]

From Individual Struggle to Group Rights

Judge Clemons's adverse ruling did not end Ozawa's quest to become naturalized. He was determined to push on. What Ozawa could not have known was that his efforts would intersect with a broader political struggle within the Japanese community to advance members' civil rights. Arguments against Japanese naturalization figured into anti-Japanese agitation as early as the 1900s, but the issue did not come to a

---

[205] Knaefler, *supra* note 52.

[206] Charles Clemons, Editorial, *Race Lines and Color Lines: An Editorial Inspired by the Ozawa Case*, Honolulu Star–Bull. (date unknown) (copy on file with author).

[207] *Id.*

[208] *Id.*

[209] *Id.*

[210] *Id.*

head until the San Francisco school board affair. The resulting controversy prompted President Roosevelt to urge Congress to pass legislation
granting naturalization rights to the Japanese. Whether this proposal
was an empty diplomatic gesture or an authentic demand for change,
Roosevelt's "Gentleman's Agreement" with Japan ultimately settled the
problem with the school board but left the question of naturalization
unresolved. Efforts on the part of immigrant newspapers such as the
Nichibei Shimbun and the *Shin Sekai* to keep the issue alive were
largely unsuccessful. Even the Japanese Association of America failed to
prioritize Japanese naturalization. While the JAA explicitly made the
right to naturalization a part of its organizational mission, ultimately
the matter was "referred . . . to a study committee where it languished
from want of action."[211]

It was not until 1913, after California passed the Alien Land Law of
1913, which, among other things, prevented Japanese from purchasing
agricultural land, that Japanese naturalization became a significant
political issue for leaders within the Japanese community.[212] Although
the law contained a number of loopholes,[213] it remained an assault on the
civil rights and dignity of the Japanese community. Because the prohibition applied to "aliens ineligible for citizenship," the right to naturalize
was the solution. On this point, there was consensus among Japanese
newspapers, community leaders, and organizations. The difficult question was how to push for naturalization rights. At least three options
were available: first, wait for Japanese diplomats to take the initiative on
behalf of their nationals in the United States; second, "lobby for Congressional legislation" allowing them to be naturalized; and third, secure
the right to naturalize through litigation in the Supreme Court in order
to "get a final judicial ruling regarding their eligibility under existing
statutes."[214] The last choice seemed most likely to get a favorable result

---

[211] Ichioka, *supra* note 85, at 5.

[212] Laws aimed at limiting or denying land ownership by Japanese immigrants were
first debated by the California Legislature in 1907. Takaki, *supra* note 19, at 203. The bill
introduced during this session was reintroduced over a period of several years and was
finally adopted in 1913 by an overwhelming majority. While the law was facially neutral
with respect to the Japanese, supporters of the legislation openly acknowledged its
intended object. Under its terms, real property acquired by "aliens ineligible to citizenship" would escheat to the State following a successful escheat action brought by the state
Attorney General. The law also limited leasehold arrangements to periods of not more than
three years. *Id.* Similar laws were enacted in many western states as well as states
reaching as far east and north as Louisiana and Minnesota, respectively. *Id.* at 206–07.

[213] These loopholes allowed "aliens ineligible to citizenship": to place lands in trust for
their American born children; form corporations holding land; hold property in the names
of American born relatives; and renew leases after the maximum three-year period ended.
Id. at 205.

[214] Ichioka, *supra* note 85, at 7–8.

because it did not hinge on either "the initiative of Japanese diplomats or on the state of American public opinion."[215]

The founding of the Pacific Coast Japanese Association's Deliberative Council in July 1914 played an important role in advancing the Japanese community's interest in naturalization. The organization functioned as the "higher coordinating organ" of the central bodies of all other Japanese associations. It "embrac[ed] at least all immigrants on the Pacific Coast and in the western states," plus Canada.[216] The Deliberative Council made clear, during its very first meeting, that its fundamental aim was to solve the naturalization problem, resolving that: "Whereas, recognizing the present urgency of solving the naturalization question, be it hereby resolved that a test case be instituted at an appropriate time in pursuit of the just legal goal of acquiring the right of naturalization for the Japanese."[217]

Politically and legally, Ozawa's case presented a real opportunity to pursue the issue. From a political standpoint, Ozawa was fully assimilated and his "character was beyond reproach."[218] To put the point slightly differently, Ozawa was as racially palatable as a person of Japanese descent could hope to be. Anti-Japanese agitators would be hard-pressed to attribute the "funny ways of the Japanese" to him. From a legal standpoint, "Ozawa fulfilled all the nonracial requirements for naturalization set by the Act of 1906."[219] In particular, an immigrant who wanted to naturalize had to file a petition of intent at least two years before filing a formal application—Ozawa had filed his petition of intent twelve years prior. Additionally, he met the requirements of five years of continuous residency, moral fitness, and knowledge of the English language.

At the district court level, Ozawa had represented himself without any backing from Japanese organizations or civic leaders. His quest for naturalization was a personal one, an individual struggle to become in law what he maintained he was in life—an American. But things were about to change. When Ozawa decided to appeal his case to the Ninth Circuit Court of Appeals, he hired David L. Withington as his counsel. The appeal received a fair amount of attention in the press—at the precise moment that the Deliberative Council determined to look for a test case. So extensive was the press coverage that Ozawa's daughter recalls wondering: "Ooh. What did he do? . . . I was kind of ashamed [of

---

[215] *Id.*

[216] *Id.* at 9–10.

[217] *Id.* at 10.

[218] *Id.* at 10–11.

[219] *Id.* at 11.

all the media attention]."[220] Part of this media frenzy included immigrant newspapers urging the Deliberative Council to support the case, arguing that the civil rights of the entire Japanese community were at stake.[221]

The Council discussed Ozawa's appeal in August 1916 but chose not to pursue it. Then, on May 31, 1917, the Ninth Circuit referred the case to the Supreme Court. Two months later, the Deliberative Council voted unanimously to assist Ozawa and appointed a four-man naturalization committee to plan a strategy. The committee kept Ozawa's attorney but made clear that it was important to retain as principal counsel "a man familiar with the procedure of the Supreme Court and one who is recognized as a leader in his profession."[222] George W. Wickersham fit the bill. As the former U.S. Attorney General, Wickersham had meaningful Supreme Court litigation experience. Moreover, as a past president of the Japan Society and Chairman of the National Committee on American–Japanese Relations, he had relationships with several leaders within the Japanese community. After the Committee agreed to Wickersham's $1000 retainer, Wickersham joined Ozawa's litigation team.[223]

Significantly, the naturalization committee decided to pursue Ozawa's litigation despite the fact that "Japanese diplomats were opposed unalterably to the Ozawa case," which meant that the Council could not depend on the Japanese government for help.[224] From the Japanese government's perspective, the timing was simply not right; America was not ready to grant Japanese the right to naturalize. Rather than pursue the matter in courts, the Japanese government thought it best to engage in an aggressive public relations campaign, one that would make Americans better understand Japan as a nation and the Japanese immigrants residing in the States as a community.

At the same time, for political and diplomatic reasons, the federal government did not want the Supreme Court to issue an opinion. Indeed, Secretary of State Robert Lansing urged Solicitor General John W. Davis to delay the case until the end of the First World War. "Japan and the United States are co-belligerents in the present war, in which, as you know, Japan has given and is giving consistent and essential assistance

---

[220] *Race: The Power of an Illusion, supra,* note 72.

[221] Ichioka, *supra* note 85, at 13.

[222] Letter from Kanzaki Kiichi to David L.Withington, Attorney for Ozawa (Aug. 7, 1917) (on file with author).

[223] Letter from Kanzaki Kiichi to George W. Wickersham, Attorney for Ozawa (July 22, 1918) (on file with author).

[224] Ichioka, *supra* note 85, at 13–14.

to the common cause," wrote Lansing in a letter dated June 3, 1918.[225] When Solicitor General Alex King took over the case, he wrote to the Secretary of State on February 3, 1919, to confirm the government's interest in delaying the litigation:

> From the correspondence in the files I understand that last summer it was not the desire of the State Department nor the Japanese Embassy to have the case argued at the then approaching term of the Supreme Court; also that the Embassy had endeavored to bring some pressure upon the applicant to delay or abandon the case but that this had been unsuccessful.

> The Supreme Court will be in recess from today, February 3, until March 3, and this case will probably be reached within a week after the court reconvenes. I would be glad to be advised whether the State Department still thinks the argument of this in the Supreme Court and a decision from that tribunal undesirable under existing conditions.

> I do not know that a postponement can be obtained, but it will be my desire to carry out the wishes of your Department in this matter as far as I properly can.[226]

Although the end of the war resolved one set of diplomatic concerns, it introduced another: America's interest in managing Japan's growing military power, especially its influence in the Far East. The worry was that a definitive answer from the Supreme Court on the question of Japanese naturalization would complicate arms control negotiations that were scheduled to take place in November 1921.[227]

While Ozawa's litigation team may not have been surprised by the American and the Japanese government's interest in delaying (if not derailing) the litigation, they may have been surprised by the opposition from a former ally: *Nichibei Shimbun,* which lodged a legal objection based on a Supreme Court decision handed down after the Council decided to take over the case. In *United States v. Morena,*[228] the Court upheld the constitutionality of a procedural provision of the 1906 act requiring that the petition of intent to naturalize be filed no less than

---

[225] Letter from Robert Lansing, United States Secretary of State, to John W. Davis, United States Solicitor General (June 3, 1918) (on file with author). "Moreover," Lansing continued, "the Japanese land question in California, which aroused considerable feeling in Japan, has not been definitely settled, and would, I fear, be opened, or at least a public discussion of it renewed if the Takao Ozawa case were argued in the Supreme Court." *Id.*

[226] Letter from Alex C. King, United States Solicitor General, to Robert Lansing, United States Secretary of State (Feb. 3, 1919) (on file with author).

[227] *Id.*

[228] 245 U.S. 392 (1918).

two years, but no more than seven years, prior to the official petition to naturalize. Because Ozawa had waited twelve years, the act presented a potential procedural obstacle to his case. Ozawa was determined to go forward, however. He made clear that he was not going to withdraw his petition. According to Ozawa, "I have filed my petition in conformity with [the] law in force at the date of my petition, and I consider it absolutely unjust to dismiss my case without a hearing on account of the Moreno [sic] case."[229]

But withdrawal and postponement were not the same thing. Wickersham thought it best to take the procedural issue seriously. He advised the committee to defer the case temporarily out of a concern that the Court would declare Ozawa's case moot (that is, not a live case or controversy) because it failed to meet the requirement set forth in *Morena*.[230] Following this advice, Ototaka Yamaoka, the head of the committee, looked for a second test case and found Takuji Yamashita and Hyosaburo Kono, two Japanese men who had been naturalized in 1902 in Washington. When they filed articles of incorporation to form a real estate company in 1921, the Secretary of State refused to accept them "on the grounds that the two men had not been naturalized legally and were unable consequently to form such a company under the laws of the state."[231] The Washington Supreme Court declined to issue a writ of mandate to compel the acceptance of the articles of incorporation, so Yamashita and Kono appealed to the U.S. Supreme Court.[232] The case was brought as a companion case to *Ozawa* to expedite review. The moment Ozawa had been waiting for was now a little more than a year away. In November 1922, Ozawa would have his answer from the Supreme Court—and so would the rest of America: People of Japanese descent were not "free white persons" and therefore were ineligible for naturalization.

The Supreme Court Litigation

Justice Taft and His Court

At the time that Ozawa's case was heard, William Howard Taft was the Chief Justice of the United States Supreme Court. In this sense, *Ozawa* is a part of the Taft Court's legacy. Any "discussion of ... [this]

---

[229] Letter from Takao Ozawa to Gerorge W. Wickersham, Attorney for Ozawa (Jan. 10, 1921) (on file with author).

[230] Letter from George W, Wickersham, Attorney for Ozawa, to Kanzaki Kiichi (Oct. 31, 1918) (on file with author). Wickersham believed that the Supreme Court would declare "the legal questions moot."

[231] Ichioka, *supra* note 85, at 16.

[232] Yamashita v. Hinkle, 260 U.S. 199 (1922).

legacy must begin with ... Taft [himself]."[233] Because "[o]n the great constitutional questions of his day, ... Taft displayed a generally consistent conservatism,"[234] his appointment as Chief Justice and the subsequent appointments of Justices Pierce Butler, Edward T. Sanford and George Sutherland, who would write the *Ozawa* opinion, created within the Court an "insurmountable conservative majority" at a time when "conservative Republicans were safely in control of the executive and legislative branches of the federal government."[235] A strong believer in the Court's exercise of political discretion,[236] Taft's influence over the Court's jurisprudence during his tenure as Chief justice was undeniable.

The Taft Court was comfortable engaging in judicial activism.[237] According to Alpheus Mason, "Taft considered the shaping of law to meet new situations the Court's 'highest and most useful function.' "[238] The Taft Court therefore has been characterized as a "Super-legislature."[239] One need only look at the number of federal laws and state statutes invalidated by the Court (twelve and 131, respectively) to see this judicial philosophy at work.[240] Taft also was suspicious of challenges to precedents. Mason notes that he harbored and "adhered to his conviction that sanctity of the judicial process is best preserved by maintenance of a line of judicial precedents against challenge by both court and legislature."[241] While sometimes deferential to the "right of

---

[233] Peter Renstrom, *The Taft Court: Justices, Rulings, and Legacy* 183 (ABC–Clio, 2003). According to Renstrom, Taft "dominated his Court for most of the decade," and "wrote almost 20% of his Court's opinions." *Id.* at 184, 186. Other scholars have noted, however, that "[p]itifully few of Taft's more than 250 opinions have survived as living presences in the Law." Robert Post, *William Howard Taft*, in *The Supreme Court Justices: A Biographical Dictionary* 460 (Melvin I. Urofsky, ed., 1994). However, because of his active role in buttressing the nominations of politically like-minded, conservative candidates after his appointment to the Court, Taft had an enormous influence on the composition of the Court itself. Renstrom, *supra*, at 187.

[234] *Supreme Court Justices: A Biographical Dictionary* 277 (Timothy L. Hall ed., 2001). This is not to say that this conservatism brought anything new to the table: Renstrom characterizes the Court prior to Taft's arrival as "already a conservative tribunal." Renstrom, *supra* note 232, at 183. Taft's appointment, he posits, "reinforced this conservatism." *Id.*

[235] Renstrom, *supra* note 233, at 183. The author also notes that this "had the effect of marginalizing Holmes and Brandeis in cases in which the court was not unanimous." *Id.*

[236] *Id.* at 185.

[237] *Id.* at 187.

[238] Alpheus Thomas Mason, *The Supreme Court from Taft to Burger* 48 (1979).

[239] *Id.* at 40–73 (using a term employed by Brandeis in Jay Burns Baking Co. v. Bryan, 264 U.S. 504, 534 (1924)).

[240] Renstrom, *supra* note 233, at 187.

[241] Mason, *supra* note 238, at 53.

Congress to define the scope of its own power and to choose the means of carrying out its express powers into execution,"[242] his belief in the limits of national power was deeply rooted.[243]

"Taft's absorbing ambition was ... to 'mass' the Court."[244] He brought a degree of collegiality to the Court, and "pressed hard for unanimity."[245] In this respect, perhaps it is not surprising that there were no dissents in *Ozawa*. Among others, Justices Louis Brandeis and Oliver Wendell Holmes joined the unanimous opinion of the newly appointed Justice Sutherland.

Sutherland was himself an immigrant to this country. Born in England, he arrived in Springville, Utah at the age of one after his father and perhaps mother had converted to Mormonism.[246] Like Ozawa, Sutherland's life was marked by hard work and accomplishment. Having left school at the age of twelve to earn a living, Sutherland entered Brigham Young Academy in 1879 "entirely as a result of his own industry and frugality."[247]

Prior to his appointment to the bench, Sutherland's career was largely in politics. This career provided some clues to the decision he would ultimately reach in *Ozawa*. In 1900, Sutherland won Utah's single congressional seat. Before leaving for the capital, Sutherland gave an interview in which he discussed his likely stance on issues of interest to his constituency. Notably, Sutherland was committed to the extension of the Chinese Exclusion Act and to nativist economic protections: "The Chinese laborers, who would naturally come to this country would be brought into unhealthy competition with our own laborers. We already have one race problem in the South with the negroes, and to open our doors to the unrestricted immigration of Mongolians would be to invite another and more serious race problem into the West." [248]

Despite the comments in this interview, Sutherland mostly focused on laissez faire policies while in Congress. By the time he reached the Court, his conservative philosophy of government was well-entrenched and ultimately earned him his appointment and record-speed confirma-

---

[242] *Id*. at 58–59.

[243] See Bailey v. Drexel Furniture Co., 259 U.S. 20 (1922) (invalidating a burdensome tax on the employment children imposed to end child labor as an impermissible exercise of legislative power under the Tenth Amendment).

[244] Mason, *supra* note 238, at 60.

[245] *Id*. at 61.

[246] *Id*. at 3.

[247] *Id*. at 5.

[248] *Id*. at 41.

tion to the Court.[249] After losing his Senate seat in 1916, Sutherland maintained his ties with Republican party officials. He served as a confidential advisor to Warren Harding during his presidential campaign in 1920. Although one scholar refers to Harding as "the man who is universally regarded as [the presidency's] crassest failure,"[250] Sutherland's close relationship with Harding was fortuitous. On September 5, 1922, one day after Justice John Clarke withdrew from the bench, Harding nominated his friend to the Court; that same day Sutherland was affirmed by the Senate.

During his sixteen years on the bench, Sutherland drew on his earlier commitment to laissez faire policies to become the intellectual leader of a group of conservative Justices who consistently overturned social welfare legislation.[251] *Ozawa*, however, was one of Sutherland's first opinions. After having been put on hold for several years, arguments in the case were finally held on October 3 and 4, 1922, less than two weeks after Sutherland arrived at the Court.[252] Though his conservative politics up to this point were clearly developed, there was little on record to indicate the nature of his jurisprudence. In particular, prior to *Ozawa*, there was almost nothing to suggest his likely take on issues of race and naturalization.[253]

Sutherland's Opinion for the Supreme Court: White Skin, White Mask

Justice Sutherland began his opinion by sketching a brief biography of Ozawa, whom he described as "a person of the Japanese race born in Japan." He then moved on to engage the central question the case presented: Whether Ozawa was "a free white person" within the meaning of the naturalization statute. Answering the question in the negative, Sutherland concluded that Ozawa was ineligible for naturalization.

Like Judge Clemons, Sutherland rejected the claim that the 1790 naturalization statute was "employed for the *sole* purpose of excluding

---

[249] Joel Francis Paschal, *Mr. Justice Sutherland: A Man Against the State* 87–100 (1951).

[250] Henry J. Abraham, *Justices and Presidents: A Political History of Appointments to the Supreme Court* 185 (3d ed. Oxford University Press 1992).

[251] *Id.* at 189.

[252] *See* Ozawa v. U.S., 260 U.S. 178 (1922).

[253] Sutherland's later opinions were decidedly unfriendly to immigrants. Although people of Asian ancestry were most frequently the victims of Sutherland's brand of strict statutory interpretation, they were not alone. *See, e.g.,* United States v. Mcintosh, 283 U.S. 605 (1931) (Canadian émigré). That said, Asians were most frequently the subject of Sutherland's alien and naturalization opinions. *See, e.g.,* Chung Fook v. White, 264 U.S. 443 (1924) (denying eligibility for citizenship to wife of native-born Chinese).

black or African race and the Indians then inhabiting th[e] country."[254]
For Sutherland, the key issue was not one of exclusion but one of
inclusion:

> The provision is not that Negroes and Indians shall be excluded, but
> it is, in effect, that only free white persons shall be included. The
> intention was to confer the privilege of citizenship to that class of
> persons whom the fathers knew as white, and to deny it to all who
> could not be so classified.[255]

Sutherland's claim that being white was the test for naturalization still
begged a crucial question: What were the criteria for determining who is
white? According to Sutherland, "[m]anifestly, the test afforded by the
mere color of the skin of each individual is impractical, as that differs
greatly among persons of the same race."[256] This was true, Sutherland
reasoned, even of the "Anglo–Saxon," whose skin color ranges "from the
fair blond to the swarthy brunette, the latter being darker than many of
the lighter hued persons of the brown or yellow races."[257] In this sense,
one could be dark in color and white in terms of race—and white in color
and dark in terms of race. A test based on skin color therefore would
produce "a confused overlapping of races."[258] Moreover, it could function
to mask a person's "true" racial identity.

But if skin color was an unreliable guide to whiteness, did a
workable standard exist? A careful reading of Justice Sutherland's
opinion reveals three interrelated formulations.

> Formulation 1: "[t]he words 'white person' were meant to indicate
> only a person of what is popularly known as the Caucasian race."[259]
> Here, Sutherland is relying both on science (by employing the term
> "Caucasian") and common knowledge (by employing the expression
> "popularly known as").

> Formulation 2: "The determination that the words 'white person'
> are synonymous with the words 'a person of the Caucasian race'
> simplifies the problem, although it does not entirely dispose of it."[260]
> Here, Sutherland seems to be suggesting that there are potential

---

[254] 260 U.S. 178, 195 (1922) (emphasis added).

[255] *Id.*

[256] *Id.* at 197.

[257] *Id.*

[258] *Id.*

[259] *Id.*

[260] *Id.* at 198.

pitfalls that will arise from equating the terms "Caucasian" and "white."

Formulation 3: "The effect of the conclusion that the words 'white person' means a Caucasian is not to establish a sharp line of demarcation between those who are entitled and those who are not entitled to naturalization, but rather a zone of more or less debatable ground outside of which, upon the one hand, are those clearly eligible, and outside of which, upon the other hand, are those clearly ineligible for citizenship. Individual cases falling within this zone must be determined as they arise from time to time by what this court has called, in another connection, 'the gradual process of judicial inclusion and exclusion.' "[261] Here, Sutherland makes clear that the fact that equating "white" with "Caucasian" does not create a definitive line for ascertaining who is and is not eligible for naturalization; it creates "a zone of more or less debatable ground."[262] According to Sutherland, some cases are clear, though he does not explain why. Ozawa's is one of these: he "is clearly of a race which is not Caucasian and therefore belongs entirely outside the zone on the negative side."[263]

There is some slippage from the first formulation to the third. As I will show, paying attention to this slippage is crucial to understanding the relationship among race, science and common knowledge not only in *Ozawa*, but in the only other naturalization case to reach the Supreme Court, *United States v. Thind*. Decided in 1923, a few months after Ozawa, *Thind* is an important part of *Ozawa's* aftermath—as is *Webb v. O'Brien*, an Alien Land law case litigated that very year.[264]

Ozawa's Aftermath: Ineligible for Citizenship and Property

Ironically, the *Ozawa* case not only cemented the racialized identity of the Japanese but also subjected them to exclusionary treatment under purportedly race-neutral provisions. California's Alien Land Laws offer a particularly instructive example of the decision's pernicious effects. Recall that as early as 1907, the California legislature discussed the propriety and feasibility of passing legislation restricting the rights of people of Japanese ancestry to own land; six years later the legislature

---

[261] *Id.* (citing Davidson v. New Orleans, 96 U.S. 97, 104 (1877)).

[262] *Id.*

[263] *Id.*

[264] 263 U.S. 313 (1923).

passed such a bill, prohibiting "aliens ineligible for citizenship" from owning real property in California.[265]

In two ways, these laws are an important part of *Ozawa's* constitutional history. First, but for the existence of a race-based naturalization regime, the regulatory effect of the Alien Land Laws on people of Japanese ancestry would have been minimal. Had the Supreme Court rendered people of Japanese ancestry "aliens *eligible* for citizenship," they would have been beyond the reach of these purportedly race-neutral restrictions. Second, one year after deciding *Ozawa*, the Supreme Court, in *Webb v. O'Brien*[266] upheld the Alien Land Laws. Together, these rulings locked Japanese people out of an aspect of formal citizenship (naturalization) and one of citizenship's crucial social markers (property). In the absence of these exclusions, the project of internment—which came more than twenty years later and which might itself be understood as a dispossession of both citizenship and property—would have been more difficult to sustain—ideologically, politically, and jurisprudentially.

The *Ozawa* decision also laid the foundation for a narrow definition of whiteness. During the same year that the Court upheld the Alien Land Laws, it decided the case of *United States v. Thind*.[267] Dr. Bhagat Singh Thind was born in the Punjab region of India on October 3, 1892 into a Sikh community. In August 1912, shortly before his twentieth birthday, Thind left India for the United States, where he hoped to become a spiritual teacher. Like Ozawa, he attended the University of California at Berkeley, working during the summers to pay for his education. When World War I started, he joined the United States Army and fought honorably until his discharge in 1918. He applied for U.S. citizenship in 1920 in Oregon, and the district court granted his petition. The Bureau of Naturalization appealed to the Ninth Circuit Court of Appeals.[268] As with Ozawa's case, the Ninth Circuit sent the case to the Supreme Court with the following question: "Is a high-caste Hindu, of full Indian blood, born at Amritsar, Punjab, India, a white person?"[269] This "question presented" could not have been more racially loaded.

Thind's oral argument was scheduled to take place on January 11, 1923, roughly two months after the Supreme Court decided Ozawa's case. According to Ian Haney López,

---

[265] Act of May 19, 1913 (California Alien Land Law), ch. 113, §§ 1–8, 1913 Cal. Stat. 206–208 (1913). This act was intended both as a punitive measure and to limit the extent to which Japanese could farm their own land.

[266] 263 U.S. 313 (1923).

[267] 261 U.S. 204 (1923).

[268] Public Broadcasting System, *Bhagat Singh Thind* (2000), *available at* http://www.pbs.org/rootsinthesand/i_bhagat1.html.

[269] 261 U.S. at 206.

It must have seemed to Thind that he could not lose, for the Supreme Court itself had made Caucasian status the test for whether one was White, and every major anthropological study classified Asian Indians as Caucasians. In addition to the apparent precedential value of Ozawa, four lower courts had specifically ruled that Asian Indians were White, while only one had held to the contrary. Moreover, Thind was a veteran of the U.S. Army, and though he had served only six months, he perhaps thought that his service to the country, as well as the congressional decision to make citizenship available to those who had served in the military for three years, might favorably affect his case.[270]

But the "precedential value" of *Ozawa* was far from decisive in granting Thind's petition. True, Sutherland equated Caucasian with white, but he made clear that, in terms of eligibility for naturalization, there was "a zone of more or less debatable ground," not "a sharp line of demarcation."

Nothing in *Ozawa* suggested that Asian Indians were "clearly eligible" for naturalization. Indeed, one could reach just the opposite conclusion if by white Sutherland meant "what is *popularly known* as Caucasian" and by "popularly known" he meant common knowledge or broad public consciousness. Thind, of course, saw things differently. From his perspective, *Ozawa* had opened the door to Asian Indian whiteness by relying on scientific classification schemes. These schemes had excluded the Japanese from the racial class of "Caucasian," but had included Asian Indians in that category. Thind believed that the Court would treat these scientific racial taxonomies as binding in defining whiteness; from his perspective, that was precisely what the Court had done in *Ozawa*.[271]

Sutherland, however, was not persuaded. He made clear that *Ozawa* had not treated "Caucasian" and "white" as synonymous terms: "[A]s ... pointed out [in *Ozawa*], the conclusion that the phrase 'white persons' and the word 'Caucasian' are synonymous does not end the matter. It enabled us to dispose of the problem as it was there presented, since the applicant for citizenship clearly fell outside the zone of debatable ground on the negative side; but the decision still left the question to be dealt with, in doubtful and different cases, by the 'process of judicial inclusion and exclusion.' "[272] For Sutherland, Thind's application was one of those "doubtful and different cases."

---

[270] Haney López, *supra* note 1, at 88.

[271] See Devon W. Carbado, *Racial Naturalization*, 57 Am. Q. 633 (2005) (discussing Giorgio Agamben's notion of "bare life" and how it relates to inclusive exclusions).

[272] 261 U.S. at 208.

Significantly, Thind presented a "doubtful and different case" not only in terms of the bottom-line question of whether he was eligible for naturalization, but also in terms of whether he was Caucasian—in the strict scientific classificatory sense. According to Sutherland:

> [T]he term "race" is one which, for the practical purposes of the statute, must be applied to a group of living persons now possessing in common the requisite characteristics, not to groups of persons who are supposed to be or really are descended from some remote, common ancestor, but who, whether they both resemble him to a greater or less extent, have, at any rate, ceased altogether to resemble one another. It may be true that the blond Scandinavian and the brown Hindu have a common ancestor in the dim reaches of antiquity, but the average man knows perfectly well that there are unmistakable and profound differences between them to-day; and it is not impossible, if that common ancestor could be materialized in the flesh, we should discover that he was himself sufficiently differentiated from both of his descendants to preclude his racial classification with either.[273]

Although Ozawa had contended in his brief that racial taxonomies were unreliable, Sutherland did not credit this point until formal science appeared to be at loggerheads with the racial conclusion he sought to reach: that Asian Indians were not white. As he wrote, "[t]he various [scientific] authorities are in irreconcilable disagreement as to what constitutes a proper racial division."[274] He then added that:

> It may be, therefore, that a given group cannot be properly assigned to any of the enumerated grand racial divisions. The type may have been so changed by intermixture of blood as to justify an intermediate classification. Something very like this has actually taken place in India. Thus, in Hindustan and Berar there was such an intermixture of the "Aryan" invader with the darkskinned Dravidian.

> In the Punjab and Rajputana, while the invaders seem to have met with more success in the effort to preserve their racial purity, intermarriages did occur producing an intermingling of the two and destroying to a greater or less degree the purity of the "Aryan" blood. The rules of caste, while calculated to prevent this intermixture, seem not to have been entirely successful.

> It does not seem necessary to pursue the matter of scientific classification further.[275]

---

[273] *Id.* at 209 (emphasis added).

[274] 261 U.S. at 211–12.

[275] *Id.* at 212.

In the foregoing passages, Sutherland was not simply rejecting science. He was suggesting as well that science is a contested field in which, by some accounts, the "supposed" or "real" Caucasian roots of Asian Indians no longer grew. To put the point slightly differently, Asian Indians had intermixed their way out of their Caucasian ancestral ground.[276] Consequently, they would be unrecognized by and unrecognizable to their "common [Caucasian] ancestor."

The broader point here is that Sutherland both repudiated scientific knowledge, on the one hand, and engaged and applied it, on the other. This is reflected in the very way in which Sutherland articulates his holding: "What we now hold is that the words 'free white persons' are words of common speech, to be interpreted in accordance with the understanding of the common man, synonymous with the word 'Caucasian' only as that word is popularly understood."[277] In effect, this holding is a re-articulation of one of the ways in which he formulates whiteness in *Ozawa*: "[t]he words 'white person' were meant to indicate only a person of what is popularly known as the Caucasian race."[278] Both formulations include the term "Caucasian" and in both formulations that term is modified by a common knowledge signifier: "popularly."

Still, Sutherland understood that his holding in *Thind* begged a significant question: What precisely is "Caucasian ... popularly understood"? He concluded that common knowledge dictated that Thind was not white because "[i]t is matter of familiar observation and knowledge that the physical group characteristics of the Hindus render then readily distinguishable from the various groups of persons in this country commonly recognized as white."[279] As a result, "the great body of our people instinctively recognize [Thind's racial difference] and reject the thought of assimilation."[280]

Sutherland then linked his reliance on common knowledge to the conditions surrounding immigration to the United States at the time Congress passed the naturalization statute:

> The immigration of that day [1790] was almost exclusively from the British Isles and Northwestern Europe, whence they and their forebears had come. When they extended the privilege of American citizenship to "any alien being a free white person" it was these immigrants—bone of their bone and flesh of their flesh—and their

---

[276] Sutherland might add: assuming the historical existence of this ground.

[277] 261 U.S. at 214–15.

[278] 260 U.S. at 197.

[279] 261 U.S. at 214–15.

[280] *Id.*

kind whom they must have had affirmatively in mind. The succeeding years brought immigrants from Eastern, Southern and Middle Europe, among them the Slavs and the dark-eyed, swarthy people of Alpine and Mediterranean stock, and these were received as unquestionably akin to those already here and readily amalgamated with them. It was the descendants of these, and other immigrants of like origin, who constituted the white population of the country when section 2169, re-enacting the naturalization test of 1790, was adopted, and, there is no reason to doubt, with like intent and meaning.[281]

Because Thind was not among the Europeans who populated the country in 1790, he like Ozawa was ineligible for citizenship.

In the aftermath of the *Thind* decision, the government targeted Asian Indians for denaturalization. So aggressive was this campaign that by 1924, at least sixty Asian Indians lost their citizenship.[282] Like the Japanese and the Chinese, they became aliens ineligible for citizenship—perpetual foreigners as a matter of law.

Classification, Caste, and Critical Perspectives on Ozawa and Thind

The existing literature on *Ozawa* and *Thind* often portrays the cases as adopting inconsistent approaches to racial classification. Ian Haney López, a leading scholar on race and naturalization, contends that the Court in *Ozawa* "ran together the rationales of common knowledge, evident in the reference to what was 'popularly known' and scientific evidence, exemplified in the Court's reliance on the term 'Caucasian.' "[283] Because the Japanese were not scientifically classified as Caucasian, they could not be white under the naturalization law. He then suggests that Sutherland's conclusion that Asian Indians were not white is an about face, a "reversal"[284] because "[t]he Court in *Thind* repudiated its earlier equation in *Ozawa* of Caucasian with White."[285]

Haney López's account, though partially right, puts the point too strongly. His interpretation treats Sutherland's language in Thind's case as a concession—"albeit tangentially and without grace"—"that, as an Asian Indian, he was a 'Caucasian.' "[286] Although this is a perfectly

---

[281] *Id*. at 213–14.

[282] Haney López, *supra* note 1, at 91.

[283] *Id*., at 79.

[284] *Id*. at 92.

[285] *Id*. at 89.

[286] Haney López, *supra* note 1, at 88–89.

plausible reading, the case also can be understood as evidence of Sutherland's difficulty in grappling with the question of whether Thind was Caucasian. In Thind, Sutherland struggled to reconcile the indeterminacy and unmanageability of science ("[t]he various authorities are in irreconcilable disagreement as to what constitutes a proper racial division"[287]), on the one hand, and the ostensible determinacy and manageability of common knowledge, on the other (the "racial difference" of Asian Indians "is of such character and extent that the great body of our people instinctively recognize it."[288]). To resolve the conflict, Sutherland distinguished between scientific views that can be manipulated and distorted and common knowledge that offered clarity and certainty in interpreting the naturalization statute.

Read in this way, *Ozawa* and *Thind* do not present us with two Justice Sutherlands—one (in *Ozawa*) who engages racial science and another (in *Thind*) who is indifferent to or unengaged by it. Rather, in both opinions, Sutherland puts racial science to work. In *Ozawa*, Sutherland employs science to reproduce and instantiate extant racial categories; in *Thind* he draws on debates within science both to challenge the validity of racial taxonomies and to question whether, according to these taxonomies, Thind was undeniably Caucasian.

Sutherland's interest in science should not surprise us. After all, the problem of racial classification is essentially epistemological: How do we come to know what is white and what is yellow, for example, and who gets to define what these words mean? The insistence on the "popular" formulation of the "common man" and the "ordinary" sense of the word "white" assumes that the term's meaning is self-evident and readily available to the members of Congress who enacted the naturalization law. Moreover, the emphasis on popular understanding already assumes an incompatibility with scientific formulations, which presumably are less commonly known, more varied in their tests and measurement of races, and less widely agreed upon.

This dichotomy between science and common knowledge is problematic—more specifically, it is ahistorical, arbitrary, and deceptive. It is ahistorical because it ignores the socio-historical and socio-linguistic context within which white and Caucasian, as European descriptors, emerged. It was not the idea of the common man but the ideas of Blumenbach and other physical anthropologists in the nineteenth century that established once and for all different categories of people who exhibited ostensibly similar characteristics. At the same time, this emerging field of physical anthropology did not exist in a social, political, or historical vacuum. Instead, the "laws, hypotheses and theories of

---

[287] 261 U.S. at 212.

[288] *Id.* at 215.

[racial] science 'necessarily reflect[ed] in large part the general non-scientific intellectual atmosphere of the time.' "[289] Some history of science scholars would go farther, describing science as an ideology.[290] Under this view, "scientists go into their laboratories to meet the needs of society." If so, the deployment of racial science was, at least in part, an effort to make sense of and even legitimize the physical anthropologists' own social world, a world within which differences had already been hierarchically marked.[291]

Of course, difference and hierarchy do not inevitably go together, notwithstanding that, historically, they have comfortably co-existed. Thus, the fact that even before Blumenbach the common white man could recognize differences in appearance between himself and an African does not dictate that any strictly "racial" identification would follow nor that this identification would take a hierarchical form. Both consequences are socially contingent, shaped by science, common knowledge, and the interaction between the two. Understood in this way, the line between common knowledge and racial science is very much blurred because of the popularization of scientific terms and because of the role of non-scientific discourses and political projects in shaping race-based scientific inquiries.[292]

The dichotomy between science and common knowledge is arbitrary and deceptive because it obscures the fact that the project of racial classification—both inside and outside of the Supreme Court—is ultimately a normative one. Recall the popular definition of "white person" from *In re Young*, invoked in Clemons's District Court Opinion:

> As commonly understood, the expression includes all European races and those *Caucasians* belonging to the races around the Mediterranean sea, whether they are considered as *"fair whites"* or *"dark*

---

[289] D. Raghunandan, *Walking on Three Legs: Science, Common Sense, and Ideology*, 17 Soc. Scientist 92, 96 (1989) (quoting John Desmond Bernal, *Science in History* 51–52 (1969)).

[290] See Raghunandan, *supra* note 289. According to Raghunandan, science is an ideology in the sense that "the system of ideas in a society is to be understood as arising from, and acting upon, the social structure and as expressing the effort by society to understand, explain the relationship with nature and between people so as to at least sustain society as it is known." *Id.* at 96.

[291] Because science emerged in the context of a culture where "war was already a cultural pattern; political and religious conflicts were well established; the idea of exploitation was not new [and] there were already ancient prejudices, hatreds and many misconceptions about life," these phenomena formed part of the "social life that was ready to be expressed through science." L. Guy Brown, *The Social Nature of Science*, 55 Sci. Monthly 361, 365 (1942).

[292] See Michael Mulkay, *Knowledge and Utility: Implications for the Sociology of Knowledge*, 9 Soc. Stud. of Sci. 63, 64–68 (1979).

whites," as classified by Huxley, and notwithstanding that certain of the southern and eastern European races are *technically* classified as of Mongolian or Tartar origin.[293]

Clemons's very invocation of formal taxonomies to elucidate a common-sense interpretation of race belies any clear divide between scientific and popular spheres of knowledge. It is doubtful that people commonly made technical scientific distinctions between "fair" and "dark" whites or that they drew precise geographical and ethnological parameters to define the white race—save, of course, that they were educated upon these matters by technicians like Huxley. In short, the commitment to common knowledge notwithstanding, the district court's estimation is far from being purely a product of widespread popular understandings.

Moreover, the focus on a pan-European conception of whiteness in Clemons's opinion in *Ozawa* and later Sutherland's opinion in *Thind* obfuscated the extent to which Southern and Eastern Europeans were not easily folded into white identity. The same can be said of Jews— across national origin. Americans had not naturally perceived Europeans to be an undifferentiated mass of whiteness; on the contrary, the "common [American] man" made intra-European distinctions along a white/non-white axis. At different historical moments, these Europeans groups became white by law. Indeed, their exclusion and eventual assimilation have prompted numerous historical accounts of "How the Irish Became White" and "How the Jews Became White."[294] In short, contrary to the simplified accounts in *Ozawa* and *Thind*, Europeans were not always white.

In fact, then, the common knowledge test was never an empirical investigation into what the "common man" (or the Congress that promulgated the naturalization statute) thought. Nor was this test unmediated by science. Despite the formal judicial wavering between vox populi and the voice of science in *Ozawa* and *Thind*, the epistemic foundation of these two discourses remained intertextual and co-consti-

---

[293] In re Young, 198 F. 715 (W.D. Wash. 1912) (quoted in *District Court Opinion, supra* note 158, at 26).

[294] *See, e.g.,* Karen Brodkin, *How the Jews Became White Folks and What That Says about Race in America* (1998); Noel Ignatiev, *How the Irish Became White* (1995). In this respect, John Tehranian is right to challenge the manageability of the common knowledge test. *See* John Tehranian, *Performing Whiteness: Naturalization Litigation and the Construction of Racial Identity in America*, 109 Yale L.J. (2000). His sense that Sutherland's account of immigration integration into whiteness is "revisionist" is persuasive. *Id.* at 826. Less persuasive is his claim that an accurate common knowledge test would utilize color, and that because *Ozawa* and *Thind* rejected a color test, "the common knowledge test never really triumphed." *Id.* at 827. Tehranian's reasoning here elides the extent to which anxieties about various groups (and particularly blacks) passing for white led the "common man" not to over-rely on physicality as a basis for racial categorization.

tutive. That is, the validation and application of racial terms required the input—collaboration—of both the scientific community and laypersons.[295] Put another way, science was one of several "social habits" through which human nature and social organization (in this case, through racial classification), "in their interactive relationship, could become functional."[296] In truth, then, the Supreme Court's express repudiation of racial science could never be complete.

Nor could the Court's repudiation of the term "Caucasian." Consider, again, *Thind*, which, according to Haney López, marked the "end[] [of] the reign of the term 'Caucasian,' "[297] so that "[w]ith this decision, the use of scientific evidence as an arbiter of race ceased in the racial prerequisite cases."[298] I would put the point slightly differently. *Thind* invited us to read Caucasian in two ways—in a formal scientific classificatory way (which I have suggested is mediated by common knowledge) and in a popularly understood way (which I have suggested is mediated by science). *Ozawa* relied on science that was confirmed by popular understanding; because Ozawa was not "Caucasian," Sutherland easily concluded that he was not white. *Thind* invoked common knowledge that was informed by but not subservient to science. This case was more difficult, however. Because Asian Indians were categorized as Caucasian, Sutherland had to ascertain whether that categorization comported with the common understanding of "Caucasian," an inquiry that could never be cleanly disentangled from racial science.

Sutherland's reliance on "familiar" racial classificatory regimes demonstrated that the law's racial epistemology was created by a combination of scientific and common knowledge: Non-scientific people (including judges) engaged in the process of observation and knowledge-production, but depended on physical group characteristics largely overdetermined by scientific categories, theories, and terminology. Indeed, observing the body by dividing it into physical characteristics—such as hair, facial features, and skin color—was a social practice derived at least in part from science, even if not recognized as such by Sutherland.

And we can see the influence of common knowledge on scientific knowledge as well. Sutherland made clear in *Thind* that "Caucasian" was not just a scientific term; it was "a conventional term,"[299] that "in this country, during the last half century especially, the word by common usage has acquired a popular meaning, not clearly defined to be

---

[295] L. Guy Brown, *The Social Nature of Science*, 55 Sci. Monthly 361, 362 (1942).

[296] *Id.*

[297] Haney López, *supra* note 1, at 90.

[298] *Id.*

[299] 261 U.S. at 211.

sure, but sufficiently so to enable us to say that its popular as distinguished from its scientific application is of appreciably narrower scope."[300] These two understandings of "Caucasian" allow for a more coherent doctrinal connection between *Ozawa* and *Thind*. Read together, these cases set forth a test for naturalization that might be articulated this way: Being Caucasian in a formal scientific sense is a necessary but insufficient condition for naturalization. While Ozawa lacked this necessary condition, for Thind it was insufficient. In no post-*Thind* naturalization case did a court grant naturalization to a person whose origins placed him outside the scientific borders of the term "Caucasian."

This is not to say that *Thind* and *Ozawa* were thoroughly consistent with each other. They are not. Unlike *Ozawa*, *Thind*, as Haney López suggests, spent some time discrediting racial science.[301] Sutherland's discussion of the Aryan theory of race, for example, was scathing.[302] Moreover, whereas in *Ozawa* Sutherland rejected the idea of a color (and implicitly a physical difference) test for race, in *Thind* the notion of bodily difference performed significant racial work. For example, Sutherland found the Aryan theory of race problematic in part because

> [t]he term "Aryan" has to do with linguistic, and not at all with *physical, characteristics* ... Our own history has witnessed the adoption of the English tongue by millions of negroes, whose descendants can never be classified racially with the descendants of white persons, notwithstanding both may speak a common root language.[303]

It was precisely the idea that physical difference (specifically skin color) was a manageable basis upon which to make racial determinations that Sutherland had rejected in *Ozawa*. In Thind, these phenotypical distinctions become dispositive and could not be overridden by assimilation, for instance, through acquisition of a common language. The contradictions and tensions between *Ozawa* and *Thind* should not blind us to the normative and doctrinal continuity between the two cases, a continuity facilitated by the fact that both relied on (somewhat differently, to be sure) common knowledge *and* racial science, even when they expressly disavowed one or the other. Both cases evidenced a negotiation, not a hard polarization, of popular and scientific categories of racial difference.[304]

---

[300] *Id.* at 209.

[301] Haney López, *supra* note 1, at 94.

[302] 261 U.S at 210–13.

[303] *Id.* at 210–11.

[304] The debate over the respective roles of common knowledge and science in defining race does not exhaust the critical perspectives on *Ozawa* and *Thind*. For example, John

Conclusion: The Legal Construction of Race

The significance of *Ozawa v. United States* is not just that it evidences a judicial moment in which the Supreme Court employed both scientific and common knowledge to pave a racialized path to American citizenship, though noting this dynamic is important given the existing literature on the case. Nor does the significance of the case lie solely in its role in creating a broader social web of exclusion within which people of Japanese descent were caught. Another significant reason for paying attention to *Ozawa* is that it helps, particularly when discussed alongside *Thind*, to make concrete an argument critical race theorists have been advancing for more than two decades—namely, that race is a social construction and that the law plays a key role in that process.[305]

In neither *Ozawa* nor *Thind* was the Court merely reflecting on and applying a set of pre-existing criteria for racial classifications. In both cases, Justice Sutherland instantiated whiteness as a racial boundary and articulated a set of rules—about phenotype, about science, about common knowledge—that was to govern the policing of this border. These rules were not in the "nature" of things. They were socially contingent and, more particularly, the product of judicial agency. Understood in this way, Ozawa was not "naturally" non-white. His non-white identity was the effect of and endogenous to a set of juridical moves. The same, of course, is true of Bhagat Thind. These moves were never just about science. Nor were they just about common sense. The construction of whiteness in *Ozawa* and *Thind* was about both.

Ozawa remains an enormously productive resource for Critical Race Theorists. The case and its progeny are a clear window on the legal construction of race. This legal construction is not just discursive; it is also material and ontological. Which is to say: In setting forth a test for whiteness, the *Ozawa* Court helped to create both a racial category and a racial people—both a racial classification and a racial experience. By the end of Justice Sutherland's opinion Ozawa was not only non-white, he was also a non-citizen—irreducibly foreign. This race-making function of *Ozawa* is a critical part of its legacy.

*

Tehranian has argued that there is a performative element to whiteness in these cases. John Tehranian, *supra* note 294, at 820. Although I agree that this is a significant dynamic in the naturalization cases, I also believe that no amount of "dramaturgy of whiteness" would have satisfied Justice Sutherland that either Ozawa or Thind was white. In fact, after *Thind*, it seems that the performance of whiteness mattered most in evaluating the claims of individuals with some credible claim to Caucasian identity.

[305] In a forthcoming article, I offer a detailed account of the process by which race is socially constructed. Devon W. Carbado, The Phenotype/Race Distinction: Or What Exactly Is Discrimination on the Basis of Race? (draft manuscript on file with author).

7

Carole Goldberg

What's Race Got to Do With It?: The Story of *Morton v. Mancari*

Introduction

Timing is everything, so the saying goes. *Morton v. Mancari*[1] is a case in point. This lawsuit, which reached the Supreme Court in 1974, pitted a longstanding, if underenforced, preference for employment of Indians within the federal Bureau of Indian Affairs ("BIA") against federal statutory and constitutional laws prohibiting racial discrimination. At that time, the Court had yet to reach a position on the legality of affirmative action, or so-called "reverse discrimination." Eager to avoid the issue, the Court chose to characterize the BIA preference as political rather than racial. As a consequence, the Indian preference law survived, as did hundreds of other federal Indian statutes and regulations differentiating Indians from non-Indians. Had *Morton v. Mancari* been decided twenty years later, when the Court was more confidently striking down race-based affirmative action laws, the BIA's Indian preference could well have fallen, causing an abrupt shift in federal Indian policy. Instead, the 1974 Court gave Congress a relatively free hand to pursue a policy of tribal self-determination, which eventually included special opportunities for Indian gaming, contracting, and education. However, opponents of race-based affirmative action continue to view *Morton v. Mancari* as a troubling decision. And the Court's distinction between political and racial classifications still generates uncertainty and confusion, contributing to the difficulty of labeling any classification as racial.

For those who wanted the case to rest on a racial analysis of federal Indian law, there was ample fodder in earlier decisions of the United

---

[1] 417 U.S. 535 (1974).

States Supreme Court. These cases had adopted the view of Indian-ness as a natural or biological characteristic, rather than a social or political construct. For example, in its 1846 decision in *United States v. Rogers*,[2] the Court had refused to extend federal jurisdiction over reservation crimes to an offense committed on tribal land by a non-Indian who had been adopted through marriage into the Cherokee Nation. According to the Court, the statute's reference to crimes committed by Indians could refer only to individuals of a particular race. Four decades later, the Court described Indians as "a race once powerful, now weak and diminished in numbers."[3] And in 1913, in *United States v. Sandoval*,[4] the Court had ruled that the federal government's power over Indian affairs extended to tribes because of their "racial" characteristics, including intellectual and moral inferiority.

On the road to the ultimate Supreme Court holding in *Morton v. Mancari* that the BIA's classification was political rather than racial, both racial and non-racial analyses were argued and accepted at different points in the litigation. Looking back, we can see that litigants and judges in the case were grappling with three distinct theories for upholding the constitutionality of the Indian preference: 1) The classification is political rather than racial, resting on tribal membership or citizenship (the "political-not-racial" theory); 2) The classification is partly racial and partly political, but the racial part is justified because of Congress's Article I power over Indian affairs, which necessarily encompasses the power to pass laws directed at people of Indian ancestry (the "Indian Commerce Clause" theory);[5] and 3) The classification is racial, but nonetheless survives analysis under principles of equal protection (the "valid-under-equal-protection" theory). Each had its drawbacks. But these positions claim our interest not merely as a matter of abstract legal or constitutional theory: Investigating which groups and litigants supported which positions also reveals fascinating biographies and backgrounds that sometimes defy our expectations.

---

[2] 45 U.S. (4 How.) 567 (1846). *See generally* Bethany R. Berger, *"Power Over this Unfortunate Race": Race, Politics and Indian Law in* United States v. Rogers, 45 Wm. & Mary L. Rev. 1957 (2004).

[3] United States v. Kagama, 118 U.S. 375, 384 (1886).

[4] 231 U.S. 28 (1913).

[5] A much earlier decision, *Simmons v. Eagle Seelatsee*, 244 F. Supp. 808 (E.D. Wash. 1965), *aff'd*, 384 U.S. 209 (1966), had adopted a similar approach. That case had involved a federal statute that limited the inheritability of Indian trust allotments to individuals who were tribal members *and* of one-quarter or more Indian ancestry. This position is elaborated in Carole Goldberg, *American Indians and "Preferential" Treatment*, 49 UCLA L. Rev. 943, 966–74 (2002).

Origins of the Case: The BIA Is Challenged from Both Sides

Ever since 1822, when Congress transferred management of Indian affairs from the War Department to the Indian Service (later renamed the Bureau of Indian Affairs), that agency has been deeply insinuated into tribal governments and economies. In the second half of the nineteenth century, as the federal government confined Indians on reservations and destroyed their traditional means of subsistence, agents of the BIA began to designate leaders; allocate vital food supplies, so as to maximize their own control; punish traditional practices; and dictate the leasing of tribal resources to non-Indians. By the 1920s, it was evident that tribes were suffering economically and culturally from the BIA's pervasive involvement in tribal affairs. So in 1934, Congress passed the Indian Reorganization Act ("IRA"), empowering tribes to create constitutions that would shift some control from the BIA to tribally-elected officials. Nevertheless, the BIA retained a significant role, even on reservations that had opted to enact an IRA constitution. Many IRA constitutions, for example, required the approval of the BIA before any tribally-enacted law could become effective. And the BIA still had to approve all attorney contracts and any leases or other conveyances involving land held in trust by the federal government for a tribe or an individual Indian. Moreover, on many reservations the BIA provided the schools and maintained the only law enforcement presence. It was not until a few years after *Morton v. Mancari* began that Congress directed the BIA to contract out its functions to tribal governments and hand its budgets over to tribal leaders.[6]

At the time of *Morton v. Mancari*, the structure of the BIA included a central office in Washington, D.C., headed by the Commissioner of Indian Affairs; five to ten regional area offices; and "agency" offices serving individual reservations or small groups of tribes. The superintendent of each agency was typically the most powerful person on the reservation, controlling resources, a staff, and major decision-making. For example, the superintendent typically appointed the reservation police officer and Court of Indian Offenses personnel, negotiated and approved all leases of tribal land, determined whether federal funds would come to the reservation for irrigation projects or range improvement, and supervised any reservation schools for Indian children.[7]

The prominent role of the BIA, its notoriously paternalistic, bureaucratic, and inefficient methods, and its unaccountability to tribal communities made it an obvious target for Indian activists of the 1960s and early 1970s. Fueled by indigenous organizing initiatives and community

---

[6] *See* Indian Self–Determination and Education Assistance Act of 1975, 25 U.S.C. § 450 et seq.

[7] *See* Theodore W. Taylor, *The Bureau of Indian Affairs* 45–76 (1984).

mobilization programs of the War on Poverty, and borrowing strategies from the Civil Rights Movement of that era, Indian activists began to mount protest marches, sit-ins, fish-ins, and takeovers of government offices.[8] Some of these actions were symbolic, such as marches at museums and archaeological digs, while others involved direct confrontation. Though the occupation of Alcatraz Island by members of the American Indian Movement was the most spectacular protest of this latter type, it was hardly the only one.[9]

One of these less notorious sit-ins set in motion the events that led to *Morton v. Mancari*. In March 1970, members of the National Indian Youth Council ("NIYC"), a group of young, mainly urban Indians, staged a sit-in at the BIA Area Office in Denver, charging discrimination in hiring and advancement of Indian employees. All of the senior positions in that BIA office were occupied by non-Indians, and the NIYC activists charged that Indians were effectively shut out of opportunities for training and promotion. In fact, the BIA's own statistics from late 1969 revealed that Indians represented 62% of the employees in the General Schedule ("GS") grades of 4 and below, and only 17% of those in the four highest grades of 14–17.[10] The sit-in began while the Commissioner of Indian Affairs was visiting Denver, but after he left, the activists refused to leave. All of the demonstrators were arrested and tried for trespass and other offenses. Harris D. Sherman, a Colorado native who had just returned to Denver with a freshly minted degree from Columbia Law School, represented the demonstrators. It was his first jury trial, and to the activists' delight, he succeeded in securing acquittals for all of the defendants.[11]

Not long thereafter, a delegation of Indians came to meet with Sherman at his law office. They were from an organization called United Scholarship Service, led by Tillie Walker, a Mandan Indian from the Fort Berthold reservation. While they were excited about the acquittals, they

---

[8] For excellent discussions of this period, see Charles Wilkinson, *Blood Struggle: The Rise of Modern Indian Nations* (2005), and Joane Nagel, *American Indian Ethnic Renewal: Red Power and the Resurgence of Identity and Culture* (1996).

[9] *See* Joane Nagel, *American Indian Ethnic Renewal: Red Power and the Resurgence of Identity and Culture* 159–75 (1996).

[10] Answer, Exhibit E, Morton v. Mancari, 417 U.S. 535 (1974) (Nos. 73–362, 73–364). In his testimony at the *Morton v. Mancari* trial, BIA Personnel Director Raymond Gunter noted that as of 1972, 57% of the BIA's approximately 16,500 employees were Indian. At the GS–7 level and below, 76% of the employees were Indian. At the level of GS–9 and above, only 20% were Indian. Cross-Examination of Raymond Gunter by Victor Ortega, Final Hearing on the Merits, Morton v. Mancari, Nov. 29, 1972, in Appendix (Trial Record), Morton v. Mancari, 417 U.S. 535 (1974) (No. 73–362) at 191.

[11] Telephone interview with Harris Sherman, former counsel for Amerind and now Executive Director, Colorado Department of Natural Resources, Oct. 7, 2005.

wanted to discuss longer-range strategies for changing the policies and practices of the BIA. Sherman agreed to help and began researching the problem. What he turned up was a provision of the Indian Reorganization Act, dating back to the 1930s, that read as follows:

> The Secretary of the Interior is directed to establish standards of health, age, character, experience, knowledge, and ability for Indians who may be appointed, [without regard to civil service laws,] to the various positions maintained, now or hereafter, by the Indian Office, in the administration of functions or services affecting any Indian Tribe. Such qualified Indians shall hereafter have the preference to appointment to vacancies in any such positions.[12]

Under the Act, "Indians" included "all persons of Indian descent who are members of any recognized Indian tribe now under Federal jurisdiction ... [and] all other persons of one-half or more Indian blood."[13]

This preference provision in the IRA was only one manifestation of the Act's general purpose, which was to restore tribal cultures, economies, and self-government.[14] John Collier, President Franklin Roosevelt's Commissioner of Indian Affairs, had crafted and brokered this legislation because of his admiration for tribal cultures and his conviction that those cultures could flourish only if tribal land bases were protected and tribal governments empowered.[15] The IRA's Indian preference provision was not the only such federal law on the books. There were some earlier preference statutes as well, but none as mandatory and comprehensive as the one found in the IRA.[16] Indeed, inadequate implementation of those earlier laws was one of the reasons why the IRA provision was so categorical. As Senator Peter Norbeck stated during hearings on the bill that became the IRA, "I think we have utterly fallen down in the present system. The Indian has been excluded. The reservation has been filled up with white people who live off the Indians."[17]

Based on this history, Sherman began contacting Bureau officials to find out how they had been implementing this provision. The answer

---

[12] 25 U.S.C. § 472.

[13] 25 U.S.C. § 479.

[14] The legislative history of the IRA is examined in Elmer R. Rusco, *A Fateful Time: The Background and Legislative History of the Indian Reorganization Act* (2000).

[15] *See* Kenneth Philp, *John Collier's Crusade for Indian Reform 1920–1954* (1977).

[16] *See* 25 U.S.C. §§ 44–46. (granting preference to Indians as herders, teamsters, laborers, translators, clerical workers, and mechanics).

[17] *To Grant Indians Living Under Federal Tutelage the Freedom to Organize for Purposes of Local Self–Government and Economic Enterprise: Hearings on S. 2755 and S. 3645 Before the S. Comm. on Indian Affairs*, 73d Cong. 259 (1934) (statement of Sen. Norbeck, Member, Comm. on Indian Affairs).

was that they had not been, except for some initial hiring decisions from outside the agency. A legal opinion from the Solicitor of the Department of the Interior issued in the mid–1940s had interpreted the IRA to require preferences for promotions as well as initial hires. But the BIA had never followed the Solicitor's recommendation.[18] Furthermore, the BIA had created its own definition of an eligible Indian that did not conform to the statutory definition. According to BIA regulations, to be eligible for their limited preference one had to have at least one-quarter Indian ancestry in a federally recognized tribe.[19] In contrast, the federal statutory definition extended the preference to anyone who was of Indian ancestry and a tribal member, regardless of percentage of ancestry, as well as to anyone of one-half or more Indian "blood," regardless of eligibility for membership in a federally recognized tribe.[20] Thus, for example, someone who had one-eighth ancestry from each of four different tribes, but eligible for membership in none of them, was entitled to a preference under the statute, but not under the BIA regulations. And someone who was not a tribal member, but had one-quarter Indian ancestry from a federally recognized tribe, would be ineligible under the statutory requirement but could receive the preference under the BIA rules. The Supreme Court later glossed over this divergence between the statute and the BIA regulations, choosing to focus on the BIA's rules because they favored the characterization of the classification as political rather than racial. In truth, neither set of rules established a strictly political requirement of citizenship in a federally recognized tribe.

For Sherman and his clients, however, there was little need to probe the significance of the BIA's rules in relation to the statute, because there were plenty of prospective plaintiffs who met the BIA's requirement. In *Freeman v. Morton*,[21] Sherman filed suit against the BIA in the United States District Court for the District of Columbia, challenging the Bureau's failure to implement the Indian preference provision of the IRA in the full range of appointment and training situations. The named plaintiff in this suit alleged that she qualified for the preference because she had at least one-quarter Indian ancestry in a federally recognized

---

[18] Telephone Interview with Harris Sherman, *supra* note 11.

[19] The requirement of one-quarter Indian ancestry or "blood" was a standard BIA requirement for federal benefits at that time. For example, in 1957, the Bureau had published regulations stating that "funds appropriated by Congress for the education of Indians may be used for making educational loans and grants to aid students of one-fourth or more degree of Indian blood attending accredited institutions of higher education...." 25 C.F.R. § 40.1. The statute authorizing such benefits, 25 U.S.C. § 13, contained no definition of eligible Indians. *See* Zarr v. Barlow, 800 F.2d 1484 (9th Cir. 1986).

[20] 25 U.S.C. § 479.

[21] No. 327–71, 1972 WL 258 (D.D.C. Dec. 21, 1972), *aff'd*, 499 F.2d 494 (D.C. Cir. 1974).

tribe. The district court ruled for the plaintiffs on summary judgment, finding that the language of the IRA's Indian preference provision was mandatory, not discretionary, and that it applied to all initial hirings, promotions, lateral transfers, and reassignments, as well as any other personnel movement intended to fill vacancies within the BIA. Only training programs were excluded, as they did not involve "positions" maintained by the BIA. Judge Howard Corcoran of the district court justified his decision by pointing to the legislative history of the preference provision, which indicated a congressional purpose "that the BIA [become] an 'Indian' agency in the sense that it [is] to be staffed by Indians wherever possible."[22]

Importantly, however, none of the parties in *Freeman v. Morton* questioned the constitutionality of the preference provision. The district court opinion included a footnote indicating first that the court would not address the issue, but nevertheless offering up the following view:

> Certainly not all classifications based on race are invalid. *Contractors Ass'n of Eastern Pa. v. Secretary of Labor*, 442 F.2d 159 (3rd Cir. 1971); and Congress has broad powers to "do all that [is] required ... to prepare the Indians to take their place as independent, qualified members of the modern body politic." *Board of County Commissioners v. Seber*, 318 U.S. 705 (1943). These Indian preference statutes appear to be a rational exercise of that power.[23]

This footnote proved prophetic of the later Supreme Court decision in *Morton v. Mancari*.

The district court's sweeping order in *Freeman v. Morton* mandated dramatic, across-the-board reform of the BIA. At first the Bureau vacillated about whether to appeal the major holding in the case, application of the preference to promotions; but eventually the agency chose to abide by the court's decision.[24] On June 26, 1972, the Secretary of the Interior announced that he had approved the Bureau's new policy to extend the Indian preference to training and filling vacancies by initial appointment, reinstatement, and promotions wherever two or more available candidates "meet the established requirements."[25] Eligible Indians were

---

[22] *Id.* at *7.

[23] *Id.* at *2 n.3.

[24] The BIA did appeal the ruling insofar as it extended the preference to lateral transfers and denied the BIA the right to make exceptions in certain cases. On both accounts, the D.C. Circuit affirmed the district court's order. Freeman v. Morton, 499 F.2d 494 (D.C. Cir. 1974), *aff'g* 1972 WL 258 (D.D.C. Dec. 21, 1972).

[25] United States Department of the Interior, Bureau of Indian Affairs, Personnel Management Letter No. 72–12, Jun. 28, 1972, Appendix (Trial Record), Morton v. Mancari, 417 U.S. 535 (1974) (No. 73–362) at 52.

described as those with more than one-quarter Indian "blood" or ancestry from a federally recognized tribe.[26]

When Senator Bob Packwood questioned the policy change on behalf of three non-Indian constituents, the Bureau responded that it regretted the concerns of non-Indian employees that their jobs were in jeopardy and assured him that the new policy would not affect "their current jobs or employment status."[27] The BIA defended its decision by pointing to both the federal legislative mandate and President Richard Nixon's "announced policy of increased self-determination in Federal and local matters affecting Indian people."[28] A relatively little known fact about Nixon is that he was a champion of Native rights. In 1970, he issued a formal statement that repudiated the disastrous 1950s policy of termination, affirmed the "solemn obligations" of the United States to Indian people, and declared that "the Indian community should have the right to take over the control and operation of federally funded programs."[29] Nixon's message was both eloquent and forceful:

> Both as a matter of justice and as a matter of enlightened social policy, we must begin to act on the basis of what the Indians themselves have long been telling us. The time has come to break decisively with the past and to create the conditions for a new era in which the Indian future is determined by Indian acts and Indian decisions.[30]

Indeed, it launched one of those periodic tectonic shifts in federal Indian policy, this time in favor of broad self-determination for Indians.

Despite assurances that no jobs were threatened, the Bureau's decision to give full effect to the Indian preference nonetheless provoked a swift and angry response from non-Indian employees of the BIA, as well as those who worked in its companion agency within the Department of Health and Human Services, the Indian Health Service.[31] These

---

[26] *Id.*

[27] Complaint, Exhibit 6, Transcript of Record at 61, Mancari v. Morton, 359 F. Supp. 585 (D.N.M. 1973) (No. 9626) (letter from John D. Crow, Deputy Commissioner of the BIA, to Senator Bob Packwood, September 1, 1972).

[28] *Id.*

[29] Message from the President of the United States Transmitting Recommendations for Indian Policy, H.R. Doc. No. 91–363 (1970). Nixon also facilitated and implemented affirmative actions policies. Dean J. Kotlowski, *Richard Nixon and the Origins of Affirmative Action*, 60 The Historian 523 (1998).

[30] Message from the President of the United States Transmitting Recommendations for Indian Policy, H.R. Doc. No. 91–363 (1970).

[31] In 1954, Congress ended BIA responsibility for Indian health care and transferred the entire Indian health program to the United States Public Health Service in what was

civil servants were understandably distraught by the government's sudden decision to adhere to the preference law. And their position could draw force from the recently enacted Equal Employment Opportunity Act of 1972,[32] which extended the federal ban on race discrimination in employment to the federal government.

Morton v. Mancari *Before the Three–Judge District Court*

Carla Mancari, Anthony Franco, Wilbert Garrett, and Jules Cooper, the plaintiffs in *Morton v. Mancari*, were all non-Indian employees of the BIA, who publicly identified themselves by the acronym "DART"— Dedicated Americans Revealing the Truth. One of them was African-American and another was Latino, each from a group that constituted only 1.7% of the BIA's employees at that time.[33] All four were teachers at the Southwest Indian Polytechnic Institute in Albuquerque, New Mexico, commonly referred to as SIPI. SIPI had opened its doors in the fall semester of 1971, fulfilling the dreams and vision of the All–Indian Pueblo Council, which had first proposed the Indian training school in 1960. The school board at SIPI was all Indian. Mancari and Cooper had received positive assessments from the faculty and deans at SIPI, but had been passed over for training and promotions because of the preference policy.

Carla Mancari relates that DART held many meetings before resolving to sue the United States government, and that she eventually emerged as the group's leader. Mancari's personal experience with issues of race had primed her to react to perceived reverse discrimination. As she recounts in her published memoir,[34] she went from a segregated upbringing in Delaware to become the only white student at South Carolina State College, an historically all-black institution. She had enrolled there in 1967 because it was the only nearby school that would accept her into a master's program in counseling and because she needed the degree to retain her job as a state vocational youth counselor. Her narrative is filled with accounts of the isolation she felt, the hostility she encountered from African–American students and faculty, and her own uplifting transformation from a segregationist to a believer in racial

---

then the Department of Health, Education, and Welfare. In the Department's view, the Indian preference requirement remained binding on the Indian Health Service, notwithstanding its new administrative home. 43 Fed. Reg. 29,783 (July 11, 1978).

[32] 42 U.S.C. § 2000e–16 (2003 & Supp. 2006).

[33] Transcript of Record at 22–23, 142, Mancari v. Morton, 359 F. Supp. 585 (D.N.M. 1973) (No. 9626).

[34] Carla Mancari, *Walking on the Grass: A White Woman in a Black World* (2001).

equality. She reported in her memoir that "working with black causes for equality led me to work with young Native Americans."[35]

Convinced that racial segregation was wrong and committed to the welfare of Indian students, Mancari was appalled to find that, in her view, the United States was condoning segregation, rather than opposing it. As she saw it, the federal government was pitting one minority group against others, sending Indians into jobs for which they were not prepared, and denying Indian students the benefits of interacting with non-Indians at SIPI. The absence of such interaction, she believed, would hurt Indians' social skills and prevent them from learning how to communicate with people different from themselves. As a vocational education teacher, she was concerned that her SIPI students were not successful in job placement for that very reason.[36]

Mancari and the other plaintiffs did not have the resources to mount a major legal challenge to the BIA's preference policy, although DART had created an eponymous newspaper to inform and raise money from the 15,000 non-Indian BIA employees potentially threatened by wider application and enforcement of the Indian preference.[37] Instead, Mancari's group found a private practitioner in Albuquerque willing to take the case pro bono, John Kulikowski. The complaint that Kulikowski drafted alleged that the newly promulgated BIA preference policy was unconstitutional under the Due Process Clause of the Fifth Amendment and in conflict with the federal employment discrimination laws. Furthermore, the complaint claimed that the policy exceeded statutory requirements in its application to training, reinstatement, and promotions. Kulikowski filed the suit as a class action, and because the plaintiffs were attempting to invalidate a federal statute, he requested a three-judge panel from the federal district court, which was the mandatory procedure for suits of this type.[38]

Reaction to the suit from the National Indian Youth Council was swift and strong.[39] NIYC charged that "[t]hese non-Indians protesting

---

[35] *Id.* at 209.

[36] Telephone Interview with Carla Mancari (Nov. 14, 2005).

[37] *Id.*

[38] Complaint, Transcript of Record at 14–15, Mancari v. Morton, 359 F. Supp. 585 (D.N.M. 1973) (No. 9626). Under the prescribed procedure for three-judge courts, the panel had to include at least one circuit court judge. Congress ended the use of such courts for constitutional challenges to state and federal laws in 1976. *See* Act of June 25, 1948, ch. 646, 62 Stat. 968 (establishing three-judge court procedure), *repealed by* Act of Aug. 12, 1976, 90 Stat. 1119. The composition of three-judge courts is specified at 28 U.S.C. § 2284 (2001).

[39] *BIA Employees Oppose Preference Policy*, Am. Indian L. Newsl. (Indian Law Center, Univ. of N.M. Sch. of Law), Sept. 27, 1972, at 232.

the new policy have been discriminating against Indian employees for years.... Ironically, these same racists are now appealing to a sense of justice and fair play."[40] Noting that the BIA had long ignored the preference requirement in the Indian Reorganization Act, NIYC declared that "[t]he interest of the law was to give Indian people self-government. Control of the BIA was essential to this concept. One cannot control his future if he cannot make policy."[41] NIYC launched its own national campaign to rally Indian employees in defense of the strengthened preference policy and promised to report all instances of failure to comply.[42]

Indian people did not fully trust the United States to represent their interests. Tillie Walker, who had initially pressed Harris Sherman to bring the *Freeman v. Morton* case, organized a new nonprofit group called Amerind, which was comprised of BIA Indian employees and established with the express purpose of representing their rights. Sherman became counsel for the organization, which moved successfully to intervene as a defendant in the litigation. Joining him were two young lawyers from DNA–People's Legal Services, which provided legal assistance to individuals on the Navajo reservation. Alan Taradash, based in DNA's Window Rock office, later became a partner at a top Albuquerque law firm, with a successful practice representing Indian nations. Rick Collins, then situated in DNA's Crownpoint office, went on to litigate at the Native American Rights Fund, and to write important scholarly works in the field of Indian law. He joined the University of Colorado Law School faculty in 1982. It was quite a team, as Sherman himself later became Executive Director of Colorado's Department of Natural Resources. As counsel for intervenor Amerind, Sherman, Taradash, and Collins worked closely with Victor Ortega, the Assistant United States Attorney assigned to represent the federal government. Together, they coordinated brief writing and oral arguments.[43]

The three-judge court, consisting of Tenth Circuit Judge Oliver Seth and District Court Judges Howard Bratton and E. L. Meechem, first granted class action status, and then proceeded, on November 29, 1972, to hear testimony in the case. Most of the facts were actually uncontested as the new policy was well documented. But plaintiffs wanted to demonstrate that the policy was being applied on a widespread basis and

---

[40] *Id.* at 233.

[41] *Id.*

[42] Carla Mancari relates that militant Indian groups were so incensed at the litigation that she received life-threatening notes, and her boss sent her to Washington, D.C. for two weeks to get her out of harm's way. Telephone Interview with Carla Mancari, *supra* note 36.

[43] Telephone Interview with Harris Sherman, *supra* note 11.

that they had been adversely affected by its implementation. Eliciting testimony for the plaintiffs, Kulikowski stressed the racial dimension of the case. For example, when questioning a BIA supervisor about his implementation of the preference policy in a case involving clerical work, Kulikowski asked whether there really was any basis for preferring the Indians over the non-Indians, all of whom had been certified as "best qualified" for the particular promotion in question. "Based on your experience," he asked, "is there any reason why an Indian individual is better qualified to perform voucher examining work as opposed to a non-Indian ... because of the racial background?" Interestingly, as the testimony of plaintiffs' witnesses unfolded, it appeared that many of the disappointed non-Indian BIA employees had failed to received promotions because of hiring freezes or budget cuts, not because the jobs were filled by Indian candidates. But instances still remained of non-Indians who were undercut in consideration for promotions because of the Indian preference.[44]

Neither the United States nor the intervenor Amerind offered evidence showing that the preference served an important government purpose. Toward the end of the trial, Amerind's attorney, Harris Sherman, apologized to the court when the witness he had intended to call, Navajo Nation Chairman Peter McDonald, could not attend because he had to preside over the opening session of the Tribal Council. Sherman noted that McDonald's testimony would have focused on how the BIA's unresponsiveness to tribal needs could be remedied by increased Indian participation, particularly in high-level positions. Sherman offered to have this testimony presented via deposition, and the court agreed to let him submit such testimony if he could obtain it within ten days. The deposition was never introduced.[45]

The three-judge court ruled unanimously for the plaintiffs, enjoining enforcement of the preference policy. Without reaching the constitutional question,[46] the court found that the preference provision in the IRA was in direct conflict with Title VII's ban on race discrimination in employment, as amended in 1972 to apply to all "executive agencies" of the federal government. As the court noted, nothing in the 1972 amendments carved out an exception for the BIA or Indian preferences. Several

---

[44] Final Hearing on the Merits, Morton v. Mancari, Nov. 29, 1972, in Appendix (Trial Record), Morton v. Mancari, 417 U.S. 535 (1974) (No. 73–362) at 136–78.

[45] *Id.* at 207.

[46] Noting that the defendants had the burden of coming forward with evidence of an important governmental objective but had offered no such evidence, the court observed that "we could well hold that the statute must fail on constitutional grounds, but instead we hold ... that the preference statutes must give way to the Civil Rights Acts." Mancari v. Morton, 359 F. Supp. 585, 591 (D.N.M. 1973).

Senators testifying in favor of the measure had used absolute, all-encompassing terms to describe the range of discrimination addressed. In the words of West Virginia Senator Robert Byrd, "Wherever there is such discrimination in employment [on the basis of race or sex], it is violative of the Constitution of the United States.... Every qualified individual—black, white or else—should be given an equal chance—not preferential treatment—at employment."[47] Senator Hubert Humphrey had declared, "We must make absolutely clear the obligation of the Federal Government to make all personnel actions free from discrimination based on race, color, sex, religion, or national origin."[48] The court also observed that courts had interpreted Title VII as generally forbidding reverse discrimination.[49]

Throughout this analysis, the court assumed that the IRA created a preference based on race. In describing the preference, the court mentioned only the blood quantum or ancestry requirement, not the provision for membership in a federally recognized tribe. Apparently no one had questioned whether a preference for Indians was the same as a racial preference. But even conceding that the preference was race-based, what about the general principle of statutory construction disfavoring repeals by implication? Although "reluctant" to find such a repeal, the court determined that one was effected in this case. First, the 1972 amendments to Title VII did exclude some federal agencies other than the BIA, leading the court to conclude that Congress must have intended to override BIA-specific preferences. In reaching this conclusion, the judges ignored Title VII's original provision exempting businesses on or near reservations that provided a preference to Indians living in the area.[50] Second, the court refused to find that the Indian preference provision was more specific than the Title VII ban because "[e]ach statute purports to cover the same particular subject of personnel actions relating to, as [Title VII's 1972 amendments] described them, '... discrimination based on race....' "[51] With an identical reach, the statutes were in direct contradiction to one another. Third, with no evidence to show that "having seventy-five per cent non-Indian blood and twenty-five per cent Indian blood was in any way a job-related criterion," the court could see no way to view the Indian preference statutes as an exception to Title VII's ban on federal government

---

[47] Mancari v. Morton, 359 F. Supp. 585, 589–90 (D.N.M. 1973) (quoting statement of Sen. Byrd).

[48] Mancari v. Morton, 359 F. Supp. 585, 590 (D.N.M. 1973) (quoting statement of Sen. Humphrey).

[49] Id. at 590.

[50] See 42 U.S.C. § 2000e–2(i).

[51] Mancari, 359 F. Supp. at 590.

employment discrimination based on race.[52] The court did not refer to the extensive legislative history of the IRA preference, which defendants had introduced to demonstrate that the preference advanced Indian self-determination.

The fact that Congress often had singled out Indian tribes for special treatment did not move the court either, as this was "no reason for a different treatment of Indians generally."[53] Indians had the same rights as other citizens. No principle of special Indian rights could resist application of Title VII's general ban on reverse discrimination. To underscore its point, the three-judge court cited the Supreme Court's then-recent decision in *Griggs v. Duke Power Co.*,[54] in which the Court had insisted that Title VII prohibited all race discrimination, however benign the underlying motive, and that no person acquired a right to be hired "simply because he was formerly the subject of discrimination, or because he is a member of a minority group."[55]

Both the attorneys and the judges involved in this three-judge court proceeding assumed that the BIA's preference was race-based. They merely differed in their views about Congress's authority and objectives in granting Indians a favored position in competition for BIA jobs. Similarly, no one questioned the differences between the IRA's eligibility criteria, which looked at both ancestry and tribal membership, and the BIA's regulations, which emphasized only ancestry. As we will see, one recurring feature of the litigation over the Indian preference provision is that lawyers or judges who focused on the ancestry components of the preference requirement found the classification to be racial and invalid, while those who focused on the tribal membership component found it to be political and therefore legally permissible. Both the statutory and initial BIA versions of the preference contain references to ancestry and membership. But it is possible to perceive only one or the other, with significant consequences. At the three-judge court level, the focus was exclusively on the ancestry component and the result was a victory for Carla Mancari and the other non-Indian plaintiffs. By the time of the United States Supreme Court's consideration of the case, the BIA would defend its preference policy by amending the regulations to highlight membership requirements as well as ancestry.

Morton v. Mancari *Before the United States Supreme Court*

As the losing party before a three-judge court, the BIA could bring a direct appeal to the United States Supreme Court, without the need for a

---

[52] *Id.*

[53] *Id.* at 591.

[54] *Id.* at 590.

[55] *Id.* (quoting 401 U.S. 424, 431 (1971)).

writ of *certiorari* and regardless of whether the court below resolved a constitutional question. When the BIA appealed, the Court had three options: to summarily affirm, summarily reverse, or note probable jurisdiction and schedule the case for full briefing and oral argument. The Court ultimately voted to note probable jurisdiction after some behind-the-scenes maneuvering. In his papers, Justice Lewis Powell noted that he was inclined to reverse summarily, but "[o]ne or two Justices may . . . want to hear the case to try to reach the question of the constitutionality of benign treatment of racial minorities."[56]

Powell went on to cite *DeFunis v. Odegaard*,[57] a case in which a white student had challenged a public law school's policy of taking race into account in admissions. Both opponents and supporters of affirmative action had expected *DeFunis* to be the showdown on the constitutionality of racial classifications favoring historically disadvantaged minorities. However, by a 5–4 vote, the Court avoided the issue on mootness grounds, over the protests of the liberal wing.[58] *Morton v. Mancari* attracted some interest on the Court from those eager for the battle averted in *DeFunis*, but a majority of the Justices were in no mood to take on the affirmative action controversy. In assessing the validity of Indian preferences, the Court would try to sidestep the question of whether considering race in hiring and promotion was impermissible reverse discrimination.

While the appeal was pending, the United States sought and obtained a stay of the injunction from Justice Thurgood Marshall, leaving the preference policy in place. At that point, some changes occurred in representation. John Kulikowski was not licensed to practice before the United States Supreme Court, so Carla Mancari sought a referral from one of the few female attorneys in Albuquerque and obtained the name of Gene Franchini. Franchini, who went on to serve on the New Mexico District Court and later the state's Supreme Court, agreed to take the case pro bono. At the time, Franchini was a member of the board of a Navajo-controlled bank in Farmington, New Mexico, only the second Indian-controlled national bank in the United States. Most of the other board members were Navajo tribal leaders. Franchini did not think that challenging the Indian preference provision would harm his Indian colleagues. To the contrary, his view was that the preference law

---

[56] Justice Powell's Notes (Dec. 20, 1973) (Morton v. Mancari, No. 73–362), Box 162, Lewis F. Powell Papers, Manuscript Division, Library of Congress, Washington, D.C.

[57] 416 U.S. 312 (1974).

[58] The decision was issued on April 23, 1974. The University of Washington Law School had agreed to allow DeFunis to enroll and to earn a diploma. Thus DeFunis would be able to complete his legal studies irrespective of any Supreme Court decision. 416 U.S. at 316–17.

"imprisoned" Native Americans because it kept them from acquiring
sufficient skills to compete. In other words, in the guise of helping them,
it kept them in their place. To this day, Franchini says he has never felt
so strongly that he was on the right side of a case.[59]

For the United States, the Solicitor General was none other than
Robert Bork, whose opposition to affirmative action has been no secret.
In a December 31, 1990 column in the *National Review*, Bork wrote, "If
racial discrimination is to be tolerated whenever the government has
some purpose in mind, however trivial the purpose and however attenuated the connection between the purpose and the discrimination, the
courts will be in for some very ugly tasks."[60] But Bork himself did not
take on the case. Responsibility fell instead to Assistant Solicitor Harry
R. Sachse, who had already argued several path-breaking Indian law
cases before the Supreme Court.[61]

Now a name partner in a boutique law firm in Washington, D.C.
specializing in high-level litigation for Indian tribes, Sachse says that the
winning argument in *Morton v. Mancari* came to him while on a train
trip from Albuquerque to Gallup, New Mexico. Sachse was working on
another case but *Morton v. Mancari* was on his mind as well that day.[62]
It was the middle of the Civil Rights Movement, and Sachse, a white
Louisiana native who was fiercely committed to racial equality, worried
that the government's position in *Mancari* would compromise the civil
rights laws. Around that same time, the University of New Mexico had
republished Felix Cohen's magisterial 1942 treatise, the *Handbook of
Federal Indian Law*,[63] in a large blue volume. While riding the train,
Harry Sachse spied a young man reading the *Handbook*. The man
appeared to be Indian, and Sachse struck up a conversation with him.
Not long into the conversation, Sachse learned that the young man was

---

[59] Telephone Interview with Gene Franchini, former Justice, New Mexico Supreme
Court (Oct. 7, 2005).

[60] Robert H. Bork, *An End to Political Judging?*, Nat'l Rev., Dec. 31, 1990, at 30.
Although Bork had not written directly on the subject of affirmative action as of 1974, a
law review article he published in 1971 signaled what his views would be. In that article, he
characterized the absolute prohibition on race discrimination as the only substantive
neutral principle embodied in the Equal Protection Clause of the Fourteenth Amendment.
Robert H. Bork, *Neutral Principles and Some First Amendment Problems*, 47 Ind. L. J. 1,
11 (1971).

[61] Those cases included McClanahan v. Arizona State Tax Comm'n, 411 U.S. 164
(1973) (state taxation of reservation income), Washington Department of Game v. Puyallup
Tribe, 414 U.S. 44 (1973) (Indian fishing rights), and Mattz v. Arnett, 412 U.S. 481 (1973)
(reservation boundaries).

[62] Telephone Interview with Harry Sachse, former Assistant to the Solicitor General of
the United States (Oct. 7, 2005).

[63] Felix Cohen, *Handbook of Federal Indian Law* (Univ. of N.M. Press 1971) (1942).

Latino, not Indian. Although Sachse's fellow passenger in all likelihood could claim some indigenous ancestry, his background was not formally recognized in the United States because the relevant tribes were from Latin America.[64]

It dawned on Sachse that there were many people like this man, who did not qualify as Indians for purposes of the BIA preference because neither they nor their ancestors were members of federally recognized tribes. At that time, Sachse was also working with Indians from the St. Regis Mohawk Tribe, some of whom lacked eligibility for rights under federal Indian law because their tribal membership was exclusively Canadian. Something clicked, and Sachse hatched the idea that the BIA preference was a political classification rather than race-based discrimination. In its brief, the United States wasted no time in announcing that "[t]he Indian preference statutes ... are based on participation by the governed in the governing agency, rather than race...."[65] The BIA's requirement of one-quarter Indian descent (or the statute's provision for Indians of one-half or more Indian "blood") received no attention at all, emphasis being placed instead on the requirement that preferred Indians be members of federally recognized tribes.

Harris Sherman, who had represented the intervenor Amerind before the three-judge court, got in touch with the prestigious Washington, D.C. law firm of Arnold & Porter, which agreed to provide representation before the Supreme Court on a pro bono basis. But Sherman was not about to surrender the oral argument, which meant that Arnold & Porter mainly handled the brief writing and argument preparation.[66] In their briefs to the court, Sherman and his co-counsel from Arnold & Porter, Stuart Land,[67] emphasized Congress's broad control over Indian

---

[64] Given the mixed Indian/Spanish population in much of Latin America, it is not so surprising that Sachse would find phenotypical similarity. However, Sachse's error in identifying the "race" of this young man exposes the flaw in assuming that such outward characteristics are the sole determinants of socially constricted racial categories. Sachse reports that the attorney was reading the *Handbook* because he practiced with a large Albuquerque law firm that regularly represented clients opposed to the tribes. Telephone Interview with Harry Sachse, *supra* note 62.

[65] Brief for the Appellants at *6, Morton v. Mancari, 417 U.S. 535 (1974) (Nos. 73-362, 73-364).

[66] Sherman later became a partner of that firm, and was reappointed to the position of Executive Director of the Colorado Department of Natural Resources in January, 2007. *See* Lynn Bartels, *Ritter Fills 3 More Posts for Cabinet*, Rocky Mountain News (Denver, CO) January 5, 2007 at 15A.

[67] Stuart Land later went on to become chairman of the firm, and a leader in the firm's renowned pro bono program. In June 2004, the Washington Lawyers' Committee for Civil Rights and Urban Affairs presented its Wiley A. Branton Award to Land in recognition of

affairs and the unique nature of the BIA as a federal agency holding vast governing power over Indian resources and people. A recurring theme in their briefs was the imperative behind the preference provision, which was to hand the governing power of the BIA over to Indian people themselves so that they could enjoy self-determination.[68]

The idea that the BIA preference was not even a race-based classification was only a minor theme for the intervenor in its jurisdictional statement. Near the end, the statement mentioned that the Bureau dealt predominantly with reservation Indians who owned their lands and dropped a footnote suggesting that "[i]n effect . . . the preference is not so much based upon race, but upon land ownership. We do not believe that the Constitution would bar a municipal ordinance giving preference in employment in municipal government to residents of the municipality."[69] How land ownership could be analogized to municipal citizenship was never explained.

The intervenor's brief on the merits discussed the nature of the classification more prominently, if not more clearly. At one point the brief explained that the classification was "primarily a *political* designation rather than a purely racial classification."[70] Congress enacted the preference provision "not because Indians belong to a different race, but because they owe allegiance to the Tribes."[71] To support this point, the brief noted that Indians of terminated tribes could not qualify for the preference.[72] Yet in the same brief, the intervenor acknowledged that there was some inevitable element of race in all legislation implementing Congress's power under the provision in Article I, Section 8, Clause 3 of the Constitution to "regulate Commerce . . . with the Indian Tribes,"[73] that not all race-based classifications are constitutionally impermissible,

---

his exceptional pro bono service and advocacy of civil rights. *See* Press Release, Washington Lawyers' Committee, *Washington Lawyers' Committee to Honor NAACP, John Payton, Stuart Land at 36th Annual Branton Awards* (June 7, 2004), *available at* http://www.wash law.org/news/releases/060704.htm.

[68] Jurisdictional Statement on Behalf of Intervenor–Appellant Amerind, *Morton*, 417 U.S. 535 (No. 73–364); Brief of Intervenor–Appellant Amerind, *Morton*, 417 U.S. 535 (Nos. 73–362, 73–364).

[69] Jurisdictional Statement on Behalf of Intervenor–Appellant Amerind at *20, *Morton*, 417 U.S. 535 (No. 73–364).

[70] Brief of Intervenor–Appellant Amerind at *26, *Morton*, 417 U.S. 535 (Nos. 73–362, 73–364) (emphasis added).

[71] *Id.* at *25.

[72] Whether they could qualify under the language of the IRA itself was not addressed.

[73] U.S. Const. art. I, § 8, cl. 3.

and that the BIA preference provision was "vital to an important governmental purpose."[74]

If the United States and Amerind were emphasizing the tribal membership requirement under the BIA's preference, attorney Gene Franchini's brief on behalf of Carla Mancari hammered on the ancestry requirement. Echoing arguments that had prevailed before the three-judge court, he contended that having a specific percentage of Indian blood had not been shown to be related to performance of federal jobs, even those involving relations with Indian nations.[75] In addition, Franchini zeroed in on the divergence between the BIA's requirement of one-quarter ancestry from a federally recognized tribe and the IRA's alternative requirements of tribal membership or one-half "Indian blood." The comparison highlighted the race-like dimension of the BIA's preference, with eligibility based exclusively on ancestry.[76]

In its reply brief, Amerind argued that any difference between the statutory and BIA eligibility criteria was not before the Court. In any event, the BIA's rules were "narrower than the statute would allow"[77] and therefore easier to justify as political rather than racial. Of course, the BIA's rules did allow for someone who had one-quarter Indian ancestry to receive the preference even if that person did not qualify for tribal citizenship or membership. But Amerind glossed over that fact by mentioning in a footnote that "[o]ne reason for selecting the quarter-blood test is that many tribes require one quarter Indian blood for tribal membership."[78] Even though that may have been true, there could still be individuals who met the BIA's requirement but were not citizens of Indian nations.

Two of the three amicus briefs before the United States Supreme Court took predictable positions. The National Federation of Federal Employees supported the BIA's old reading of the Indian preference law, urging the Court to interpret it as applying only to initial hires to the Indian service, not to promotions.[79] The National Congress of American Indians as well as other local and national intertribal groups provided legal support and social context for the position taken by the appellants,

---

[74] Brief of Intervenor–Appellant Amerind, *supra* note 70, at *22, *34.

[75] Brief for the Appellees at *14, *Morton*, 417 U.S. 535 (Nos. 73–362, 73–364).

[76] *Id.* at *9. *See also supra* text accompanying notes 12–19.

[77] Reply Brief for Intervenor–Appellant Amerind at *3, *Morton*, 417 U.S. 535 (Nos. 73–362, 73–364).

[78] *Id.* at *3 n.3.

[79] Brief of Amicus Curiae National Federation of Federal Employees at *6, *Morton*, 417 U.S. 535 (No. 73–362).

documenting the utter failure of the BIA to fulfill its role as guardian of the Indians.[80]

The most interesting amicus brief, however, came from the Mexican American Legal Defense and Educational Fund ("MALDEF"). Despite the fact that one of the plaintiffs in the case was Mexican–American, MALDEF sided with the United States and Amerind in defending the preference. MALDEF's statement of interest in the case made it evident that MALDEF saw the future of affirmative action potentially at stake,[81] and the brief itself equates the preference with permissible affirmative action programs. As Vilma Martinez and other MALDEF attorneys wrote, the Indian preference could not violate Title VII because

> [b]oth Title VII as amended and the Indian Preference Statutes were intended to protect minorities from employment discrimination, and generally to improve the status of minorities who have been subject to historic and pervasive discrimination and deprivation. Implementation of these policies may frequently require preference of qualified minorities over similarly qualified whites in order to remedy practices which have resulted in discrimination against minorities.[82]

The BIA's history of discrimination against Native American employees was therefore sufficient to justify the preference statute under Title VII. Similarly, in its discussion of the constitutional issue in the case, MALDEF argued that the Fifth Amendment's equal protection guarantee "does not require that all governmental programs be 'color blind' nor does it prohibit consideration of race or ethnic background in attempts by government to correct racial or ethnic inequalities."[83] In short, MALDEF's position was that the classification was indeed one based on race or national origin, but that it was constitutional nonetheless because the test of "strict scrutiny" should not apply to such classifications when they are established for the benefit of groups subject to "historic and pervasive discrimination and deprivations."[84]

Briefs for the appellants thus offered all three of the pro-preference theories identified at the outset of this chapter—the political-not-racial

---

[80] Brief of Amici Curiae Montana Inter–Tribal Policy Board, National Congress of American Indians, and National Tribal Chairmen's Association at *10, *Morton*, 417 U.S. 535 (Nos. 73–362, 73–364).

[81] Motion of the Mexican American Legal Defense and Educational Fund for Leave to File Brief Amicus Curiae at *4, *Morton*, 417 U.S. 535 (Nos. 73–362, 73–364).

[82] Brief of Amicus Curiae Mexican American Legal Defense and Educational Fund at *8, *Morton*, 417 U.S. 535 (Nos. 73–362, 73–364).

[83] *Id.* at *16.

[84] *Id.* at *20.

theory, the partly racial but necessary under the Indian Commerce Clause theory, and the racial but valid-under-equal-protection theory.[85] Each theory had its drawbacks. The first position, taken by the United States, was arguably inconsistent with the IRA itself, which allowed some non-tribal citizens of sufficient Indian ancestry to qualify for the preference. This approach also ignored the ancestry element in tribal membership criteria and the fact that ancestry was still one requirement under the BIA rules.[86] The second position, taken by Amerind, accepted that the Indian preference was at least partly racial in nature. However, the explicit recognition of ancestry was seen as an essential element of discharging the United States government's obligations to the tribes. This approach required the Court to acknowledge that the Constitution allows racial classifications in some circumstances, a step some of the Justices might have been reluctant to take. And the third position, taken by MALDEF, would embroil the Court in the messy and larger controversy over affirmative action.

The case was argued before the Supreme Court on April 24, 1974, with Chief Justice Burger absent. Indian protesters affiliated with the American Indian Movement ("AIM") picketed outside the Supreme Court building, demanding that the preference be upheld. According to Franchini, Russell Means, one of the AIM leaders, actually kidnapped the Commissioner of Indian Affairs, holding him in the Carolina Hotel until the oral argument was over and releasing him afterwards.[87] Means's action may have been prompted by public statements by the Secretary of the Interior who, according to Franchini, had suggested that the Indian preference was an illegal racial classification.[88] In fact, during oral argument, Franchini tried to assert that the Secretary of the Interior actually agreed with his clients' position.[89] Given that the official stance of the United States was to the contrary, however, the Justices refused to take that possibility seriously.[90]

In oral argument, Harry Sachse, representing the United States, clearly framed the preference as political not racial, claiming that he could show "that it is not a racial discrimination involved in this case at all, but a determination to have the people whose property and lives are affected by the Bureau of Indian Affairs have prominent roles in the

---

[85] See supra text accompanying note 5.

[86] For a more thorough critique of this position, see Goldberg, supra note 5, at 958–66.

[87] Telephone Interview with Gene Franchini, supra note 59.

[88] Id.

[89] Transcript of Oral Argument at *46, Morton v. Mancari, 417 U.S. 535 (1974) (Nos. 73–362, 73–364).

[90] Id. at *45–47.

Bureau of Indian Affairs."[91] He also affirmed that the BIA was limiting the preference to members of federally recognized tribes, despite the fact that both the statute and the earlier BIA rules seemed to allow some persons who were of Indian descent but not tribal members to qualify. His argument stressed the fact that many persons of Indian descent could not qualify for the preference, though he failed to mention that Indian descent was also a sine qua non for receiving the preference and that Indian ancestry was almost invariably a criterion for tribal membership.[92] Sachse also reassured the Justices, in response to questioning, that although the terms of the statute might be broader than the BIA's practice, that issue was not before the Court. Yet he muddied the water when he argued that the 1972 amendments to Title VII could not have repealed the Indian preference because "it is inconceivable ... that Congress, in an act setting out to increase minority participation in government, would have abolished the Indian preference without a word saying that they are doing it."[93] That point, of course, implied that Indians were a minority group potentially covered by Title VII's ban on racial or ethnic discrimination.

Harris Sherman's portion of the oral argument, representing the Indian employees of the BIA, focused on the statutory question in the case, namely the relationship between Title VII and the Indian preference statute. He demonstrated that Congress and the executive branch had long operated on the principle that the two provisions were compatible, and that Congress had even enacted preference measures after Title VII was amended in 1972 to apply to federal employers. Why, Sherman asked, would Congress have believed this to be the case? It is likely, he answered, that Congress viewed the Indian preference statutes as "basically not racial statutes."[94] When the Justices tried to pin him down on why this was so, he reiterated Sachse's position that the BIA was limiting the preference to individuals who were presently tribal members *and* at least one-quarter Indian ancestry. Neither Sachse nor Sherman received many skeptical questions from the Justices.[95]

Gene Franchini, representing the appellees, had a far rougher time in oral argument. Justices Byron White and Thurgood Marshall pep-

---

[91] *Id.* at *5.

[92] This feature of the preference arguably placed the law in the category of a "race plus" classification. *See, e.g.,* Phillips v. Martin Marietta Corp., 400 U.S. 542 (1971) ("sex plus" classification). For an argument that Indian classifications should not be treated as "race plus," see Carole E. Goldberg–Ambrose, *Not "Strictly" Racial: A Response to "Indians as Peoples,"* 39 UCLA L. Rev. 169, 181 & n.65 (1991).

[93] Transcript of Oral Argument, *supra* note 89, at *14–15.

[94] *Id.* at *21.

[95] *Id.* at *4–27.

pered him with questions exploring the implications of a constitutional ruling against the Indian preference. In particular, they asked how any federal services to Indians could survive such a holding. Franchini tried to argue that the two situations were different, but the Justices seemed unpersuaded and reluctant to render any holding that would invalidate centuries of federal Indian policy. Franchini was also caught off guard when one of the Justices questioned him about the permissibility of veterans' preferences, an analogy that suggested the Court's ultimate view of the case. Franchini appeared to evoke no sympathy when he characterized the Indian preference as harmful rather than helpful to Indians, calling it a "prison" and a denial of equal citizenship.[96] While his argument was a familiar trope of anti-affirmative action rhetoric, none of the Justices made statements or asked questions pursuing this line of attack. Instead, Justice William Rehnquist asked Franchini whether the United States, having mandate authority over American Samoa, could afford a local employment preference to Samoans. The clear implication of this question was that the BIA preference performed a similar, and wholly permissible, function. By this time, the ancestry element in the BIA's regulation had wholly disappeared from the scene, both in the representations of the United States and the Justices' questioning.[97]

Justice Harry Blackmun wrote the opinion for a unanimous Court. His notes and papers indicate that his view of the case immediately before oral argument was that the Indian preference and the 1972 amendments to Title VII could be reconciled in part because "the preference statutes deal mainly with tribes and not race. The EEO Act deals with race, although, of course, it does mention national origin."[98] His law clerk's bench memorandum pointed out the same basis for reconciliation, noting that "national origin might enter in, but appellee does not argue this."[99] The memorandum suggested further that "[e]ven if the 1934 Act was considered as dealing with race, ... it could stand in light of the historical and other constitutional factors present in this case."[100] Thus, both the theory that the classification is not racial and

---

[96] *Id.* at *40.

[97] *Id.* at *4–27.

[98] Justice Blackmun's Conference Notes, at 6 (Apr. 23, 1974) (Morton v. Mancari, No. 73–362; Amerind v. Mancari, No. 73–364), Box 186, Harry A. Blackmun Papers, Manuscript Division, Library of Congress, Washington, D.C.

[99] Memorandum from James J. Knicely, Law Clerk, U.S. Sup. Ct., to Justice Harry A. Blackmun, U.S. Sup. Ct., at 2 (April 20, 1974) (Morton v. Mancari, No. 73–362; Amerind v. Mancari, No. 73–364), Box 186, Harry A. Blackmun Papers, Manuscript Division, Library of Congress, Washington, D.C.

[100] *Id.*

the separate theory that the classification is racial and constitutionally justifiable appear in this early analysis of the case.

Before the opinion was issued on June 17, 1974, there was much jockeying, both by the attorneys and the Justices, to avoid confronting the racial preference issue. On May 8, 1974, the Solicitor General himself, Robert Bork, wrote to the Court, bringing to the Justices' attention a motion that had been made to amend the opinion of the D.C. Circuit in *Freeman v. Morton*, Harris Sherman's original case that had triggered the BIA's policy change and Carla Mancari's lawsuit.[101] This motion, jointly made by the United States and Amerind, had requested a change in the court of appeals' language describing those eligible for the BIA preference, which indicated that all those "of one-quarter or more Indian blood" would qualify.[102] The motion pointed out that the current version of the BIA's Manual[103] *also* required membership in a federally recognized tribe, and any omission of that requirement "would be misleading, particularly to Indians of terminated tribes or unrecognized tribes."[104] Thus, the United States wanted to reinforce its representation, made at oral argument, that no racial classification was involved, even if that meant omitting reference to the ancestry component of the preference. And when Justice Blackmun circulated his first draft of the opinion in *Morton v. Mancari*, the only critical response he received from his brethren was about the brief reference to *DeFunis*. Blackmun had written "[w]hatever may be the constitutional consequences of a case of purely benign racial discrimination, cf. *DeFunis v. Odegaard*, ... this is not such a case."[105] Both Justice Potter Stewart, who had sided with the majority in vacating *DeFunis*, and Justice William O. Douglas, who had written a dissent, urged Blackmun to delete that reference. As Justice

---

[101] Letter from Robert H. Bork to Michael Rodak, Jr., Clerk, Supreme Court of the United States (May 8, 1974), (Morton v. Mancari, No. 73–362; Amerind v. Mancari, No. 73–364), Box 186, Harry A. Blackmun Papers, Manuscript Division, Library of Congress, Washington, D.C.

[102] Joint Motion to Amend Opinion, Freeman v. Morton, No. 73–1490, United States Court of Appeals for the District of Columbia Circuit, May 8, 1974.

[103] 44 Bureau of Indian Affairs Manual 335 (1972).

[104] Joint Motion to Amend Opinion, Freeman v. Morton, No. 73–1490, United States Court of Appeals for the District of Columbia Circuit, May 8, 1974, at *2. In a subsequent case, *Zarr v. Barlow*, 800 F.2d 1484 (9th Cir. 1986), the Ninth Circuit invalidated the one-quarter ancestry requirement as inconsistent with statutory law. *See also* Malone v. Bureau of Indian Affairs, 38 F.3d 433 (9th Cir. 1994).

[105] Justice Blackmun's First Draft, at 16 (circulated June 11, 1974) (*Morton*, 417 U.S. 535 (1974)), Box 1621, William O. Douglas Papers, Manuscript Division, Library of Congress, Washington, D.C.

Douglas noted, "You really do not need it: and my characterization of [*DeFunis*] would be different."[106]

So by the time Blackmun's opinion was filed in *Morton v. Mancari*, the United States had limited the preference to tribal members (of at least one-quarter Indian descent); the potential statutory issue of preference based on one-half tribal ancestry had been cleared from the case; national origin discrimination was not a relevant issue; and the Justices were determined to keep the affirmative action debate out of sight, probably because both liberals and conservatives feared that they lacked a decisive majority on that issue. That set the stage for the Court's resolution of the race issue and the appeal.

Much of Blackmun's opinion is devoted to overturning the ruling of the three-judge court that the 1972 amendments to Title VII repealed the Indian preference dating from the IRA of 1934. After observing that the 1972 amendments did not expressly repeal the earlier statute and listing several pieces of evidence suggesting that Congress did not intend to repeal the Indian preference, Blackmun pointed out that absent such intent, "the only permissible justification for a repeal by implication is when the earlier and later statutes are irreconcilable."[107] However, reconciliation was entirely possible, he noted. Without expressly denying that the Indian preference was a racial classification, he made an equivalent claim: "A provision aimed at furthering Indian self-government by according an employment preference within the BIA for qualified members of the governed group can readily co-exist with a general rule prohibiting employment discrimination on the basis of race."[108]

The constitutional issue was dispatched in a mere six paragraphs. At the outset, it appeared that Justice Blackmun was opting for the second theory favoring the preference, namely that Congress' Commerce Clause power over Indian affairs justified the classification, even if it was partly racial in nature. Justice Blackmun emphasized the "unique legal status of Indian tribes under federal law" and Congress's plenary power, "based on a history of treaties and the assumption of a 'guardian-ward' status, to legislate on behalf of federally recognized Indian tribes."[109] He noted that nearly all of Title 25 of the United States Code, composed of laws directed at Indians, would be wiped out if Indian-specific legislation were treated as invidious racial discrimination. But then midway into

---

[106] Handwritten Note from Justice William O. Douglas, U.S. Sup. Ct., to Justice Harry A. Blackmun, U.S. Sup. Ct. (undated) (regarding Morton v. Mancari, No. 73–362), Box 1621, William O. Douglas Papers, Manuscript Division, Library of Congress, Washington, D.C.

[107] Morton v. Mancari, 417 U.S. 535, 550 (1974).

[108] *Id.*

[109] *Id.* at 551.

the analysis he abruptly switched gears in favor of the first theory, asserting that the Indian preference constituted neither racial discrimination nor a racial preference, but instead a political classification based on tribal citizenship. In a footnote, he observed,

> The preference is not directed towards a "racial" group consisting of "Indians"; instead, it applies only to members of "federally recognized" tribes. This operates to exclude many individuals who are racially to be classified as "Indians." In this sense, the preference is political rather than racial in nature.[110]

Later, Blackmun reinforced this point by noting, "The preference, as applied, is granted to Indians not as a discrete racial group, but, rather, as members of quasi-sovereign tribal entities whose lives and activities are governed by the BIA in a unique fashion."[111] He analogized the classification to a non-racial requirement that an elected official come from the community that he or she will govern, although the analogy was far from perfect.[112] Then, in a nod toward the third theory, namely that the discrimination is racial but justifiable in equal protection terms, Justice Blackmun opined, "Here, the preference is reasonably and directly related to a legitimate, nonracially based goal [of increasing participation of Indians in the agency that affects their lives]. This is the principal characteristic that generally is absent from proscribed forms of racial discrimination."[113] In connection with this point, he emphasized that the preference was limited to the BIA, an agency whose legal status is *"sui generis"* because of its governing role in Indian country, and that a broader Indian exemption from civil service examinations would pose an "obviously more difficult question."[114]

After listing a number of earlier decisions where the Court had upheld legislation singling Indians out for special treatment, Justice Blackmun concluded the opinion with an oft-quoted statement that "[a]s long as the special treatment can be tied rationally to the fulfillment of Congress' unique obligation toward the Indians, such legislative judg-

---

[110] *Id.* at 554 n.24.

[111] *Id.* at 554.

[112] The tribal membership component made no distinction among the Indian nations. Thus, for example, a Navajo would have a preference for BIA employment on the Colville reservation, with questionable benefits for Colville self-governance. As one commentator noted, "A closer analogy might be a requirement that a senatorial candidate be a resident of 'a state,' but not necessarily the state in which he is running for office, or a requirement that a city council candidate need only live in a city—any city." Wayne R. Farnsworth, Note, *Bureau of Indian Affairs Hiring Preferences After* Adarand Constructors, Inc. v. Peña, 1996 BYU L. Rev. 503, 510.

[113] *Morton*, 417 U.S. at 554.

[114] *Id.*

ments will not be disturbed."[115] This affirmation of a unique form of equal protection scrutiny did nothing to clarify the Court's underlying theory for deciding the case. For example, if the classification is truly political and not racial, then it is unclear why anything other than standard "rational basis" analysis would be called for under equal protection analysis.[116] Any connection with "Congress' unique obligation toward the Indians"[117] would be irrelevant, and an exemption for all Indians from civil service examinations would be perfectly allowable so long as any rational justification was available. Nonetheless, *Morton v. Mancari* became widely known as the case that declared Indian classifications to be political rather than racial.

The Practical and Legal Impact of Morton v. Mancari

Morton v. Mancari ushered in a new era of opportunity for Indians within the BIA. Today, more than 95% of the BIA's 12,000 employees are Indian. My own father-in-law's experience dramatizes this development. Before *Morton v. Mancari*, he held a series of low-GS jobs as a mechanic within the BIA on his own Turtle Mountain Chippewa reservation and others. Following the Court's decision, he rose quickly through the BIA ranks, eventually becoming the widely respected supervisor of maintenance for the many school buildings and other BIA facilities at Turtle Mountain.

The Court's decision also coincided with—and reflected—a wave of Indian policy favoring tribal self-determination, a policy that resulted in the transfer of many BIA functions to the Indian nations themselves.[118] This broader self-determination policy, combined with new tribal political initiatives, spawned congressional legislation addressing Indian issues and raised the question of how far *Morton v. Mancari* would extend. Statutes such as the Indian Child Welfare Act[119] and the Indian Gaming Regulatory Act[120] acknowledged and created special legal rights for individual Indians and tribes. For example, in a state child welfare proceeding relating to foster care, the parent of an Indian child and the child's tribe were entitled to the application of certain placement prefer-

---

[115] *Id.* at 555.

[116] *See* Goldberg, *supra* note 5, at 959.

[117] *Morton,* 417 U.S. at 555.

[118] A year after the decision in *Morton v. Mancari,* for example, Congress passed the Indian Self–Determination and Education Assistance Act, 25 U.S.C. §§ 450–450l, which directed the BIA to contract with tribes to perform BIA services. *See also* Wilkinson, *supra* note 8 at 197–98.

[119] 25 U.S.C. §§ 1901–1963 (2001).

[120] 25 U.S.C. §§ 2701–2721 (2001).

ences favoring the child's Indian relatives and other Indian foster families.[121] Would provisions like that survive equal protection challenge on race discrimination grounds? That depended in part on whether *Morton v. Mancari* was a narrow decision confined to favorable treatment for Indians within the BIA, or a broader statement about federal power over Indian affairs. Other questions remained as well. Would *Morton v. Mancari* apply to classifications that appeared to disadvantage individual Indians as well as to those that preferred them? Would it extend to classifications made by state governments as well as by the United States? And what would be its relationship to affirmative action, an area of law which the Court had so assiduously tried to avoid?

Within five years of its decision in *Morton v. Mancari*, the Supreme Court decided several cases that firmed up some contours of the doctrine but still left important questions unanswered. In *Fisher v. District Court*[122] and *United States v. Antelope*,[123] the Court established that *Mancari* could spread beyond the BIA, encompassing even some laws that worked to the detriment of individual Indians. In *Fisher*, the Court reviewed a principle of federal Indian law making tribal jurisdiction exclusive and thus denying states jurisdiction over domestic relations matters involving only tribal Indians living in Indian country.[124] The losing party before the tribal court challenged the rule denying access to state court, claiming racial discrimination. The Court rejected the challenge, citing *Mancari*, and found that so long as the classification was designed to benefit Indians as a class, it mattered not that some individual Indians might be disadvantaged by denial of access to a state court. In *Antelope*, the detriment to the individual Indian as a result of special federal Indian laws was even graver. Under the federal Major Crimes Act,[125] an Indian who killed a non-Indian on a reservation was subject to the federal law of homicide, which included a felony-murder rule. In contrast, a non-Indian who killed a non-Indian under identical circumstances would be subject to state homicide law, which in Antelope's case meant no state felony-murder rule. But the Court again relied on *Mancari* to reject the defendant's predictable equal protection claim.

Scholars and others have questioned whether the extension of *Mancari* to situations disadvantaging individual Indians means that the

---

[121] 25 U.S.C. § 1915(b) (2001).

[122] 424 U.S. 382 (1976).

[123] 430 U.S. 641 (1977).

[124] "Indian country" is a term of art within Indian law, referring to those areas subject to special rules of federal, tribal, and state jurisdiction. The formal definition of Indian country is found in 18 U.S.C. § 1151 (2000), and includes all reservations.

[125] 18 U.S.C. § 1153 (2000).

federal government can use its Indian affairs power to subjugate tribes and their members, certainly a troubling implication.[126] *Mancari*'s critics contend that only consistent application of strict equal protection scrutiny to all Indian classifications can afford adequate safeguards to Indians.[127] But *Mancari* did not put an end to the application of strict scrutiny to Indian classifications. Courts and scholars adhering to *Mancari* remain willing to call Indian classifications racial when it is apparent that the intent behind the treatment of Indians is connected to race or ancestry, not tribal relations.[128] While most of the cases adopting this view have involved state rather than federal discrimination,[129] if classifications involving Indians were truly based on political status rather than race, it would make no difference which government had established the classification.

In fact, the early post-*Mancari* cases addressed not only the range of federal actions to which the decision would apply, but also whether the relaxed *Mancari* standard would apply at all to state classifications. The greatest guidance on this question came from the Court's 1979 decision in *Washington v. Confederated Bands and Tribes of the Yakima Indian Nation*,[130] which held that a state classification could be measured against the *Mancari* standard only if Congress had directed or at least envisioned the state law under review to be in furtherance of federal Indian policy. As an example, the Court cited state laws assuming jurisdiction over Indian country in accordance with Congress's authorization. Lower courts later extended this application of *Mancari* to any state classification that advances federal Indian policy, such as a state exemption for Indian practitioners of peyote religion, mirroring a similar federal exemption.[131] While these applications of *Mancari* to state classifications answered an important question about the scope of the precedent, they did little to clarify the principle underlying *Mancari*. Specifi-

---

[126] See David C. Williams, *The Borders of the Equal Protection Clause: Indians as Peoples*, 38 UCLA L. Rev. 759 (1991).

[127] See, e.g., Nell Jessup Newton, *Federal Power over Indians: Its Sources, Scope, and Limitations*, 132 U. Pa. L. Rev. 195, 241–47 (1984).

[128] See, e.g., Eugene Volokh, *The California Civil Rights Initiative: An Interpretive Guide*, 44 UCLA L. Rev. 1335, 1358–59 (1997).

[129] See, e.g., Pyke v. Cuomo, 258 F.3d 107, 109 (2d Cir. 2001) (law does not permit denial of police protection to reservation Indians "on the basis of discriminatory anti-Indian animus"); Navajo Nation v. New Mexico, 975 F.2d 741 (10th Cir. 1992) (state may not cut health care funds to tribal provider when the motive is at least in part to discriminate against Indians); Fallon Paiute–Shoshone Tribe v. City of Fallon, 174 F. Supp. 2d 1088 (D. Nev. 2001) (city may not violate equal protection by denying utility services to reservation Indians).

[130] 439 U.S. 463, 500–02 (1979).

[131] See, e.g., Peyote Way Church of God, Inc. v. Thornburgh, 922 F.2d 1210 (5th Cir. 1991) (application of the *Mancari* standard to state law exempting only Native American practitioners of peyote religion from state-controlled substances law).

cally, *Yakima*'s limitation of *Mancari* to state laws effectuating federal policy is difficult to reconcile with the political-not-racial theory of *Mancari*. For if the state classification is truly nonracial, relaxed scrutiny should apply without regard to any relationship between state law and federal policies.

As of 1980, the lower *Mancari* standard of review had spread far beyond the BIA, encompassing federal laws unrelated to Indian representation in the governance of their communities, as well as laws disadvantaging individual Indians and state laws effectuating federal policies. Not long after *Mancari*, Congress felt confident enough about the constitutionality of Indian preferences to enact several more, including a preference for Indians in employment and subcontracting under tribal contracts to perform federal Indian services;[132] a preference for Indians to receive scholarships or internships to prepare to teach in Indian communities or to train for professions such as law;[133] and a preference for adoptive and foster care placements for Indian children.[134] Several of these provisions resembled the kinds of preferences—especially in employment and education—that were conventionally described as "race-based affirmative action."

By this time, however, the political and legal assault on affirmative action had shifted into high gear.[135] *Mancari*'s ready acceptance of preferential treatment seemed at odds with that movement, and some of the opponents of affirmative action came to view Indian law, and *Mancari*'s protection of it, as threatening to their ultimate agenda of overthrowing government-sponsored racial and ethnic preferences. The tendency to see *all* federal Indian law classifications through the affirmative action lens was magnified by the fact that Native Americans or American Indians were typically included among the groups benefited by conventional state and federal affirmative action in education, employment, and contracting, along with African Americans and Latinos. The upshot of this conflation of Indian law with affirmative action has been an effort by affirmative action opponents to confine or to overturn *Mancari* through scholarly work,[136] litigation,[137] and legislation.[138] For

---

[132] 25 U.S.C. §§ 450–458 (2001).

[133] 25 U.S.C. §§ 2622, 2623(a), 3371 (2001).

[134] 25 U.S.C. § 1915 (2001).

[135] For insight into this agenda, see Ward Connerly, *Creating Equal: My Fight Against Race Preferences* (2000); Dinesh D'Souza, *The End of Racism: Principles for a Multiracial Society* (1995); Terry Eastland, *Ending Affirmative Action: The Case for Colorblind Justice* (1996).

[136] *See, e.g.*, Stuart Minor Benjamin, *Equal Protection and the Special Relationship: The Case of Native Hawaiians*, 106 Yale L.J. 537 (1996); L. Scott Gould, *Mixing Bodies and Beliefs: The Predicament of Tribes*, 101 Colum. L. Rev. 702 (2001).

[137] *See, e.g.*, Am. Fed'n of Gov't Employees v. United States, 104 F. Supp. 2d 58 (D.D.C. 2000), *aff'd*, 330 F.3d 513 (D.C. Cir. 2003) (upholding federal contracting preference for Indians against claim that it was impermissible race-based discrimination).

[138] *See, e.g.*, Native American Equal Rights Act of 2000, 146 Cong. Rec. E1864 (daily ed. Oct. 19, 2000) (statement of Rep. Weldon).

example, the sponsor of the Native American Equal Rights Act, a measure that would have repealed Indian preferences in employment and contracting, announced that most Americans, believing in a color-blind society, "would be surprised . . . to learn that non-Indians may be lawfully discriminated against under what are known as 'Indian preference laws.' "[139] He insisted that even though "what motivated the Congress to pass the Indian preference laws was not racism, but rather political favoritism" the ultimate effect of such laws "is . . . to favor one race over all others."[140] For him, the *Mancari* political-not-racial analysis was just a pretext for labeling a racial preference as something else.

The Supreme Court at first refused to allow Indian preferences to get mixed up with affirmative action. In the 1978 case of *Regents of the University of California v. Bakke*,[141] a white applicant denied admission to a public medical school challenged the set-aside of seats for underrepresented racial and ethnic groups as impermissible reverse discrimination. In defending its policy, the University tried to cite *Mancari* for the proposition that states may pass laws preferring members of traditionally disadvantaged groups.[142] But the Court would have none of that, pointing out that *Mancari* had emphasized the sui generis character of the BIA and had found "that the preference was not racial at all."[143]

Then, in 1995, the Court decided *Adarand Constructors, Inc. v. Pena*,[144] a challenge to affirmative action in federal contracting. In finding the consideration of race unconstitutional, Justice Sandra Day O'Connor wrote that "all racial classifications, imposed by whatever federal, state, or local governmental actor, must be analyzed . . . under strict scrutiny. In other words, such classifications are constitutional only if they are narrowly tailored measures that further compelling governmental interests."[145] The federal law invalidated in *Adarand* had

---

[139] *Id.*

[140] *Id.*

[141] 438 U.S. 265 (1978).

[142] *Id.* at 304 n.42.

[143] *Id.*

[144] 515 U.S. 200 (1995).

[145] *Id.* at 227. This opinion overturned an earlier decision by the Court that had allowed use of a lower level of equal protection scrutiny for federal classifications benefiting traditionally disadvantaged groups. *See* Metro Broad., Inc. v. F.C.C., 497 U.S. 547 (1990).

included Native Americans along with Blacks, Hispanics, and Asian Pacific and subcontinent Asian Americans in granting a preference for subcontracts on federally contracted projects. Justice O'Connor's insistence that the standard of equal protection review not be "dependent on the race of those burdened or benefited by a particular classification"[146] left many, including Justice Stevens in dissent, wondering whether *Mancari* had been fatally undermined.[147] As Professor L. Scott Gould wrote, "[f]or Congress and tribes, *Mancari* is a refuge for race-conscious legislation in an *Adarand* world of race neutrality."[148]

The perception that *Mancari* was on the ropes led a panel of the Ninth Circuit, in *Williams v. Babbitt*,[149] to sharply curtail *Mancari*'s application. *Williams* involved a challenge by a non-Indian to the Interior Department's interpretation of the Reindeer Industry Act of 1937, which gave certain advantages and support to Native Alaskans in carrying on the business of reindeer herding.[150] While the Act did not expressly prohibit non-Natives from engaging in such activity, the Interior Department interpreted the Act to bar non-Indian herding.[151] In rejecting the Department's interpretation, the Ninth Circuit invoked concerns that a federally conferred Native monopoly on reindeer herding would violate guarantees of equal protection. To avoid the force of *Mancari*, the panel observed that unlike the BIA employment preference, the classification made by the Interior Department was a "naked preference for Indians unrelated to unique Indian concerns."[152]

For the panel, the fact that Congress had passed the Reindeer Act in order to reestablish a land-based way of life for Alaska Natives was not a unique enough Indian interest because reindeers were not indigenous to Alaska and reindeer herding was not a traditional Native Alaskan

---

[146] *Adarand*, 515 U.S. at 222 (citing Richmond v. J.A. Croson Co., 488 U.S. 469, 494 (1989)).

[147] Citing *Mancari*, Justice Stevens wrote, "We should reject a concept of 'consistency' that would view the special preferences that the National Government has provided to Native Americans since 1834 as comparable to the official discrimination against African–Americans that was prevalent for much of our history." *Adarand*, 515 U.S. at 244–45 (Stevens, J., dissenting) (footnote omitted). In Stevens' view, the *Mancari* Court had found that the Indian preference was not racial because it did not apply to all Native Americans. *Id.* at 244 n.3. *See also* Farnsworth, *supra* note 112 at 522–24 (indicating that application of *Adarand* to the current BIA hiring preference could well lead to a conclusion that the preference is unconstitutional).

[148] Gould, *supra* note 136, at 717.

[149] 115 F.3d 657 (9th Cir. 1997).

[150] *See* 25 U.S.C. § 500 (2001).

[151] *See* Reindeer Herders Ass'n v. Juneau Area Dir., 23 IBIA 28 (1992).

[152] *Williams*, 115 F.3d at 664.

pursuit.[153] Drawing analogies, the panel expressed "serious[] doubt that Congress could give Indians a complete monopoly on the casino industry or on Space Shuttle contracts."[154] The *Williams* court expressly sought to reframe *Mancari* as a decision resting on something akin to the valid-under-equal-protection theory of MALDEF. Judge Alex Kozinski, writing for the panel, wanted heavy scrutiny applied to Indian preferences, believing that preferences tied to traditional Indian self-government and lands, and *only* such preferences, would survive judicial review because they serve the compelling interest of the United States in fulfilling its trust responsibility. The panel was emboldened to confine *Mancari* so tightly, despite later decisions expanding its reach, because of *Adarand*. As Judge Kozinski wrote for the *Williams* panel, "If Justice Stevens is right about the logical implications of *Adarand*, *Mancari*'s days are numbered."[155]

Remarkably, however, *Mancari* remains good law, despite its equivocal foundation, the weakness of its reasoning, and the attacks from opponents of affirmative action. In 2000, in *Rice v. Cayetano*,[156] the Supreme Court had a golden opportunity to repudiate or severely restrict *Mancari*, but ultimately backed away. As Eric Yamamoto and Catherine Betts discuss more fully in chapter 14, the plaintiff in *Rice v. Cayetano* was challenging a Hawaiian statute that allowed only descendents of indigenous Hawaiians to vote for the trustees of the state's Office of Hawaiian Affairs. This office had been established under federal direction to administer state laws and obligations toward Native Hawaiians, among others. A threshold question was whether *Mancari* even applied, given that Native Hawaiians were not organized into a tribe and had no formally recognized government-to-government relationship with the United States. Rather than skirting the question of *Mancari*'s applicability on that basis, the *Rice* Court chose instead to contrast the particular circumstances in *Mancari* (involvement of the BIA, the main federal agency responsible for Indian affairs) with those in *Rice* itself (a state-sponsored election). According to the Court, "[t]o extend *Mancari* to this context would be to permit a State, by racial classification, to fence out whole classes of its citizens from decisionmaking in critical state affairs. The Fifteenth Amendment forbids this result."[157] Thus the Court's relatively narrow reliance on the Fifteenth Amendment in *Rice* served to protect *Mancari* against erosion.

---

[153] *See* Carole Goldberg, *Descent Into Race*, 49 UCLA L. Rev. 1373, 1376–80 (2002).

[154] *Williams*, 115 F.3d at 665.

[155] *Id.*

[156] 528 U.S. 495 (2000).

[157] *Id.* at 522.

Several reasons help to explain *Mancari*'s survival, especially after *Adarand*. First is the narrow survival of affirmative action itself, as reflected in another case featured in this book: the Supreme Court's 2003 decision in *Grutter v. Bollinger*.[158] Second is a recent indication by the Court in *United States v. Lara*[159] of its general inclination to defer broadly to Congress in matters affecting Indians.[160] Third is the multiple rationales or theories upon which the case rests, even if one or more of them is unstable. The political-not-racial theory is the most vulnerable but also the one that appeals most to opponents of race-based affirmative action.[161] Its ascendance has produced a preponderance of federal statutory and administrative schemes that limit benefits to members of federally recognized tribes, excluding members of non-federally recognized tribes as well as individuals who may have considerable Indian ancestry but cannot qualify under particular tribal membership requirements.[162] The Indian Commerce Clause theory is the most defensible, historically and legally, but also the most obscure, resting as it does on the not very well known body of Indian law. And the valid-under-equal protection theory appeals to advocates of racial justice, who think all race-based preferences should be judged according to a more relaxed standard of review.[163]

Conclusion: The Significance of Mancari for Issues of Race

The United States Supreme Court could have chosen to analyze *Morton v. Mancari* as a race case, as the lower court had done. Instead, it viewed the individuals receiving Indian preference as members of political bodies. What difference did that choice make for the broader corpus of race-related law and for other racial groups? This question—an invitation to speculation—can be addressed at both the doctrinal level and a more theoretical level.

As a doctrinal matter, if the Court had acknowledged the racial dimension in *Morton v. Mancari*, it might have felt compelled to apply a

---

[158] 539 U.S. 306 (2003).

[159] 541 U.S. 193 (2004).

[160] In *Lara*, the Court upheld a federal statute recognizing inherent powers of Indian nations to exercise criminal jurisdiction over nonmember Indians, even though the Court itself, in an earlier decision, had found that such tribal jurisdiction did not exist because it had been implicitly divested when Indian nations became dependent on the United States. *Id.* at 197–200.

[161] *See, e.g.,* Volokh, *supra* note 128, at 1358–59.

[162] For a discussion of this phenomenon, see Robert N. Clinton et al., *American Indian Law: Native Nations and the Federal System* 132–37 (Lexis, rev. 4th ed. 2005).

[163] *See* Brief of Amicus Curiae Mexican American Legal Defense and Educational Fund, *supra* note 82, at *19.

"strict scrutiny" analysis. Whether taking that road would have aided racial groups seeking to uphold affirmative action is not so clear, however. On the one hand, a Court unwilling to overturn the huge body of federal Indian legislation might have felt pressed to water down strict scrutiny, enabling affirmative action to survive as well with a stronger foundation than the equivocal *Bakke* later afforded. On the other hand, as the Court's struggle over *DeFunis* and *Bakke* suggests, no clear majority was ready to choose that path. Certainly the other alternative available to the Court, if it felt compelled to apply strict scrutiny to a classification it viewed as racial, was to let Indian legislation fall along with affirmative action, at least when the Indian legislation fit the affirmative action mold of employment, education, or contracting preferences.

The racial road not taken in *Mancari* has implications for race and law theory as well. By emphasizing the political dimension of Indian societies and ignoring the role of kinship and ancestry, the Court may have underscored a natural and biological conception of race over a conception that emphasizes social construction and meaning. Today, critical race theory leans strongly toward the view of race as socially and politically constructed, with law playing a crucial role in that process.[164] In other words, the law does not simply operate upon naturally existing racial differences, but rather shapes peoples' understanding and experience of those very differences.

In contrast, *Mancari* sharply separated the legal and political framework surrounding Native people from their "racial" characteristics, suggesting that the two were completely different. This move obscures not only the legal or political construction of race for other people of color, but also the extent to which the law and broader political dynamics have racialized Native peoples. Had the Court adopted the Indian Commerce Clause theory, with its acknowledgment that the Constitution expressly approves of Indian-specific legislation, even with its inevitable mixture of racial and political components, the message emanating from *Mancari* might have been more consistent with a theory of the social construction of race. But whatever one may say about the impact of *Mancari* on race law, there is no denying the effect that broader racial issues have had on *Mancari*. Wider controversies over affirmative action swirled about the case from the beginning, when it was up for argument and decision; and the currents of that controversy continue to bring waves of challenge and defense to the Court's decision.

Certainly Carla Mancari viewed the litigation as part of a broader crusade for an integrated society in which all races would be accepted,

---

[164] *See, e.g., Introduction, Critical Race Theory: The Key Writings That Formed the Movement*, at xxv (Kimberlé Crenshaw et al. eds., 1995).

and she sought a repudiation of affirmative action which she believes benefits one minority at the expense of others. In the wake of the Court's decision, Mancari changed direction in her career. She moved away from social service toward more spiritual and metaphysical preoccupations. For her the Supreme Court's decision was a sad and life-changing experience.[165] But for Indian people like my father-in-law, who were able to march through the door of opportunity the Court opened, it was an unquestionable benefit. And for Indian nations as a whole, it dispelled any constitutional clouds that may have darkened Congress' tribal self-determination policy, which reached its apex in the decades following *Mancari*.

---

[165] Telephone Interview with Carla Mancari, *supra* note 36.

8

Ian Haney López & Michael A. Olivas

Jim Crow, Mexican Americans, and the Anti–Subordination Constitution: The Story of *Hernandez v. Texas*

Introduction

Brown v. Board of Education has been widely celebrated as the first decision in which the Supreme Court, newly unified under the leadership of Chief Justice Earl Warren, set out to dismantle Jim Crow segregation.[1] But it was not. That distinction belongs to an almost entirely forgotten jury exclusion case decided two weeks earlier: *Hernandez v. Texas*.[2] *Hernandez* deserves the honor of being recognized as the first civil rights decision of the Warren Court.[3] It is also the first Supreme

---

[1] Even the meticulous Richard Kluger describes *Brown* as "Warren's first major opinion as Chief Justice." Richard Kluger, *Simple Justice: The History of* Brown v. Board of Education *and Black America's Struggle for Equality* 702 (Vintage Books 1977) (1975).

[2] 347 U.S. 475 (1954).

[3] *See "Colored Men" and "Hombres Aqui": Hernandez v. Texas and the Emergence of Mexican–American Lawyering* (Michael A. Olivas ed., 2006); Ian Haney López, *Race and Colorblindness after* Hernandez *and* Brown, 25 Chicano–Latino L. Rev. 61 (2005) (hereinafter Hernandez *and* Brown); Ian F. Haney López, *Race, Ethnicity, Erasure: The Salience of Race to LatCrit Theory*, 85 Cal. L. Rev. 1143 (1997). *See also* Symposium, *Commemorating the 50th Anniversary of* Hernandez v. Texas, 25 Chicano–Latino L. Rev. 1 (2005); Symposium, Hernandez v. Texas*: A 50th Anniversary Celebration*, 11 Tex. Hisp. J.L. & Pol'y 11 (2005); Clare Sheridan, *"Another White Race": Mexican Americans and the Paradox of Whiteness in Jury Selection*, 21 Law & Hist. Rev. 109 (2003); George A. Martinez, *Legal Indeterminacy, Judicial Discretion and the Mexican–American Litigation Experience: 1930–*

Court case to extend the protections of the Fourteenth Amendment to
Latinos, as well as the most resounding early triumph in the Latino
struggle for civil rights.[4] But *Hernandez* deserves attention not simply as
a case that should be rescued from oblivion and installed into its rightful
place in the pantheon of "great cases" from the past. *Hernandez* has
contemporary doctrinal relevance today. *Hernandez* helps demonstrate
that the Warren Court declared constitutional war not on racial classifications per se, but on group subordination. *Hernandez*, when read
together with *Brown*, pushes towards an anti-subordination rather than
anti-classification conception of the Equal Protection Clause. Put differently, *Hernandez* stands in opposition to the claim that the Constitution
should be colorblind, in the sense of treating all governmental uses of
racial classifications with equal hostility.

This chapter puts *Hernandez* in context, while also suggesting that
this case, long overshadowed, may yet have tremendous doctrinal significance. We first provide a litigation history, describing the path to the
Supreme Court and the professional identities and personal biographies
of the lawyers who represented Hernández.[5] Next, we turn to the
Supreme Court opinion, paying particular attention to a central paradox.
Though the Court struck down Jim Crow practices that barred Latinos
from jury participation, the Justices did not analyze the case as if it
involved race relations but instead focused on "other differences from
the community norm" that sometimes formed the basis of social hierarchy. We then explain this paradox, attributing it to the fact that the
parties on both sides of the litigation classified people of Mexican
ancestry as white. After detailing how this consensus emerged, we
elaborate on why the classification of Mexicans as white restricted the
extent to which Chief Justice Warren could adjudicate Hernández's
Fourteenth Amendment claim explicitly in racial terms. In the context of
this discussion, we suggest that the contemporary relevance of *Hernandez* derives precisely from the fact that while the opinion centrally
concerned an aspect of Jim Crow stratification, it reasoned generally in
terms of group mistreatment.

1980, 27 U.C. Davis L. Rev. 555 (1994); and Ricardo Romo, *Southern California and the
Origins of Latino Civil–Rights Activism*, 3 W. Legal Hist. 379 (1990).

[4] For an overview of Mexican–American civil rights litigation, see Martinez, *supra* note
3.

[5] A quick note on accent marks: as a name, Hernández carries an accented "a"
indicating that emphasis should be placed on this vowel. For purposes of grammatical
accuracy and to encourage the correct pronunciation of this case name, we have opted to
include the accent when referring to Hernández as an individual. On the other hand,
because the accent is not used in the case title before the Texas courts or in the *United
States Reports*, we do not use an accent in referencing *Hernandez* as a case.

The Path to the Supreme Court

Hernandez traveled an unlikely route to the Supreme Court. With roots in an angry exchange of words that led to a tragic shooting, the significance of the case was far from obvious at the outset. On August 4, 1951, twenty-four-year-old service station attendant Pedro (Pete) Hernández shot and killed tenant farmer Joe Espinosa, apparently during a barroom brawl in Chinco Sánchez's Tavern, located in Sprung's Grocery in Edna, the county seat for Jackson County, Texas.[6] Within twenty-four hours, Hernández was indicted for murder by an all-white grand jury,[7] and four days later he was denied bail.[8] His family scraped together the resources to hire Johnny Herrera, one of the very few experienced Mexican–American lawyers in the Houston area. Herrera had graduated from the South Texas College of Law, a freestanding law school in Houston, and at the time the only law school in what was then Texas' largest city.[9] He had worked a number of jobs, gone to law school at night, and driven a cab until he became a licensed attorney in 1943. Herrera had carved out a general civil practice, but increasingly had taken on criminal cases, in large part because there was such a need and there were so few Mexican–American lawyers in Texas. At the time, the Houston area had fewer than half a dozen Mexican–American attorneys, and Herrera took two of them, James deAnda and Arnulfo Azios, into his firm. James deAnda had graduated from Texas A & M University and the University of Texas Law School when it was still a segregated institution. DeAnda later speculated that he was able to matriculate only because he was "guero" (light-skinned) and because the school officials had likely thought he was Italian.[10] When law firms and city offices

---

[6] The facts of the case are spelled out in the various published opinions, while the entire trial record is available in microfilm in the District Clerk Office, Jackson County, Edna, Texas. *See* Transcript of Record, State v. Hernandez (Dist. Ct., Jackson Co., Tex. 1951) (No. 2091), *reprinted in "Colored Men" and "Hombres Aqui," supra* note 3, at App. V. Additional facts about the arrest and trial are taken from the contemporaneous news stories that appeared on the front page of the *Edna Herald*. *See Bond Is Denied, Edna Youth Charged in Rifle Slaying,* Edna Herald, Aug. 5, 1951, at 1; *Jury to Get Hernandez Case Today,* Edna Herald, Oct. 11, 1951, at 1; *Hernandez Life Term Appealed,* Edna Herald, Oct. 18, 1951, at 1.

[7] Interview with James deAnda, retired judge and lawyer, in Houston, Texas (Nov. 6, 2005).

[8] *Bond Is Denied, supra* note 6.

[9] Although Herrera graduated from law school in 1940, it took him several attempts to pass the Texas bar examination; he did not receive his license to practice law until 1943. *See Handbook of Texas,* Entry for Herrera, John J., *available at* http://www.tsha.utexas. edu/handbook/online/articles/HH/fhe63.html (last visited Nov. 20, 2006) (providing a biography of Herrera); Hernandez v. Texas: *A 50th Anniversary Celebration, supra* note 3, at 28 (statement of Judge James deAnda).

[10] Interview with James deAnda, *supra* note 7. *See also* Steven H. Wilson, Brown *over "Other White": Mexican Americans' Legal Arguments and Litigation Strategy in School*

found out he was Mexican American, he was unable to otherwise secure employment in Houston, making him grateful for the offer to hang his shingle with the more experienced Herrera.

When the *Hernandez* case came in, Herrera and deAnda were in the midst of litigating another jury exclusion case. The central legal claim in *Hernandez*—that Mexican Americans were entitled to a "jury of their peers" that included other Mexican Americans—had an established pedigree in Texas. With the encouragement of the League of United Latin American Citizens ("LULAC"), the leading Hispanic civil rights organization of the day, lawyers for Mexican Americans had brought similar challenges at least seven times between 1931 and the trial court decision in *Hernandez v. State* in 1952. However, they had consistently lost on this claim before the Texas courts.[11] Herrera and deAnda first litigated the jury exclusion claim not in *Hernandez*, but in *Aniceto Sanchez v. State*.[12] The appellate court in *Sanchez* would later pithily summarize the alleged crime:

> The appellant was convicted for murder and assessed a penalty of ten years in the penitentiary. The evidence discloses that appellant, a Mexican, was a farm worker and lived on a large plantation in a cottage within a few feet of that occupied by the deceased. On the night of the tragedy [April 23, 1950], shortly after twelve o'clock, the deceased came up to the residence of appellant where he was engaged with others in drinking beer. He was singing a song in Mexican which, interpreted, is entitled "You, Only You" and is said to be a Mexican love song. Apparently this incensed appellant who, without any words, went into his house, got his gun, came out and shot, killing the deceased a short distance from his front door steps. About this there is no controversy.[13]

Aniceto Sánchez had shot Hylario Smershy, whose Czech surname hid his Mexican ancestry.[14] Sánchez and Smershy worked side by side for Imperial Sugar, plowing fields with large mules, and living in shanties

---

Desegregation Lawsuits, 21 Law & Hist. Rev. 145, 149–150 (2003) (reviewing deAnda's role in *Hernandez*).

[11] *See* Ramirez v. State, 40 S.W.2d 138 (Tex. Crim. App. 1931); Carrasco v. State, 95 S.W.2d 433 (Tex. Crim. App. 1936); Serapio Sanchez v. State, 181 S.W.2d 87 (Tex. Crim. App. 1944); Salazar v. State, 193 S.W.2d 211 (Tex. Crim. App. 1946); Bustillos v. State, 213 S.W.2d 837 (Tex. Crim. App. 1948); Rogers v. State, 236 S.W.2d 141 (Tex. Crim. App. 1951); Aniceto Sanchez v. State, 243 S.W.2d 700 (Tex. Crim. App. 1951).

[12] 243 S.W.2d 700.

[13] *Id.* at 701.

[14] Marie-Theresa Hernandez, *Reconditioning History: Adapting Knowledge from the Past into the Realities of the Present: A Mexican–American Graveyard*, 3 *Rethinking History* 289, 298–99 (1999) (history of San Isidro Cemetery, Richmond, Texas, by daughter of the man [Jose F. Hernandez] who served as the translator in the *Aniceto Sanchez* trial).

near each other in the part of a company town called "El Gran Centro." Although the two knew each other well and often drank together after work, that evening Sánchez apparently felt that Smershy was acting inappropriately towards his wife by trying to woo her, as the love song "Tu Solo Tu" portrays a drunken and passionate man lusting after a woman ("borracho y apasionado no mas por tu amor").[15]

When the *Sanchez* case came into the office in the summer of 1950, Herrera had tried a number of cases before juries, for whom he had a genuine feel, and deAnda had just received his license to practice law. Herrera and deAnda discussed the fact that no Mexican-origin jurors had been called at the grand jury or the petit jury stages, and familiarized themselves with earlier cases challenging the exclusion of Mexican Americans from Texas juries.[16] They agreed that Herrera would prepare a general defense, while deAnda would focus on the jury exclusion claim by gathering available data on the demographics of Texas and specifically of the area where the case arose, Fort Bend County.[17] To document the exclusion of Mexican Americans from local juries, deAnda went to the area's public libraries, inquired of state and local government agencies, and read available studies and newspapers to gather data on jury selection practices.

The economic and social conditions in Fort Bend laid the foundation for Jim Crow segregation and stratification. The county lay an hour southwest of Houston and in the 1950s was essentially rural, dominated by sugar and rice plantations.[18] Agricultural production in the area relied

---

Otherwise quite accurate, she mistakenly reverses the parties: "A man named Hylario Smershy had killed another man, Aniceto Sanchez." *Id.* at 298. We gratefully acknowledge the assistance of Professor Hernandez.

[15] The full verse reads: "Woman, look how I am, Due to your loving/ I am drunk and passionate due to your love/ Look how I am given over to drunkenness and perdition." (trans. Michael A. Olivas).

[16] Interview with James deAnda, *supra* note 7. *See generally* James deAnda, *Hernandez at Fifty, A Personal History*, in *"Colored Men" and "Hombres Aqui," supra* note 3, at 199–208 (oral history of *Hernandez* lawsuit). Unfortunately, deAnda's personal and professional papers from the *Hernandez* era were lost in a fire in the Houston federal courthouse when deAnda was a federal judge. For a list of earlier cases, see *supra* note 11. DeAnda and Herrera were particularly influenced by the *Serapio Sanchez* case, tried in El Paso in 1944 by attorney A. L. Carlton. *Serapio Sanchez*, 181 S.W.2d at 87. Importantly, Carlton agreed to share his case files with deAnda and Herrera. Interview with James deAnda, *supra* note 7.

[17] James deAnda did the research in part because he had not yet tried a case, having just received his bar membership in December 1950. DeAnda and Herrera agreed that the latter would try their cases until deAnda gained experience by observing trials. Interview with James deAnda, *supra* note 7.

[18] The town of Sugar Land dominated the area, later made famous by the early Stephen Spielberg movie about a caravan that led there. *The Sugarland Express* (Universal Pictures 1974).

on a stable and dependent workforce, sharply stratified by race and class, with blacks, Mexican Americans, and state prisoners of all races laboring under an Anglo managerial elite.[19] Until 1914, the Texas Department of Corrections had contracted prison labor with Imperial Sugar and other area companies.[20] After that, the companies recruited and maintained their own workforces, using a traditional Southern corporate racial strategy of separate housing and occupational segregation, complete with ethnic churches, separate graveyards, company stores, and scrip rather than currency—all of which combined to accentuate the different racial groupings and to maintain the subordinate status of minority workers and their families.[21] Harold Hyman's classic study of the area, *Oleander Odyssey*, largely criticized labor practices employed by the companies, but appeared to take the segregation and stratification of Mexican-origin workers for granted. When one new manager removed the shacks in the Mexican part of town, Hyman simply commented that the demolition of "the noisome shanties of 'Mexico' (as that part of town was dubbed)," prompted no "known complaints by the unsalubrious residents" of the barrio.[22] Fort Bend County was, in other words, the Deep Jim Crow South, but with Mexicans occupying the bottom rungs of the ladder along with blacks.[23]

DeAnda submitted his research in the *Sanchez* case to the court on March 19, 1951. In a six-page brief that argued for quashing the indictment, the defense charged that the all-white grand jury and petit jury had violated Sánchez's equal protection rights.[24] The brief noted that there had been a rush to indict Sánchez, that Sánchez spoke no English and did not understand any rights he might have asserted, and that he had been "under severe mental strain" when arrested and indicted.[25] On the question of jury discrimination, deAnda and Herrera

---

[19] Hernandez, *supra* note 14, at 291–292; Harold M. Hyman, *Oleander Odyssey: The Kempners of Galveston, Texas, 1854–1980s*, at 305 (1st ed. 1990).

[20] Hernandez, *supra* note 14, at 3.

[21] *Id.*

[22] *Hyman, supra* note 19, at 305.

[23] On May 4, 1953, the U.S. Supreme Court, in *Terry v. Adams*, would strike down the Fort Bend County practice of using a segregated surrogate party, the Jaybird Party, to thwart African American voting in the Democratic Party. Terry v. Adams, 345 U.S. 461 (1953). *See* Hernandez, *supra* note 14, at 292–294. *See also* Hyman, *supra* note 19; Randolph B. Campbell, *An Empire for Slavery: The Peculiar Institution in Texas, 1821–1865*, at 57–58 (reprint ed. 1991). *See generally* David Montejano, *Anglos and Mexicans in the Making of Texas, 1836–1986* (1st ed. 1987); Arnoldo de León, *They Called Them Greasers: Anglo Attitudes Toward Mexicans in Texas, 1821–1900*, at 104 (1st ed. 1983).

[24] Bill of Exception No. 1, State v. Hernandez (Dist. Ct., Jackson Co., Tex. 1951) (No. 2091), *reprinted in "Colored Men" and "Hombres Aqui," supra* note 3, at App. II, at 1.

[25] *Id.* at App. II, at 2.

pointed out that in thirty-five years no Mexican American had been called to jury duty in any capacity in the county, which was home to more than 6,000 Mexican Americans, constituting approximately one-quarter of the county population. The brief concluded:

> [T]here has prevailed in Fort Bend County, Texas for a period of over thirty-five years, a systematic, continual and un-interrupted practice of discrimination against Mexican–Americans as a race, and people of Mexican extraction and ancestry as a class separate from other white Americans, a class to which this Defendant belongs, in the selection of Grand Jury Commissioners and Grand Jurors solely because of membership within that class.[26]

Nevertheless, on March 20, 1951 the jury convicted Sánchez of murder and on April 7, 1951 he was sentenced to ten years in prison.[27] On November 21, 1951 the Texas Court of Criminal Appeals, Texas' highest court for criminal matters, affirmed the verdict and sentence.[28] Sánchez would not let his lawyers appeal his case any further, apparently calculating that he had received a relatively light sentence and worrying that he might fare much worse, possibly even risking the death penalty, if he were to be retried.

While Herrera and deAnda awaited the decision from the Texas appellate court in *Sanchez,* they were asked to represent Pete Hernández. Jackson County was even farther southwest from Houston than was Fort Bend County, though both areas shared an intense pattern of Southern agricultural segregation. Encouraged by progressive colleagues like Maury Maverick, a San Antonio lawyer and legislator, Herrera and deAnda decided once again to press the jury selection challenge.[29] This time, though, they planned to make this a central element of the defense and to focus on the jury challenge from the very beginning of the case. In September 1951, San Antonio attorneys Gustavo García and Carlos Cadena joined the defense team in order to bolster the challenge against Texas jury practices. García was known as a talented litigator, and Cadena had already established a reputation as a skilled appellate lawyer and something of an intellectual. Herrera and García had known each other through LULAC and other circles, but had not maintained close

---

[26] *Id.* at 2–5.

[27] *Sanchez,* 243 S.W.2d 700; Copy of Sentence, No. 7103, Sanchez v. State, 243 S.W.2d 700 (Tex. Crim. App. 1951), *reprinted in "Colored Men" and "Hombres Aqui," supra* note 3, at App. II, at 7.

[28] *Sanchez,* 243 S.W.2d at 700.

[29] Interview with James deAnda, *supra* note 7. Maverick, who died a month after the case was decided, signed the brief that was eventually filed with the United States Supreme Court. *See generally* Richard B. Henderson, *Maury Maverick: A Political Biography* (1970). *See infra* note 53 (naming the signatories to the brief).

ties, as each struggled to establish a law practice. In 1951, their experience was typical of the fewer than two dozen Mexican–American lawyers practicing in Texas, who were frequently too geographically isolated from each other and too busy to interact on a regular basis.

On October 4, 1951, not unexpectedly, the district court rejected the initial allegation of jury discrimination and refused to quash the Hernández indictment.[30] Between October 8 and 11, 1951, Hernández was tried by an all-white jury. His lawyers pressed the claim that Mexican Americans were unfairly excluded from jury service, tying their absence to a larger pattern of discrimination. In one of the most dramatic episodes in the trial, García introduced evidence regarding the segregated courthouse bathrooms by calling to the stand co-counsel John Herrera. As excerpted from the trial court transcript, the exchange between García and Herrera proceeded as follows:

Q. During the noon recess I will ask you if you had occasion to go back there to a public privy, right in back of the courthouse square?

A. Yes, sir.

Q. The one designated for men?

A. Yes, sir.

Q. Now did you find one toilet there or more?

A. I found two.

Q. Did the one on the right have any lettering on it?

A. No, sir.

Q. Did the one on the left have any lettering on it?

A. Yes, it did.

Q. What did it have?

A. It had the lettering "Colored Men" and right under "Colored Men" it had two Spanish words.

Q. What were those words?

A. The first word was "Hombres."

Q. What does that mean?

A. That means "Men."

Q. And the second one?

A. "Aqui," meaning "Here."

---

[30] Memorandum Denying Motion to Quash Indictments, State v. Hernandez (Dist. Ct., Jackson Co., Tex. 1951) (No. 2091), *reprinted in "Colored Men" and "Hombres Aqui," supra* note 3, at App. V, at 261.

Q. Right under the words "Colored Men" was "Hombres Aqui" in Spanish, which means "Men Here"?

A. Yes, sir.[31]

Under cross-examination by the district attorney, Herrera continued:

Q. There was not a lock on this unmarked door to the privy?

A. No, sir.

Q. It was open to the public?

A. They were both open to the public, yes, sir.

Q. And didn't have on it "For Americans Only," or "For English Only," or "For Whites Only"?

A. No, sir.

Q. Did you undertake to use either one of these toilets while you were down here?

A. I did feel like it, but the feeling went away when I saw the sign.

Q. So you did not?

A. No, sir, I did not.[32]

As this colloquy made clear, the racial caste system which degraded Mexican Americans was not simply an abstraction for the defense counsel, who served both as advocates for a despised group and as members of that group. In this context, García would later report that "it was necessary ... to travel a hundred miles to and from Houston each morning and evening to attend Court [in Jackson County] because, for obvious reasons, it would have been ill advised to stay overnight in Edna."[33]

On October 11, 1951, the jury convicted Hernández of murder with malice aforethought and sentenced him to life imprisonment.[34] The attorneys for Hernández now faced two critical decisions: Should they appeal and, more importantly, should they begin planning to take this case to the United States Supreme Court? An appeal to the Texas courts alone would yield little. No state appellate court was likely to overturn

---

[31] Transcript of Record for Hearing on Motion to Quash Jury Panel and Motion to Quash the Indictment at 74–75, State v. Hernandez (Dist. Ct., Jackson Co., Tex. 1951) (No. 2091), *reprinted in "Colored Men" and "Hombres Aqui,"* supra note 3, at App. V, at 300–302.

[32] *Id.* at 76.

[33] Gustavo C. García, *An Informal Report to the People, in A Cotton Picker Finds Justice: The Saga of the* Hernandez *Case* (Ruben Munguia ed., 1954) (no page numbers in original); *reprinted in "Colored Men" and "Hombres Aqui,"* supra note 3, at 356–72.

[34] Hernandez v. State, 251 S.W.2d 531 (Tex. Crim. App. 1952).

the exclusion of Mexican Americans from jury service. If Jim Crow juries were to be declared unconstitutional in Texas, the United States Supreme Court would have to intervene. In contemplating a Supreme Court challenge, though, the lawyers could not wait for a negative decision from the Texas court before attempting to raise the funds to cover the significant expenses that would be involved, nor could they procrastinate if they were to marshal the strongest arguments and evidence they could for a case of probable national significance.

In making this decision, the attorneys carefully weighed the pros and cons of Supreme Court review. Among the negatives, the facts of the case did not generate much sympathy, turning on a barroom murder; Norman Rockwell would not be painting Pete Hernández. Also, if defense counsel prevailed and the original verdict was thrown out, Hernández would be retried and might receive not life in prison but a death sentence. Then there was the question of resources. The filing fees, printing costs, and travel expenses associated with an appeal to the Supreme Court would be significant. Who would cover them? In addition, there was the simple fact that not a single Mexican–American lawyer was admitted to practice before the Supreme Court. Hernández's lawyers did not practice on a national scale, nor did they have access to a team of Mexican–American civil rights lawyers who did. Instead, they were regional lawyers in Texas with busy, diverse local practices.[35] Finally, there was the fear of failure. If the Supreme Court did agree to hear the case, that might be the best opportunity in a generation not only to overturn the exclusion of Mexican Americans from Texas juries but to establish the civic equality of Mexican Americans as a national principle. But if the lawyers failed to make the best possible arguments, they might doom their community to further decades of social marginalization.

The lawyers who took and argued *Hernandez* were not long-time collaborators, but general practitioners subject to a racial caste system, which offered only dim promises and few opportunities to them and their largely Mexican-origin clients. *Hernandez* would not be part of a series of carefully chosen and litigated cases, and so stood in marked contrast to the systematic assault on school segregation being waged by the National Association for the Advancement of Colored People's Legal Defense Fund ("LDF"). LULAC was a decentralized organization with no official capacity to hire lawyers, bring lawsuits, or undertake legal actions.[36]

---

[35] For a fascinating account of the relationship between daily practice and civil rights litigation among black lawyers during the 1920s and 1930s, see Kenneth W. Mack, *Rethinking Civil Rights Lawyering and Politics in the Era before* Brown, 115 Yale L.J. 256 (2005). Mack's analysis might provide a model for the type of research necessary to fully flesh out the legal history of Mexican–American civil rights lawyering.

[36] There are discrepancies in the narratives regarding the extent to which this was a "LULAC case." In large part, this reflects the fact that the records from this era are

Many of its local chapters were, moreover, leery of throwing their support behind a murder trial. Not until 1968 would deAnda along with other Mexican–American lawyers, and with assistance from the Ford Foundation, organize to establish the Mexican American Legal Defense and Educational Fund ("MALDEF"). Modeled on the LDF, MALDEF would later provide the structure and resources for strategic litigation on behalf of the larger Latino community, including *San Antonio Independent School District v. Rodriguez* in 1973, challenging school financing in Texas, and *Plyler v. Doe* in 1982, a victory for undocumented children.[37]

Despite these obstacles, there were compelling reasons to pursue Supreme Court review. The timing seemed propitious. By 1951, the Court already had given the NAACP several prominent victories eroding the American apartheid system, for instance by requiring the University of Texas and Oklahoma State University to admit black students.[38] Hernández's attorneys had watched with great interest as the University of Texas Law School was forced to accept a black applicant, especially because three of the team's four attorneys had themselves attended that

incomplete and almost all the parties have died without leaving full oral histories. Neil Foley, a careful scholar who has consulted the archival materials surrounding *Hernandez*, has suggested that "two Mexican American civil rights organizations, LULAC (League of United Latin American Citizens) and the American GI Forum, challenged lower court rulings." Neil Foley, *Straddling the Color Line: The Legal Construction of Hispanic Identity in Texas*, in *Not Just Black and White: Contemporary Perspectives on Immigration, Race, and Ethnicity in the United States* 345 (Nancy Foner & George M. Frederickson eds., 2004). Benjamin Marquez, who has written the authoritative history of LULAC, characterized the case as having been brought by "LULAC lawyers" who "volunteered their time and effort for LULAC." Benjamin Marquez, *LULAC, The Evolution of a Mexican American Political Organization* 55 (1st ed. 1993). The litigation record suggests, however, that *Hernandez* was not a LULAC nor still less a GI Forum case, though it was litigated by lawyers loosely associated with LULAC and to a lesser extent the Forum. Guadalupe San Miguel, Jr., makes a compelling argument that LULAC and other Mexican–American organizations played a more formal role in bringing education cases generally, but the evidence does not make *Hernandez* part of this tradition. Guadalupe San Miguel, Jr., *"Let Them All Take Heed": Mexican Americans and the Campaign for Educational Equality in Texas, 1910–1981*, at 54–55 (1st ed. 1987).

[37] San Antonio Indep. Sch. Dist. v. Rodriguez, 411 U.S. 980 (1973); Plyler v. Doe, 457 U.S. 202 (1982). For a detailed study in the *Law Stories* series that focuses on *Plyler*, see Michael A. Olivas, Plyler v. Doe: *The Education of Undocumented Children, and the Polity*, in *Immigration Stories* 197 (David A. Martin & Peter H. Schuck eds., 2005). MALDEF had a minor role in *Rodriguez*, submitting a brief.

[38] McLaurin v. Okla. State Regents for Higher Educ., 339 U.S. 637 (1950); Sweatt v. Painter, 339 U.S. 629 (1950). *See generally* Michael A. Olivas, Brown *and the Desegregative Ideal: Location, Race, and College Attendance Policies*, 90 Cornell L. Rev. 391 (2005) (reviewing higher education cases leading to *Brown*). There are dozens of excellent works detailing the history of *Brown*, but none of these meticulous studies mentions *Hernandez*, except perhaps in passing.

school, in whatever fashion.[39] But *Hernandez* was a case about jury exclusion. Was jury exclusion on a par with school segregation? To be sure, all-white juries imperiled Mexican–American defendants who, like Hernández himself, risked hostile and biased convictions. Moreover, the Mexican–American community suffered because white juries rarely and reluctantly convicted whites for depredations against Mexican Americans.[40]

Beyond these practical concerns, many Mexican Americans saw jury exclusion as glaring proof of their second-class status. In fact, LULAC's determined opposition to jury exclusion arose first and foremost because of this stigmatizing effect.[41] Trial by jury rests on the idea of defendants being judged by their peers. In the context of Texas race politics, however, to put Mexican Americans on juries was tantamount to elevating such persons to equal status with whites. The idea that "Mexicans" might judge whites deeply violated Texas' racial caste system—and placing Mexican Americans on juries became critical to the caste system's demise. LULAC hoped *Hernandez* would topple a key pillar of Jim Crow: the belief that whites should judge all but be judged by none but themselves.

To the extent that it was important to litigate the racial exclusivity of the jury system in Texas, the facts of *Hernandez* were perfect: In a county more than 14% Mexican American, there had been no Hispanic jurors in over a quarter-century. Moreover, Gus García in particular was anxious to take the case further. Although he had a serious problem with alcoholism and was often volatile, he was a brilliant orator and driven to pursue equality for Mexican Americans as far as he could. The lawyers also felt that the *Sanchez* case had been good practice, and that with time and work they could hone their arguments. Finally, initial discussions with local LULAC groups indicated possible support for a Supreme Court appeal—support that might mature into help in financing the

---

[39] Gus García had graduated from the University of Texas Law School in 1938; Carlos Cadena in 1940 (summa cum laude, with what was at the time the highest grade point average ever accumulated there); and James deAnda in 1950. For a review of the University of Texas Law School experience for Mexican Americans at the time, see Lisa Lizette Barrera, *Minorities and the University of Texas School of Law (1950–1980)*, 4 Tex. Hisp. J.L. & Pol. 99 (1998) (noting, among other things, that fewer than twenty Mexicans Americans graduated from that school before 1950, including the first two in 1932).

[40] United States Comm'n on Civil Rights, *Mexican Americans and the Administration of Justice in the Southwest* 88–89 (1970). A very different scenario existed in late nineteenth-century New Mexico, where majority-Mexican jurors often sat in judgment of whites. *See* Laura E. Gomez, *Race, Colonialism, and Criminal Law: Mexicans and the American Criminal Justice System in Territorial New Mexico*, 34 Law & Soc. Rev. 1129 (2000).

[41] Sheridan, *supra* note 3, at 138–39.

case. The team reached the decision to push forward with the state appeal with a plan to prepare for a possible Supreme Court challenge.

Moving to renew the jury exclusion claim at the Texas appellate level, deAnda sent his research materials to Cadena in San Antonio. Using the *Aniceto Sanchez* brief as a starting point, Cadena included the Jackson County demographics and added data he obtained with the assistance of Dr. George I. Sánchez, an education professor at the University of Texas.[42] Although not an attorney, Sánchez, a native of New Mexico, had been an expert witness and general resource for Mexican–American lawyers in Texas cases, particularly those involving desegregation, housing, and elementary and secondary schooling issues.[43] Sánchez also oversaw some general support funds, which he used to encourage civil rights litigation, and he was corresponding with Thurgood Marshall as both Mexican–American and African–American legal strategies were progressing on parallel tracks in Texas.[44]

Despite the efforts to strengthen the jury exclusion claim, the Texas Court of Criminal Appeals affirmed Hernández's murder conviction and life sentence on June 18, 1952.[45] Then, on October 22, 1952, that court refused a rehearing on the jury selection issue.[46] The time had come to decide whether to file a petition for *certiorari* with the United States Supreme Court. After consulting with local LULAC councils and community members for a few months, the attorneys decided to file. LULAC

---

[42] George I. Sánchez had been active in the *Delgado* case in which a federal court in 1948 ruled that school segregation in four central Texas counties violated the Fourteenth Amendment. *See* Delgado v. Bastrop Ind. Sch. Dist., Civ. Cause No. 338 (W.D. Tex. 1948) (unpublished). This case is discussed in San Miguel, *supra* note 36, at 123–26. Drawing on his experience with *Delgado*, Sánchez encouraged the lawyers to mount the same systematic attack on the segregation and caste status of Mexican Americans in Texas that the NAACP Legal Defense Fund was mounting on a national basis for African Americans. Neil Foley, *Over the Rainbow:* Hernandez v. Texas, Brown v. Board of Education, *and* Black v. Brown, 25 Chicano–Latino L. Rev. 139, 146–148 (2005).

[43] For an appraisal of Sánchez's record in his native New Mexico, see Phillip B. Gonzales, *Forced Sacrifice as Ethnic Protest: The Hispano Cause in New Mexico & The Racial Attitude Confrontation of 1933*, at 174–80 (2001) (recounting University of New Mexico protest involving Sánchez and others). *See also Humanidad: Essays in Honor of George I. Sanchez* (Americo Paredes ed., 1977).

[44] Foley, *supra* note 42, at 146–47. *See generally* San Miguel, *supra* note 36; Ruben Donato, *The Other Struggle for Equal Schools: Mexican Americans During the Civil Rights Era* (1997). For an interesting comparison of Gustavo García and Thurgood Marshall, see Lupe S. Salinas, *Gus Garcia and Thurgood Marshall: Two Legal Giants Fighting for Justice*, 28 T. Marshall L. Rev. 145 (2003). Salinas notes that García also had a general commercial practice in San Antonio. *Id.* at 146 n.8.

[45] *Hernandez*, 251 S.W.2d 531 (Tex. Crim. App. 1952), *supra* note 34.

[46] Order Overriding Motion for Rehearing, *reprinted in "Colored Men" and "Hombres Aqui," supra* note 3, at App. V, at 323.

and others in the community promised to raise money for the effort. For example, Albert Armendariz, one of the few Mexican–American lawyers in El Paso, offered to use LULAC funds to help with the appeal.[47] Additionally, Professor Sánchez, who was in charge of disbursing funds for the Marshall Trust, which had donated $5,000 for civil rights trials in October 1953, was already committed to supporting an appeal in *Hernandez*.[48] On January 21, 1953, Hernández's lawyers filed a petition for a writ of *certiorari* with the Supreme Court, including the $900 filing fee.[49] As they waited to hear whether their petition would be granted, all the lawyers went about their regular business, continuing to represent civil and criminal clients in courts across Texas. The attorneys knew that if the case was accepted for argument, it would be on a fast track and would require their full attention. The legal team also discussed other possible test cases, in the event that this case was not accepted. There was no need to find another case, however, for on October 12, 1953 the Supreme Court granted *certiorari* and calendared *Hernandez* to be heard that term.[50]

With the invitation to argue the case before the country's highest court, worries about García's alcoholism resurfaced. In a heartbreaking letter to George Sánchez, Carlos Cadena wrote in early December 1953:

[47] Interview with Albert Armendariz, in San Antonio, Texas (Sept. 20, 2004). *See also* Foley, *supra* note 42, at 146–47. The various files of the attorneys in this case contain many references to fundraising. For one representative example, John Herrera wrote to a national LULAC official recounting various costs and quotidian details of the case and its preparation. Letter from John Herrera to Luciano Santoscoy (May 15, 1954) (on file at Houston Metropolitan Research Center, John J. Herrera papers, Box 2, Folder 24). Carlos Cadena and George Sánchez also corresponded about this issue, as Cadena had arranged to get the briefs filed and the court costs paid, with money from the Marshall Trust. Letter from George I. Sánchez to Carlos Cadena (Oct. 2, 1953) (on file at University of Texas Benson Latin American Collection, George I. Sánchez papers, Box 9, Folder 2); Letter from Carlos Cadena to George I. Sánchez (May 6, 1954) (on file at University of Texas Benson Latin American Collection, George I. Sánchez papers, Box 9, Folder 2).

[48] Letter from George I. Sánchez to Carlos Cadena (May 13, 1954) (on file at University of Texas Benson Latin American Collection, George I. Sánchez papers, Box 9, Folder 2) (conveying check for $500).

[49] Letter from George I. Sánchez to Carlos Cadena (Oct. 2, 1953) (on file at Houston Metropolitan Research Center, John J. Herrera papers, Box 2, Folder 24); Letter from Carlos Cadena to George I. Sánchez (May 6, 1954) (on file at Houston Metropolitan Research Center, John J. Herrera papers, Box 2, Folder 24).

[50] Hernandez v. Texas, 346 U.S. 811 (1953) (granting *certiorari*). The Court had simultaneously granted *certiorari* for a rehearing of *Brown v. Board of Education*. *Hernandez* remained in *Brown*'s shadow, not attracting the massive attention accorded the Legal Defense Fund's longstanding and meticulous campaign against public school segregation. For a review of the publicity regarding *Brown*, see Robert J. Cottrol, Raymond T. Diamond & Leland B. Ware, *Brown v. Board of Education: Caste, Culture, and the Constitution* 101–18 (2003).

Gus is apparently on the wagon, at least for the time being. He told
me that he was not going to touch a drop until after January 4 [the
day of the Supreme Court arguments] ... Some time back I had a
long talk with Nora [Gus García's then-wife]. That was during the
time that Gus was off on a toot, and she was quite worried about
him. Anyway, somebody gave him a little lecture, because he told me
of his plan to stay sober, he mentioned that things had reach[ed] a
horrible state when your own family was afraid that you would
make a jackass out of yourself before the Supreme Court. Of course,
I don't know how long he will continue in his present frame of
mind.[51]

When it was time to fly to Washington, D.C. for the arguments, the
Hernandez team only had funds to send three attorneys. Despite the
concerns about his trouble with the bottle, García was widely regarded
as the most talented orator on the team. It was decided he would go to
Washington, along with the more senior lawyers, Cadena and Herrera;
deAnda, as the most junior, remained in Texas to mind the store and
continue the trials that were ongoing. Once in Washington, the lawyers
scrambled to find someone to sponsor their membership in the Supreme
Court bar.[52] Herrera would write that it was "a very proud moment"
when he was sworn in, having been sponsored by one of the United
States Senators from Texas, Price Daniel, who also sponsored García
and, for purposes of submitting the brief, deAnda.[53]

---

[51] Letter from Carlos Cadena to George I. Sánchez (Dec. 1953) (on file at University of
Texas Benson Latin American Collection, George I. Sánchez papers, Box 9, Folder 2).

[52] Letter from James deAnda to Clerk, U.S. Supreme Court (Dec. 1, 1953) (on file at
Houston Metropolitan Research Center, John J. Herrera papers, Box 2, Folder 24).

[53] Letter from John Herrera to J.C. Machuca (Jan. 19, 1954) (on file at Houston
Metropolitan Research Center, John J. Herrera papers, Box 2, Folder 24); Letter from John
Herrera to J.C. Machuca (May 15, 1954) (on file at Houston Metropolitan Research Center,
John J. Herrera papers, Box 2, Folder 24); Letter from John Herrera to Luciano Santoscoy
(on file at Houston Metropolitan Research Center, John J. Herrera papers, Box 2, Folder
24). Carlos Cadena had been sponsored by U.S. Rep. Paul Kilday. *Group Seeks Latins on
Jury*, San Antonio Light, Jan. 5, 1954, at 6.

The signatories to the brief included García and Cadena as the Attorneys of Record,
while Herrera and deAnda signed as being Of Counsel. It is this formal arrangement and
the fact that García argued the case that have led some observers to characterize the case
as solely the efforts of the more flamboyant García and the more scholarly Cadena. In
addition, the brief was also signed by Maury Maverick, who died a month after the case
was decided. *See generally* Richard B. Henderson, *Maury Maverick: A Political Biography*
(1970). Finally, Cristóbal (Cris) Aldrete, a 1951 South Texas College of Law graduate, was
also Of Counsel on the brief. He was a Del Rio, Texas, lawyer whose family had been
involved in a 1930 case challenging segregation in the Del Rio school district. See
Handbook of Texas, Entry for Aldrete, Cristóbal, *available at* http://www.tsha.utexas.edu/
handbook/online/articles/AA/falwl.html (last visited Nov. 20, 2006) (biography of Aldrete).

In a later pamphlet designed to publicize the case, García wrote about their journey with a sense of posterity:

> The following country bumpkins went to Washington: Attorneys (1) Cadena, (2) Herrera and (3) Garcia participated in this case before the Supreme Court of the U.S. Messrs. Cadena and Garcia presented the oral arguments, and Mr. Herrera, sitting at counsel table, assisted in the organization of the arguments and the preparation of the notes, made suggestions and rendered memoes [sic] as the case progressed before the Court.
>
> (4) Mr. Abel Cisneros, courageous radio commentator of Wharton, Texas, who went along because the substantial sum contributed by his home town was conditioned upon his accompanying Mr. Herrera. He took copious notes and, after he came home, rendered a lengthy report over the radio to the people of East Texas.
>
> (5) Mr. Manuel B. Lopez, of San Antonio, a graduate attorney, who is at present serving his hitch in the Army in Virginia, was very helpful to us, guiding us around Washington, and faithfully carrying out all the duties of an all-round "leg man."
>
> (6) Mr. Anthony (Tony) Garcia, Director of Municipal Markets of San Antonio, attended as an observer for the Lulacs, on his vacation time and at his own personal expense. His moral support, his encouragement, and his timely suggestions were invaluable to us.
>
> (7) Mr. Chris Aldrete, Chairman of the American G. I. Forum. Though too recent a law graduate to be presented to the Court, he, too, was very helpful.
>
> We all stayed at the Mayflower Hotel, which is neither higher nor cheaper than any other first class hospice in Washington. The average rate per person is $10.00 a day. After Tony Garcia, Johnny Herrera, and Abel Cisneros arrived, the writer moved into a suite with them, which cost us $36.00 per day. The undersigned slept on a couch in the living room, which, however, was far more comfortable and luxurious than many a bed in which he has slept in his day. Tony Garcia stretched out his hefty frame on a rollaway bed. By obtaining this suite, we actually saved at least a dollar per person per day and at the same time had a decent place to hold meetings among ourselves, with members of the press, and with some friends from Washington, who guided us and assisted us, and who deserve our sincerest thanks.[54]

On January 11, 1954, Gus García and Carlos Cadena argued the *Hernandez* case before the Supreme Court, with Herrera joining them at

---

[54] García, *supra* note 33.

the counsel's table. In a highly unusual gesture, Chief Justice Warren invited García to continue speaking for twelve minutes more than was typically allocated for oral arguments. According to observers, García performed brilliantly.[55] A San Antonio newspaper took particular glee in later recalling the following exchange between García and Justice Tom Clark, who hailed originally from Texas:

> Garcia [is] best remembered in the case before the Supreme Court for his remark to Texas' Justice Clark in which he said, "in the way of assimilation, if there is any assimilating to be done, it seems to me the other people have to do it. After all, Gen. Sam Houston was nothing but a wetback from Tennessee."[56]

Unfortunately, no transcript of the oral arguments seems to exist for *Hernandez*, and there was little contemporary coverage. What was said, and how the Justices responded, has largely been lost to history. Two weeks later, Thurgood Marshall argued *Brown* before the same Court with a much larger audience and international attention devoted to the case. On May 3, 1954, two weeks before handing down *Brown v. Board of Education*, Chief Justice Warren delivered the unanimous opinion of the Court in *Hernandez*, overturning the trial result and the Texas Court of Criminal Appeals decision.[57] To that opinion we now turn our attention.

The Supreme Court Opinion: A Jim Crow Case

In holding that the Texas practice of excluding Mexican Americans from juries violated the Equal Protection Clause of the Fourteenth Amendment, the Supreme Court focused on the treatment of that group in Jackson County. Setting up the case, Chief Justice Warren noted that though "race and color" formed the usual basis for discrimination prohibited under the Fourteenth Amendment, "from time to time other differences from the community norm may define other groups which need the same protection."[58] He then went on to specify the test for

---

[55] John J. Herrera, Letter to the Editor, Houston Post, Feb. 22, 1972, at 27 (on file at Houston Metropolitan Research Center, John J. Herrera papers, Box 2, Folder 24) (setting out details of the case). At the Supreme Court hearing, Herrera served as timekeeper for Cadena and García. Only the three of them were at the *Hernandez* table.

[56] *Pete Hernandez Due Parole*, La Prensa (San Antonio), June 15, 1960, at 1. There was one published story on the argument. Sarah McLendon, *Jury Bias Put to High Court*, San Antonio Light, Jan. 12, 1954, at A1. Both García and Herrera had family ties to that area stretching back past Texas' independence. Indeed, Herrera's great-great-grandfather, Colonel Francisco Ruiz, was one of two Mexican signatories to the 1836 Texas Declaration of Independence. Maury Maverick, Foreword *to A Cotton Picker Finds Justice: The Saga of the* Hernandez *Case* (Ruben Munguia ed., 1954); García, *supra* note 33.

[57] Hernandez v. Texas, 347 U.S. 475 (1954).

[58] *Id.* at 478.

when the Constitution required intervention: "When the existence of a distinct class is demonstrated, and it is further shown that the laws, as written or as applied, single out that class for different treatment not based on some reasonable classification, the guarantees of the Constitution have been violated."[59] *Hernandez* in effect adopted a two-step approach: first, an inquiry into whether a group existed as a "distinct class"; and second, some demonstration that the class was subject to "different treatment" that was unreasonable. This formulation, while generic as initially expressed, gained concrete meaning as applied in the case.

Regarding whether Mexican Americans constituted a distinct group, Chief Justice Warren wrote that "[w]hether such a group exists within a community is a question of fact,"[60] something that may be "demonstrated ... by showing the attitude of the community."[61] To satisfy this inquiry, Chief Justice Warren recapitulated the evidence presented in the case of a Jim Crow hierarchy that placed Mexican Americans in an inferior position in Jackson County. In a long paragraph chronicling the mistreatment of Mexicans, Chief Justice Warren noted the following: Community members regularly "distinguished between 'white' and 'Mexican' "; "business and community groups" largely excluded persons of "Mexican descent"; "children of Mexican descent were required to attend a segregated school"; "[a]t least one restaurant in town prominently displayed a sign announcing 'No Mexicans Served' "; and two men's bathrooms sat side by side on the courthouse grounds, "one unmarked, and the other marked 'Colored Men' and 'Hombres Aqui' ('Men Here')."[62] On the first question of whether Mexican Americans existed as a "distinct class," Chief Justice Warren turned to evidence demonstrating a history of group subordination. He did not ask whether Mexican Americans constituted a racial group, or even some analog, such as a national origin or ethnic group. His focus was not on categories per se, but on processes of social differentiation and, more particularly, social stratification. As applied, the question of the "existence of a distinct class"[63] turned out to be an inquiry into whether a group existed under social practices of group subordination.

Having concluded that Mexican Americans constituted a subordinated group, Chief Justice Warren turned to the question of whether the challenged practice singled out that class "for different treatment." He

---

[59] *Id.*

[60] *Id.* at 478.

[61] *Id.* at 479.

[62] *Id.* at 479–80.

[63] *Id.* at 478.

offered, though, a new formulation: To meet this prong, Hernández would have "the burden of proving discrimination."[64] Chief Justice Warren then applied precedents centered on the exclusion of African Americans from juries, affording Hernández the opportunity to prove discrimination in the same manner used by that quintessential constitutional out-group. Here, the Court pointed out that Mexican Americans constituted 14% of Jackson County's population and that Texas had stipulated that in the last twenty-five years no person from that community had served on a grand or petit jury.[65] Chief Justice Warren then dismissed Texas' defense that the jury commissioners had sought only to empanel "those whom they thought were best qualified."[66] The lack of intentional discrimination, *Hernandez* ruled, was irrelevant:

> Circumstances or chance may well dictate that no persons in a certain class will serve on a particular jury or during some particular period. But it taxes our credulity to say that mere chance resulted in there being no members of this class among the over six thousand jurors called in the past 25 years. The result bespeaks discrimination, whether or not it was a conscious decision on the part of any individual jury commissioner. The judgment of conviction must be reversed.[67]

In addressing the question of "different treatment," Chief Justice Warren sought evidence of "discrimination" and used as his model for ferreting out such mistreatment the case law elaborated to protect the core group subject to systematic subordination, African Americans. Moreover, he dispensed with any pretense that the issue was one of intentional discrimination and focused instead on patterns of mistreatment, whether consciously enforced or not. The concern with "different treatment" turned out to be more accurately a focus on whether the challenged practice formed part of a larger pattern of oppressive "discrimination," intentionally or otherwise. Chief Justice Warren asked two questions: if there existed "a distinct class," and if the challenged practiced amounted to "different treatment." As applied, though, the Supreme Court in *Hernandez* asked, first, whether the group seeking constitutional protection suffered from subordination generally and, second, whether the challenged practice amounted to a specific aspect of such oppression. The *Hernandez* test rests on opposition to group hierarchy: It focuses on status and subordination, without being distracted by

---

[64] *Id.* at 480.

[65] *Id.* at 480–81.

[66] *Id.* at 481.

[67] *Id.* at 482.

the irrelevant questions of the exact nature of the group identity or the presence of discriminatory intent.

The Paradox of Race: Mexican Americans and Whiteness

The facts cited in *Hernandez*, especially when read against the background of Texas' Jim Crow practices targeting Mexican Americans, show that the case was centrally about racial hierarchy. But it should be noted that the Court did not analyze the case in specifically racial terms. True, the opinion acknowledged that "[t]hroughout our history differences in race and color have defined easily identifiable groups which have at times required the aid of the courts in securing equal treatment under the laws."[68] But the Court then went on to say that "from time to time *other differences* from the community norm may define other groups which need the same protection."[69] According to Chief Justice Warren, for Hernández to prevail he had to show that he was discriminated against not as a member of a group defined by race or color, but as a member of a group marked by inchoate "other differences."[70] In the face of the Court's heavy reliance on evidence of racial discrimination, the search for "other differences" and the refusal to treat Mexican Americans as a race seem surprising. This elision of racial difference startles all the more when one recalls that at the time the Court decided *Hernandez*, national hysteria regarding Mexican immigration pervaded public discourse.[71] Moreover, there exists evidence of negative racial beliefs about Mexican Americans even among members of the Supreme Court itself. In examining the origins of the Court's opinion in *Brown*, Mark Tushnet brings to light revealing comments regarding Mexican Americans made by Justice Tom Clark, who was originally from Texas, during a 1952 conference discussion of the segregation decisions. According to Tushnet:

---

[68] *Id.* at 478.

[69] *Id.* (emphasis added).

[70] *Id.* at 479. The Court declined to reach the question of "whether or not the Court might take judicial notice that persons of Mexican descent are there considered as a separate class." *Id.* at 479 n.9. Instead, *Hernandez* provided that the question of distinct class status would have to be answered on a case-by-case basis.

[71] In the wake of a sharp economic recession in 1953, national attention focused on the purported dangers posed by the porous border with Mexico. Juan Ramon García, *Operation Wetback: The Mass Deportation of Mexican Undocumented Workers in 1954*, at 143–44 (1980). On June 9, 1954, a little over a month after the Court decided *Hernandez*, Attorney General Herbert Brownell launched "Operation Wetback," a detention and repatriation campaign orchestrated by the Border Patrol that expelled from this country in the course of several months over one million persons of Mexican descent. Kitty Calavita, *Inside the State: The Bracero Program, Immigration, and the I.N.S.* 54–55 (1992).

Clark, in a statement which, apart from its racism, is quite difficult to figure out, said that Texas "also has the Mexican problem" which was "more serious" because the Mexicans were "more retarded," and mentioned the problem of a "Mexican boy of 15 . . . in a class with a negro girl of 12," when "some negro girls [would] get in trouble."[72]

The racial dynamic of the case and of the times makes the Court's focus on "other differences," rather than directly on racial hierarchy, quite perplexing.

To understand this aspect of the case requires returning to *Hernandez*, not with a focus on the particular lawyers involved, but with an eye to the case as part of social history centered on the racial rules governing Mexican–American lives in Texas. Paradoxical as it may seem, Chief Justice Warren could not approach *Hernandez* as a racial case because the various parties involved all insisted that race did not set Mexican Americans apart from the majority, for both ostensibly shared a racial identity as white. This aspect of the case constitutes not simply an anomalous footnote, but centrally informs the history as well as the contemporary salience of *Hernandez*. As this section shows, the classification of Mexican Americans as white explains the arguments made by the parties before the Court, and as the next section demonstrates, underlies the emergence of *Hernandez* as a powerful complement to *Brown*.

When the all-white grand jury indicted Pete Hernández for murder in 1951, Mexican Americans in Texas suffered under a Jim Crow regime of racial subordination.[73] The specific practices identified by Chief Justice Warren in *Hernandez* had developed in Texas over the course of more than a century of Anglo–Mexican conflict. In the early years of the nineteenth century, white settlers from the United States moved westward into what was then Spanish territory, which became the independent country of Mexico in 1821. The new arrivals clashed with the local people and eventually precipitated a war between Mexico and the United States in 1846. During this period, whites in Texas and across the nation depicted Mexicans as an innately and insuperably inferior race. According to historian Reginald Horsman,

---

[72] Mark V. Tushnet, *Making Civil Rights Law: Thurgood Marshall and the Supreme Court, 1936–1961*, at 194 (1994).

[73] For an in-depth account of the early racialization of Mexicans, see Ian F. Haney López, *Racism on Trial: The Chicano Fight for Justice* (2003), especially chapter three. *See also* Tomás Almaguer, *Racial Fault Lines: The Historical Origins of White Supremacy in California* (1994); Laura E. Gomez, *Manifest Destinies: The Making of the Mexican American Race* (2007); Robert F. Heizer & Alan J. Almquist, *The Other Californians: Prejudice and Discrimination Under Spain, Mexico, and the United States to 1920* (1971).

By the time of the Mexican War, America had placed the Mexicans firmly within the rapidly emerging hierarchy of superior and inferior races. While the Anglo–Saxons were depicted as the purest of the pure—the finest Caucasians—the Mexicans who stood in the way of southwestern expansion were depicted as a mongrel race, adulterated by extensive intermarriage with an inferior [Native American] race.[74]

These views continued, and became institutionalized, over the remainder of the nineteenth century and well into the twentieth. According to another historian, Arnoldo de León,

> in different parts of [Texas], and deep into the 1900s, Anglos were more or less still parroting the comments of their forbears.... They regarded Mexicans as a colored people, discerned the Indian ancestry in them, identified them socially with blacks. In principle and in fact, Mexicans were regarded not as a nationality related to whites, but as a race apart.[75]

The facts underlying *Hernandez* stand as evidence of the racialization of Mexican Americans as biological inferiors in Texas.[76]

This degraded image of Mexican Americans helps to explain the school segregation that Chief Justice Warren referenced. According to the testimony of one frustrated mother, the "Latin American school" consisted of a decaying one-room wooden building that flooded repeatedly during the rains, with only a wood stove for heat and outside bathroom facilities and with just one teacher for the four grades taught there.[77] This separate and unequal scholastic segregation of whites and Mexican Americans typified the practices of Texas school boards. Although not mandated by state law, from the turn of the twentieth century, school officials in Texas customarily separated Mexican Ameri-

---

[74] Reginald Horsman, *Race and Manifest Destiny: The Origins of American Racial Anglo–Saxonism* 210 (1981).

[75] de Leon, *supra* note 23, at 104.

[76] In this vein, it is no accident that *Hernandez* originated in Texas, where perhaps more than anywhere else Mexican Americans have been unyieldingly constructed as innately and irremediably inferior. David Montejano, in an excellent history of Anglo–Mexican relations in Texas, argues that these relations did not develop uniformly, but within "a patchwork or mosaic of distinct local societies." *See* Montejano, *supra* note 23, at 7.

[77] Transcript of Record for Hearing on Motion to Quash Jury Panel and Motion to Quash the Indictment, *supra* note 31, at 84–87, *reprinted in "Colored Men" and "Hombres Aqui," supra* note 3, at 307–10. This testimony relates to experiences with the school in the early 1940s. By 1948, there were apparently two teachers and two rooms in the Edna district's "Latin American school." *Id.* at 51, *reprinted in "Colored Men" and "Hombres Aqui," supra* note 3, at 282–86. The Court relies on these latter figures. *Hernandez*, 347 U.S. at 479 n.10.

can and white students.[78] That racism drove this process was clear. A school superintendent explained it this way: "Some Mexicans are very bright, but you can't compare their brightest with the average white children. They are an inferior race."[79] According to the historian Guadalupe San Miguel, many whites "simply felt that public education would not benefit [Mexican Americans] since they were intellectually inferior to Anglos."[80] To be sure, as in Jackson County, school segregation in the rest of Texas was most pronounced in the lower grades.[81] But also, as in that county, this fact reflected not a lack of concern with segregation at the higher grades, but rather the practice of forcing Mexican–American children out of the educational system altogether after only a few years of school.[82] The segregated schooling noted in *Hernandez* constitutes but one instance of rampant educational discrimination against Mexican Americans in Texas and across the Southwest.[83]

Though Anglos in Texas came to understand and treat Mexicans as racial inferiors over the course of the nineteenth and well into the twentieth century (with vestiges of such treatment persisting even today), the Mexican community did not acquiesce in this view. Instead, using various strategies, Mexicans in Texas crafted alternative identities for themselves to counteract the degrading stereotypes espoused by Anglos. During the nineteenth century, it was common for members of this community to understand themselves as exiles from Mexico, and so not part of the United States and therefore not appropriately subject to the American racial hierarchy. Rather than directly challenging the racial logic that depicted them as inferiors, these early generations sought to evade it by considering themselves separate from American

---

[78] San Miguel, *supra* note 36, at 47. *See also* Guadalupe Salinas, *Mexican–Americans and the Desegregation of Schools in the Southwest*, 8 Hous. L. Rev. 929 (1971).

[79] San Miguel, *supra* note 36, at 32 (citing Paul S. Taylor, *An American–Mexican Frontier: Nueces County, Texas* (1934) (specific page attribution not given)).

[80] San Miguel, *supra* note 36, at 51.

[81] A study conducted in 1944 found that 90% of 122 widely dispersed school districts in Texas segregated students through the first two grades or above, 50% separated these students through the sixth grade or above, and 17% continued segregation through the eighth grade or higher. U.S. Comm'n on Civil Rights, Mexican American Education Study, *Report 1: Ethnic Isolation of Mexican Americans in the Public Schools of the Southwest* 13 (1971) (citing Wilson Little, *Spanish-Speaking Children in Texas* 60 (1944)).

[82] Jorge C. Rangel & Carlos M. Alcala, *Project Report: De Jure Segregation of Chicanos in Texas Schools*, 7 Harv. C.R.-C.L. L. Rev. 307, 314–315 (1972).

[83] Jackson County's segregation of Mexican–American school children came to an official end only in 1948, after a federal court ruled that similar segregation in four central Texas counties violated the Fourteenth Amendment. See the discussion of *Delgado v. Bastrop* in note 42, *supra*.

society.[84] This strategy has remained popular with each new wave of immigrants. Beginning in the 1920s and 1930s, however, broad segments of the Mexican-origin community in the United States came to see themselves as Americans. During this epoch, Mexican community leaders embraced an assimilationist ideology; indeed, the label "Mexican American" emerges from this period and encapsulated the effort to both retain pride in one's Mexican cultural origins and to express an American national identity. The civil rights groups that supported the challenge in *Hernandez* reflected the efforts of this new generation of "Mexican Americans"—indeed, one could not be a member of LULAC unless one was in fact a citizen of the United States, and LULAC actively campaigned for restrictions on Mexican immigration.[85]

Inseparable from this new assimilationist identity was an engagement with American racial logic. On this score, many community leaders, representing the most elite among the Mexican Americans, began to argue that they were white. The elite's ability to claim a white identity partly reflected their elevated class standing and their relatively fair features, attributes that stemmed from race politics not only in the Southwest but also in Mexico. In both countries, white was alright: There had been a strong connection between color and presumptions of worth or worthlessness for centuries, ensuring a close correlation between phenotypical whiteness and elevated class standing. Correspondingly, working-class Mexicans or those with dark features (and again, these categories substantially overlapped) were much less likely either to achieve middle-class status or to insist on a white identity.[86] Thus, no homogeneous racial identity existed within the Mexican community in the United States, especially where, as mentioned, recent immigrants more often identified in cultural or national, rather than racial terms. Nevertheless, whiteness formed a central component of elite Mexican identity in the mid-twentieth century Southwest.

---

[84] Haney López, *supra* note 73, at 70–82. *See also* Neil Foley, *Becoming Hispanic: Mexican Americans and the Faustian Pact with Whiteness, in Reflexiones 1997: New Directions In Mexican American Studies* 53 (Neil Foley ed., annual ed. 1997).

[85] David G. Gutierrez, *Walls and Mirrors: Mexican Americans, Mexican Immigrants, and the Politics of Ethnicity* 85–86 (1995).

[86] The range of somatic differences in the Mexican–American community significantly affects the way individual Mexican Americans are racialized. As Jorge Klor de Alva explains, "In the extremely race-conscious environment of the United States ... different shades of humanity translate into different experiences of reality. Light-skinned Mexicans face fewer obstacles than their darker compatriots; they are less likely to be conscious of discrimination and more likely to look favorably upon American society." Jorge Klor de Alva, *Telling Hispanics Apart: Latino Sociocultural Diversity, in The Hispanic Experience in the United States: Contemporary Issues and Perspectives* 107, 114 (Edna Acosta–Belén & Barbara R. Sjostrom eds., 1988).

In this context, *Hernandez* may have evolved as it did partly because the case was litigated by middle-class Mexican Americans of generally lighter skin color. Middle-class and fair-featured, LULAC members may have been more able than most to embrace the notion of a white identity as the price and reward of assimilation into American society.[87] In turn, a self-conception as white influenced the position taken by lawyers associated with LULAC in a range of cases. Lawsuits frequently adopted what LULAC termed its "other white" legal strategy, protesting not segregation generally, but only the lawfulness of segregating the putatively white Mexican–American group.[88] This strategy seemed to have played out in *Hernandez* too. In their brief to the Supreme Court, Hernández's lawyers complained that "while legally white," in Jackson County "frequently the term white excludes the Mexicans and is reserved for the rest of the non-Negro population."[89]

In the wake of *Hernandez*, some members of the Mexican–American community became concerned that the decision did not adequately preserve their status as white. Though the decision helped to end discrimination against them, it associated Mexican Americans with the black civil rights movement and thus threatened a white identity.[90] García would respond angrily to such criticism, insisting in strident terms that Mexican Americans were typical white ethnics experiencing temporary disfavor before their full assimilation:

> We are not passing through anything different from that endured at one time or another by other unassimilated population groups: the Irish in Boston (damned micks, they were derisively called); the Polish in the Detroit area (their designation was bohunks and polackers); the Italians in New York (referred to as stinking little wops, dagoes and guineas); the Germans in many sections of the country (called dumb square-heads and krauts); and our much maligned friends of the Jewish faith, who have been persecuted even here, in the land of the free, because to the bigoted they were just "lousy kikes."[91]

Co-counsel Carlos Cadena also insisted on a white ethnic identity, reminding critics that "[i]t must be remembered that this decision is based strictly on a question of national origin—not race. Those of

---

[87] Mario T. García, *Mexican Americans: Leadership, Ideology, & Identity, 1930–1960*, at 47 (1989).

[88] On the "other white" legal strategy, see Wilson, *supra* note 10, passim.

[89] Brief for the Petitioner at 38, Hernandez v. Texas, 347 U.S. 475 (1954) (No. 406).

[90] Carlos C. Cadena, *Legal Ramifications of the* Hernandez *Case, in A Cotton Picker Finds Justice: The Saga of the* Hernandez *Case* (Ruben Munguia ed., 1954).

[91] García, *supra* note 33.

Mexican descent who decry it as classifying 'our people' as non-white should keep this in mind."[92] The sense of possessing a white ethnic identity, as opposed to a nonwhite racial status, informed how Hernández's lawyers understood the oppression of Mexicans in Texas. The *Hernandez* team's efforts to secure equal treatment for Mexican Americans were founded on a claim that Mexican Americans were white.

Before the Supreme Court, Texas also argued that Mexican Americans formed part of the white race. It most likely did so because, among the Texas courts, acceptance of the claim that Mexican Americans were white had emerged as a means to defeat their equal protection claims. The Texas criminal court had addressed discrimination against Mexican Americans in the selection of juries on at least seven previous occasions between 1931 and its decision in *Hernandez* in 1952, consistently ruling against the Mexican–American defendant. The court had not, however, been consistent in its racial characterization of Mexican Americans. In its initial decisions, and as late as 1948, the court construed Mexican–American challenges to jury exclusion as involving discrimination against members of the "Mexican race." For example, *Ramirez v. State* involved, according to the court, a challenge to "unjust discrimination against the Mexican race in Menard county,"[93] while *Carrasco v. State* raised a question of "alleged discrimination against the Mexican race on the part of the jury commission."[94] In these initial cases, the court denied that racial discrimination had occurred. Instead, the court concluded that the absence of Mexican Americans on local juries reflected a lack of Mexican Americans qualified under Texas law to serve.

This line of reasoning eventually proved troublesome for the courts, though, because often the evidence used to demonstrate the dearth of suitable Mexican Americans instead seemed to prove the prevalence of racial stereotypes. In 1931 in *Ramirez*, for example, the Texas Criminal Court of Appeals cited the testimony of several local officials to establish that no Mexican Americans qualified for jury service. First, the county attorney: "Joe Flack testified that he ... [did] not know[] a person of the Mexican race ... qualified to sit on the jury, as those in the county did not know English well enough and were otherwise ignorant."[95] Next, the sheriff:

> The sheriff and tax collector of Menard county testified that ... he did not think the Mexicans of Menard county were intelligent enough or spoke English well enough or knew enough about the law

---

[92] Cadena, *supra* note 90.

[93] 40 S.W.2d 138, 139 (Tex. Crim. App. 1931).

[94] 95 S.W.2d 433, 434 (Tex. Crim. App. 1936).

[95] *Ramirez*, 40 S.W.2d at 139.

to make good jurors, besides their customs and ways were different from ours, and for that reason he did not consider them well enough qualified to serve as jurors.[96]

Finally, a jury commissioner:

Albert Nauwald testified that he ... would not select a negro to sit on the grand jury or petit jury while acting in the capacity of jury commissioner, even though the negro was as well qualified in every way to serve as a juror as any white man; that he was opposed to Mexicans serving on the jury; that he did not consider any individual Mexican's name in connection with making up the jury list; [and] that he did not consider the Mexicans in Menard county as being intelligent enough to make good jurors, so that the jury commission just disregarded the whole Mexican list and did not consider any of them when making up their jury list. . . .[97]

Strikingly, the trial court in *Ramirez* cited this evidence not to uphold the discrimination claim but to buttress the assertion that Mexican Americans were unfit for jury service existed: "The proof did not show that there had been a discrimination against the Mexican race ... there was no evidence that there was any Mexican in the County who possessed the statutory qualifications of a juror."[98] The Texas appellate court agreed,[99] and the U.S. Supreme Court refused to hear an appeal.[100] The Texas appellate court would dismiss three more challenges to "racial" discrimination in jury selection on the ground that no Mexican Americans were qualified to serve.[101]

In sharp contrast to these four decisions, however, one decision by the appellate court in 1946 and two others handed down in 1951 characterized Mexican Americans as white and construed challenges to their exclusion from juries not in terms of race but in terms of nationality.[102] In these decisions—which anticipated the state court's approach in *Hernandez* in 1952—the court quickly rejected the defendants' claims of

---

[96] *Id.*

[97] *Id.*

[98] *Id.* at 140 (internal quotations omitted).

[99] *Id.*

[100] Ramirez v. Texas, 284 U.S. 659 (1931).

[101] Carrasco v. State, 95 S.W.2d 433, 434 (Tex. Crim. App. 1936); Serapio Sanchez v. State, 181 S.W.2d 87, 88 (Tex. Crim. App. 1944); Bustillos v. State, 213 S.W.2d 837, 841 (Tex. Crim. App. 1948).

[102] Salazar v. State, 193 S.W.2d 211 (Tex. Crim. App. 1946); Rogers v. State, 236 S.W.2d 141 (Tex. Crim. App. 1951); Aniceto Sanchez v. State, 243 S.W.2d 700 (Tex. Crim. App. 1951).

discrimination in jury selection by noting their supposed membership in the white race. For example, in *Salazar v. State*, the court wrote:

> The Mexican people are of the same race as the grand jurors. We see no question presented for our discussion under the Fourteenth Amendment to the Constitution of the United States and the decisions relied upon by appellant, dealing with discrimination against race.[103]

Similarly, in *Aniceto Sanchez v. State*, the court ruled against the jury exclusion claim by tersely postulating that "[Mexicans] are not a separate race but are white people of Spanish descent, as has often been said by this court. We find no ground for discussing the question further and the complaint raised by this bill will not be sustained."[104] With these quick comments, the court dismissed the defendants' Fourteenth Amendment challenge, dispensing with not only the question of discrimination, but also of qualifications. The Texas courts no longer felt compelled to answer these questions. Instead, state judges relied solely on the assertion of Mexican–Americans' whiteness in order to reject contentions of impermissible discrimination in jury selection. The state court in *Hernandez* took exactly this approach.[105]

One cannot know the particular motivations behind the Texas appellate court's shift to categorizing Mexican Americans as white. It seems quite likely, however, that the desire of the court to find some basis for neatly disposing of Mexican American claims of jury discrimination formed a primary motive. At the time that the appellate court in *Hernandez* adopted a white conceptualization of Mexican Americans, the judicial rationales for rejecting claims of racial discrimination against members of that community were wearing thin. By 1952, persons challenging the exclusion of Mexican Americans from juries could point, as Hernández's lawyers did, to research indicating that in at least fifty Texas counties with large Mexican–American populations, no Mexican American had ever been called for jury service.[106] They also could demonstrate convincingly that many Mexican Americans qualified for jury service, a point the state stipulated in *Hernandez*.[107] Finally, a full panoply of Supreme Court cases held that the Fourteenth Amendment prohibited racial jury discrimination of the sort apparently practiced against Mexican Americans—a roll call of cases in which, as Hernández's

---

[103] *Salazar*, 193 S.W.2d at 212.

[104] *Aniceto Sanchez*, 243 S.W.2d at 701.

[105] The *Hernandez* court cited *Sanchez* with approval. Hernandez v. State, 251 S.W.2d 531, 535 (Tex. Crim. App. 1952).

[106] Brief for the Petitioner, *supra* note 89, at 14.

[107] Hernandez v. Texas, 347 U.S. 475, 481 (1954).

lawyers noted in their brief to the Court, "the State of Texas is more than proportionately represented."[108] Against this backdrop of massive discrimination, purposeful and directed litigation, fast accumulating evidence, and clear constitutional law, the local practices of jury exclusion in Texas counties seemed increasingly difficult to uphold. Declaring that the Fourteenth Amendment did not protect Mexican Americans in the context of jury selection because they were white may simply have been the most expedient manner by which the appellate court could immunize local discriminatory practices.

Hernandez, Brown, *and the Anti–Subordination Constitution*

The consensus among the parties in *Hernandez* that Mexican Americans were white precluded a racial analysis for what was otherwise evidently a racial case. The Court could not decide *Hernandez* by applying the logic it would use two weeks later in *Brown*, for as a matter of historical contingency the parties did not frame the case in terms of racial mistreatment. This was no small detail, for this happenstance produced a momentous difference between *Brown* and *Hernandez*.[109] In *Brown*, it was obvious that the Constitution protected African Americans; the troubling question was whether it prohibited de jure school segregation. The mistreatment of black Americans indisputably constituted the core concern of the Fourteenth Amendment, and their legal protection required no particular justification. At issue instead was the constitutionality of the widespread practice of segregating schools, and the Court hesitated to condemn such practices in strong terms for fear of engendering a backlash. The result was a decision that neither discussed why the Constitution protected blacks nor explained exactly what was wrong with school segregation.[110] By contrast, in *Hernandez* the issue was whether the Fourteenth Amendment protected the targeted group at all; if it did, their exclusion from juries was clearly prohibited as this practice was one of the few forms of segregation struck down by the Reconstruction Court.[111] But in addressing whether the Constitution protected Mexican Americans, the Court could not simply rely on the presumption of coverage in the black cases, for the parties had insisted that Mexican Americans were white. Thus, the paradoxical racial posture

---

[108] Brief for the Petitioner, *supra* note 89, at 29.

[109] This thesis is discussed generally in Haney López, Hernandez *and* Brown, *supra* note 3, and Ian Haney López, Hernandez v. Brown, N.Y. Times, May 21, 2004, at A17.

[110] For efforts to rewrite *Brown* in a manner that would achieve clarity on these and other issues, see *What Brown v. Board of Education Should Have Said: The Nation's Top Legal Experts Rewrite America's Landmark Civil Rights Decision* (Jack M. Balkin ed., 2001).

[111] *See Hernandez*, 347 U.S. at 477 (citing Strauder v. West Virginia, 100 U.S. 303 (1880)).

of *Hernandez* forced the Justices to explain in more general terms which groups deserved particular constitutional protection, and to specify as well the nature of the practices prohibited under equal protection, without recourse to the overdetermined language of race.

Doubtless Chief Justice Warren's basic approach in *Hernandez* paralleled his underlying sense of the correct analysis regarding *Brown v. Board of Education*. The Warren Court clearly understood the Fourteenth Amendment to protect blacks because a vicious racial hierarchy relegated blacks to an inferior position, and the Justices unanimously struck down school segregation because that practice represented a particularly insidious instance of racial subordination. And yet, Chief Justice Warren did not write this in *Brown*. Instead, the decision simply assumed that it was well settled that equal protection applied to African Americans. Moreover, most likely because the Court feared a backlash, the Justices tempered their criticism of Jim Crow segregation, speaking not of segregated schools as aspects of racial domination but instead of unspecified harms to the "hearts and minds" of black children. Lest even this prove too much, the Court forbore explaining from whence such harms arose—whether from the simple fact of separation or the virulence of white hostility. Again, any fair reading would conclude that *Brown* struck down school segregation because it oppressed blacks. But *Brown* did not strongly and unambiguously ground its decision on an anti-subordination rationale. This shortcoming has opened the door to the misreading of *Brown* that now dominates constitutional race law: *Brown*, the contemporary Court insists, stands for the proposition that the Constitution prohibits not subordination, but only explicit state invocations of race.[112] *Hernandez* deserves renewed attention because, when read with *Brown*, it strongly demonstrates that the Warren Court understood full well that the issue was not classification, but hierarchy.

Under contemporary Fourteenth Amendment jurisprudence, the Court now regards with constitutional indifference any subordination not predicated on an express use of a racial classification, while it

---

[112] Consider Justice Clarence Thomas's interpretation of *Brown*:

Segregation was not unconstitutional because it might have caused psychological feelings of inferiority. Public school systems that separated blacks and provided them with superior educational resources—making blacks "feel" superior to whites sent to lesser schools—would violate the Fourteenth Amendment, whether or not the white students felt stigmatized, just as do school systems in which the positions of the races are reversed. Psychological injury or benefit is irrelevant to the question whether state actors have engaged in intentional discrimination—the critical inquiry for ascertaining violations of the Equal Protection Clause. . . .

Regardless of the relative quality of the schools, segregation violated the Constitution because the State classified students based on their race.

Missouri v. Jenkins, 515 U.S. 70, 121 (1995) (Thomas, J., concurring).

regards with equal hostility all uses of race, whether designed to perpet-uate or dismantle racial hierarchy. Because the Court could find no explicit references to race in Georgia's capital punishment law, *McCles-key v. Kemp* upheld the system as constitutional. The Court reached this result, even though it was uncontroverted that the state sentenced to death blacks who murdered whites at twenty-two times the rate for blacks who killed blacks.[113] Because of a fixation on racial classifications as illicit in themselves, the Court now wields the Constitution to strike down almost every effort to ameliorate racism's legacy. *Richmond v. J.A. Croson Co.* insists that when the former capital of the Confederacy adopts an affirmative action program to steer some of its construction dollars to minority-owned firms, it engages in impermissible discrimina-tion—even when, without that program, less than two-thirds of 1% of construction contracts had gone to minorities in a city that was over 50% African–American.[114] It is not too strong to say that the current Court uses the Constitution to protect the racial status quo: It principally condones discrimination against minorities, and virtually always con-demns efforts to achieve greater racial equality.

Underlying the contemporary Court's insistence on proscribing all, but only, explicit racial classifications lies a particular conception of race evident in a more recent decision, this one too entitled *Hernandez* and again involving jury discrimination.[115] *Hernandez v. New York*, in com-parison to cases like *McCleskey* and *Croson*, is a minor case, but it puts into sharp relief the understanding of race that undergirds the Court's contemporary colorblind jurisprudence. In *Hernandez v. New York*, the prosecutor peremptorily struck from the jury every Latino in a case involving a Hispanic defendant. Because some witnesses did not speak English, jurors were expected to abide by the translation provided by a Spanish-language interpreter. The prosecutor struck bilingual members of the jury pool because he did not believe that they "could" set aside their familiarity with Spanish. The phrase "could," rather than "would," is telling, for while the latter term suggests concern about individual temperament, the former invokes a sense of group disability.[116] Also raising concern, the prosecutor questioned only potential jurors who

---

[113] McCleskey v. Kemp, 481 U.S. 279 (1987).

[114] Richmond v. J.A. Croson Co., 488 U.S. 469 (1989).

[115] Hernandez v. New York, 500 U.S. 352 (1991).

[116] *Id.* at 404 (The prosecutor testified: "I felt there was a great deal of uncertainty as to whether they could accept the interpreter as the final arbiter of what was said by each of the witnesses, especially where there were going to be Spanish-speaking witnesses, and I didn't feel, when I asked them whether or not they could accept the interpreter's translation of it, I didn't feel that they could.").

were Hispanic but no others about their ability to speak Spanish.[117]

Nevertheless, the Court upheld the exclusion, finding no bias on the part of the prosecutor. Justice O'Connor's rationale, offered in a concurring opinion, is particularly revealing. Justice O'Connor thought it irrelevant that the basis for exclusion correlated closely with Hispanic identity and operated to exclude all and only Latinos. Because the prosecutor did not justify the strikes in explicitly racial terms, Justice O'Connor reasoned, no basis existed for constitutional intervention. The strikes "may have acted like strikes based on race," Justice O'Connor conceded, "but they were *not* based on race. *No matter how closely tied or significantly correlated to race* the explanation for a peremptory strike may be, the strike does not implicate the Equal Protection Clause unless it is based on race."[118] According to Justice O'Connor, race does not factor into social relations until and unless someone utters that term. Race exists in this conception almost as a magic word: Say it, and race suddenly springs into being, but not otherwise. This talismanic formalism strips race of all social meaning and of any connection to social practices of group conflict and subordination. It also forms the cornerstone of the Court's colorblind jurisprudence.

The Court's resistance to connecting disparate treatment to racial discrimination, evident in *McCleskey*, ties back to the Court's narrow conception of race. If race reduces to a question of mere physical difference unconnected in any way to social hierarchy or history, then mistreatment on any basis not explicitly tied to physical difference or descent is, by definition, not racial discrimination. Race becomes the basis for discrimination only when a party intends that result; otherwise, there is no discrimination, only the "discrepancies" of social life. But in *Hernandez v. Texas*, the Court unanimously held that constitutional harm could be demonstrated absent a showing of intentional discrimination. Responding to the state's contention that no purposeful racism could be shown, Chief Justice Warren pointedly noted that "it taxes our credulity" to say discrimination was not at issue, concluding that the "result bespeaks discrimination, whether or not it was a conscious decision on the part of any individual jury commissioner."[119] Cannot we say the same? Does it not tax our credulity to say that the racial disparities in Georgia's death penalty system resulted from mere chance? Is it not clear that, when blacks convicted of killing whites are sentenced to death *twenty-two* times as often as blacks convicted of murdering

---

[117] Sheri Lynn Johnson, *The Language and Culture (Not To Say Race) of Peremptory Challenges*, 35 Wm. & Mary L. Rev. 21, 53 (1993).

[118] *Hernandez v. New York*, at 375 (O'Connor, J., concurring) (emphasis in second sentence added).

[119] Hernandez v. Texas, 347 U.S. 475, 482 (1954).

blacks, this result bespeaks discrimination, whether or not we can identify a particular biased actor? Race is not merely a word or a skin pigment, but a social identity deeply connected to history and power, privilege and disadvantage. It makes a travesty of the Fourteenth Amendment to refuse to see McCleskey's case as rooted in the context of a Georgia penal system steeped in racial oppression.

If the Court's pinched conception of race lends support to an intent test, it also allows the Court to equate race-conscious remedies with racism. Under a colorblind standard, nothing differentiates racism from affirmative action, Jim Crow from racial remediation. Witness Justice Clarence Thomas's declaration that "there is a 'moral [and] constitutional equivalence' between laws designed to subjugate a race and those that distribute benefits on the basis of race in order to foster some current notion of equality."[120] How can affirmative action be the equivalent of the segregated juries, schools, restaurants, and bathrooms in Jackson County, Texas? The answer again lies in the colorblind Court's artificially empty conception of race. When the Court abstracts race from social context and group conflict, it reduces the harm of racism to a violation of liberal norms. Under this conception, to treat someone differently on the basis of race amounts to favoring or disfavoring individuals on the basis of criteria over which they have little or no control. This is, to be sure, a potential issue with affirmative action, as it is with a wide range of distinctions our society commonly makes—most commonly, those associated with wealth. But a more impoverished understanding of the harms of Jim Crow can scarcely be conjured. The lawyers for Hernández spent hours on the road every morning traveling to the Jackson County seat to argue the case; they left every evening, for lack of accommodations available to Mexican Americans and because they feared for their safety should they remain.[121] As *Hernandez* emphatically demonstrates, the principal harm of racism involves violent subordination, not the transgression of meritocratic norms.

Today's Court gets racism backwards. The Justices deny that racism operates, no matter how stark the impact, if no state actor specifically invokes race, even though most racism now occurs through institutionalized practices.[122] At the same time, under strict scrutiny the Court concludes that virtually any explicit use of race amounts to racism. In fact, though, efforts to counteract racial oppression's extensive harms

---

[120] Adarand Constructors, Inc. v. Pena, 515 U.S. 200, 240 (1995) (Thomas, J., concurring) (citation omitted).

[121] García, *supra* note 33.

[122] *See generally* Ian F. Haney López, *Institutional Racism: Judicial Conduct and a New Theory of Racial Discrimination*, 109 Yale L.J. 1717 (2000) (discussing the operation of institutional racism in the judicial system).

must refer to race and should not be presumptively suspect. This misunderstanding of racism is anchored by a narrow conception of race. It is race-as-a-word-that-must-be-uttered-for-it-to-exist, race-as-skin-color-disconnected-from-social-practice-or-national-history, which undergirds colorblindness. We can best oppose this understanding of race, and the perverse constitutional results it justifies, by insisting on the deep connection between race and social inequality. Herein lies the single most important insight of *Hernandez v. Texas*. The core issue is not whether officers of the state directly invoked race, as the current Court would require. In considering whether equal protection commands the Court's intervention, Chief Justice Warren clearly stated in *Hernandez* that the key constitutional questions centered on whether "a distinct class" suffered "different treatment"—which is to say, whether the group seeking protection was treated as inferior by community practices, and whether the challenged practice formed part of that larger web of subordination. The Fourteenth Amendment cannot be returned to the task of racial emancipation until the Supreme Court recognizes that *Hernandez v. Texas* raised the correct concerns and begins asking these questions anew.

Epilogue

Just as the important lessons of *Hernandez* have been largely forgotten, so too has the fate of the defendant Pete Hernández. On May 7, 1954, four days after the Supreme Court issued its decision, the Texas Department of Corrections notified the Jackson County Sheriff that Hernández, prisoner number 124147, was to be remanded to Jackson County for retrial.[123] Because he suffered from a severely clubbed foot, Hernández had never been handed over to a state prison or put into the general population; instead, he had been sequestered in the Jackson County jail during the entire appeal process. On September 28, 1954, Hernández was re-indicted, and on October 16, Gus García filed a motion for a change of venue. When he prevailed, the new trial was moved to Refugio County, near Corpus Christi.[124] On November 15, 1954, the second trial was held, with García arguing the case.[125] Despite the

---

[123] *Pete Hernandez is Re–Indicted By Jury*, Edna Herald, Sept. 28, 1954, at 1. On June 10, 1954, the case was formally remanded to the Texas Court of Criminal Appeals, and four days later the remanded case was filed there. *Id.*

[124] *Id.*; *Garcia Will Ask For Venue Change in Pete Hernandez Trial*, Edna Herald, May 27, 1954, at 1. The article lists all the indictments handed down by that grand jury, which included twelve persons, two of them with Hispanic names (Ysabel Barron and Sesoria Rodriguez). *See also Murder Trial May Be Nov. 15*, Edna Herald, Oct. 21, 1954, at 1. Refugio County is near Corpus Christi, and has a long history of anti-Mexican prejudice. *See generally* Hobart Huson, *Refugio: A Comprehensive History of Refugio County from Aboriginal Times to 1953* (1953 & 1955).

[125] *Hernandez Due Parole*, La Prensa (San Antonio), June 15, 1960, at 1.

changed venue and a more representative jury, Pete Hernández was again found guilty, though he did receive a lower sentence of twenty years instead of life. Some evidence exists that this trial may have been decided by a "pickup-jury" aware of an arrangement to reduce Hernández's sentence; if so, the official proceeding was largely for show.[126] Hernández began serving his sentence in Harlem State Prison Farm as inmate number 136125.

Over the next few years, Hernández's attorneys moved on with their practices. Hernández, who had arguably risked his life by agreeing to appeal the case and thus subjecting himself to a retrial at which the death penalty might have been imposed, was largely forgotten. But in 1960, Gus García tracked him down. On February 1, 1960, he wrote to John Herrera: "I would like to know when Hernández was released and what he is doing now. Don't put this off, John."[127] Upon learning that Hernández was locked up in the Harlem State Prison Farm, on February 12, García wrote to the head of the State Board of Pardons and Paroles, Jack Ross:

> I feel really conscience-stricken, Jack, about this matter, and I would like to do everything possible within my power to gain freedom for this boy who was willing to risk a possible death sentence upon the second trial of his case in order to help us establish a very important principle of law and civil rights for Latin Americans everywhere.[128]

Spurred by García's appeal, the parole board made an affirmative recommendation on June 7, 1960, and the next day Hernández was paroled and released by order of Governor Price Daniel, who, as a Senator, had sponsored several of the *Hernandez* lawyers before the Supreme Court bar.[129]

---

[126] James deAnda characterized the 1954 re-trial as a "pickup-jury," one designed to effectuate a plea bargain. Inasmuch as the U.S. Supreme Court had ordered the defendant tried by a more representative jury, state officials were likely more conscientious in this retrial than would have ordinarily been the case. Interview with James deAnda, retired judge and lawyer, at Houston, Texas, (Feb. 17, 2006). In a 1977 interview, Herrera was quoted as saying that Hernández had received a ten-year sentence and that he had served only eight months of the sentence. Richard Vara, *Dedicated Defendant, Lawyers Made Constitutional History*, Houston Post, Nov. 27, 1977, at 9. The parole correspondence records reveal that Hernández was in jail until 1960. *Hernandez Due Parole, supra* note 119.

[127] Letter from Gus García to John J. Herrera (Feb. 1, 1960) (on file at Houston Metropolitan Research Center, John J. Herrera papers, Box 2, Folder 24).

[128] Letter from Gus García to State Board of Pardons and Paroles (Feb. 12, 1960) (on file at Houston Metropolitan Research Center, John J. Herrera papers, Box 2, Folder 24).

[129] John J. Herrera, Letter to the Editor, Houston Post, Feb. 22, 1972 (setting out many details of the case) (on file at Houston Metropolitan Research Center, John J. Herrera papers, Box 2, Folder 24); *Group Seeks Latins on Jury, supra* note 52, at 6.

With Hernández's release, García wrote a batch of letters. Some went to various friends and colleagues, announcing the victory. "While I do not wish to claim credit for the final conclusion of our historical issue, I have pestered Jack Ross for several months now via letters, long distance calls, and two personal visits in Austin. I can now truthfully say that my conscience is clear in this matter."[130] But García wrote one letter to Hernández directly, offering paternal advice:

> We all make mistakes in this life, Pete, and yours was a terrible one. But I do not want you to think of the past. You are still young and your whole life is ahead of you.... More than anything else, I want you to hold that temper of yours in check. If you feel that you are starting to get mad, just think of all those long years in jail and in prison and RUN, don't walk, away from trouble.[131]

Of the trajectory of Hernández's life after his release, nothing official survives in recorded form.[132] García was under the impression that Hernández planned to move to Port LaVaca, Texas after being released from prison.[133] Many years later, James deAnda recalled hearing from Jackson County residents that Hernández, who had become a prison barber, practiced his trade after his release until he died in the 1970s.[134]

The *Hernandez* case augured illustrious careers for some but not all members of the legal team. Hernández's lawyers had few ties to each other before they tried the case, and they never tried a major case together again afterwards. Among the lawyers, Carlos Cadena became the first Mexican–American law professor in the country, joining the St. Mary's law faculty in San Antonio in 1954, and then later becoming its City Attorney. In 1964, he again argued before the Supreme Court in a case involving a Puerto Rican, *Lopez v. Texas*.[135] John Herrera and James deAnda returned to their practice in Houston. Later in the 1950s, Herrera became the National President of LULAC, and remained a

---

[130] Letter from Gus García to John J. Herrera, *supra* note 121; Letter from Gus García to State Board of Pardons and Paroles, *supra* note 122.

[131] García also offered to assist Hernández should he get into trouble, providing home and office phone numbers to Hernández. Letter from Gus García to Pete Hernández (June 8, 1960) (on file at Houston Metropolitan Research Center, John J. Herrera papers, Box 2, Folder 24).

[132] Tad Walch, *Anti-Bias Ruling Hailed*, Deseret Morning News (Salt Lake City), May 3, 2004, at B1 (interview with Ignacio García, who notes that no authoritative record exists of Hernández's death).

[133] Letter from Gus García to Pete Hernández, *supra* note 125.

[134] Interview with James deAnda, *supra* note 7.

[135] 378 U.S. 567 (1964) (per curiam). In another case in which the Court denied *certiorari*, Cadena was co-counsel for the respondent. Congregation of Sisters of Charity of the Incarnate Word v. San Antonio, 372 U.S. 967 (1963).

longtime civic leader in Houston. In 1955, deAnda moved to Corpus Christi, where he established a very successful civil practice.[136] In 1979, President Jimmy Carter appointed deAnda to serve as a federal judge, the second Mexican American to serve in that position (after Reynaldo Garza).[137] DeAnda eventually became the first Mexican American to rise to the position of Chief Judge in 1988, presiding over the Southern District of Texas until he retired in 1992.[138] He then returned to private practice in Houston, not fully retiring until 2002; he passed away at the age of eighty-one in 2006.[139]

Meanwhile, García's struggle with alcoholism pushed him into hard times even during the 1950s, though he continued to practice law in San Antonio and other cities, including a brief stint in Houston, where he partnered with Herrera. In what may have been among his final letters to Herrera, García wrote in January 1963: "This is the final turning point in my life, and whether I choose the right road or end up in the gutter or a suicide depends largely on the few friends I have left."[140] Over the next eighteen months, García was hospitalized in Waco, Texas, lost his law license, and finally expired on a bench in a San Antonio park, where he sat dead for hours, unnoticed. He was 48 years old.[141]

Unlike its more well-known companion case, *Brown v. Board of Education*, *Hernandez v. Texas* had more pedestrian, more *campesino* roots: a drunken barroom brawl and a shooting in the backwater agricultural town of Edna, Texas; lawyers committed to civil rights but responsible for maintaining private practices; civic organizations dedicated to advancing the community but without a specialized advocacy program; and funds scraped together to pay the fees and to get some lawyers to Washington, D.C. There had been earlier efforts to diversify juries, reaching back at least to the trial of Gregorio Cortez in 1901, and there would be later efforts to strike down unrepresentative juries, including efforts by the legendary Oscar Zeta Acosta in Los Angeles in

---

[136] James deAnda and Gus García later tried an important school desegregation case together, Hernandez v. Driscoll Indep. Sch. Dist., 2 Race Rel. L. Rep. 329 (1957) (unpublished opinion, S.D. Tex. Civ. No. 1384). García so antagonized the federal judge in this case that he was not allowed to speak in court, so James deAnda made objections on the record. The formal filings also listed Richard Casillas and Albert Pena, Jr. as co-counsel. 2 Race Rel. L. Rep. 34 (1957).

[137] Dennis Hevesi, *James deAnda, 81, Lawyer in Case for Hispanic Jurors, Dies*, N.Y. Times, Sept. 9, 2006.

[138] *Id.*

[139] *Id.*

[140] Letter from Gus García to John Herrera (Jan. 28, 1963) (on file at Houston Metropolitan Research Center, John J. Herrera papers, Box 5, Folder 5).

[141] Paul Thompson, San Antonio Evening News, June 14, 1964, at 2A.

the 1960s.[142] Still, in the new millennium Latinos remain substantially underrepresented in the Texas jury system.[143] Nevertheless, in a brief and shining moment in 1954, Mexican–American lawyers prevailed in a system that accorded their community little legal status or respect. Through sheer tenacity, brilliance, and some luck, they showed that it was possible to tilt against windmills and to slay the dragon of Jim Crow. These attorneys changed history. But they did more than that: They also prodded the Supreme Court to articulate exactly why and when some groups deserved special concern under the Equal Protection Clause. Chief Justice Warren made clear in *Hernandez*, in a way he occluded in *Brown*, that the touchstone for constitutional protection is group subordination, not the abstract fact of racial classification. More than fifty years after *Hernandez v. Texas* was handed down, the country as a whole must bring this decision out of *Brown*'s shadow, and the Supreme Court should reread *Brown* in light of the critically important lessons taught by the first Warren Court decision that took on Jim Crow.

---

[142] As early as 1901, the lawyer for Gregorio Córtez called attention to the jury pool in this famous case. *Gregorio Cortez's Trial. Motion for a Change of Venue Being Heard*, Dallas Morning News, Oct. 5, 1901, p.1; *see generally* Richard J. Mertz, *"No One Can Arrest Me": The Story of Gregorio Cortez*, 1 J. S. Tex. 1 (1974). On Acosta's challenges to the exclusion of Mexican Americans from juries in Los Angeles, see Haney López, *supra* note 73, at 32, 36–38, 41–50, 94–103; *see also* Michael A. Olivas, *"Breaking the Law" on Principle: An Essay on Lawyers' Dilemmas, Unpopular Causes, and Legal Regimes*, 52 U. Pitt. L. Rev. 815, 846–54 (1991).

[143] For a recent study of Houston-area juries and the problems of underrepresentation, see Larry Karson, *The Implications of a Key–Man System for Selecting a Grand Jury: An Exploratory Study*, 3 Sw. J. of Crim. Just. 3 (2006), *available at* http://swjcj.cjcenter.org/arc hives/3.1/Karson.pdf.

9

Jerry Kang

Dodging Responsibility: The Story of *Hirabayashi v. United States*

Introduction

"Strict scrutiny" for race-based classifications is typically traced back to *Korematsu v. United States*,[1] the Japanese–American internment case in which the Supreme Court trumpeted that "all legal restrictions which curtail the civil rights of a single racial group are immediately suspect."[2] But the link can be made one year earlier, to the first of the internment cases: *Hirabayashi v. United States*.[3] Although less well-known, *Hirabayashi* is arguably the more important case because it created the procedural and precedential foundation upon which *Korematsu* was built.[4]

To complicate matters, we must take account of two *Hirabayashi* cases: one decided during World War II, and the other a part of the 1980s *coram nobis* cases. In these latter cases, the men whose convictions the Supreme Court affirmed in the 1940s marched back into federal district court, and on the basis of "smoking gun" evidence discovered in the National Archives, they achieved vindication four decades after their initial defeat. Although these cases are rightly cele-

---

[1] 323 U.S. 214 (1944).

[2] *Id.* at 216.

[3] 320 U.S. 81 (1943).

[4] *See, e.g.,* Regents of the Univ. of Cal. v. Bakke, 438 U.S. 265, 290–91 (1978) (citing to *Hirabayashi*, then *Korematsu* for strict scrutiny standard); Simon & Schuster, Inc. v. Members of the N.Y. State Crime Victims Bd., 502 U.S. 105, 124 (1991) (Kennedy, J. concurring) (citing to *Hirabayashi* for equal protection principles).

brated, a closer review of Hirabayashi's victory reveals a troublesome tale about judicial accountability and evasion of responsibility.

Hirabayashi at War

The Internment

The Juggernaut

Prior to the terrorist attacks on September 11, 2001, the day of infamy for the United States was December 7, 1941.[5] The attack on Pearl Harbor left approximately 2,300 dead and nearly twenty Navy ships destroyed. Immediately, the United States declared war on Japan. Beginning that very day, the Federal Bureau of Investigation ("FBI") arrested over 2,000 Japanese resident aliens who had been kept on a special list of people marked as potentially subversive and dangerous. This "ABC" list included nearly all first-generation Japanese American leaders.

In January 1942, a report authored by Supreme Court Justice Owen Roberts concluded that espionage by sleeper cells in Hawai'i had aided the enemy attack. That same month, pressure increased for radical solutions. For example, West Coast politicians, such as Congressman Leland Ford of California, urged mass internment of the Japanese; prominent editorialists, like Westbrook Pegler, did the same. Seeing a convenient opportunity to eliminate competition from Japanese farmers, whites with agricultural interests inflamed public sentiment. Even Earl Warren, then Attorney General of California, lobbied aggressively in favor of mass removal of Japanese Americans.

On February 14, 1942, General John L. DeWitt, who was in charge of the Western Defense Command, made his final recommendation in favor of mass evacuation of Japanese Americans from the West Coast. Five days later, President Franklin Delano Roosevelt issued Executive Order ("E.O.") 9066, which authorized commanders in the United States to designate military areas and exclude any person from those areas.[6] Although aware of the racially targeted evacuation to come,

---

[5] *See generally* Eric K. Yamamoto et al., *Race, Rights and Reparation: Law and the Japanese American Internment* 38–40, 96–102 (2001); Comm'n on Wartime Relocation and Internment of Civilians, *Personal Justice Denied* (1982) [hereinafter *Personal Justice Denied*]; and various books written by Roger Daniels. *See, e.g.,* Roger Daniels, *Concentration Camps, North America: Japanese in the United States and Canada During World War II* (1981) [hereinafter *Concentration Camps*]; Roger Daniels, Prisoners Without Trial: Japanese Americans in World War II (Eric Foner ed., 1993) [hereinafter *Prisoners*]; Roger Daniels, *The Politics of Prejudice: The Anti–Japanese Movement in California and the Struggle for Japanese Exclusion* (1962).

[6] The relevant language read: "I hereby authorize and direct the Secretary of War, and the Military Commanders whom he may from time to time designate, whenever he or any

President Roosevelt made no explicit mention of the Japanese.[7]

In late February, Congress also began to hold regional hearings, which were chaired by Representative John Tolan of California.[8] Most witnesses at these "National Defense Migration" hearings spoke ill of the Japanese; in sharp contrast, well-known witnesses sympathized with those of German or Italian descent. For example, author Thomas Mann spoke for anti-Nazi refugees.[9] The mayor of San Francisco, Angelo Rossi, was an Italian American.[10] Reprentative Tolan himself encouraged testimony about Joe DiMaggio's honest and law-abiding parents, who lived in the San Francisco area.[11]

In the first half of March, General DeWitt issued Proclamations 1 and 2,[12] which designated military areas in all West Coast states, as well as Arizona, and warned of future evacuation. On March 21, 1942, Congress passed Public Law ("P.L.") 503,[13] which criminalized disobedience of duly authorized military regulations. This was the federal law under which Gordon Hirabayashi would later be convicted. On March 24, DeWitt's Proclamation 3 instituted a *curfew* for all alien enemies and anyone of Japanese descent—alien and citizen alike.[14] Three days later, DeWitt's Proclamation 4[15] prohibited Japanese from relocating out of the military areas at their own discretion. This "freeze order" made certain that they would leave only as the military dictated. Beginning on March 24 and proceeding throughout the year, General DeWitt eventually issued 108 civilian *exclusion* orders.[16] These orders required all Japanese

---

designated Commander deems such action necessary or desirable, to prescribe military areas in such places and of such extent as he or the appropriate Military Commander may determine, from which any or all persons may be excluded, and with respect to which, the right of any person to enter, remain in, or leave shall be subject to whatever restrictions the Secretary of War or the appropriate Military Commander may impose in his discretion." Exec. Order No. 9066, 7 Fed. Reg. 1407 (Feb. 19, 1942).

[7] *See* Greg Robinson, *By Order of the President: FDR and the Internment of Japanese Americans* 108 (2001).

[8] *See National Defense Migration: Hearings Before the House of Representatives Select Comm. Investigating Nat'l Defense Migration*, H.R. Res. 113, 77th Cong. (1942).

[9] *Concentration Camps, supra* note 5, at 79.

[10] *See* Allan R. Bosworth, *America's Concentration Camps* 68 (1967).

[11] *Prisoners, supra* note 5, at 51.

[12] Public Proclamation No. 1, 7 Fed. Reg. 2320 (Mar. 26, 1942); Public Proclamation No. 2, 7 Fed. Reg. 2405 (Mar. 28, 1942).

[13] Act of Mar. 21, 1942, Pub. L. No. 77–503, 56 Stat. 173 (1942).

[14] Pub. Proclamation No. 3, 7 Fed. Reg. 2543 (Mar. 24, 1942).

[15] Public Proclamation No. 4, 7 Fed. Reg. 2601 (Apr. 4, 1942).

[16] *See Ex parte Endo*, 323 U.S. 283, 288 (1944) ("Beginning on March 24, 1942, a series of 108 Civil Exclusion Orders were issued by General DeWitt pursuant to Public Proclamation Nos. 1 and 2.").

Americans, both aliens and "non-aliens" (i.e. American citizens), living in certain territories to report to specified evacuation centers.

The evacuees were then warehoused for months in assembly centers run by the Army. The centers often were nothing more than quickly converted fairgrounds and racetrack stalls, more fit for animals than families, especially those with infants, small children, and elderly relatives. As of April 7, 1942, after mountain and Midwestern state governors rejected the idea of resettlement—some warning of mass lynchings[17] —it became clear that the assembled Japanese would be funneled indefinitely into "relocation centers"—euphemisms for concentration camps. By June 1942, just six months into the war, 97,000 Japanese Americans had been rounded up, and most were held in assembly centers.[18]

It was in the first week of June that the United States' victory in the Battle of Midway made any West Coast invasion highly improbable. Still, the internment juggernaut churned on. By November, over 100,000 persons were forced from assembly centers into relocation camps.[19] Of these, approximately 70% were U.S. citizens based on their birth in the United States.[20] The others were indeed aliens, as is often mentioned by internment apologists, but at the time, federal law only allowed "free white persons" and persons of African descent to naturalize. In 1922, the Supreme Court had made clear in *Ozawa v. United States*[21] that regardless of how fair the flesh and how absolute the cultural assimilation, Japanese were not white.

These ten "relocation" centers were located in deserts and swamps, surrounded by barbed wire and armed sentries. Although obviously not Nazi death camps, conditions were deplorable, and there were numerous incidents of physical brutality by military guards.[22] Without adequate medical care, many elderly, infirm, and infant prisoners needlessly suffered and died. The situation was ironic and Kafkaesque. For instance, Japanese Americans were forcibly drafted out of camps to fight in

---

[17] *See* Yamamoto et al., *supra* note 5, at 196.

[18] *See* Peter Irons, *Justice at War: The Story of the Japanese American Internment Cases* 73 (1983).

[19] *See Personal Justice Denied, supra* note 5, at 149.

[20] Birthright citizenship was secured by a Chinese litigant at the end of the nineteenth century. *See* United States v. Wong Kim Ark, 169 U.S. 649 (1898) (holding that Chinese persons born in the United States were citizens under the Fourteenth Amendment's Citizenship Clause).

[21] 260 U.S. 178 (1922).

[22] *See, e.g.*, Eric L. Muller, *All the Themes but One*, 66 U. Chi. L. Rev. 1395, 1408–09 (2001) (describing beatings, tear gas, and shootings).

Europe, albeit in segregated battalions; they were disloyal enough to imprison, but loyal enough to kill, and to die, for their country.[23] Those who resisted the draft because of their families' imprisonment in concentration camps were stigmatized, prosecuted, and imprisoned.[24] Japanese Americans also were expected to be productive and compliant citizens within the camps. Internees were to demonstrate patriotism under duress and to work to make each camp self-sufficient.[25] Children behind barbed wire had to pledge allegiance to the flag.[26]

The internees—many of them very young—were imprisoned for an average of 900 days. Family structures dissolved; family savings evaporated; real and personal property was lost; lives were shattered; spirits were broken. Yet for the internees, no individualized findings of guilt or disloyalty were made. Instead, military necessity under exigent circumstances was the blanket justification for their confinement.[27] By contrast, in Hawai'i where Pearl Harbor was bombed, and where far more Japanese Americans resided, both in relative and absolute numbers, martial law was declared but there was no internment.[28]

The Stand

Although the Supreme Court titled the case *Kiyoshi* Hirabayashi v. United States, Hirabayashi's 1918 birth certificate reads far more plainly "Gordon Hirabayashi."[29] Born in the city of Pontiac, near Seattle, Hirabayashi was raised in a small Japanese–American farming community in the White River Valley. His parents had migrated from Japan to

---

[23] On January 20, 1944, the Department of War announced that it would draft Japanese Americans out of the internment camps into segregated combat units. *See id.* at 64. They were drafted into the 442nd Regimental Combat Team, which had merged with the 100th Battalion (originally from Hawai'i). This unit, which included volunteers and draftees, "became the most decorated unit of its size and length of service in U.S. military history." Mitchell T. Maki et al., *Achieving the Impossible Dream: How Japanese Americans Obtained Redress* 43 (1999).

[24] *See generally* Eric L. Muller, *Free to Die for Their Country: The Story of the Japanese American Draft Resisters in World War II* (2001).

[25] Richard S. Nishimoto, *Inside An American Concentration Camp: Japanese American Resistance at Poston, Arizona* 34–35 (Lane Ryo Hirabayashi ed., 1995) (qutoing labor and loyalty oath that Poston internees were required to sign).

[26] *See* Doris Kearns Goodwin, *No Ordinary Time: Franklin and Eleanor Roosevelt: The Home Front in World War II* 429 (1994).

[27] *See, e.g.*, Yamamoto, et al., *supra* note 5, at 193–230.

[28] *See* Robinson, *supra* note 7, at 156–57; David M. Kennedy, *Freedom from Fear: The American People in Depression and War, 1929–1945*, at 748 (C. Vann Woodward ed., 1999) (suggesting that "wholesale evacuation" was infeasible).

[29] I thank Greg Robinson for this observation.

join a unique farming cooperative made up of four families who shared a "non-denominational Christian outlook that emphasized principled lives and personal integrity."[30] This religious outlook was part of the "grass-roots Japanese *Mukyokai* movement," which has "often [been] compared to the Society of Friends ('Quakers')."[31]

Life on the cooperative helped forge the moral character that led Hirabayashi to take a stand. As he put it:

> The living co-op was where their beliefs were truly lived. That is, they didn't preach something, and practice something else. So that kind of straightforward living had an impact on me. That made it difficult for me to compromise some things. You always compromise to make out, you know. But when it comes to fundamental things, you either accept them, or you don't. And when it comes to being true to yourself, you're not trying to fool somebody else, and you can't fool yourself. You've got to be true to something. That's the sort of thing that I learned: if something is valuable, be true to that.[32]

One example of being true to one's values is worth specific mention. When Gordon Hirabayashi was just a child, the cooperative resisted an escheat action pursued by the State of Washington under its 1921 Alien Land Law. This law prohibited aliens ineligble for citizenship, which included Japanese immigrants, from owning real property. In this escheat action, the government claimed that although title was formally held by the White River Gardens corporation, the law was still being violated in spirit; accordingly, the land should be forfeited to the state. The cooperative pursued its losing case not only up through the Washington Supreme Court but all the way to the United States Supreme Court.[33]

Given Hirabayashi's upbringing, it is not entirely surprising that as a child he was a Boy Scout, indeed one of the "highest achievers" of his racially mixed troop. In what would foreshadow far more vicious discrimination, the troop visited Washington, DC in 1936 with plans to meet President Roosevelt. However, when the President refused to meet the

---

[30] Stan Flewelling, Shirakawa: *Stories from a Pacific Northwest Japanese American Community* 62 (2002).

[31] *Id.* at 63.

[32] *Id.* at 64 (quoting Gordon Hirabayashi).

[33] *See* State of Washington v. Taka Hirabayashi, 133 Wash. 462 (1925) (affirming escheat action), *aff'd sub nom.* White River Gardens, Inc. v. State of Washington, 277 U.S. 572 (1928) (per curiam). For an oral history of this litigation by Shoichiro Katsuno, the head of one of the four families, see Kazuo Ito, *Issei: A History of Japanese Immigrants in North America* 173–75 (1973).

scoutmaster because he was Japanese, the entire troop declined the invitation.[34]

When the curfew and evacuation orders came down, Hirabayashi was a twenty-four-year-old senior at the University of Washington. In contrast to Fred Korematsu who was avoiding internment in order to stay with his Italian–American girlfriend,[35] Hirabayashi's resistance was more self-consciously moral and political. He already had made the unpopular decision to be a conscientious objector during the war. Although he initially planned to comply with the curfew, he eventually concluded that going along with the orders would be inconsistent with his "fundamental principles" and that he would have to take a stand, even if it was a lonely and unpopular one. As he later recalled:

> Regarding the curfew, I just took a citizen's position and felt that I'm not going to have anything more to do with it, which is the position that all non-Japanese took. I mean, they didn't have to abide by it, so they didn't do anything about it. So I just said, I'm going to live like an ordinary American, and left it up to the government; if they wanted to pick me up, okay. We'll face it then. So I just ignored it, and nothing happened. The exclusion order is something different, because everybody's being removed. If I was roaming the streets, sooner or later—sooner probably—I'd be accosted and picked up. So rather than to run into that . . . I just made arrangements with Arthur Barnett [a friend and a Quaker] to meet me the morning after the last busload of Japanese left, and he'd drive me over to the FBI.[36]

This was no easy decision. Hirabayashi's mother was the family's driving force, a woman he described as being "two generations early to be [called] a feminist."[37] Still, she did not want the family divided in a time of crisis. Weeping, she begged him—her eldest son—not to challenge internment. She pointed out that no one knew whether he would be jailed, exiled to Japan, or even killed.[38] Notwithstanding these intense

---

[34] See Flewelling, supra note 30, at 126.

[35] Korematsu had been arrested on May 30, 1942, trying to pass as a Spanish–Hawaiian, under the alias "Clyde Sarah." Keen on staying in Northern California, Fred Korematsu had surgery on his nose and eyes to try to alter his physical features. See Korematsu v. United States, 140 F.2d 289, 293 (9th Cir. 1943) (describing plastic surgery attempt), aff'd, 323 U.S. 214 (1944).

[36] Interview with Gordon Hirabayashi (Feb. 9, 1981), (on file with the University of Washington Libraries).

[37] Yasuko I. Takezawa, Breaking the Silence: Redress and Japanese American Ethnicity 81 (1995) (quoting Gordon Hirabayashi).

[38] See id. at 81–82.

familial pressures, Hirabayashi chose to take a stand. As he explained later:

> If I went with [my parents], I'd have to give up something to make myself go, and what I'd have to give up was what made me an objector to what I considered injustice. And if I went along, that meant defending myself, and it would affect me. I wouldn't be the same person [my mother's] got beside her. And later she realized this . . . .[39]

After refusing to comply with an exclusion order,[40] Hirabayashi turned himself in to the FBI on May 16, 1942. He brought along a four-page statement explaining the constitutional and moral grounds for his civil disobedience. The FBI soon learned that Hirabayashi also had violated curfew.[41] Arthur Barnett advised Hirabayashi and accompanied him when he went to the FBI. Acquainted with Barnett, Mary Farquharson, an Oregon attorney, state senator, and member of the Seattle chapter of the American Civil Liberties Union ("ACLU"), organized a defense fund for Hirabayashi and hired Frank Walters to represent him at trial. Although the local chapter of the ACLU participated, the national ACLU declined to assist because of its strong support for President Roosevelt. Nor did the second-generation Japanese American Citizens League (JACL), the most influential community organization, initially come to Hirabayashi's defense. Instead, JACL leaders insisted on cooperation with, not defiance of, the government as evidence of loyalty.[42]

The Case

Trial and Appeal

Hirabayashi's trial began on October 20, 1942. Because he admitted both the curfew and exclusion violations, the case was cut and dried. Although his lawyer appealed to the jury to nullify the discriminatory military orders, it returned with a guilty verdict in ten minutes. Hirabayashi was originally given consecutive sentences that ran for less than ninety days. Because a ninety-day sentence would allow him to serve

---

[39] *Id.* at 82.

[40] Civilian Exclusion Order No. 57, 7 Fed. Reg. 3725 (May 10, 1942).

[41] According to Peter Irons, Hirabayashi brought along his diary, which showed that he obeyed the curfew until May 4, 1942 but subsequently disobeyed it until he turned himself in on May 16, 1942. Irons, *supra* note 18, at 92, 106–07. Hirabayashi's recollection differs slightly, and he explained that this information was revealed in the FBI interrogation. *See* Flewelling, *supra* note 30, at 229 (quoting Gordon Hirabayashi).

[42] *See, e.g.*, Maki et al., *supra* note 23, at 33–34 (describing national JACL policy to urge full cooperation with the government to demonstrate loyalty).

time outside doing menial labor, instead of remaining inside a jail cell, Hirabayashi requested a longer sentence. The judge obliged and granted him a ninety-day sentence for each offense, to run *concurrently* instead of *consecutively*.[43] This seemingly trivial difference would later prove to have extraordinary consequences.

The Ninth Circuit Court of Appeals, en banc, heard Hirabayashi's appeal, as well as those of Minoru Yasui[44] and Fred Korematsu, on February 19, 1943. All three cases related to convictions for violating curfew and evacuation orders related to the internment process. However, instead of ruling on the cases, the court certified the relevant legal questions to the Supreme Court.[45] The Court took the unusual step of requesting that the record in each case be transmitted in its entirety so that the Justices could decide the lawsuits as if they had been brought on direct appeal.[46]

The Supreme Court

By the time the case reached the Supreme Court, Hirabayashi's attorneys had ceded control to the national ACLU, which had adopted a policy against any direct constitutional attack on Executive Order 9066. The brief thus focused on the non-delegation doctrine, which forbade Congress from delegating its authority to agencies without providing adequate standards. The ACLU argued that the broad grant of authority to the military violated this requirement. By comparison, the racial discrimination argument took up only two pages in the petitioner's brief and was left for the local ACLU chapter and JACL to elaborate in their amicus briefs.

Procedure

The Supreme Court heard argument in *Hirabayashi* (and its companion case *Yasui*) on May 10 and 11, 1943. By this time, internment was a *fait accompli*. Yet, in its published opinion, the Court found a way to ignore this painful reality by adopting what I call a *segmentation* technique. To avoid discussing the detention of Japanese Americans, the Court parsed the entire internment process into three separate parts: (1) curfew, (2) exclusion, and (3) relocation.

---

[43] *See* Irons, *supra* note 18, at 159.

[44] United States v. Minoru Yasui, 48 F. Supp. 40 (D. Or. 1942).

[45] According to Irons, this was done at the suggestion of the Attorney General Francis Biddle, without knowledge of the defendants or the Supreme Court. *See* Irons, *supra* note 18, at 182.

[46] The current version of the certification statute can be found at 28 U.S.C. § 1254(2) (2000).

Recall that Hirabayashi's convictions in the district court were for violating curfew and an exclusion order. According to historian Peter Irons, Chief Justice Harlan F. Stone was keen on avoiding the exclusion issue. He feared that such a challenge could open up a difficult review of the entire internment process, including the continuing incarceration of tens of thousands of people. So, through reasoning argued by neither party,[47] Chief Justice Stone took advantage of Hirabayashi's concurrent sentences. He wrote:

> Since the sentences of three months each imposed by the district court on the two counts were ordered to run concurrently, it will be unnecessary to consider questions raised with respect to the first count [the exclusion violation] if we find that the conviction on the second count, for violation of the curfew order, must be sustained.[48]

Through this sentencing fortuity, the Court sua sponte found a convenient way to segment off the narrow issue of curfew as the sole question presented. This segmentation technique was not a simple, necessary application of some established doctrine regarding appellate review of concurrent sentencing. Instead, the Court was making new law. In subsequent invocations of the concurrent sentencing doctrine, the Court has repeatedly cited *Hirabayashi* as the foundational precedent.[49]

With this procedural tactic, the question presented became much more manageable: during a time of national peril, was the military's adoption of a mere curfew lawful? The Court made clear that it was "decid[ing] only the issue as we have defined it"[50] and that it would be "unnecessary to consider whether or to what extent such findings would support orders differing from the curfew order."[51] By limiting the decision strictly to curfew, the Justices made clear that *Hirabayashi* would not necessarily be decisive precedent in cases that involved evacuation and internment.

---

[47] The government made no mention of this argument in its brief. To avoid the larger discussion of the internment, the government instead had argued that Hirabayashi lacked standing to question the constitutionality of any restraint placed on other persons because Hirabayashi himself, after making bail, was allowed to proceed inland in order to accept employment found by religious friends. Brief for the United States at 36, 72–73, Hirabayashi v. United States, 320 U.S. 81 (1943) (No. 870).

[48] *Hirabayashi*, 320 U.S. at 85.

[49] *See, e.g.*, Benton v. Maryland, 395 U.S. 784, 789 (1969) ("The most widely cited application of this approach to cases where concurrent sentences, rather than a single general sentence, have been imposed is *Hirabayashi v. United States....*"); Lanza v. New York, 370 U.S. 139, 151 n.1 (1962) (Brennan, J., concurring); Roviaro v. United States, 353 U.S. 53, 59 n.6 (1957); Pinkerton v. United States, 328 U.S. 640, 641 n.1 (1946).

[50] *Hirabayashi*, 320 U.S. at 102.

[51] *Id.* at 105.

Substance

(1) Power

In *Hirabayashi*, the Court started its substantive analysis by asking who had granted General DeWitt the power to declare a curfew. The Justices pointed out that this power had been conferred by both Congress, in P.L. 503, and the Executive Branch, in E.O. 9066.[52] Accordingly, DeWitt was not acting as some rogue agent without official authorization. Because the federal government is one of limited powers, the next logical question is: where did Congress and the President get *their* power? Although state governments enjoy a general "police power" to act in the public interest, all federal government actions must (at least ostensibly) stem from some specific grant of power identified in the Constitution. The Court concluded that both P.L. 503 and E.O. 9066 were "exercise[s] of the power to wage war conferred on the Congress and on the President, as Commander in Chief of the armed forces, by Articles I and II of the Constitution."[53] According to the Court, given the threat assessment, curfew was a perfectly reasonable exercise of that war power.

Interestingly, in making this case, the Court noted that those of Japanese origin might be disloyal because American society discriminated against them:

> There is support for the view that social, economic and political conditions which have prevailed since the close of the last century, when the Japanese began to come to this country in substantial numbers, have intensified their solidarity and have in large measure prevented their assimilation as an integral part of the white population.[54]

Indeed, in a footnote, the Court provided an exhaustive inventory of the various laws that treated individuals of Japanese descent as second-class citizens and perpetual foreigners: federal laws that prevented their immigration and naturalization; state laws that restricted property ownership and intermarriage with whites; and economic discrimination that limited professional and employment opportunities.[55] No doubt, these observations were prompted by the government's brief, which specifically suggested that discriminatory practices might lead the Japanese to become detached and disloyal:

---

[52] *Id.* at 91–92.

[53] *Id.* at 92.

[54] *Id.* at 96.

[55] *Id.* at 96 n.4.

The reaction of the Japanese to their lack of assimilation and to their treatment is a question which of course does not admit of any precise answer. It is entirely possible that an unknown number of the Japanese may lack to some extent a feeling of loyalty toward the United States as a result of their treatment, and may feel a consequent tie to Japan, a heightened sense of racial solidarity, and a compensatory feeling of racial pride or pride in Japan's achievements.[56]

The Court went on to explain—without seeing the Catch–22—that, therefore, the Japanese posed a greater national security risk than other groups:

The restrictions, both practical and legal, affecting the privileges and opportunities afforded to persons of Japanese extraction residing in the United States, have been sources of irritation and may well have tended to increase their isolation, and in many instances their attachments to Japan and its institutions.

Viewing these data in all their aspects, Congress and the Executive could reasonably have concluded that these conditions have encouraged the continued attachment of members of this group to Japan and Japanese institutions. These are only some of the many considerations which those charged with the responsibility for the national defense could take into account in determining the nature and extent of the danger of espionage and sabotage, in the event of invasion or air raid attack.[57]

The Court had no sense of either the ironic or the absurd. The opinion made no mention of the fact that, along with state judiciaries, the Court had itself sanctioned the very discrimination that was now being used to justify further oppression of the Japanese.

And it was not as if the Court was clueless. The JACL, which joined the litigation at the Supreme Court level, pointed out explicitly in its amicus brief that accepting such reasoning would put this country on "a treadmill of intolerance from which there is no escape."[58] In making its case, the JACL pulled no punches: "By [this line of reasoning], the Nazi

---

[56] Brief for the United States, *supra* note 47, at 21 (citations omitted); *see also* Brief of the States of California, Oregon and Washington as Amici Curiae at 11, Hirabayashi v. United States, 320 U.S. 81 (1943) (No. 870) ("The Japanese of the Pacific Coast area on the whole have remained a group apart and inscrutable to their neighbors. As they represent an unassimilated, homogenous [sic] element which in varying degrees is closely related through ties of race, language, religion, custom and ideology to the Japanese Empire.") (citations omitted).

[57] *Hirabayashi*, 320 U.S. at 98–99.

[58] Brief Amicus Curiae (Japanese American Citizens League) at 64, Hirabayashi v. United States, 320 U.S. 81 (1943) (No. 870).

treatment of the Jews is vindicated, for the Jews of Germany had suffered civil and social disabilities and therefore, by the sadistic turn of logic, should have been ripe for treason to the Reich precisely as Herr Hitler declared."[59]

In his arguments, Hirabayashi had suggested a different line of analysis, based not on race or ethnicity but on citizenship. In other words, military orders should distinguish between enemy aliens and U.S. citizens. Accordingly, if citizens of Japanese descent had to suffer curfew in the name of national security, so should all citizens. The Court responded that the Constitution required no such irrationality:

> In a case of threatened danger requiring prompt action, it is a choice between inflicting obviously needless hardship on the many, or sitting passive and unresisting in the presence of the threat. We think that constitutional government, in time of war, is not so powerless and does not compel so hard a choice if those charged with responsibility of our national defense have reasonable ground for believing that the threat is real.[60]

The final issue of power that the Court addressed was the *nondelegation doctrine*.[61] At the time, this doctrine prevented Congress from delegating broad, unspecified legislative powers to an agency (in this case, the military); the delegation had to be constrained by sufficiently specific substantive standards. The Court conceded that P.L. 503 contained no explicit substantive standard; however, when read in light of E.O. 9066 as well as DeWitt's Public Proclamations issued before the statute's passage, a sufficiently clear implicit substantive standard could be divined:

> It is true that the Act does not in terms establish a particular standard to which orders of the military commander are to conform, or require findings to be made as a prerequisite to any order. But the Executive Order, the Proclamations and the statute are not to be read in isolation from each other. They were parts of a single program and must be judged as such. The Act of March 21, 1942, was an adoption by Congress of the Executive Order and of the Proclamations. The Proclamations themselves followed a standard authorized by the Executive Order—the necessity of protecting military resources in the designated areas against *espionage and sabotage*. And by the Act, Congress gave its approval to that standard.[62]

---

[59] *Id.* at 64–65.

[60] *Hirabayashi*, 320 U.S. at 95.

[61] *Id.* at 102–03.

[62] *Id.* at 103 (emphasis added).

Of course, viewing the Executive Order, Public Proclamations, and the statute as parts of a coordinated, indivisible program clashes with the segmentation technique, which methodically severed curfew from evacuation. By relying on executive and military pronouncements as a kind of surrogate legislative history, the Court held that, pursuant to war-making powers granted by the Constitution to Congress and the President, these political branches delegated their authority to the military, with adequately clear instructions to make the institution of a curfew lawful.

(2) Equality

Even if the military had the affirmative power to issue curfews, officers might nonetheless exercise that power in a way that violated some other constitutional injunction, such as the right to equality. The obvious source of that right is the Fourteenth Amendment's Equal Protection Clause; however, that Amendment applies only to the states. Not until *Bolling v. Sharpe*,[63] a companion case to *Brown v. Board of Education*,[64] did the Court hold that the Fifth Amendment's Due Process Clause contained a substantially equivalent equal protection component. Still, even back in 1943, the Court understood that a racially (or ethnically) targeted curfew could pose constitutional problems sounding in equality even if articulated in terms of due process.

The Court's equality analysis was paradoxical. On the one hand, as a matter of theory, the Court waxed eloquent against racism, prejudice, and racial discrimination. Indeed in *Hirabayashi*, the Court laid the doctrinal foundation for what we now call strict scrutiny for governmental racial classifications. The Court wrote:

> Distinctions between citizens solely because of their ancestry are by their very nature odious to a free people whose institutions are founded upon the doctrine of equality. For that reason, legislative classification or discrimination based on race alone has often been held to be a denial of equal protection.[65]

---

[63] 347 U.S. 497 (1954). *Bolling* cited to both *Korematsu* and *Hirabayashi* for the proposition that "[c]lassifications based solely upon race must be scrutinized with particular care, since they are contrary to our traditions and hence constitutionally suspect." *Id.* at 499 & n.3.

[64] 347 U.S. 483 (1954).

[65] *Hirabayashi*, 320 U.S. at 100 (citing, among others, *Yick Wo v. Hopkins*, 118 U.S. 356 (1886)). Five years earlier, Justice Stone had authored footnote 4 of *Carolene Products*, commonly noted as a precursor to the "strict scrutiny" doctrine announced in *Korematsu*. *See* United States v. Carolene Products Co., 304 U.S. 144, 152 n.4 (1938) (suggesting perhaps a stricter review of statutes evincing "prejudice against discrete and insular minorities").

On the other hand, as a matter of practice, the Court was extremely deferential to claims of military necessity. As the Court explained, "reasonably prudent men" had "ample ground" and "substantial basis" to believe that the Japanese in America "might reasonably be expected to aid a threatened enemy invasion."[66]

This type of analysis appeared earlier in the *Hirabayashi* opinion when the Court defended the curfew as a clearly reasonable exercise of the war power. Without specific evidence that individuals of Japanese origin posed a threat to national security, this approach amounted to nothing more than racial profiling. The Court thought it was rational to assume that the Japanese posed greater security threats than Americans of other races and ethnicities. As the Court explained, there was good reason to target the Japanese: "[t]he fact alone that attack on our shores was threatened by Japan rather than another enemy power set these citizens apart from others who have no particular associations with Japan."[67] Indeed, the Court felt bound to follow this racialized common sense. The Justices wrote that "[w]e cannot close our eyes to the fact, demonstrated by experience, that in time of war residents having ethnic affiliations with an invading enemy may be a greater source of danger than those of a different ancestry."[68]

In the end, through segmentation, the *Hirabayashi* case was framed as solely about curfew, about staying home between the hours of eight o'clock in the evening and six o'clock in the morning. And curfew in a time of war—even if ethnically targeted—did not seem too gross a burden when it was so commonsensical to target the Japanese. After all, according to this racial logic, *they* had already targeted *us*.[69]

The Significance

Hirabayashi's true significance can be appreciated only in the context of the other three Supreme Court internment opinions. Its impact on *Yasui* was dispositive insofar as that case also presented the curfew issue.[70] In an opinion issued the same day, the Court simply relied on *Hirabayashi* to affirm Yasui's conviction. Much more interesting, howev-

---

[66] *Hirabayashi*, 320 U.S. at 94–95.

[67] *Id.* at 101.

[68] *Id.*

[69] Three separate concurrences were written in *Hirabayashi*, one each by Justices Douglas, Murphy, and Rutledge. Both Justices Douglas and Murphy originally penned their concurrences as dissents until Justice Felix Frankfurter persuaded them otherwise. *See* Irons, *supra* note 18, at 243–47.

[70] *See* Minoru Yasui v. United States, 320 U.S. 115, 116–17 (1943).

er, is *Hirabayashi*'s relationship to *Korematsu* and *Endo,* the two cases decided the following year.

Opening Korematsu*'s Door*

In *Korematsu,* the Court, in an opinion by Justice Hugo Black, began by replicating the segmentation technique introduced in *Hirabayashi.* Ignoring the government's own concession to the contrary,[71] the Court speculated that, had Korematsu obeyed the evacuation order, he might not have ended up in a relocation camp after all.[72] Accordingly, the Court would focus exclusively on the legality of *evacuation* and ignore questions related to detention. Cloaking itself in the mantle of self-restraint, the Court exclaimed: "To do more would be to go beyond the issues raised, and to decide momentous questions not contained within the framework of the pleadings or the evidence in this case."[73]

Through segmentation, then, the only question presented was whether the government could require Japanese Americans to evacuate their homes temporarily—as if a hurricane were coming—for personal safety and the good of the country. In answering this narrowly framed question, the Court announced that

> All legal restrictions which curtail the civil rights of a single racial group are immediately suspect. That is not to say that all such restrictions are unconstitutional. It is to say that courts must subject them to the most rigid scrutiny. Pressing public necessity may sometimes justify the existence of such restrictions; racial antagonism never can.[74]

This language marks *Korematsu* as the fount of strict scrutiny. In application, however, the flowery rhetoric wilted into limp acceptance of crude, time-worn racial stereotypes. In the Court's view, "pressing public necessity" included assumptions of disloyalty based on race; such generalizations were not seen as evidence of "racial antagonism."[75]

The payoff of the segmentation technique executed in *Hirabayashi* was substantial. Reneging on its promise not to use *Hirabayashi* as

---

[71] *See* Brief for the United States at 28–29, Korematsu v. United States, 323 U.S. 214 (1944) (No. 22), *reprinted in* 42 *Landmark Briefs and Arguments of the Supreme Court of the United States: Constitutional Law* 197, 230–31 (Philip B. Kurland & Gerhard Casper eds., 1975) [hereinafter *Landmark Briefs*] ("[H]ad [Korematsu] obeyed all of the provisions of the order and the accompanying Instructions, [he] would have found himself for a period of time, the length of which was not then ascertainable, in a place of detention.").

[72] *See Korematsu,* 323 U.S. at 221.

[73] *Id.* at 222.

[74] *Id.* at 216.

[75] *See id.* at 219.

precedent for the next case, the *Korematsu* Court wrote: "In the light of the principles we announced in the *Hirabayashi* case, *we are unable to conclude* that it was beyond the war power of Congress and the Executive to exclude those of Japanese ancestry from the West Coast war area at the time they did."[76] Through segmentation, the Court was able to frame the evacuation question as a minor extension of a practice recently upheld as constitutional. Indeed the precedent was so squarely on point that the Court, employing its double-negative circumlocutions, protested that it could not rule otherwise. The segmentation technique allowed the Court to obscure its own agency and thereby minimize responsibility for its choice. It ceded responsibility to a Supreme Court of the past (admittedly only one year past), which had established guidance squarely on point (even though the earlier Court had disclaimed that it was doing so).

Of course, invoking *Hirabayashi* in this way broke the promise that the Court made in that very opinion—namely, that it was deciding only the narrow issue of curfew and nothing else. As Justice Robert H. Jackson pointed out in his celebrated *Korematsu* dissent, the majority took a carefully limited *Hirabayashi* opinion, which repeatedly emphasized that it was deciding only the curfew issue, as precedent for far greater burdens. Jackson lamented that "[t]he Court is now saying that in *Hirabayashi* we did decide the very things we there said we were not deciding."[77] From this experience, Justice Jackson emphasized how a judicial imprimatur of military action was more dangerous than the military action itself: the official approval would have "a generative power of its own, and all that it creates will be in its own image."[78] Just as *Hirabayashi* acted as a "loaded weapon" ready to be picked up and used by the *Korematsu* Court one year later, Justice Jackson worried out loud what *Korematsu* might trigger in the years to come.[79]

Justice Jackson's concerns can be understood in terms of the segmentation technique: segmentation not only allowed the Court to isolate easier issues for decision, but also allowed the decisions to be made in installments, which fostered the appearance of a reserved, reasoned, and precedent-guided incrementalism. Through segmentation, the Court was able to create precedent on the easier issue (curfew) that drew no dissents. This precedent could then be invoked to decide the next and harder issue (only slightly harder because evacuation had been segment-

---

[76] *Id.* at 217–18 (emphasis added).

[77] *Id.* at 247 (Jackson, J., dissenting).

[78] *Id.* at 246.

[79] *Id.*

ed from indefinite detention). This reliance on precedent in turn enabled the Court to treat its conclusions as inevitable applications of the law.

Framed this way, evacuation did not raise a novel legal question. The difference from the facts in *Hirabayashi* was a matter of quantitative degree of burden, not a qualitative difference of legal moment. And, as the Court explained, because the curfew order had been upheld, only a small extension of constitutional interpretation was required to affirm the evacuation order as well.

Showing Endo's *Dodge*

Hirabayashi also illuminates the fourth and final case, *Endo*,[80] which was released on the same day as *Korematsu*. In *Endo*, the question presented was whether the government could indefinitely detain a concededly loyal Japanese–American citizen. In this final case, Mitsuye Endo won her habeas corpus petition, but there was never any holding that her constitutional rights had been violated. Rather, the Court decided the case on administrative law grounds. Astonishingly, the Justices held that the War Relocation Authority ("WRA"), which maintained the camps, was never authorized to keep people like Endo locked up in the first place.[81]

After reviewing E.O. 9066 (delegating power to the military to bar access to military areas), E.O. 9012 (creating the WRA), and P.L. 503 (authorizing criminal penalties for violating duly issued military regulations),[82] the Court could see no literal mention of detention in any of these documents.[83] The Court further invoked the minimalist doctrine of constitutional avoidance: steer clear of statutory readings that raise constitutional questions. Accordingly, the Court created a presumption that the political branches were "sensitive to and respectful of the liberties of the citizen."[84] Indeed, the Court assumed that "law makers intended to place no greater restraint on the citizen than was clearly and unmistakably indicated by the language they used."[85] To read the relevant documents otherwise

---

[80] *Ex parte* Mitsuye Endo, 323 U.S. 283 (1944).

[81] *Id.* at 302–04.

[82] *Id.* at 285–90.

[83] *Id.* at 300–01. The Court made an explicit finding that "[n]either the Act nor the orders use the language of detention." *Id.* at 300.

[84] *See id.* at 299–300 ("We have likewise favored that interpretation of legislation which gives it the greater chance of surviving the test of constitutionality.... We must assume that the Chief Executive and members of Congress, as well as the courts, are sensitive to and respectful of the liberties of the citizen.").

[85] *Id.* at 300.

would be to assume that the Congress and the President intended that this discriminatory action should be taken against these people wholly on account of their ancestry even though the government conceded their loyalty to this country. *We cannot make such an assumption.*[86]

In concurring in the result, Justice Owen Roberts sharply criticized the majority for "ignor[ing] patent facts" and for "hiding [its] head in the sand."[87] The hypocrisy is patent if we recall how the Court addressed similar authorization questions only one year before in *Hirabayashi*. There, the Court saw authorization of curfew as applied to citizens, even though E.O. 9066 and P.L. 503 did not explicitly mention such authority and were extraordinarily vague in their delegation of power to the military.[88] In other words, when it was convenient to see authorization for curfew, the Court could read between the lines; when the picture grew more embarrassing because indefinite detention was at issue, the Court was blind.[89]

Hirabayashi at Peace

Four decades later comes a very different story. Indeed, the successful Japanese American redress movement of the 1970s and 1980s is as uplifting as the 1940s internment is depressing. The executive branch apologized,[90] Congress paid reparations,[91] and the federal courts vacated the convictions of Korematsu, Yasui, and Hirabayashi in the coram nobis cases.[92] These reversals were based on "smoking gun" evidence,[93] unearthed at the National Archives, which demonstrated the lack of military necessity for the internment. At first glance, the story of redress

---

[86] *Id.* at 303–04 (emphasis added).

[87] *Id.* at 309 (Roberts, J., concurring in result).

[88] Hirabayashi v. United States, 320 U.S. 81, 89–90 (1943).

[89] Patrick Gudridge and I disagree sharply, but respectfully, about the proper interpretation of *Endo. See, e.g.,* Patrick O. Gudridge, *Remember* Endo?, 116 Harv. L. Rev. 1933 (2003); Jerry Kang, *Watching the Watchers: Enemy Combatants in the Internment's Shadow*, 68 Law & Contemp. Probs. 255 (2005); Patrick O. Gudridge, *The Constitution Glimpsed from Tule Lake*, 68 Law & Contemp. Probs 81 (2005).

[90] Proclamation No. 4417, 41 Fed. Reg. 7741 (Feb. 20, 1976) (known as "An American Promise").

[91] Civil Liberties Act of 1988, Pub L. No. 100–383, 102 Stat. 903 (codified as amended at 50 U.S.C. app. §§ 1989–1989d (2000)).

[92] *See* Hirabayashi v. United States, 828 F.2d 591, 608 (9th Cir. 1987); *see also* Yasui v. United States, 772 F.2d 1496, 1499–1500 (9th Cir. 1985); Korematsu v. United States, 584 F. Supp. 1406, 1420 (N.D. Cal. 1984).

[93] Reproductions of the suppressed evidence can be found in Yamamoto et al., *supra* note 5, at 300–09.

warrants unqualified celebration. But a closer examination reveals a grey lining to that silver cloud.

Smoking Guns

In 1981, government researcher Aiko Yoshinaga–Herzig and historian Peter Irons uncovered remarkable evidence of government wrongdoing during the wartime litigation. First, they located the original copy of General DeWitt's Final Report, which was not the copy generally distributed or made available to the Court in the internment cases. This original copy included the following language:

> It was impossible to establish the identity of the loyal and the disloyal with any degree of safety. *It was not that there was insufficient time* in which to make such a determination; it was simply a matter of facing the realities that a positive determination could not be made, that an exact separation of the "sheep from the goats" was unfeasible.[94]

When officials at the War Department received the original report in April 1943, they forced General DeWitt to change the language. After some protest, he complied and altered the report to read as follows:

> To complicate the situation *no ready means* existed for determining the loyal and the disloyal with any degree of safety. It was necessary to face the realities—a positive determination could not have been made.[95]

All copies of the original report (except the one found in the National Archives) were destroyed. The revised version was dated June 1943, but was not made public until January 1944. Attorneys at the Department of Justice, who eagerly awaited the Final Report in preparation for the 1943 *Hirabayashi* and *Yasui* curfew cases, did not receive a copy until after these cases were decided.[96]

Second, various memoranda from intelligence agencies refuting any threat of espionage or sabotage were uncovered. The Office of Naval Intelligence ("ONI") produced a report that concluded that the potentially disloyal were fewer than 3500, and that most of these were already in custody after the ABC list arrests made immediately after Pearl Harbor.[97] The FBI expressly rejected General DeWitt's assertion in the

---

[94] Petition for Writ of Coram Nobis, Korematsu v. United States, 584 F. Supp. 1406 (N.D. Cal. 1984) (No. CR–27635 W) (emphasis added), *reprinted in Justice Delayed: The Record of the Japanese American Internment Cases* 125, 140 (Peter Irons ed., 1989) [hereinafter *Justice Delayed*].

[95] *Justice Delayed, supra* note 94, at 141 (emphasis added).

[96] *See* Irons, *supra* note 18, at 211.

[97] *See id.* at 203. *See generally* Memorandum from Lieutenant Commander K.D. Ringle, Office of Naval Intelligence, re Japanese Question (Jan. 26, 1942) ("the entire

Final Report that there was any shore-to-ship signaling to aid attacks on the United States after Pearl Harbor.[98] J. Edgar Hoover's FBI found that the call for evacuation was based primarily upon public and political pressure, not good data. The Federal Communications Commission ("FCC") confirmed the FBI's finding on signaling and chided the Army for incompetently attributing broadcasts picked up all the way from Japan to sources in California.[99] The federal government provided none of these memoranda to the Court in any of the litigation.

Finally, the original *Korematsu* brief had been altered to mislead the Court. As originally drafted, a critical footnote in the government's brief took the following position on General DeWitt's controversial Final Report:

The Final Report of General DeWitt ... is relied on in this brief for statistics and other details concerning the actual evacuation and the events that took place subsequent thereto. *The recital of the circumstances justifying the evacuation as a matter of military necessity, however, is in several respects, particularly with reference to the use of illegal radio transmitters and to shore-to-ship signaling by persons of Japanese ancestry, in conflict with information in the possession of the Department of Justice.* In view of the contrariety of the reports on this matter we do not ask the Court to take judicial notice of the recital of those facts contained in the Report.[100]

This language alerted the Court that there was reason to question the Final Report's accuracy. Any reliance whatsoever on the Final Report was questionable because it was not part of the record below, either at the district court trial or on the Ninth Circuit appeal. Instead, the Report was transmitted to the Supreme Court directly in the *Korematsu* litigation, and the facts cited could be accepted only under the doctrine

---

'Japanese Problem' has been magnified out of its true proportion, largely because of the physical characteristics of the people"), *reprinted in* Yamamoto et al., *supra* note 5, at 300.

[98] *See* Memorandum from J. Edgar Hoover, Director, Federal Bureau of Investigation, to Att'y General, U.S. Dep't of Justice (Feb. 7, 1944), *reprinted in* Yamamoto et al., *supra* note 5, at 301 ("there is no information in the possession of this Bureau ... which would indicate that the attacks made on ships or shores in the area immediately after Pearl Harbor have been associated with any espionage activity ashore or that there has been any illicit shore-to-ship signaling, either by radio or lights.").

[99] Letter from James Lawrence Fly, Chairman, Fed. Comm. Comm'n, to Francis Biddle, Att'y General, U.S. Dep't of Justice, at 2 (Apr. 4, 1944) ("In the early months of the war, the Commission's field offices and stations on the West Coast were deluged with calls, particularly from the Army and Navy, reporting suspicious radio signaling.... In no case was the transmission other than legitimate."), *reprinted in* Yamamoto et al., *supra* note 5, at 304.

[100] *See* Yamamoto et al., *supra* note 5, at 310 (quoting Memorandum of John L. Burling to Assistant Attorney General Herbert Wechsler, September 11, 1944).

of judicial notice. Even under the widest interpretation of judicial notice, the government's cautionary footnote would have made it difficult for a fair-minded Court to accept the entire document without reservation.

But after intervention by the Department of War, the presses printing the *Korematsu* brief were literally stopped[101] and the footnote was revised to read:

> The Final Report of General DeWitt is relied on in this brief for statistics and other details concerning the actual evacuation and the events that took place subsequent thereto. We have specifically recited in this brief the facts relating to the justification for the evacuation, of which we ask the Court to take judicial notice; and *we rely upon the Final Report only to the extent that it relates to such facts.*[102]

This mealy-mouthed lawyerism concealed the Justice Department's grave doubts about General DeWitt's exaggerated claims.

On the basis of the newly discovered evidence in the National Archives—the suppressed original Final Report, exculpatory intelligence memoranda, and the revised footnote in the *Korematsu* brief—Fred Korematsu, Minoru Yasui, and Gordon Hirabayashi returned to the federal district courts that had convicted them. With the help of young, smart, passionate *sansei* (third-generation) lawyers, the three defendants petitioned for the obscure writ of error coram nobis, which permits courts to correct factual errors in criminal convictions to avoid manifest injustice.[103] The closest analogy is the writ of habeas corpus, which did not apply because the petitioners were no longer in custody. The petitioners knew that the coram nobis writ required a showing of extraordinary circumstances amounting to a complete miscarriage of justice.[104] What was less certain was whether the defendants also had to demonstrate actual prejudice—that, but for the suppression of evidence, the wartime Court would have ruled otherwise.

---

[101] *See* Irons, *supra* note 18, at 287–88.

[102] Brief for the United States, *supra* note 71, at 11 n.2 (emphasis added), *reprinted in* 42 *Landmark Briefs, supra* note 71, at 203, 213 n.2.

[103] District courts are granted the authority to issue such writs through the All Writs Act, 28 U.S.C. § 1651 (2002). This writ was not destroyed by Federal Rule of Civil Procedure 60(b), which ends all common law writs, because although the coram nobis writ is litigated pursuant to the civil rules, it relates to a criminal proceeding. Further, the writ is not preempted by the federal "motion to vacate" (habeas corpus) statute, 28 U.S.C. § 2255 (2002), which requires the petitioner to be in custody.

[104] *See* United States v. Morgan, 346 U.S. 502, 512 (1954) (stating that coram nobis "included errors 'of the most fundamental character,'" such that "[o]therwise a wrong may stand uncorrected which the available remedy would right").

The Coram Nobis Cases

Brought in 1984, *Korematsu* was the first of the three coram nobis cases to be heard. Uncertain about what to do, the government filed a nonresponsive two-page letter suggesting that the federal district court simply vacate the conviction, without granting the writ, and simply "put behind us the controversy."[105] Judge Marilyn Patel declined this invitation and instead granted Korematsu's petition.[106] For her, the gross miscarriage of justice was obvious. As for actual prejudice, Judge Patel concluded that it was not necessary as a matter of law: "Whether a fuller, more accurate record would have prompted a different decision cannot be determined. Nor need it be determined. Where relevant evidence has been withheld, it is ample justification ... that the conviction should be set aside."[107] This was an extraordinary victory.

By contrast, in *Yasui*, the next coram nobis case to be decided, District Court Judge Robert Belloni complied with the government's request.[108] With the now familiar rhetoric of self-restraint, he simply vacated Yasui's criminal conviction without granting the writ. Minoru Yasui died in November 1986, before his appeal could be heard.

The final coram nobis case was Hirabayashi's, which the federal government litigated vigorously in sharp contrast to the prior cases. After a full evidentiary hearing, the district court vacated Hirabayashi's conviction on evacuation, but not on curfew. The different results turned on the question of prejudice. The gross miscarriage of justice was clear, but, contrary to and completely silent on Judge Patel's prior reading of the law, Judge Donald Voorhees held summarily that actual prejudice had to be shown.[109] In his estimation, the suppressed evidence would have altered how the Supreme Court reviewed the evacuation, but not the curfew, conviction.[110]

Hirabayashi's appeal was heard in the Ninth Circuit Court of Appeals by Judges Mary Schroeder, Alfred Goodwin, and Jerome Farris.[111] On the question of whether actual prejudice was required, the

---

[105] Government's Response and Motion, Korematsu v. United States, 584 F. Supp. 1406 (N.D. Cal. 1984) (No. CR–27635W), *reprinted in Justice Delayed, supra* note 95, at 210–12.

[106] *Korematsu*, 584 F. Supp. at 1420.

[107] *Id*. at 1419.

[108] Yamamoto et al., *supra* note 5, at 318.

[109] Hirabayashi v. United States, 627 F. Supp. 1445, 1454 (W.D. Wash. 1986) (citing United States v. Dellinger, 657 F.2d 140, 144 n.9 (7th Cir. 1981)), *rev'd in part*, 828 F.2d 591 (9th Cir. 1987).

[110] *See id*. at 1457.

[111] Hirabayashi v. United States, 828 F.2d 591 (9th Cir. 1987).

court declined to answer. In its view, regardless of whether prejudice was necessary as a matter of law, prejudice had been amply shown in this case as a matter of fact.[112] Thus, the court affirmed the trial court's vacation of Hirabayashi's evacuation conviction. It then reversed the trial court' refusal to set aside the curfew conviction as clearly erroneous, because a fully informed Supreme Court would have vacated that conviction as well.

Denying Prejudice

By finding prejudice as a matter of fact (even though, as a matter of law, this was not deemed a necessary element), the Ninth Circuit adopted the official story that the wartime Supreme Court was an innocent, misled by duplicitous lawyers. The Court did nothing wrong; it was merely tricked. In the 1940s *Endo* opinion, the Court avoided holding President Roosevelt and Congress accountable; in the 1980s *Hirabayashi* opinion, the Ninth Circuit completed the "circle of absolution,"[113] ensuring that the wartime Court would not be called to account.

But, this exculpatory story is revisionist.[114] As damning as the "smoking gun" evidence uncovered in the 1980s was, the Court would *not* have ruled otherwise on the question of evacuation, and certainly not on that of curfew. Since these are serious charges, I prosecute them carefully.

Evacuation

Recall that the district court in the *Hirabayashi* coram nobis case had found prejudice on the evacuation issue. In other words, the Supreme Court would have vacated this conviction if only it had the full story. The Ninth Circuit heartily affirmed this finding for the following reasons.

DeWitt's Racism: Who Knew?

First, the court of appeals suggested that the Supreme Court had no reason to believe that General DeWitt was racist. Evidence regarding his attitude "was limited primarily to a newspaper clipping."[115] Moreover, this evidence was presented by the Japanese Americans and their amici, who were partisans in the litigation. Although we now know that this

---

[112] *Id.* at 603–04.

[113] Jerry Kang, *Denying Prejudice: Internment, Redress, and Denial*, 51 UCLA L. Rev. 933, 986 (2004).

[114] *See id.* at 985–95 (arguing at length why this conception of the wartime Court is revisionist).

[115] *Hirabayashi*, 828 F.2d at 601.

was "objective and irrefutable proof" of racial bias, according to the Ninth Circuit, the Supreme Court back in the 1940s did not.

This is preposterous. Here is the text of the newspaper clipping quoting General DeWitt's comments before a House of Representatives Subcommittee on Naval Affairs, as reported in *The San Francisco News* on April 13, 1943:

> I don't want any Jap back on the Coast.... There is no way to determine their loyalty.... It makes no difference whether the Japanese is theoretically a citizen—he is still a Japanese. Giving him a piece of paper won't change him.... I don't care what they do with the Japs as long as they don't send them back here. A Jap is a Jap.[116]

During the wartime litigation, this article appeared in full in the Appendix of Hirabayashi's reply brief, was quoted prominently in Yasui's opening brief,[117] and was also quoted in Korematsu's brief.[118] It was specifically mentioned by attorney Al Wirin during Yasui's oral argument.[119] In the *Korematsu* dissent, Justice Frank Murphy quoted long portions.[120] This passage was not a partisan "spin" of Army policy. Instead, it was a verbatim account by a prominent newspaper, published just one month prior to Supreme Court oral argument and never disclaimed by General DeWitt.

In addition, *Korematsu* referred explicitly to another, equally damning document letter from General DeWitt to the Secretary of War one and a half months prior to evacuation. In it, General DeWitt wrote that "the Japanese race is an enemy race" and that regardless of being born in the United States, their "racial strains are undiluted." Further, "[t]he very fact that no sabotage has taken place to date is a disturbing and confirming indication that such action will be taken."[121]

To avoid confusion, we must remember that the question is not whether the newspaper transcript and the personal letter provide conclu-

---

[116] H.R. Rep. No. 77-1911, at 13-14 (1942) (Tolan Committee Report).

[117] *See* Appellant's Reply Brief at 25-26, Hirabayashi v. United States, 320 U.S. 81 (1943) (No. 870); Appellant's Brief at 55, Minoru Yasui v. United States, 320 U.S. 115 (1943) (No. 871).

[118] *See* Petition for Writ of Certiorari at 32-33, Korematsu v. United States, 323 U.S. 214 (1944) (No. 22), *reprinted in* 42 Landmark Briefs, *supra* note 71, at 39-40.

[119] *See* Irons, *supra* note 18, at 222-23.

[120] *See Korematsu*, 323 U.S. at 236 n.2 (Murphy, J., dissenting).

[121] Brief for Appellant at 63, Korematsu v. United States, 323 U.S. 214 (1944) (No. 22) (quoting Letter from General DeWitt to Henry Stimson, secretary of War (Feb. 13, 1942)), *reprinted in* 42 Landmark Briefs, *supra* note 71, at 161.

sive evidence of General DeWitt's racism by the standards of the 1940s or the 1980s or even today. The proper question instead is whether these materials reveal as much about the attitude and reasons for General DeWitt's actions as the original version of the Final Report. Put another way, given that the Supreme Court was made aware of these virulent sentiments, would the language in the original Final Report have altered the Court's fundamental assessment of General DeWitt's fairness or bias? No, it would not. As President Ronald Reagan's Department of Justice put it to the Ninth Circuit: "General DeWitt's beliefs were not concealed from anyone, including the Supreme Court, in 1943 or thereafter."[122]

The Solicitor General's Protestations

Second, the Ninth Circuit pointed out that the Supreme Court relied heavily on the claims of Solicitor General Charles Fahy, who argued exigency as justification. The court of appeals thought it unlikely that the Supreme Court "would have reached the same result even if the Solicitor General had advised ... the Court of the true basis for General DeWitt's orders...."[123]

On the one hand, this must be right: if the Solicitor General, in oral argument, confessed that the entire internment juggernaut was manufactured by a racist cabal, without a scintilla of military justification, the Supreme Court would have had great difficulty allowing internment to proceed. This much is revealed by the following exchange between Justice Felix Frankfurter and Solicitor General Fahy in the *Korematsu* oral argument, quoted by the Ninth Circuit.

> MR. JUSTICE FRANKFURTER: Suppose the commanding general, when he issued Order No. 34, had said, in effect, "It is my judgment that, as a matter of security, there is no danger from the Japanese operations; but under cover of war, I had authority to take advantage of my hostility and clear the Japanese from this area." Suppose he had said that, with that kind of crude candor. It would not have been within his authority, would it?
>
> MR. FAHY: It would not have been.
>
> MR. JUSTICE FRANKFURTER: As I understand the suggestion, it is that, as a matter of law, the report of General DeWitt two years later proved that that was exactly what the situation was. As I understand, that is the legal significance of the argument.

---

[122] Brief for Government at 31, Hirabayashi v. United States, 828 F.2d 591 (1987) (No. 86–3853).

[123] *Id.*

MR. FAHY: That is correct, Your Honor; and the report simply does nothing of the kind.[124]

On the other hand, this is a red herring—the wrong counterfactual. The proper question is what would the Supreme Court have done if the suppressed evidence were made available and if the Solicitor General answered questions during oral argument in ways that nevertheless furthered his client's position. Even if the original Final Report were entered into evidence, and even if the memoranda from the FBI, the FCC, and the ONI were also admitted, Solicitor General Fahy likely would have been clever enough to discredit that evidence as irrelevant, not probative, taken out of context, not sufficiently expert, or simply a minority report. In any event, the Solicitor General's remarks came *after* Hirabayashi's conviction was affirmed, too late to influence the disposition of his case.

The *Korematsu* Footnote

Third, the Ninth Circuit emphasized the bowdlerized footnote in the *Korematsu* brief. It pointed out that the Court asked specific questions about that footnote during oral argument, which supposedly demonstrated the Court's sensitivity to the facts of military exigency. But again, the question is not whether exigency was an important variable to the wartime Court. Of course it was. The question is whether the suppressed evidence would have reversed the Court's judgment about the existence of that exigency. As I have already argued, the Court would have turned a blind eye to this information just as it did to proof of General DeWitt's racist assumptions about Japanese Americans. More important, the timing once again is wrong. Hirabayashi's case came before *Korematsu*. This means that the *Korematsu* brief was not even in existence when Hirabayashi's case was litigated. So, how could a future misleading edit to a footnote that had not yet been written have prejudiced him?

The Relevance of the Dissent in *Korematsu*

Fourth, the Ninth Circuit stated that the "divided opinions ... demonstrate beyond question the importance which the Justices ... placed upon the position of the government that there was a perceived military necessity...."[125] The Ninth Circuit was suggesting that because three Justices in *Korematsu* dissented even without seeing the suppressed evidence, even more Justices would have dissented and constituted a new majority (back in *Hirabayashi*) if the evidence had been revealed.

But precisely the opposite inference can be drawn from the existence of these dissents. Notwithstanding the suppressed evidence, Justice

[124] *Hirabayashi*, 828 F.2d at 600.

[125] *Id.* at 603.

Murphy knew enough to call the opinion in *Korematsu* a "legalization of racism."[126] In his well-crafted, fully-documented opinion, he demolished any arguments based on military necessity under exigent circumstances. He also made explicit mention of evidence and sources that should have carried probative weight comparable to the suppressed materials. The suppressed evidence would not have added substantially to the persuasive power of Murphy's opinion.

Right Decision in *Endo*

Last, the Ninth Circuit asserted that the right outcome in *Endo* "clearly evidence[s]" that military exigency was critical to the Court's *Hirabayashi* and *Korematsu* decisions.[127] Yet again, this is the wrong question. Instead, the court of appeals should have asked whether the *Endo* decision demonstrates that the suppressed evidence would have altered the results in the other two cases. My discussion of *Endo* suggests just the opposite. All the machinations that the Court deployed to make certain that responsibility would be thrust upon the "rogue" WRA reveals not the genuine honesty of the Court, but its political connivance. *Endo*'s victory in no way reveals a sincere but simple-minded Court duped by government attorneys.

Apart from the arguments made by the Ninth Circuit, there are other reasons to doubt that the Supreme Court was misled into finding military exigency because of the suppressed evidence. Consider all the other points expressly raised both by Hirabayashi and the government as early as 1943. To make clear that wholesale internment of Japanese Americans on the West Coast was not necessary, Hirabayashi offered evidence of two types of differential treatment.

Hirabayashi first focused attention on Japanese Americans in Hawai'i, which was 1,500 miles closer to the Pacific theater of operations and which had actually been bombed. He provided persuasive details about the Hawaiian population, which, if the government's theory was to be believed, posed a far greater threat because persons of Japanese ancestry comprised 34.2% of the total population.[128] Hirabayashi cited laudatory comments about the Japanese made by General Delos C. Emmons, in charge of Hawai'i, as early as January 28, 1943.[129] Based on this evidence, Hirabayashi argued that "the experience in Hawaii dem-

---

[126] *Korematsu*, 323 U.S. at 242 (Murphy, J., dissenting).

[127] *Hirabayashi*, 828 F.2d at 603.

[128] Brief for Appellant at 6 n.4, Hirabayashi v. United States, 320 U.S. 81 (1943) (No. 870) (providing population statistics as of 1941).

[129] *Id.* at 7.

onstrates" that the fear of West Coast invasion was "pure fantasy. . . . beyond a shadow of a doubt."[130]

Hirabayashi then compared the treatment of the Japanese Americans to that of Italian and German resident aliens. Specifically, he claimed that the Attorney General successfully provided individualized loyalty hearings to Italian aliens. Within ten months, the Attorney General deemed 600,000 aliens of Italian origin to be a non-threat;[131] there was no reason why the same could not have been done with the far smaller Japanese–American population, which was comprised mostly of citizens. In addition, Hirabayashi provided examples of individualized suits to revoke the citizenship of naturalized Germans,[132] as well as evidence of how European allies treated enemy aliens without mass internment.[133] Given this evidence that individualized loyalty hearings could have been conducted at a brisk pace, it seems unlikely that the Supreme Court was genuinely misled about exigent circumstances.[134]

---

[130] *Id.* at 19. Similar arguments, not surprisingly, were raised by Korematsu. *See, e.g.,* Petition for Writ of Certiorari, *supra* note 118, at 34, *reprinted in* 42 *Landmark Briefs, supra* note 71, at 41; Brief for Appellant, *supra* note 121, at 73, *reprinted in* 42 *Landmark Briefs, supra* note 71, at 171 (noting that in Hawai'i, as of March 1944, there were 6,678 citizens of Japanese ancestry and 743 aliens of Japanese ancestry continued to work on military installations).

[131] Brief for Appellant, *supra* note 128, at 20. This should not be read to suggest that there were in fact 600,000 individual hearings. Instead, there were approximately 600,000 Italian aliens in the United States at the time of war, and of that total, only a few hundred were placed on special enemy alien lists, prompting their arrest by the Department of Justice soon after Pearl Harbor. Subsequently, these individuals were given individual hearings in front of enemy alien review boards.

According to historian Roger Daniels, the DOJ interned approximately 1,500 aliens of European descent, mostly German and Italian. *Prisoners, supra* note 5, at 26. The Commission on Wartime Relocation and Internment of Civilians reported slightly different numbers, that by mid-February, the DOJ "had interned 2,192 Japanese; 1,393 Germans and 264 Italians." *Personal Justice Denied, supra* note 5, at 284. Adversarial loyalty hearings were, however, granted to all those interned in these special DOJ camps. *Id.* at 285.

By October 1942 (ten months after Pearl Harbor), the Attorney General had removed all restrictions on Italian aliens. *See* Harrop A. Freeman, *Genesis, Exodus, and Leviticus: Genealogy, Evacuation, and Law,* 28 Cornell L.Q. 414, 417, 455 (1943). In December, the same was done for German aliens. *See* Bosworth, *supra* note 10, at 211.

[132] Appellant's Reply Brief, *supra* note 117, at 13.

[133] The ACLU, in its amicus brief, made specific comparisons to the England, where 112 alien tribunals were set up and, in six months, provided individual hearings to 74,220 individuals. Only 2,000 were interned. Brief Amicus Curiae (American Civil Liberties Union) at 16, Hirabayashi v. United States, 320 U.S. 81 (1943) (No. 870).

[134] The Japanese American Citizens League's amicus brief also made very strong arguments that the various factors that apparently made Japanese Americans suspect similarly applied to Italian and German Americans. These arguments were cross-referenced

Compare this argument about the possibility of individual hearings with what the government explicitly said in its 1940s *Hirabayashi* brief: in telling portions, the government argued that individualized hearings would have been "virtually worthless" unless they were preceded by a thorough investigation, and even then, they would be of "doubtful utility" because they would have required the hearing board to "look deep into the mind of a particular Japanese" in making nearly impossible judgments about loyalty.[135] It would be hard work indeed to examine those "inscrutable" Orientals.[136]

In addition, in a remarkable embrace of group liabilities (if not rights), the government argued that what was at issue was not individual loyalty. "It is entirely irrelevant, therefore, to assert that the majority of individuals evacuated were perfectly loyal citizens of the United States."[137] Instead, it was action against the entire group, which collectively posed a danger. Having read these arguments explicitly in the government's briefs, would the Supreme Court really have learned something new from the original language of the Final Report?

If the Supreme Court had wanted to find that the circumstances were not sufficiently exigent as to require mass internment, there was sufficient material in the government's own brief to support that finding. In addition, there were numerous arguments provided by the Japanese–American litigants as well as the amici.[138] Put another way, the Supreme Court was not *actually* blind to what was going on. It was *willfully* so. Even if the original version of the Final Report and the suppressed

---

by Hirabayashi in his reply brief. *See* Brief Amicus Curiae (Japanese American Citizens League), *supra* note 58, at 2, 12–20, Hirabayashi v. United States, 320 U.S. 81 (1943) (No. 870); Appellant's Reply Brief, *supra* note 117, at 2–3.

[135] Brief for the United States, *supra* note 47, at 62–63. *Cf.* Brief of the States of California, Oregon and Washington as Amici Curiae, *supra* note 56, at 43 (citing H.R. Rep. No. 77–1911, at 13–14 (1942) (Tolan Committee Report) ("Most commonly it was said that homogeneity of racial and cultural traits made it impossible to distinguish between the loyal and the disloyal.")).

[136] California, Oregon, and Washington, all West Coast states subject to the curfew and exclusion orders, filed an amicus brief in *Hirabayashi* and *Yasui*. They explained that the Japanese "have remained a group apart and *inscrutable* to their neighbors ... an unassimilated, homogeneous element...." Brief of the States of California, Oregon and Washington as Amici Curiae, *supra* note 56, at 11 (emphasis added). *See also id.* at 44 ("[I]nscrutability is a definite racial characteristic.").

[137] Brief for the United States, *supra* note 47, at 64.

[138] For instance, Korematsu explicitly argued that exigency was not credible given the delay between December 7, 1941 and March 30, 1942, when the first groups of people were forced into assembly centers. Brief for Appellant, *supra* note 121, at 21, *reprinted in* 42 *Landmark Briefs, supra* note 71, at 119. Also, Korematsu noted the strange delay of two years before the Final Report was publicly released. *Id.* at 55, *reprinted in* 42 *Landmark Briefs, supra* note 71, at 153.

intelligence memoranda had been made available in *Hirabayashi*, and even if the original *Korematsu* brief footnote had appeared in the *Hirabayashi* litigation, there is overwhelming evidence that the Supreme Court would have applied the same techniques of segmentation and selective interpretation in order to affirm the convictions and not interfere with the internment machine.

Curfew

So far I have argued that the suppressed evidence would not have altered the Court's approval of exclusion. For the same reasons, the Court would have been even less inclined to strike down curfew. This is why even Judge Voorhees refused to vacate that conviction. However, the Ninth Circuit Court of Appeals, in a breezy five paragraphs, found clear error. Essentially, it suggested that the wartime Court did not distinguish between curfew and exclusion and viewed both as serious deprivations of liberty requiring military exigency.[139]

Reagan's Department of Justice argued that the dissenting Justices in *Korematsu*, who had concurred in *Hirabayashi*, clearly distinguished curfew from evacuation. But the court of appeals retorted that the beliefs of a dissenting minority of Justices were irrelevant and that the majority in *Korematsu* followed "exactly the same rationale that was followed in *Hirabayashi* and made no such distinction...."[140] The court of appeals found that both curfew and evacuation were "tried together, briefed together, and decided together."[141] Accordingly, if there was prejudice for one, there must be prejudice for the other.

This analysis willfully ignores the wartime Court's use of segmentation to parse the various steps in the internment process.[142] Recall that the Court, sua sponte, relied on the fortuity of Hirabayashi's concurrent sentencing to segment off curfew from evacuation. If the Court had actually thought the issues to be identical, as the Ninth Circuit would contend four decades later, then there would have been no reason for segmentation. Moreover, in *Korematsu*, the Court went to great lengths to distinguish evacuation from detention. After careful examination of the Supreme Court's tactics, it seems implausible that the suppressed

---

[139] Hirabayashi v. United States, 828 F.2d 591, 608 (9th Cir. 1987).

[140] *Id.*

[141] *Id.*

[142] I say "willfully" because the Department of Justice clearly pointed out this segmentation strategy in its brief. *See* Brief for Government, *supra* note 122, at 19. To be clear, the United States was not renouncing segmentation as a bad or inappropriate strategy in the 1940s or in the 1980s. *See, e.g., id.* at 22–23 (arguing that Judge Voorhees had erred by not carefully distinguishing evacuation from detention in granting the writ as to the evacuation conviction).

evidence would have led the Court to call off something as "trivial" as curfew as early as 1943.

The Ninth Circuit did not have to reach this result. Given the precedent of the time, the court of appeals could simply have said that prejudice was not necessary to the coram nobis writ, allowing Hirabayashi to win without any comment on, much less whitewashing of, history. This is, in fact, current coram nobis law in the Ninth Circuit, post-*Hirabayashi*.[143] In the alternative, the court of appeals could have held that actual prejudice was necessary, but since the Supreme Court would have affirmed Hirabayashi's convictions even with the suppressed evidence, no relief could be granted. This would have produced a loss for Hirabayashi but exposed the truth. If this medicine was too bitter to swallow, still another possibility would have allowed the court to speak the truth about history while ultimately vacating Hirabayashi's convictions—to establish a rule of law that "actual prejudice is normally required [to issue the writ of coram nobis; however,] in cases of extraordinary manifest injustice, the writ will nonetheless issue."[144]

Conclusion

In its wartime incarnation, *Hirabayashi* created the beginnings of what we now call strict scrutiny. Abstractly, that doctrinal commitment is worth celebrating. However, *Hirabayashi* was also the first, crucial step in a judicial strategy that rubberstamped mass internment while withholding official judicial imprimatur, and absolved the political branches while blaming convenient bureaucratic scapegoats. In the coram nobis cases, *Hirabayashi* continues this story of evading institutional responsibility. The Ninth Circuit in the 1980s adopted a farcical version of the historical record in order to absolve the wartime Court of any wrongdoing.

The internment cases often are taught as proof that the rule of law can work itself pure by correcting errors made by a few bad apples—as *Endo* corrected *Korematsu*, as the coram nobis opinions corrected the wartime cases, and so on. But more critical examination uncovers a counter-story of a judiciary that has concealed its transgressions through deft legal exegesis and manipulative reasoning. That counter-symbol— *not of law working itself pure, but of judges dodging responsibility*—is what we must remember during these tortured times.

---

[143] Under current Ninth Circuit coram nobis law, actual prejudice is not a legal requirement. *See* Kang, *supra* note 113, at 996.

[144] *Id*. The full argument appears at *id*. app. at 1006–13.

10

R.A. Lenhardt

Forgotten Lessons on Race, Law, and Marriage: The Story of *Perez v. Sharp*

Introduction

June 2007 marked the fortieth anniversary of the U.S. Supreme Court's decision in *Loving v. Virginia*.[1] In four decades, the story of the plaintiffs in that case—Mildred Jeter and Richard Loving—has become common lore. Articles and textbooks now tell of the couple's secret marriage and flight from Virginia under fear of prosecution for the crime of being a black woman and a white man in love.[2] We know, too, of their multi-year exile in nearby Washington, D.C., and, finally, of their lawsuit challenging the law that kept them from the life of which they dreamed.[3]

In the field of law, *Loving* has achieved what many call canonical status.[4] It is, among other things, a case included in most legal curricula and is thought to be crucial to an understanding of equal protection law and race in American society.[5] Even more than this, however, *Loving* has entered the national consciousness to an extent achieved by few other

---

[1] 388 U.S. 1 (1967).

[2] *See, e.g.,* D. Kelly Weisberg & Susan Frelich Appleton, *Modern Family Law: Cases and Materials* 154–55 (2d ed. 2002); Robert A. Pratt, *Crossing the Color Line: A Historical Assessment and Personal Narrative of* Loving v. Virginia, 41 How. L.J. 229 (1998); Peter Wallenstein, *Tell the Court I Love My Wife: Race, Marriage, and Law—An American History* (2002).

[3] Weisberg and Appleton, *supra* note 2, at 154–55.

[4] *See* J.M. Balkin & Sanford Levinson, *The Canons of Constitutional Law*, 111 Harv. L. Rev. 963, 970–1002 (1998).

[5] *Id.* at 975–78 (setting out the factors associated with canonical status in law).

cases. Many people—including those without a legal background—could identify it as an important "first," a landmark case in the area of racial equality and marriage.

What few people recognize, however, is that *Loving* was not, in fact, the first case to deem antimiscegenation laws unconstitutional. The first post-Reconstruction case to reach such a conclusion came nearly twenty years before *Loving*, when the California Supreme Court decided *Perez v. Sharp* in 1948.[6] The story of the plaintiffs in that case—Andrea Pérez and Sylvester Davis—has, however, rarely been told. Indeed, with only a few exceptions, scholars have not regarded *Perez* as a decision worthy of study,[7] and few people have even heard of it. Only recently—with the advent of litigation regarding the right of gays and lesbians to marry— has *Perez* attracted notice.[8]

This chapter tells the story of *Perez*, beginning with how Andrea and Sylvester met, fell in love, and came to challenge the California law barring interracial marriage. Their romance is put in context through a brief overview of American antimiscegenation statutes (with a specific focus on California) and a review of early judicial decisions in this area. The story then turns to the case as it entered the judicial system, reviewing the innovative strategies adopted both by Andrea and Sylvester's attorney and by the State of California in defending its policy of racial exclusion. The California Supreme Court's decision in *Perez* was the culmination of this legal battle and the chapter explains how the case divided the justices. Finally, the story closes with the aftermath of *Perez*,

---

[6] Perez v. Sharp, 198 P.2d 17 (Cal. 1948). At various times, the case was alternatively known as *Perez v. Moroney* and *Perez v. Lippold*, the latter of which is the case title in the Pacific Law Reporter. The name changes reflect shifts in management at the office of the Los Angeles County Clerk. W.G. Sharp was the head of the office when the court handed down its decision in October of 1948. *See* Peggy Pascoe, *Miscegenation Law, Court Cases, and Ideologies of "Race" in Twentieth-Century America*, 83 J. Am. Hist. 44, 61 n.42 (1996).

[7] I am aware of only four other legal scholars who have explored the case in detail. *See* Rachel F. Moran, *Interracial Intimacy: The Regulation of Race and Romance* 85–88 (2001); Randall Kennedy, *Interracial Intimacies: Sex, Marriage, Identity, and Adoption* 259–66, 269 (2003); Kevin R. Johnson & Kristina L. Burrows, *Struck by Lightning? Interracial Intimacy and Racial Justice* (reviewing Rachel F. Moran, *supra*), 25 Hum. Rts. Q. 528 (2003). A handful of scholars in other disciplines also have studied the case. *See, e.g.*, Peter Wallenstein, *supra* note 2, at 192–99; Pascoe, *supra* note 6; Fay Botham, "Almighty God Created the Races": Theologies of Marriage and Race in Anti–Miscegenation Cases, 1865– 1967, at 25 (2005) (unpublished Ph.D. dissertation, Claremont Graduate University); Mark Robert Brilliant, Color Lines: Civil Rights Struggles on America's "Racial Frontier," 1945– 1975 (Aug. 2002) (unpublished Ph.D. dissertation, Stanford University). Additionally, historian Dara Orenstein has compiled an excellent oral history of the case. *See* Dara Orenstein, *Void for Vagueness: Mexicans and the Collapse of Miscegenation Law in California*, 74 Pac. Hist. Rev. 367 (2005).

[8] *See, e.g.*, Goodridge v. Dep't of Pub. Health, 798 N.E.2d 941, 958 (Mass. 2003) (discussing *Perez*).

tracing its effect on the plaintiffs and chronicling the responses of state legislatures and courts.

The chapter concludes with an analysis of the *Perez* story, first exploring how the case—despite having all the hallmarks of a landmark decision—came to be ignored and eclipsed by the much later decision in *Loving*. Next, the discussion addresses what we might gain from devoting more attention to *Perez* and its place in equal protection law. *Perez*, like *Loving*, provides an important narrative about intimacy and marriage—as well as the right to enjoy both on one's own terms. But the California decision offers much more. Unique, in part because it highlights early efforts to grapple with notions of colorblindness that are now enshrined in equal protection law, *Perez* tells us things that *Loving* on its own could never convey. The California high court's path-breaking opinion provides an insufficiently explored perspective on racial formation in the United States and underscores the illogic of biological accounts of racial difference in ways that few others can. Further, *Perez* highlights the limitations of the black-white paradigm that is typically employed when considering antimiscegenation laws, and, in doing so, opens additional avenues for exploring such laws and examining the nature of associations among a range of groups.

Work and Romance

Andrea Pérez and Sylvester Davis, Jr. met and fell in love in 1940s Los Angeles, a city in the midst of both racial entrenchment and change. On the one hand, efforts by whites to segregate and discriminate against racial minorities were commonplace.[9] On the other hand, even as white Angelenos solidified their privileged social and economic status through discriminatory practices and policies, new opportunities became available to racial minorities.[10] As the federal government called on corporations to increase production to meet World War II needs, businesses like Lockheed Aviation expanded operations and made available to minorities jobs previously reserved for whites.[11] The availability of these new and often lucrative positions in Los Angeles spurred the migration of throngs of new workers (many of whom were blacks leaving the South[12]), and

---

[9] *See, e.g.*, Kevin R. Johnson, Hernandez v. Texas: *Legacies of Justice and Injustice*, 25 Chicano–Latino L. Rev. 153, 174 (2005) (discussing instances of racial bias); Josh Sides, *L.A. City Limits: African American Los Angeles from the Great Depression to the Present* 16–18, 48–49 (same).

[10] Sides, *supra* note 9, at 57.

[11] Orenstein, *supra* note 7, at 371 n.10; Sides, *supra* note 9, at 36 (discussing the effect of World War II on the availability of jobs for African Americans).

[12] Sides, *supra* note 9, at 36–56; John Valery White, *The Turner Thesis, Black Migration, and the (Misapplied) Immigrant Explanation of Black Inequality*, 5 Nev. L.J. 6, 12–13, 21–24 (2004).

changed the terms on which the city's racial terrain would be navigated.[13]

Sylvester Davis, Jr., the eldest child of a truck driver and a homemaker, was the product of the first wave of black migration.[14] After World War I, his parents moved to the Central Avenue district of Los Angeles, an area that was racially diverse, but was nevertheless called "the Black Belt."[15] Devout Catholics, the Davises attended mass nearby at the progressive St. Patrick's Church, a congregation that included Mexicans, blacks, and even some whites,[16] and the four Davis children attended racially diverse Catholic schools.[17] Sylvester grew into adulthood in this melting pot, and, after graduating from college, still lived there with his family.[18] In 1941, he obtained a position working the assembly line at Lockheed's Burbank plant.[19]

For Sylvester, being hired at Lockheed was a triumph;[20] the company had been notorious for excluding blacks from jobs, hiring only one or two in Sylvester's cohort.[21] Lockheed adhered to this pattern until 1942, when demand for war-related products required the company to hire minorities and women in substantial numbers. It was this change in hiring policy that made it possible for Sylvester and Andrea to meet.[22] One day in 1942, shortly after Andrea had begun working at the plant, Sylvester glanced up from his work on the assembly line and saw her.[23] Knowing that Andrea would need an orientation to the assembly line's operation, Sylvester asked for and got permission from his supervisor to train her.[24] Before long, Andrea and Sylvester were driving home together and then dating.[25]

---

[13] *See* Moran, *supra* note 7, at xi, 74, 185 (discussing the effects of segregation on interracial intimacy). *See also* Botham, *supra* note 7, at 25 (discussing statistics on migration of members of racial groups).

[14] Orenstein, *supra* note 7, at 372.

[15] *Id.*

[16] Botham, *supra* note 7, at 28; *see also* Orenstein, *supra* note 7, at 372.

[17] Orenstein, *supra* note 7, at 372.

[18] *Id.*

[19] *Id.*

[20] *See id.* at 372 n.10.

[21] *Id.* at 372.

[22] *Id.* at 372, 372 n.10, 404 n.82.

[23] *Id.* at 367.

[24] *Id.*

[25] *Id.* at 367–68.

Andrea Pérez lived with her Mexican immigrant parents in a small *barrio* in central Los Angeles known as Dogtown.[26] The second oldest in a family of nine children, Andrea grew up speaking Spanish and proudly embracing her Mexican heritage.[27] Like Sylvester, Andrea attended racially and ethnically diverse schools. She enrolled at Lincoln High School, which took pride in including students "from every race—Germans, Mexicans, Chinese, French, Japanese, English, Scandinavians, Dutch, [and] Portuguese."[28] Although a wide variety of ethnic groups was represented at Lincoln, African Americans were "strikingly absent" from the student body.[29]

As a result of racial segregation in Los Angeles, relationships (and marriages) between Mexican Americans and blacks were somewhat unusual.[30] Nevertheless, Andrea and Sylvester dated steadily for more than a year, until Sylvester was drafted into the Army and sent to fight in France in 1944.[31] The couple resumed the relationship upon his return a year later and eventually decided to marry—a decision that was unpopular with Andrea's father, Fermín, who "exploded" at the idea of Andrea marrying a "Negro."[32] As a Mexican, Fermín occupied a social and economic space that was below white Angelenos but well above blacks,[33] and he did not look forward to the decline in racial standing that Andrea's marriage to Sylvester would bring.[34] Andrea and Sylvester were nonetheless determined to follow through with their plans.

In 1947 (nearly five years after they first met) Andrea and Sylvester went to the office of the Los Angeles County Clerk to get a marriage license.[35] As it happened, Fermín's objection to the marriage was not the

---

[26] *Id.* at 372.

[27] *Id.* at 368 n.4. Her parents were also proud of this heritage. *Id.* at 374.

[28] *See id.*

[29] *Id.* The absence of a meaningful number of blacks was reflective of race relations and segregation levels in the city at that time. *Id.* at 374–75.

[30] *Id.* at 374.

[31] *Id.*

[32] *Id.*

[33] *Id.* at 374–75; Sides, *supra* note 9, at 24, 27 (discussing, inter alia, differential treatment of blacks and Latinos in area of work and union membership).

[34] Orenstein, *supra* note 7, at 374–75. Andrea's mother, Serafina, reportedly felt differently, but she declined to openly disagree with her husband on this issue. *Id.*

[35] *Id.* at 368. Some disagreement exists over whether Andrea and Sylvester went to the county clerk on their own or with some prompting from Dan Marshall. Fay Botham and Mark Brilliant both suggest that Marshall orchestrated this part of the case. *See* Botham, *supra* note 7, at 42; Brilliant, *supra* note 7, at 132–33.

most significant obstacle they would have to overcome; standing solidly in their path was California law, which had made access to marriage contingent upon race since California attained statehood in 1850. Under the California Code, "white persons" were expressly precluded from marrying "Negroes, Mongolians, members of the Malay race, or mulattoes."[36] The statute did not, however, say anything explicit about Mexicans, and it had been longstanding practice in California to treat Mexicans as white under the law.[37] From a legal perspective, therefore, it was irrelevant that Andrea strongly identified as Mexican, and, as a mestiza, could not easily be mistaken for white.[38] Still, she was surprised when the county clerk concluded that she was legally white and therefore barred from marrying Sylvester.[39]

In California, as in many jurisdictions at the time, county clerks served as the gatekeepers to marriage,[40] making independent determinations about a person's racial status when it was not evident from his or her skin color.[41] One clerk explained how a colleague exercised this discretion: "When she set her eyes on people, she just knew."[42] On many occasions, however, clerks had been known to grant licenses to individuals even when this "sixth sense" made clear that they should not be legally permitted to marry.[43] In some regions, for example, clerks regularly permitted Mexican women "deemed suitably dark in complexion" to marry Punjabi Indian men, who were non-white under the Code.[44] Even judges had occasionally been known to permit Mexicans to circum-

---

[36] Cal. Civ. Code § 60 (West 1941), *invalidated by* Perez v. Sharp, 198 P.2d 17 (Cal. 1948).

[37] Orenstein, *supra* note 7, at 369.

[38] *See infra* text accompanying notes 45–49.

[39] Orenstein, *supra* note 7, at 368. Andrea's classification as white was more than a little ironic given that so much effort had been made at earlier points in the state's history to classify individuals of Mexican heritage as non-white. *See* Ian F. Haney López, *Racism on Trial: The Chicano Fight for Justice* (2003).

[40] Orenstein, *supra* note 7, at 386.

[41] *See* Moran, *supra* note 7, at 5 (discussing the role of clerks in implementing antimiscegenation statutes); *see also* Brilliant, *supra* note 7, at 128 (quoting clerk Rosalind Rice, explaining that she did not "just sit here and look at people and say, 'You're white,' or 'You're Negro.' . . . I took time to study these things.").

[42] *See* Jean Simon, *Marriage Recorder Uses "Sixth Sense" to Determine Race*, L.A. Sentinel, Dec. 23, 1948, at 2 (discussing, inter alia, the methods employed by clerk Rosamond Rice in determining the racial identity of applicants).

[43] Orenstein, *supra* note 7, at 402.

[44] *Id.* at 387; Karen Isaksen Leonard, *Making Ethnic Choices: California's Punjabi Mexican Americans* 62–73 (1992). *See also* Moran, *supra* note 7, at 5 (noting that in some cases, Latinos who "appeared 'too dark' to marry whites" were denied marriage licenses).

vent color lines.[45] Andrea thus might have argued that, as a mestiza, she was American Indian, not white,[46] but she chose not to, making no attempt to classify herself as anything other than white.[47] Why she did not remains unclear. The only thing evident from reports is that, in the eyes of the clerk, Andrea was white,[48] and at the end of the day, that was all that mattered. Years after the *Perez* litigation ended, Sylvester Davis declared Andrea's classification as "white" to be "horse manure"[49] because the race ascribed to Andrea clearly did not fit with her experience as a Mexican American. Sylvester and Andrea both knew that the clerk's determination was wrong, but they were ensnared in the thicket of California's rather complicated racial categories.[50]

Limitations on Interracial Intimacy and Marriage

The power the Los Angeles county clerk had under California law to block Sylvester and Andrea's marriage on the basis of race can be understood only by reviewing the history of antimiscegenation laws as a whole. The laws were first enacted in the South and were most common there. But the statutes also became a way for frontier states like California to regulate increasingly complex and dynamic race relations. White supremacy and the legacy of slavery are very much a part of the story of Sylvester and Andrea's romance.

---

[45] Orenstein, *supra* note 7, at 386 & n.40 (describing Judge Walter Guerin's later-overruled decision to permit Ruth Salas, a woman of mixed Irish and Mexican descent, essentially to create a new racial category not enshrined in law—Irish Indian—in order to marry Gavino Visco, who, as a Filipino, was prohibited from marrying whites under California law).

[46] The advantage of claiming native ancestry was that marriages between American Indians and blacks were not prohibited. Indeed, marriages between whites and American Indians were not problematic, as they had been deemed permissible under the California Code. *See* Orenstein, *supra* note 7, at 387 n.40 (citing a California Attorney General opinion concluding that such marriages did not violate state law). Significantly, though, claiming native ancestry might have posed some difficulties for Andrea, as she could not have pointed to a background linked to American Indian tribes per se. For Andrea and other Latinos of native ancestry, "racial mixing primarily involved Spaniards and the indigenous peoples of South and Central America." Moran, *supra* note 7, at 168.

[47] *Id.* at 388. Mexicans in similar cases had, for example, successfully gotten themselves classified as "Negro." *Id.* at 388 n.43.

[48] *See id.* at 388 (describing the clerk as "unwilling to interpret the law loosely").

[49] *Id.* at 394.

[50] *See id.* at 375 (describing California's antimiscegenation laws as " 'labyrinthine' ").

California's Antimiscegenation Law in Context

The first American antimiscegenation law was enacted in 1664 in the colony of Maryland.[51] The law required the enslavement of any white woman who intermarried with a slave, and it functioned to reinforce the boundary between free and slave status and to clarify the line between whiteness and blackness.[52] In later years, states in both the South and the North adopted interracial marriage bans at one time or another.[53] This attempt to establish the contours of racial difference resulted in a web of antimiscegenation measures that far outlasted slavery.

When Andrea and Sylvester decided to marry in 1947, California was one of thirty states with antimiscegenation laws.[54] Section 69 of the California Code provided that "no license may be issued authorizing the marriage of a white person with a Negro, mulatto, Mongolian or member of the Malay race."[55] Section 60 implemented section 69, providing that "[a]ll marriages of white persons with negroes, Mongolians, members of the Malay race, or mulattoes are illegal and void."[56]

Racial complexity of the sort evident in sections 60 and 69 was uncommon in statutes enacted in the South, which primarily targeted marriages between whites and blacks.[57] But references to multiple racial groups were a regular fixture in western states such as California, where lawmakers used legislation to assuage the white public's fears about the influx of Chinese, Japanese, and Filipino workers.[58] Under California's law, which was amended as late as 1933,[59] the groups with the strictest constraints on their intimate choices were blacks, mulattoes, and individuals of Chinese, Japanese, and Filipino descent;[60] in contrast, Native Americans enjoyed the greatest degree of personal autonomy in this arena, as sections 60 and 69 were never read to apply to them.[61] Ironically, although Mexicans were regarded as white under the antimis-

---

[51] Wallenstein, *supra* note 2, at 3.

[52] *See* Moran, *supra* note 7, at 4.

[53] Kennedy, *supra* 7, at 18–26 ("Between the 1660s and the 1960s, forty-one colonies or states enacted racial laws regulating sex or marriage.").

[54] Wallenstein, *supra* note 2, at 199.

[55] Cal. Civ. Code § 69 (West 1941), *invalidated by* Perez v. Sharp, 198 P.2d 17 (Cal. 1948).

[56] Cal. Civ. Code § 60 (West 1941), *invalidated by* Perez v. Sharp, 198 P.2d 17 (Cal. 1948).

[57] Moran, *supra* note 7, at 17.

[58] *Id.* at 28–31.

[59] Leti Volpp, *American Mestizo: Filipinos and Antimiscegenation Laws in California*, 33 U.C. Davis L. Rev. 795, 801–02, 822 n.109 (2000).

[60] *Id.* at 822 n.109.

[61] Orenstein, *supra* note 7, at 386–87 and n.40.

cegenation law, they were classified as non-white to exclude them from places such as public schools and swimming pools.[62]

The consequences of transgressing the racial lines established by California's sections 60 and 69 were relatively minor; other states, however, imposed severe punishments for violating interracial marriage bans.[63] In Virginia, for example, a couple could, as the Lovings did, face criminal prosecution for violating the prohibition.[64] Indeed, in some jurisdictions, mere interracial sexual intimacy or cohabitation was enough to merit sanction.[65] In California, however, marriage, not sex, was the target, and entering into a proscribed interracial marriage simply meant that the marriage would be deemed void. No other penalties were imposed, even in cases where couples sought to evade California law by leaving the jurisdiction to marry.[66]

This comparative leniency aside, California's statutory scheme was fundamentally no different than those in other states. All the laws attempted to further a white supremacist agenda by demeaning and stigmatizing racial minorities.[67] To that end, sections 60 and 69 "set the boundaries of sexual decency and marital propriety,"[68] defining who could safely be loved and who was too spoiled to be the object of anyone's affection.[69] By limiting blacks and other minorities in the pursuit of rights deemed essential to full citizenship, such as marriage and the

---

[62] *See* Ian F. Haney López, *Race, Ethnicity, Erasure: The Salience of Race to LatCrit Theory*, 10 La Raza L.J. 57, 84 n.87 (1998) (citing Lopez v. Seccombe, 71 F. Supp. 769 (S.D. Cal. 1944)) (discussing the exclusion of Mexican Americans from pools); Sides, *supra* note 9, at 14–15 (discussing segregation in schools).

[63] *See* Statutory Ban on Interracial Marriage Invalidated By Fourteenth Amendment, 1 Stan. L. Rev. 289, 289 n.4 (1949).

[64] *See* Loving v. Virginia, 388 U.S. 1 (1967).

[65] *See, e.g.*, McLaughlin v. Florida, 379 U.S. 184 (1964) (considering the constitutionality of a Florida statute penalizing overnight interracial cohabitation).

[66] *See* Pearson v. Pearson, 51 Cal. 120 (1875).

[67] *See* Loving v. Virginia, 388 U.S. 1, 11 (1967) ("[T]hat Virginia prohibits only interracial marriages involving white persons demonstrates that the racial classifications ... stand ... as measures designed to maintain White Supremacy."); *see also The Supreme Court in Conference (1940–1985)*, at 695 (Del Dickson ed., 2001) (excerpting Chief Justice Warren's comments during Court conference on *Loving*) ("Miscegenation statutes maintain white supremacy. They should go down the drain. I reverse.").

[68] Rachel F. Moran, *Love with a Proper Stranger: What Anti–Miscegenation Laws Can Tell Us About the Meaning of Race, Sex, and Marriage*, 32 Hofstra L. Rev. 1663, 1664–66 (2004).

[69] Moran, *supra* note 7, at 61.

formation of stable families, California's antimiscegenation law marked them as individuals on the very margins of society.[70]

Judicial Review of Antimiscegenation Statutes

Prior to 1948, laws like California's received universally favorable treatment in the federal and state court systems. During Reconstruction, three state courts did declare antimiscegenation statutes invalid,[71] but these provisions were soon reinstated and the wholesale use of racial rules regulating intimacy and family again became the norm and remained so for almost a century.[72]

The maintenance of this norm was at least partially due to the U.S. Supreme Court's endorsement of antimiscegenation statutes in the 1883 case of *Pace v. Alabama*.[73] As others have noted, however, the Supreme Court had occasion to consider the significance of antimiscegenation laws prior to 1883.[74] In *Dred Scott v. Sandford*, for example, Justice Taney, used the existence of prohibitions on intermarriage as evidence that blacks were considered inferior to whites and thus could not properly be regarded as citizens of the United States.[75] Then, in 1883, *Pace v. Alabama* asked the Court to address the constitutionality of the punishment meted out to Tony Pace and Mary J. Cox, an unmarried interracial couple engaged in an intimate relationship.[76] Alabama law at the time punished same-race adultery with a fine and up to six months imprisonment for first offenders, but took a harsher view of adultery across racial lines, punishing the latter with imprisonment of two to seven years.[77] Emphasizing the power of the State to regulate in this area, the Court held that the disparate treatment of the offenses posed no Fourteenth Amendment problem because the individuals *within* each category of offense were treated equally. "Whatever discrimination is made in the punishment prescribed in the two sections," the Court explained, "is

---

[70] R.A. Lenhardt, *Understanding the Mark: Race, Stigma, and Equality in Context*, 79 N.Y.U. L. Rev. 803, 810 (2004).

[71] *See* Burns v. State, 48 Ala. 195 (1872); *Ex parte* Francois, 9 F. Cas. 699 (C.C.W.D. Tex. 1879) (No. 5,047); Hart v. Hoss & Elder, 26 La. Ann. 90 (1874). A number of state legislatures also temporarily suspended their antimiscegenation statutes as well. *See* Moran, *supra* note 7, at 77.

[72] *See, e.g.*, Green v. State, 59 Ala. 68 (1877) (reversing the Alabama court's earlier determination invalidating an antimiscegenation statute in *Burns v. State*).

[73] 106 U.S. 583 (1883).

[74] *See* Wallenstein, *supra* note 2, at 53.

[75] Dred Scott v. Sandford, 60 U.S. (19 How.) 393 (1856). *See also* Lenhardt, *supra* note 70, at 845.

[76] *Pace*, 106 U.S. 583.

[77] *See* Cheryl I. Harris, *In the Shadow of* Plessy, 7 U. Pa. J. Const. L. 867, 881 (2005).

directed against the offense designated and not against the person of any particular color or race. The punishment of each offending person, whether white or black, is the same."[78]

Perhaps even more than the Court's later decision in *Plessy v. Ferguson*,[79] the *Pace* decision helped to usher in the separate-but-equal policies that were prevalent in the South until well after *Brown v. Board of Education*.[80] *Pace* also cemented the role of interracial marriage bans in regulating intimacy and family formation.[81] A spate of legal decisions affirming the importance of antimiscegenation laws in preventing interracial marriage followed the *Pace* Court's ruling.[82] The sentiments expressed in *Scott v. State* by a Georgia Supreme Court judge reflect those articulated in these and other pre-*Loving* decisions:

> It is our duty to declare what the law is, not to make law. For myself, however, I ... say that it was dictated by wise statesmanship, and has a broad and solid foundation in enlightened policy.... The amalgamation of the races is not only unnatural, but is always productive of deplorable results....
>
> . . .
>
> ... The Legislature certainly had as much right to regulate the marriage relation by prohibiting it between persons of different races as they had to prohibit it between persons within the Levitical degrees, or between idiots. Both are necessary and proper regulations. And the [instant] regulation ... is equally so.[83]

Using language like this, courts consistently upheld antimiscegenation laws by imposing criminal penalties for intermarriage,[84] granting annulments to individuals who claimed that they inadvertently married across the color line,[85] and invalidating wills that required recognition of interracial marriages.[86] Courts were quick to void even longstanding

---

[78] *Pace*, 106 U.S. at 639.

[79] 163 U.S. 537 (1896).

[80] 347 U.S. 483 (1954). Professor Peggy Cooper Davis has discussed *Pace* as an important "doctrinal antecedent to *Plessy*." Peggy Cooper Davis, *Neglected Stories: The Constitution and Family Values* 67 (1997). See also Wallenstein, *supra* note 2, at 121.

[81] Wallenstein, *supra* note 2, at 120.

[82] *Id.* at 120, 173, 177–78, 180–83, 189, 198 (discussing precedents following *Pace*).

[83] Scott v. State, 39 Ga. 321, 323–24 (1869).

[84] *See* Loving v. Virginia, 388 U.S. 1, 1 (1967).

[85] *See* People v. Godines, 62 P.2d 787 (Cal. Ct. App. 1936).

[86] *See* Lee v. Giraudo (In re Monks' Estate), 120 P.2d 167 (Cal. Dist. Ct. App. 1941) (invalidating a will because, inter alia, the decedent's marriage to his wife was invalid

marriages if one spouse was a member of a race proscribed from marrying whites.[87]

A Test (Case) of Faith

In 1947, Andrea and Sylvester faced a legal regime set squarely against interracial marriage. Still, the couple had a number of options available to them, including cohabitation or leaving the state to marry, as others had done.[88] But these alternatives were not real options for the devoutly Catholic couple because they wanted to receive the sacrament of marriage in their home church.[89] So, instead, they pursued the only other viable option: litigation.

Developing a Strategy for Justice

Among the white families who worshipped at St. Patrick's, Sylvester's childhood church, were the Marshalls. After high school, Andrea had worked for the Marshalls as a babysitter and housekeeper, and she knew that Dan Marshall was a progressive attorney involved in anti-racist causes.[90] Andrea and Sylvester met with Marshall to discuss their dilemma, and he quickly agreed to represent them.[91] By the time Andrea and Sylvester approached Marshall, the law firm that he operated with two law school friends had been involved in a number of cutting-edge civil rights battles, including one challenging the use of racially restrictive covenants and ensuring the admission of the first black to the Los Angeles Bar Association.[92] Marshall arguably knew that plaintiffs in antimiscegenation cases, perhaps out a sense of futility, typically declined to challenge the statutes directly. Instead, couples merely contested the statute's application to particular racial categories.[93] That is, if the

---

because she was part African American); Gregory Michael Dorr, *Principled Expediency: Eugenics,* Naim v. Naim, *and the Supreme Court,* 42 Am. J. Legal Hist. 119, 120 (1998).

[87] Pascoe, *supra* note 6, at 51–52.

[88] Orenstein, *supra* note 7, at 386. Other states, such as Florida, prohibited interracial cohabitation, or punished those who procured marriage outside of their borders. *See supra* notes 65–66 and accompanying text; *see also* Loving v. Virginia, 388 U.S. 1 (1967); McLaughlin v. Florida, 379 U.S. 184 (1964).

[89] Orenstein, *supra* note 7, at 386; Petition for Writ of Mandamus, Mem. of Points and Authorities, and Proof of Service at 4, Perez v. Sharp, 198 P.2d 17 (Cal. 1948) (No. L.A. 20305).

[90] Orenstein, *supra* note 7, at 388.

[91] *Id.* at 389.

[92] *Id.* at 388–89.

[93] *See, e.g.,* Pascoe, *supra* note 6, at 44–45 (discussing Arizona's *Kirby v. Kirby* and efforts to disprove a racial classification).

law barred marriages between whites and blacks alone, the plaintiff, in a move reminiscent of that employed in cases challenging slave classifications might, for example, argue that he or she was Native American.[94] Though Marshall could have argued that Andrea was not white, he preferred to strike a blow, not at the margins, but at the very heart of California's laws.[95]

Marshall's Catholic faith accounted for his view that racism was antithetical to the laws of humanity, a view that arguably shaped his ultimate strategy in *Perez*.[96] He eventually decided that any challenge to California's antimiscegenation statute should be made, not on the basis of race, but on religious grounds.[97] In particular, Marshall argued that the law violated the couple's religious freedom because Catholic dogma did not prohibit interracial marriage.[98] Though ordinarily a lawsuit goes through the lower courts before ever being considered by the state's highest court, Marshall was hopeful that the California Supreme Court would exercise its original jurisdiction to hear the case without a trial.[99]

Marshall's approach had advantages. From a legal standpoint, his argument not only circumvented unfavorable equal protection law, but also subjected the state to a higher burden than ordinary reasonableness. Officials would have to show the existence of a grave danger justifying limits on the free exercise of religion.[100] Also, on the level of strategy, Marshall's theory carried the possibility of appealing both to judges who were very religious and to judges who were members of a religious minority, as were California Supreme Court Justices Douglas Edmonds, a "devoted Christian Scientist," and Roger Traynor, a fellow Catholic.[101]

Still, Marshall was taking a risk. In 1947, no one could easily have predicted how the court, later regarded among the most prestigious in the nation, would respond. At the time, the state's race jurisprudence

---

[94] To avoid enslavement, individuals would often challenge the racial classification applied to them at trial. *See, e.g.*, Hudgins v. Wrights, 11 Va. (1 Hen. & M.) 134 (1806); Gobu v. Gobu, 1 N.C. (Tay.) 188 (1802). For more, see Ariela J. Gross, *Litigating Whiteness: Trials of Racial Determination in the Nineteenth–Century South*, 108 Yale L.J. 109 (1998).

[95] Orenstein, *supra* note 7, at 390.

[96] *See id.* at 388.

[97] *Id.* at 390.

[98] *See* Orenstein, *supra* note 7, at 389–90.

[99] Brilliant, *supra* note 7, at 134.

[100] *See* W. Va. Bd. of Educ. v. Barnette, 319 U.S. 624 (1943).

[101] *See* Orenstein, *supra* note 7, at 390; Ben Field, *Activism in Pursuit of the Public Interest: The Jurisprudence of Chief Justice Roger J. Traynor* 36 (2003).

had not produced significant victories for minorities. Amidst the furor of World War II, the justices had, for example, upheld prohibitions on land ownership and procurement of commercial fishing licenses for non-citizen Japanese.[102] The court did decline to enforce a racially restrictive covenant in *Fairchild v. Raines*,[103] but, as of 1947, had not yet concluded that such covenants were *per se* invalid.[104]

Moreover, Marshall could not expect support from civil rights groups like the National Association for the Advancement of Colored People ("NAACP"), with which he had worked in prior cases. The NAACP was in disarray at the local level and had decided at the national level that, given the current social and political climate, a conservative approach focused on issues such as residential segregation and education was more prudent than a direct attack on antimiscegenation laws.[105] Similarly, the Catholic Church refused to lend assistance, even though its teachings had inspired Marshall and his friend Ted LeBerthon to found the Los Angeles chapter of the Catholic Interracial Council ("LACIC"), an anti-racist group established in the 1930s by Father John LaFarge, Jr. Indeed, when Marshall contacted an area church official about the possibility of testifying in the case,[106] the official sent a short and discouraging written reply.[107] His response suggested that the *Perez* lawsuit was ill advised because it would "stir up more passion and prejudice."[108] In sum, Marshall was on his own.

Briefs and Oral Argument in the California Supreme Court

As hoped, the arguments Marshall advanced in his August 1947 petition for mandamus persuaded the California Supreme Court to exercise its original jurisdiction.[109] During preparations for an October oral argument, the case proceeded much as Marshall had envisioned, with matters of religious freedom at center stage. By conceding the "fact" that Andrea was "a white female person" and Sylvester "a Negro

---

[102] *See* People v. Oyama, 173 P.2d 794 (Cal. 1946), *rev'd*, 332 U.S. 633 (1948); Torao Takahashi v. Fish & Game Comm'n, 185 P.2d 805 (Cal. 1947), *rev'd*, 334 U.S. 410 (1948).

[103] 151 P.2d 260 (Cal. 1944).

[104] *See, e.g.*, Shideler v. Roberts, 160 P.2d 67 (Cal. Dist. Ct. App. 1945). Of course, the U.S. Supreme Court, in *Shelley v. Kraemer*, 334 U.S. 1 (1948), later held that restrictive covenants violated equal protection guarantees.

[105] Orenstein, *supra* note 7, at 391, 392 & n.56.

[106] *See* Letter from Daniel G. Marshall to the Reverend Joseph T. McGuken (Apr. 23, 1947); *see also* Orenstein, *supra* note 7, at 390–91.

[107] *See* Orenstein, *supra* note 7, at 390–91.

[108] *Id.*

[109] *Id.* at 394.

male person," Marshall at first seemed to avoid the focus on race that characterized early challenges to antimiscegenation laws.[110]

Deputy County Counsel Charles C. Stanley's initial submissions for the defense focused on Marshall's religious claims. For example, the State's demurrer rejected the argument that a higher standard of review applied.[111] According to Stanley, interracial marriage constituted conduct, not religious belief, and so did not enjoy heightened constitutional protection.[112] Even if the court applied a higher standard, he argued, California had a strong interest in regulating miscegenous conduct because, like bigamy, interracial marriage had a "tendency to disturb the public peace or corrupt the public morals."[113] Similarly, to support the contention that no question of religious liberty was at issue, the State's return by way of answer seized upon the writings of Father John La Farge—the priest who had assisted Marshall in creating the LACIC— that could be read to say Catholics should not enter mixed marriages.[114]

But the State would later change the trajectory of argument in the case by filing—on the day of oral argument—a supplemental brief dealing primarily with issues of race.[115] A virtual eugenicist treatise, the 120–page brief sought to highlight evidence showing the reasonableness of the State's policies. In ways that later prompted Marshall to question how "a servant of the people ... [could be] bold enough to argue for the validity of a statute upon [white superiority] grounds,"[116] Stanley used disputed eugenics-based social science to argue that interracial marriages resulted in social problems, including the birth of interracial children who, as the offspring of parents "lost to shame," would be " 'social outcasts.' "[117] He also maintained that such marriages—especially with

---

[110] Petition for Writ of Mandamus, Mem. of Points and Authorities at 2, 5, Perez v. Sharp, 198 P.2d 17 (Cal. 1948) (No. L.A. 20305).

[111] Orenstein, *supra* note 7, at 394 & n.61.

[112] Return by Way of Demurrer, Points and Authorities in Support of Demurrer at 8–9, *Perez*, 198 P.2d 17 (No. L.A. 20305).

[113] *Id.* at 5.

[114] Return By Way of Answer at 3–4, *Perez*, 198 P.2d 17 (No. L.A. 20305). Marshall would later confirm, however, that LaFarge was not actually opposed to interracial marriage. Letter from Reverend John LaFarge, S.J. to Daniel G. Marshall 1 (Sept. 26, 1947) ("The Church will urge people not to enter such unions not because of anything wrong in interracial marriage but simply because of the dangers ... to people's peace of mind....").

[115] *See* Respondent's Supplemental Brief in Opposition to Writ of Mandate, *Perez*, 198 P.2d 17 (No. L.A. 20305).

[116] Petitioners' Reply Brief at 24, *Perez*, 198 P.2d 17 (No. L.A. 20305).

[117] *Id.* at 110.

respect to the "Negro race," which he deemed "biologically inferior to the white"—produced "undesirable biological results."[118]

At oral argument, the judicial focus was exclusively on these and other similar arguments. Marshall delivered an eloquent argument about religious freedom, which, based on the oral argument transcript, appears to have inspired no questions.[119] Only Stanley was subjected to questioning, and from an arguably unlikely source: Justice Roger Traynor. Traynor, who would later be appointed Chief Justice, was in only the seventh of what would be a thirty-year tenure on the court. His expertise was not in civil rights, but in tax, having taught that subject at UC Berkeley's Boalt Hall School of Law.[120] Nevertheless, Justice Traynor was troubled by several aspects of the case, including the State's choice of racial categories:

Mr. Justice Traynor: What is a negro?

Mr. Stanley: We have not the benefit of any judicial interpretation. The statute states that a negro [sic] cannot marry a negro, which can be construed to mean a full-blooded negro, since the statute also says mulatto, Mongolian, or Malay.

Mr. Justice Traynor: What is a mulatto? One-sixteenth blood?

Mr. Stanley: Certainly certain states have seen fit to state what a mulatto is.

Mr. Justice Traynor: If there is 1/8 blood, can they marry? If you can marry with 1/8, why not with 1/16, 1/32, 1/64? And then don't you get in the ridiculous position where a negro cannot marry anybody? If he is white, he cannot marry black, or if he is black, he cannot marry white.

Mr. Stanley: I agree that it would be better for the legislature to lay down an exact amount of blood, but I do not think that the statute should be declared unconstitutional as indefinite on this ground.

Mr. Justice Traynor: That is something anthropologists have not been able to furnish, although they say ... there is no such thing as race.[121]

Marshall no doubt understood from this questioning that his case could be won on a theory focused on race after all.[122] Asserting that

---

[118] *Id.* at 62.

[119] *See* Transcript of Oral Argument, *Perez*, 198 P.2d 17 (No. L.A. 20305), Brilliant, *supra* note 7, at 137.

[120] Field, *supra* note 101, at 5; *see also* Orenstein, *supra* note 7, at 395.

[121] Transcript of Oral Argument at 3–4, *Perez*, 198 P.2d 17 (No. L.A. 20305).

[122] *See* Orenstein, *supra* note 7, at 396.

"prejudice" best explained California's prohibition, Marshall's reply brief thus emphasized the extent to which the State's concerns about social consequences had no logical stopping point and noted that, in 1947, reputable social scientists were of the opinion that the concept of race on which the State relied was "popularly understood, [a]s a myth."[123] Given this doubt about the State's "science," Marshall cautioned the court against "allow[ing] a biological experiment to be continued at the expense of the dignity ... of these two decent citizens and other equally worthy citizens...."[124]

The California Supreme Court's Decision

On October 1, 1948, almost a year after oral argument, the court issued its decision.[125] By a 4–3 vote, the court ruled for Andrea and Sylvester,[126] marking the first invalidation of an antimiscegenation statute since Reconstruction.[127]

The Majority Opinion

The majority opinion was drafted by Justice Roger Traynor, who in future years would emerge as one of the "ablest judge[s] of his generation,"[128] a committed pragmatist who believed that his duty as a jurist was to "search out and eliminate legal rules that ... no longer served their purpose."[129] This philosophy placed him at the forefront of fundamental shifts in popular understanding of matters ranging from product liability to individual rights.[130]

Traynor cast the issues in the case in an inspired light from the outset. *Perez* was not, he suggested, merely about race or religion; it was also about what he, citing early U.S. Supreme Court due process cases such as *Meyer v. Nebraska*,[131] called the fundamental right "to marry ... the person of one's choice...."[132] This formulation of the rights at stake

---

[123] Petitioner's Reply Brief at 4, *Perez*, 198 P.2d 17 (No. L.A. 20305).

[124] *Id.* at 31.

[125] Orenstein, *supra* note 7, at 397; *Perez*, 198 P.2d at 17.

[126] *See Perez*, 198 P.2d at 29.

[127] *See* Moran, *supra* note 7, at 84.

[128] Henry J. Friendly, *Ablest Judge of His Generation*, 71 Cal. L. Rev. 1039, 1039 (1983); *see also* Warren E. Burger, *A Tribute*, 71 Cal. L. Rev. 1037, 1037 (1983) (describing Traynor as "a splendid judge, a fine scholar, and an effective administrator").

[129] Field, *supra* note 101, at 7.

[130] *Id.* at 45–119.

[131] 262 U.S. 390 (1923).

[132] Perez v. Sharp, 198 P.2d 17, 19 (Cal. 1948).

in the case was very much ahead of its time. Although the importance of marriage in society would figure prominently in later privacy cases like *Griswold v. Connecticut*,[133] it would not formally be recognized as a fundamental right until *Loving* in 1967.[134] Casting the issues this way allowed Traynor to circumvent the doctrine of separate but equal by announcing that cases involving access to segregated trains and education were "inapplicable."[135] "Since the essence of the right to marry is freedom to join in marriage with the person of one's choice," he explained, "a segregation statute for marriage necessarily impairs the right to marry."[136] A person consigned to segregated facilities might still ride a railway car or be educated in a public school, but for the individual prevented "by law from marrying the person of his choice ... that [other] person to him may be irreplaceable."[137]

The central issue in the case thus became not whether whites and blacks received equal treatment, but whether the impairment of rights the statute effectuated was justified. At the time Justice Traynor wrote, the principle of colorblindness—now regularly articulated in Supreme Court decisions on race—was just taking root, and the Court's regrettable decisions in Japanese curfew and relocation cases, such as *Hirabayashi v. United States*[138] and *Korematsu v. United States*,[139] were only a few years old. As a result, courts were still in the process of determining how judicial review in race cases should proceed. It was not at all obvious what to make of the notion that "all legal restrictions which curtail the ... rights of a ... racial group are immediately suspect.... [and] must [be subjected] ... to the most rigid scrutiny."[140]

Traynor had already embraced what seems, in part, to have motivated the Court in its later holdings: the idea of race as biologically

---

[133] 381 U.S. 479 (1965).

[134] *See* Loving v. Virginia, 388 U.S. 1, 1 (1967). Some scholars argue that, because of the dual grounds—race and marriage—on which *Loving* was decided, the first clear articulation of the due process right to marry did not come until *Zablocki v. Redhail*, 434 U.S. 374 (1978) (declaring unconstitutional a Wisconsin statute requiring any person with child-support obligations to get court approval before being permitted to marry). *See, e.g.,* Joseph A. Pull, *Questioning the Fundamental Right to Marry*, 90 Marq. L. Rev. 21, 31 (2006).

[135] *Perez*, 198 P.2d at 20–21.

[136] *Id.*

[137] *Id.* at 25.

[138] 320 U.S. 81 (1943); *see also* Orenstein, *supra* note 7, at 397.

[139] 323 U.S. 214 (1944). Of course, the term *colorblindness* was itself not at all new. *See* Plessy v. Ferguson, 163 U.S. 537, 559 (1896) (Harlan, J., dissenting) ("Our Constitution is color-blind, and neither knows nor tolerates classes among citizens.").

[140] *Korematsu*, 323 U.S. at 216.

irrelevant. His majority opinion, which analyzed the relevant statutes under federal rather than state constitutional law, reviewed in great detail what was then new social science research on race by scholars like Gunnar Myrdal and Otto Kleinberg. This research repudiated eugenicist conclusions about race and racial difference that had been cited by the State and, for Traynor, also demonstrated that any scientific foundation for California's law had been thoroughly discredited.[141]

Traynor found preposterous the idea that that the statutes "prevent[ed] the Caucasian race from being contaminated by [inferior] races,"[142] noting that many individual differences were due to "environmental factors," rather than hereditary ones.[143] Indeed, he found that the reasons offered by the State were, in the new language of strict scrutiny, insufficiently "compelling."[144] This groundbreaking conclusion alone could have ended the analysis, as it was all that was needed to carry out the required review. But Traynor felt compelled to add more.

Perhaps to underscore that California's laws had "outlived their purpose," Traynor asserted that they relied on racial categories that were "illogical and discriminatory" and arguably rendered the state's statutes "void for vagueness."[145] Sections 60 and 69 never clarified how determinations about race should be made, nor did they deal explicitly with persons of mixed ancestry. As a result, the provisions were too vague to put individuals on notice of the prohibited behavior. If nothing else, it was certainly absurd that white and black persons could be barred from marrying, but that a "Mulatto [could] marry a Negro" and "[a] person having five-eighths Mongolian blood and three-eighths white blood could properly marry anoth[e]r person of preponderantly Mongolian blood."[146]

These questions of racial ambiguity and vagueness were arguably salient to Traynor because of Andrea's tenuous hold on white identity.

---

[141] See Field, supra note 101, at 38–40; see also Carter G. Woodson, The Beginnings of the Miscegenation of the Whites and Blacks, 3 J. of Negro Hist. 335 (1918); W.E. Burghardt DuBois, Social Equality and Racial Intermarriage, The World Tomorrow 83 (1922) (critiquing eugenics).

[142] Perez v. Sharp, 198 P.2d 17, 23 (Cal. 1948).

[143] Id.

[144] Id. at 27.

[145] Id. at 26. For an early discussion of the vagueness doctrine, see, e.g., Connally v. General Construction Co., 269 U.S. 385 (1926). Perez arguably marks the first time that the concept of vagueness had been used in the antimiscegenation context. Prior to 1948, litigants had employed it in the residential segregation context. See infra note 233 and accompanying text.

[146] Perez, 198 P.2d at 23.

After all, she might plausibly have avoided the law's application altogether by asserting that she was non-white. Justice Traynor had to accept that Andrea was white because that "fact" was not in dispute; however, he no doubt suspected, or perhaps even knew, that Andrea was not someone likely to enjoy the privileges of whiteness.[147] That he referred to Mexican Americans several times in his opinion,[148] even noting that some had skin as dark as blacks, arguably bears this theory out.[149] Oddly enough, Traynor's vagueness holding may have been the one time that Andrea's racial identity was addressed head on. How best to understand her identity had, from the start, been an important issue that was artificially suppressed by Marshall's framing of the case.

The Concurrences

Vast differences of opinion existed among the justices in the majority with respect to rationale. Justice Edmonds, adopting the approach advocated by Marshall in his initial court filings, separately concurred on the ground that the case turned on issues of religious freedom, not race.[150] Justice Jesse W. Carter, joined by Chief Justice Phil Gibson, maintained that the validity of the state's antimiscegenation law was not merely an empirical question, as Traynor had suggested.[151] Their concurrence argued that California's law had never, at any point in history, been constitutional.[152] This was so, they contended, because of normative principles of equality set forth in the Fourteenth Amendment, the Declaration of Independence, and the recently enacted Charter of the United Nations.[153] In their view, California's statutes "violate[d] the very premise on which [the United States] and its Constitution were built...."[154] This concurrence devoted comparatively little space to discussion of California's eugenics-based evidence. Indeed, the evidence was used only to question the State's articulated interests and to suggest—by quoting Hitler's *Mein Kampf*—that the court could "take judicial notice of the fact ... that steady inroads ha[d] been made on the

---

[147] Orenstein, *supra* note 7, at 370, 397.

[148] *See id.* at 397–98 (discussing Traynor's use of *Westminster Sch. Dist. v. Mendez*, 161 F.2d 774 (9th Cir. 1947)).

[149] *Perez*, 198 P.2d at 23.

[150] *Id.* at 34–35 (Edmonds, J., concurring). *See also* Orenstein, *supra* note 7, at 399, Botham, *supra* note 7, at 73–76.

[151] *Perez*, 198 P.2d at 29–34 (Carter, J., concurring).

[152] *Id.* at 29.

[153] *Id.* at 34.

[154] *Id.*

myth of racial superiority...."[155] Instead of resting on empirical grounds, Justice Carter's opinion emphasized the normative imperative of colorblindness on the part of the State.

In contrast to Justice Traynor, who appeared to appreciate the ways in which colorblindness ignored certain social realities about race, Justice Carter seemed to embrace the concept completely. He was intent on correcting California's erroneous assumption that, after *Korematsu*, the State merely had to produce "some" evidence of a legitimate purpose in order to survive judicial review of a racial classification. Carter seems to have written separately partially in order to clarify that such evidence, though arguably adequate in most cases, could not suffice in a race case. As he explained, " '[p]ressing public necessity may sometimes justify the existence of [legal restrictions based on race]; racial antagonism never can.' "[156]

The Dissent

The three justices in dissent—Justice John W. Schenk, B. Rey Schauer, and Homer R. Spence—spoke with a unified voice. Schenk, who drafted the opinion for his fellow dissenters, offered a very traditional defense of California's antimiscegenation statute. Noting that twenty-nine other states had similar statutes on the books, he argued that there was nothing to support the majority's invalidation of the statute. After all, every federal and state court to consider the issue since Reconstruction had upheld laws prohibiting interracial sex and marriage.[157] Moreover, Schenk argued, California had been consistent in its support of antimiscegenation policies. Over time, its statutes had expanded, not reduced, the range of prohibited marriages.[158]

In any event, it was enough for Justice Schenk that the State had some evidence supporting its determinations. He dismissed out of hand the notion that, under U.S. Supreme Court precedent, the state legislature might need to prove more than was ordinarily required to sustain its policy. He argued that only equal treatment was required, a standard clearly met in his view because "[e]ach petitioner has the right and the privilege of marrying within his or her own group."[159] "It is not within

---

[155] *Id.* Marshall had also cited Mein Kampf in refuting the race-based arguments advanced by the State. Petitioners' Reply Brief at 23–24, *Perez*, 198 P.2d 17 (No. L.A. 20305).

[156] *Id.* at 33 (quoting *Korematsu v. United States*, 323 U.S. 214, 216 (1944)).

[157] *Id.* at 39 (Shenk, J., dissenting).

[158] *Id.* at 38.

[159] *Id.* at 46.

the province of the courts," he explained, to second-guess "findings of the legislature. . . ."[160]

Perez *and Its Aftermath*

The decision in *Perez* made headline news[161] but did not result in immediate relief for Andrea and Sylvester. Because of the possibility that state officials would petition the Supreme Court to review the California high court's decision, the couple waited a year to marry.[162] Likewise, the county clerk did not begin to issue marriage licenses to interracial couples until after the threat of an appeal had passed.[163] Once the county clerk resumed its regular administrative practices, however, a number of interracial couples sought and obtained licenses; in fact, "during the 30 months following *Perez*, the L.A. County Clerk issued . . . 455 licenses" to such couples.[164]

Outside of California, *Perez*'s immediate impact was much harder to detect. Legislators in other states with antimiscegenation statutes did not begin to revisit their earlier policy judgments until 1951.[165] Oklahoma and Montana, in 1951 and 1953, respectively, became the first states to remove race-based barriers to marrying "the person of one's choice."[166] They were followed by North Dakota in 1955, Nevada and California in 1959, and then Arizona in 1962. Remarkably, it took other states even longer to repeal their statutes.[167] Alabama, the last state to

---

[160] *Id.* at 42. Justice Schenk also objected to Justice Traynor's vagueness holding. He argued that Andrea and Sylvester lacked standing to raise a vagueness challenge since, based on their declaration that they were a white woman and a black man, neither was a member of a race that could be seen as uncertain under the statute. *Id.* at 47.

[161] Articles about the decision appeared in national and local California newspapers. *See* Field, *supra* note 101, at 40–41; Orenstein, *supra* note 7, at 401–03; Brilliant, *supra* note 7, at 148.

[162] Orenstein, *supra* note 7, at 404. They were eventually married in a private wedding ceremony at St. Patrick's Church. The marriage, before Andrea's death in 2002, lasted more than fifty years and produced several children. *Id.* at 404, 407.

[163] The State had unsuccessfully sought rehearing and ultimately declined to petition for *certiorari* in the U.S. Supreme Court. *See* Brilliant, *supra* note 7, at 128.

[164] Field, *supra* note 101, at 41.

[165] California's legislature did not remove its statutes from the Code until 1959, and only then after a multi-year lobbying effort by African–American assemblyman August Hawkins. Orenstein, *supra* note 7, at 401. Earl Warren, who was governor of California at the time *Perez* was decided, heeded advice not to remove the laws from the books. *Id.* at 401.

[166] Wallenstein, *supra* note 2, at 8.

[167] *See id.* at fig.10 (illustrating a map with the states that still had anti-miscegenation laws in 1966).

do so, did not act until 2000, over opposition from a number of legislators.[168]

State courts also largely ignored *Perez*. Few even cited it, let alone determined that they would follow it. The Virginia Supreme Court's treatment of *Perez* in *Naim v. Naim*[169] is typical. The *Naim* opinion recognized *Perez*, but regarded it as "contrary to the otherwise uninterrupted course of judicial decision."[170] The U.S. Supreme Court briefly considered *Naim*, but ultimately concluded that there was no jurisdiction over the case.[171] The *Perez* decision did not embolden the Justices to intervene in Virginia's regulation of interracial marriage, and *Naim* may have cemented the marginalization of the California Supreme Court's pathbreaking opinion.

Because California officials declined to seek certiorari in *Perez*, the U.S. Supreme Court never had any occasion directly to consider that decision. This was quite likely a welcome fact for many of the Justices.[172] With the many challenges to racially segregated educational and housing opportunities advanced by the NAACP in the 1940s and early 1950s, which culminated in the Court's rejection of the separate-but-equal doctrine in *Brown*, the Justices undoubtedly felt that they had more than their share of controversy. The Court was in no hurry to touch what many regarded as the explosive question of interracial relations.[173] In fact, the Court did not address matters of interracial intimacy until 1964, when, in *McLaughlin v. Florida*, the Justices struck down a Florida statute that exacted harsher penalties for interracial than intraracial adultery.[174] Only after *McLaughlin* did the Court take up the question of interracial marriage in *Loving*.

---

[168] *See* Jeff Amy, *Voters Strike Ban on Interracial Marriage*, Mobile Reg. (Ala.), Oct. 8, 2000, at A24.

[169] 87 S.E.2d 749 (Va. 1955). *Naim* concerned a marriage between a white woman and a Chinese man, which was voided on the grounds that it violated Virginia's antimiscegenation law. *Id.* at 750.

[170] *Id.* at 753. This reception helps to explain the relatively scant attention *Perez* received in law reviews at the time. Field, *supra* note 101, at 41. Articles addressing *Perez* appeared in the California and Harvard law reviews in 1953 and 1957, respectively. *See The Supreme Court, 1956 Term*, 71 Harv. L. Rev. 94 (1957); David Bruce Harriman, Comment, *The Void for Vagueness Rule in California*, 41 Cal. L. Rev. 523 (1953). Other citations do not appear until later. Field, *supra* note 101, at 41–42.

[171] Dorr, *supra* note 86, at 120.

[172] *See* Philip Elman & Norman Silber, *The Solicitor General's Office, Justice Frankfurter, and Civil Rights Litigation, 1946–1960: An Oral History*, 100 Harv. L. Rev. 817 (1987) (on avoidance of antimiscegenation issues).

[173] *See id.* at 845.

[174] McLaughlin v. Florida, 379 U.S. 184 (1964). Significantly, the male in *McLaughlin* asserted that he was not Black, as authorities contended, but Latino. Moran, *supra* note 7, at 92.

Chief Justice Earl Warren, who had been governor of California at the time *Perez* was decided in 1948, authored the Court's decision in *Loving*. Relying on the Fourteenth Amendment, a unanimous Court struck down the statute as violative of the Equal Protection Clause.[175] Additionally, all but one Justice concluded that the law denied individuals due process of law by interfering with their fundamental right to marry.[176] In explaining the judgment of the Court, Chief Justice Warren took an approach very different from that employed by Justice Traynor. He devoted very little attention to social scientific evidence, focusing instead on normative matters of racial equality and personal choice.[177]

Nevertheless, Chief Justice Warren included a citation to *Perez* in his opinion.[178] Without some discussion or analysis of *Perez*, it is difficult to know exactly what, if anything, Warren hoped to convey in employing this citation. The similarities in the way *Loving* and *Perez* discuss race and marriage are, however, especially noteworthy and should not be overlooked. Although Warren never referred to the "person of one's choice" in analyzing the questions presented to him, as Justice Traynor had, the Chief Justice did take care to emphasize the important function marriage serves in society and its hallowed place as a prerequisite of full citizenship. In concluding that race-based limitations on marriage were grounded in white superiority and thus could not be constitutionally condoned, Warren explained that "[m]arriage is one of the 'basic civil rights of man,' fundamental to our very existence and survival."[179] This language and, in many ways, the substance of the *Loving* opinion itself, track key aspects of *Perez*; both decisions reveal "a commitment to racial equality and a commitment to marital autonomy."[180] And, yet, it is *Loving*, not *Perez*, that stands out in the minds of most individuals; in fact, *Perez* rarely receives mention.

---

[175] Loving v. Virginia, 388 U.S. 1, 11–12 (1967).

[176] *Id.* at 12. Justice Potter Stewart wrote a short concurrence to express his view that an act's criminality could not constitutionally turn on matters of race. *Id.* at 13 (Stewart, J., concurring).

[177] Moran, *supra* note 7, at 6.

[178] *Loving*, 388 U.S. at 6 n.5 (majority opinion).

[179] *Loving*, 388 U.S. at 12 (quoting Skinner v. Oklahoma, 316 U.S. 535, 541 (1942)). Interestingly, notes on *Loving* indicate that Warren omitted a reference to *Meyer v. Nebraska*, a due process case, to ensure that Hugo Black joined his opinion. *See Supreme Court in Conference, supra* note 67, at 696.

[180] Moran, *supra* note 7, at 6.

Understanding Perez *and Its Place in Race Law*

The story of *Perez v. Sharp*—of Andrea and Sylvester's struggle to love, marry, and build a family across racial boundaries—makes clear the decision's importance for students and scholars of race and the legal system in the United States. In rescuing *Perez* from the land of lost cases,[181] same-sex marriage advocates have provided race scholars with a rare gift. *Perez* offers a unique snapshot of the early stages of the colorblindness doctrine that is now so embedded in race jurisprudence that it seems always to have existed. The case also offers important insights into antimiscegenation law and its role in erecting what some call the "cruel lunacy of American pigmentocracy."[182] Given these contributions, it is a wonder *Perez* remained unknown to so many people for so long. Why has it been thoroughly eclipsed by *Loving*? The following sections explore this question and discuss what greater attention to *Perez* could offer the study of race.

Why Are We Not "Loving" Perez?

In stark contrast to *Perez, Loving v. Virginia* holds an exalted, canonical status in the American law.[183] Forty years after it was decided, scholars continue to mine *Loving* for insights,[184] and law schools regard it as a necessary fixture in introductory constitutional law classes.[185] Perhaps because of the oddly appropriate surname of the lead plaintiffs, *Loving* also enjoys wide recognition within the non-legal community and has even been the subject of a television movie;[186] the decision seems accessible to the broader public to an extent few constitutional cases beyond *Brown v. Board of Education*,[187] or perhaps *Roe v. Wade*,[188] can claim.

---

[181] *See* Randall Kennedy, Lecture, *Race Relations Law in the Canon of Legal Academia*, 68 Fordham L. Rev. 1985, 1997 (2000).

[182] *Id.* at 1990.

[183] *See supra* note and accompanying text. Professors Jack Balkin and Sanford Levinson classify canonical legal cases as ones deemed essential to pedagogy, cultural literacy, and academic theory. *See* Balkin & Levinson, *supra* note 4, at 970–1002 (describing a canonical case as one that "reproduces" itself in "successive generations of human minds," such that it becomes seen as central to an understanding of our legal system and society).

[184] *See, e.g.*, Symposium, *Intimacy, Marriage, Race, and the Meanings of Equality: Perspectives on the 40th Anniversary of* Loving v. Virginia, 2007 Wisc. L. Rev. (2007).

[185] *See, e.g.*, Paul Brest et al., *Processes of Constitutional Decisionmaking: Cases and Materials* (4th ed. 2000); Walter F. Murphy et al., *American Constitutional Interpretation* (3d ed. 2003); Geoffrey R. Stone et al., *Constitutional Law* 529 (5th ed. 2005).

[186] *See* Mr. and Mrs. Loving (DLP Productions 1996) (starring, among others, Ruby Dee, Timothy Hutton, and Lela Rochon).

[187] 347 U.S. 483 (1954).

[188] 410 U.S. 113 (1973).

No one could seriously characterize *Loving*'s special position as undeserved. After all, *Loving* crystallized the strict scrutiny analysis under the Equal Protection Clause after the Supreme Court's important, but yet still ill-defined statements regarding the standard of review in cases such as *Brown*.[189] And *Loving* also provides the Supreme Court's first statement that the institution of marriage ranks as not only important, as decisions such as *Griswold v. Connecticut*[190] suggested, but as a fundamental right guaranteed by the Due Process Clause of the Fourteenth Amendment.[191] Still, even one who concurs fully in current assessments of *Loving*'s importance in the area of race might well ask why *Perez* has not also gained the attention of legal scholars studying issues of race and identity.

Conventional wisdom would suggest that *Perez*'s early and near complete disappearance from race law can be explained by the fact that it is the decision of a state court rather than the U.S. Supreme Court.[192] Certainly, the legal canon, particularly in the area of constitutional law, tends to be extremely Supreme Court-centered.[193] But, without more, this does not provide a complete explanation for how *Perez* has been regarded or, more appropriately, disregarded these many years.[194] Given the void created by the Supreme Court's stubborn refusal to hear matters relating to interracial marriage,[195] one could reasonably have

---

[189] Loving v. Virginia, 388 U.S. 1, 11 (1967).

[190] 381 U.S. 479 (1965).

[191] *Loving*, 388 U.S. at 12.

[192] *See* Balkin & Levinson, *supra* note 4, at 1003.

[193] *Id.*; *see also* Jill Elaine Hasday, *The Canon of Family Law*, 57 Stan. L. Rev. 825, 828 (2004). Moreover, the canon appears to be focused on a relatively small number of Supreme Court cases. Political scientist Jerry Goldman explored this issue in his article entitled *Is There a Canon of Constitutional Law?*, which surveys legal casebooks in order to identify canonical decisions. He found that although approximately twenty-two Supreme Court cases appeared regularly in most of the casebooks he surveyed, only a subset of the casebooks included each of these decisions as important or "principal" cases. Jerry Goldman, *Is There a Canon of Constitutional Law?*, 2 L. & Pol. Book Rev. 134 (1992), *available at* http://www.bsos.umd.edu/gvpt/lpbr/subpages/reviews/goldman2.htm.

[194] After all, unlike *Perez*, not all state or lower federal court cases get consigned to Never–Never Land. With respect to the common law, *Palsgraf v. Long Island R.R. Co.*, 162 N.E. 99 (N.Y. 1928), taught in most law school torts courses, provides an illustrative counterpoint to the accepted wisdom that only U.S. Supreme Court cases can tell us something about our law and our legal system. *See also* Williams v. Walker–Thomas Furniture Co., 350 F.2d 445 (D.C. Cir. 1965); Greenman v. Yuba Power Prods., Inc., 377 P.2d 897 (Cal. 1963) (en banc); Goodridge v. Dep't of Pub. Health, 798 N.E.2d 941 (Mass. 2003).

[195] *See supra* notes 171–180 and accompanying text.

expected *Perez*, which focuses on questions of federal constitutional law, to emerge as at least a significant case in the area of antimiscegenation law.

Goodridge v. Department of Public Health,[196] the Massachusetts Supreme Judicial Court's 2003 decision granting marriage rights to same-sex couples on grounds of state constitutional law, arguably plays such a role currently, as the U.S. Supreme Court has not yet addressed the issue of same-sex marriage. Even when other state courts have declined to extend similar rights to lesbian and gay couples, judges have felt compelled, at least minimally, to engage *Goodridge* as a significant decision from a sister court.[197] As previously noted, *Perez*, which is discussed in the *Goodridge* opinion, was largely denied similar recognition by other courts immediately after the California Supreme Court issued the decision.[198]

The fact that *Perez* was decided before the Supreme Court's landmark 1954 decision in *Brown* also does not provide a compelling explanation for *Perez*'s treatment. That *Perez* did not have the full benefit of the tremendous legal and moral momentum created by the civil rights strategy implemented by former Justice Thurgood Marshall and the NAACP during the 1940s and 1950s no doubt matters at some level.[199] *Loving* and its endorsement of freedom and equality in the area of interracial intimacy certainly would not have been possible without the strategic and doctrinal groundwork laid by *Brown* over a decade earlier.[200] Even so, the absence of the civil rights movement does not, for example, explain the forces that kept *Perez* from being canonized once *Brown* was decided or elucidate what keeps *Perez* from wider recognition today. Likewise, *Perez*'s limited impact on efforts to dismantle antimiscegenation laws only explains so much. After all, even *Loving* has not done all one might have expected in this area.[201]

---

[196] 798 N.E.2d 941 (Mass. 2003).

[197] *See, e.g.*, Lewis v. Harris, 908 A.2d 196 (N.J. 2006); Hernandez v. Robles, 855 N.E.2d 1 (N.Y. 2006); Andersen v. King County, 138 P.3d 963 (Wash. 2006) (en banc).

[198] *See supra* notes 169–170 and accompanying text.

[199] For a discussion of *Brown* and the NAACP's strategy in litigating that and other similar cases, see Genna Rae McNeil, *Groundwork: Charles Hamilton Houston and the Struggle for Civil Rights* 218–19 (1983).

[200] Ironically, *Loving* also might not have been possible without the foundation laid by *Perez*. Having *Perez* as a precedent obviously did not impede the Supreme Court's decision in *Loving* and may very well have inspired Chief Justice Earl Warren as he drafted his opinion.

[201] *See* Randall Kennedy, *Interracial Intimacy*, Atlantic Monthly, Dec. 2002, at 103–04. Some commentators report that public opinion remains against interracial marriage. *See* John G. Culhane, *Uprooting the Arguments Against Same-Sex Marriage*, 20 Cardozo L.

Other factors, in my view, better account for *Perez*'s virtual obscurity in legal study. One such factor relates to the opinion's failure to make
a stronger normative statement about the inherently stigmatizing effects
of California's white supremacist antimiscegenation law.[202] As already
noted, Justice Traynor focused in large part on social scientific evidence
contradicting the State's arguments concerning white intellectual and
physical superiority. In doing so, he endeavored to show that the
empirical basis for statutes limiting intimacy on racial grounds had
disappeared. This was, of course, not an entirely unworthy purpose, but
the opinion implicitly suggested that at one time there had been credible
support for the law. Justice Traynor's approach neglected the more
important principle that state laws grounded in generalizations about
the inferiority of certain races are inherently illegitimate because they
stigmatize minorities, marking them not only as sexually undesirable,
but also as unfit for full membership in the broader community.[203] In
contrast, Justice Carter's concurrence, with its contention that California's statutes had never been legitimate, avoids this pitfall.

Had Justice Traynor sought to articulate the normative concerns
that underlay his obsessive focus on the admittedly appalling sociological
evidence produced by California, *Perez* might have been viewed as a
leading case.[204] At the very least, it might have generated more of a
response from courts in other states. *Loving* itself provides indirect
support for this. Chief Justice Warren's opinion in that case has been
criticized by scholars for its inadequate articulation of the normative
reasons for the judgment.[205] In my view, however, *Loving*, for all its
deficiencies, articulates those reasons more effectively than *Perez*. With
Loving, one understands that the legal foundations of white privilege
had somehow collapsed, not merely shifted.

Rev. 1119, 1170–71 & n.243 (1999) ("[O]pinion polls . . . show that more Americans still
oppose than support interracial marriages.").

[202] For more on the problem of racial stigmatization through law, see Lenhardt, *supra*
note 70, at 852–63.

[203] *See id.* at 809.

[204] Professor Suzanne Goldberg has written persuasively about the need for courts to
articulate broader normative justifications for their decisions in cases involving civil rights.
See Suzanne B. Goldberg, *Constitutional Tipping Points: Civil Rights, Social Change, and
Fact–Based Adjudication*, 106 Colum. L. Rev. 1955 (2006).

[205] *See* Ronald J. Krotoszynski, Jr., *Dumbo's Feather: An Examination and Critique of
the Supreme Court's Use, Misuse, and Abuse of Tradition in Protecting Fundamental
Rights*, 48 Wm. & Mary L. Rev. 923, 939 (2006). The Massachusetts Supreme Judicial
Court in *Goodridge* provides a more recent example of a court's unwillingness to pull
normative punches on a controversial social issue, namely same-sex marriage. *See* Goodridge v. Dep't of Pub. Health, 798 N.E.2d 941 (Mass. 2003); Marc Spindelman, *Homosexu-
ality's Horizon*, 54 Emory L.J. 1361, 1362 (2005).

Another factor bearing on *Perez*'s obscurity concerns the extent to which it might be viewed as a case that tests the limits of the black-white paradigm.[206] For reasons that relate, among other things, to the history of slavery, Reconstruction, and the reign of Jim Crow in the United States, cases and much of the scholarship in the area of race have focused largely on the legal relationships between whites and blacks. Even though *Perez* was presented to the California Supreme Court as such a case, Andrea and Sylvester's lawsuit did not really fit this mold. *Loving*, admittedly, likely struck some people as an unusual case to the extent that it involved a black woman and a white man, rather than a romantic pairing between a black man and a white woman, the kind of interracial relationship regarded as most threatening to the white social order, particularly in the South.[207] However, it fell squarely within the ambit of the black-white paradigm.

Andrea and Sylvester constitute an altogether different story. Romantic interactions between Mexican Americans and African Americans have not been thoroughly researched. Indeed, Mexican Americans as a separate racial or cultural group have not been adequately understood.[208] As Professor Kevin Johnson recently noted, it was not until the Supreme Court's 1954 decision in *Hernandez v. Texas*,[209] holding that the Equal Protection Clause prohibited the exclusion of individuals of Mexican heritage from juries, that "the law began to recognize the social reality of Mexican Americans in the United States."[210] The unique questions about race and culture presented by California's treatment of Mexicans as white for the purposes of bans on interracial marriage are not ones that have been adequately explored.[211] What were the legal, economic, and social mechanisms by which Mexicans became white in the United States? Through what means and to what extent have they become other than white? My sense is that had these and other latent issues, such as the treatment that should be accorded so-called mixed-race individuals,[212]

---

[206] For a discussion of the black-white paradigm and its prevalence in thinking about interracial relations, see, for example, Juan F. Perea, *The Black/White Binary Paradigm of Race: The "Normal Science" of American Racial Thought*, 85 Cal. L. Rev. 1213 (1997).

[207] *See* Barbara Holden–Smith, *Lynching, Federalism, and the Intersection of Race and Gender in the Progressive Era*, 8 Yale J.L. & Feminism 31, 32 (1996).

[208] Johnson, *supra* note 9, at 171–73.

[209] 347 U.S. 475 (1954).

[210] Johnson, *supra* note 9, at 156.

[211] *But see, e.g.*, Ian Haney López, *White By Law* (10th anniv. ed. 2006).

[212] Traynor raised the mixed-race issue in trying to address the arbitrariness of the categories drawn by California and, I think, in indirectly referencing Andrea Pérez's racial background. For more on the treatment of mixed-race individuals, see Lee v. Giraudo (*In re*

not been present, *Perez* might have received the attention that it deserves.[213]

What Would "*Loving*" Perez *Teach Us That* Loving *Cannot*

The previous discussion of *Perez*'s failure to gain broader recognition as an important race case begs the question whether "loving" *Perez* at this point would have any rewards. In other words, should we regard *Perez* as a landmark case about race in the same league as *Loving*; and, if so, what would doing so tell us about antimiscegenation laws and race that *Loving* itself has not already taught us? The answer to the first question seems clear: *Perez* merits attention, if only because it provides a unique window on early applications of the Supreme Court's colorblindness principle.[214] The answer to the second question, however, may be less obvious, particularly given that *Loving* seems to have defined issues of race and antimiscegenation law for so long.

Nevertheless, there are plainly lessons *Perez* can impart to students and scholars of race that are distinct from those already conveyed by *Loving*. Ironically, initial proof of this fact may lie in some of the obstacles to *Perez*'s acceptance discussed in the previous section. As an initial matter, that *Perez* involved an African–American man and Mexican–American woman, and, thus, does not fit neatly into the black-white

---

Monks' Estate), 120 P.2d 167 (Cal. Dist. Ct. App. 1941) (rejecting plaintiff's argument that California's antimiscegenation statute effectively prohibiting any mixed-race person from marrying at all was unconstitutional); Richard R.W. Brooks, *Incorporating Race*, 106 Colum. L. Rev. 2023, 2045 n.83 (2006) (quoting Jack M. Balkin, Plessy, Brown, *and* Grutter: *A Play in Three Acts*, 26 Cardozo L. Rev. 101, 107 (2005)); Ken Nakasu Davison, *The Mixed–Race Experience: Treatment of Racially Miscategorized Individuals Under Title VII*, 12 Asian L.J. 161 (2005); Marie–Amélie George, *The Modern Mulatto: A Comparative Analysis of the Social and Legal Positions of Mulattoes in the Antebellum South and the Intersex in Contemporary America*, 15 Colum. J. Gender & L. 665 (2006).

[213] Not insignificantly, the attention *Perez* garners today in same-sex marriage cases relates primarily to the California Supreme Court's statements about marriage and not about the portions of Justice Traynor's opinion discussing issues of race. *See, e.g.,* Goodridge v. Dep't of Pub. Health, 798 N.E.2d 941, 953, 957–58 (Mass. 2003). For more on *Perez* in recent marriage litigation, see R.A. Lenhardt, *Beyond Analogy*: Perez v. Sharp, *Antimiscegenation Laws, and the Fight for Same–Sex Marriage*, 76 Cal. L. Rev. ___ (forthcoming 2008).

[214] It bears noting that in some ways, Justice Traynor arguably moved the Court's strict scrutiny analysis beyond where it had historically been taken. While the notion that race is a biological irrelevancy underlies the colorblindness principle on which strict scrutiny relies, the Court does not discuss this issue in its cases, focusing instead on the terrible history of racial discrimination in this country and the normative problems presented by governmental reliance on race. *See, e.g.,* Johnson v. California, 543 U.S. 499 (2005). In contrast, Justice Traynor, as this section explains in more detail, focused primarily on the illogic of biological accounts of race and the flaws in social science research on which such accounts depend. *See supra* notes 141–146 and accompanying text.

paradigm for race cases, focuses us on black-Latino intimate associations in ways that *Loving* never would. Even today, relationships like the one between Sylvester and Andrea are relatively rare.[215] *Perez* invites us to explore why interracial marriages involving African Americans and Latinos have not occurred at higher rates and to identify the racial norms or structural obstacles that impede such couplings.[216] Likewise, *Perez* opens the door to discussions about the nature of interactions between African Americans and Latinos more generally—for example, at work, in schools and residential neighborhoods, and in places of worship—that *Loving* seems unlikely to generate.[217] Recent tensions between African American and Latino residents in neighborhoods of Los Angeles, the place where Sylvester and Andrea's romance first took root, underscore both that such interactions are complex and that they are ripe for further study.[218]

Even more fundamentally, though, *Perez* also tells us something about race and the operation of antimiscegenation law prior to *Loving*. Although arguably less daring than the concurrence drafted by Justice Carter,[219] Justice Traynor's opinion in *Perez* was groundbreaking for more than just the conclusion it reached. His vagueness holding, in particular, seizes on an aspect of antimiscegenation law overlooked by most cases, including *Loving*—namely, the various processes by which racial identity was determined for the purposes of assessing compliance with interracial marriage restrictions.[220] In doing so, Traynor artfully

---

[215] *See* Michael J. Rosenfeld, *Measures of Assimilation in the Marriage Market: Mexican Americans 1970–1990*, 64 J. Marriage & Fam. 152, 153 (2002), *available at* http://www.stanford.edu/?mrosenfe/marital"assimilation.pdf (indicating that in 1990 only 1.4% of Mexican–American women married black men).

[216] One commentator recently noted that in recent surveys "Latinos identified African Americans as their least desirable marriage partners, whereas African Americans proved to be more accepting of intermarriage with Latinos." *See* Tanya K. Hernandez, Editorial, *Roots of Latino/Black Anger: Longtime Prejudices, Not Economic Rivalry, Fuel Tensions*, L.A. Times, Jan. 7, 2007, at M1.

[217] For a discussion of conflicts between African Americans and new immigrants, including Latinos, at work, see Jennifer Gordon & R.A. Lenhardt, *Rethinking Work and Citizenship*, 55 UCLA L. Rev. ___ (forthcoming 2008); Jennifer Gordon & R.A. Lenhardt, *Citizenship Talk: Bridging the Gap Between Race and Immigration Perspectives*, 75 Fordham L. Rev. 2493, 2516–19 (2007) [hereinafter *Citizenship Talk*].

[218] *See* Hernandez, *supra* note 216 (discussing acrimony between African Americans and Latinos in Los Angeles today); *see also* Yolanda Woodlee, *The Hunt for Work Fosters Tension: Black Residents, Latino Laborers in the Middle*, Wash. Post, Jan. 26, 2007, at B1 (discussing tensions between Latino immigrants and residents of a predominantly African–American neighborhood in Washington, D.C.).

[219] *See supra* notes 151–156 and accompanying text.

[220] The issue of how to define race was present—as it arguably was in all antimiscegenation cases—but somewhat latent in *Loving*. Virginia's adoption of the one-drop rule meant

revealed the arbitrariness of the racial hierarchy antimiscegenation laws helped to erect. His vagueness holding illustrates not only the fallacy of biological accounts of race—a theme deeply embedded in the colorblindness principle Traynor sought to apply—but also serves to underscore the critical role law has played in effecting the social construction of race in American society. In this sense, that portion of *Perez*'s majority opinion may well entitle Justice Traynor to billing as an early critical race theorist, as well as a leader in torts and other areas of the law.[221]

As indicated previously, it seems likely that Andrea's attenuated connection to whiteness prompted Traynor to consider the problem of racial definition and to reach an issue—the vagueness of California's chosen categories—not even remotely necessary to deciding the case. The discussion of "persons of mixed ancestry" in the majority opinion is probably the best evidence of Traynor's discomfort with how Andrea had been classified:

> If the statute is to be applied generally to persons of mixed ancestry the question arises whether it is to be applied on the basis of the physical appearance of the individual or on the basis of a genealogical research as to his ancestry. If the physical appearance of the individual is to be the test, the statute would have to be applied on the basis of subjective impressions of various persons. Persons having the same parents and consequently the same hereditary background could be classified differently. On the other hand, if the application of the statute to persons of mixed ancestry is to be based on genealogical research, the question immediately arises what proportions of Caucasian, Mongolian, or Malayan ancestors govern the applicability of the statute. Is it any trace of Mongolian or Malayan ancestry, or is it some unspecified proportion of such ancestry that makes a person a Mongolian or Malayan within the meaning of section 60?[222]

Obviously, Traynor focused here on the deficiencies inherent in the categories included in California law. At some level, however, the opinion is really also an indictment of the race-related rules established by other

---

that no serious inquiry into Mildred Loving's racial heritage was ever undertaken, as it was presumably clear that the requirement of "one drop" had been satisfied in Mildred's case.

[221] *See* Email from Kevin Johnson, Associate Dean for Academic Affairs & Mabie–Apallas Professor of Public Interest Law, U.C. Davis School of Law, to Robin A. Lenhardt, Associate Professor of Law, Fordham University School of Law (March 17, 2006) (on file with the author). Critical race scholars have long emphasized the role of law in constructing notions of race in the United States. *See* López, *supra* note 211.

[222] Perez v. Sharp, 198 P.2d 17, 28 (Cal. 1948).

states, and the role they played in erecting the "American pigmentocracy."[223]

As a 1948 law review article noted, states employed widely divergent and sometimes conflicting mechanisms in this area.[224] For example, in determining whether an individual was African American, some states, including Kentucky, which did not have a statute defining blackness, concentrated on the individual's "physical characteristics," like hair texture or coloring, and whether he or she could be said to have an "appreciable mixture" of black and white blood.[225] Other states identified, by statute, the precise quantum of African heritage necessary to classify someone as black.[226] At one point, Maryland used the "third generation" measure, while Florida settled on 1/16th African ancestry.[227] As time went on and interracial births increased, some Southern states applied more general tests of blackness. Louisiana at one point used what was referred to as the "appreciable degree" test.[228] Other states simply said that any African ancestry at all was enough to constitute blackness for the purposes of antimiscegenation, school segregation, or public conveyances legislation.[229] How could race mean anything at all, Justice Traynor seemed to ask, if it meant so many different and sometimes irreconcilable things to so many different people?

In registering his dissatisfaction with the methods employed by California in determining race for the purposes of antimiscegenation law,

---

[223] Kennedy, *supra* note 181, at 1990.

[224] *See* Harold Cohen, Comment, *An Appraisal of the Legal Tests Used to Determine Who Is a Negro*, 34 Cornell L.Q. 246, 247 (1948); *see also* George H. Cohen, *Who Is Legally a Negro?*, 3 Intramural L. Rev. of N.Y.U. 93–96 (April 1948) (discussing various definitions of race). It was not uncommon for states to apply one test of race in one context, say that of public school segregation, and to apply a different test in another area, such as antimiscegenation. *Id.* at 91.

[225] Harold Cohen, *supra* note 224, at 250.

[226] *Id.* at 250–51.

[227] *Id.* at 250. In contrast, Maine, in the pre-Civil War case of *Bailey v. Fiske*, decided that being 1/16th or even 1/8th African American was not enough to qualify as "Negro." *Id.* at 248 (citing Bailey v. Fiske, 34 Me. 77 (1852)).

[228] Harold Cohen, *supra* note 224, at 249.

[229] *Id.* at 250–51. Not insignificantly, each of these tests raised complex questions about the kind of evidence that could be permitted to prove or disprove blackness under the relevant measure. George Cohen, *supra* note 224, at 99. Typically, courts entertained a wide range of evidence, including ethnological research, testimony about a subject's habits and social relations (including whether the individual "sits in the white section of public conveyances or theatres"), and even physical evaluations. Harold Cohen, *supra* note 224, at 251. One researcher reports that one court, "after testimony that the formation of the Negro's foot is peculiar, . . . held [that it was] proper to require the man suspected of being colored to remove his shoes and show his bare feet to the jury." *Id.* (discussing *Daniel v. Guy*, 19 Ark. 121 (1857)).

Justice Traynor arguably endeavored to prove what he had first suggested in his oral argument colloquy with Stanley, the lawyer defending
California's antimiscegenation policy—that "there is no such thing as
race."[230] The decision to couch this truth in the language of the vagueness doctrine was, quite simply, inspired. Justice Traynor may well be,
as others have suggested, the first judge to apply notions of vagueness in
a race case.[231] That said, it bears noting that he was not the first to
conceptualize the problem of racial identification in these terms. That
honor seems to belong to the defendant in a little-known New York
Superior Court case from 1937.[232]

Ridgway v. Cockburn involved a suit by a white land owner to
enforce a restrictive covenant in the suburb of Westchester, New York,
that forbade the sale of land to African Americans.[233] Facing unfavorable
precedent—the U.S. Supreme Court's decision in *Shelley v. Kraemer*
invalidating such covenants would not be decided until 1948[234]—the
defendant, Patricia Cockburn, took one of the few options available to
her: She challenged the legality of the application of the covenant to her
particular circumstances. Cockburn's contention was that the category of
"Negro" was vague, could not be determined "without constant aid of an
anthropologist," and, in any event, arguably did not describe her racial
background.[235] More specifically, the defense, submitting an affidavit
from anthropologist Franz Boas attesting that a " 'Negro' is a person of
full West or Central African racial descent from those regions where no
admixture of foreign blood has occurred,"[236] advanced the argument that
the "defendant did not know whether or not she was a 'Negro,' although
she admitted that she had some colored blood, possibly as much as one
eighth."[237] For his part, however, the *Ridgway* judge was untroubled by
the instability of the distinctions among racial categories; he dismissed
the defendant's argument and contention that he should decide, "whether or not, as a matter of public policy, there should be any definition [of
blackness] whatsoever"[238] with barely a mention, concluding that the

---

[230] Transcript of Oral Argument at 3–4, Perez v. Sharp, 198 P.2d 17 (Cal. 1948) (No.
L.A. 20305).

[231] Orenstein, *supra* note 7, at 397.

[232] George Cohen, *supra* note 224, at 95–96.

[233] Ridgway v. Cockburn, 296 N.Y.S. 936 (N.Y. Sup. Ct. 1937). The couple purchased
the lot and then sought to construct a home on it. George Cohen, *supra* note 224, at 95.

[234] Shelley v. Kraemer, 334 U.S. 1 (1948).

[235] *Ridgway*, 296 N.Y.S. at 940; George Cohen, *supra* note 224, at 95.

[236] George Cohen, *supra* note 224, at 95.

[237] *Id.*

[238] *Id.*

blackness of both the defendant and her husband, Joshua Cockburn, had been established.[239] But the point had been made and, arguably, in a way that had repercussions as far away as California.[240]

Whatever its origins, Traynor's vagueness holding stands as a searing comment on the state of antimiscegenation law in the mid-twentieth century, a time when World War II prompted new social science research as well as changes in law and social conditions that fundamentally altered the nature of American race relations. *Perez* is an important artifact of the past. At the same time, though, the decision also suggests a future direction for students and scholars of race and its role in modern society.

Critical race theory ("CRT") has long embraced the central insight reflected in Justice Traynor's opinion in *Perez*—that the state is intimately involved in the formation of race and racial structures in our society.[241] Professor Ian Haney López's important work on the social construction of race effected through, among other things, judicial decisions in the area of immigration, provides a notable example.[242] As much as current CRT scholarship reflects this thesis about the nature of racial formation, however, there remain many as yet unexplored dimensions of race in American society. Justice Traynor's vagueness holding invites an inquiry into the particular mechanisms through which race is defined and understood today, when interracial marriage is more common than it has ever been and multiracialism has become prevalent.[243] For the most part, however, legal scholars have not yet undertaken this study. With the exception of exciting new work by Professors Devon Carbado and Mitu Gulati, few critical race scholars in the field of law have explored the precise methods by which race is currently defined and thus constructed.[244] When do determinations turn on an individual's physical

---

[239] *Ridgway*, 296 N.Y.S. at 939–42.

[240] Not insignificantly, the strategy employed in *Ridgway* ultimately had tangible benefits for the plaintiffs in that case. Events unfolded in a way that permitted them to remain in the Westchester neighborhood and home they had chosen for themselves. George Cohen, *supra* note 224, at 95–96.

[241] *See* Michael Omi & Howard Winant, *Racial Formation in the United States* 82 (2d ed. 1994).

[242] López, *supra* note 211.

[243] Mackenzie Carpenter, *Are You Melungeon, Nuyorican or What? Racial Identities Spawn New Tags*, Pittsburgh Post–Gazette (Pa.), Mar. 8, 2006, at A1.

[244] *See* Devon W. Carbado & Mitu Gulati, *Acting White* (2007) (unpublished manuscript, on file with author). Carbado and Gulati expound on notions and theories advanced in the following works: Devon W. Carbado & Mitu Gulati, *Working Identity*, 85 Cornell L. Rev. 1257 (2000); Devon W. Carbado & Mitu Gulati, *The Law and Economics of Critical Race Theory*, 112 Yale L.J. 1757 (2003).

characteristics, such as hair texture or skin coloring? When do they hinge on an individual's racial reputation or social relations? The debate now raging in the media about whether presidential candidate Senator Barack Obama, a mixed-race individual of African and white heritage, can properly be regarded as African American or merely black under-scores the salience of these and other questions, which must be explored if we are to understand what race now means in American society.

Perez requires that scholars, in trying to complicate the current picture of racial formation in the United States, also pay special atten-tion to the situation of Mexican Americans. As already noted, the unique questions about race and culture presented by California's treatment of Mexicans as white for the purposes of bans on interracial marriage are not ones that have been adequately explored.[245] A number of scholars have provided in-depth explorations of, for example, the role of the Treaty of Guadalupe Hidalgo—which, in the wake of the Mexican American War "stipulated ... that Mexica[n] [nationals] who lived within the newly annexed territory of the Southwest would be 'incorpo-rated into the Union of the United States' with the 'enjoyment of all the rights of citizens' "—in the racialization of Mexican Americans.[246] But scholars have not yet fully interrogated the issues inherent in the process by which Mexican Americans became white for some purposes (for example, marriage, as in *Perez*) and "colored" for others (for example, school segregation, as in *Westminster School District of Orange County v. Mendez*[247]). *Loving*, of course, provides little insight into such matters.

Recently, legal scholars like Ariela Gross have offered perceptive accounts of the way the law operated to racialize Mexicans in jurisdic-tions such as Texas.[248] Professors George Martinez, Kevin Johnson, and Ian Haney López also have made significant contributions on the issue of Mexican racialization.[249] Additional research, however, is required to

---

[245] *See supra* notes 41–50 and accompanying text.

[246] *See, e.g.*, Martha Menchaca, *Recovering History, Constructing Race: The Indian, Black, and White Roots of Mexican Americans* 215 (2001).

[247] 161 F.2d 774 (9th Cir. 1947) (invalidating efforts to segregate students of Mexican descent in public schools).

[248] *See* Ariela J. Gross, Comment, *Texas Mexicans and the Politics of Whiteness*, 21 L. & Hist. Rev. 195 (2003); *see also* Johnson, *supra* note 9 (discussing *Hernandez* and issues of race in Texas).

[249] *See, e.g.*, Kevin R. Johnson, *"Melting Pot" or "Ring of Fire"?: Assimilation and the Mexican–American Experience*, 85 Cal. L. Rev. 1259 (1997); López, *supra* note 39; George A. Martinez, *The Legal Construction of Race: Mexican–Americans and Whiteness*, 2 Harv. Latino L. Rev. 321 (1997). *See also* Tanya Katerí Hernández, *Afro–Mexicans and the*

obtain a more complete understanding of the ways in which the law has operated to construct the race of Mexican Americans. Besides antimiscegenation laws, what other laws or policies operated to effect Mexican whiteness? Did laws or policies pertaining to the status of Mexican Americans operate differently in the many jurisdictions where individuals of Mexican descent could be found? What benefits and disadvantages did racialization bring for Mexican Americans? How did Mexicans respond to this racialization? What tests or standards did courts and legislators apply in defining the racial status of Mexicans?

The answers to such questions will enhance our understanding of the past and the significance of the treatment Andrea Pérez received in 1947 when she sought to marry Sylvester Davis. Understanding the past in turn will lay the foundation for current debates about the place of individuals of Mexican descent in traditional racial hierarchies in the United States. The protest marches in which many Latino immigrant workers participated in the spring of 2006 demonstrate that the post–9/11 context has emerged as an important site for the racialization of Mexicans and other Latinos.[250] These events, however, fit into a larger historical pattern, one in which the racial identity of Latinos has been deeply ambiguous and hotly contested.

Conclusion

The story of Andrea Pérez and Sylvester Davis is a tale about love and its triumph over prejudice and bigotry. In this chapter, however, I have endeavored to demonstrate that it is also much more. Legal scholars should be "loving" *Perez v. Sharp*, as well as the U.S. Supreme Court's landmark decision in *Loving*. *Perez* offers new insights into antimiscegenation law and into the history of the principle of colorblindness that is now so dominant in constitutional equal protection doctrine. Justice Roger Traynor's vagueness holding in *Perez*, in particular, maps out a path that courts applying strict scrutiny have not yet followed. Further, *Perez* provides a unique window through which new or understudied questions about race and the experience of African Americans and Latinos can be accessed. *Perez* is clearly a significant decision worthy of serious study in its own right and not merely as a footnote to *Loving*.

*

Chicano Movement: The Unknown Story, 92 Cal. L. Rev. 1537 (2004) (reviewing López, *supra* note 39); Kevin R. Johnson, *How Did You Get to Be Mexican?* (1999).

250 *See* Jennifer Gordon & R.A. Lenhardt, *Citizenship Talk*, *supra* note 217. On 9/11 and race more generally, see Leti Volpp, *The Citizen and the Terrorist*, 49 UCLA L. Rev. 1575 (2002).

11

Reginald Oh & Thomas Ross

Judicial Opinions as Racial Narratives: The Story of *Richmond v. Croson*

Introduction

In *City of Richmond v. J.A. Croson Co.*,[1] a majority of the Supreme Court struck down a Richmond ordinance which set aside thirty percent of the subcontracting work on city construction jobs for minority firms.[2] The majority concluded that the ordinance denied white contractors "equal protection of the laws."[3] Justice Thurgood Marshall, dissenting, characterized the Richmond decision as "a deliberate and giant step backward in the Court's affirmative action jurisprudence."[4]

The *Croson* decision is one of the most important chapters in the Court's evolving jurisprudence on colorblindness and color-conscious remedies. The case is an important turning point, in which the imperative of colorblindness is used both to dismantle the legacy of slavery and Jim Crow segregation and to question the legitimacy of government initiatives to mitigate racial inequality. The case's importance derives not only from the doctrinal position the Court stakes out but also from competing narratives about race in the opinions. The "*Croson* narratives" tell stories that reveal a great deal, and not just about affirmative action. They reveal, with special clarity, the deeper nature of our struggle to move to a world in which discriminatory subordination on the basis of race truly has no place, no purpose, no logic.

---

[1] 488 U.S. 469 (1989).

[2] *See id.* at 486 (plurality opinion).

[3] *Id.* at 493.

[4] *Id.* at 529 (Marshall, J., dissenting).

After setting forth the procedural history of the litigation, the chapter discusses the importance of the *Croson* decision for the evolution of affirmative action jurisprudence. Next, the analysis draws on narrative theory to argue that opinions tell stories. The chapter then unpacks the legal narratives that constitute the *Croson* opinions. More specifically, Justice Sandra Day O'Connor's plurality opinion is contrasted with the differing legal narratives that Justice Antonin Scalia and Justice Marshall constructed. While Justice Scalia's abstract narrative relies on rhetorical devices to reinforce prevailing views about the dangers of affirmative action, Marshall's narrative provides historical detail to inform readers about the racism experienced by African Americans in Richmond.

Notwithstanding the normative power of Justice Marshall's dissent, the narrative he articulates is limited in at least one respect: the geographic boundary within which it is situated. His narrative could have told an even richer, more edificatory story about racism if the geographic scale of his narrative had been expanded beyond the jurisdictional boundaries of the city of Richmond. When the narratives in *Croson* are understood as not just about race relations within the city of Richmond but also about race relations between blacks in the city of Richmond and whites in the Richmond suburbs, a much fuller account of the racism experienced by African Americans emerges. The chapter concludes with some final observations about the important role that the *Croson* decision has played in undermining the possibility of truly achieving a colorblind society.

Croson *and the Story of Affirmative Action*

As Rachel Moran's contribution to this volume attests, the constitutionality of affirmative action has been perhaps the most divisive and difficult question of contemporary constitutional jurisprudence. Affirmative action demands the paradoxical solution of first taking account of race in order to get to a world in which it is not taken into account. *Richmond v. Croson* is a pivotal case in the Court's evolving approach to this paradox. Prior to the *Croson* decision, the Court through its decisions in *Regents of the University of California v. Bakke*,[5] *United Steelworkers of America v. Weber*,[6] and *Fullilove v. Klutznick*,[7] gave some measure of deference to government-sponsored race-conscious programs aimed at remedying the continuing effects of past and present racial subordination and segregation.

---

[5] 438 U.S. 265, 284–87 (1978).

[6] 443 U.S. 193, 204–09 (1979).

[7] 448 U.S. 448, 490–492 (1980).

However, in *Wygant v. Jackson Board of Education*,[8] a plurality of the Court struck down an affirmative action program. In doing so, these Justices suggested that strict scrutiny ought to apply, not only to invidious racial classifications targeting discrete and insular racial minorities, but even to "benign racial classifications"—that is, racial classifications intended to help rather than harm people of color. Under strict scrutiny, a governmental decision is constitutional only if it serves a "compelling state interest" and the means chosen to achieve those interests are "narrowly tailored" to minimize the harms associated with the government's explicit use of race. As the most rigorous standard of review under equal protection, the Court rarely upholds laws that it reviews under strict scrutiny.

In *Croson*, a majority of the Court took heed of the *Wygant* Court's reasoning and held that race-conscious affirmative action programs, at least those enacted by state and local governments, should not receive deference but instead must be subject to the most rigorous judicial scrutiny. Before explaining why the Court reached this conclusion, it is helpful to know how the case got to the Supreme Court.

The Procedural History of Richmond v. Croson

The lawsuit began when the J.A. Croson Company, a corporation with its principal place of business in Ohio, filed a lawsuit challenging the constitutionality of the City of Richmond's refusal to accept its bid on a plumbing contract. Although Croson was the only bidder on the construction project, the City declared that Croson's bid was a nonresponsive bid because it had failed to comply with the City of Richmond's Minority Business Utilization Plan. The plan required that prime contractors who were awarded city construction contracts had to subcontract at least thirty percent of the dollar amount of each contract to "minority business enterprises."[9] A "minority business enterprise" was defined as any business at least fifty-one percent owned or controlled by "citizens of the United States who are Blacks, Spanish-speaking, Orientals, Indians, Eskimos, or Aleuts."[10] In its complaint, Croson contended that the City of Richmond's minority set-aside program exceeded the scope of its powers under state law, and that it violated the Fourteenth Amendment Equal Protection Clause because the ordinance discriminated on the basis of race.

Croson filed its lawsuit in the Commonwealth of Virginia before the Circuit Court of the City of Richmond. Pursuant to the federal removal

---

[8] 476 U.S. 267, 274–76 (1986).

[9] *Id.* at 477.

[10] *Id.* at 478 (quoting Richmond, Va., City Code § 12–23 (Apr. 11, 1983)).

statute, the defendant City of Richmond removed the case to the United States District Court for the Eastern District of Virginia. The Honorable Robert R. Merhige heard the case. He was the same judge who had presided over the Richmond school desegregation lawsuit in the early 1970s and ruled that the proper remedy for school segregation was interdistrict busing between city and suburban schools.[11] The United States Court of Appeals for the Fourth Circuit overruled his desegregation decision and the Supreme Court, in a 4–4 per curiam decision, affirmed the Fourth Circuit's opinion.[12]

Once again protective of color-conscious remedies, Judge Merhige rejected Croson's equal protection challenge and upheld the set-aside program. He reasoned that the set-aside was a constitutional means of remedying racial exclusion in the Richmond construction industry. Croson appealed the district court's decision to the Fourth Circuit Court of Appeals; a divided 2–1 panel affirmed the district court's ruling.[13] Croson then petitioned for a writ of *certiorari* in the United States Supreme Court. The Supreme Court granted the writ, vacated the Fourth Circuit's decision, and remanded the case. The Supreme Court directed the court of appeals to reconsider its decision in light of the recent Supreme Court decision in *Wygant v. Jackson Board of Education,* a case in which a plurality of the Court struck down a local school district's affirmative action plan under strict scrutiny.[14] On remand, a divided panel of the Fourth Circuit Court of Appeals reversed its earlier ruling and held that, under *Wygant,* the City of Richmond's plan must be reviewed under strict scrutiny. Under this standard, the plan failed because it was not narrowly tailored to promote a compelling state interest.[15]

The City of Richmond petitioned for writ of *certiorari* in the United States Supreme Court. The Court granted the petition, and in 1989, the Court upheld the Fourth Circuit's ruling, holding that the plan violated equal protection.

The Importance of the Croson Decision

Croson marked the first time that a majority of the Court agreed upon strict scrutiny as the standard of review when determining the constitutionality of race-conscious affirmative action programs. In justifying its holding, the Court laid down the doctrinal and rhetorical foundation for its current colorblind affirmative action jurisprudence. In

---

[11] Bradley v. Richmond Sch. Bd., 325 F. Supp. 828 (E.D. Va. 1971).

[12] School Bd. of Richmond v. State Bd. of Ed., 412 U.S. 92 (1973).

[13] J.A. Croson Co. v. City of Richmond, 779 F.2d 181 (4th Cir. 1985).

[14] 478 U.S. 1016 (1986).

[15] 822 F.2d 1355, 1357 (4th Cir. 1987).

Adarand v. Pena, the Court applied *Croson* to federal government set-asides and held that the principle of consistency required that they too must be subject to strict scrutiny.[16] In *Grutter v. Bollinger*[17] and *Gratz v. Bollinger,*[18] the Court again reaffirmed the *Croson* Court's emphatic declaration that any race-conscious affirmative action plan must be subject to strict scrutiny, whether the program seeks to aid struggling minority owned businesses, or whether it seeks to racially integrate institutions of higher education. More recently in *Parents Involved in Community Schools v. Seattle School District,* the Supreme Court relied on the reasoning of *Croson* and it progeny to subject voluntary school desegregation programs in elementary and secondary public schools to strict scrutiny.[19]

The fact that the doctrinal approach the Court took in *Croson* is now firmly a part of affirmative action jurisprudence should not obscure the fact that *Croson* deeply fractured the Court and spawned six separate opinions with six separate narratives. Each narrative is rich. Justice O'Connor's opinion provides the primary justification for the majority's decision, but the most powerful, complex, and important narratives are the concurring opinion by Justice Scalia[20] and the dissenting opinion by Justice Marshall.[21] For over a decade, Scalia and Marshall occupied the contemporary Court's most extreme positions on the issue of affirmative action: Scalia consistently opposed the programs and Marshall consistently supported them.[22] On doctrinal grounds alone, their divergent approaches to affirmative action deserve careful attention. But there is another reason for paying attention to their opinions. They exemplify two forms of narrative that run through contemporary affirmative action cases: a contextual narrative that attends to the present and historical specificities of race; and a decontextualized narrative in which race is abstracted from its material realities. Before revealing the precise form that these narratives take in Scalia's and Marshall's opinions, the next section draws on narrative theory to explain why it is important to conceptualize judicial opinions as narratives.

---

[16] Adarand v. Pena, 515 U.S. 200 (1995).

[17] Grutter v. Bollinger, 539 U.S. 306 (2003).

[18] Gratz v. Bollinger, 539 U.S. 244 (2003).

[19] Parents Involved in Comty. Sch. v. Seattle School Dist., No. 1, 127 S.Ct. 2738 (2007).

[20] *See* Croson, 488 U.S. at 520–28 (Scalia, J., concurring).

[21] *See id.* at 528–61 (Marshall, J., dissenting).

[22] Justice Scalia's absolute opposition to affirmative action predates his judicial career. "I am, in short, opposed to racial affirmative action for reasons of both principle and practicality." Antonin Scalia, *The Disease as Cure,* 1979 *Wash. U. L.Q.* 147, 156.

Judicial Opinions as Narrative

In the desperate struggle to make sense of a world in which the very idea and possibility of "making sense" is questioned, people latch on to various ideas that somehow may provide meaning, even in the post-everything world. "Hermeneutics,"[23] "metaphor,"[24] and even forms of "hopeful nihilism"[25] are embraced. Narrative is yet another potential mooring.[26] A narrative is an account of events, a story. The telling of a narrative is "someone telling someone else that something happened."[27]

The question of what it is that makes a list of events into a narrative is central to narrative theorizing.[28] A list of apparently random

---

[23] *See generally* Richard Bernstein, *Beyond Objectivism and Relativism: Science, Hermeneutics, and Praxis* 109–69 (1983) (discussing how philosophic hermeneutics help to clarify and deepen understanding of lessons learned from the post-empiricist philosophy and history of science); Hans Gadamer, *Truth and Method* 146 (1975) (proposing that a hermeneutical understanding of art is part of the aesthetic experience); David Hoy, *The Critical Circle: Literature, History, and Philosophical Hermeneutics passim* (1978) (an investigation of the development of the hermeneutic circle and the influence that the development and changes in meaning of this concept have had on philosophical inquiry); David Hoy, *Interpreting the Law: Hermeneutical and Post Structuralist Perspectives,* 58 S. Cal. L. Rev. 136, 136–137 (1985) (discussing the practical limits of the hermeneutics in legal interpretation).

[24] *See generally* Milner Ball, *Lying Down Together: Law, Metaphor, and Theology* 21–36 (1985) (examining numerous conceptual metaphors for the legal system); Max Black, *Models and Metaphors* 25–47 (1962) (discussing modern methods of interpreting metaphors); Ivor Armstrong Richards, *The Philosophy of Rhetoric* 89–138 (1936) (discussing the uses and limitations of metaphors); James B. White, *When Words Lose Their Meaning: Constitutions and Reconstitutions of Language, Character, and Community* [hereinafter James B. White, *When Words*] 205–08 (1984) (examining the use and significance of metaphor in Edmund Burke's *Reflections on the Revolution in France*); Paul Ricoeur, *The Metaphorical Process as Cognition, Imagination, and Feeling,* 5 Critical Inquiry 143, 143 (1978) (discussing the role imagination and feeling in the interpretation of metaphor); Thomas Ross, *Metaphor and Paradox,* 23 Ga. L. Rev. 1053, 1083–84 (1989) (discussing the need to confront legal metaphors in order to comprehend the power and effects of the law).

[25] *See generally* Joseph Singer, *The Player and the Cards: Nihilism and Legal Theory* 94 Yale L.J. 1, 9, 66–70 (1984) (discussing "hopeful nihilism" and the critical legal studies movement).

[26] *See, e.g., On Narrative* (W.J.T. Mitchell ed. 1980) (a collection of essays exploring the role of narrative in social and psychological formations). The work of Hayden White on historical narrativity is especially powerful. *See* Hayden White, *Metahistory: The Historical Imagination in Nineteenth Century Europe* (1973); *see also* Paul Ricoeur, *Time and Narrative* ix (1984) (viewing narrative as a means of unifying and understanding the world).

[27] "Accordingly, we might conceive of narrative discourse most minimally and most generally as verbal acts consisting of *someone telling someone else that something happened.*" Barbara Herrnstein Smith, *Narrative Versions, Narrative Theories,* in *On Narrative, supra* note 26, at 209.

[28] *See* Paul Ricoeur, *Time and Narrative* ix (1984) (viewing narrative as a means of

events: "I drove to the office; my friend, Welsh, went to a chess tournament last weekend; there was a bird outside my window a moment ago," is not a story. Of course, in a different context, between a particular storyteller and a particular story reader—for example, between me and my analyst—this list might become narrative. Yet, in the context of reading this chapter, the list of events lacks that essential something that might make it a narrative. Whatever that essential something is, the narrativity is in the reading, in a shared context. Thus, the possibility of narrative, as well as the texture of the narrative, arises in the reading, and hence, in part from the reader.

Reading opinions as narratives is not a new idea. James Boyd White has pushed this interpretational approach for some time.[29] According to White, "the narrative is the archetypal legal and rhetorical form, as it is the archetypal form of human thought in ordinary life as well."[30] It is through narrative, says White, that a community constitutes itself.[31] Robert Cover powerfully expressed the place of narrative in law:

> In [the] normative world, law and narrative are inseparably related. Every prescription is insistent in its demand to be located in discourse—to be supplied with history and destiny, beginning and end, explanation and purpose. And every narrative is insistent in its demand for its prescriptive point, its moral. History and literature cannot escape their location in a normative universe, nor can prescription, even when embodied in a legal text, escape its origin and its end in experience, in the narratives that are the trajectories plotted upon material reality by our imaginations.[32]

Opinions are, and are not, narratives. They are, after all, formal texts located in a particular process. Opinions are not literature, or some other sort of fictional story; neither are opinions historical expositions,

---

unifying and understanding the world).

[29] *See, e.g.,* James B. White, *Heracles' Bow: Essays on the Rhetoric and Poetics of Law* 139–91 (1985) [hereinafter *Heracles' Bow*] (arguing that "ostensibly 'factual' narratives are also necessarily 'fictional' and . . . necessarily express 'values' as well"); James B. White, *The Legal Imagination: Studies in the Nature of Legal Thought and Expression* 430–501, 858–925 (1973) (discussing the legal use of the language of race and the narrative imagination); James B. White, *When Words, supra* note 24, at 264–70 (discussing the conversational process of the law); James B. White, *Thinking About Our Language*, 96 Yale L.J. 1960, 1961 (1987) (asserting "the value and primacy of . . . literary discourse over a certain kind of academic language").

[30] *See Heracles' Bow, supra* note 29, at 175.

[31] *See id.* at 172 ("I say the process of storytelling is both collective and individual. One could go further and say that the idea of community itself depends upon both language and story: a community is a group of people who tell a shared story in a shared language.").

[32] *Id.* at 175.

or some other form of factual storytelling. An opinion often contains what most would call a story—a recitation of the facts. Yet, we do not naturally read opinions as narratives. To do so takes conscious intellectual effort.

On the other hand, one can read opinions as narratives without a substantial distortion of either the idea of "narrative," or the function and apparent nature of the judicial opinion. Judges, as storytellers, tell their audiences that something happened. The "something" that happened is the process of choice. Judges choose to exercise their power in a particular way and tell the story of their choice—a story that readers are asked to understand as inevitable rather than contingent. Society generally accepts the notion of judges (or lawyers) crafting their version of the "facts," telling the story their way, yet pretending that the events speak for themselves.[33] To this extent, we have known for some time that opinions are, in part, stories.

In organizing and interpreting events according to a narrative structure, courts actively construct and produce their versions of social reality, versions which then become codified in legal doctrine.[34] Contrary to the conventional view of judicial lawmaking, instead of taking established facts and mechanically applying the law to them, courts actually create narrative accounts of social reality and then make legal judgments and decisions based on their narrative accounts.[35]

When we understand that courts engage in the invisible process of constructing narratives as a precondition to making legal decisions, we can better understand how law actively constructs dominant, inequality-reinforcing visions of social reality.[36] Social reality can be defined as "the bundle of presuppositions, received wisdom, and shared understandings against a background of which legal and political discourse takes place."[37] A narrative construction of social reality makes sense of human

---

[33] " '[T]he objectivity of narrative is defined by the absence of all reference to the narrator.' . . . The events are chronologically recorded as they appear on the horizon of the story. Here no one speaks. The events seem to tell themselves." Hayden White, *The Value of Narrativity in the Representation of Reality, in On Narrative, supra* note 26, (quoting Emile Benveniste, *Problems in General Linguistics* 208 (Mary Elizabeth Meek trans. 1971)).

[34] *See* Mark Kelman, *Interpretative Construction in Substantive Criminal Law*, 33 Stan. L. Rev. 591, 593 (1981).

[35] *Id.*

[36] *See* Peter Kollock & Jodi O'Brien, *The Production of Reality: Essays and Readings on Social Interaction* 541–42 (2d ed. 1997) (realizing that judges and juries are limited in their search for the truth and thus are merely able to reconstruct the truth within the confines of the law).

[37] Richard Delgado, *Storytelling for Oppositionists and Others: A Plea for Narrative*, 87 Mich. L. Rev. 2411, 2413 (1989).

behavior and the structures of everyday life.[38] Certain narratives operate to rationalize and justify existing institutions and structures of inequality and subordination.[39] For example, narratives about the relationship between unregulated markets and the accumulation of societal wealth help to rationalize socioeconomic inequality as a natural and necessary by-product of economic efficiency.[40]

Legal narratives, in particular, can be especially powerful in reinforcing dominant constructions of social reality, because they have the weight and imprimatur of state authority behind them.[41] In a legal dispute, a judge has to choose between competing narrative constructions of what happened in the past, declare one story over another as the definitively true version, and create rights or impose liability on a party based on the story that he or she has chosen to be the "truth."[42] When a court chooses a particular narrative over another, the chosen narrative becomes the official government truth, and therefore becomes even more powerful as rhetoric in public discourse precisely because that particular narrative now has the sanction and force of the law. In short, law consists of stories given authority and truth by virtue of being told and validated by a judge.

Do all legal narratives operate to reinforce prevailing, status quo-reinforcing views of social reality? The answer is no. As Critical Race Scholars contend, outsider narratives have the power and potential to challenge dominant views of social reality. Outsider narratives are stories told by members of subordinated groups whose voices have historically been silenced and marginalized.[43] Such stories carry the potential for social transformation, because they educate people about how racism and subordination operate and thus they can provide a map for dismantling structures of inequality and for constructing new, more egalitarian institutions.

---

[38] *See id.* at 2412–15 (interpreting stories told by different groups within the population to demonstrate how each version of the same story presents a different reality).

[39] Patrick Ewick & Susan S. Silbey, *Subversive Stories and Hegemonic Tales: Toward Sociology of Narrative*, 29 Law & Soc'y Rev. 197, 212 (1995).

[40] *See id.* at 213 ("finding that in society, narratives further the existing structures of meaning and power").

[41] *Cf. id.* at 208–09 (noting that judges exercise control over the law by the use of limited narratives as a means to convey a certain side of a story that only advances certain goals, while ignoring other facts or characterizations that change the story).

[42] *See id.* at 209 (noting also that lawyers only allow witnesses to tell facts that enhance the lawyer's version of the story, and that the lawyer intervenes when a witness continues to speak beyond what the lawyer requires).

[43] *See* Delgado, *supra* note 37, at 2412; see also Angela P. Harris, *The Jurisprudence of Reconstruction*, 82 Cal. L. Rev. 741 (1994).

Two forms of narrative are relevant to the discussion of *Richmond v. Croson*. Those forms are abstract legal narratives and contextual legal narratives. An abstract narrative lacks historical detail and instead is filled with formal principles and metaphors. This type of narrative does not actually tell stories, but instead invites readers to fill in the abstractions and metaphors with their own beliefs, assumptions, and stories. Because readers must draw on their own experience and imagination to interpret the narrative, it rationalizes pre-existing beliefs and assumptions. As a result, an abstract narrative tends not to produce new information or knowledge.

On the other hand, a well-told contextual legal narrative provides rich factual and historical detail of people and events as a way to illuminate understanding of a particular doctrinal issue. This kind of narrative tells a story about specific people in particular places in particular times. Because the story provides information that readers previously did not have, the narrative educates them. In educating readers about events, people, and places with which they are not familiar, a contextual narrative can help readers to empathize with the story's "characters." A contextual legal narrative produces new knowledge for the reader, new ways of understanding the world and the law. And, to the extent that these stories produce new knowledge that challenges status quo-reinforcing beliefs, contextual narratives have the power to raise awareness about racial subordination and the law's role in rectifying or reinforcing this injustice.

The Legal Narratives in Croson[44]

It is with this understanding of abstract legal narratives and contextual legal narratives that we now turn to the opinions in *Richmond v. Croson.*

Justice O'Connor's Narrative

Notwithstanding the choice to focus on Scalia's and Marshall's narratives, the backdrop to their stories must be built. Although each of the opinions teaches something about its author, neither can be properly understood without an explication of the plurality opinion by Justice O'Connor.[45] Justice O'Connor's opinion failed to garner the full support of a majority of the Justices, even though it became the controlling view of the case. That said, her narrative struggles to find a cohesive center and actually creates the void that Scalia's and Marshall's stories seek to fill. Beyond its essential plurality status on the headcount, one cannot make sense of O'Connor's opinion as "the voice" of the Court. It is a

---

[44] This part of the chapter borrows heavily from Thomas Ross's *The Richmond Narratives*, 68 Tex. L. Rev. 381 (1989).

[45] *See Croson*, 488 U.S. at 476–511 (plurality opinion).

remarkably tortured piece of work. The opinion divides the Court so deeply that it is essentially impossible to discern a coherent legal structure to which a majority of the Court commits.[46] The fact that a majority joined only O'Connor's recitation of the facts and her application of strict scrutiny to these facts is itself revealing. She could hold the center only when making highly fact-dependent assertions that turned on the particularities of the Richmond set-aside program. The splintering of the Justices is partly a product of the twisted narrative that O'Connor tells.

After the initial recitation of the facts, which is rhetorically crafted in a fairly ordinary way, O'Connor's opinion addresses a somewhat peripheral issue, namely, whether the city of Richmond has the "power" to enact affirmative action legislation.[47] This then leads to the second part of her opinion: an inquiry into legislative power, as distinguished from the constitutionality of the enacted law.[48] In particular, she asks whether the political branches can enforce the mandate of equal protection by going further than the Constitution requires. More specifically, she analyzes whether political actors can employ race-conscious remedies despite a formal norm of colorblindness under the Fourteenth Amendment's guarantee of equal protection.

The quarrel, for Justice O'Connor, is over whether *Fullilove* or *Wygant* controls.[49] She concludes that neither case is dispositive.[50] *Fullilove*'s apparent concession of legislative power is not controlling for O'Connor because that case concerned federal statutes, and Congress, she concludes, is especially empowered under the Fourteenth Amendment.[51] *Wygant* does not control Richmond because that lawsuit involved

---

[46] Only Justices William Rehnquist and Byron White joined in O'Connor's entire opinion. Justices John Paul Stevens and Anthony Kennedy joined to create a majority for parts I, III(B), and IV only. Justice Kennedy also joined parts III(A) and V. Justice Scalia concurred in the judgment. Justices Marshall, William Brennan, and Harry Blackmun dissented, with Marshall and Blackmun writing dissenting opinions. *See id.* at 475.

[47] *See id.* at 486. "The parties and their supporting amici fight an initial battle over the scope of the city's power to adopt legislation designed to address the effects of past discrimination." *Id.*

[48] *See id.* at 486–93.

[49] *See, e.g.,* Wygant v. Jackson Bd. Of Educ., 476 U.S. 267, 284 (1986) (holding school board policy giving preferential protection to minority personnel during layoffs was unconstitutional); Fullilove v. Klutznick, 448 U.S. 448, 492 (1980) (holding requirement that specified percentage of federal public works funds go to minority owned businesses was not unconstitutional).

[50] *See Croson,* 488 U.S. at 486 (plurality opinion). "We find that neither of these two rather stark alternatives can withstand analysis." *Id.*

[51] *See id* at 488. "What appellant ignores is that Congress, unlike any State or political subdivision, has a specific constitutional mandate to enforce the dictates of the fourteenth

the action of a school board, presumably a less-empowered body than a city council.[52] Justice O'Connor concludes that a "local subdivision (if delegated the authority from the state) has the authority to eradicate the effects of private discrimination within its own legislative jurisdiction."[53] She also concludes that "if the city could show that it had essentially become a 'passive participant' in a system of racial exclusion practiced by elements of the local construction industry, . . . it is clear that the city could take affirmative steps to dismantle such a system."[54]

In the third part of her opinion, O'Connor directly addresses the equal protection issue.[55] Her formal discourse on the appropriate level of judicial review does not win the support of a majority of the Justices.[56] O'Connor concludes that strict scrutiny is the appropriate standard of review for the Richmond ordinance.[57] In doing so, she offers the common arguments of paternalism ("preferential programs may only reinforce common stereotypes")[58] and equality as symmetry ("the guarantee of equal protection cannot mean one thing when applied to one individual and something else when applied to a person of another color").[59]

O'Connor also makes a special argument for strict scrutiny in Richmond—one built around the phrase, "simple racial politics,"[60] and the fact that "blacks comprise approximately fifty percent of the population of the city of Richmond . . . and five of the nine seats on the City

---

Amendment. . . . Thus our treatment of an exercise of congressional power in Fullilove cannot be dispositive here." *Id*. at 490 (citing Fullilove v. Klutznick, 448 U.S. 448 (1980)).

[52] *See id*. at 491–92. "As a matter of state law, the city of Richmond has legislative authority over its procurement policies, and can use its spending powers to remedy private discrimination, if it identifies that discrimination with the particularity required by the Fourteenth Amendment. To this extent, on the question of the city's competence, the Court of Appeals erred in following *Wygant* by rote in a case involving a state entity which has state-law authority to address discriminatory practices within local commerce under its jurisdiction." *Id*. at 492.

[53] *Id*. at 491–92.

[54] *Id*. at 492.

[55] *See id*. at 493–506.

[56] *Id*.

[57] *See id*. at 493–94. Justice O'Connor refers to the need for "searching judicial inquiry" and "strict scrutiny." *Id*. at 493. She criticizes Justice Marshall's alternative intermediate scrutiny test, calling it a "watered-down" version of equal protection review. *Id*. at 494–95 (plurality opinion).

[58] *Id*. at 494 (quoting Regents of the Univ. of Cal. v. Bakke, 438 U.S. 265, 298 (1978)).

[59] *Id*. (quoting Regents of the Univ. of Cal. v. Bakke, 438 U.S. 265, 298–90 (1978)).

[60] She refers in two passages to the special danger of "racial politics" in this case. *Id*. at 493–94, 510.

Council are held by blacks."[61] O'Connor concludes that "the concern that a political majority black will more easily act to the disadvantage of a minority white ... would seem to militate for ... the application of heightened judicial scrutiny."[62] For O'Connor, the presence of five blacks on the Richmond city council justifies strict judicial scrutiny to smoke out simple racial politics.[63]

O'Connor's version of strict scrutiny requires a "factual predicate" of past discrimination in the Richmond construction industry; such a showing would constitute a compelling state interest.[64] A majority of the Court joins the portion of her opinion that focuses on this question.[65] O'Connor argues that Richmond merely offered a "generalized assertion" and an "amorphous claim" of past discrimination in the Richmond construction industry.[66] She dismisses the reliance on the huge statistical disparity between the black population of Richmond and the black community's participation in public contracting as the wrong comparison.[67] The relevant comparison, according to O'Connor, is between the number of qualified black contractors in the Richmond market and the amount of the city construction work in which they participate—evidence that the Richmond city council failed to gather.[68] With regard to the demonstrated absence of blacks in the Richmond contractors' associations, O'Connor says:

> [S]tanding alone this evidence is not probative of any discrimination in the local construction industry. There are numerous explanations for this dearth of minority participation, including past societal

---

[61] Id. at 495.

[62] Id. at 496.

[63] See id. at 493 ("[T]he purpose of strict scrutiny is to 'smoke out' illegitimate uses of race...."). Justice Marshall characterizes this argument as insulting and unworthy of a place in constitutional jurisprudence. See id. at 554–55 (Marshall, J., dissenting).

[64] "In sum, none of the evidence presented by the city points to any identified discrimination in the Richmond construction industry. We, therefore, hold that the city has failed to demonstrate a compelling interest in apportioning public contract opportunities on the basis of race." Croson, 488 U.S. at 505 (plurality opinion).

[65] See id. at 498–506.

[66] See id. at 498–99. "[A] generalized assertion that there has been past discrimination in an entire industry provides no guidance for a legislative body to determine the precise scope of the injury it seeks to remedy.... [A]n amorphous claim that there has been past discrimination in a particular industry cannot justify the use of an unyielding racial quota." Id.

[67] See id. at 501.

[68] See id. at 501–02 ("[W]here special qualifications are necessary, the relevant statistical pool for purposes of demonstrating discriminatory exclusion must be the number of minorities qualified to undertake the particular task.").

discrimination in education and economic opportunities as well as both black and white career and entrepreneurial choices. Blacks may be disproportionately attracted to industries other than construction.[69]

This statement permits her to reason that "none of the evidence presented by the city points to any identified discrimination in the Richmond construction industry."[70] Therefore, she concludes, no compelling interest was demonstrated to justify the ordinance's burdening of the white contractors.[71]

Although the absence of a compelling interest might have terminated the equal protection analysis, in the fourth part of the opinion, O'Connor again writes for a majority in addressing the "means" or "narrow tailoring" question.[72] She observes that there is no evidence that the Richmond city council considered "race neutral" measures to increase minority participation.[73] Moreover, because Richmond awards its construction contracts on a case-by-case basis, she does not understand why a racial quota is needed.[74] The city, she says, could investigate the need for remedial action in each individual contracting process.[75] O'Connor suggests that a quota is merely a device being used to avoid

---

[69] *Id.* at 503.

[70] *Id.* at 505.

[71] *Id.*

[72] *See id.* at 507.

[73] *See id.*

[74] *See id.* at 508.

[75] *See id.* "Given the existence of an individualized procedure, the city's only interest in maintaining a quota system rather than investigating the need for remedial action in particular cases would seem to be simple administrative convenience." *Id.* In this discussion of the "means" issue, Justice O'Connor reiterates her concern about the ordinance's inclusion of non-black minorities, "under Richmond's scheme, a successful black, Hispanic, or Oriental entrepreneur from anywhere in the country enjoys an absolute preference over other citizens based solely on their race. We think it obvious that such a program is not narrowly tailored to remedy the effects of prior discrimination." *Id.* In her earlier reference to the ordinance's inclusion of non-black minorities as beneficiaries she remarks, "[i]t may well be that Richmond has never had an Aleut or Eskimo citizen." *Id.* at 506. While these observations support the rather obvious point that Richmond's set-aside ordinance was not structured to assure that only actual victims of specific racial discrimination would benefit, they may undercut her "racial politics" specter. If the blacks on Richmond's city council were engaged in simple racial politics, they might have chosen to limit the beneficiaries to their own race. Moreover, O'Connor must know that this feature of the Richmond ordinance was obviously patterned after the federal scheme validated in *Fullilove. See Croson*, 488 U.S. at 486–87 (plurality opinion).

the bureaucratic effort of looking for real discrimination in particular cases.[76]

The fifth and final part of O'Connor's opinion is noteworthy in two respects. Moving away from her fact-specific analysis of the Richmond program, she again loses her majority. O'Connor initially seems to leave room for the possibility of constitutional affirmative action programs.[77] "In the extreme case, some form of narrowly tailored racial preference might be necessary to break down patterns of deliberate exclusion."[78] However, she reiterates that any affirmative action measure must be supported by ample findings to ensure that it is not the product of racial politics.[79]

As a whole, Justice O'Connor's opinion is extraordinary. Only several disconnected pieces of the opinion commanded a majority, thus producing one of the most complex "scorecards" of the Justices in history. The opinion relies mostly on the idea of racial politics to justify a nigh impassable conception of strict scrutiny.[80] O'Connor not only invokes the idea of racial politics, but she also discredits or ignores the evidence adduced by the city council and the judgment of the council. In effect, her opinion stands for the proposition that the city council members cannot be trusted because they are black people voting on an affirmative action law.[81]

O'Connor's opinion splinters the Court, is hard to follow, and is unclear as to her holding on the question of affirmative action. Scalia and Marshall do not have similar problems; both express the clearest possible vision of the constitutionality of affirmative action. Scalia and Marshall want to distance themselves from O'Connor's opinion. Scalia

---

[76] *See Croson*, 488 U.S. at 508 (plurality opinion). She does not, however, explain exactly how this inquiry would proceed when, for example, all of the bids received for a city construction job might happen to come from white contractors, each using white subcontractors. *See id.*

[77] *See id.* at 509–10.

[78] *Id.* at 509.

[79] *See id.* at 510–11.

[80] *See id.* at 493.

[81] In her discussion of the council's findings, Justice O'Connor speaks of "simple legislative assurance of good intention," "the highly conclusionary statement of a proponent of the Plan," and "unsupported assumption[s]." *Id.* at 500–502. Unpersuaded by the argument that the fact-finding process of legislative bodies is entitled to some degree of judicial deference, she uses an ironic precedent to support her non-deferential posture. "The history of racial classifications in this country suggests that blind judicial deference to legislative or executive pronouncements of necessity has no place in equal protection analysis." *Id.* at 501 (citing Korematsu v. United States, 323 U.S. 214 (1944) (Murphy, J., dissenting)).

concurs only in the judgment,[82] and Marshall dissents.[83] Scalia and Marshall seem to share nothing except the strength of their respective convictions. But each opinion tells us much about the nature and power of opinions as narratives.

Justice Scalia's Abstract Legal Narrative and the White Imagination

Scalia's opinion is, in structure and purpose, straightforward. He constructs a series of arguments, each related to his central thesis that affirmative action must be severely circumscribed. "In my view there is only one circumstance in which the states may act by race 'to undo the effects of past discrimination': where that is necessary to eliminate their own maintenance of a system of unlawful racial classification."[84] In form and language the opinion seems ordinary. Virtually every paragraph is littered with cites to other cases. The rhetorical format is one of reliance on abstract principles, derived from precedents and the lessons of history.[85] All in all, it is an opinion familiar in its structure and language.

Nonetheless, Scalia's opinion, however ordinary in form and apparently abstract, has a special vividness and concrete quality that emerges in the process of reading. In the first paragraph Scalia quotes Alexander Bickel: "[D]iscrimination on the basis of race is illegal, immoral, unconstitutional, inherently wrong, and destructive of democratic society."[86] Scalia quickly follows with the language from Justice John Marshall Harlan's dissent in *Plessy* stating that " 'our Constitution is color-blind.' "[87] By linking the Bickel and Harlan

---

[82] *See id.* at 520–28 (Scalia, J., concurring).

[83] *See id.* at 528–61 (Marshall, J., dissenting).

[84] *Id.* at 524 (Scalia, J., concurring).

[85] *See id.* at 522–23.

[86] *Id.* at 521 (quoting Alexander Bickel, *The Morality of Consent* 133 (1975)).

[87] *Id.* (quoting *Plessy v. Ferguson*, 163 U.S. 537, 559 (1896) (Harlan, J., dissenting)). Professor Laurence Tribe has demonstrated the problem in wrenching this particular metaphor out of its historical context.

Consider Justice Harlan's reference to color blindness in the context of his preceding five sentences:

> The white race deems itself to be the dominant race in this country. And so it is, in prestige, in achievements, in education, in wealth and in power. So, I doubt not, it will continue to be for all time, if it remains true to its great heritage and holds fast to the principles of constitutional liberty. But in the view of the Constitution, in the eye of the law, there is in this country no superior, dominant, ruling class of citizens. There is no caste here. Our Constitution is color blind. . . .

Even for this late nineteenth-century proponent of white dominance, it appears that the colorblind ideal was only shorthand for the concept that the Fourteenth Amendment

quotes,[88] Scalia begins the process of constructing the important argument of symmetry. That is, race-based classifications are suspect, regardless of whether a government policy uses them to perpetuate or ameliorate inequality. Purportedly benign motivations can not save affirmative action; the best of intentions will not protect society against the insidious impact of color-conscious programs. As the opinion continues, the Bickel quote takes on added significance. It is the beginning of a continuing metaphor, the metaphor of the bad seed, or implicitly, the metaphor of affirmative action as a cancer.[89]

Several paragraphs later, Scalia speaks of the special danger of "oppression" from political "factions" (blacks) in "small political units" (Richmond, Virginia).[90] Subsequently, Scalia speaks the words that offer the reader a powerful sense of vividness. "The prophesy of oppression . . . came to fruition in Richmond in the enactment of a set-aside clearly and directly beneficial to the dominant political group, which happens also to be the dominant racial group."[91]

To understand the vividness of Scalia's extended metaphor, one must recall Bickel's lesson and ask what it is that makes affirmative action "destructive" to society. To say that a particular kind of law will "destroy" us is an abstraction waiting to be made real and vivid in the

---

prevents our law from enshrining and perpetuating white supremacy. Laurence Tribe, *American Constitutional Law* § 16–22, 1525, 1521–44 (2d ed. 1988) (quoting *Plessy v. Ferguson, 163 U.S. 537, 559 (1896)* (Harlan, J., dissenting) (emphasis added)) (footnote omitted).

Harlan's "colorblind" metaphor is commonly used as part of the argument for symmetry in equal protection. See Laurence Tribe, *In What Vision of the Constitution Must the Law Be Color-Blind?*, 20 J. Marshall L. Rev. 201, 203 (1986). Harlan, however, addressed the symmetry argument in *Plessy*:

It was said in argument that the statute of Louisiana does not discriminate against either race, but prescribes a rule applicable alike to white and colored citizens. But this argument does not meet the difficulty. Every one knows that the statute in question had its origin in purpose, not so much to exclude white persons from railroad cars occupied by blacks, as to exclude colored people from coaches occupied by or assigned to white persons. Railroad corporations of Louisiana did not make discrimination among whites in the matter of accommodation for travelers. The thing to accomplish was, under the guise of giving equal accommodation for whites and blacks, to compel the latter to keep to themselves while traveling in railroad passenger coaches. No one would be so wanting in candor as to assert the contrary.

Plessy v. Ferguson, 163 U.S. 537, 556–57 (1896) (Harlan, J., dissenting). Thus, Harlan himself apparently rejected the symmetry argument.

[88] *See Croson,* 488 U.S. at 521 (Scalia, J., concurring).

[89] *See generally* Susan Sontag, *Illness as Metaphor* 736–39 (1977) (arguing that using illness metaphorically distorts reality because "illness is *not* metaphor").

[90] *Croson,* 488 U.S. at 523 (Scalia, J., concurring).

[91] *Id*. at 524.

reading. The abstraction can become vivid for the white reader by imagining the oppression that white people might suffer at the hands of black people. When and where blacks are the dominant racial group, they will oppress whites unless whites act to stop them. Affirmative action is thus the seed that will destroy whites. It is the means by which whites might be oppressed in those places where whites are racially outnumbered. In the city of Richmond, the dangerous seed of affirmative action came to fruition.

Scalia draws out this metaphor by language which seems abstract, formal, and quite ordinary in legal writing.[92] The vividness is provided by the reader. This interpretation is a product of both the reader's individual imagination and the cultural influences shared by a white audience.[93] Individual imagination may lead the reader to imagined stories of personal disadvantage in the name of affirmative action, ("I did not get the appointment because I am a white male") or perhaps a brute image of the white man's fear of the black man ("I left the building late last night and a black man followed me, asking for money"). Individual imagination as part of the process of reading Scalia's opinion will take different readers to different imaginings.

Nonetheless, one can suppose that throughout the white audience there will be a large measure of consonance in the readings. The cultural influence provides meaning through a nonpictorial kind of imagining. In some way the white reader will experience associations: connecting ideas of "difference" and "dominance," "victims" and "revenge," or other nonpictorial imaginings that produce precisely the sense of unease and fear that makes Scalia's metaphor vivid and powerful. These associations are part of the cultural experience of the members of the audience. Although the precise nature and power of these associations will vary, the influence of the shared cultural heritage of most members of Scalia's audience will produce a substantial consonance in the vividness of the nonpictorial imaginings.

The metaphor of destruction takes an even more evocative turn when Scalia amplifies it by the use of the metaphor of fire.[94] "When we depart from the principle that racial discrimination is destructive of our society we play with fire, and much more than an occasional DeFunis, Johnson, or Croson [each of whom alleged reverse discrimination] burns."[95] The fear of black insurrection is part of the unbroken history

---

[92] *See id.* at 520–28.

[93] *See* Thomas Ross, *Metaphor and Paradox*, 23 Ga. L. Rev. 1053, 1083–84, 1069 (1989) (discussing the need to confront legal metaphors in order to comprehend the power and effects of the law).

[94] *See Croson*, 488 U.S. at 527 (Scalia, J., concurring).

[95] *Id.*

of the white man's imagination. Our slave laws were especially harsh.[96] Features of those laws can be linked to the understandable fears of white men who often lived in circumstances where the victims of their cruelty and oppression literally outnumbered their masters.[97] For them, the fear of insurrection and revenge was an inescapable part of their imaginings and was expressed in their formal laws.[98]

The foregoing fears constitute an unbroken part of our imagination. The history of oppression, cruelty, and humiliation imposed on the black person by the white person did not end with the Emancipation Proclamation, the enactment of the Fourteenth Amendment, or even the civil rights laws of the 1960s.[99] To live in a society with people whose great grandparents we enslaved and who are themselves the subjects of continuing humiliation must give us our own versions of the white slave master's nightmares. When and where we have been dominant, we have abused our power. What could we imagine when we are told of the fruition of the prophesy when blacks became the dominant race in Richmond? What must we envision when Scalia speaks of the black person "evening the score"?[100] The white reader will make vivid the abstraction, by individual pictorial imagination, by some version of the revenge of the black man, and by the nonpictorial imaginings of the cultural influences of white America. Behind the abstraction of Bickel's lesson and the cool rationality of the argument for equality as symmetry, the reader of Scalia's opinion can imagine a disturbing and vivid meaning.

Scalia invokes another powerful narrative, the white man's narrative of his own struggle, and thus, the whining quality of the black

---

[96] "No ante-bellum Southerner could ever forget Nat Turner. The career of this man made an impact upon the people of his section as great as that of John C. Calhoun or Jefferson Davis.... The danger that other Nat Turners might emerge ... became an enduring concern.... [T]he fear of rebellion, sometimes vague, sometimes acute, was with [Southern whites] always." Kenneth Stampp, *The Peculiar Institution: Slavery in the Ante-Bellum South* 132-34 (1956). *See generally* Derrick Bell, *Race, Racism and the American Law* §§ 1.1-.7, 2-24 (2d ed. 1980) (discussing the history of American slavery); David Brion Davis, *The Problem of Slavery in Western Culture* 125-64 (1966) (discussing the changing views of the value and dangers of American slavery); Paul Finkelman, *An Imperfect Union: Slavery, Federalism, and Comity* 3-45 (1981) (discussing the conflict between northern and southern law on slavery issues); A. Leon Higginbotham, *In the Matter of Color* 176-86 (1978) (discussing the penalties imposed on runaway and criminal slaves); Mark Tushnet, *The American Law of Slavery 1810-60* at 44-70 (1981) (discussing case studies involving slave law).

[97] *See* Higginbotham, *supra* note 96, at 152.

[98] *See* Richard Kluger, *Simple Justice* 27-28 (1975).

[99] "The battle against pernicious racial discrimination or its effects is nowhere near won." *Croson*, 488 U.S. at 561 (Marshall, J., dissenting).

[100] *Id.* at 527 (Scalia, J., concurring).

person's plea.[101] Scalia reminds the reader of discrimination against the Chinese and Hispanics.[102] And in the penultimate paragraph, he states: "The relevant proposition is not that it was blacks, or Jews, or Irish who were discriminated against, but that it was individual men and women, 'created equal,' who were discriminated against. And the relevant resolve is that that should never happen again."[103] Invoking the other victims of the prejudice and oppression of the white Anglo–American Christian man will trigger, in the audience, narratives of personal struggle and oppression. Who among us has not felt oppressed, marginalized because of our beliefs, or the subject of perceived prejudice because of our social background? Each person struggles ceaselessly. Scalia's invocation of the other oppressed categories opens up a rich, vivid narrative to the reader, a narrative and imagining which leads not to empathy for the other oppressed groups, but rather to a sense that we all have struggled. Thus, when blacks seek an advantage, we can sense a whining quality to their plea.

The last paragraph of Scalia's opinion consists of a single sentence. His closing remark is a perfect composite of the abstract and vivid: "Since I believe that the appellee [Croson] here had a constitutional right to have its bid succeed or fail under a decisionmaking process uninfected with racial bias, I concur in the judgment of the Court."[104] This sentence is abstract in several senses. First, it speaks of no names or places. It is universal in its ostensible implications. Second, the central and implicit assumption in this declaration is that once the bias of the ordinance is removed no other racial bias will exist. This assumption has compelling plausibility in an abstract conception of place and time. It becomes problematic in its real place and time. We would not realistically suppose that the public contracting process in Richmond, Virginia, or anywhere in America, would be wholly uninfected by racial bias once it is cleansed of the taint of affirmative action.

The last sentence of the Scalia opinion is also vivid and concrete in its final invocation of the metaphor of affirmative action as a societal cancer.[105] The last sentence's proclamation of the "infection" of racial bias connects the white reader to the metaphor of affirmative action as the seed of our destruction. That metaphor, in turn, can take us again to the imaginings of oppression and revenge at the hands of black citi-

---

[101] *See id.* at 520–28.

[102] *See id.* at 523.

[103] *Id.* at 528.

[104] *Id.*

[105] *See id.*

zens.[106] With this concluding sentence, Scalia has beautifully tied together his narrative. Scalia's narrative is one which, through its abstractions and metaphors, invites the reader to tell his own narratives and thereby make the abstract vivid and concrete. The individual pictorial imagination and the nonpictorial imaginings of the cultural influences are triggered again and again by Scalia's abstractions and metaphors. Scalia demands of his readers that they become more than mere readers—he demands that they become storytellers as well—and they do.

Justice Marshall's Contextual Legal Narrative

Marshall's dissenting opinion is in many respects quite ordinary. It is littered with long strings of legal citations, and is, in part, built around an abstract decisional model.[107] His model is a two-pronged standard requiring that the affirmative action ordinance pursue "important governmental objectives" and that the chosen means be "substantially related" to those objectives.[108] Referred to as "intermediate scrutiny" and applicable to gender-based classifications, this standard of review is less rigid than strict scrutiny. As a formal matter, Justice Marshall builds his analysis around this test. As a substantive matter, Marshall's opinion is much more than an application of intermediate scrutiny. As with Scalia's opinion, Marshall's contains a narrative—not an abstract narrative, but one that is laden with historical and contemporary racial specificities.

The central and powerful distinction between Marshall's and Scalia's narratives is the one between the narrative invited and the narrative given. Scalia's narrative in its abstractions and metaphors invites the reader to embellish with his narratives and imaginings, to make the abstract concrete, to provide meaning to the metaphors. Marshall's opinion, on the other hand, provides details. It names and talks of persons and places. For Marshall, history is a source of other stories more than a repository of abstract principles. Marshall is a storyteller in a very different way.

Every storyteller knows that stories have beginnings and endings and that readers often pay special attention to those places in the narrative. A reader of the Richmond narratives encounters the ending of Scalia's story juxtaposed with the beginning of Marshall's story. As the echoes of Scalia's metaphor of affirmative action as an infectious disease fades,[109] Marshall begins thus: "It is a welcome symbol of racial progress

---

[106] See supra notes 94–100 and accompanying text.

[107] See Croson, 488 U.S. at 528–61 (Marshall, J., dissenting).

[108] Id. at 535.

[109] See id. at 528 (Scalia, J., concurring).

when the former capital of the Confederacy acts forthrightly to confront the effects of racial discrimination in its midst."[110] In that first sentence, Marshall introduces a story he will not merely invite, but will also tell— the story of Richmond's "disgraceful history" of race relations.[111] Marshall tells of the "Richmond experience," an experience of "the deliberate diminution of black residents' voting rights, resistance to school desegregation, and publicly sanctioned housing discrimination."[112] Marshall speaks of the attempt to annex white suburbs to avoid the specter of a black majority in the city,[113] and uses the word "apartheid."[114]

O'Connor dismisses[115] and Scalia speaks only implicitly[116] to this story of Richmond's history. The Justices thus dispute whether the story of Richmond's history is legally relevant. For Marshall, however, as the spokesperson for affirmative action, it is a special and powerful narrative. Here Marshall is talking to the same audience as Scalia—the white audience. Unlike Scalia, Marshall cannot merely invite narratives from this audience. He must provide them. These carefully crafted narratives, coupled with the imaginings and narratives of the reader, hopefully can cultivate the empathy necessary to move beyond self-interest.[117] So, Marshall tells the white audience a story that is likely to be neither part of their actual personal experience nor part of their culture's repertoire of stories. He asks the white reader to hear this story and to empathize. It is a struggle for the reader, and one that may, for some, never succeed. Still, if Marshall fails to tell this story and other stories like it, the white reader is unlikely to tell this narrative on his own.

Marshall rejects the argument for symmetry by contrasting "governmental actions that themselves are racist, and governmental actions that seek to remedy the effects of prior racism" or, perhaps more evocatively, between "remedial classifications" and "the most brute and repugnant forms of state-sponsored racism."[118] "State-sponsored racism" is a pow-

---

[110] *Id.* (Marshall, J., dissenting).

[111] *Id.* at 529.

[112] *Id.* at 544.

[113] *See id.*

[114] *Id.* at 545.

[115] *See id.* at 499 (plurality opinion).

[116] *See id.* at 522–23 (Scalia, J., concurring).

[117] "[Human solidarity] is to be achieved not by inquiry but by imagination, the imaginative ability to see strange people as fellow sufferers. Solidarity is not discovered by reflection but created. It is created by increasing our sensitivity to the particular details of the pain and humiliation of other, unfamiliar sorts of people." Richard Rorty, *Contingency, Irony, and Solidarity* xvi (1989).

[118] *Croson*, 488 U.S. at 551–52 (Marshall, J., dissenting).

erful set of words invoking imaginings in the reader, of whatever race, of the institutions of slavery and apartheid which scar our history.

Marshall tells another story of racism that may be discerned in O'Connor's opinion, among others. He focuses on O'Connor's references to the dominant racial group in Richmond, and the specter of simple racial politics.[119] Marshall argues that cities under the leadership of members of a racial minority may often be cities with much to remedy.[120] He reminds us that this is certainly true of Richmond.[121] Thus, Marshall argues, one should assume that the political leaders of Richmond acted with sincere remedial goals in mind and not simple racial politics.[122]

This measured objection contrasts sharply with his final reaction to O'Connor's argument on simple racial politics.[123] Marshall challenges the majority's view that remedial measures undertaken by municipalities with black leadership must face a stiffer test under equal protection than remedial measures undertaken by municipalities with white leadership. The differential treatment, he argues, implies a lack of political maturity on the part of this Nation's elected minority officials that is totally unwarranted. Such insulting judgments have no place in constitutional jurisprudence.[124]

At this moment, Marshall invites the white reader to imagine the hurt and insult of racism. Marshall's charge that O'Connor and others have expressed "insulting judgments" about black elected officials is a story of racism on the Court. As such, it is a powerful move and an especially evocative moment for the reader. Marshall's charge is, in a sense, inviting a narrative about the Justices. As the white reader struggles to understand the deeper meaning of Marshall's charge, he experiences discomfort. Marshall reveals the unthinkable notion that the Justices themselves harbor racist assumptions and attitudes. For some readers, this may be the most powerful story Marshall has told.

Thus Scalia and Marshall tell different narratives. Scalia invites the reader to make his abstractions and metaphors concrete and vivid. Marshall tells stories in explicit detail, stories with history and context not likely to be provided by his audience. The forms of narrative connect in a complex way to ideology through the distinction between narrative invited and narrative told. These strategies recognize in different ways

---

[119] *Id.* at 553.

[120] *Id.* at 554.

[121] *Id.*

[122] *Id.* at 554–55.

[123] *Id.*

[124] *Id.* at 555.

white resistance to affirmative action. When Scalia offers the abstract principle of symmetry, the white reader will have little difficulty providing narratives and imaginings that permit him to reject affirmative action. The rejection appears to occur only at a formal level on the field of the cool syllogism; in fact, it goes on in the hot and vivid world of the imagining reader. White readers immediately appreciate that affirmative action is hard to accept because it works against their self-interest. Abstract arguments about building a better world—a world in which we have taken account of race and thereby successfully moved past race— may not be wholly sufficient. The essential byproduct of affirmative action is some disadvantage to the white person. This is not an easy thing to accept. Affirmative action must be grounded in the historical fact and continuing reality of racial discrimination. This too is not an easy truth to accept. Whites feel guilty and fear the consequences of their oppression of blacks, including the prospect of political revenge by black majorities in cities like Richmond.

By contrast, Marshall offers stories more richly told. His stories are not the stories of whites, but he seeks to make them their stories. His success depends upon the narrative's capacity to reconstruct the imaginings and narratives of his white audience. When Marshall tells of Richmond's disgraceful history, white readers may imagine, with more or less vivid imagery, the stories of the black victims. These readers may seek to move past their cultural heritage, or they may fall back on their counter-narratives. They could imagine the oppression of other minority groups, or their own personal struggle. They could imagine the specter of revenge in permitting a response to historical oppression.

Marshall's stories quite obviously do not necessarily persuade the white reader. But his stories make possible the essential move for any white reader who might embrace affirmative action—the move to empathy. Only if a white audience can join, in some imperfect way, in the feelings and circumstances of the beneficiaries of affirmative action can this audience accept the program's legitimacy. Marshall attempts to elicit empathy by telling stories emphasizing the connection between past racial discrimination and the set-aside. He believes that if readers understand and accept that connection, then they would realize that the Richmond city council was not engaging in racial politics when they enacted the program, but in good faith carrying out the ongoing process of undoing the effects of past racial discrimination.

The *Croson* Narratives as Narratives Justifying the Principle of Colorblindness

Marshall's narrative, however, failed to address directly the Court's concerns about reverse majoritarian racial discrimination, and instead, may only have confirmed them. Both Marshall and Scalia agree about the history of white oppression of blacks in Richmond. However, from that history, they draw radically different implications. For Scalia, the long and horrific history of white oppression of blacks is a compelling reason to be *more*, not less suspicious of the black Richmond city council's actions. That is because the history of white oppression gave blacks a strong motive to tyrannize whites, and with control of the city council, they had acquired the means and power to do so.

Without saying so explicitly, the Court in *Croson* effectively declared that whites were now a discrete and insular minority deserving of suspect class status. Their suspect class status derives, not from their status as an inferior racial out-group, but from their status as the historical oppressor of racial minorities. Strict scrutiny of affirmative action is necessary to prevent blacks and other racial minorities from using the power of the state to "even the score" against their former oppressor. For O'Connor, the danger is that black-controlled governments enacting affirmative action plans will be motivated by racial interest group politics rather than any true desire to remedy the effects of past discrimination. In short, both Scalia and O'Connor fear that black-controlled governments will act in precisely the same racist and discriminatory ways that the white-controlled governments had acted when they were in power.

Hence, for Scalia and O'Connor, the imperative of colorblindness takes on a greater urgency in the new social reality of race relations, where blacks and other groups of color are not only equal to whites, but, in some cases, they are more powerful. As blacks and other groups of color increasingly take political control in localities throughout the United States, the number of white political minorities will grow. Since it is no longer possible to make a clear distinction between invidious and benign racial classifications, colorblind symmetry under equal protection is necessary to ensure that no one racial group or coalition of racial groups, black, Asian, Native American or Latino, can use the pretense of remedying past discrimination to enact legislation motivated by racial retribution or racial politics.

An Alternative Croson Narrative: Race Relations in Richmond as a Story of Suburban–Urban Racial Subordination[125]

O'Connor's and Scalia's stories provide powerful justifications for adopting colorblindness as the central organizing principle under equal protection. Their justifications reflect a vision of race relations that views whites and groups of color as equal. In some jurisdictions, blacks

---

[125] This part of the chapter draws heavily from Reginald Oh's *Re-Mapping Equal Protection Jurisprudence: A Legal Geography of Race and Affirmative Action*, 53 Am. U. L. Rev. 1305 (2004).

will continue to be a political minority and a suspect class. In others, whites will be the vulnerable minority. In this new social and demographic landscape, all the races are now suspect classes, and thus, the colorblind principle must be adopted to ensure the fair treatment of all racial groups, not just historically oppressed racial groups.

Although Marshall's narrative properly focused on the history of racism in Richmond, it relied unconsciously on some limiting geographic assumptions that restricted the power of his narrative to provide an alternative social reality of race. In particular, he missed the opportunity to show why the fears of racial retribution and racial politics in the narratives of O'Connor and Scalia were unfounded. In constructing a narrative, a storyteller must make implicit choices about the *geographic* context in which the story takes place. Those geographic choices shape and structure the story that is told. By including certain spaces in the story and by excluding others, or by expanding or restricting the geographic scale in which the story takes place, the storyteller makes critical decisions about what facts are relevant or irrelevant to the story.

The alternative geographical framework set forth here supports Justice Marshall's narrative and exposes some of the fallacies in O'Connor's and Scalia's narrative. Specifically, this alternative framework undermines their conclusion that blacks are the dominant racial and political majority in Richmond, and that whites in Richmond are the oppressed racial and political minority. A broadened geographic scale reveals that the story is not just about the city of Richmond, but about the city of Richmond and its relationship to outlying suburbs. This framework expands beyond Richmond's borders to make the greater Richmond metropolitan area the place in which the story unfolds.

In changing the geographic scale of the narrative, new facts become relevant, such as the fact that whites constitute the majority in the greater Richmond metropolitan area. The shift also makes urban-suburban relations a central part of the story and shows that blacks' majority status in Richmond is less a sign of rising political power and more a sign of continuing socioeconomic powerlessness. Blacks have become a majority in Richmond due to white flight to the suburbs. The city has been economically devastated by the outmigration of middle-class whites and has a strong incentive to pursue policies that attract white suburbanites and businesses to move back to Richmond. The city actually has an economic interest in enacting policies favorable to the remaining middle-class whites in Richmond as a way to protect the tax base.

This reconstructed narrative then becomes a story, not just about affirmative action and the city of Richmond, but a story about white flight, ongoing residential and school segregation, and the continuing political and economic domination of white suburbs over black central cities. It is within this context that the affirmative action program struck down in *Croson* should be understood as a modest attempt by the distressed city of Richmond to engage in economic development. Within this alternative geographic framework, it becomes more difficult to maintain the notion that blacks are now politically powerful and whites are now politically vulnerable, even in cities like Richmond. The line between invidious and benign racial classifications may not be as blurry as the Court suggests.

Geographic Constructs in Legal Narratives

One effective way of unpacking an inequality-reinforcing narrative is to uncover all the conscious and unconscious spatial or geographic constructs embedded within it. A narrative that organizes itself around a coherent plot often achieves its coherence by ignoring and obscuring the spatial or geographic dimensions of social reality.[126] John Berger argues that it is no longer possible to tell a coherent story unfolding sequentially over time, both because in today's postmodern world, we are too self-aware of events that continually disrupt the linear, temporal flow of a story-line, and because we are too self-aware of the geographic "simultaneity and extension of events and possibilities."[127]

Berger points to the increasing interconnectedness of the postmodern world as a main cause for our constantly having to take into account[128] these simultaneous developments. According to Berger:

> There are many reasons why this should be so: the range of modern means of communications; the scale of modern power: the degree of personal political responsibility that must be accepted for events all over the world; the fact that the world has become indivisible: the unevenness of economic development within that world: the scale of exploitation. All these play a part. Prophecy now involves a geographical rather than historical projection; *it is space not time that hides consequences from us*.... Any contemporary narrative which ignores the urgency of this dimension is incomplete and acquires the oversimplified character of a fable.[129]

In this remarkable passage, Berger contends that any narrative, legal or historical, that ignores the full range of geographic relationships is more likely to be a construct of a storyteller's imagination than a representa-

---

[126] *Id.* at 110–11.

[127] Edward W. Soja, *Thirdspace: Journeys to Los Angeles and Other Real-and-Imagined Places* 165–66 (1996) (quoting John Berger, *The Look of Things* 40 (1974)).

[128] *Id.*

[129] *Id.* (emphasis added).

tion of reality.[130] Such a narrative actually hides from the reader the consequences and conditions of the material world.[131]

Moreover, in terms of the role that narratives play in the law, these choices about which spaces and places to include or exclude can obscure power relations and power dynamics. As geographer Doreen Massey explains, "Social space can helpfully be understood as a social product, as constituted out of social relations, and social interactions."[132] Precisely because it is constituted out of social relations, spatiality is always and to everywhere an expression and medium of power.[133]

How does one go about uncovering and critically examining the embedded spatial constructs in a legal narrative? To examine and to deconstruct the spaces and places of a narrative mean at least two things. First, there must be a critical examination of the geographic scale or setting of a narrative. This inquiry asks: What is the geographic setting for the story? What are alternative settings? In *Croson*, all of the justices' narratives assumed that the geographic scale for their stories had to be the city of Richmond. Accordingly, in constructing their narratives, the justices examined only the facts and processes occurring within the city limits. However, there were alternative choices. For example, the justices could have set the scale at the state level and discussed the conflict over the set-aside as a story about race relations in Virginia.

Second, there must be an exploration of how people move within the narrative domain—that is, the place within which the narrative takes place. The latter line of geographic inquiry assumes that where people are located has great significance, and that questioning, in a particular story, people's location at any given time and place can disrupt and deconstruct the plot of a legal narrative. This inquiry asks: Where are the "characters" from? Where are they now? How did they get from there to here?

---

[130] *Id.* at 66 (arguing that any narrative which disregards the spatial dimension is insufficient in conveying meaning and is similar to the oversimplified narrative of a fable).

[131] *See id.* at 165 (asserting that the use of spatial narrative and chronological narrative is necessary to reveal the critical perspective needed to practically and theoretically evaluate the present world).

[132] *See* Doreen Massey, *Space/Power, Identity/Difference: Tensions in the City, in* The Urbanization of Injustice 100, 104 (Andy Merrifield & Erik Swyngedouw eds., 1997) (using the influence that major trade policies, such as the North American Free Trade Agreement and General Agreement on Tariffs and Trades, have over the reorganization of the population of major world cities to illustrate that social space in the modern world is defined by constant changing social forces and interactions).

[133] *See id.* (arguing the size of a city's population is a reflection of powerful social forces, such as global trade agreements and national agricultural policies, which have influenced change in the city's social structure).

Croson *as a Narrative about Race Relations in the Greater Richmond Metropolitan Area*

The contextual narrative set forth here challenges an unconscious assumption that O'Connor's, Scalia's and Marshall's narratives share— that the proper geographic scale for their stories was the boundary lines of Richmond. Their narratives presume that race relations in Richmond can be understood by examining what takes place solely within the city's borders.

The alternative narrative presupposes that to better understand race relations in Richmond, it is necessary to look outside jurisdictional lines and expand the geographic scale of the story. Specifically, the alternative detailed narrative interrogates a critical theme in O'Connor's and Scalia's legal narratives: Regardless of the city's formal status as a state entity, Blacks now are a numerical majority on the Richmond city council and thus have become the dominant racial and political group in Richmond.[134] Once black political power in the city of Richmond is analyzed in the context of urban-suburban relations, however, black control of elected municipal offices in Richmond is actually evidence of the continuing political and socioeconomic powerlessness of African Americans.

In *Croson*, the Court recognized the demographic change in the city of Richmond from majority white to majority black.[135] In doing so, both Justices O'Connor and Scalia used the majority status of African Americans to support their conclusion that the city council had engaged in invidious racial discrimination against whites. With control of the city council, blacks in Richmond now had the will and power to enact laws that harmed white interests in order to benefit black interests.

However, in Scalia's legal narrative, he assumes, without question, that numerical majority status in the city's population and on the city council means that blacks are the clear "dominant political and racial group" in Richmond. The reality is that the status of African Americans in Richmond when *Croson* was decided cannot be so easily characterized. Rather, paradoxically, the formal political power that African Americans obtained in Richmond actually reflects their position of relative political powerlessness in relation to whites in Richmond, in the Richmond metropolitan area, and in the state of Virginia.

The continuing, actual political powerlessness experienced by African Americans in Richmond becomes clear only when a simple question about geography and demography is asked: How did blacks end up becoming a majority in the city of Richmond? This simple question opens

---

[134] *See Croson*, 488 U.S. at 524.

[135] *See id.* at 479.

up the *Croson* analysis from its restricted geographic setting, the city of Richmond, and directs it to an analysis of race relations between whites and blacks in the Richmond metropolitan area. None of the justices raised this question. Underlying the inquiry is the notion that where people are located, where they have been, where they are now, and where they will be in the future, is of great social (and narrative) significance.

The rise of the black majority in Richmond occurred for primarily one reason—the outward migration of whites from the city to the suburbs.[136] In Richmond, beginning in the 1960s, white residents exercised their exit option not to flee local racial politics, but to escape from the court-ordered racial integration of public schools.[137] As previously noted, this strategy succeeded precisely because the Supreme Court thwarted a federal district court's efforts to order interdistrict busing in Richmond. Despite the Court's own role in precipitating this demographic transformation, the changes in the metropolitan area figured not at all in the discussion of Richmond's set-aside program.

A similar pattern of white flight occurred throughout the country, contributing to the problems of central cities such as Richmond.[138] In fact, the election of black mayors and city council members in cities across the United States stems from this demographic shift.[139] The rise of black majorities in central cities, the base of support for black political officials, does not reflect growing influence and socioeconomic gains, but more accurately reflects white exit to the suburbs and the resulting concentration of poverty in central cities.[140]

The consequences of white flight from the central city of Richmond have been dramatic. The city's population has declined by 19% since

---

[136] *See* Christopher Silver & John V. Moeser, *The Separate City: Black Communities in the Urban South, 1940–1968* 42 (1995) (explaining that whites began moving West from the city in the 1940's, establishing homogenous suburban neighborhoods, while blacks began to predominate census tracks in most areas of central Richmond).

[137] *See* Robert Pratt, *Simple Justice Denied: The Supreme Court's Retreat from School Desegregation in Richmond, Virginia,* 24 Rutgers L.J. 709, 710 (1993) (stating that whites were able to prevent de facto integration through passive resistance techniques, but by the time of court-ordered busing in 1970, whites had already begun to exit Richmond in large numbers). *See generally* Bradley v. Richmond Sch. Bd., 325 F. Supp. 828 (E.D. Va. 1971) (holding that attendance figures may be used to determine if a Richmond school integration plan is working practice and not simply on paper).

[138] *See* Silver & Moeser, *supra* note 136, at 167 (observing that post-1960s, a population loss resulted in a weakening economy, drastic drops in home ownership and a substantial decline in the supply of habitable housing in Richmond).

[139] *See id.*

[140] Pratt, *supra* note 137, at 710, 723.

1970, and in 1996, Richmond's population dipped below 200,000.[141] In stark contrast, the three adjacent, predominantly white counties have doubled in population, growing by 220,000 new residents.[142] The black majority in the city had grown from 50% in the mid–1970s to nearly 60% in the mid–1990s.[143] Thus, the black rise to political power in Richmond primarily occurred through the attrition of whites rather than through gains in the black population.[144] Because the socioeconomic health of a city depends on population gain and economic growth,[145] the demographic shift was a major signal that the city of Richmond was in distress.

While the metropolitan area's population growth mirrors its economic growth, the city of Richmond's population decline mirrors its economic decline. From 1979 to 1994, total employment opportunities in the Richmond metropolitan area increased by 34%.[146] During that same period, total employment opportunities in the city of Richmond declined by 6%, representing a loss of 11,000 jobs.[147] In 1979, 53% of all jobs in the Richmond metropolitan area were located in the city of Richmond.[148] By 1994, only 37% of the jobs were located there. And between 1980 and 1993, the time period when the set-aside was enacted, 90% of business investment in the metropolitan area was in the suburbs.[149] In 1980, white median household income in the city was 42% higher than black median household income.[150] Ten years later, in 1990, white median household income in the city was 65% higher than black median household income.[151] Moreover, by 1990, over 63% of all the poor in the Richmond metropolitan area resided within the city of Richmond.[152]

---

[141] David Rusk, *Cities Without Suburbs* 37 (1995).

[142] *Id.*

[143] Anthony Downs, *New Visions for a Metropolitan Area* (1994).

[144] *See id.* at 27 (identifying a cycle where a rise to black political dominance traps poor blacks in cities of declining economic opportunity while simultaneously accelerating the flight of middle-class residents).

[145] *See id.* at 47 (explaining that cities that have experienced a flight of middle-class families to the suburbs, and thus encountered a steady population drop, typically stagnate economically and reliance on federal and state aid).

[146] John W. Moeser, *Spirit of Community Can Rescue Richmond*, Richmond Times Dispatch, July 14, 1996, at F1.

[147] *Id.*

[148] *Id.*

[149] *Id.*

[150] *Id.*

[151] *Id.*

[152] *Id.*

With regard to the Richmond public schools, in 1954, white children constituted 57% of the Richmond city public school population.[153] By 1989, blacks constituted more than 87% of the public school population and whites only 13%.[154] Presently, black children make up 95% of the public school population in the Richmond city schools.[155] These statistics show that school segregation has increased over the past several decades. Moreover, the segregation is occurring on both a race and a class level, as the children in the Richmond public schools also tend to be low-income students.[156]

Once the geographic context of Richmond's population is understood, the way in which blacks became a majority and rose to power undercuts a narrative that racial progress has advanced in a steady, linear fashion.[157] Since the late 1960s, while the Richmond metropolitan area has been flourishing, the city of Richmond has been dying. Instead of moving into a position of power, Richmond's black community has obtained political control of "a depreciating asset."[158]

Richard Hatcher, the first African–American mayor of Gary, Indiana, recognizes the "paradox" of black political gain in America.[159] Specifically, the number of black elected officials grew from 200 to 300 in 1972 to over 6,000 by 1989.[160] Despite these gains in black political power, the economic status of black communities during this period continued to decline.[161] Moreover, the prospects for African Americans residing in areas controlled by African–American political leaders have

---

[153] Pratt, *supra* note 137, at 710.

[154] *Id.*; Jennifer E. Spreng, *Scenes from the Southside: A Desegregation Drama in Five Acts*, 19 U. Ark. Little Rock L. J. 327, 390 (1997).

[155] Pratt, *supra* note 137, at 710.

[156] *Id.*

[157] *See* William E. Nelson, Jr. & Philip J. Meranto, *Electing Black Mayors: Political Action in the Black Community* 337 (1997) (countering a theory of black political dominance and alternatively maintaining that the demographic conditions that result in an increase of black political power may also restrict black leaders' abilities to govern effectively).

[158] Rusk, *supra* note 141, at 27; see Silver & Moeser, *supra* note 136, at 166–69 (asserting that Richmond in the 1990's "lacked the means to attract and to sustain population densities necessary to support vital urban institutions").

[159] See Richard Hatcher, *Conclusion to Race, Politics, and Economic Development: Community Perspectives* 175 (James Jennings ed., 1992) (noting that political power in the hands of American ethnic groups does not always translate into the achievement of economic power for these groups).

[160] *Id.*

[161] *Id.* at 175–76.

worsened.[162] When white middle-class residents leave the cities for the suburbs, they take with them the cities' most valuable taxable assets. Thus, black mayors are faced with an increased demand for government services yet lack the basic fiscal resources to effect change within their communities.[163] As political scientists William Nelson and Philip Meranto observed in 1977:

> It is undoubtedly true that in the foreseeable future most black mayors will be elected in dead or dying cities. . . . These cities will bear only a modest resemblance to the financially secure governmental structures captured by white ethnics. The election of black mayors signals instead the onset of black takeover of bankrupt cities consumed by social conflict, physical decay, and enormous financial problems.[164]

Understood in this way, the worsening socioeconomic conditions of African Americans residing in localities ruled by black political leaders are due not to a failure of political will but to structural conditions affecting the vast majority of localities under African–American control. The phenomenon of white flight not only has contributed to the socioeconomic distress of African Americans residing in a central city like Richmond, but also has represented a form of geopolitical power that challenges formal, liberal territorial conceptions of political influence. The power of "geographic exit" helps to explain the structural factors that make it very difficult for African–American political leaders of cities like Richmond to remedy the socioeconomic conditions of their African–American constituents.

Once urban-suburban race relations in Richmond and other American metropolitan areas are understood in terms of the power of geographic exit, a seeming paradox emerges regarding the nature of political power in the United States. For African Americans in particular, the attainment of political power is no longer a means of achieving socioeconomic power. Nor is it a reflection of the attainment of such power. In fact, the precise opposite can be true: at the local level, African Ameri-

---

[162] See Douglas S. Massey & Nancy A. Denton, *American Apartheid* 153–60 (4th ed. 1994) (illustrating that despite the existence of black leadership in central cities, the resulting political and residential isolation of these communities undermines black politicians' ability to promote their citizens' welfare); Paul E. Peterson, *City Limits* 88 (1981) ("Unfortunately, improved access to local politics did not thereby radically alter the socioeconomic well-being of racial minorities and low-income groups.").

[163] See Nelson & Meranto, *supra* note 157, at 337.

[164] *Id.*; see also Richard Briffault, *Our Localism: Part II-Localism & Legal Theory*, 90 Colum. L. Rev. 346, 408–09 (1990) (arguing that, although the rise of minority mayors has increased the role of minority and neighborhood interests, urban politics continues to focus on the protection of the local tax base and the maintenance of access to capital markets).

cans' hold on formal political power now often depends on their continual socioeconomic distress and intense socioeconomic racial segregation.

Moreover, at the local level, the threat of geographic exit gives both the white Richmond suburban majority and the white Richmond city minority the ability to influence and control the city's policymaking. Whites in Richmond have this power because they as a group are largely middle-class and the city has a strong economic incentive to keep them as residents to preserve the city's property tax base.[165] Thus, the Richmond City Council policies have a bias in favor of whites, and low-income African Americans living in the city are not privileged simply because they are a numerical majority.[166] As Richard Briffault observes, "[c]ontemporary cities, as a rule, do not engage in innovative re-distributive programs, not because they lack the legal authority, but rather because they fear that initiating such programs would cause residential and commercial taxpayers to depart."[167]

Furthermore, white Richmond suburban business and political leaders continue to exercise enormous political influence over the black-controlled Richmond city council. During the 1980s, the black city council often aligned itself with white suburban business interests at the expense of the interests of poor blacks in Richmond.[168] The city council sought to restore "economic superiority to the central city and to encourage the return of the [mostly white] middle class [to Richmond], if only as visitors."[169] As a result, the black city council made downtown redevelopment the cornerstone of its policies while eschewing redistributive policies that would more directly help African–American residents. Thus, in 1982, the city council diverted $1.25 million in federal funds intended for community development to provide seed funding for the Richmond Renaissance downtown revitalization project.[170]

The significance of the de-linking of formal political power from economic power, particularly in Richmond, is made abundantly clear by

---

[165] *Id.*

[166] Gerald Frug, *City Services*, 73 N.Y.U. L. Rev. 23, 25–27 (1998).

[167] Briffault, *supra* note 164, at 408; see also Frug, *supra* 166, at 25–26 (summarizing public goods theory that central cities have economic incentives to keep middle class residents from exiting); Clayton P. Gillette, *Equality and Variety of Municipal Services*, 100 Harv. L. Rev. 946, 961 (1987) (reviewing Charles H. Haar & Daniel W. Fessler, *The Wrong Side of the Tracks: A Revolutionary Rediscovery of the Common Law Tradition of Fairness in the Struggle Against Inequality* (1986) and asserting that poor central cities have incentive to offer "bribes" to keep middle-class residents from leaving).

[168] Christopher Silver, *Twentieth–Century Richmond: Planning, Politics, and Race* 316–19 (1984).

[169] *Id.* at 316.

[170] *Id.*

a 1986 study examining the socioeconomic characteristics of forty-three medium-sized cities in the United States.[171] That study revealed that Richmond was both the richest and poorest city among those examined.[172] The most affluent neighborhood of all forty-three cities was Richmond's predominantly white, West End neighborhood, while the second poorest area among all forty-three cities consisted of Richmond's predominantly African–American neighborhoods.[173]

Despite the fears of the *Croson* majority, the city of Richmond was acting in concert with and on behalf of the interests of white, middle-class business and political elites, and not engaging in local racial tyranny—or "simple racial politics." Arguably, the city council was not doing enough to serve the needs and interests of its black constituents. Against this backdrop, the set-aside program challenged in *Croson* looks like a rather modest effort to enact a policy focused on the economic interests of African Americans.[174] In the context of urban-suburban relations in the greater Richmond metropolitan area, the operational purpose of redevelopment is clear—to stem the flow of jobs and industry out of the city and to foster economic growth within Richmond. Given these underlying purposes, the *Croson* Court's assertions regarding the "dominant political and racial group in Richmond" are exposed as groundless.

The *Croson* legal narratives, by circumscribing the geographic scale to the city limits of Richmond, obscured the workings of power that flow across metropolitan boundaries and essentially rendered invisible racialized suburban-urban political and economic conflict. The *Croson* narratives, in justifying the decision to strike down the city of Richmond's set-aside program, obfuscated the very tensions that gave rise to the set-aside program, a limited effort to ameliorate some of the devastating effects caused by white flight and by suburban domination of metropolitan politics in the Richmond area.

Conclusion

Croson tells not one race law story but several. Contained in its opinions are narratives about winners and losers, victims and perpetrators, innocence and guilt. This is not to say that the narratives take the same rhetorical form. They do not. Marshall's narrative is contextual while Scalia's is abstract. But even Marshall's narrative reflects a certain

---

[171] Silver & Moeser, *supra* note 136, at 183–84.

[172] *Id.*

[173] *See id.* at 184 (noting the Atlanta, Georgia had the poorest neighborhoods among the forty-three cities surveyed).

[174] *Id.* at 183–84.

degree of formalism. More particularly, his opinion acquiesces in the idea that the relevant location for the story is the city of Richmond. A legal narrator must make choices about the geographic setting in which the story takes place, and those choices are neither neutral nor inconsequential but instead have a dramatic effect on the representation of "reality" in that narrative.

The story of *Richmond v. Croson* transcends the boundaries of the city. By restricting the geographic scale of its narrative to the city lines of Richmond, the *Croson* Court not only obscured power dynamics and relations between the Richmond suburbs and the central city, but also rendered invisible the phenomenon of white suburban political and socioeconomic dominance over the predominantly black central city. The disappearance of these structural phenomena in the case is all the more disturbing when one considers the wealth of social science literature examining the phenomena of political, economic, and race relations between suburbs and inner cities in metropolitan areas across the United States.[175] Legal scholars and social scientists clearly understand that formal legal notions of political power bounded by neat distinctions between city and suburban governments do not comport with the reality of modern metropolitan areas. Yet, legal narratives like the ones told in *Croson* are so powerful that they make us forget about what is actually happening at the concrete level, and they pull us into a self-contained, nonexistent world where power is neatly contained within the jurisdictional borders of a local government, where power neatly corresponds with numerical superiority, and where the abuse of power takes the form of set-asides for people of color.

In the end, the narratives of race relations in the Richmond metropolitan area are stories about race relations throughout the United States. The racial subordination in Richmond is typical of major cities across America. Conceptualizing judicial opinions as narratives, exposing the narratives in *Croson*, and expanding the geographic scope of the stories in *Croson* show that the continuing subordination of African Americans is a national phenomenon, one justifying constitutional support for, rather than distrust of, affirmative action. Yet, the Court's stories, though at times conflicting and incomplete, have enabled it to convert colorblindness into a fiction of fair play, casting doubt on color-conscious remedies in the name of false symmetry and formal equality.

In the name of colorblindness, the Court struck down a modest attempt by the Richmond City Council to integrate the Richmond construction industry, further entrenching patterns of racial segregation that reinforce the subordination of distressed central cities in Richmond

---

[175] *See, e.g.*, Rusk, *supra* note 141; Anthony Downs, *New Visions for Metropolitan America* 169 (1994).

and in metropolitan areas throughout the United States. These patterns perpetuate race consciousness, because people find it difficult to conceive of only one race of "Americans" if racially separate and unequal neighborhoods, schools, universities, suburbs, cities, workplaces, and industries still dominate the American social landscape.

To create a nation in which persons are judged by the content of their character, racialized spaces signifying white racial superiority and black racial inferiority must be dismantled. Yet, through blind allegiance to the imperative of colorblindness, some members of the Court are protecting the racially stratified social structures and spaces that perpetuate the race consciousness they profess to abhor.

*

12

Kevin R. Johnson

The Song Remains the Same: The Story of *Whren v. United States*

Introduction

Long before the "war on terror" commenced after the tragic events of September 11, 2001, police across the United States aggressively pursued the "war on drugs." For more than two decades, Congress and state legislatures stiffened criminal penalties for drug crimes and increased law enforcement budgets, as politicians of all political persuasions embraced "tough on crime" measures. State and federal governments spent millions of dollars to build prisons. Not coincidentally, the U.S. prison population increased six fold from 1972 to 2000, with about 1.3 million men incarcerated in state and federal prisons at the dawn of the new millennium.[1] As of 1997, about 60 percent of the federal prisoners and 20 percent of the state prisoners had been convicted of drug crimes.[2]

The war on drugs did not calm the public's fears about crime. Indeed, in the early 1990s, the perception among the general public was that crime was out of control on the streets of urban America.[3] Legislators and law enforcement officers responded aggressively. In 1994, for example, President William Jefferson Clinton, a Democrat who supported a firm anti-crime platform, signed into law a comprehensive crime

---

[1] *See* Becky Pettit & Bruce Western, *Mass Imprisonment and the Life Course: Race and Class Inequality in U.S. Incarceration*, 69 Am. Soc. Rev. 151, 151 (2004).

[2] *See id.* at 152.

[3] *See* David S. Broder, *Clinton's Approval Rating Weakens; Poll Shows Rising Public Concern Over Crime, Health Care Plan*, Wash. Post, Nov. 16, 1993, at A1.

bill, filled with anti-drug measures and authorizing the imposition of the death penalty for certain federal criminal offenses.[4]

Even though the available statistical data suggest that whites, Latina/os, blacks, and Asian Americans have roughly similar rates of illicit drug use,[5] the war on drugs has had devastating impacts on minority communities.[6] One particularly egregious example occurred in the small rural town of Tulia, Texas where an undercover narcotics officer framed more than twenty percent of the adult African–American population.[7] Many observers claimed that African Americans and Latina/os were the true targets of the war on drugs. Some have gone so far as to label the drug war as the new Jim Crow,[8] tapping into memories of a long period in U.S. history when criminal laws enforced white supremacy.

In fighting the drug war, federal, state, and local law enforcement agencies developed profiles to identify likely offenders. Police, in their investigatory activities, commonly employed drug courier[9] and gang member profiles, which almost invariably focused attention on young African–American and Latino males.[10] Racial profiling of young African–American and Latino men in traffic stops on the American roads and highways emerged as a central law enforcement tool in the war on drugs.[11] Blacks and Latina/os have been stopped in numbers dispropor-

---

[4] *See* Violent Crime Control and Law Enforcement Act of 1994, Pub. L. No. 103–322, 108 Stat. 1796.

[5] *See* Nat'l Inst. on Drug Abuse, *Drug Use Among Racial/Ethnic Minorities* 29–57 (rev. ed. 2003).

[6] *See generally* Michael H. Tonry, *Malign Neglect—Race, Crime, and Punishment in America* 81–123 (1995).

[7] *See generally* Nate Blakeslee, *Tulia: Race, Cocaine, and Corruption in a Small Texas Town* (2005) (documenting the sting operation in Tulia, Texas in which corrupt narcotics officer framed a group of African Americans for selling cocaine).

[8] *See* Ira Glasser, *American Drug Laws: The New Jim Crow*, 63 Alb. L. Rev. 703 (2000); William H. Buckman & John Lamberth, *Challenging Racial Profiles: Attacking Jim Crow on the Interstate*, Champion, Sept./Oct. 1999, at 14.

[9] *See* Morgan Cloud, *Search and Seizure by the Numbers: The Drug Courier Profile and Judicial Review of Investigative Formulas*, 65 B.U. L. Rev. 843 (1985).

[10] *See* Frank Rudy Cooper, *The Un–Balanced Fourth Amendment: A Cultural Study of the Drug War, Racial Profiling and Arvizu*, 47 Vill. L. Rev. 851, 869–76 (2002); Margaret M. Russell, *Entering Great America: Reflections on Race and the Convergence of Progressive Legal Theory and Practice*, 43 Hastings L.J. 749 (1992).

[11] *See* Kevin R. Johnson, *U.S. Border Enforcement: Drugs, Migrants, and the Rule of Law*, 47 Vill. L. Rev. 897, 902–03 (2002); Lisa Walter, Comment, *Eradicating Racial Stereotyping From Terry Stops: The Case for an Equal Protection Exclusionary Rule*, 71 U. Colo. L. Rev. 255, 258–66 (2000). *See generally* Floyd D. Weatherspoon, *Racial Profiling of*

tionately large compared to their percentage of the general population. A study by the New Jersey Attorney General found that, in the sample studied, these minority groups represented the "overwhelming majority of searches (77.2%)."[12] Minorities often complain of being stopped for "driving while black" and "driving while brown."

Racially disparate policing has had consequences. Blacks and Latina/os today are disproportionately represented among prison populations across the country. "By 2002, around 12 percent of black men in their twenties were in prison or jail."[13] The impacts of the drug war were so racially disproportionate that one law professor and former federal prosecutor advocated that jurors should, as a matter of principle, acquit black defendants on drug charges because of the harms imposed on the African–American community by the mass imprisonment of blacks.[14] As the call for jury nullification of the drug laws suggests, minority communities deeply distrust the criminal justice system.[15] Profiling has contributed to this distrust by singling out blacks and Latina/os for the humiliation and emotional distress of race-based traffic stops. To make matters worse, it is not even clear that profiling is an effective law enforcement tool.[16]

Racial profiling has not been limited to criminal law enforcement. Border Patrol officers have long employed crude racial profiles, which include "Mexican appearance," as the basis for immigration and drug stops. The Supreme Court in 1975 sanctioned reliance on race in this way, so long as it was one of many factors relied upon by immigration

---

African–American Males: Stopped, Searched, and Stripped of Constitutional Protection, 38 J. Marshall L. Rev. 439 (2004).

[12] Peter Verniero & Paul H. Zoubek, *Interim Report of the State Police Review Team Regarding Allegations of Racial Profiling* 27 (1999).

[13] Pettit & Western, *supra* note 1, at 151 (citation omitted).

[14] *See* Paul Butler, Essay, *Racially Based Jury Nullification: Black Power in the Criminal Justice System*, 105 Yale L.J. 677 (1995). Professor Butler became interested in jury nullification because of the African American community's reaction to the sting operation that resulted in the indictment of District of Columbia Mayor Marion Barry, an African American, in 1990 on crack cocaine charges. Many African Americans differ from other racial groups in their view of black lawbreakers. *See* Regina Austin, *"The Black Community," Its Lawbreakers, and a Politics of Identification*, 65 S. Cal. L. Rev. 1769, 1776–87 (1992).

[15] *See* Illinois v. Wardlow, 528 U.S. 119, 132–36 (2000) (Stevens, J., dissenting) (summarizing reasons why African Americans might reasonably fear interacting with the police in the United States).

[16] *See* Samuel R. Gross & Katherine Y. Barnes, *Road Work: Racial Profiling and Drug Interdiction on the Highway*, 101 Mich. L. Rev. 651 (2002) (reviewing statistical data on traffic stops and costs and benefits of such stops).

authorities.[17] Evidence unfortunately suggests that the Border Patrol relies predominantly on race in making immigration stops.[18] Namely, many civil rights suits have been brought contending that the federal government unduly considers physical appearance in immigration stops to the detriment of lawful immigrants and U.S. citizens who "fit" the profile.[19]

The war on drugs is not the first time that the criminal laws in the United States have had distinct racial impacts. From the days of the slave codes, the criminal justice systems throughout the nation have had racially disparate impacts on African Americans.[20] *Brown v. Board of Education*[21] and the civil rights movement helped to remove explicit racism from the law. The war on drugs, despite its disparate impacts, was facially neutral; its stated purpose was to eradicate the drug trade and the use of illegal drugs in the United States, with no mention of race.

Despite the claims of neutrality, profiling will intuitively strike many observers as contrary to the law. Law enforcement measures based on alleged group propensities for criminal conduct, such as racial profiling, appear to run afoul of the U.S. Constitution, which is generally premised on the view that individualized suspicion is necessary for police action.[22] Racial profiling also seems to run counter to the Fourteenth Amendment's guarantee of equal protection of the law.

So far, these constitutional concerns have not weighed heavily on the United States Supreme Court. Since at least 1970, the Court has played a central role in the war on drugs. In case after case, it has consistently deferred to police practices in fighting crime and greatly increased the discretion afforded police officers.[23] In 2005, for example,

---

[17] *See* United States v. Brignoni–Ponce, 422 U.S. 873, 886–87 (1975) (holding that "Mexican appearance" was one relevant factor in, but not enough by itself to justify, an immigration stop). *See generally* Kevin R. Johnson, *The Case Against Race Profiling in Immigration Enforcement*, 78 Wash. U.L. Q. 675 (2000) (criticizing racial profiling in immigration enforcement).

[18] *See* Johnson, *supra* note 17, at 688–716.

[19] *See, e.g.*, Hodgers–Durgin v. de la Vina, 199 F.3d 1037 (9th Cir. 1999) (en banc); Murillo v. Musegades, 809 F. Supp. 487 (W.D. Tex. 1992).

[20] *See* Randall Kennedy, Race, Crime, and the Law 76–135 (1997).

[21] 347 U.S. 483 (1954).

[22] *See, e.g.*, United States v. Sokolow, 490 U.S. 1, 7 (1989); Terry v. Ohio, 392 U.S. 1, 27 (1968).

[23] *See, e.g.*, United States v. Flores–Montano, 541 U.S. 149 (2004) (allowing fuel tank search at border to search for drugs absent reasonable suspicion); United States v. Arvizu, 534 U.S. 266 (2002) (permitting stop of vehicle in search of drugs even though law

the Court ruled that the use of a dog to sniff for drugs during an ordinary traffic stop did not violate the Fourth Amendment.[24] Some commentators contend that the Court has developed a jurisprudence of "drug exceptionalism" in which the Bill of Rights gives way when it reviews the exercise of police power within the war on drugs.[25] None other than Supreme Court Justice John Paul Stevens observed that "[n]o impartial observer could criticize [the] Court for hindering the progress of the war on drugs. On the contrary, decisions like the one the Court makes today [which authorized a search of a closed container in an automobile] will support the conclusion that *this Court has become a loyal foot soldier in the Executive's fight against crime.*"[26]

Not long before the declaration of the war on drugs, the Supreme Court had made it more difficult to protect racial minorities from discrimination. In *Washington v. Davis*,[27] the Court held that proof of a discriminatory *intent*, not simply a discriminatory *impact*, of a facially neutral governmental policy, was necessary to establish a violation of the Equal Protection Clause of the Fourteenth Amendment. Because the discriminatory intent requirement poses a formidable evidentiary barrier to equal protection claims,[28] it has been the subject of sustained academic criticism.[29]

---

enforcement officers relied on numerous factors that alone were insufficient to justify the stop): Illinois v. Wardlow, 528 U.S. 119 (2000) (holding that flight from the police could be a factor justifying a stop); Ohio v. Robinette, 519 U.S. 33 (1996) (ruling that police need not tell a person that he or she can leave before securing consent to a search); Florida v. Bostick, 501 U.S. 429 (1991) (finding that police officers in drug interdiction effort could board buses and request searches of bags).

[24] *See* Illinois v. Caballes, 543 U.S. 405 (2005).

[25] *See* Erik Luna, *Drug Exceptionalism*, 47 Vill. L. Rev. 753 (2002). One federal appeals judge went so far as to exclaim that "I sense that history is likely to judge the judiciary's evisceration of the Fourth Amendment in the vicinity of the Mexican border [in the war on drugs] as yet another jurisprudential nadir, joining *Korematsu*, *Dred Scott*, and even *Plessy* on the list of our most shameful failures to discharge our duty of defending constitutional civil liberties...." United States v. Zapata–Ibarra, 223 F.3d 281, 282 (5th Cir. 2000) (Weiner, J., dissenting) (footnotes omitted).

[26] California v. Acevedo, 500 U.S. 565, 601 (1991) (Stevens, J., dissenting) (emphasis added).

[27] 426 U.S. 229, 238–39 (1976).

[28] *See generally* Theodore Eisenberg & Sheri Lynn Johnson, *The Effects of Intent: Do We Know How Legal Standards Work?*, 76 Cornell L. Rev. 1151 (1991) (empirical study concluding that discriminatory intent standard has deterred filing of civil rights lawsuits).

[29] *See, e.g.,* Linda Hamilton Krieger, *The Content of Our Categories: A Cognitive Bias Approach to Discrimination and Equal Employment Opportunity*, 47 Stan. L. Rev. 1161 (1995); Charles R. Lawrence III, *The Id, the Ego, and Equal Protection: Reckoning with*

In certain respects, the link between criminal procedure and civil rights is clear-cut. Under the leadership of Chief Justice Earl Warren, the Supreme Court issued path-breaking decisions in both areas of law, with the rulings informed by the quest for racial equality.[30] In contrast, since the Supreme Court adopted the discriminatory intent requirement for equal protection violations in 1976, it has been difficult for criminal defendants to establish that police conduct violated the Fourteenth Amendment.[31]

Before 1996, many defendants unsuccessfully pursued claims that police made traffic stops based on race.[32] More generally, in *McCleskey v. Kemp*,[33] the Supreme Court rejected an equal protection claim alleging racial discrimination in the imposition of the death penalty. Despite overwhelming empirical evidence supporting the claim, the Court found that it had not been established that the state actors possessed the requisite discriminatory intent. One influential commentator opined that "[i]t is nearly impossible to make [the] showing" required by the Court.[34]

Similarly, although over a century ago the Court held that selective enforcement of the laws based on race is unconstitutional,[35] the case of *United States v. Armstrong*,[36] decided the same year as *Whren v. United States*, demonstrates the difficulty in obtaining the evidence necessary to establish selective enforcement of the drug laws. According to the Court, even though the jurisdiction prosecuted only African Americans for crack-related offenses that year, the black defendants failed to make the threshold showing that similarly situated whites had not been prosecut-

---

Unconscious Racism, 39 Stan. L. Rev. 317 (1987); R.A. Lenhardt, *Understanding the Mark: Race, Stigma, and Equality in Context*, 79 N.Y.U. L. Rev. 803 (2004).

[30] *See* Yale Kamisar, *The Warren Court and Criminal Justice: A Quarter–Century Retrospective*, 31 Tulsa L.J. 1, 6–8 (1995).

[31] Angela P. Harris, *Equality Trouble: Sameness and Difference in Twentieth–Century Race Law*, 88 Cal. L. Rev. 1923, 2011–12 (2000) (suggesting that the Supreme Court may have desired to reduce the number of equal protection claims by adopting the intent requirement).

[32] *See* David Cole, *No Equal Justice: Race and Class in the American Criminal Justice System* 40 (1999) (reporting results of computer search of federal court of appeals decisions from August 1993 to February 1996).

[33] 481 U.S. 279, 291–99 (1987).

[34] Cole, *supra* note 32, at 135.

[35] *See* Yick Wo v. Hopkins, 118 U.S. 356 (1886).

[36] 517 U.S. 456 (1996). The Court's decision in *Armstrong* has been roundly criticized. *See, e.g.*, Richard H. McAdams, *Race and Selective Prosecution: Discovering the Pitfalls of Armstrong*, 73 Chi.-Kent L. Rev. 605 (1998) (contending that standard established by the Court in *Armstrong* is nearly impossible for any individual defendant to satisfy).

ed and therefore could not obtain the discovery from the U.S. government they sought to prove their discrimination claim.

This is the background against which the Supreme Court considered and decided *Whren v. United States* in 1996.[37]

The Case

In the early 1990s, the District of Columbia, the nation's capital, had a reputation as a high-crime city with a booming drug trade. Even its mayor, Marion Barry, was arrested in 1990 for crack cocaine use (albeit in a controversial sting operation). In 1993, homicides—many drug-related—were near an all-time high in the District. The mayor considered calling in the National Guard to patrol the streets, a drastic move ordinarily reserved for quelling mass civil unrest. Rejecting that option, President Clinton increased federal support to local law enforcement authorities.[38]

June 1993 was an especially crime-filled month in Washington. A rash of murders, with ten people killed in one thirty-six hour period, made the headlines.[39] Metropolitan Police Department Chief Fred Thomas "outlined a short-term revival of Operation Clean Sweep, an expensive anti-crime initiative of the mid–1980s. *He said the department's narcotics and special investigations division will be focusing more on arresting smaller-time drug dealers on the streets instead of larger, more sophisticated rings.*"[40] Needless to say, D.C. police in the summer of 1993 must have felt pressure to act, clean up the streets, and put the full court press on small- as well as big-time drug dealers. Not surprisingly, the number of arrests increased.[41]

At the same time, troubling reports surfaced that D.C. police officers had engaged in criminal conduct, possibly even the selling of drugs. Minority citizens often complained of abuse at the hands of the local police.[42] Such reports, of course, were not limited to the District of

---

[37] 517 U.S. 806 (1996).

[38] *See* Yolanda Woodlee, *U.S. Police Agencies to Help District; Kelly Receives Commitment from Clinton Cabinet Members*, Wash. Post, Oct. 27, 1993, at A1; Ruben Castaneda, *Year Ranks with D.C.'s Deadliest; Drugs, Guns, Poverty Blamed as Homicides Keep Pace With '91*, Wash. Post, Aug. 12, 1993, at A1.

[39] *See* Keith A. Harriston & Ruben Castaneda, *Violent 36 Hours Leaves 10 Slain Across District*, Wash. Post, June 24, 1993, at D1.

[40] Serge F. Kovaleski, *D.C. Moves to Stem Tide of Violence; More Police Planned for Affected Areas*, Wash. Post, June 26, 1993, at A10 (emphasis added).

[41] *See* Ruben Castaneda, *Extra Officers, Neighbors' Aid Stave Off Violence in District*, Wash. Post, June 29, 1993, at B3.

[42] *See* Mary McGrory, *The Thinnest Blue Line*, Wash. Post, Dec. 26, 1993, at C1; Op-Ed., *Policing the D.C. Police*, Wash. Post, May 4, 1993, at A20.

Columbia. Los Angeles had seen riots in 1992 after the acquittal of police officers for the beating of African American Rodney King. In 1995, a racist Los Angeles Police Department officer undermined the prosecution's murder case against O.J. Simpson.[43] Later in the 1990s, a public outcry followed the revelations that New York police officers, in the midst of a crackdown on crime in the city under the direction of Mayor Rudy Giuliani, tortured Abner Louima and killed the unarmed Amadou Diallo; both were black immigrants.

These examples indicate that the case of *Whren v. United States* could have arisen in any large urban center in the United States during the 1990s. Events in the District of Columbia, however, increased the likelihood that young African–American men would be stopped on the streets at night in June 1993. In the end, two young African–American men were arrested, convicted, and sentenced to many years in prison. As the Supreme Court later characterized it, the prosecution was a "run-of-the-mine" case.[44] This certainly is one perspective. However, the arrest, prosecution, and conviction on federal drug charges resulted in lengthy prison sentences that forever changed the lives of those two young African–American men. The fact that the Court could label this case as ordinary shows how far the war on drugs had progressed.

The Traffic Stop

On the night of June 10, 1993, District of Columbia police vice officers Efrain Soto, Jr. and Homer Littlejohn along with other plain clothes vice officers were patrolling the area of Minnesota Avenue and Ely Place, in Southeast Washington, in two unmarked cars. The Supreme Court later described this as a " 'high drug area' of the city."[45] The two vehicles held a total of nine or ten officers. Investigator Tony Howard drove the car in which Officers Soto and Littlejohn were passengers.

The vice officers were from the Metropolitan Police Department's Sixth District station, known locally as 6D. Years later, this precinct's vice squad was the subject of a newspaper exposé reporting that the officers, including Littlejohn and Soto, had engaged in excessive use of force, planted evidence, and perjured themselves to secure drug convictions.[46]

---

[43] *See* Devon W. Carbado, *The Construction of O.J. Simpson as a Racial Victim*, 32 Harv. C.R.-C.L. L. Rev. 49, 71–72 (1997).

[44] *Whren*, 517 U.S. at 819.

[45] *Id.* at 808.

[46] *See* Jason Cherkis, *Rough Justice: How Four Vice Officers Served as Judge and Jury on the Streets of MPD's 6th District*, Wash. City Paper, Jan. 7, 2000,

Importantly, these were vice officers, not traffic cops, who were on the look out for drug dealing. Vice officers ordinarily would not concern themselves with such mundane matters as the traffic laws. Instead, uniformed police officers ordinarily made traffic stops because plain-clothes officers tended to provoke alarm and resistance from drivers who were pulled over. Indeed, District of Columbia police regulations permit plainclothes officers to make traffic stops "only in the case of a violation that is so grave as to pose an *immediate threat* to the safety of others."[47]

Soto testified that as the officers turned left off of Ely Place onto 37th Place heading north, he noticed a dark Nissan Pathfinder with temporary tags at a stop sign. Two young African–American men were in the vehicle. Soto observed the driver, later identified as James Brown, looking down into the lap of the passenger, Michael Whren. A car was stopped behind the vehicle at the stop sign. Soto watched the Pathfinder, which, he later testified, remained stopped at the intersection for more than twenty seconds. Howard was making a U-turn to follow the vehicle, when Brown turned west without signaling and, as Soto testified, "sped off quickly."

The officers followed the Nissan Pathfinder and pulled into the lane of traffic next to it. After noticing that Brown could not pull over because of cars parked to the vehicle's right, Soto told Brown to put the Pathfinder in park. Followed by Littlejohn, Soto exited his vehicle and approached the driver's side of the Pathfinder, identifying himself as a police officer. The traffic stop was near an elementary school, a fact that later led to a separate and enhanced criminal charge for possession of crack cocaine for sale near a school.

Soto testified that, as he approached the Pathfinder, he saw that Whren was holding a large clear plastic bag of what the officer suspected to be crack cocaine in each hand. Soto yelled "C.S.A." to notify the other officers that he had observed a Controlled Substances Act violation. Soto would later testify that, as he reached for the driver's side door, he heard Whren yell "pull off, pull off," and observed him pull off the cover of a power window control panel in the passenger door and put one of the large bags into a hidden compartment. Soto opened the door, dove across Brown, and grabbed the other bag from Whren's left hand. Littlejohn pinned Brown to the back of the driver's seat so that he could not move.

---

available at https: //secure.washingtoncitypaper.com/cgi-bin/Archive/abridged2.bat?path= q:/DocRoot/2000/000107/4VICE & search= & SearchString = & AuthorLastName=cherk is & IssueDate=mm®dd®yyyy & SelectYear=2000 & next.x =95 & next.y=18 (subscription required), last visited Nov. 30, 2006. Perjury by police officers to secure convictions is so common that officers refer to the practice as "testilying." *See* Christopher Slobogin, *Testilying: Police Perjury and What to Do About It*, 67 U. Colo. L. Rev. 1037 (1996).

[47] Metropolitan Police Department, Washington, D.C., General Order 303.1, pt.1, Objectives and Policies (A)(2)(4) (Apr. 30, 1992) (emphasis in original).

Officers then converged on the suspects, placed them under arrest, and searched the Nissan Pathfinder. The officers recovered two tinfoils containing marijuana laced with PCP, a bag of chunky white rocks and a large white rock of crack cocaine from the hidden compartment on the passenger side door, unused ziplock bags, a portable phone, and personal papers. What had been a routine stop for a traffic violation ended in a drug bust.

As mentioned previously, District of Columbia traffic regulations permitted plainclothes officers to make traffic stops "only in the case of a violation that is so grave as to pose an *immediate threat* to the safety of others."[48] The officers never claimed that the driving of James Brown constituted a traffic violation that was so grave as to pose an immediate safety threat and in effect admitted that they had violated regulations. Either the police just got lucky when they found drugs in plain view while violating departmental policy, or one of the vice officers had a hunch that the occupants of the vehicle were engaged in drug activity and used an alleged violation of the traffic laws as a pretext to stop the sports utility vehicle.

The District Court

On July 8, 1993, a federal grand jury returned an indictment against Michael Whren and James Brown charging them with possession with intent to distribute 50 grams or more of crack cocaine in violation of a variety of federal statutes. The district court judge assigned to the case was Norma Holloway Johnson, an African–American jurist appointed to the federal bench by President Jimmy Carter in 1980.[49] Over the years, Judge Johnson had earned a reputation as being somewhat unpredictable on the bench.

Michael Whren and James Brown each had counsel, both of whom were experienced private criminal defense lawyers. Defense counsel brought a motion to suppress the drug evidence on the ground that the stop violated the Fourth Amendment's prohibition of unreasonable searches and seizures. The district court held a hearing to consider the suppression motion. At the hearing, defense counsel pressed the arresting officers to explain their reasons for making the traffic stop. Officer Efrain Soto testified that the driver of the vehicle, James Brown, was

---

[48] *Id.*

[49] Before becoming a federal judge, Judge Johnson previously served as a trial judge for ten years in the District of Columbia courts. As Chief Judge, Johnson later decided a number of matters involving Independent Counsel Kenneth Starr's investigation of President Bill Clinton. *See In re* Grand Jury Proceedings, 5 F. Supp. 2d 21 (D.D.C. 1998); *In re* Grand Jury Proceedings, No. 98–228, 1998 U.S. Dist. LEXIS 17290 (D.D.C. Sept. 24, 1998); *In re* Grand Jury Proceedings, 5 F.Supp. 2d 21 (D.D.C. 1998).

"not paying full time and attention to his driving."[50] Soto admitted that he did not intend to issue a ticket to the driver for stopping too long at the stop sign; rather, he wanted to inquire about why Brown was obstructing traffic and sped off without signaling in a school area. He denied that the decision to stop the Nissan Pathfinder was based on a "racial profile." Littlejohn's testimony confirmed Soto's but differed with respect to the hand from which Soto seized the drug from Whren.

This testimony notwithstanding, the judge had real doubts about the motive for stopping the Pathfinder. As counsel for Whren and Brown later explained,

> [t]he court had been concerned by the "lengthy pause" before Officer Soto answered "no" to the following question from Mr. Brown's counsel:
>
> Q ... [I]sn't it true that your decision to stop that Pathfinder was because you believed that two young black men in a Pathfinder with temporary tags were suspicious; isn't that true?
>
> When the court asked Officer Soto why he had "hesitate[d] a long time" before answering that "very straightforward question," Soto stated that he had "wanted to really think" and "analyze the question." He denied basing the stop on any "racial profile."[51]

Despite her doubts, Judge Johnson denied the motion to suppress. Although noting some discrepancies between the testimony of Soto and Littlejohn, she ruled that

> the one thing that was not controverted ... is the facts surrounding the stop. There may be different ways in which one can interpret it but, truly, the facts of the stop were not controverted. There was nothing to really demonstrate that the actions of the officers were contrary to a normal traffic stop. It may not be what some of us believe should be done, or when it should be done, or how it should be done, but the facts stand uncontroverted, and the court is going to accept the testimony of Officer Soto.
>
> I was indeed concerned primarily with the manner in which he responded to a question more ... so than his response to the question. But I do believe that the government has demonstrated through the evidence presented that the police conduct was appropriate and, therefore, there is no need to suppress the evidence. And it is so ordered. The motions to suppress will be denied.[52]

---

[50] United States v. Whren, 53 F.3d 371, 373 (D.C. Cir. 1995).

[51] Brief for the Petitioners at 10 n.11, Whren v. United States, 517 U.S. 806 (1996) (No. 95–5841) (citations omitted).

[52] Transcript of Motions and Trial Before the Honorable Norma Holloway Johnson at 138–39, United States v. Whren, Crim. No. 93–0273 (1993).

A trial was subsequently held. One of the defense attorneys recalls the case as one in which the deck was stacked against their clients, with the judge antagonistic to the defense at every turn.[53] A jury convicted Whren and Brown on all counts of the indictment. Judge Johnson sentenced Whren and Brown to fourteen years in prison, along with supervised release and fines.[54] With nothing to lose, the defendants appealed their convictions to the U.S. Court of Appeals for the District of Columbia Circuit.

The Court of Appeals

On appeal, Lisa Burget of the Federal Public Defenders Office represented Whren and G. Allen Dale represented Brown. Margaret Lawton, Assistant U.S. Attorney, represented the government. The case was argued in February 1995 and decided in May of that year.

The panel assigned to the case consisted of three appointees of Republican President Ronald Reagan—former Conservative Party (a short-lived offshoot of the Republican Party) U.S. Senator James Buckley, who is the brother of conservative pundit William F. Buckley, and former federal prosecutors Stephen Williams[55] and David Sentelle.

In the D.C. Circuit, Whren and Brown contended that the police officers obtained evidence through an illegal search and seizure in violation of the Fourth Amendment.[56] They specifically argued that the police officers used the traffic violations as a pretext for a search for drugs without probable cause and that the search was objectively unreasonable under the Fourth Amendment. As the court of appeals summarized the argument in a published opinion written by Judge Sentelle,

> Appellants argue that this court should borrow from the law of other circuits in determining whether "objective circumstances" warrant a search. While several circuits hold that an alleged pretextual stop is valid as long as an officer legally "could have" stopped

---

[53] *See* Telephone Interview of Christian Camenisch by Kevin R. Johnson, June 2005.

[54] *See Whren*, 53 F.3d at 373.

[55] Williams is also a former law professor, most recently at the University of Colorado School of Law.

[56] Whren and Brown also challenged their convictions and sentences for possession and intent to distribute cocaine base under 21 U.S.C. § 841, arguing that the crime was a lesser included offense of their separate convictions for possession with intent to distribute cocaine base within 1000 feet of a school under 21 U.S.C. § 860(a). The government ultimately agreed with the appellants on this issue and the court of appeals remanded for entry of an amended judgment and resentencing. *See Whren*, 53 F.3d at 372. For a subsequent appeal of the sentencing in the case holding that a defendant on remand generally cannot raise new challenges to sentencing, see United States v. Whren, 111 F.3d 956 (D.C. Cir. 1997), *cert. denied*, 522 U.S. 1119 (1998).

the car in question because of a suspected traffic violation ...,
appellants urge the court to adopt the test laid out by the Tenth and
Eleventh Circuits, which have held that a stop is valid only if "under
the same circumstances a reasonable officer *would have* made the
stop in the absence of the invalid purpose." Appellants contend that
the "would have" test is superior to the "could have" test because
the latter fails to place any reasonable limitations on discretionary
police conduct, thus "cut[ting] at the heart of the Fourth Amendment." Brief of Appellant Whren at 22.[57]

The D.C. Circuit found that its previous decision in *United States v.
Mitchell*[58] had "implicitly adopt[ed]"[59] the "could have" test. In *Mitchell*,
the court of appeals, in an opinion written by Judge Buckley and joined
by Judge Williams, two of the judges on the panel in *Whren*, held that a
stop was reasonable so long as an officer had observed a traffic violation.[60] In *Mitchell*, a police stop for speeding and failing to signal led to a
search that uncovered drugs and firearms. According to the court of
appeals in *Whren*, one virtue of the "could have" test is that it avoided
inquiry into the officer's state of mind; in the court's view, the probable
cause required for the traffic stop sufficiently limited police discretion.
Applying the test to the facts at hand, the D.C. Circuit found that Soto
and Littlejohn had grounds to stop Whren and Brown and affirmed the
denial of the motion to suppress the evidence and the convictions.[61]

The Supreme Court Litigation

Whren and Brown next sought review of their convictions in the
United States Supreme Court. They contended that the Court needed to
reconcile a split in the lower courts about the appropriate Fourth
Amendment test to apply in evaluating the lawfulness of traffic stops.[62]
In urging the Court not to hear the case, the Solicitor General contended
that the disagreement over the appropriate Fourth Amendment test was
not significant because the "minority" view would not change the result
in many cases. As the Solicitor General noted, "to date, pretext claims

---

[57] *Whren*, 53 F.3d at 374 (citations omitted) (emphasis in original).

[58] 951 F.2d 1291 (D.C. Cir. 1991).

[59] *Whren*, 53 F.3d at 375.

[60] *See Mitchell*, 951 F.2d at 1295–96.

[61] *See Whren*, 53 F.3d at 376.

[62] *See* Petition for Writ of Certiorari to the United States Court of Appeals for the
District of Columbia Circuit at 7–9, Whren v. United States, 517 U.S. 806 (1996) (No. 95–
5841).

have rarely succeeded in any circuit. Far more typical are cases finding that the stop was undertaken pursuant to routine police practice."[63]

On January 5, 1996, the Supreme Court agreed to hear *Whren v. United States*.[64] Until then, the "Court had not explicitly decided whether the police could use the legal justification of a minor crime as a pretext to stop a person in order to search or interrogate that person for an unrelated, more serious crime for which the police did not have reasonable suspicion—a so-called pretextual stop."[65]

The Briefs

Whren and Brown's brief emphasized the need for the "would have" test—that is, that a stop is valid only if under the same circumstances a reasonable officer *would have* made the stop absent an impermissible purpose—to circumscribe police discretion and curtail pretextual stops based on race.[66]

Whren and Brown argued that any alternative would offer "carte blanche" to the police to stop automobiles based on the race of the driver. Their argument found support in some precedent and leading authorities.[67] As one court of appeals judge had forcefully put it, "[g]iven the 'multitude of applicable traffic and equipment regulations' in any jurisdiction, ... upholding a stop on the basis of a regulation seldom enforced opens the door to the arbitrary exercise of police discretion.... The ['could have'] standard ... allows virtually unfettered discretion by upholding a stop even if ... motivated by an illegal purpose...."[68]

The opening salvo of the brief for Whren and Brown played on the theme that police discretion must be limited, as well as emphasizing the role of race in traffic stops:

> *This case arose because the sight of two young black men in a Nissan Pathfinder with temporary tags, pausing at a stop sign in Southeast Washington, D.C., aroused the suspicion of plainclothes vice officers*

---

[63] Brief for the United States in Opposition to the Petition for Writ of Certiorari to the United States Court of Appeals for the District of Columbia Circuit at 9, Whren v. United States, 517 U.S. 806 (1996) (No. 95–5841).

[64] 516 U.S. 1036 (1996).

[65] Christopher R. Dillon, Note, Whren v. United States *and Pretextual Traffic Stops: The Supreme Court Declines to Plumb the Collective Conscience of Police*, 38 B.C. L. Rev. 737, 753 (1997) (footnote omitted).

[66] *See* Brief for the Petitioners, *supra* note 51, at 15–37.

[67] *See* Wayne R. LaFave, Jerold H. Israel, & Nancy J. King, *Criminal Procedure* § 3.1, at 113–14 (4th ed. 2004); David A. Sklansky, *Traffic Stops, Minority Motorists, and the Future of the Fourth Amendment*, 1997 Sup. Ct. Rev. 271, 283 n.73.

[68] United States v. Botero–Ospina, 71 F.3d 783, 790–91 (10th Cir. 1995) (en banc) (Seymour, C.J., dissenting).

patrolling for narcotics violations in an unmarked car. The officers decided to stop the Pathfinder and "investigate" why the driver was stopped so long at the stop sign—ostensibly a violation of the District of Columbia Municipal Regulation requiring drivers to pay "full time and attention" to operating their vehicle.... Turning around to make the stop, one of the officers claimed to see the Pathfinder commit two other minor traffic infractions. Without any intention of issuing a ticket, and in violation of police regulations, the officers then seized the Pathfinder at a stoplight a few blocks away and discovered illegal drugs in plain view.[69]

To bolster the argument, the brief summarized studies establishing the racially disparate impacts of traffic stops on African Americans.[70]

The United States countered that the "could have" test, by which a traffic stop is valid under the Fourth Amendment so long as an officer lawfully "could have" stopped the car in question because of a suspected traffic violation, offered the only workable standard for police officers. According to the Solicitor General, that test did not afford unbridled discretion to police officers to rely on race to stop an automobile: "Any decision to single out a suspect or suspects on the basis of [race or ethnicity] ... would be unlawful under the Equal Protection Clause."[71] This elaboration of the government's argument was apparently made for the first time in the Supreme Court. Importantly, the Solicitor General did not engage in any attempt to justify a race-based traffic stop by police officers; such an argument would have been difficult for the Court to accept in light of its consistent view that the Constitution bans state action motivated by discriminatory intent.

Whren and Brown countered that regardless of whether the police violated the Equal Protection Clause, the traffic stop was impermissible under the Fourth Amendment. Their brief further argued that equal protection claims were inherently difficult to prove and failed to offer a full remedy for a race-based stop by police officers:

---

[69] Brief for the Petitioners, *supra* note 51, at 2–3.

[70] *See id.* at 21–27.

[71] Brief for the United States at 28, *Whren*, 517 U.S. 806 (No. 95–5841) (citing, inter alia, Yick Wo v. Hopkins, 118 U.S. 356, 373–74 (1886)). The brief quoted a concurring opinion of Chief Judge Jon Newman in a Second Circuit decision adopting the "could have" test in which he emphasized that " 'the Equal Protection Clause has sufficient vitality to curb most of the abuses that the [defendant] apprehends. Police officers who misuse the authority we approve today may expect to be defendants in civil suits seeking substantial damages for discriminatory enforcement of the law.' " *Id.* at 28 (quoting United States v. Scopo, 19 F.3d 777, 786 (2d Cir. 1994)) (Newman, C.J., concurring); *see* Brief of the California District Attorney's Association, as Amicus Curiae in Support of Respondent at 27–29, *Whren*, 517 U.S. 806 (No. 95–5841) (making similar argument).

[T]he Equal Protection Clause cannot be relied upon to curb the systemic abuses petitioners have documented. An equal protection claim in the selective traffic enforcement setting would require determination of the very subjective intent of the officer that the government agrees is so difficult to establish. Any individual motorist ... might have a "gut instinct" that his race played a role in his stop, but would be hard-pressed to gather even the minimal amount of information needed ... to file a complaint. Even if the claim survived [a motion to dismiss], the kind of data required to prove intentional discrimination is not generally available.[72]

Friends of the court filed briefs in support of both sides. The American Civil Liberties Union and National Association of Criminal Defense Lawyers aligned themselves with the defendants, while various state attorney generals and the conservative Criminal Justice Legal Foundation sided with the U.S. government. The briefs in support of the defendants repeatedly expressed concern with the use of pretextual traffic stops to investigate other crimes. In contrast, the briefs supporting the government's position emphasized the difficulty and impropriety of interrogating the intent of police officers who made a valid traffic stop. The war on drugs almost assuredly was on the minds of all parties.[73]

Oral Argument

In April 1996, the Supreme Court heard oral argument in *Whren v. United States*. Lisa Wright, who had married and changed her last name from Burget since arguing the case in the D.C. Circuit, argued on behalf of the defendants. An experienced Assistant to the Solicitor General (and former President of the *Harvard Law Review*), James A. Feldman, argued for the United States. As expected, the arguments centered on the contrasting tests for judging the validity of a traffic stop. At one point, the questioning by the Court allowed Feldman to reiterate the U.S. government's proposed remedy for police reliance on race in a traffic stop:

QUESTION: ... [Y]ou wouldn't say selective enforcement based on race or religion would be permissible.

---

[72] Reply Brief for the Petitioners, at 8–9, *Whren*, 517 U.S. 806 (No. 95–5841) (citations omitted); *see* Brief Amicus Curiae of the American Civil Liberties Union in Support of Petitioners at 10–11, *Whren*, 517 U.S. 806 (No. 95–5841) (making a similar argument).

[73] *See* Brief for the Petitioners, *supra* note 51 at 13–29; Reply Brief, *supra* note 72, at 2–5; Brief Amicus Curiae of the American Civil Liberties Union in Support of Petitioners, *supra* note 72, at 6–12; Brief of Amicus Curiae National Association of Criminal Defense Lawyers in Support of Petitioners at 10–11, *Whren*, 517 U.S. 806 (No. 95–5841).

MR. FELDMAN: Our view would be that those would be unconstitutional—

QUESTION: For a different reason.

MR. FELDMAN:—but they would be unconstitutional under the Equal Protection Clause—

QUESTION: Right.

MR. FELDMAN: —and there would be different standards applied to them.

Later, Feldman went on to emphasize that the defendants' "arguments are primarily directed towards interests that are not protected by the Fourth Amendment. Insofar as there's an equal protection claim, that claim should be made under the Equal Protection Clause."[74]

The Supreme Court Opinion

Less than three months after oral argument in June 1996—at the end of the term when the Court rushes to file many decisions—it handed down the opinion in *Whren v. United States.*[75] The unanimous Court affirmed the D.C. Circuit's decision. In an opinion written by Justice Antonin Scalia (formerly a member of the D.C. Circuit himself), the Justices framed the question as "whether the temporary detention of a motorist who the police have probable cause to believe has committed a civil traffic violation is inconsistent with the Fourth Amendment's prohibition against unreasonable seizures unless a reasonable officer would have been motivated to stop the car by a desire to enforce the traffic laws."[76]

As previously discussed, the problem of pretextual stops based on race came up in the briefs and oral argument. Nevertheless, in restating the facts of the case, the Court failed to mention that Whren and Brown were African American. The Court instead delayed mentioning this most salient fact until later in the opinion in introducing the Fourth Amendment argument: "Petitioners [Whren and Brown], who are both black, ... contend that police officers might decide which motorists to stop based on decidedly impermissible factors, such as the race of the car's occupants."[77]

---

[74] Transcript of Oral Argument at *42, *47, 1996 U.S. TRANS LEXIS 20, *Whren,* 517 U.S. 806 (1996) (No. 95–5841).

[75] 517 U.S. 806 (1996).

[76] *Id.* at 808.

[77] *Id.* at 810; *see* Anthony C. Thompson, *Stopping the Usual Suspects: Race and the Fourth Amendment,* 74 N.Y.U. L. Rev. 956, 978 (1999) (noting that "the [Supreme] Court in *Whren* presented the facts of the case without any mention of race" and explaining that

The Court began its legal analysis by reciting standard Fourth Amendment law that an automobile stop must be "reasonable."[78] The Court seized on the admission of Whren and Brown that the officers had probable cause to believe that Brown's driving of the Nissan Pathfinder violated various provisions of the District of Columbia traffic code.[79] This admission was the linchpin of the Court's opinion and critical to the ultimate disposition of the case.

The Court addressed directly the argument that, because a police officer could almost invariably find a technical traffic code violation for virtually anyone driving on the roads, upholding Whren and Brown's stop would allow police to use pretextual grounds to investigate other crimes. The Court reviewed cases in which it had rejected searches as unconstitutional pretexts under the Fourth Amendment.[80] Justice Scalia found that those decisions were limited to searches in which officers lacked probable cause and thus were distinguishable from Whren and Brown's stop.

In *Colorado v. Bannister,*[81] the Court had upheld a traffic stop that was followed by the plain view sighting of contraband and an arrest for unrelated charges. The Court had remarked that "[t]here was no evidence whatsoever that the officer's presence to issue a traffic citation was a pretext to confirm any other previous suspicion about the occupants."[82] However, the Court rejected Whren and Brown's argument that, because the stop in question was pretextual, the decision in *Colorado v. Bannister* was distinguishable. Rather, the Court, according to Justice Scalia, had "repeatedly" rejected the argument "that an officer's motive invalidates objectively justifiable behavior under the Fourth Amendment."[83]

The Court would not accept the defendants' proposed Fourth Amendment test that called for determining "whether the officer's conduct deviated materially from usual police practices, so that a reason-

---

the current Court's criminal decisions often seek to downplay the importance of the race of the defendants).

[78] *See Whren,* 517 U.S. at 809–10 (citing Delaware v. Prouse, 440 U.S. 648, 653 (1979); United States v. Martinez–Fuerte, 428 U.S. 543 (1976); United States v. Brignoni–Ponce, 422 U.S. 873, 878 (1975)).

[79] *See Whren,* 517 U.S. at 810.

[80] *See* Florida v. Wells, 495 U.S. 1 (1990); Colorado v. Bertine, 479 U.S. 367 (1987).

[81] 449 U.S. 1 (1980).

[82] *Id.* at 4 n.4.

[83] *Whren,* 517 U.S. at 812. For this proposition, the Court cited United States v. Villamonte–Marquez, 462 U.S. 579 (1983); Scott v. United States, 436 U.S. 128 (1978); and United States v. Robinson, 414 U.S. 218 (1973).

able officer in the same circumstances would not have made the stop for the reasons given."[84] It understood the proposed standard to ask whether a police officer had the proper state of mind based on what a reasonable officer might believe given the same set of facts. Snidely denigrating any such inquiry, Justice Scalia saw it as reducing a reviewing court "to speculating about the hypothetical reaction of a hypothetical constable—an exercise that might be called virtual subjectivity."[85] As the Court recognized in finding that drug checkpoints to interdict unlawful drugs violated the Constitution, however, reasonableness of police conduct is the touchstone of the Fourth Amendment.[86] The Court offered no reason why it could not apply a reasonableness standard to a traffic stop.

Besides the problem of discerning the state of mind of a police officer, a standard the Justices were unwilling to import from the Equal Protection Clause, the Court expressed concern about local variation in the Fourth Amendment standard. In the case before it, the officers' conduct was alleged to be unreasonable because District of Columbia police regulations permitted plainclothes officers to make traffic stops " 'only in the case of a violation that is so grave as to pose an *immediate threat* to the safety of others.' "[87] Because different police departments are subject to different rules and regulations, in the Court's view, incorporation of local rules and regulations into its Fourth Amendment analysis could lead to divergent interpretations of whether the same traffic stop was unconstitutional. As a result, a most troubling fact in the case—that the officers had in fact deviated from the local regulations in making the stop—did not warrant analysis in the Court's opinion. That fact was irrelevant to the application of the Fourth Amendment, and any violation of police department policy presumably had to be addressed by local authorities.

The Court also rejected any claim that it should balance competing interests in deciding whether plainclothes officers could lawfully make traffic stops in the circumstances before the Court. Generally opposed to multifactored balancing tests as a matter of principle,[88] Justice Scalia

---

[84] *Whren*, 517 U.S. at 814.

[85] *Id.* at 815.

[86] *See* City of Indianapolis v. Edmond, 531 U.S. 32, 37 (2000) ("The Fourth Amendment requires that searches and seizures be reasonable.").

[87] *Whren*, 517 U.S. at 815 (quoting Metropolitan Police Department, Washington, D.C., General Order 303.1, pt. 1, Objectives and Policies (A)(2)(4) (Apr. 30, 1992)) (emphasis in original).

[88] *See* Antonin Scalia, *The Rule of Law as a Law of Rules*, 56 U. Chi. L. Rev. 1175 (1989); *see, e.g.*, Burnham v. Superior Court of California, 495 U.S. 604, 622–27 (1990) (plurality) (Scalia, J.) (criticizing freewheeling fairness analysis in evaluating the constitu-

reasoned that the cases that balanced the interests at stake were inapplicable to the case at hand "because they involved seizures without probable cause."[89] The Court emphasized once again that, in contrast to its balancing cases, the police in this case had the requisite probable cause for the traffic stop.

The Court rejected the argument that, because traffic regulations are so comprehensive, police under the "could have" test can stop whomever they want for a technical violation of the law. The Court could not identify a standard that it might apply to evaluate such conduct and emphasized that "[f]or the run-of-the-mine case, which this surely is, we think there is no realistic alternative to the traditional common-law rule that probable cause justifies a search and seizure."[90] In a brief, yet critically important, passage of the opinion, the Court accepted the Solicitor General's argument about the proper remedy for race-based traffic stops:

> We of course agree with petitioners that the Constitution prohibits selective enforcement of the law based on considerations such as race. But the constitutional basis for objecting to intentionally discriminatory application of laws is the Equal Protection Clause, not the Fourth Amendment.[91]

The Court failed to cite any cases supporting its conclusion that the Equal Protection Clause offered the exclusive constitutional remedy for the alleged pretextual stop. Nor did it acknowledge the formidable difficulties facing criminal defendants who attempt to prove an equal protection claim. The Court must have been aware of the heavy evidentiary burden on a party seeking to prove discriminatory intent, especially given that about one month before deciding *Whren*, *United States v. Armstrong* barred the discovery of evidence that African–American defendants claimed was necessary to prove racially discriminatory enforcement of the crack cocaine laws.[92] Applying " 'ordinary equal protection standards,' "[93] the Court required a showing that the prosecution of the individual defendant was motivated by racial animus. Such a state of

---

tionality under the Due Process Clause of state court exercise of personal jurisdiction over non-resident defendants).

[89] *Whren*, 517 U.S. at 817–18. In this regard, the Court referred to Delaware v. Prouse, 440 U.S. 648 (1979) (random traffic stop); United States v. Martinez–Fuerte, 428 U.S. 543 (1976) (checkpoint stops); United States v. Brignoni–Ponce, 422 U.S. 873 (1975) (roving patrols).

[90] *Whren*, 517 U.S. at 819.

[91] *Id.* at 813.

[92] 517 U.S. 456 (1996).

[93] *Id.* at 465 (citing Wayte v. United States, 470 U.S. 598, 608 (1985)).

mind, of course, is difficult, if not impossible, to establish without the information about other criminal prosecutions sought from the government. Racial bias in the enforcement of the crack cocaine laws is well-documented,[94] and the *Armstrong* data showed that for an entire year, *all* crack cocaine arrests in that district involved black defendants, despite comparable rates of drug usage by whites. Nevertheless, the Court in *Armstrong* found that the defendants were not entitled to discovery from the government to secure the evidence necessary to prove a selective prosecution claim.

Under the Equal Protection Clause, Whren and Brown would have to pursue a civil action for damages based on the discriminatory conduct. For criminal defendants, this remedy is far less appealing than the suppression of illegally obtained evidence. The Fourth Amendment's exclusionary rule bars the use of unlawfully seized evidence against a defendant; there is no counterpart in the Fourteenth Amendment. The inability to exclude the fruits of a stop based on impermissible factors under the Equal Protection Clause makes any such claim of limited value to defendants like Whren and Brown, who wanted to avoid conviction and a jail sentence. To criminal defendants, the hope is to escape conviction and imprisonment, not to recover damages in a civil action for a violation of their constitutional rights.

The Fallout

Having lost their case in the Supreme Court, Michael Whren and James Brown went to prison. Both were released after nearly a decade. As of February 2006, Whren was working his way through school as a licensed commercial truck driver. He also took the Maryland real estate examination. Brown's former attorney did not know his whereabouts after release from prison.

Nothing appears to have come of the fact that Metropolitan Police Department vice officers Efrain Soto and Homer Littlejohn stopped Brown and Whren in violation of departmental regulations. Both officers continued serving on the vice squad for many years. However, their stories are more surprising than those of Whren and Brown.

For at least a decade, allegations of serious misconduct dogged the 6D vice division. In 2000, an article in a local District of Columbia newspaper reported that, among other things, Littlejohn had been accused of planting evidence. Both Littlejohn and Soto had been the subject of citizen complaints of alleged misconduct, although none had been upheld. Soto was sued for false arrest and beating a suspect in 1995, which ended in a settlement. Local judges raised questions about

---

[94] *See* David A. Sklansky, *Cocaine, Race, and Equal Protection*, 47 Stan. L. Rev. 1283 (1995); William J. Stuntz, *Race, Class, and Drugs*, 98 Colum. L. Rev. 1795 (1998).

whether Soto and Littlejohn testified truthfully in drug cases. Moreover, according to the newspaper article, Soto and Littlejohn had their own personal legal problems. In 1996 and 1998, Soto's wife was granted temporary restraining orders because he battered her. Littlejohn was charged with drunk driving in 1998 and 1999.[95]

In one criminal appeal in 2004, the D.C. Circuit reversed a drug and firearms conviction because the trial court had denied the defendant the opportunity to put on witnesses willing to testify that Soto had a reputation within the local legal community as untruthful.[96] The defendant, who claimed that Soto had planted a gun at the scene of the arrest, sought to introduce the testimony of a local defense attorney who believed that Soto had lied in other cases. The defendant also proffered another witness who would testify that Soto and other officers wrongly arrested him on a drug charge in 1995.

Although accused of excessive use of force, planting evidence, perjury, and being part of a squad of lawless vice officers, Soto received a departmental award in December 2004.[97] Additionally, in 2002, the Mayor of the District of Columbia honored Littlejohn for his police service.[98] The very next year, he was indicted for perjury for allegedly lying to a grand jury about contacting another grand jury witness (a police officer).[99]

Soto and Littlejohn apparently continued to make traffic stops as pretexts to search for drugs. In May 1999, a judge heard testimony "from Littlejohn that he along with Soto and [another officer], had stopped [a suspect] after they spotted him from a block away driving without a seat belt. After learning that [he] didn't have a driver's license, they arrested and searched him and found drugs."[100] The continued use of pretextual stops should hardly be surprising in light of the fact that Littlejohn and Soto's previous efforts in *Whren* resulted in successful convictions. The Supreme Court in *Whren* effectively sanctioned such stops and, by so doing, encouraged officers to use them as a

---

[95] *See* Cherkis, *supra* note 46.

[96] *See* United States v. Whitmore, 359 F.3d 609, 613–15 (D.C. Cir. 2004) (discussing allegations of Soto's misconduct).

[97] *See* Metropolitan Police Department, Fifth Annual Awards Ceremony program 9 (2004), *available at* http://mpdc.dc.gov/mpdc/LIB/mpdc/about/heroes/awards/awardsprog_04.pdf, last visited Nov. 30, 2006.

[98] *See* Karlyn Barker, *City, Chamber Honor Public–Safety Heroes*, Wash. Post, Mar. 21, 2002, at T6.

[99] *See Crime & Justice*, Wash. Post, Dec. 5, 2003, at B2.

[100] Cherkis, *supra* note 46.

tool in the war on drugs. No one can say how many similar stops have been made across the country after the *Whren* decision.

From a legal perspective, the early effort to curtail racial profiling through the Fourth Amendment failed. However, profiling emerged as an issue of public concern,[101] particularly as the twentieth century drew to a close. The Supreme Court left it to the political process—and growing minority political power—to address the problems of race-based policing on the streets of the United States. Although political action initially brought progress, efforts to end racial profiling by law enforcement were derailed by the so-called war on terror that followed the tragic events of September 11, 2001.

The Immediate Legal Response to Whren v. United States

Unquestionably, the Supreme Court's decisions in *Whren v. United States* and *United States v. Armstrong*, taken together, have made it exceedingly difficult to challenge police practices as constituting racial discrimination. In *Whren*, the Court foreclosed inquiry into the subjective intent of police officers in evaluating a traffic stop under the Fourth Amendment and allowed police officers to base a stop for investigation of drug and other crimes on a violation of the traffic laws. By effectively sanctioning pretextual traffic stops under the Fourth Amendment and relegating defendants to a toothless Equal Protection remedy, the Court increased the vast powers that police officers possess in the war on drugs. Moreover, *Armstrong* made it difficult to collect the basic evidence necessary to establish a claim of discriminatory enforcement of the criminal laws. Together, *Armstrong* and *Whren* effectively immunize police from any challenges for race-based law enforcement conduct; only the most egregious police misconduct will likely be subject to sanction.

Whren v. United States quickly emerged as the leading traffic stop case in both the Supreme Court and the lower courts. The Court later relied on the decision in finding that the motivations of police officers were irrelevant to Fourth Amendment analysis.[102] Lower courts fastidiously follow *Whren v. United States* and prosecutors frequently invoke the holding in attempts to immunize the conduct of police officers. Today, the decision is the boilerplate citation for the proposition that the subjective motive of the police in making a stop is irrelevant in evaluating the stop's constitutionality under the Fourth Amendment.[103] State

---

[101] *See, e.g.,* Robert D. McFadden, *Police Singled Out Black Drivers in Drug Crackdown, Judge Says,* N.Y. TIMES, Mar. 10, 1996, § 1, at 33; Jon Nordheimer, *Troopers Are Accused of Stopping Drivers Based on Race,* N.Y. TIMES, Dec. 23, 1994, at B5.

[102] *See* Devenpeck v. Alford, 543 U.S. 146, 153–54 (2004); Arkansas v. Sullivan, 532 U.S. 769, 771 (2001); United States v. Knights, 534 U.S. 112, 122 (2001).

[103] *See, e.g.,* United States v. Brigham, 382 F.3d 500, 510 (5th Cir. 2004) (en banc); United States v. Serena, 368 F.3d 1037, 1041 (8th Cir. 2004); United States v. Jones, 377

courts have also wholeheartedly adopted *Whren* in interpreting the Fourth Amendment and its counterparts in state constitutions.[104]

The lower courts have also relied on *Whren* for the bolder proposition that, so long as there was an objectively reasonable basis for the stop, it is justified even if it was admittedly a pretext.[105] One court of appeals bluntly stated that "traffic stops, in practice, may be used as a pretext to investigate other crimes because courts will not usually inquire into the actual motives of the police."[106]

Although the Court unanimously decided *Whren v. United States*, a couple of Justices soon appeared to have second thoughts. A year after the decision, Justice Anthony Kennedy dissented from the majority's holding in *Maryland v. Wilson*[107] that police could order a passenger from the vehicle even though he was not suspected of any crime. In his view,

> [t]he practical effect of our holding in *Whren*, of course, is to allow the police to stop vehicles in almost countless circumstances. When *Whren* is coupled with today's holding, the Court puts tens of millions of passengers at risk of arbitrary control by police. If the command to exit were to become commonplace, the Constitution would be diminished in a most public way.[108]

In the controversial 2001 decision of *Atwater v. City of Lago Vista*,[109] which found that the arrest of a driver for a minor traffic violation did not violate the Fourth Amendment, the Court relied on *Whren* in rejecting a balancing test. Justice Sandra Day O'Connor dissented, claiming that the Court in *Whren* had not addressed the particular issue

---

F.3d 1313, 1314 (11th Cir. 2004) (per curiam); United States v. Ibarra, 345 F.3d 711, 713–16 (9th Cir. 2003); United States v. Bookhardt, 277 F.3d 558, 565 (D.C. Cir. 2002); United States v. Saucedo, 226 F.3d 782, 789 (6th Cir. 2000); Hernandez v. United States, 531 U.S. 1102 (2001); United States v. Dhinsa, 171 F.3d 721, 724–25 (2d Cir. 1998); United States v. Williams, 106 F.3d 1362, 1365 (7th Cir. 1997).

[104] *See* Abraham Abramovsky & Jonathan I. Edelstein, *Pretext Stops and Racial Profiling After* Whren v. United States*: The New York and New Jersey Responses Compared*, 63 Alb. L. Rev. 725 (2000); *see, e.g.*, Gama v. Nevada, 920 P.2d 1010, 1013–14 (Nev. 1996). *But see* Washington v. Ladson, 979 P.2d 833, 842 (Wash. 1999) (finding that Washington state constitution prohibited pretextual stop).

[105] *See, e.g.*, United States v. Linkous, 285 F.3d 716, 719–20 (8th Cir. 2002); United States v. Escalante, 239 F.3d 678, 680–81 (5th Cir. 2001); United States v. Wellman, 185 F.3d 651, 655–56 (6th Cir. 1999).

[106] United States v. Woodrum, 208 F.3d 8, 10 (1st Cir. 2000) (citation omitted).

[107] 519 U.S. 408 (1997).

[108] *Id.* at 423 (Kennedy, J., dissenting).

[109] 532 U.S. 318 (2001).

currently before the Court and that the "unbounded discretion" given police officers to arrest a person by the Court

> carries with it grave potential for abuse. The majority takes comfort in the lack of evidence of "an epidemic of unnecessary minor-offense arrests." ... But the relatively small number of published cases dealing with such arrests proves little and should provide little solace. Indeed, as the recent debate over racial profiling demonstrates all too clearly, a relatively minor traffic infraction may often serve as an excuse for stopping and harassing an individual. After today, the arsenal available to any officer extends to a full arrest and the searches permissible concomitant to that arrest. An officer's subjective motivations for making a traffic stop are not relevant considerations in determining the reasonableness of the stop. *See Whren v. United States....* But it is precisely because these motivations are beyond our purview that we must vigilantly ensure that officers' poststop actions—which are properly within our reach—comport with the Fourth Amendment's guarantee of reasonableness.[110]

Some lower court judges have expressed specific concerns about how *Whren* shields racial profiling. In one case, a court of appeals judge asserted unequivocally that "[i]f there ever was a clear case of racial profiling, it is [the present] case. By affirming these convictions, the majority gives support to police officers in this circuit who seize and search individuals because of their race."[111] In another case, a dissenting court of appeals judge observed that

> [i]n this case there is the unspoken issue of racial profiling.... [I]n my view, the obvious facts of this case, i.e., four young African–Americans traveling in a vehicle with out-of-state license plates stopped on a public highway in East Texas by a white highway patrolman for "following too closely" and then interrogated for 20 minutes about matters unrelated to the reasons for that stop, are so suggestive of circumstances in which racial profiling typically occurs that the [courts] fail in our responsibility to the hundreds of our minority citizens who daily exercise their constitutional right to travel ... without harassment when we close our eyes and minds to the reality of these circumstances.[112]

The Supreme Court in *Whren* emphasized that, even if the stop did not violate the Fourth Amendment, there was an equal protection

---

[110] *Id.* at 363–64, 372 (O'Connor, J., dissenting).

[111] United States v. Martinez, 354 F.3d 932, 935 (8th Cir. 2004) (Lay, J., dissenting).

[112] United States v. Brigham, 382 F.3d 500, 520 n.27 (5th Cir. 2004) (en banc) (DeMoss, J., dissenting).

remedy for a race-based traffic stop. As discussed previously, such claims face many barriers. The problems with enforcing an equal protection claim based on a pretextual traffic stop can be seen vividly in the post-*Whren* case of *Brown v. City of Oneonta*.[113] In that case, the U.S. Court of Appeals for the Second Circuit held that, despite the fact that the police questioned every young African–American man (and one African–American woman) in a small college town after a robbery victim told police that a Black man had committed the crime, the class action plaintiffs failed to demonstrate that the police had acted with a discriminatory intent. The facts of *Oneonta* are extreme, yet the plaintiffs still failed to prevail on their equal protection claim. It therefore seems that it would be extremely difficult to succeed on this theory in a "run-of-the-mine" case like that of Whren and Brown. Not surprisingly, after *Whren*, there has been a long string of defeats in lawsuits claiming that unconstitutional racial profiling led to a traffic stop.[114]

In contrast to the enthusiastic application of *Whren* to vindicate traffic stops and shield police officers' motives from scrutiny by the courts, the academic criticism of the Supreme Court's decision has been harsh[115] with defenders few and far between.[116] The criticisms run the gamut, from the claim that the ruling blunted any efforts to eradicate racial profiling through the Fourth Amendment[117] to the argument that the equal protection remedy for racial discrimination suggested by the

[113] 221 F.3d 329, 338–39 (2d Cir. 1999). For critical analysis of the *Oneonta* decision, see R. Richard Banks, *Race-Based Suspect Selection and Colorblind Equal Protection Doctrine and Discourse*, 48 UCLA L. Rev. 1075 (2001), and Bela August Walker, Note, *The Color of Crime: The Case Against Race–Based Suspect Descriptions*, 103 Colum. L. Rev. 662 (2003).

[114] *See, e.g.,* Flowers v. Fiore, 359 F.3d 24, 34–35 (1st Cir. 2004); Bingham v. City of Manhattan Beach, 341 F.3d 939, 948–49 (9th Cir. 2003); Chavez v. Illinois State Police, 251 F.3d 612, 634–48 (7th Cir. 2001); United States v. Avery, 137 F.3d 343, 354–58 (6th Cir. 1997); United States v. Duque–Nava, 315 F. Supp. 2d 1144 (D. Kan. 2004). Some racial profiling claims, however, have been successful. *See, e.g.,* Marshall v. Columbia Lea Reg'l Hosp., 345 F.3d 1157, 1166–1171 (10th Cir. 2003); Price v. Kramer, 200 F.3d 1237 (9th Cir. 2000).

[115] *See, e.g.,* Devon W. Carbado, *(E)Racing the Fourth Amendment*, 100 Mich. L. Rev. 946, 1032–34 (2002); Andrew D. Leipold, *Objective Tests and Subjective Bias: Some Problems of Discriminatory Intent in the Criminal Law*, 73 Chi.-Kent L. Rev. 559, 566–69 (1998); David Rudovsky, *Law Enforcement by Stereotypes and Serendipity: Racial Profiling and Stops and Searches Without Cause*, 3 U. Pa. J. Const. L. 296, 319–21 (2001).

[116] *See, e.g.,* Steve Holbert & Lisa Rose, *The Color of Guilt & Innocence: Racial Profiling and Police Practices in America* 172 (2004) ("[P]retext stops [as permitted by *Whren*] can be a useful means of apprehending those who violate the law.").

[117] *See* Alberto B. Lopez, *Racial Profiling and* Whren: *Searching for Objective Evidence of the Fourth Amendment on the Nation's Roads*, 90 Ky. L.J. 75 (2001–2002).

Court is not full and effective.[118] Many commentators find problematic the wide-ranging discretion that the Supreme Court's Fourth Amendment analysis has afforded police, which in turn hinders efforts to end race-based law enforcement. The Equal Protection Clause, with its difficult proof problems, simply has not proven to be a viable method for criminal defendants to address systemic reliance on race by local police. Leading criminal procedure authority Wayne LaFave, for example, suggests that the decision in *Whren v. United States* encourages police to act on a "hunch."[119] In his view, the Court's Fourth Amendment ruling does not adequately limit police discretion, and a race-based equal protection challenge to a traffic stop is next to impossible to prove.[120] LaFave sees *Whren* as undermining other settled search and seizure precedent that limits law enforcement officers' authority.[121]

In sum, the Supreme Court's decision in *Whren v. United States* authorized and encouraged police to employ traffic stops as a tool in the war on drugs. The Court's refusal to consider the intent of police officers in its Fourth Amendment analysis created a safe haven for racial profiling. Lower courts seized on the decision to justify pretextual traffic stops. And Equal Protection claims challenging racial profiling, the only legal avenue of relief that remained, have been notoriously difficult to prove.

Political Fallout—The Fall and Rise of Racial Profiling

Not long after the Supreme Court's decision in *Whren v. United States*, racial profiling emerged as a national issue of pressing concern. A practice that was part and parcel of the war on drugs finally came under sustained public scrutiny. Scholars and policymakers critically examined racial profiling in criminal law enforcement, which in its most extreme form bases police stops of African Americans, Latina/os, and other racial minorities on their perceived group propensities for criminal conduct.[122]

---

[118] *See* Pamela S. Karlan, *Race, Rights, and Remedies in Criminal Adjudication*, 96 MICH. L. REV. 2001, 2005–14 (1998).

[119] LaFave et al., *supra* note 67, at § 12.5, at 676.

[120] *See* 1 Wayne R. LaFave, *Search and Seizure: A Treatise on the Fourth Amendment* § 1.4(f), at 136–55 (4th ed. 2004); Wayne R. LaFave, *The "Routine Traffic Stop" From Start to Finish: Too Much "Routine," Not Enough Fourth Amendment*, 102 Mich. L. Rev. 1843, 1852–61 (2004).

[121] *See* 3 LaFave, *supra* note 120, at § 6.7(d), at 497, § 7.2(d), at 591.

[122] *See, e.g.*, Angela J. Davis, *Race, Cops, and Traffic Stops*, 51 U. Miami L. Rev. 425, 442–43 (1997); David A. Harris, *The Stories, the Statistics, and the Law: Why "Driving While Black" Matters*, 84 Minn. L. Rev. 265 (1999); Tracey Maclin, *Race and the Fourth Amendment*, 51 Vand. L. Rev. 333, 342–62 (1998); Floyd Weatherspoon, *Ending Racial*

Prominent federal officials condemned the use of racial profiling to stop African Americans on the nation's highways. In 1999, President Clinton issued an Executive Order condemning racial profiling and requiring federal law enforcement agencies to collect statistical data to determine whether abuses were occurring.[123] In the 2000 Democratic Presidential primary campaign, candidates Bill Bradley and Al Gore each claimed to be tougher on racial profiling than the other in a debate at a famous African–American landmark—the Apollo Theater in Harlem.

As Professor Albert Alschuler summarized,

> Until September 11, 2001, almost everyone condemned racial profiling. President Bill Clinton called the practice "morally indefensible" and "deeply corrosive." President George W. Bush pledged, "[W]e will end it." A federal court observed, "Racial profiling of any kind is anathema to our criminal justice system." 81 percent of the respondents to a 1999 Gallup poll declared their opposition.[124]

One influential criminal procedure scholar went so far as to state that "profiling is the great issue of our time."[125]

Although the movement to end racial profiling had begun before 1996, public awareness of the problem of racial profiling grew significantly after *Whren v. United States*. Criminal defendants' losses in the Supreme Court effectively shifted efforts from the courts to legislatures to address the problem. African American, Latina/o, and civil rights groups pressed to make this a significant political issue.

Despite the doctrinal difficulties, lawsuits continue to challenge racial profiling by state law enforcement agencies, including those in New Jersey and California.[126] State legislatures passed laws requiring state and local police departments to adopt policies on profiling. Some state laws required the collection of demographic and other data on drivers stopped by police, with the hope of uncovering evidence of

---

Profiling of African–Americans in the Selective Enforcement of Laws: In Search of Viable Remedies, 65 U. Pitt. L. Rev. 721 (2004).

[123] *See* Memorandum on Fairness in Law Enforcement, 35 WEEKLY COMP. PRES. DOC. 1067 (June 9, 1999).

[124] Albert W. Alschuler, *Racial Profiling and the Constitution*, 2002 U. Chi. Legal F. 163, 163 (footnotes omitted). The court opinion quoted by Professor Alschuler was Martinez v. Village of Mount Prospect, 92 F. Supp. 2d 780, 782 (N.D. Ill. 2000).

[125] William J. Stuntz, Essay, *Local Policing After the Terror*, 111 Yale L.J.. 2137, 2142 (2002) (discussing regulation of police).

[126] *See New Jersey Enters Into Consent Decree on Racial Issues in Highway Stops*, 66 Crim. L. Rep. 251 (2000); Rodriguez v. California Highway Patrol, 89 F. Supp. 2d 1131 (N.D. Cal. 2000).

impermissible profiling.[127] Many states and localities conducted studies on traffic stops in their jurisdictions. If nothing else, political action shed light on racial profiling as a national problem that deserved attention. This growing public awareness may have begun to influence judicial decisions. One court of appeals barred the reliance on race in making an immigration stop, finding that it was of little probative value in evaluating citizenship status.[128]

Unfortunately, the horrible events of September 11, 2001 resurrected governmental reliance on statistical probabilities that are at the core of racial profiling. Law enforcement authorities began to question persons who appeared Arab or Muslim, with no suggestion that there was evidence linking them to terrorist activity. Persons who "looked" Arab or Muslim were removed from airplanes, arrested, detained, interrogated, and sometimes physically and psychologically abused, often while denied access to counsel and family.[129] The federal government also imposed special immigration procedures, including registration with federal authorities, on noncitizens from select Arab and Muslim nations.

Many commentators proclaimed that the reconsideration of the use of race in law enforcement made perfect sense. Public opinion shifted in favor of racial profiling, which does not affect the vast majority of American citizens, as a tool in the war on terror.[130]

> Shortly after [September 11, 2001], 58 percent of the respondents to a Gallup poll said that airlines should screen passengers who appeared to be Arabs more intensely than other passengers. Half the respondents who voiced an opinion favored requiring people of Arab ethnicity, including United States citizens, to carry special identification cards.[131]

The federal government's policies were in line with, and tended to confirm the wisdom of, the new-found public support for racial profiling.

---

[127] See Matthew J. Hickman, U.S. Dep't of Justice, Traffic Stop Data Collection Policies for State Police, 2004 (2005).

[128] See United States v. Montero–Camargo, 208 F.3d 1122, 1135 (9th Cir. 2000) (en banc) ("Hispanic appearance is, in general, of such little probative value that it may not be considered as a relevant factor where particularized or individualized suspicion is required.").

[129] See, e.g., Susan M. Akram & Kevin R. Johnson, Race, Civil Rights, and Immigration Law After September 11, 2001: The Targeting of Arabs and Muslims, 58 N.Y.U. Ann. Surv. Am. Law 295, 351–55 (2002); David Cole, Enemy Aliens, 54 Stan. L. Rev. 953 (2002); Leti Volpp, The Citizen and the Terrorist, 49 UCLA L. Rev. 1575 (2002).

[130] See Samuel R. Gross & Debra Livingston, Essay, Racial Profiling Under Attack, 102 Colum. L. Rev. 1413, 1413–14 (2002); see, e.g., Peter H. Schuck, A Case for Profiling, Am. Law., Jan. 2002, at 59.

[131] Alschuler, supra note 124, at 163 (footnotes omitted).

The federal government's profiling of Arabs and Muslims in the dragnet after September 11th promoted the legitimacy of racial profiling. It also undermined federal efforts to pressure state and local law enforcement agencies to end profiling in criminal law enforcement, which had been a federal priority during Clinton's presidency. In keeping with the pre-September 11th policy, a handful of local law enforcement agencies refused the Attorney General's request to interview Arabs and Muslims as part of the war on terror because this tactic constituted impermissible racial profiling.[132]

Once government embraces the use of race-based statistical probabilities as a law enforcement tool in one area, the argument logically follows that the probabilities justify similar law enforcement techniques across the board—from combating terrorism to fighting crime on the streets to apprehending undocumented immigrants. As was true for many years, statistical probabilities also can be employed to justify focusing police action on African Americans, Latina/os, and Asian Americans, in cities across the United States. The federal government, for example, relied on probabilities to justify the internment of persons of Japanese ancestry during World War II.[133] Ultimately, the logic of profiling threatens all minority communities in all areas of law enforcement.

Immediately after September 11th, the political wherewithal for eradicating racial profiling in law enforcement waned. Although the federal government officially condemns profiling in ordinary criminal law enforcement,[134] the efforts to end racial profiling by state and local police have lost steam. Thus, the impact of the profiling adopted after September 11th was felt not only by Arabs and Muslims but also by African Americans, Latina/os, and other racial minorities resisting race-based law enforcement.

Conclusion

In supporting law enforcement in the war on drugs, the Supreme Court's decision in *Whren v. United States* was one of a string of Fourth Amendment decisions that disadvantaged criminal defendants, and had

---

[132] *See* Fox Butterfield, *A Nation Challenged: The Interviews; Police Are Split on Questioning of Mideast Men*, N.Y. Times, Nov. 22, 2001, at A1; Jim Adams, *Twin Cities Police Undecided on Helping FBI; They Fear Interviewing Mideast Men Would Be Profiling*, Star Trib. (Minneapolis, Minn.), Nov. 22, 2001, at 7B.

[133] *See* Korematsu v. United States, 323 U.S. 214 (1944) (upholding the internment of persons of Japanese ancestry during World War II).

[134] *See* Kevin R. Johnson, *Racial Profiling After September 11: The Department of Justice's 2003 Guidelines*, 50 Loy. L. Rev. 67 (2004) (reviewing Department of Justice policy attempting to reconcile the ban on racial profiling in criminal law enforcement with profiling in the war on terror).

disparate impacts on minority communities. The drug war has clear racial overtones and its enforcement has further estranged African Americans and Latina/os from the police. In this way, the drug war fits comfortably in a long history of the enforcement of the criminal laws in ways that punish racial minorities.

The story behind *Whren v. United States* reveals much about the war on drugs. Two small-time African–American drug offenders both spent almost a decade in prison. Drug use continued while prison populations swelled beyond capacity. The police officers certainly bent the rules and violated departmental policy in stopping Michael Whren and James Brown. No disciplinary action came of it and the same officers later stood accused of lying, planting evidence, and brutality. Unfortunately, the conduct of Officers Soto and Littlejohn is not un-heard of: claims of police abuse of authority were prevalent throughout the 1990s.

The Supreme Court's decision, however, provides fascinating lessons about legal change and social reform. *Whren* made any challenge to a pretextual stop based in large part on race extremely difficult under the Fourth Amendment, with standard equal protection doctrine placing an onerous burden on plaintiffs seeking to prove a claim of racial discrimi-nation. Following *Whren v. United States*, advocacy efforts to end racial profiling focused on political, not legal, solutions. A growing movement challenged race-based policing and brought the problem to the attention of the nation. For a time, that movement achieved success as lawmakers and police criticized racial profiling and adopted policies designed to eradicate the practice. The tragedy of September 11, 2001, however, noticeably slowed the efforts to end racial profiling, as the nation relied heavily on racial, national origin, and religious profiles, in the newly proclaimed war on terror. This retrenchment reveals the difficulty racial minorities face in relying on the political process to ensure racial justice and suggests the need for different minority groups to work together to eliminate racial profiling.[135] Currently, we see a criminal justice system that has disparate impacts on minority communities, much as in the days of Jim Crow. Times have changed, as has the legal discourse, but the song remains the same.

*

---

[135] *See* Kevin R. Johnson, *The Case for African American and Latina/o Cooperation in Challenging Racial Profiling in Law Enforcement*, 55 Fla. L. Rev. 341 (2003).

13

Rachel F. Moran

The Heirs of *Brown*: The Story of *Grutter v. Bollinger*

Perhaps no case better exemplifies the tensions between colorblind-ness and color-consciousness than *Grutter v. Bollinger*,[1] the lawsuit that challenged affirmative action in admissions at the University of Michi-gan Law School. Before the litigation began, the federal courts were deeply divided over the legitimacy of weighing race in deciding whether to offer applicants a seat in the entering class of a college or university. When the lawsuit was filed, the parties took dramatically different positions on whether affirmative action was a blight on individual fairness or a boon to racial justice. Intense disagreements about the legitimacy of affirmative action in turn led to split decisions and judicial in-fighting. Even the United States Supreme Court's ruling ultimately could not resolve the controversy. *Grutter* is the story of a jurisprudence of fragmentation, fraught with the ambiguity and ambivalence born of unresolved conflict.

The Roots of the Controversy

Grutter and its companion case, *Gratz v. Bollinger*,[2] were challenges to the use of race in admissions by both the law school and undergradu-ate program at Michigan. A bare majority of the Justices upheld the law school's process of holistic review, but a clear majority struck down the point system used to evaluate undergraduate applicants.[3] The divergent outcomes led Justice Antonin Scalia to term the cases a constitutional "split double header."[4] In fact, though, the Michigan cases were not the

---

[1] 539 U.S. 306 (2003).

[2] 539 U.S. 244 (2003).

[3] *Grutter*, 539 U.S. at 343; *Gratz*, 539 U.S. at 275–76.

[4] *Grutter*, 539 U.S. at 346, 348 (Scalia, J., dissenting).

first to reflect a deep ambivalence about remedies for racial injustice. In the 1950s, the Court's landmark school desegregation decisions in *Brown I*[5] and *Brown II*[6] reflected a similar inconstancy. Although the Court issued unanimous opinions, a wide gulf yawned between the resounding pronouncement that "separate educational facilities are inherently unequal" in *Brown I* and the willingness to brook "all deliberate speed" in *Brown II*. In *Brown I*, the Court recited a history of official discrimination and identified the resulting harms. Black students had been treated not as individuals but as members of a racial caste. Public schools were segregated by law, and they afforded unequal educational opportunities.[7] The remedy for these wrongs was not clear. Should school districts simply eliminate the practice of assigning students on the basis of race? Or should they affirmatively seek to integrate the public schools and equalize educational opportunities? *Brown II* left these questions unanswered, instead delegating to the lower federal courts the daunting task of fashioning judicially enforceable remedies.[8]

In the wake of the *Brown* decisions, "freedom of choice"[9] plans demonstrated the potential for conflicting interpretations of how to remedy past discrimination. These plans let students and parents choose where to go to school but did not explicitly address entrenched segregation and inequality. Not surprisingly, the results simply replicated the pattern of racially identifiable schools.[10] The Court struck down this formalistic approach as ineffective, but the federal courts would struggle for decades to identify race-conscious remedies that "promise[] realistically to work, and promise[] realistically to work now"[11] in achieving desegregation. Throughout the years following *Brown*, the federal courts justified the use of race as a way to overcome past discrimination, to do the corrective justice that was long overdue.[12]

Before the *Brown* decisions, the Court had decided a series of cases that declared racial barriers to access in higher education unconstitu-

---

[5] 347 U.S. 483 (1954).

[6] 349 U.S. 294 (1955).

[7] 347 U.S. at 493–95.

[8] 349 U.S. at 299–300.

[9] Green v. County Sch. Bd., 391 U.S. 430, 431–32 (1968).

[10] *Id.* at 437–39.

[11] *Id.* at 439.

[12] *See* J. Harvie Wilkinson, *From* Brown *to* Bakke: *The Supreme Court and School Integration, 1954–1978* at 139 (paperback ed. 1981) (describing "the language of violation-remedy" as "the framework for all future Court decisions involving student busing").

tional.[13] Black applicants could not be denied admission to public colleges and universities solely on the basis of race. Once enrolled, non-white students could not be subjected to humiliating, segregative practices.[14] Unlike compulsory programs of public elementary and secondary education, undergraduate and graduate study were earned privileges. So, the Court did not assert that public colleges and universities had to engage in vigorous outreach, recruitment, or targeted admissions. Instead, all that was required was a race-neutral process of granting admission and access to resources, such as assignment of space in the classroom, the cafeteria, and the library.[15] Under the Court's approach, the number of minority students in higher education remained small.[16] The Justices did not aspire to the kind of racial balance designed to desegregate elementary and secondary schools. Instead, the Court opted for the individualized, colorblind treatment rejected under "freedom of choice" plans as chimerical after years of harsh, exclusionary treatment.

In the 1960s and 1970s, this picture began to change in response to activism and civil unrest.[17] With federal support, colleges and universities instituted affirmative action by factoring race into the admissions process and markedly expanding minority enrollments. Race-conscious practices became pervasive not just in admissions but elsewhere, as targeted efforts were made to recruit non-white students, to offer race-based financial aid, to hire faculty of color, to develop ethnic studies programs, and to support race-based student organizations and theme houses.[18] These color-conscious initiatives were a sharp departure from traditional practices, and as the competition for scarce seats in selective

---

[13] Missouri. *ex rel.* Gaines v. Can., 305 U.S. 337 (1938); Sipuel v. Bd. of Regents of Univ. of Okla., 332 U.S. 631 (1948); McLaurin v. Okla. State Regents for Higher Educ., 339 U.S. 637 (1950); Sweatt v. Painter, 339 U.S. 629 (1950). *See generally* Richard Kluger, *Simple Justice: The History of* Brown v. Board of Education *and Black America's Struggle for Equality*, 239–86 (paperback ed. 1975).

[14] *McLaurin*, 339 U.S. at 639–42.

[15] *Missouri. ex rel. Gaines*, 305 U.S. at 350–52 (admissions); *Sipuel*, 332 U.S. at 632–33 (admissions); *McLaurin*, 339 U.S. at 639–40 (segregated seating in classroom, cafeteria, and library); *Sweatt*, 339 U.S. at 636 (admissions).

[16] William G. Bowen, et al., *Equity and Excellence in American Higher Education*, 140–42 (2005) (in 1951, blacks on average made up less than 1% of students entering colleges and universities in the College and Beyond database; only in the 1960s did affirmative action and active recruitment begin); *see also* William G. Bowen & Derek Bok, *The Shape of the River: Long–Term Consequences of Considering Race in College and University Admissions*, 1–5 (1998).

[17] Jerome Karabel, *The Chosen: The Hidden History of Admission and Exclusion at Harvard, Yale, and Princeton*, 380–409 (2005).

[18] Bowen et al., *supra* note 16, at 142–43; Bowen & Bok, *supra* note 16, at 5–8.

institutions grew, affirmative action became a subject of high-profile controversy.[19]

In 1978, the United States Supreme Court made its first attempt to quell the increasingly contentious debate over the use of race in admissions. In *Regents of the University of California v. Bakke*,[20] the Justices considered a program at the University of California at Davis Medical School that set aside sixteen seats in the entering class for black and Latino students. Allan Bakke, a rejected white applicant, sued on the ground that Davis had violated his constitutional rights by engaging in reverse discrimination.[21] The lower courts found that Davis was barred from using quotas or set-asides under equal protection law, however laudable the objective of enhancing minority access to the medical profession might be.[22]

On appeal, the *Bakke* case badly fractured the Court. The Justices could not even agree as to whether any constitutional questions needed to be reached. Justice John Paul Stevens wrote for four Justices who concluded that Title VI, like the Equal Protection Clause, was colorblind except when race-conscious remedies were needed to address past discrimination. In all other circumstances, "[r]ace cannot be the basis of excluding anyone from participating in a federally funded program."[23] By setting aside seats based on race, the Davis program clearly violated the statutory requirement, and there was no need to reach the equal protection analysis.

Justice William Brennan wrote for another four Justices who found that Title VI and equal protection were co-extensive but concluded that neither required colorblindness.[24] In determining whether the Davis program satisfied federal anti-discrimination law and the Constitution, these Justices refused to apply strict scrutiny, the most exacting level of

---

[19] Bowen et al., *supra* note 16, at 143–44; Bowen & Bok, *supra* note 16, at 8–9, 13–14.

[20] 438 U.S. 265 (1978). The Court previously had declined to hear a challenge to the consideration of race in admissions at a public law school. The plaintiff had been admitted by order of the trial court, and by the time the case reached the Justices, he was in his third and final year of the program. With four Justices dissenting, the Court found that there was no longer a live case or controversy. DeFunis v. Odegaard, 416 U.S. 312 (1974).

[21] *See* Bernard Schwartz, *Behind* Bakke*: Affirmative Action and the Supreme Court* 5–11 (1988).

[22] Bakke v. Regents of the Univ. of Cal., 553 P.2d 1152 (Cal. 1976); Schwartz, *supra* note 21, at 17–25.

[23] 438 U.S. at 418 (Stevens, Stewart, and Rehnquist, JJ. and Burger, C.J., concurring in part and dissenting in part).

[24] *Id.* at 336–40 (Brennan, White, Marshall, and Blackmun, JJ., concurring in part and dissenting in part).

review under equal protection.[25] Under this standard, the government's use of a suspect classification like race passes constitutional muster only when necessary to promote a compelling state interest. This demanding requirement traditionally has meant that nearly all such classifications are deemed invalid. Because the Davis program was motivated by a desire to benefit racial minorities, Justice Brennan argued that it should not be subject to the rigid requirement of strict scrutiny.

Two other standards of review were available to Justice Brennan. One was the rational basis test, which asks whether there is any plausible justification for a governmental policy. Because the Davis program explicitly relied on race, Justice Brennan was unwilling to apply this extremely lenient approach. Instead, he opted for an intermediate standard, which looks at whether the policy substantially advances an important governmental objective. Under this test, Justice Brennan concluded that the medical school had sound reasons for believing that "minority underrepresentation is substantial and chronic,"[26] that the admissions program did not stigmatize applicants like Allan Bakke as inferior, and that the quota did not operate as an invidious ceiling on minority enrollments.[27]

With the 4–4 split, Justice Lewis Powell cast the deciding vote. He determined that, because Davis's affirmative action program relied on a racial classification, strict scrutiny was the appropriate standard to apply. Although Powell ultimately rejected Davis's two-track system, he made clear that race could be used to promote diversity in higher education as well as to make amends for an institution's past discrimination. By diversity, Powell did not mean racial balance for its own sake; instead, he emphasized the First Amendment interest in a diversity of ideas. To the extent that race relates to a person's background, experience, and outlook, colleges and universities could use this factor to ensure that the student body included the mix of perspectives necessary to prompt "speculation, experiment, and creation."[28]

In Powell's view, even though the Davis medical school had articulated a compelling justification for its affirmative action program, the means chosen to achieve diversity were not narrowly tailored. He characterized the Davis program as a quota system in which a specified number of seats were reserved for students of color. He concluded that quotas were not necessary to advance diversity. Instead, the admissions process

---

[25] *Id.* at 356–62.

[26] *Id.* at 362.

[27] *Id.* at 369–76.

[28] *Id.* at 312 (opinion of Powell, J.) (citing Sweezy v. N.H., 354 U.S. 234, 236 (1957)).

could rely on a comprehensive system of individualized review.[29] As an example of a plan that satisfied strict scrutiny, Powell offered Harvard's admissions program, which accorded a plus for race along with other characteristics such as geographic origin, musical talent, socioeconomic disadvantage, and unique personal experience. Under this plan, all applicants competed against each other based on individual characteristics, including race, that could enrich the program.[30]

After *Bakke,* colleges and universities continued to consider race in admissions despite ongoing popular opposition. By the 1990s, attacks on these programs had intensified.[31] The Court itself fueled much of the controversy by striking down affirmative action efforts in employment and government contracting.[32] In doing so, the Justices cast doubt on the constitutional legitimacy of diversity as a compelling interest.[33] Although *Bakke* remained good law, the lower federal courts began to question whether it was still binding precedent. These doubts culminated in the Fifth Circuit Court of Appeals' decision in *Hopwood v. Texas.*[34] The plaintiff, Cheryl Hopwood, a disappointed white applicant, had challenged the admissions process at the University of Texas Law School. In finding in Hopwood's favor, the Fifth Circuit went out of its way to discredit Justice Powell's opinion in *Bakke.* The *Hopwood* court concluded that Powell had spoken only for himself and that subsequent Court opinions had undermined his reasoning. According to the Fifth Circuit, only remediation of a defendant's past discrimination could qualify as a compelling interest; diversity could not.[35] The state of Texas sought *certiorari,* but the Court refused to take the case even though the Fifth Circuit had rejected *Bakke* outright.[36]

The turmoil continued as lower federal courts reached different conclusions about *Bakke*'s implications. In a lawsuit alleging that affir-

---

[29] *Id.* at 315, 319–20.

[30] *Id.* at 316–17, 321–24.

[31] Rachel F. Moran, *Diversity and Its Discontents: The End of Affirmative Action at Boalt Hall,* 88 Cal. L. Rev. 2241, 2253 (2000).

[32] *See, e.g.,* Adarand Constr., Inc., v. Pena, 515 U.S. 200 (1995); City of Richmond v. J.A. Croson Co., 488 U.S. 469 (1989) (plurality opinion).

[33] In particular, the Court in *Adarand* seemed to retreat from an earlier decision in *Metro Broad., Inc. v. Fed. Comm. Comm'n,* 497 U.S. 547 (1990), in which it had indicated that diversity was an appropriate justification for granting minority-owned businesses a preference in the award of broadcast licenses. *Adarand,* 515 U.S. at 226–27 (overruling *Metro Broadcasting* on other grounds).

[34] 78 F.3d 932 (5th Cir. 1996), *cert. denied,* 518 U.S. 1033 (1996).

[35] *Id.* at 944–55.

[36] *Hopwood,* 518 U.S. 1033 (1996).

mative action in admissions at the University of Washington Law School was unconstitutional, the Ninth Circuit concluded that *Bakke* was controlling and that diversity could be a compelling interest.[37] In a case arguing that the University of Georgia impermissibly considered race in undergraduate admissions, the Eleventh Circuit hinted that diversity was not a compelling interest but refrained from reaching the issue because Georgia's program was not narrowly tailored to serve that goal.[38] With the courts in disarray, some opponents of affirmative action turned to the political process for vindication. In California, the Board of Regents banned any consideration of race or gender in admissions at the state's top tier of public universities.[39] Shortly thereafter, voters in California and Washington approved popular initiatives that outlawed affirmative action in all government decision-making, not just public university admissions.[40] Following the lead of these two states, Governor Jeb Bush instituted a similar policy on admissions in Florida by executive order.[41]

In short, by the time the Michigan litigation was filed, the battle over colorblindness and color-consciousness was being waged in both the judicial and political arenas. Although the Court had upheld the constitutionality of affirmative action in higher education, the programs remained vulnerable. Opponents insisted that *Bakke* had been rendered a dead letter and that race-based admissions were anathema to the American people. These claims had so much force that colleges and universities were banned from weighing race in admissions in California, Florida, Louisiana, Mississippi, Texas, and Washington. Among these states were some of the most racially and ethnically diverse in the nation. Clearly, there was no consensus—not even a fragile one—on the future of affirmative action in higher education.

The Heirs of Brown: The Struggle Over a Constitutional Legacy

Beginning in the late 1980s, the Center for Individual Rights ("CIR") had waged a steady campaign against affirmative action. In the field of higher education, that campaign had culminated in the *Hopwood*

---

[37] Smith v. Univ. of Wash. Law Sch., 233 F.3d 1188 (9th Cir. 2000), *cert. denied*, 532 U.S. 1051 (2001).

[38] Johnson v. Bd. of Regents of the Univ. of Ga., 263 F.3d 1234 (11th Cir. 2001).

[39] Regents of the University of California, *Policy Ensuring Equal Treatment–Admissions* (SP–1) (July 20, 1995), *available at* http://www.berkeley.edu/news/berkeleyan/1995/0830/text.html.

[40] Proposition 209 (Nov. 5, 1996) (codified at Cal. Const. art. I, § 31); Initiative 200 (Nov. 3, 1998) (codified at Rev. Code Wash. 49.60.400).

[41] One Florida Initiative, Exec. Order 99–281 (Nov. 9, 1999).

decision.[42] Despite this high-profile success, CIR was not satisfied. Colleges and universities throughout much of the country continued to operate affirmative action programs, and CIR longed for a decisive victory that would end these practices altogether.[43] Because undergraduate admissions at Michigan already had attracted intense scrutiny, CIR concluded that this elite public campus would make an excellent target in the ongoing war on affirmative action.[44] Michigan's highly selective public law school was another program that relied on race to diversify the student body. When CIR solicited potential plaintiffs, Barbara Grutter came forward to be interviewed.[45] A mother of two, she ran a health-care consulting business from her suburban home in the Detroit area. She had a 3.8 undergraduate grade point average from Michigan State, and her Law School Admissions Test ("LSAT") placed her in the 86th percentile of all test-takers. Grutter had applied to the law school, been wait-listed, and ultimately was rejected.[46] To CIR, she seemed like an ideal plaintiff. Her age and experience set her apart from many other applicants, and her academic credentials were competitive.

With Grutter as a plaintiff, CIR drew on the expertise of its Washington-based team, Michael Greve and Michael McDonald, to frame the case. Both Greve and McDonald had spent time working at the Washington Legal Foundation ("WLF"), a conservative advocacy group, before founding CIR. Greve was a philosopher not a lawyer, but McDonald had devoted much of his time as a WLF attorney to fighting affirmative action in the award of broadcast licenses at the Federal Communications Commission.[47] Greve and McDonald both became restive at WLF, believing that it took on too many issues and relied too heavily on amicus (that is, friend of the court) briefs. The two decided to strike out on their own by establishing a public interest law firm that would bring suits in a few select areas and pursue them from start to finish. To magnify the firm's influence, Greve and McDonald planned to draw on the talents of lawyers in the Reagan administration who were reentering private practice throughout the country. The result was CIR, founded in 1988 with Greve handling fundraising and general strategy

---

[42] Greg Stohr, *A Black and White Case: How Affirmative Action Survived Its Greatest Legal Challenge* 27, 30 (2004).

[43] *Id.* at 31.

[44] *Id.* at 33–37.

[45] *Id.* at 47–48.

[46] *Id.* at 47–48.

[47] *Id.* at 25–27.

and McDonald scouting out potential lawsuits and offering his legal expertise.[48]

When CIR targeted Michigan as the site for an affirmative action challenge, McDonald reached out to an old friend and former classmate from George Washington University Law School, Kirk Kolbo. After law school, Kolbo had gone to Minneapolis to work as a litigator in a large law firm. A Democrat in his younger days, Kolbo had grown increasingly conservative during his years in practice. Eventually, in 1994, Kolbo handled his first case for CIR, defending a male professor against sexual harassment charges.[49] Kolbo had wanted to take another case, involving race-based financial aid at the University of Minnesota, but his law firm partners refused to sue their state's flagship campus because of potential conflicts of interest. When the opportunity to sue Michigan over its admissions practices arose, however, Kolbo's partners gave him the green light.[50]

In suing the University of Michigan Law School, CIR confronted worthy adversaries. The President of Michigan, Lee Bollinger, had previously served as dean of the law school. A graduate of Columbia, Bollinger specialized in First Amendment doctrine after clerking on the United States Supreme Court and joining the Michigan faculty.[51] As dean of the law school, he had overseen efforts in the early 1990s to revamp the admissions policy to ensure compliance with *Bakke*'s mandate. He even replaced the admissions director so that the program modifications would be properly implemented. The resulting 1992 policy became the basis for the litigation in *Grutter*.[52] Jeffrey Lehman, who succeeded Bollinger as dean, had a similarly distinguished record. Himself a graduate of the law school, Lehman was a former Supreme Court clerk who began his teaching career at Michigan. There, he became a specialist in tax and welfare law. Before becoming dean, Lehman had served on the committee that developed the new admissions standards.[53]

The 1992 policy relied on holistic review that took into account not just grades and LSAT scores but other characteristics of applicants relevant to law study. The law school expressed its commitment to "racial and ethnic diversity with special reference to the inclusion of students from groups which have been historically discriminated against, like African Americans, Hispanics and Native Americans, who without

---

[48] *Id.* at 27–28.

[49] *Id.* at 37–38.

[50] *Id.* at 38.

[51] *Id.* at 13–14.

[52] 539 U.S. at 312–16; Stohr, *supra* note 42, at 14–15.

[53] Stohr, *supra* note 42, at 15.

this commitment might not be represented in our student body in meaningful numbers."[54] The policy was designed to achieve a "critical mass" of these students to enable them to excel and to contribute to the exchange of ideas.[55]

When looking for counsel to represent the law school, Bollinger and Lehman turned to an alumnus, John Pickering, a name partner at the prominent Washington law firm of Wilmer, Cutler & Pickering.[56] Pickering suggested that his colleague John Payton serve as lead attorney. After graduating from Harvard Law School, Payton had become one of the few black partners at a major law firm. He split his time between commercial litigation and civil rights work.[57] Payton had been one of the lawyers who unsuccessfully argued in defense of affirmative action in government contracting in *City of Richmond v. J.A. Croson Co.*, a Supreme Court case that dealt a serious blow to the consideration of race in this area.[58] The Michigan litigation afforded Payton an opportunity to revisit these issues in the field of higher education, hopefully with a better outcome. In fact, though, Payton did not wind up arguing *Grutter* before the Supreme Court. After he represented the law school in the lower courts, Michigan brought in Maureen Mahoney, another well-known Washington litigator, to handle the final stage of the litigation.[59] The move was a controversial one. Although Mahoney was widely admired for her thorough preparation and skills as an advocate, some observers grumbled that the decision had been politically motivated because Mahoney was white, Republican, and a former clerk of conservative Chief Justice William Rehnquist.[60]

Michigan's counsel might have seemed like a dream team, but a group of students nevertheless insisted that the law school would not adequately represent their interests. According to the students, they were "the direct beneficiaries of affirmative action and the direct targets of this lawsuit."[61] In their view, the University would defend itself "by invoking—and by only invoking—the most clearly established legal principles that do not potentially subject it to liability, in particular the

---

[54] 539 U.S. at 316.

[55] *Id.*

[56] Stohr, *supra* note 42, at 39.

[57] *Id.* at 39–41.

[58] *Id.* at 41–42.

[59] *Id.* at 200.

[60] *Id.* at 200–01.

[61] Memorandum of Law in Support of Motion for Intervention at 4, Grutter v. Bollinger, 137 F. Supp. 2d 821 (E.D. Mich. 2001) (No. 97–CV–75928).

compelling state interest in diversity upheld in *Bakke*," while the students were prepared to "raise fundamental questions of equality."[62] The students were represented by a recent New York University School of Law graduate, Miranda Massie. Massie worked at Scheff and Washington, a small law firm in Detroit that served clients alleging sexual harassment, police brutality, and racial discrimination. Like the students she represented, Massie was a young activist, and she saw the *Grutter* case as a way to reinvigorate the civil rights movement.[63]

In the Michigan litigation, all of the parties claimed to be the true heirs of *Brown*'s legacy. For Barbara Grutter, *Brown*'s defining principle was that government officials must refrain from differential treatment on the basis of race except to correct a past wrong. Powell's opinion was simply a diversion from this fundamental truth: "Justice Powell's lonely opinion, with its non-remedial analysis, remains just that: alone. It did not command the allegiance of anyone on the Court but him, and it never has."[64] CIR, on Grutter's behalf, called on the courts to be true to *Brown* by rejecting Powell's assertion that diversity is a compelling interest.

The University of Michigan contended that *Bakke* was a legitimate part of *Brown*'s legacy because the commitment to a diverse student body fully integrated students of all races and ethnicities. Indeed, diversity in higher education was especially important because "in some areas, such as housing and elementary and secondary education, our society is as racially separate today as it was before *Brown v. Board of Education*, before the Civil Rights Act of 1964 and the Voting Rights Act of 1965, and before the *Bakke* decision."[65] Without affirmative action, black, Latino, and Native American students would be present in only token numbers at selective institutions like Michigan.[66]

---

[62] *Id.* at 22.

[63] Stohr, *supra* note 42, at 85–88; Miranda Massie, *Litigators and Communities Working Together:* Grutter v. Bollinger *and the New Civil Rights Movement*, 19 Berkeley Women's L.J. 437, 442 (2004).

[64] Plaintiff's Memorandum of Law in Support of Motion for Partial Summary Judgment on Liability at 37, Grutter v. Bollinger, 137 F. Supp. 2d 821 (E.D. Mich. 2001) (No. 97–CV–75928).

[65] Defendants' Memorandum of Law in Support of Motion for Summary Judgment at 14, Grutter v. Bollinger, 137 F. Supp. 2d 821 (E.D. Mich. 2001) (No. 97–CV–75928); Defendants' Memorandum of Law in Support of Renewed Motion for Summary Judgment at 10–14, Grutter v. Bollinger, 137 F. Supp. 2d 821 (E.D. Mich. 2001) (No. 97–CV–75928).

[66] Defendants' Memorandum of Law in Support of Motion for Summary Judgment, *supra* note 65, at 17; Defendants' Memorandum of Law in Support of Renewed Motion for Summary Judgment, *supra* note 65, at 10–11.

The student-intervenors insisted that *Brown* was a resounding call to rectify past racial injustice by overcoming the vestiges of subordination and stratification. According to their brief, the case presented "a choice between two traditions in American life and law: the tradition of *Plessy v. Ferguson* and the tradition of *Brown v. Board of Education.* To choose *Plessy* would be to espouse the fiction of formal equality while abandoning the goal of real equality, cleaving the law from the truth of our society."[67] Affirmative action was but a modest step in addressing the problems inherent in "a society stymied and disfigured by ongoing inequality" in the quest "to move forward to genuine democracy and pluralism...."[68] It would be up to the federal courts to decide which of these parties was *Brown*'s true heir.

Strict Scrutiny, Diversity, and Critical Mass: The Battle over Bakke

The *Grutter* case came to be framed as a referendum on Justice Powell's opinion in *Bakke*. Because the student-intervenors wanted to move beyond *Bakke*, they struggled without success to paint a broader picture of racial injustice. Instead, Michigan and CIR dominated the litigation as they brought their divergent views of *Brown*'s legacy to bear in addressing the rigors of strict scrutiny. Recall that to survive strict scrutiny, an admissions policy must be necessary to promote a compelling state interest.[69] The debate over whether diversity qualifies as a compelling interest could be traced back to *Brown I*. In its stirring rhetoric, the Court had focused only on remedying past discrimination by schools that had adopted official policies of racial segregation. By contrast, Powell's opinion in *Bakke* rested on a wholly different foundation: the importance of academic freedom and the need for a vigorous exchange of ideas in colleges and universities. Moreover, he had singled out a particular approach, the Harvard plan, as an appropriate way to advance this interest. This race-based decision-making was not clearly limited in the ways that temporary remedies for past discrimination were. The result was an epic battle over whether *Bakke* was true to *Brown*'s principles.

Diversity: Compelling or Merely Sound Educational Policy?

CIR's legal team was deeply committed to refuting diversity's status as a compelling interest, yet the task was a delicate one. A diverse student body was closely identified with desegregation in many people's

---

[67] Defendant-Intervenors' Brief in Support of Defendants' Motion for Summary Judgment at 1, Grutter v. Bollinger, 137 F. Supp. 2d 821 (E.D. Mich. 2001) (No. 97–CV–75928).

[68] *Id.* at 37.

[69] *See Adarand*, 515 U.S. at 227 (1995).

minds, so rejecting diversity bordered on a racist rejection of the integrationist ideal. As a result, Kolbo admitted that diversity might be beneficial, a concession that Michigan's defense counsel mentioned repeatedly during the *Grutter* litigation.[70] From CIR's perspective, though, the question of whether diversity offered some educational advantages was beside the point.

Kolbo argued that despite decades of diversity-based admissions, the United States Supreme Court had never recognized this rationale. Powell wrote only for himself, and his focus on diversity and academic freedom did not command the support of any of his colleagues. The four Justices who supported race-based programs had relied on corrective justice, not the First Amendment. So, Powell's analysis was not the narrowest approach; it was a wholly different one.[71] Kolbo also contended that because the Harvard plan was not before the Court, Powell's comments on it were merely advisory. Therefore, the Court had never upheld the constitutionality of any race-based admissions program.[72]

For CIR, the only clear principle established by *Bakke* was that race-based set-asides are illegal. Without Powell's opinion as binding precedent, Michigan had to make an independent case for diversity as a compelling interest. Kolbo contended that no such case could be made. Even if a diverse pedagogy yielded some benefits, it was not comparable to the remedial justification at the heart of *Brown*. First Amendment freedom of speech could not trump an individual's right to equal treatment under law.[73]

According to Payton, these arguments were readily rebutted. Colleges and universities had treated the Powell opinion as controlling for decades, relying on it in fashioning affirmative action programs. The Supreme Court had never disavowed this interpretation, and only the

---

[70] Trial Transcript at 24, Grutter v. Bollinger, 137 F. Supp. 2d 821 (E.D. Mich. 2001) (97–CV–75928) (testimony on Feb. 16, 2001) (closing argument of Kirk Kolbo) ("... we have said many times before and I will say it again today that we don't stand here, the plaintiffs don't stand here as opponents of diversity."); *id.* at 46 (closing argument of John Payton) ("In fact, Mr. Kolbo and Mr. Purdy [Kolbo's co-counsel] have throughout the trial and Mr. Kolbo has today agreed that having a racially and ethnically diversed [sic] student body is important and educationally valuable. The point is not disputed.").

[71] Plaintiff's Memorandum of Law in Support of Motion for Partial Summary Judgment on Liability, *supra* note 64, at 27–35; Plaintiff's Renewed Motion for Partial Summary Judgment on Liability at 3–10, Grutter v. Bollinger, 137 F. Supp. 2d 821 (E.D. Mich. 2001) (No. 97–CV–75928).

[72] Grutter v. Bollinger, 288 F.3d 732, 785–87 (6th Cir. 2002) (Boggs, J., dissenting) ("Any speculation regarding the circumstances under which race could be used was little more than an advisory opinion, as those circumstances were not before the court....").

[73] Plaintiff's Memorandum of Law in Support of Motion for Partial Summary Judgment on Liability, *supra* note 64, at 27–35.

Hopwood decision had outright rejected the claim that diversity is compelling.[74] Powell provided the crucial swing vote in applying strict scrutiny and holding Davis's program unconstitutional. He also was the key fifth vote for the view that some affirmative action programs could meet this exacting standard. As a result, Powell's diversity rationale was the narrowest one consistent with the outcome in the case and therefore was controlling.[75]

Assuming that the district court recognized that diversity could be a compelling interest, Michigan was prepared to offer proof of its programs' educational benefits. The most direct evidence was an expert report prepared by Dr. Patricia Gurin, a professor of psychology and women's studies at Michigan, who had been working on diversity issues since the early 1990s.[76] Her work distinguished structural diversity, that is, the number of students of color on campus, from classroom diversity and informal interactional diversity. Classroom diversity measured the opportunity to engage with issues of race in the formal curriculum. Informal interactional diversity reflected the amount of interracial socializing that occurred outside of class. According to Gurin, classroom dialogue and informal contact outside of class were the key links that allowed structural diversity to yield desirable pedagogical outcomes.[77]

Relying on survey research data, Gurin concluded that enhanced classroom and interactional diversity correlated positively and significantly with intellectual engagement and active learning, especially for white students. These forms of diversity also generated greater citizenship engagement, particularly with those of other races and ethnicities, and once again, the effect was largest for white students. Finally, experiences with classroom and interactional diversity resulted in a greater willingness to live racially and ethnically integrated lives after college with an effect on whites that was "especially impressive."[78] Michigan offered other expert reports on the history of discrimination in America, the persistence of segregation, and the dangers of stereotyping, as well as some anecdotal accounts of the benefits of diversity in law

---

[74] Defendants' Memorandum of Law in Support of Motion for Summary Judgment, *supra* note 65, at 37–41; Defendants' Memorandum of Law in Support of Renewed Motion for Summary Judgment, *supra* note 65, at 32–36; Defendants' Opposition to Plaintiff's Renewed Motion for Partial Summary Judgment at 2–4, Grutter v. Bollinger, 137 F. Supp. 2d 821 (E.D. Mich. 2001) (No. 97–CV–75928).

[75] Defendants' Memorandum of Law in Support of Motion for Summary Judgment, *supra* note 65, at 39–41; Defendants' Memorandum of Law in Support of Renewed Motion for Summary Judgment, *supra* note 65, at 32–36.

[76] Expert Report of Patricia Gurin at 1, Grutter v. Bollinger, 137 F. Supp. 2d 821 (E.D. Mich. 2001) (No. 97–CV–75928).

[77] *Id.* at V.D.

[78] *Id.* at V.E.

study.[79] Clearly, however, Gurin's study offered the most direct and systematic evidence that diversity yielded educational benefits not just in general but at Michigan, particularly for undergraduates.

Not surprisingly, Gurin's research prompted sharp attacks from organizations and researchers opposed to affirmative action. Some critics questioned her findings on methodological grounds. For instance, was taking an ethnic studies course an appropriate way to operationalize classroom diversity? Was student self-reporting without objective data on academic performance sufficient?[80] Others subjected her social science evidence to a legalistic test of relevance. These critics demanded that Gurin show a direct and positive relationship between structural diversity and educational benefits because Michigan's use of race in admissions was on trial, not the legitimacy of classes on race or interracial socializing on campus.[81] Gurin defended her findings on the ground that the mere presence of minority students on campus was necessary but not sufficient to achieve a vigorous exchange of ideas.[82] Of course, had Gurin focused exclusively on structural diversity, these same critics might very well have alleged that her research supported the adoption of illicit quotas. Along the same lines, some took Gurin to task because she had not established causal connections between diversity and positive outcomes, but merely interactions and correlations.[83] According to these

---

[79] Expert Report of Derek Bok, Grutter v. Bollinger, 137 F. Supp. 821 (E.D. Mich. 2001) (No. 97–CV–75928); Expert Report of William Bowen, Grutter v. Bollinger, 137 F. Supp. 821 (E.D. Mich. 2001) (No. 97–CV–75928); Expert Report of Albert Camarillo, Grutter v. Bollinger, 137 F. Supp. 821 (E.D. Mich. 2001) (No. 97–CV–75928); Expert Report of Eric Foner, Grutter v. Bollinger, 137 F. Supp. 821 (E.D. Mich. 2001) (No. 97–CV–75928); Expert Report of Claude M. Steele, Grutter v. Bollinger, 137 F. Supp. 821 (E.D. Mich. 2001) (No. 97–CV–75928); Expert Report of Thomas J. Sugrue, Grutter v. Bollinger, 137 F. Supp. 821 (E.D. Mich. 2001) (No. 97–CV–75928); Expert Report of Kent D. Syverud, Grutter v. Bollinger, 137 F. Supp. 821 (E.D. Mich. 2001) (No. 97–CV–75928); Expert Report of Robert B. Webster, Grutter v. Bollinger, 137 F. Supp. 821 (E.D. Mich. 2001) (No. 97–CV–75928).

[80] See, e.g., Robert Lerner & Althea K. Nagai, A Critique of the Expert Report of Patricia Gurin in Gratz v. Bollinger, 21–34 (2001).

[81] See, e.g., Thomas E. Wood & Malcolm J. Sherman, Response to Patricia Gurin and to Ewart A.C. Thomas and Richard J. Shavelson 2 (June 2, 2001).

[82] Patricia Gurin, Wood & Sherman: Evidence for the Educational Benefits of Diversity in Higher Education: Response to the Critique by the National Association of Scholars of the Expert Witness Report of Patricia Gurin in Gratz, et al. v. Bollinger and Grutter v. Bollinger, 9–13 (2001); Patricia Gurin, Evidence for the Educational Benefits of Diversity in Higher Education: Response to the Continuing Critique by the National Association of Scholars of the Expert Witness Report of Patricia Gurin in Gratz, et al. v. Bollinger and Grutter v. Bollinger, et al. (2003); Patricia Gurin, Lerner & Nagai: Evidence for the Educational Benefits of Diversity in Higher Education: An Addendum (2001).

[83] John Staddon, Have Race–Based Admissions Improved American Higher Education?, 2–3 (2003); Wood & Sherman, supra note 81, at 4–6.

critics, the statistical relationships, while significant, were not large enough to merit substantial policy changes, much less constitutionally protected ones.[84] If these critics were correct, Michigan bore the impossible burden of demonstrating that diversity generated direct and substantial educational benefits at a level of certainty well beyond that typically achieved by social science survey research. Should diversity become an empirical question rather than a normative ideal, Michigan would face real evidentiary challenges.

Critical Mass: Forbidden Quota or Permissible Plus?

Even if diversity qualified as a compelling interest, the requirement of narrow tailoring remained. The narrow tailoring requirement stems from a preoccupation with the harms that race-based classifications can inflict. The notion is that affirmative action programs can burden whites like Barbara Grutter as well as stigmatize and stereotype non-whites, so any use of race must be carefully calibrated to minimize these injuries. A concern about potential harms exists notwithstanding the fact that plaintiffs like Grutter need not demonstrate that, but for the existence of the affirmative action program, they would have been admitted to the university. To some extent, Powell's rejection of quotas and his insistence on individualized review of applicants reflected a desire to reduce these burdens. Kolbo had marginalized Powell's opinion as authority for finding diversity to be compelling, but he nevertheless relied on its discussion of the Harvard plan to attack the mechanics of Michigan's law school program. According to Kolbo, Powell rejected any program that attached a heavy weight to race because the result would be a two-track system, one in which a plus for race became the functional equivalent of a quota.

Based on the stability of the racial composition of the entering class, CIR's team contended that critical mass in fact set a fixed minimum of minority enrollments.[85] To show that applicants to Michigan's law school did not compete on an equal footing, Kolbo introduced statistical evidence prepared by Dr. Kinley Larntz. Larntz's grids revealed that in the middle range of the applicant pool, blacks enjoyed much higher odds of being admitted than whites (or even Latinos) with comparable creden-

---

[84] *See, e.g.*, Lerner & Nagai, *supra* note 80, at 44–45; Wood & Sherman, *supra* note 81, at 4.

[85] Plaintiff's Memorandum of Law in Support of Motion for Partial Summary Judgment on Liability, *supra* note 64, at 20–23; Plaintiff's Renewed Motion for Partial Summary Judgment on Liability, *supra* note 71, at 3–4; Plaintiff's Memorandum in Opposition to Defendants' Renewed Motion for Summary Judgment at 2–4, Grutter v. Bollinger, 137 F. Supp. 2d 821 (E.D. Mich. 2001) (No. 97–CV–75928); Trial Transcript, *supra* note 70, at 6–24 (closing argument of Kirk Kolbo).

tials.[86] In addition, Kolbo argued that the law school's diversity admissions program could continue indefinitely once it received constitutional approval. The judiciary therefore would be endorsing a permanent, balkanized racial spoils system in higher education.[87] According to CIR, this tragic step was unnecessary because race-neutral alternatives were available to achieve a diverse student body. In particular, Kolbo pointed to experiences in states like California, Texas, and Florida, where public institutions (including highly selective ones) had enrolled students of all races and ethnicities despite a ban on affirmative action in admissions.[88]

For Michigan, the narrow tailoring requirement was a significant stumbling block. The law school insisted that critical mass was not tantamount to a quota. There was no fixed set-aside, and the number of students enrolled each year fluctuated within a significant range.[89] Payton had to rebut Larntz's data decisively. Dr. Joel Raudenbush, a statistician who specialized in the area of higher education, testified about the limits of the grids CIR had presented.[90] According to Payton, this testimony showed that there were no systematic racial differences in the law school's treatment of the most highly qualified and least qualified applicants. The former were uniformly admitted and the latter uniformly rejected. Only in the middle range of applicants did race play a role; this outcome was wholly predictable because Michigan acknowledged that it used race as a plus in the process.[91] Larntz's data simply confirmed that Michigan was following its policy. Even if race received only a slight plus, the odds of admission for underrepresented groups would substantially exceed those for whites because the grids focused on

---

[86] Report of Dr. Kinley Larntz, Deposition Exhibit 68, Grutter v. Bollinger, 137 F. Supp. 2d 821 (E.D. Mich. 2001) (No. 97–CV–75928); Trial Transcript at 7–116, Grutter v. Bollinger, 137 F. Supp. 2d 821 (E.D. Mich. 2001) (No. 97–CV–75928) (testimony on Jan. 17, 2001); Trial Transcript at 19–56, Grutter v. Bollinger, 137 F. Supp. 2d 821 (E.D. Mich. 2001) (No. 97–CV–75928) (testimony of Dr. Kinley Larntz on Feb. 10, 2001); Trial Transcript, *supra* note 70, at 8–12 (closing argument of Kirk Kolbo).

[87] Plaintiff's Memorandum in Opposition to Defendants' Renewed Motion for Summary Judgment, *supra* note 85, at 4.

[88] *Id.*

[89] Defendants' Memorandum of Law in Support of Motion for Summary Judgment, *supra* note 65, at 20–23; Defendants' Post–Trial Memorandum Regarding Proposed Findings of Fact and Conclusions of Law at 2–3, 14–26, Grutter v. Bollinger, 137 F. Supp. 2d 821 (E.D. Mich. 2001) (No. 97–CV–75928).

[90] Trial Transcript at 5–118, Grutter v. Bollinger, 137 F. Supp. 2d 821 (E.D. Mich. 2001) (No. 97–CV–75928) (testimony on Jan. 19, 2001); Trial Transcript at 6–24, Grutter v. Bollinger, 137 F. Supp. 2d 821 (E.D. Mich. 2001) (No. 97–CV–75928) (testimony of Dr. Stephen W. Raudensbush on Feb. 12, 2001).

[91] Trial Transcript, *supra* note 70, at 40, 51–57 (closing argument of John Payton).

applicants with comparable grades and LSAT scores.[92] In fact, race did not play a dispositive role, Payton argued, given that a higher proportion of non-white than white applicants was rejected.[93]

As for when the program would end, Michigan would stop considering race when it was no longer necessary to achieve a diverse student body. Racial disparities in LSAT scores and, to a lesser extent, grades had prompted Michigan to weigh race in the admissions process, but the gap had narrowed and would eventually close.[94] Meanwhile, forcing the law school to abandon affirmative action could lead to a dramatic drop in black, Latino, and Native American enrollments, a de facto re-segregation of elite legal education.[95] The law school had explored race-neutral options and found them wanting. A lottery system would abandon academic standards, while percentages focused too heavily on geography, were rooted in residential segregation, and did not apply to law school as opposed to undergraduate admissions.[96]

Both CIR and Michigan claimed to be the heirs of *Brown*, but the debate over *Bakke* demonstrated how malleable and uncertain that legacy was. Despite decades of affirmative action in colleges and universities, there was no consensus that diversity was a compelling interest, even if it might be sound educational policy. Nor was it clear whether Michigan had to prove that diversity yielded benefits or whether *Bakke* simply presumed these benefits. Even if diversity did qualify as compelling, CIR believed that race should receive little, if any, weight to achieve this goal. Michigan, by contrast, thought race should be accorded enough weight to achieve critical mass in the entering class, so that students of color would be present in more than token numbers. These sharp divisions were in turn reflected in the fractured decisions that dogged the *Grutter* litigation as it wended its way up to the Supreme Court.

The Least Dangerous Branch

Alexander Bickel once called the federal judiciary "the least dangerous branch" because even though it has become the final arbiter of constitutional principle, it must generate the assent of Congress and the

---

[92] *Id.* at 57–60.

[93] *Id.* at 38.

[94] *Id.* at 36–37.

[95] Defendants' Post–Trial Memorandum Regarding Proposed Findings of Fact and Conclusions of Law, *supra* note 89, at 27; Trial Transcript, *supra* note 70, at 35–36, 66.

[96] Defendants' Post–Trial Memorandum Regarding Proposed Findings of Fact and Conclusions of Law, *supra* note 89, at 26–29; Trial Transcript, *supra* note 70, at 49–50, 62–65.

executive branch to preserve its legitimacy.[97] The *Grutter* case reveals that external constraints are not the only source of an enfeebled judicial branch that struggles to win popular assent. At times, the wounds are self-inflicted. In the Michigan litigation, judges not only reached widely divergent conclusions about the constitutionality of the law school's admissions policy, but they also engaged in captious sniping and harsh in-fighting. Under the stress of the raw realities of race, the unanimous but fragile decisions in *Brown I* and *II* degenerated into a crippling jurisprudence of fragmentation.

Forum Shopping in the District Court

The first skirmishes occurred in the district court. Judge Bernard Friedman was assigned to hear the law school case, while Judge Patrick Duggan sat on the undergraduate case.[98] Friedman had arrived at the bench in an unorthodox way. Without finishing college or taking the LSAT, he applied to and was accepted by the Detroit College of Law, an institution committed to access for a wide variety of students. Friedman excelled in his studies and joined the local prosecutor's office after graduation.[99] Though born into a family of Democrats, he switched to the Republican Party while serving as a prosecutor. When he left government service, he created one of the first racially integrated law firms in the state.[100] Eventually, the Governor of Michigan appointed Friedman to the state bench in the early 1980s. There, he had a reputation for making the workings of the judiciary accessible to the public. In 1988, President Ronald Reagan named Friedman to the federal district court.[101]

Friedman immediately recognized that *Grutter* could be the case of a lifetime for him. Early on, though, the Michigan defense team sensed that Friedman was deeply unsympathetic to their arguments. As a result, the lawyers suggested to Friedman that the undergraduate and law school cases were companion lawsuits that should be tried together, presumably under Duggan. Friedman told the attorneys that he and Duggan agreed that the cases should be tried separately.[102] Seven months after the lawsuit began, one of Payton's associates took the highly unusual step of filing a motion with the district court asking that the law school case be reassigned to Duggan. The formal reasons proffered in the

---

[97] Alexander M. Bickel, *The Least Dangerous Branch: The Supreme Court at the Bar of Politics* 1, 247–54 (2d ed. 1986).

[98] Stohr, *supra* note 42, at 75–76, 77.

[99] *Id.* at 77–78.

[100] *Id.* at 78.

[101] *Id.*

[102] *Id.* at 95–96.

motion were "docket efficiency" and the need to try companion cases together.[103] CIR opposed the motion as thinly disguised forum shopping.

In response to the motion, Chief Judge Anna Diggs Taylor consulted Friedman, who once again refused to give up the case. Taylor then disqualified herself on the ground that her husband, as a Regent, was a defendant in the litigation.[104] She reassigned the matter to two former chief judges, who concluded that the lawsuits were companion cases.[105] Friedman responded with an opinion that blasted the judges for acting without proper authority. He characterized their decision as a "nullity" that was "void" because it was merely an "advisory opinion."[106] Friedman considered the decision "an affront to the dignity and independence of the court and an unlawful intrusion upon and interference and meddling with this court's business."[107] In addition, Friedman charged Taylor with a breach of ethics that "tarnishes this court's appearance of fairness and appears to place the court's imprimatur upon a judge-shopping practice which we, collectively as a bench, in the past always have denounced."[108] After the fireworks, Friedman stayed on the case.[109]

To minimize the possibility that Friedman would enter adverse findings of fact that could damage Michigan's chances on appeal, Payton moved for summary judgment. He argued that the only issues in genuine dispute were questions of law, while the key facts were uncontested.[110] CIR also moved for summary judgment, a somewhat surprising strategy given that Friedman was likely to make highly favorable factual findings for Grutter.[111] Perhaps CIR's lawyers hoped for an unequivocal statement of principle universally condemning affirmative action. Whatever the reasons, both sides appeared willing to dispense with trial proceedings by treating the lawsuit as a referendum on whether Powell's legal analysis in *Bakke* remained controlling.

---

[103] *Id.* at 96.

[104] *Id.* at 97.

[105] *Id.*

[106] Grutter v. Bollinger, 16 F. Supp. 2d 797, 800, 803 (E.D. Mich. 1998).

[107] *Id.* at 802.

[108] *Id.*

[109] Stohr, *supra* note 42, at 95–100.

[110] Defendants' Memorandum of Law in Support of Motion for Summary Judgment, *supra* note 65, at 3; Defendants' Post–Trial Memorandum Regarding Proposed Findings of Fact and Conclusions of Law, *supra* note 89, at 1–3.

[111] Plaintiff's Memorandum of Law in Support of Motion for Partial Summary Judgment on Liability, *supra* note 64, at 2; Plaintiff's Renewed Motion for Partial Summary Judgment on Liability, *supra* note 71, at 1, 6.

Only Massie and the student-intervenors seemed eager to air their alternative theories of stratification and subordination by presenting expert witnesses in court. Despite the parties' cross-motions for summary judgment, Friedman held a fifteen-day bench trial to address issues related to the narrow tailoring requirement. At trial, the student-intervenors used the bulk of the time. They introduced testimony covering a wide array of topics, including the discriminatory impact of grades and standardized tests, hostile campus climate, and the history of racial discrimination in America. Despite these efforts, Judge Friedman largely ignored the student-intervenors' evidence and theories in disposing of the case. Instead, he focused on the arguments that Michigan and CIR had made about *Bakke*.[112]

Michigan's intuitions about judicial sympathies were confirmed when Judge Duggan upheld the undergraduate point system, while Judge Friedman roundly rejected every facet of the law school program.[113] In condemning the use of race in admissions, Friedman found that diversity was not a compelling interest. In his view, Powell's diversity rationale was "neither narrower nor broader than the remedial rationale" but instead they were "completely different rationales, neither one of which is subsumed within the other."[114] As a result, "Justice Powell's discussion of the diversity rationale was not among the governing standards to be gleaned from *Bakke*."[115] Citing expert evidence submitted by Michigan, Friedman acknowledged that diversity could produce "benefits [that] are important and laudable,"[116] a point undisputed by the parties. Even so, the evidence was irrelevant because the diversity rationale had never been recognized by a majority of the Court.[117]

Even assuming that diversity qualified as a compelling interest, Friedman held that the law school's program was not narrowly tailored. He was especially critical of the amorphous concept of critical mass, writing that "defendants know it when they see it, but it cannot be quantified."[118] In his view, critical mass was tantamount to a quota system because each year, the law school enrolled an entering class with

---

[112] *Grutter*, 137 F. Supp. 2d at 825, 855–56. See infra notes 194–196 and accompanying text.

[113] Stohr, *supra* note 42, at 149–52, 166–67.

[114] 137 F. Supp.2d at 847.

[115] *Id.*

[116] *Id.* at 850.

[117] *Id.*

[118] *Id.* at 851.

at least 10–12% underrepresented students.[119] Moreover, Friedman concluded that there was no logical basis for selecting some groups for preferential treatment and omitting others that had experienced discrimination. For instance, Mexican Americans as well as Puerto Ricans from the mainland received special consideration, but other Latinos did not.[120] Friedman also expressed concern that there was no time limit on the use of affirmative action.[121] Finally, he concluded that the law school had not adequately explored race-neutral alternatives because it failed "to consider them, and perhaps experiment with them, prior to implementing an explicitly race-conscious system."[122] As a result, Friedman struck down the admissions policy as unconstitutional.

None of these rulings was necessarily indicative of a lack of even-handedness. However, there are two features of Friedman's handling of the case that cast some doubt on his impartiality. First, the judge repeatedly rejected requests to grant qualified immunity to Bollinger, Lehman, and the director of admissions, Dennis Shields. The defendants argued that they had acted in good faith in implementing the 1992 admissions policy and so were protected from liability in a personal capacity.[123] In opposing the motion for qualified immunity, CIR argued that the defendants had relinquished any protection by intentionally discriminating on the basis of race.[124] Friedman left this issue unresolved for almost two years and granted the immunity only when he issued his final opinion.[125] Despite CIR's argument about intentional misconduct, the case for qualified immunity seems to have been clear, and typically such requests are granted as promptly as possible to avoid chilling

---

[119] *Id.*

[120] *Id.* at 851–52

[121] *Id.* at 851.

[122] *Id.* at 853.

[123] Defendants' Memorandum of Law in Support of Motion for Summary Judgment, *supra* note 65; Renewed Motion by Defendants Bollinger, Lehman, and Shields for Summary Judgment on Grounds of Qualified Immunity at 1–2, Grutter v. Bollinger, 137 F. Supp. 2d 821 (E.D. Mich. 2001) (No. 97–CV–75928); Memorandum of Law in Support of Renewed Motion by Defendants Bollinger, Lehman, and Shields for Summary Judgment on Grounds of Qualified Immunity at 11–28, Grutter v. Bollinger, 137 F. Supp. 2d 821 (E.D. Mich. 2001) (No. 97–CV–75928); Reply in Support of Renewed Motion by Defendants Bollinger, Lehman, and Shields for Summary Judgment on Grounds of Qualified Immunity at 15–19, Grutter v. Bollinger, 137 F. Supp. 2d 821 (E.D. Mich. 2001) (No. 97–CV–75928).

[124] Plaintiff's Memorandum in Opposition to the Renewed Motion by Defendants Bollinger, Lehman, and Shields for Summary Judgment on Grounds of Qualified Immunity at 17, 19, 21–22, Grutter v. Bollinger, 137 F. Supp. 2d 821 (E.D. Mich. 2001) (No. 97–CV–75928).

[125] 137 F. Supp. 2d at 853–54.

government officials' ability to carry out their duties.[126] Friedman's foot-dragging on questions of immunity is hard to square with a norm of fairness and impartiality.

In addition, once the decision had been entered, Friedman denied the defendants' request for a stay, even though the admissions process was already well under way. The law school had extended 826 offers and still had to make at least 300 more to generate a first-year entering class. Moving quickly was essential because of the intense competition for highly qualified students. Friedman's ruling brought the admissions process to a standstill by requiring that Michigan immediately implement a new system of colorblind review.[127] Under the circumstances, it certainly would have been reasonable to issue a stay so that Michigan could have time to develop appropriate policies and practices for the following year. Moreover, the likelihood of an appeal reinforced the need for a stay, given the resulting doubts about the standards that ultimately would apply. In denying the stay, Friedman evinced little sympathy for Michigan's plight. Indeed, he cited the defendants' "extensive experience in reviewing law school applications" as a basis for concluding that they "should have no difficulty identifying 100 excellent candidates within this time frame without considering race."[128] Ultimately, the Sixth Circuit granted the stay in light of the uncertainties and disruption that the order imposed, and Michigan proceeded under the 1992 admissions policy.[129]

Public Squabbling on the Sixth Circuit

In the Sixth Circuit, a new round of judicial squabbling broke out. Again, the in-fighting related to which judges should decide the case. Initially, the appeal from Friedman's decision was assigned to the three-judge panel that had determined whether the students could intervene. The three judges declared themselves a "must panel" that would hear all future appeals. The original panel included a Florida district court judge sitting temporarily on the court of appeals. Because this judge was no longer available, Chief Judge Boyce Martin added himself to the panel. With Martin's addition, the panel consisted entirely of jurists sympathetic to affirmative action.[130] Realizing that it would lose, CIR filed a motion to have Grutter heard en banc, that is, before the entire court, rather

---

[126] See Hunter v. Bryant, 502 U.S. 224, 227 (1991); Mitchell v. Forsyth, 472 U.S. 511, 525–29 (1985); Harlow v. Fitzgerald, 457 U.S. 800, 817–18 (1982).

[127] Stohr, supra note 42, at 169–70.

[128] Grutter, 137 F. Supp.2d at 874, 878–79; Stohr, supra note 42, at 170.

[129] Grutter v. Bollinger, 247 F.3d 631 (6th Cir. 2001); Stohr, supra note 42, at 174–75.

[130] Stohr, supra note 42, at 175.

than before the three-judge panel. Proceeding directly to en banc review was an unusual step, but CIR argued that the case was of such significance that it would ultimately be heard by the entire court anyway.[131] In response, Martin informed CIR that its petition would not be considered until the briefs in the case could be reviewed.[132] Five months later and on the eve of oral argument, the parties were notified that the case would be heard en banc. Oral argument was postponed to allow all of the judges to familiarize themselves with the record.[133]

The Sixth Circuit's handling of the en banc petition led to shrill and very public division among members of the court. Judge Danny Boggs and Chief Judge Martin already were deeply estranged, and despite norms of judicial collegiality, they never spoke to one another.[134] Boggs published a procedural appendix that accused Martin of playing politics by assigning himself to the panel when the Florida judge became unavailable.[135] Boggs also accused Martin of failing to circulate the en banc petition promptly, either to other members of the three-judge panel or the court as a whole.[136] Boggs's ire was fueled by the way in which the problems came to light shortly before the originally scheduled oral argument. Apparently, a government attorney told a senior judge that "the Michigan cases were 'being taken care of.' "[137] As a result, the judge investigated the situation and concluded that the original panel should not have declared itself a "must panel" and that the case should be reassigned through a random selection process. At this point, Martin circulated the en banc petition along with a note that a "question ... has been raised regarding the composition of the panel."[138]

During the delay in considering the en banc petition, two members of the Sixth Circuit retired, arguably tipping the balance in Michigan's favor.[139] Later, a Senate Judiciary Committee memorandum revealed that Elaine Jones of the National Association for the Advancement of Colored People ("NAACP") had asked an aide to Senator Ted Kennedy

---

[131] Petition for En Banc Hearing, Grutter v. Bollinger, 288 F.3d 732 (6th Cir. 2002) (No. 01–1447).

[132] Stohr, *supra* note 42, at 176.

[133] Gratz v. Bollinger, 277 F.3d 803 (6th Cir. 2001) (disposition of petition for en banc review in *Gratz* and *Grutter*); Stohr, *supra* note 42, at 204–05.

[134] Stohr, *supra* note 42, at 203.

[135] 288 F.3d at 810–11, 813–14.

[136] *Id.* at 811–13.

[137] Stohr, *supra* note 42, at 205.

[138] *Id.*

[139] *Id.* at 205, 209.

to delay an appointment to the Sixth Circuit until *Grutter* was decided. Eventually, four conservative organizations lodged an ethical complaint against Jones before the Virginia State Bar Association. Although the Bar rejected the complaint, this episode fueled suspicions that the Sixth Circuit had been playing games with the en banc process.[140]

Martin did not formally respond to Boggs's allegations of misconduct. Later, he said that doing so "would have been like getting into 'a pissing match with a skunk.' "[141] Boggs's remarks did prompt an impassioned reply from Judge Karen Nelson Moore, one of the two Sixth Circuit judges originally assigned to *Grutter*. She insisted that standard procedures had been followed throughout the litigation.[142] She found Boggs's allegations "shameful" and concluded that they marked "a new low point in the history of the Sixth Circuit."[143] Moore worried that the scathing indictment would "irreparably damage the already strained working relationships among the judges of this court" as well as "undermine public confidence in our ability to perform our important role in American democracy."[144] Judge Eric Clay also chided Boggs for his "embarrassing and incomprehensible attack on the integrity of the Chief Judge and this Court as a whole."[145] If, indeed, the judiciary was the least dangerous branch, it appeared to be doing an effective job of crippling itself.

The Sixth Circuit split 5–4 in deciding *Grutter*. The court of appeals first had to determine how much deference to give the trial court's conclusions. At trial, CIR had savored the prospect of a clear-cut normative victory, but now it saw the benefits of characterizing Friedman's conclusions as findings of fact that could not be overturned unless clearly erroneous.[146] Michigan insisted that in seeking summary judgment, the parties had agreed that the material facts were undisputed.[147] Consequently, all of the holdings involved matters of law that should be reviewed de novo, that is, as questions that did not merit deference to the trial court. The intervenors also wanted de novo review, in part

---

[140] *Id.* at 313–14.

[141] *Id.* at 210.

[142] 288 F.3d at 752, 753–57 (Moore, J., concurring).

[143] *Id.* at 753, 758.

[144] *Id.* at 758.

[145] *Id.* at 758, 772 (Clay, J., concurring).

[146] Final Brief of Appellee at 18–19, Grutter v. Bollinger, 288 F.3d 732 (6th Cir. 2002) (No. 01–1447).

[147] Proof Brief of Defendants–Appellants at 19, Grutter v. Bollinger, 288 F.3d 732 (6th Cir. 2002) (No. 01–1447).

because they hoped that their legal theories of the case, largely ignored by Judge Friedman, might be given some weight in the decision-making process.[148]

Writing for the majority, Martin held that the trial court's decision raised mixed questions of law and fact that required de novo review.[149] Although not bound to defer to Friedman's findings, Martin did adopt a similar legal framework. Like Friedman, Martin treated *Grutter* as a referendum on *Bakke* and defined the Sixth Circuit's task in carefully circumscribed, jurisprudential terms. Applying this approach, Martin found that Friedman had wrongly disregarded the diversity rationale because it was binding precedent.[150] His approach had two important consequences. First, Martin's opinion simply assumed that diversity was a compelling interest, so the expert evidence that Michigan had amassed to show the pedagogical benefits became largely irrelevant. Apparently, Martin privately harbored doubts about the reliability and integrity of the research, and he worried that a lengthy evaluation of it would damage the chances for Supreme Court review.[151] Second, because Martin was committed to punctilious compliance with Powell's opinion in *Bakke*, the concerns of the student-intervenors largely disappeared from the case. Massie had argued that the diversity rationale did not go far enough in redressing the subordination and stratification that slavery and segregation had wrought. Because Martin used his analysis to reaffirm *Bakke*, his opinion did not look beyond pedagogy to exclusion and inequality.

For these reasons, it fell to Judge Clay to offer a strong defense of diversity in his concurring opinion. He embraced Michigan's research and highlighted the intervenors' arguments that diversity was linked to desegregation. He found that:

> While it is true that the law school's policy is based upon its desire to achieve a diverse student body, the very reason that the law school is in need of a program to *create* a diverse environment is because the discrimination faced by African Americans and other minorities throughout the educational process has not produced a diverse student body in the normal course of things. Diversity in education, at its base, is the desegregation of a historically segregated population.... [152]

---

[148] Defendant–Interveners' Final Brief at 53–68, Grutter v. Bollinger, 288 F.3d 732 (6th Cir. 2002) (No. 01–1447).

[149] 288 F.3d at 738.

[150] *Id.* at 738–44.

[151] Stohr, *supra* note 42, at 206.

[152] 288 F.3d at 768 (Clay, J., concurring) (emphasis in original).

Yet, like Powell, Clay wrote only for himself.

In dissent, Boggs asserted that the Supreme Court had never endorsed the diversity rationale. Adopting CIR's reasoning, he concluded that Powell's opinion was not controlling, that subsequent Supreme Court decisions had not endorsed the diversity rationale, and that any references to the Harvard plan were merely advisory.[153] Boggs also blasted the diversity rationale on the merits, arguing that the law school's willingness to equate race with rare and remarkable achievements, such as an Olympic gold medal, showed that the object was not in fact experiential diversity. As he put it: "After reading the description of [the] admissions criteria, a Michigan law student might yearn to meet the mere Olympian who failed to medal and was thus considered insufficiently interesting by the Law School."[154] Because "the only type of diversity that is given more than modest, if any, weight is based on assigned racial categories," Boggs concluded that "the Law School grants preferences to race, not as a proxy for a unique set of experiences, but as *a proxy for race itself.*"[155] To Boggs, the case was unambiguous: Michigan's admissions process wrongly relied on race in the absence of any compelling constitutional justification.

Once the Sixth Circuit had decided the case en banc, the parties split over whether to seek Supreme Court review. When CIR petitioned for *certiorari*,[156] Michigan opposed the motion in order to preserve its victory in the court of appeals and continue its programs.[157] The intervenors, however, sided with CIR in seeking *certiorari* because they still hoped for a decisive, national vindication of affirmative action programs.[158] When the Court ultimately agreed to hear the case,[159] Michigan assumed responsibility for defending its programs. The law school's counsel refused to cede any of its precious time for oral argument to

---

[153] *Id.* at 776–88 (Boggs, J., dissenting).

[154] *Id.* at 790.

[155] *Id.* at 791–92 (emphasis in original).

[156] Petition for Writ of Certiorari, Grutter v. Bollinger, 539 U.S. 306 (2003) (No. 02–241).

[157] Brief in Opposition at 14, Grutter v. Bollinger, 539 U.S. 306 (2003) (No. 02–241). However, Michigan asked that if the Court did grant *certiorari*, the Justices should also hear the undergraduate case, even if the Sixth Circuit had not yet issued a decision. *Id.* at 30.

[158] Response to the Petition for Certiorari by Respondents Kimberly James, et al., at 3, Grutter v. Bollinger, 539 U.S. 306 (2003) (No. 02–241) ("to correct erroneous appellate decisions striking down efforts at integration and fairness in education, and to rebuff decisively this extreme and dangerous attack on our best and hardest-gained achievements, the student defendants urge the Court to grant certiorari.").

[159] 537 U.S. 1043 (2002).

Massie to make arguments about subordination, stratification, and social justice. Having already largely disappeared from the opinions in the Sixth Circuit, the intervenors became further marginalized. Ironically, the give-and-take with the Justices was precisely the kind of showcase that Massie had hoped to use in mobilizing a civil rights constituency. Yet, the bully pulpit of oral argument was closed to her.[160]

Both Michigan and CIR recognized that *Grutter* would be a close and hard-fought case in the Supreme Court. Each side worked with amici to bolster its position. In addition, the law school made a controversial decision to replace Payton, who had handled the case since its inception, with Maureen Mahoney, another experienced Washington litigator and a former clerk to Chief Justice Rehnquist. Ultimately, Payton argued the undergraduate case, while Mahoney represented the law school. Michigan hoped that as a moderate Republican and white woman, Mahoney would enjoy special credibility with key swing Justices.[161] Whether the substitution of counsel in the final stages of litigation made any difference to the outcome is hard to say. Yet, this unusual last-minute switch certainly demonstrated how high the stakes were for the future of affirmative action.

The High Court Has Its Say

By contrast to the machinations in the Sixth Circuit, the Supreme Court appeared to be a model of civility and decorum. The Justices did not seem eager to game the process by manipulating which of them would hear the case. At one point, Justice John Paul Stevens considered recusing himself from *Grutter* because his former law clerk, Jeffrey Lehman, was a defendant. Stevens had been among the dissenters in *Bakke*, but in the intervening years, he had become increasingly sympathetic to affirmative action, a shift that he attributed to learning on the job. Without Stevens's vote, the odds were that the Court would deadlock or reject affirmative action altogether. Whatever their ideological differences, all of Stevens's colleagues firmly supported his decision to remain on the case.[162]

Indeed, Stevens's participation proved vitally important, as the Justices split 5–4 on the constitutionality of the law school's admissions practices. Despite sharp differences of opinion, there was none of the open rancor that marked the lower court proceedings. Although Justice Sandra Day O'Connor reportedly struggled to find "the middle of the

---

[160] Motion for Enlargement of Argument Time and for Divided Argument or in the Alternative, Divided Argument at 1–6, Grutter v. Bollinger, 539 U.S. 306 (2003) (No. 02–241); *Grutter*, 538 U.S. at 904; Stohr, *supra* note 42, at 256–57.

[161] Stohr, *supra* note 42, at 200–03.

[162] *Id.* at 220–21.

road" on affirmative action in higher education, she ultimately concluded that the Michigan cases were about "whether Powell's ruling [in
Bakke] should remain on the books."[163] In her opinion for the Court, she
made clear that it was unnecessary to decide whether Powell's opinion,
written only for himself, constituted binding precedent because a majority of the Court was now willing to endorse a diversity rationale.[164]

Rejecting arguments that the Court's earlier decisions recognized
affirmative action only as a remedy for past discrimination, O'Connor
noted that "[t]he Law School's educational mission is one to which we
defer."[165] Based on a longstanding tradition of academic freedom, she
found that Michigan acted well within the scope of its educational
autonomy in seeking a diverse student body.[166] Describing the benefits of
diversity as "substantial," she mentioned the expert testimony and other
research in passing before focusing on amicus briefs filed on Michigan's
behalf by major corporations and a group of retired military generals.[167]
These briefs, which addressed the benefits of a diverse workforce,
enabled O'Connor to go beyond the pedagogical process to include the
goal of cultivating "a set of leaders with legitimacy in the eyes of the
citizenry."[168] Particularly at selective institutions like Michigan's law
school, she wrote, "it is necessary that the path to leadership be visibly
open to talented and qualified individuals of every race and ethnicity."[169]

The holding that diversity is compelling prompted sharp dissent.
Justices Clarence Thomas and Antonin Scalia insisted that states did not
have a compelling interest in offering any legal education at public
universities, much less a diverse one.[170] The law school did not contribute
significantly to leadership in the state. In fact, as an elite national
institution, Michigan served a large number of out-of-state residents,
and few of its graduates even remained in the area.[171] Perhaps most
significantly, the dissent questioned whether preserving selective public
education was a compelling state interest. Thomas and Scalia insisted
that Michigan could easily diversify the law school by lowering its
academic requirements for admission. For this reason, "[t]he majority's

---

[163] Jeffrey Toobin, *The Nine: Inside the Secret World of the Supreme Court* 217 (2007).

[164] 539 U.S. at 325.

[165] *Id.* at 328.

[166] *Id.* at 330.

[167] *Id.* at 331.

[168] *Id.* at 332.

[169] *Id.*

[170] *Id.* at 349, 357–58 (Thomas, J., dissenting).

[171] *Id.* at 359–60.

broad deference to both the Law School's judgment that racial aesthetics leads to educational benefits and its stubborn refusal to alter the status quo in admissions methods finds no basis in the Constitution or decisions of this Court."[172]

Having upheld the diversity rationale as compelling, O'Connor turned to whether the law school's admissions policy was narrowly tailored. She found that holistic review resulted in individualized consideration of each applicant, that all those admitted were academically qualified, and that diversity factors other than race received substantial weight in the process.[173] According to O'Connor, narrow tailoring did not require "exhaustion of every conceivable race-neutral alternative," nor did it "require a university to choose between maintaining a reputation for excellence or fulfilling a commitment to provide educational opportunities to members of all racial groups...."[174] As a result, the law school properly rejected options like a lottery system, lowered standards for admissions, and percentage plans because they were inconsistent with the institutional mission and precluded individualized review.[175] Even so, the Justices were concerned about the lack of a clear timetable for phasing out affirmative action,[176] and so O'Connor expressed the hope "that 25 years from now, the use of racial preferences will no longer be necessary to further the interest approved today."[177]

Chief Justice Rehnquist offered the most penetrating critique of this narrow tailoring analysis. Looking at past admissions statistics, he pointed out that the critical mass of African–American students was twice as large as for Hispanics and six times as large as for Native Americans. Although Michigan had described Hispanics as one of "the groups most isolated by racial barriers in our country,"[178] the law school was considerably more likely to reject them than African Americans with similar credentials. For Rehnquist, this type of differential treatment demonstrated that the law school's real objective was to enroll students in numbers proportionate to their representation in the applicant pool, not to achieve some mythical critical mass.[179]

---

[172] *Id.* at 364.

[173] *Id.* at 334–39 (opinion of O'Connor, J.).

[174] *Id.* at 339.

[175] *Id.* at 339–40.

[176] Id. at 341–43.

[177] *Id.* at 343.

[178] *Id.* at 383 (Rehnquist, J., dissenting).

[179] *Id.* at 383–86.

After its defeat, CIR petitioned for rehearing. Grutter's counsel argued that the Court had nowhere addressed the standard of review on appeal. In particular, the majority did not indicate the degree of deference that should be accorded to Friedman's finding that the law school's program in practice weighed race so heavily that pluses became tantamount to quotas.[180] CIR was certainly correct that O'Connor did not explicitly address this issue. Nor did any of the other Justices. Plainly, the Court did not feel bound by Friedman's rulings, and the petition for rehearing predictably was denied.[181] CIR's high hopes for a clear-cut normative victory after *Hopwood* had been dashed, and it was not even able to make the most of a sympathetic district court's fact-finding to salvage its position.

Law and Politics: The Role of the Student–Intervenors and the Amici Curiae

The *Grutter* case clearly fragmented the federal courts. Yet, their points of disagreement should not conceal some areas of consensus. The judges, adopting the stance taken by CIR and Michigan, treated the litigation as a referendum on *Bakke* and not as an invitation to engage broader questions of race and equality. As such, there was no dispute about whether strict scrutiny was the relevant standard of review, no dispute about whether societal discrimination can function as a compelling justification for affirmative action, no dispute about whether affirmative action can be conceptualized as an anti-discrimination measure rather than a preference, and no dispute about whether affirmative action was a necessary outgrowth of *Brown*'s desegregation imperative. Although each of these issues continues to be debated in the public and political arenas as well as in legal scholarship, the judges were in accord that the *Grutter* litigation raised none of them. The strength of the courts' commitment to this narrowly legalistic framework is illustrated by the very different influence wielded by the student-intervenors on the one hand and the amicus curiae on the other. The students were increasingly marginalized as they called for a recognition of the realities of racial subordination in America. The amici provided a sense of how elite leaders understood the future of race, and the Court accorded significant weight to their views in part because they were addressed to the ongoing vitality of *Bakke*.

The Student–Intervenors: From Participants to Bystanders

For the students who intervened in the litigation, the debate over *Bakke* was itself a diversion from what was really at stake. In their view,

---

[180] Petition for Rehearing at 1–4, Grutter v. Bollinger, 539 U.S. 306 (2003) (No. 02–241).

[181] 539 U.S. 982 (2003).

Grutter was part of an epic struggle to overcome racial oppression. The intervenors wanted politics front and center in the courtroom, whether or not it fit the doctrinal contours of the diversity rationale.[182] Even though the students challenged the law school's willingness to confront a history of exclusion and racism, Michigan did not oppose their motion to intervene. Instead, Payton simply observed that intervention "could significantly complicate discovery and possibly other aspects of these cases."[183] Michigan's defense team undoubtedly worried that the students would interfere with their efforts to bolster *Bakke*, but university officials were hard-pressed to object to their own students getting involved, particularly when they appeared to share the common objective of preserving affirmative action programs. CIR was not similarly reticent. Kolbo contended that the students' participation would lead to substantial delay by "expand[ing] the scope of this lawsuit well beyond anything put in issue by the complaint and answer," particularly given the "breathtaking" range of "extraneous issues that would entangle the Court, parties and lawsuit if intervention is allowed."[184] CIR, already having devoted a substantial amount of its resources to the Michigan litigation, surely did not look forward to an even greater drain on the organization's time, energy, and funds. The district court denied the motion to intervene, but the Sixth Circuit Court of Appeals ultimately held that the students could participate in the case.[185]

Both CIR and Michigan had moved for summary judgment before the district court.[186] The intervenors supported the law school's motion, but in fact they welcomed the prospect of a trial. The trial could serve as a platform to air the ideological and political concerns that they had about the narrow, legalistic framing of the case.[187] The students' brief indicted Michigan and the *Bakke* decision as well as Barbara Grutter. The intervenors chided the law school, a purported ally, for its history of de facto segregation, its use of biased measures like the LSAT and undergraduate grade point average, and its failure to achieve critical

---

[182] Stohr, *supra* note 42, at 161–64.

[183] Response of Defendants Regents of the University of Michigan et al. at 1, Grutter v. Bollinger, 137 F. Supp. 2d 821 (E.D. Mich. 2001) (No. 97–CV–75928).

[184] Plaintiffs' Memorandum in Opposition to Motion for Intervention at 12, Grutter v. Bollinger, 137 F. Supp. 2d 821 (E.D. Mich. 2001) (No. 97–CV–75928).

[185] Opinion and Order Denying Motion to Intervene, Grutter v. Bollinger, No. 97–CV–75928 (E.D. Mich. filed July 6, 1998), *rev'd*, 188 F.3d 394 (6th Cir. 1999).

[186] Plaintiff's Memorandum of Law in Support of Motion for Partial Summary Judgment on Liability, *supra* note 64, at 2; Defendants' Memorandum of Law in Support of Motion for Summary Judgment, *supra* note 65, at 3.

[187] Defendant–Intervenors' Brief in Support of Defendants' Motion for Summary Judgment, *supra* note 67, at 1.

mass under a modest program of affirmative action.[188] The students attributed the lackluster performance in part to Powell's decision in *Bakke,* which strayed from *Brown* by "reject[ing] the clear, measurable, and publicly-accountable standards contained in the UC Davis plan."[189] By impugning even the law school's limited commitment to diversity, the intervenors argued, Grutter's lawsuit offered a "perverse, even racist, view of equality" that harkened back to *Plessy v. Ferguson,* with its mythical claim that separate facilities could be equal. The students warned that CIR was asking the Court once again to elevate form over substance.[190]

To thwart the triumph of empty legalisms, the intervenors invoked a legacy of civil rights activism, insisting that "[t]he tradition of mass mobilization and progressive legal action must be upheld in this case."[191] As part of this strategy, Miranda Massie introduced student petitions and took steps to insure that students would be seated in the audience during trial and oral arguments.[192] Before the Sixth Circuit, her efforts prompted a lecture from the court about the need for the judiciary to resist political influences in applying the rule of law. As the court explained, "We decide the case on the law and the facts and we want it very clear that we are not policymakers. We are not a legislative body. We are not the executive branch. We are the judiciary."[193]

In fact, the intervenors became increasingly marginalized as the case made its way up to the United States Supreme Court. Before the district court, Massie was able to introduce expert reports and testimony on the history of racial discrimination in America, the bias inherent in standardized tests like the LSAT, and the hostile climate that students of color faced on college campuses.[194] The trial judge devoted the last part

---

[188] *Id*. at 6–8, 26–27, 28–35, 38.

[189] *Id*. at 18–19.

[190] *Id*. at 24–25.

[191] *Id*. at 13.

[192] Trial Transcript, *supra* note 70, at 32–33 (remarks of Miranda Massie); Transcript of Oral Argument at 7, Grutter v. Bollinger, 288 F.3d 732 (6th Cir. 2002) (No. 01–1441) (oral argument by Miranda Massie); Stohr, *supra* note 42, at 164, 196.

[193] Transcript of Oral Argument, *supra* note 192, at 7 (remarks of Chief Judge Boyce Martin); Stohr, *supra* note 42, at 196.

[194] Trial Transcript, Grutter v. Bollinger, 137 F. Supp. 2d 821 (E.D. Mich. 2001) (No. 97–CV–75928) (testimony on Jan. 23–24, 2001; Feb. 6–9, 12, 15, 2001); Expert Report of Walter Allen and Daniel Solorzano, Grutter v. Bollinger, 137 F. Supp. 2d 821 (E.D. Mich. 2001) (No. 97–CV–75928); Expert Report of Marcus Feldman, Grutter v. Bollinger, 137 F. Supp. 2d 821 (E.D. Mich. 2001) (No. 97–CV–75928); Expert Report of John Hope Franklin, Grutter v. Bollinger, 137 F. Supp. 2d 821 (E.D. Mich. 2001) (No. 97–CV–75928); Expert Report of Gary Orfield, Grutter v. Bollinger, 137 F. Supp. 2d 821 (E.D. Mich. 2001) (No.

of his opinion to addressing the intervenors' case. Although their arguments were largely irrelevant to the outcome, the district court did credit some of their evidence about the gap in test scores and grade point averages.[195] Ironically, Judge Friedman's opinion cited one of the intervenors' witnesses, who described race-neutral initiatives in California, to refute Michigan's concern that ending affirmative action would lead to re-segregation.[196] Although not the desired impact, the intervenors at least were a part of the discussion.

At the Sixth Circuit level, Massie participated during oral argument, but her arguments did not receive much attention in the judges' opinions. In a concurring opinion, Judge Clay noted that "as the intervenors essentially argue, *Bakke* and *Brown* must ... be read together so as to allow a school to consider race or ethnicity in its admissions for many reasons, including to remedy past discrimination or present racial bias in the educational system."[197] Judge Boggs simply responded that remedying societal discrimination was not a justification recognized by the Court and, in any event, was not "the question litigated (except by intervenors), either at the trial level or the appellate level...."[198] Boggs's comment made clear that he did not see the students as real parties to the case.

By the time the case reached the United States Supreme Court, Massie did not even get her requested ten minutes of time to participate in oral argument, although she did obtain a coveted ticket to attend the proceedings.[199] Massie must have found her exclusion a perverse omission. She had supported Grutter's petition for *certiorari* in hopes that

---

97–CV–75928); Expert Report of Jay Rosner, Grutter v. Bollinger, 137 F. Supp. 2d 821 (E.D. Mich. 2001) (No. 97–CV–75928); Expert Report of Martin Shapiro, Grutter v. Bollinger, 137 F. Supp. 2d 821 (E.D. Mich. 2001) (No. 97–CV–75928); Expert Report of Faith Smith, Grutter v. Bollinger, 137 F. Supp. 2d 821 (E.D. Mich. 2001) (No. 97–CV–75928); Expert Report of Stephanie Wildman, Grutter v. Bollinger, 137 F. Supp. 2d 821 (E.D. Mich. 2001) (No. 97–CV–75928); Expert Report of David White, Grutter v. Bollinger, 137 F. Supp. 2d 821 (E.D. Mich. 2001) (No. 97–CV–75928); Expert Report of Frank Wu, Grutter v. Bollinger, 137 F. Supp. 2d 821 (E.D. Mich. 2001) (No. 97–CV–75928); Expert Report of Richard Lempert, Grutter v. Bollinger, 137 F. Supp. 2d 821 (E.D. Mich. 2001) (No. 97–CV–75928); Stohr, *supra* note 42, at 161–64.

[195] Grutter v. Bollinger, 137 F. Supp. 2d 821, 869–70 (E.D. Mich. 2001).

[196] *Id.*

[197] Grutter, 288 F.3d at 768 (Clay, J., concurring).

[198] *Id.* at 809 (Boggs, J., dissenting).

[199] Motion for Enlargement of Argument Time and for Divided Argument or in the Alternative, Divided Argument, *supra* note 160, at 1; Grutter v. Bollinger, 538 U.S. 904 (2003) (denying interveners' motion to expand time and participate in oral argument); Stohr, *supra* note 42, at 256–57, 263.

the Court would vindicate affirmative action throughout the nation.[200] Michigan, on the other hand, was happy to leave its victory before the Sixth Circuit intact and opposed high court review.[201] Yet, it was Michigan's defense team, with its close attention to the particularities of the law school's situation under *Bakke,* which got to argue the case. In the Supreme Court opinions, the intervenors again were largely missing in action. Even when Justice Sandra Day O'Connor cited research by one of the intervenors' expert witnesses, she described it as material "[i]n addition to the expert studies and reports entered into evidence at trial."[202] For all intents and purposes, the intervenors had disappeared from the case along with their broad concerns about racial stratification and subordination.

The Amici: From Bystanders to Participants

As the intervenors' role waned, the influence of the amici curiae grew. Despite judicial lectures to Massie about the need to keep politics out of the courtroom, the battle of the amicus briefs was clearly a way to signal power and status in the contentious debate over affirmative action. At the district court level, only a few organizations filed briefs. These were generally groups with a strong interest in higher education, like the American Council on Education and the Association of American Law Schools, although some major businesses and the Michigan Attorney General expressed support for the law school's position as well.[203] Before the Sixth Circuit, the number of amicus briefs multiplied substantially. The vast majority were from the business community, other colleges and universities, state officials, and higher education associations, all in support of preserving affirmative action under *Bakke.*[204] A

---

[200] Response to the Petition for Certiorari by Respondents Kimberly James, et al., *supra* note 158, at 1–3.

[201] Brief in Opposition, *supra* note 157, at 18–30.

[202] 539 U.S. at 330.

[203] *See, e.g.,* Brief of Amici Curiae American Council on Education, et al., Grutter v. Bollinger, 137 F. Supp. 2d 821 (E.D. Mich. 2001) (No. 97–CV–75928); Brief of Association of American Law Schools, et al., Grutter v. Bollinger, 137 F. Supp. 2d 821 (E.D. Mich. 2001) (No. 97–CV–75928); Brief of Amicus Curiae General Motors Corporation in Support of Defendants, Grutter v. Bollinger, 137 F. Supp. 2d 821 (E.D. Mich. 2001) (No. 97–CV–75928); Brief of Steelcase, Inc., et al. as Amici Curiae in Support of Defendants, Grutter v. Bollinger, 137 F. Supp. 2d 821 (E.D. Mich. 2001) (No. 97–CV–75928); Brief of the Attorney General as Amicus Curiae, Grutter v. Bollinger, 137 F. Supp. 2d 821 (E.D. Mich. 2001) (No. 97–CV–75928).

[204] The amici filing on Michigan's behalf that are listed in the Sixth Circuit's docket include the American Bar Association, Judith Areen (then Dean of Georgetown University Law Center), the American Council on Education, the Lawyer's Committee for Civil Rights, General Motors Corporation, the NOW Legal Defense Fund, Ohio State University, 3M

few briefs from conservative think tanks and legal advocacy organizations were filed in support of Grutter as well.[205]

In the Supreme Court, over 80 briefs were filed, of which the overwhelming majority were for Michigan. Fewer than twenty were for Grutter, and a handful were for neither side.[206] The briefs in support of Michigan emphasized the benefits of diversity in higher education and the business world. In addition to the amici who had filed on Michigan's behalf before the Sixth Circuit, the law school enjoyed a substantial boost from a brief filed by a group of retired military generals. The brief indicated that the military academies and Reserve Officer Training Corps programs relied on affirmative action to ensure integrated leadership of the armed forces. These measures were considered vital to preserving morale and trust among the enlisted ranks.[207] This brief often has been characterized as pivotally important in swaying the Court to uphold affirmative action, and the Justices certainly addressed it during oral argument.[208] Michigan began to enlist the generals' support in 2000, but by the time the brief was actually filed, national security and military preparedness had taken on a new urgency in the wake of September 11, 2001, the day that devastating terrorist attacks on American soil took place.[209]

Corporation, the Michigan Attorney General, the Harvard Civil Rights Project, Representative John Conyers, the National Asian Pacific American Bar Association, the Clinical Legal Education Association, and the International Union, United Automobile, Aerospace & Agricultural Implement Workers of America. General Docket, Grutter v. Bollinger, 288 F.3d 732 (6th Cir. 2002) (No. 01–1447) (case filed Apr. 2, 2001).

[205] The amici filing on Grutter's behalf that are listed in the Sixth Circuit's docket include the Pacific Legal Foundation, the National Association of Scholars, the Center for Equal Opportunity, the American Civil Rights Institute, the Independent Women's Forum, and the Michigan Education Association. *Id.*

[206] For a list and description of amicus briefs filed before the United States Supreme Court, see Amicus Briefs–United States Supreme Court Summary of Arguments, *available at* http://www.umich.edu/?urel/admissions/legal/gru_amicus-ussc/summary.html (updated Apr. 4, 2003); Stohr, *supra* note 42, at 253–56. In fact, one close observer of the Court remarked that: "The Michigan tactics in front of the justices came to resemble a political campaign as much as a litigation strategy...." Toobin, *supra* note 163, at 213.

[207] Consolidated Brief of Lt. Gen. Julius W. Becton, Jr., et al., Grutter v. Bollinger, 539 U.S. 306 (2003) (No. 02–241); Stohr, *supra* note 42, at 247–51.

[208] Transcript of Oral Argument at 7–10, 12–13, Grutter v. Bollinger, 539 U.S. 306 (2003) (No. 02–241) (questions to Kirk Kolbo from Justices Ruth Bader Ginsburg, John Paul Stevens, David Souter, Antonin Scalia, and Anthony Kennedy).

[209] Stohr, *supra* note 42, at 140–42, 178, 218–20, 247–51 (describing Michigan's efforts to get military officials to file an amicus brief). During the confirmation hearings for John Roberts that took place approximately two years after *Grutter*, Senator Edward Kennedy indicated that "the court expressed—expressly gave great weight to the representation by military leaders—military leaders—that said highly qualified, racially diverse office corps is

The briefs filed on behalf of Grutter painted a complicated picture of the alliance that opposed affirmative action. The aftermath of September 11th undercut CIR's position that public officials could consider race only when rectifying past discrimination. Racial profiling had been identified as a key tool in the war on terrorism, and when Norman Mineta, then Secretary of Transportation, insisted on colorblind searches at airports, he was widely ridiculed as a captive of political correctness unable to get tough on threats to the American people.[210] As a result, some amici supporting Grutter began to call for a national security exception to the requirement that the Constitution be colorblind. At the same time, Grutter's supporters argued that there was no compelling basis for the "racial profiling" of applicants to Michigan.[211]

Meanwhile, the United States filed a brief on behalf of Grutter that dodged the question of whether diversity was a compelling interest. The brief came as blow to CIR, which had expected the Bush Administration's full support.[212] Solicitor General Theodore Olsen firmly believed that the United States should openly reject the diversity rationale, but Bush was reluctant to commit himself to a hard-line position on the eve of his reelection campaign. In addition, some high-level black and Latino advisers, most notably Alberto Gonzales, Colin Powell, and Condoleezza Rice, reportedly urged Bush not to abandon affirmative action.[213] Instead,

---

essential to the military's ability to fulfill its principal mission and to provide national security." Confirmation Hearing on the Nomination of Judge John G. Roberts, Jr. to be Chief Justice of the United States: Hearings Before the Senate Committee on the Judiciary, 109th Cong., 1st Sess. (2005).

[210] *See, e.g.,* Peter Wood, *Diversity; It's Not a Small, Small World, After All*, The Am. Spectator, Mar. 2003–Apr. 2003, at 52; Karina Rollins, *No Compromises: Why We're Going to Lose the War on Terror . . . and How We Could Win*, The Am. Enterprise, Jan. 1, 2003, at 18; Heather MacDonald, *Why the FBI Didn't Stop 9/11*, 12 City J. 14 (Autumn 2002); *Profiling: Better Safe*, Nat'l Rev., Mar. 25, 2002, at 17; Stuart Taylor, Jr., *Blind to Terror: Politically Correct Concerns Make Air Travel Dangerous*, Legal Times, Mar. 18, 2002, at 67.

[211] Brief Amici Curiae of the Center for Equal Opportunity, et al. at 16, Grutter v. Bollinger, 539 U.S. 306 (2003) (No. 02–241) ("There are, perhaps, other governmental interests that might be hypothesized as compelling enough to justify temporary racial and ethnic classifications by the government—such as national security. . . ."); Brief Amicus Curiae of Pacific Legal Foundation in Support of Petitioner at 10, Grutter v. Bollinger, 539 U.S. 306 (2003) (No. 02–241) ("the University's purported interest in operating a racially diverse law school is neither remedial nor necessary to prevent imminent danger to life and limb. . . ."). Justice Thomas picked up on these concerns in his dissenting opinion. *Grutter*, 539 U.S. at 351 (citing the Court's application of strict scrutiny to Japanese internment in *Korematsu* to show that national security constitutes a "pressing public necessity" and thus is a compelling interest).

[212] Stohr, *supra* note 42, at 254–55.

[213] Carl M. Cannon, *Spinning the Court*, 35 The Nat'l J. 2110 (2003) (Bush's endorsement of diversity in higher education was necessary to appeal to moderate swing voters

the brief described diversity as a paramount goal, which nevertheless had to be achieved through narrowly tailored means.[214] Angry and disillusioned by his marginalization within the Administration, Olsen nevertheless submitted the brief and argued the case before the Court.[215]

During the argument, Olsen's deep conflicts over conceding that diversity was a compelling interest were palpable. When Justice O'Connor questioned him about Powell's rationale, he replied that "contrary to what our opponents have said, we would not believe that the single opinion, which was the only opinion, to examine the issue of diversity" commanded the Court's support.[216] When pressed by Justices Anthony Kennedy and John Paul Stevens, Olsen stated that "the word diversity means so many things to so many different people"[217] and that "the Harvard program ... wasn't examined according to any compelling governmental interest."[218] The Bush Administration's brief was consistent with others that emphasized the narrow tailoring requirement and skirted the question of whether diversity was compelling. The brief for the State of Florida, for example, highlighted the success of the One Florida Initiative, which eliminated affirmative action in admissions and substituted percentage plans, at the behest of the President's brother, Governor Jeb Bush.[219]

Although some of the most influential amicus briefs filed on Grutter's behalf did not attack the diversity rationale, a few advocacy organizations adopted a hard-hitting, polemical stance. For instance, the Claremont Institute for the Study of Statesmanship and Political Philosophy linked Michigan's use of race in admissions to the presumptions of inferiority that underlay *Plessy v. Ferguson*'s "separate but equal" rationale for segregation. According to the Institute's brief, "racial preferences, whether in hiring or contracting, the provision of government benefits, or, as here, in law school and college admissions, are ostensibly designed to shield minority group members, but in fact are

---

who wanted to "take Bush's vow of compassionate conservatism seriously and who want a chief executive who is racially sensitive"); Stohr, *supra* note 42, at 238–41.

[214] Brief of the United States as Amicus Curiae Supporting Petitioner at 12–13, Grutter v. Bollinger, 539 U.S. 306 (2003) (No. 02–241).

[215] Stohr, *supra* note 42, at 241, 270–72.

[216] Transcript of Oral Argument, *supra* note 208, at 25.

[217] *Id.* at 27.

[218] *Id.* at 26.

[219] Brief of the State of Florida and the Honorable John Ellis "Jeb" Bush, Governor, as Amicus Curiae in Support of Petitioners, Grutter v. Bollinger, 539 U.S. 306 (2003) (No. 02–241).

premised on the notion that they are incapable of competing without a brother—a white big brother—to guide them."[220]

The Institute argued that by opposing colorblindness, Michigan betrayed *Brown*'s legacy and was no better than those who had defied school integration because "today, defenders of racially discriminatory laws, as emphatic as their predecessors in the 1950s, are exhibiting the same determination to avoid the commands of the Equal Protection Clause."[221] If anything, "the defiance of today's defenders of racial classifications is ... even more pernicious, because their reliance on 'diversity' as a government interest is one that effectively assures that race will always be relevant in American life...."[222] Much like the student-intervenors, the Claremont Institute had moved beyond claiming that it was the heir of *Brown* to charging that any opponents were the bastards of *Plessy*.

There are several reasons why the odyssey through the federal courts looked so different for the intervenors and the amici. As the intervenors argued against the empty formalism of equality, their own involvement in the litigation was increasingly undermined by procedural formalism. The intervenors were best able to participate at the trial court level where their inclusion was mandatory. Even there, the students entered the case late, and their efforts to introduce independent evidence were seen more as a source of delay than of legal insight. As the prospect of Supreme Court review grew, the need for clean lines of argument in the lower courts intensified. To highlight the issues related to diversity, the district court treated the intervenors' arguments as an afterthought, and the Sixth Circuit opinions largely ignored them. The intervenors became a side show, even though they were nominally parties to the case.

The role of the amici, on the other hand, increased in importance as the case went on. Only a few organizations were willing to expend their political capital when the case was being tried before the district court. As the litigation unfolded, however, it became clear that the Michigan cases might make history. Both CIR and the law school realized that it was vitally important to have friends in high places who would impress the court with arguments that reinforced the parties' own claims. The amici were not parties to the lawsuit, so their participation was wholly optional. Yet, far from marginalizing them, their voluntary decision to

---

[220] Brief of Amicus Curiae The Claremont Institute Center for Constitutional Jurisprudence in Support of Petitioners at 14, Grutter v. Bollinger, 539 U.S. 306 (2003) (No. 02–241).

[221] *Id.* at 19.

[222] *Id.* at 23 (citing City of Richmond v. J.A. Croson Co., 488 U.S. 469 (1989) (plurality opinion)).

become involved marked the momentous nature of the case and put it in a political context.

It was the stature and sheer number of amici that really mattered. Their briefs typically adopted a highly legalistic tone, focusing on the *Bakke* paradigm and adding little to the parties' arguments. In this way, the amici brought politics into the courtroom without undermining the judiciary's claim that it was dedicated entirely to questions of law. On occasion, the briefs added a real-world dimension that had not been fully addressed before. The military brief offers perhaps the best example because it supplemented the factual record in an area that had taken on newfound significance in the wake of September 11th. The power of the briefs to enrich the Court's understanding was such that when Justice Ruth Bader Ginsburg questioned Solicitor General Olsen about affirmative action in the military academies, his response that "we haven't examined [the legality of the practice] and we haven't presented a brief with respect to the specifics of each individual academy"[223] sounded more like an evasion than a legal argument.

The Aftermath

Although the jurisprudential focus on *Bakke* limited the scope of racial politics in the courtroom during the Michigan litigation, the *Grutter* ruling was not nearly as successful in containing the persistent public debate over affirmative action afterwards. In his dissent from *Grutter*, Justice Scalia described the results of the Michigan litigation as "perversely designed to prolong the controversy and the litigation."[224] Lawsuits still could be brought to challenge "whether, in the particular setting at issue, any educational benefits flow from racial diversity."[225] According to Scalia, just as Michigan had defended itself with expert research, other colleges and universities were similarly obligated to demonstrate the proper exercise of their academic freedom. Even if institutions demonstrated that diversity was compelling, the narrow tailoring requirement would remain a significant obstacle. For instance, if officials claimed that diversity promoted interracial understanding and tolerance, Scalia could find little justification for race-specific student organizations, housing, and graduation ceremonies.[226]

Whether meant as a prediction or a provocation, Scalia's view that affirmative action would remain controversial has been confirmed in the

---

[223] Transcript of Oral Argument, *supra* note 42, at 21; Stohr, *supra* note 42, at 270–71.

[224] 539 U.S. at 348 (Scalia, J., dissenting).

[225] *Id.*

[226] *Id.* at 349.

early years following *Grutter*. The Court's deference to college and university administrators is a displacement of responsibility. Justice O'Connor's decision endorses diversity not as a moral imperative but as a pedagogical option. Without a constitutional mandate to desegregate or to undo racial stratification, university officials are free to exercise their judgment about educational matters, but they are also largely on their own in defending these judgments. Doubts about the educational benefits of diversity can seriously undermine admissions programs that consider race. In legal education, for instance, Professor Richard Sander has argued that affirmative action harms rather than helps blacks because they attend schools where they are not academically competitive.[227] As a consequence, black students suffer from the effects of an "academic mismatch" that leads them to disengage from their studies.[228] These mismatched students wind up disproportionately clustered at the bottom of the class, and they are more likely to drop out and to fail the bar than white classmates.[229] Due to these adverse effects, Sander makes the admittedly counterintuitive claim that affirmative action actually decreases rather than increases the number of black lawyers.[230]

Other scholars have taken Sander to task for the methodological assumptions underlying his conclusion that affirmative action hinders blacks' access to the legal profession.[231] These critiques blunt the claim that considering race in admissions does more harm than good, but they do not tackle the question of how to do the most good by fully capitalizing on the benefits of a diverse student body. Relatively few researchers have been willing to take on this task, despite the urgency of narrowing the achievement gap and making the most of diversity in the next twenty-five years. Michigan, recognizing its role as a leader in this area after *Grutter*, created the Center for Institutional Diversity to address issues like these in the wake of the litigation. So far, however, most colleges and universities continue to focus primarily on defending their admissions programs without systematically linking them to institutional practices that promote learning and leadership.[232] By failing to gener-

---

[227] Richard Sander, *A Systemic Analysis of Affirmative Action in American Law Schools*, 57 Stan. L. Rev. 367, 371–72 (2004).

[228] *Id.* at 449–54.

[229] *Id.* at 426–48.

[230] *Id.* at 472–75.

[231] *See, e.g.,* David Chambers, et al., *The Real Impact of Eliminating Affirmative Action in American Law Schools: An Empirical Critique of Richard Sander's Study*, 57 Stan. L. Rev. 1855 (2005); Ian Ayres & Richard Brooks, *Does Affirmative Action Reduce the Number of Black Lawyers?*, 57 Stan. L. Rev. 1807 (2005).

[232] For information on Michigan's initiative, see http://www.diversity.umich.edu/futuring/index.html (site last visited Sept. 25, 2007). For a discussion of the limited

ate evidence that diversity promotes the exchange of ideas in and out of class, university officials leave themselves vulnerable to charges that critical mass is a sham and that their project is one of "racial aesthetics" rather than real intellectual enrichment.

Without a strong image of the diverse college campus, admissions programs become easy targets for political attack. In the wake of the Michigan litigation, opponents of affirmative action successfully pushed for a ballot initiative to eliminate the very practices and policies that *Grutter* vindicated as constitutional.[233] The initiative is a direct rebuke not only of the Supreme Court's endorsement of diversity but also of the University of Michigan's claim to academic freedom. Rather than debate the pedagogical benefits of diversity, the ballot measure's backers focused on individual fairness to applicants.[234] Their campaign rhetoric adopted the perspective of a student like Barbara Grutter, who found herself on the wrong end of race-based affirmative action. Largely ignored was the position of a university president like Lee Bollinger or a law school dean like Jeffrey Lehman, who must make trade-offs among competing values. On the campaign trail, the complexities of intellectual diversity lacked the strong hold on the public imagination that individual fairness could command. Massie and colleagues from Scheff and Washington were back in federal court to seek certification of a class of students who would challenge the constitutionality of the initiative.[235] So

research in this area, see Braz Camargo, et al., Evidence About the Potential for Affirmative Action in Higher Education 2 (National Bureau of Economic Research Working Paper No. 13342, 2007), *available at* http://www.nber.org/papers/w13342; Rachel F. Moran, *Of Doubt and Diversity: The Future of Affirmative Action in Higher Education*, 67 Ohio St. L.J. 201, 227–28 (2006). *See also* Devon W. Carbado & Mitu Gulati, *What Exactly is Racial Diversity?*, 91 Cal. L. Rev. 1149, 1153–64 (2003) (offering a framework for linking the concept of diversity to particular pedagogical objectives).

[233] Proposal 2 (Nov. 7, 2006) (codified at Mich. Const. art. I, § 26). *See also* Curt A. Levey, *Colleges Should Take No Comfort in the Supreme Court's Reprieve*, Chron. of Higher Educ., July 18, 2003, at B11; Rebecca Trounson and Stuart Silverstein, *Bid to Export Prop. 209*, L.A. Times, July 8, 2003, § 2 at 1; Dana Milbank, *Affirmative Action Opponents Preparing for a Ballot Battle*, Wash. Post, July 4, 2003, at A7.

[234] *See, e.g.*, Trounson & Silverstein, *supra* note 233, § 2 at 1 (quoting sponsor Ward Connerly's claim that *Grutter* was "an aberration" that was "not consistent with where this country is or where it ought to be" so that the issue had be to be taken "back to the people"). Opponents of the initiative alleged that the sponsors had engaged in fraud and misrepresentation when collecting signatures to place the proposal on the ballot. A federal judge agreed that some voters had been wrongly informed that the measure would preserve affirmative action, but because voters of all races were misled, there was no violation of the Voting Rights Act. Operation King's Dream v. Connerly, 2006 WL 2514115, at *11–*12, *17 (E.D. Mich. 2006), *appeal dismissed as moot*, 501 F.3d 584 (6th Cir. 2007).

[235] Plaintiff Coalition to Defend Affirmative Action (BAMN's) et al.'s Motion to Certify Classes and to Be Appointed Lead Counsel, Coalition to Defend Affirmative Action v. Granholm, Nos 06–15024, 06–15637 (E.D. Mich. May 16, 2007).

far, initial decisions upholding the enforceability of the law indicate that these students face an uphill battle in the Sixth Circuit.[236]

Even in parts of the country where *Grutter* remains controlling, the narrow tailoring requirement has been used to undermine the decision's impact. Despite the Court's endorsement of holistic review, federal agencies have devoted considerable resources to investigating the illicit consideration of race in colleges and universities. The U.S. Commission on Civil Rights has used Professor Sander's research as a basis for questioning accreditation standards that require law schools to "demonstrate by concrete action" a commitment to diversity among students, faculty, and staff. In addition to raising concerns that such results-based measures of success are potentially discriminatory, the Commission's report has called for disclosure and study of racial disparities in the academic qualifications of admitted students, their performance in law school, their graduation rates, and their success in passing the bar.[237]

Meanwhile, the Office for Civil Rights ("OCR") has made clear that minorities-only programs, activities, and scholarships are unacceptable because they are not necessary to achieve diversity. The agency also has investigated admissions programs that allegedly weigh race so heavily that the results become indistinguishable from quotas or set-asides.[238] Finally, OCR has touted race-neutral alternatives, including colorblind comprehensive review, percentage plans, and socioeconomic diversity programs.[239] The implication seems to be that race-based affirmative action is no longer necessary at most institutions.

Coupled with congressional silence, OCR's enforcement practices have obscured the fact that Michigan actually prevailed in the litigation. In fact, the NAACP filed a complaint charging that OCR was actively discouraging colleges and universities from using affirmative action, despite the holding in *Grutter*.[240] After *Brown*, the Court's desegregation mandate was not self-executing but depended heavily on the actions of Congress, the President, and federal agencies. Much the same is true of diversity. So far, no federal authority has vindicated *Grutter* by issuing

---

[236] Coalition to Defend Affirmative Action v. Granholm, 473 F.3d 237, 247–51 (6th Cir. 2006).

[237] U.S. Commission on Civil Rights, Affirmative Action in American Law Schools 1–7 (April 2007), *available at* http://www.usccr.gov/pubs/AALSreport.pdf.

[238] *See, e.g.,* Peter Schmidt, *Federal Civil–Rights Officials Investigate Race–Conscious Admissions,* Chron. of Higher Educ., Dec. 17, 2004, at A26.

[239] Office for Civil Rights, *Achieving Diversity: Race–Neutral Alternatives in American Education* (2004).

[240] Peter Schmidt, *Report Criticizes Civil–Rights Office,* Chron. of Higher Educ., July 1, 2005, at 18.

guidelines or bringing enforcement actions to ensure compliance with the principles set forth in O'Connor's opinion. Despite the NAACP's protest, there seems to be little public outrage at these systematic efforts to undermine diversity in admissions.

The chances that *Grutter* would be broadly enforced were further diminished when Justice O'Connor stepped down from the Court. At about the same time that she retired, Chief Justice Rehnquist died. In 2005, John Roberts succeeded Rehnquist as Chief Justice; in 2006, Samuel Alito filled the vacancy left by O'Connor.[241] Neither of these new members of the Court seemed to be committed to the diversity rationale.[242] In 2007, the Court decided *Parents Involved in Community Schools v. Seattle School District No. 1*,[243] which addressed the constitutionality of voluntary desegregation plans in elementary and secondary schools. Writing for a plurality, Chief Justice Roberts carefully limited *Grutter* to higher education based on unique concerns about academic freedom.[244] In a section of the opinion endorsed by four Justices, Roberts went out of his way to note the doubts surrounding the concept of critical mass, in particular, whether the law school had "count[ed] back from its applicant pool to arrive at the 'meaningful number' it regarded as necessary to diversify its student body."[245] Setting aside these doubts, Roberts made clear that *Grutter* provided no support for the claim that "pure racial balancing [is] a constitutionally compelling interest."[246] Instead, *Grutter* gave a broad account of diversity that required individualized consideration of a range of characteristics, not just race.[247] In short, Roberts' opinion suggested that *Grutter* was limited not just to higher education but to the specifics of the admissions process employed by Michigan's law school.

At the same time that *Grutter* was narrowly limited to its facts, it was deployed to obscure *Brown*'s desegregation legacy. The Court characterized the voluntary plans as an illicit form of affirmative action. According to a majority of the Justices, diversity was a compelling interest, but the race-based school assignments were not narrowly tai-

---

[241] David D. Kirkpatrick, *Alito Sworn In as Justice After Senate Gives Approval*, N.Y. Times, Feb. 1, 2006, at A1; Sheryl Gay Stolberg and Elisabeth Bumiller, *Senate Confirms Roberts as 17th Chief*, N.Y. Times, Sept. 30, 2005, at A1.

[242] Peter Schmidt, *Supreme Court Shows Increased Skepticism Toward Affirmative Action*, Chron. of Higher Educ., Dec. 15, 2006, at 20.

[243] 127 S.Ct. 2738 (2007).

[244] *Id.* at 2754.

[245] *Id.* at 2757 (citation omitted).

[246] *Id.* at 2763.

[247] *Id.* at 2753, 2763–64.

lored to achieve this goal. In his opinion, Chief Justice Roberts explicitly rejected the notion that racial balancing, that is, desegregation, might be a compelling interest in its own right without a remedial rationale. Instead, he emphasized the Constitution's requirement of individualized, colorblind treatment.[248] In doing so, Roberts built upon what Justice Thurgood Marshall once termed an "artful distinction" that allowed the Court to "cordon[] off" the school desegregation cases from affirmative action "to avoid having to repudiate [them]."[249] If *Grutter* was the beneficiary of *Brown's* legacy, the heir had arguably overthrown its progenitor.

Ironically, then, O'Connor's decision in *Grutter*, so carefully rooted in a legal analysis of *Bakke's* diversity rationale, has been eclipsed by the very racial politics that the Court assiduously sought to avoid. A statewide referendum rejected affirmative action in Michigan, and federal enforcement agencies subverted race-conscious admissions elsewhere in the country. The ideological shift in the Court that came with the highly politicized appointment of two new Justices cast doubt on the continued vitality of *Grutter*. Even if the decision technically remained good law, it had not fully legitimated affirmative action and had been used to deflect desegregation. Once hailed as an important civil rights victory, *Grutter* seemed increasingly tenuous, a reminder of the provisional quality of precedent wrought by narrow majorities and a jurisprudence of fragmentation.

Conclusion

The story of *Grutter v. Bollinger* reveals that *Brown's* legacy remains deeply contested. In many ways, *Brown* itself contained the seeds of this ambiguity. *Brown I* was a short and unanimous opinion, one that created an appearance of consensus and certainty. At the same time, though, the Justices left much unsaid. *Brown II* was the opportunity to sort out priorities and resolve uncertainties, but the Court preserved its unanimity by temporizing and leaving the tough questions to district court judges. The Civil Rights Act of 1964[250] reinvigorated the desegregation campaign in the courts. So long as race-conscious remedies were directly linked to rectifying past discrimination, particularly in the South, the federal courts believed themselves to be on firm ground.

Yet, Congress, the President, and newly formed federal civil rights agencies were not content with desegregating public schools or even public beaches, public transportation, and public golf courses. Officials

---

[248] *Id.* at 2753–54, 2757–59, 2767–68.

[249] Richmond v. J.A. Croson Co., 488 U.S. 469, 558–59 (1989) (Marshall, J., dissenting).

[250] Pub. L. No. 88–352, 78 Stat. 241 (codified as amended at 42 U.S.C. § 2000 (2005)).

moved aggressively to improve racial access to the ballot box, the workplace, motels, restaurants, and even private clubs.[251] Affirmative action was vital to these efforts, but it moved well beyond corrective justice to a vision of America's future. The Court, once having been a leader in the realm of racial justice, found itself struggling to keep pace with these bold new initiatives. Affirmative action tested the fragile consensus that the Justices had cobbled together in *Brown*. Programs that expressly considered race pitted the commitment to colorblindness directly against the goals of integration and equality.

As these values came into conflict, the result was a jurisprudence of fragmentation. This jurisprudence culminated in litigation like *Grutter*, which was marked by ambivalence and ambiguity, conflict and contestation at every turn. The price has been tremendous. No longer do the Court's pronouncements vindicate a rule of law. They are simply split decisions that become further fodder for political controversy over the role of race in public life. These debates in turn require that judges be unmasked as ideological tools for one side or the other, not the fair and neutral arbiters of law that they profess to be. At times, jurists insert themselves into this polarizing discourse. Before *Grutter*, the Fifth Circuit was willing to issue a direct challenge to the validity of the *Bakke* decision by depicting Powell as a Justice without a portfolio, a voice without a constituency, and therefore a less than credible source of constitutional law. Later, in the Sixth Circuit, the judges engaged in barely concealed feuding and even open warfare. Their shrill accusations made it hard to believe that the federal judiciary was detached and deliberative, rather than partisan and polemical.

With the federal courts in disarray, it is hard to say precisely what *Grutter*'s legacy will be. Perhaps it should be remembered not for the way that it wrestled with the constitutional legitimacy of colorblindness and color-consciousness but for the way in which it epitomized the high cost of failing to acknowledge the relationship between law and politics. *Brown I* needed the majesty of the law to give force to its call for racial justice. Yet, *Brown II* quickly revealed that the Justices were acutely aware of the political consequences of their decision. *Brown I* and *Brown II* created an artificial divide between law and politics, one with devastating consequences for the jurisprudence of race. As the *Grutter* decision demonstrates, the Court has yet to bridge this profoundly troubling gap.

---

[251] *See* Philip A. Klinkner with Rogers M. Smith, *The Unsteady March: The Rise and Decline of Racial Equality in America* 275–87 (1999); Matthew J. Lindsay, *How Antidiscrimination Law Learned to Live with Racial Inequality*, 75 U. Cin. L. Rev. 87, 92–108 (2006).

14

Daniel P. Tokaji

Representation and Raceblindness: The Story of *Shaw v. Reno*

Introduction

The Voting Rights Act of 1965 ("VRA") is probably the most successful civil rights statute in the history of the United States. Although the Fourteenth and Fifteenth Amendments promised equal protection of law and equal access to the ballot, the decades between Reconstruction and the 1960s made a mockery of that promise. Throughout the states of the former Confederacy, African Americans were almost completely shut out of the political process. As late as 1964, for example, only 6.4% of black Mississippians were even registered to vote.[1] Outside of the South, blacks and other people of color enjoyed the formal right to vote but were seldom elected to office. The United States Congress and state legislative bodies remained predominantly—and many of them exclusively—white institutions. The VRA opened up the political process to people who had long been excluded, most notably African Americans in the South. By the 1980s and 1990s, the VRA was being used to integrate legislative bodies that had been almost entirely white for decades. The change was so profound that it has been called the "quiet revolution."[2]

When the United States Supreme Court decided *Shaw v. Reno*[3] (*Shaw I*) in 1993, the decision seemed to presage a reversal of the changes that the VRA had initiated. In *Shaw I*, the Supreme Court recognized a new kind of equal protection claim that was "analytically

---

[1] Samuel Issacharoff, et al., *The Law of Democracy* 546 (2d ed. 2001).

[2] *Quiet Revolution in the South: The Impact of the Voting Rights Act 1965–1990* (Chandler Davidson & Bernard Grofman eds., 1994) [hereinafter *Quiet Revolution*].

[3] 509 U.S. 630 (1993).

distinct" from any previously articulated.[4] Specifically, the decision allowed white North Carolinians to challenge their state's deliberate creation of a majority-black district that the Court deemed "bizarre" in shape.[5] *Shaw I* imported into voting rights law the raceblindness principle articulated in the Supreme Court's affirmative action cases—namely, that race-conscious practices are constitutionally suspect.[6]

The Court applied the raceblindness principle to the drawing of legislative districts, despite the fact that African Americans had been locked out of Southern politics for most of the preceding century. During Reconstruction, Southern blacks were allowed to vote, were elected to state legislatures, and even served in Congress. By the turn of the twentieth century, however, white Democrats had regained their monopoly on political power in the South, almost entirely excluding blacks from participating in elections. Notwithstanding its relatively progressive self-perception,[7] the State of North Carolina was not an exception.[8] Between 1900 and 1992, it did not send a single African American to Congress.[9] To understand the story of *Shaw v. Reno*, it is essential to review this long and ugly history of racial exclusion, as well as the VRA's phenomenal success in countering it.

Understanding this story also necessitates an examination of the post–1990 redistricting process, during which the Justice Department of President George H.W. Bush pursued an aggressive VRA enforcement policy. Federal officials demanded that Southern states increase the number of safe minority districts, a policy that concentrated the most reliably Democratic constituency (i.e., blacks) and thereby facilitated gains in Republican legislative power in surrounding districts. The Justice Department's effort to increase the number of majority-minority districts led directly to the litigation in North Carolina and, eventually, to *Shaw I*. But the most fascinating part of the story is what has transpired since the Court's 1993 opinion in *Shaw I*, including three more trips to the Supreme Court for North Carolina redistricting plans. These decisions have left the *Shaw* doctrine in a state of limbo, creating

---

[4] *Id.* at 652.

[5] *Id.* at 655–56.

[6] *See, e.g., City of Richmond v. J.A. Croson Co.*, 484 U.S. 1058 (1988).

[7] J. Morgan Kousser, *Southern Politics: Suffrage Restrictions and the Establishment of the One–Party South, 1880–1920*, at 245 (1974).

[8] William R. Keech & Michael P. Sistrom, *North Carolina, in Quiet Revolution, supra* note 2, at 154–75.

[9] J. Morgan Kousser, Shaw v. Reno *and the Real World of Redistricting and Representation*, 26 Rutgers L.J. 625, 631 (1995).

a voting rights jurisprudence that can most generously be described as muddled.

In the wake of *Shaw I*, some voting rights advocates worried that the second Reconstruction would meet the same fate as the first—that a short period of minority inclusion would be followed by yet another lengthy period of exclusion.[10] Although the worst fears expressed after *Shaw I* have not yet come to pass, the decision has spawned an internally unstable, if not self-contradictory, voting rights jurisprudence.[11] The Court has simultaneously embraced the rhetoric of raceblindness, while allowing substantial leeway for race-conscious redistricting. Its decisions have occasionally recognized this apparent contradiction, but have yet to resolve it. The legacy of *Shaw v. Reno* thus remains a murky one.

Before the Revolution

To understand the story of *Shaw v. Reno* it is first necessary to examine the history of voting rights in the South. That history is, of course, inextricably linked to the experience of African Americans as they moved from slavery to freedom and equality during Reconstruction, to subjugation and exclusion under Jim Crow, and then to greater inclusion if not equality during the second half of the twentieth century. Like the larger struggle for racial equality, the expansion of voting rights has not proceeded in a straightforward fashion. Progress has occurred by fits and starts, with brief advances followed by decades of stagnation and backsliding. Though mentioned only in passing in the Court's opinion, this experience provides an essential context for the post–1990 redistricting that gave rise to litigation in North Carolina and other states.

After ratification of the Fourteenth Amendment in 1868, federal troops supervised the voter registration of over 700,000 African Americans.[12] It quickly became apparent that this would be insufficient to ensure that newly freed slaves were afforded equal voting rights.[13] The

---

[10] Laughlin McDonald, *The Counterrevolution in Minority Voting Rights*, 65 Miss. L.J. 271, 273–74 (1995) (seeing *Shaw* cases as emblematic of a "counterrevolution" in voting rights that threatened to undo the gains won since VRA).

[11] *See* Georgia v. Ashcroft, 539 U.S. 461, 491 (2003) (Kennedy, J., concurring); Richard H. Pildes, *Is Voting–Rights Law Now at War with Itself?: Social Science and Voting Rights in the 2000s*, 80 N.C. L. Rev. 1517, 1517 (2002).

[12] Bernard Grofman et al., *Minority Representation and the Quest for Voting Equality* 8–10 (1992) [hereinafter Grofman et al., *Minority Representation*].

[13] Gabriel J. Chin, *Reconstruction, Felon Disenfranchisement, and the Right to Vote: Did the Fifteenth Amendment Repeal Section 2 of the Fourteenth Amendment?*, 92 Georgetown L.J. 259, 269 (2004) (Congress recognized "almost immediately that Section 2 [of the

Fifteenth Amendment, ratified in 1870, specifically prohibited the denial or abridgement of the right of citizens to vote "on account of race, color, or previous condition of servitude." Congress then passed a series of enforcement acts, which provided for supervision of congressional elections and proscribed the suppression of the vote through violence or intimidation.[14]

For a longer period of time than is commonly supposed, the federal laws enacted to enforce the Fourteenth and Fifteenth Amendments actually served their intended purpose, allowing African–American men to vote and even get elected to office. In 1872, there were over 300 Southern blacks serving in state legislatures and Congress, a threshold that was not again reached until the 1990s.[15] The number of black legislators decreased precipitously from 1872 to 1878,[16] and continued to drop after that.[17] Still, approximately two-thirds of black males voted in the presidential election of 1880, three years after Reconstruction ended. Blacks continued to vote through the 1890s, even as Southern states imposed increasingly burdensome restrictions on the franchise.[18]

By the start of the twentieth century, however, almost all blacks in the South had been denied the vote.[19] This was largely a consequence of states' rewriting their constitutions to "exclude blacks from the electorate without obviously violating the Fifteenth Amendment."[20] Disfranchisement was accomplished through a battery of practices including literacy tests, interpretation tests, property qualifications, criminal disenfranchisement, white primaries, poll taxes, gerrymanders, physical intimidation, and even murders.[21] The Supreme Court's decisions upholding some of these practices entrenched the continuing exclusion of blacks from democratic politics throughout the South.[22] As of 1940, only

---

Fourteenth Amendment] would protect neither northern political interests nor the rights of the freedmen.").

[14] J. Morgan Kousser, *Colorblind Injustice: Minority Voting Rights and the Undoing of the Second Reconstruction* 18 (1999).

[15] *Id.* at 19.

[16] *Id.*

[17] *Id.* at 20.

[18] *Id.* at 20–21.

[19] Grofman et al., *Minority Representation, supra* note 12, at 10.

[20] *Id.* at 8.

[21] *Id.* at 8–10; *see generally* Kousser, *supra* note 14, at 25–38.

[22] *See, e.g.,* Giles v. Harris, 189 U.S. 475 (1903) (upholding Alabama's registration scheme against constitutional challenge).

3% of voting-age blacks in the South were even registered.[23]

Although the Supreme Court in the nineteenth century declared that the right to vote was "fundamental,"[24] it did little to stop the suppression of African Americans' voting rights until the late twentieth century. Instead, the Court turned a blind eye to Southern states' actions that effectively cut blacks out of democratic politics altogether.[25]

Race and Representation in North Carolina

North Carolina's history of excluding African Americans mostly mirrored that of other Southern states. Among the peculiarities of North Carolina history is that Reconstruction was *not* the first time that African Americans in the state were allowed to vote. Free blacks in North Carolina actually voted under the first state constitution, adopted in 1776.[26] Not until the 1835 state constitutional convention were free blacks wholly deprived of the right to vote, and this prohibition remained in effect until after the Civil War.[27]

The Second Military Reconstruction Act of 1867 re-enfranchised African Americans and, by 1868, they constituted 70,444 of North Carolina's 196,872 registered voters.[28] As a condition of readmission to the Union, North Carolina and other Southern states were required to adopt constitutions giving blacks the right to vote. States also had to agree that their constitutions "shall never be so amended or changed as to deprive any citizen or class of citizens of the United States of the right to vote," except as punishment for those convicted of felonies.[29] North Carolina amended its constitution accordingly in 1868.[30]

During and after Reconstruction, a substantial number of blacks were elected to federal, state, and local office in North Carolina. Four blacks won election to the second congressional district (commonly known as the "black second") from 1874 to 1898.[31] The last was

---

[23] Chandler Davidson, *The Recent Evolution of Voting Rights Law Affecting Racial and Language Minorities, in* Quiet Revolution, *supra* note 2, at 29.

[24] Yick Wo v. Hopkins, 118 U.S. 356, 370 (1886).

[25] Kousser, *supra* note 14, at 49–53.

[26] *Equal Protection of the Laws in North Carolina* 5 (1963) [hereinafter *Equal Protection*].

[27] *Equal Protection*, *supra* note 26, at 6; William Mabry, *The Negro in North Carolina Politics Since Reconstruction* 3 (1940).

[28] *Equal Protection*, *supra* note 26, at 7.

[29] Chin, *supra* note 13, at 271.

[30] *Equal Protection*, *supra* note 26, at 7.

[31] Eric Anderson, *Race and Politics in North Carolina, 1872–1901: The Black Second* x (1981).

Representative George White, who was also the last African American to serve in Congress from *any* state until 1929 and the last to serve from any Southern state until 1973.[32] A total of fifty-nine blacks sat in the North Carolina house and eighteen in the state senate, between 1876 and 1900.[33]

At the local level, white Democrats engaged in exhaustive efforts to limit black influence, modest though it was, from 1870 through 1900. An 1875 constitutional amendment replaced the popular vote with legislative control of county government, to promote white control of eastern counties with substantial black populations.[34] Centralization of authority over elections was critical to these disenfranchisement efforts. The state board of elections supervised the appointment of local election officials, with those officials given broad discretion over the information required of voters, the time the registration books were open, and challenges to voter eligibility on election day.[35]

Still, North Carolina's blacks continued to vote in substantial numbers for over two decades after the end of Reconstruction.[36] An alliance of Populists and Republicans captured the state's general assembly in 1894, with the support of blacks.[37] Another so-called "fusion ticket" prevailed again in the 1896 elections.[38] The electoral success of the Republican–Populist fusion led to an enormous backlash on the part of white Democrats, whose successful 1898 campaign was based on an explicit platform of white supremacy.[39] But the pivotal election for black voting rights in North Carolina occurred two years later.

The 1900 election resulted in a decisive victory for the openly racist gubernatorial candidate Charles Aycock, and for a package of constitutional amendments that he supported to stop the "Negro domination" of state politics.[40] The amendments provided that, in order to be registered,

---

[32] Keech & Sistrom, *supra* note 8, at 156.

[33] *Id.* at 157.

[34] *Equal Protection*, *supra* note 26, at 9; Keech & Sistrom, *supra* note 8, at 157.

[35] Keech & Sistrom, *supra* note 8, at 157.

[36] *Equal Protection*, *supra* note 26, at 10.

[37] *Id.* at 11.

[38] Keech & Sistrom, *supra* note 8, at 158.

[39] *Equal Protection*, *supra* note 26, at 11; Brief of the Congressional Black Caucus as Amicus Curiae at 12, Shaw v. Hunt (Shaw II), 517 U.S. 899 (1996) (No. 94–923), 1995 U.S. Supreme Court Briefs LEXIS 524, at *21; *see also* Mabry, *supra* note 27, at 57–72 (1940) (detailing the steps taken by white Democrats to disenfranchise North Carolina blacks between 1899 and 1900).

[40] Helen G. Edmonds, *The Negro & Fusion Politics in North Carolina 1894–1901*, at 199–200 (1951).

voters had to pay a poll tax and "be able to read and write any section of the constitution in the English language" to the registrar's satisfaction.[41] This requirement was accompanied by a grandfather clause that allowed citizens to vote if they could trace their ancestry to someone who had voted before January 1, 1867.[42] After passing the necessary legislative hurdles, the amendments were submitted to voters for the August 2, 1900 election. Democrats forthrightly asserted that the object of the amendments was elimination of the "ignorant and irresponsible negro vote," estimating that between 80,000 and 90,000 blacks would be disfranchised by the educational clause alone.[43]

Both Aycock and the voting amendments prevailed by a wide margin in the election.[44] As in other states, "good government" was the coded term for disfranchisement of black voters. Yet after the election, Governor Aycock was remarkably candid about what he and other white North Carolinians had accomplished:

> I am proud of my State, moreover because there we have solved the Negro problem.... We have taken him out of politics and have thereby secured good government under any party and laid foundations for the future development of both races.

> I am inclined to give you our solution to this problem. It is first, as far as possible under the Fifteenth Amendment, to disfranchise him; after that let him alone, quit writing about him; quit talking about him ... let the Negro learn once and for all that there is unending separation of the races ... that they cannot intermingle; let the white man determine that no man shall by act or thought or speech cross this line, and the race problem will be at an end.[45]

The 1900 election marked the effective end of African Americans' right to vote in North Carolina for most of the twentieth century. The literacy test, requiring that voters read a section of the state constitution to the registrar's satisfaction, was the main device by which blacks were excluded from voting. North Carolina's elimination of the poll tax in 1920 made it possible for some poor whites to vote, but did little for

---

[41] Keech & Sistrom, *supra* note 8, at 158; *Equal Protection*, *supra* note 26, at 11.

[42] *Equal Protection*, *supra* note 26, at 11.

[43] Edmonds, *supra* note 40, at 203.

[44] *Id.* at 209–10.

[45] Brief of the Congressional Black Caucus as Amicus Curiae, *supra* note 39, at 13–14, 1995 U.S. Supreme Court Briefs LEXIS 524, at *22–23 (quoting Charles B. Aycock, Speech Before the North Carolina Society, Baltimore (Dec. 18, 1903)), *in The North Carolina Experience: An Interpretive and Documentary History* 415 (Lindsey S. Butler & Alan D. Watson eds., 1984).

blacks, who were still effectively kept out of politics by the literacy test.[46] Although some of North Carolina's blacks were allowed to vote before passage of the Voting Rights Act, their ability to influence elections was severely limited. Only a handful of African Americans were elected to local office in some Piedmont cities, including Winston–Salem and Durham, during the 1940s and 1950s. Once again, the election of blacks to office provoked a backlash—with whites resurrecting strategies like the at-large electoral schemes that had served them so well after Reconstruction.

The Warren Court began to show some interest in stopping the exclusion of blacks from Southern politics, even before the Voting Rights Act of 1965. Five years earlier, in *Gomillion v. Lightfoot*, the Court struck down an Alabama law that altered the City of Tuskegee's boundaries from a square to a twenty-eight-sided figure in a transparent effort to keep African Americans out of city boundaries and thus city politics.[47] A few months before enactment of the 1965 Act, the Supreme Court held that Louisiana's interpretation test violated the Fifteenth Amendment.[48]

Still, the intransigent character of white resistance to black voting rights necessitated a more comprehensive remedy than the Supreme Court could implement on its own. The Court was already struggling with the "massive resistance" to public school desegregation that had emerged in response to its 1954 decision in *Brown v. Board of Education*. Decisive congressional action on voting rights was clearly needed. In 1965, it finally came.

The Voting Rights Revolution

The VRA was not Congress' first attempt to protect African Americans' voting rights. In 1957, Congress enacted the first civil rights bill since Reconstruction.[49] The Civil Rights Act of 1957 authorized the appointment of an Assistant Attorney General for Civil Rights and allowed the Justice Department to intervene in private civil actions. The 1957 Act also allowed the Attorney General to bring actions for injunctive relief in federal district court but only four such suits were brought between 1957 and 1960, and those cases were stymied by difficulties in obtaining registration records and other dilatory tactics.[50] Congress

---

[46] Keech & Sistrom, *supra* note 8, at 158.

[47] 364 U.S. 339 (1960).

[48] Louisiana v. United States, 380 U.S. 145 (1965).

[49] Alexander Keyssar, *The Right to Vote: The Contested History of Democracy in the United States* 260 (2000).

[50] Grofman et al., *Minority Representation, supra* note 12, at 12–13; Keyssar, *supra* note 49, at 260.

passed another Civil Rights Act in 1960, which took the significant step of allowing federal district courts to vest oversight of state elections in federal referees if a "pattern and practice" of discrimination was found. But the referee provision was seldom used and the 1960 Act proved almost as ineffectual as its predecessor. A contributing factor was the reluctance of federal district judges, some of whom were unsympathetic to the plight of black voters, to stop exclusionary practices in their home states. Even when practices were declared illegal, new ones were put in their place—or, in some cases, court orders were simply disregarded.[51]

A series of events that took place between 1963 and 1965 finally made it politically feasible for Congress to enact the rigorous measures needed to overcome the intransigence of Southern states. The 1963 bombings of African–American churches in Birmingham, Alabama and the 1964 murder of three civil rights workers in Philadelphia, Mississippi transformed public opinion outside the South.[52] Northern outrage facilitated passage of the Civil Rights Act of 1964, which included some provisions regarding voting but was mainly focused on public accommodations, education, and employment. Then came Fannie Lou Hamer's riveting testimony before the Credentials Committee at the 1964 Democratic National Convention, describing how she and others had been beaten by Mississippi highway patrolmen for simply trying to register and "become first-class citizens."[53] Finally, on March 7, 1965, in an episode that would come to be known as "Bloody Sunday," the Alabama police attacked voting rights demonstrators crossing the Edmund Pettus Bridge outside Selma—beating some of them, including future Congressman John Lewis, to the point of unconsciousness.[54] Widespread horror over these events gave newly-elected President Lyndon B. Johnson the support he needed to push through Congress the "goddamndest, toughest, voting rights bill" that his staffers could devise.[55]

That bill was the Voting Rights Act of 1965.[56] Passed by an overwhelming majority of Congress, the 1965 Act included unprecedented measures to root out the practices that had kept blacks from voting since the turn of the century—and to prevent Southern states from putting new ones in their place. Section 2 prohibited practices denying or

---

[51] Grofman et al., *Minority Representation, supra* note 12, at 13–14.

[52] *Id.* at 14.

[53] Taylor Branch, *Pillar of Fire: America in the King Years 1963–65*, at 461–62 (1998).

[54] Kousser, *supra* note 14, at 12.

[55] Abigail Thernstrom, *Whose Votes Count?* 15 (1987) (quoting Washington Research Project, *The Shameful Blight: The Survival of Racial Discrimination in Voting in the South* 2 (1972)).

[56] Pub. L. No. 89–110, codified at 43 U.S.C. § 1973 *et seq.*

abridging the vote on account of race, while Section 3 strengthened the procedures available in cases brought by the Attorney General.

The Act's linchpin was the provisions in Sections 4 and 5. Under Section 4, jurisdictions were covered and subjected to special requirements if (1) they conditioned voting on a test or some other device, and (2) less than 50 percent of the voting age population was either registered or actually voted in the 1964 presidential election. Even if the state as a whole was not covered under Section 4, those counties which satisfied both criteria would be. All covered jurisdictions were required immediately to suspend their tests and devices, including literacy tests. In addition, under Section 5, covered jurisdictions were obligated to "preclear" any changes to their voting procedures, by submitting them for approval to either the Justice Department or the U.S. District Court for the District of Columbia. Proposed changes could take effect only if they were found to have neither the purpose nor the effect of weakening minority voting strength.[57] Through the Section 5 preclearance requirement, states and counties that had used a literacy test or other disenfranchising device could be prevented from adopting new measures that would have the same effect.[58]

Under Section 4, six southern states (Alabama, Georgia, Louisiana, Mississippi, South Carolina, and Virginia) were covered in their entirety, making all electoral changes subject to preclearance.[59] Although the entire state of North Carolina was not covered, forty of its 100 counties were.[60] Those jurisdictions were required to eliminate any tests or devices used to screen voters and to preclear any subsequent changes to their voting procedures.

In the immediate aftermath of the 1965 Act's passage, Southerners in Congress were most distressed by the VRA provisions eliminating the literacy test, providing for federal examiners, and requiring states to apply to the D.C. federal district court (rather than to friendlier federal judges in the South) in order to escape coverage. Attorney General Nicholas Katzenbach noted that the provisions were intended to prevent Southern legislatures from "outguess[ing]" both Congress and the federal courts by developing new disfranchising devices when old ones were struck down.[61] The focus on the ban on literacy tests and other devices is

---

[57] Under the Supreme Court's 1974 decision in *Beer v. United States*, 425 U.S. 130 (1976), Section 5 prohibits those changes that are "retrogressive"—that is, ones that weaken minority strength compared to what it had been previously.

[58] Grofman et al., *Minority Representation*, *supra* note 12, at 16–17.

[59] *Id.* at 17.

[60] Keech & Sistrom, *supra* note 8, at 160; Shaw v. Barr, 808 F. Supp. 461, 463 (E.D.N.C. 1992).

[61] Thernstrom, *supra* note 55, at 21.

understandable, given that those provisions had a much more immediate effect than the Section 5 preclearance requirement. In Alabama, Georgia, Louisiana, Mississippi, South Carolina, and Virginia, black registration increased dramatically within two years after the Act's passage. In Alabama, for example, black registration rose from 19.3% to 51.6% of all voters between 1965 and 1967, while in Mississippi it increased from 6.7% to 59.8%. Overall, black registration increased from 29.3% to 52.1% in the seven covered states in these two years.[62]

At the time of the Voting Rights Act, North Carolina had a higher percentage of blacks registered than any other Southern state. But two years later, its black registration rate was actually *lower* than every other covered state except South Carolina.[63] Although the 1965 Act would eventually have a dramatic effect on North Carolina politics as well, that effect was somewhat slower in coming. That is partly because a higher percentage of blacks were registered in North Carolina even before the Act's enactment.[64] It is also because election officials in North Carolina aggressively pursued an array of strategies designed to dilute black voting power, while failing to preclear most of the changes being implemented. Gaston County went to court in 1966, seeking to reinstate its suspended literacy test, but was rebuffed by the Supreme Court.[65] In 1966, the state legislature authorized forty-nine county boards to move from district-based to at-large election systems, making it more difficult for black voters to elect candidates of their choice. Six counties immediately moved to at-large election systems, while six others changed their boundaries.[66]

Very few of the changes that took place in North Carolina during the early years of the 1965 Act were submitted for preclearance. Between 1965 and 1971, there were eighty-eight proposed changes to the election law, but only twelve of them were submitted to the Justice Department—all of which were precleared.[67] To be fair, it was not until 1969 that the Supreme Court made clear the full range of election practices that were subject to preclearance, holding in *Allen v. State Board of Elections* that the Act was "aimed at the subtle, as well as the obvious,

---

[62] Grofman et al., *Minority Representation, supra* note 12, at 23.

[63] *Id.*

[64] Thernstrom, *supra* note 55, at 18; *see also* Grofman et al., *Minority Representation, supra* note 12, at 23 (reporting that black registration in North Carolina showed a modest increase, going from 46.8% to 51.3% between March 1965 and September 1967).

[65] Gaston County v. United States, 288 F. Supp. 678 (D.D.C. 1968), *aff'd*, 395 U.S. 285, 297 (1969).

[66] Keech & Sistrom, *supra* note 8, at 162.

[67] *Id.* at 162.

state regulations which have the effect of denying citizens their right to vote because of their race.''[68] Still, the preclearance requirement had very little effect on North Carolina politics during the early years of the VRA's life.[69]

That is not to say that the 1965 Act's effects on North Carolina were inconsequential. Particularly in the forty covered counties, there was a significant impact during the Act's first decade. The percentage of blacks registered in these counties—the ones in which election officials had most aggressively used the literacy test to prevent blacks from voting—increased from 32.4% to 54.0% between 1964 and 1976.[70] In 1968, Henry Frye became the first black elected to the state legislature in the twentieth century.[71] It was not until the 1980s and 1990s, however, that blacks in North Carolina were elected to legislative office in substantial numbers. The biggest jump in representation came after the 1982 election when the number of blacks in the state house increased from three to eleven. By 1990, there were five blacks in the fifty-person state senate, and thirteen blacks in the 120–person state house.[72] But until 1992, *no* blacks had been elected to either Congress or statewide elected office from North Carolina since Reconstruction.[73]

1992 was the pivotal year for black representation in Congress, in North Carolina as throughout the South. Black candidates Eva Clayton and Mel Watt were elected from the newly drawn First and Twelfth Congressional Districts—the two districts that would be at issue in the *Shaw* litigation. Overall, the number of blacks elected to the House from Southern states increased from five in 1990 to seventeen in 1992,[74] ''solely as a consequence of the increase in the number of black majority congressional districts.''[75] Of the seventeen blacks elected to Congress in

---

[68] 393 U.S. 544, 565 (1969).

[69] Although the Act suspended literacy tests in the covered North Carolina counties, no federal examiners were ever sent to the state. Keech & Sistrom, *supra* note 8, at 160 (citing U.S. Commission on Civil Rights, *The Voting Rights Act: Ten Years After* 31–34 (1975) and U.S. Commission on Civil Rights, *The Voting Rights Act: Unfulfilled Goals* 101–04 (1981)).

[70] Keech & Sistrom, *supra* note 8, at 160 (citing Joel A. Thompson, *The Voting Rights Act in North Carolina: An Evaluation*, in 16 Publius: The Journal of Federalism 139, 143–45 (1986)).

[71] Kousser, *supra* note 14, at 246.

[72] Keech & Sistrom, *supra* note 8, at 166.

[73] *Id.* at 163.

[74] Bernard Grofman, Lisa Handley, & David Lublin, *Drawing Effective Minority Districts: A Conceptual Framework and Some Empirical Evidence*, 79 N.C. L. Rev. 1383, 1394 (2001) [hereinafter Grofman et al., *Effective Minority Districts*].

[75] Bernard Grofman & Lisa Handley, *1990s Issues in Voting Rights*, 65 Miss. L.J. 205, 220 (1995).

1992 and 1994 from the South, *all* were elected from majority-minority districts.[76]

Three features of the VRA's implementation account for its success in increasing minority participation and representation. The first is that the original Act stopped nominally race-neutral practices like literacy tests, which were used to prevent blacks from voting. The discretion vested in local election officials had made it difficult and time-consuming to prevent these tests from being applied in a discriminatory manner. The second critical feature was its unprecedented rearrangement of state-federal power. In particular, section 5 required that covered jurisdictions preclear changes in election procedures with the Justice Department or the D.C. federal court before they could take effect. The significance of this requirement did not become fully apparent until *Allen*'s holding that preclearance applied not only to blatant obstructions of the vote, but also to more subtle means of diluting minority voting strength. After this holding, the Department of Justice began objecting to state election changes much more frequently than it previously had.[77] Third and perhaps most importantly, the VRA's ultimate success in increasing minority representation is a consequence of the fact that it was *not* raceblind, but instead was interpreted to require race-conscious action by both the courts and the Department of Justice. This approach is manifest in both the 1982 amendments to Section 2 of the Act, and in the manner that the Justice Department interpreted the preclearance requirements of Section 5, particularly in the post–1990 redistricting cycle.

The 1982 amendments were a direct response to the Supreme Court's narrow construction of the VRA's reach. In 1980, the Court held that voting rights plaintiffs must show discriminatory *intent*, and not simply discriminatory effects, in order to make out a Section 2 claim.[78] Congress reacted by amending Section 2 in 1982, to make clear that practices that "result[] in" the dilution of minority voting strength may also violate the Act. These amendments were enacted over the vigorous opposition of some conservatives within the Reagan Administration— most notably a twenty-seven-year old attorney in the Department of Justice. That attorney was the future Chief Justice John Roberts, who acknowledged that Section 2 was "an important part of what has been uniformly described as the most successful civil rights law ever enacted" but argued that incorporation of a results test "would establish essen-

---

[76] Brief for American Civil Liberties Union and Lawyers' Committee for Civil Rights Under Law as Amici Curiae at 2–3, Shaw v. Hunt (Shaw II), 517 U.S. 899 (1996) (No. 94–923), 1995 U.S. Supreme Court Briefs LEXIS 551, at *6.

[77] Davidson, *supra* note 23, at 32.

[78] Mobile v. Bolden, 446 U.S. 55 (1980).

tially a quota system for electoral politics."[79] Roberts was wrong to characterize Section 2 as a "quota." But it is certainly true that the 1982 amendments to the Act require that courts take into consideration whether minorities are able to elect candidates of their choice—and that usually means minority candidates—in determining whether Section 2 has been violated.[80]

Also critical to increasing minority representation was the Justice Department's enforcement of Section 5 of the Voting Rights Act. Under President George H.W. Bush, the Justice Department aggressively enforced Section 5's preclearance requirement to block proposed election changes that did not include an adequate number of districts in which racial minorities had the opportunity to elect a candidate of their choice.[81] At first glance, it might seem incongruous that a Republican Administration would insist upon the creation of safe black districts, given that African Americans are among the most reliably Democratic voters. From a partisan political perspective, however, the creation of districts with a supermajority of blacks made a great deal of sense for Republicans. Creating a majority-black district generally has the effect of "bleaching" its surrounding districts, making them more white and thereby depriving Democratic candidates in those districts of reliable voters. Although there is great controversy over the magnitude of this effect, the creation of safe black districts does appear to have benefited Republican candidates in the aggregate.[82] Party leaders have wryly

---

[79] Memorandum from John Roberts, Assistant to the Att'y Gen., U.S. Dep't of Justice, to Brad Reynolds, Assistant Att'y Gen., Civil Rights Div., U.S. Dep't of Justice, entitled "Why Section 2 of the Voting Rights Act Should Be Retained Unchanged" at 1–2 (Dec. 22, 1981), available at http://www.lls.edu/academics/faculty/pubs/hasen-roberts-vra–1.pdf.

[80] The Supreme Court articulated the test for section 2 vote dilution claims in *Thornburgh v. Gingles*, 478 U.S. 30 (1986), which concerned the NAACP Legal Defense Fund's challenge to North Carolina's 1982 redistricting plan. Under *Gingles*, one of the three "preconditions" for such a claim is that the minority group's preferred candidates usually have been defeated due to racial bloc voting. *Id.* at 50.

[81] Some argued that this requires a district to be at least 65% African American, to compensate for the higher percentage of voting-age citizens and turnout among whites, though the Justice Department disclaimed any rigid numerical threshold. David Lublin, *The Paradox of Representation: Racial Gerrymandering and Minority Interests in Congress* 45–46 (1997); *see also* United Jewish Organizations v. Carey, 430 U.S. 144, 152 (1977) (noting that a member of New York's legislative reapportionment committee "testified . . . he 'got the feeling [from Justice Department officials] . . . that 65 percent would probably be an approved figure'. . . .").

[82] Grant M. Hayden, *Resolving the Dilemma of Minority Representation*, 92 Calif. L. Rev. 1589, 1609–10 (2004) (noting estimates of between two and eleven congressional seats won by Republicans due to race-conscious districting).

referred to this phenomenon as the "happy coincidence" between the interests of blacks and Republicans.[83]

The Post–1990 North Carolina Redistricting

The redistricting that led to *Shaw v. Reno* took place against a backdrop of racially charged politics stretching over a century, which had continued into the very recent past. Still fresh in the minds of the state's voters was the bitter campaign for U.S. Senate in 1990 between the archconservative white Republican incumbent Jesse Helms and his black Democratic challenger Harvey Gantt. For anyone who thought that racial politics in North Carolina was a thing of the past, the Gantt–Helms campaign demonstrated otherwise. The campaign featured a notorious television advertisement that played upon the white backlash against affirmative action programs. The ad showed a pair of white hands crumpling up a job rejection notice, while in the background a narrator's voice intoned: "You needed that job and you were the best qualified, but they had to give it to a minority because of a racial quota. Is that really fair?" Although Gantt was leading in the polls until the final days, the ad helped turn the tide toward Helms, who prevailed by a narrow margin.[84]

The Helms campaign's use of the term "quota" presaged the white backlash that would emerge in the North Carolina redistricting litigation. One of the most striking aspects of this backlash, which culminated in the *Shaw* opinions, is how quickly it materialized. Even *before* the election of North Carolina's first two African–American congressional representatives in over nine decades, white voters were in court challenging the deliberate creation of majority-black districts. Such favoritism toward blacks, it was argued, violated the equal protection mandate of "colorblind" government decisionmaking.

The white voters who brought the *Shaw* case were undeniably correct that North Carolina's creation of majority-black districts was motivated in substantial part by pressure from the George H.W. Bush Justice Department. But this pressure was not the only motivation for the "bizarrely shaped" districts at issue in *Shaw*. As the tortuous saga of North Carolina's post–1990 redistricting shows, these shapes were as much the product of incumbent and partisan self-interest as they were of a desire to promote black political power. The oddly shaped districts that the Court condemned in *Shaw* reflected not only the Justice Department's demand for two majority-black districts, but also the state legislature's desire to protect Democratic incumbents.

---

[83] Thernstrom, *supra* note 55, at 234.

[84] Daniel Patrick Tokaji, *The Persistence of Prejudice: Process–Based Theory and the Retroactivity of the Civil Rights Act of 1991*, 103 Yale L.J. 567, 581–82 (1993).

It is often said that if elections are the process through which voters choose their representatives, then redistricting is the process through which representatives choose their voters. Every ten years, after the census, states must draw new district lines to account for population shifts. This requirement is a function of the Supreme Court's "one person, one vote" jurisprudence, which requires that legislative seats (other than those in the United States Senate) represent areas with approximately equal populations.[85] Special exactitude is required with respect to U.S. House districts.[86]

The 1990 census resulted in the addition of one U.S. House seat in North Carolina, increasing the state's delegation from eleven to twelve.[87] Under North Carolina law, the state's General Assembly has sole responsibility for drawing legislative districts. At the time, Democrats dominated North Carolina's legislature and enjoyed a 7–4 majority in the state's congressional delegation.[88] Democratic incumbents wanted to maintain their advantage, while Republicans generally favored the creation of majority-black districts as a way to unseat Democrats. Republican candidates would have a better chance of being elected in the "bleached" districts around majority-black ones. The state's then-Governor Jim Martin was a Republican but had no veto power over reapportionment plans.[89]

In addition to concerns about preserving safe seats for incumbents, the Democratic legislature faced another problem in creating majority-black districts. Although 22% of North Carolina's population was African American, that population was scattered among smaller urban areas such as Charlotte, Durham, Raleigh, Wilmington, Winston–Salem, and Greensboro, as well as more rural areas in the northeast. Even the creation of a single majority-black district was a challenge, given this geographic dispersal.[90] The negligible percentage of Latinos or any other minority group in North Carolina made it impossible to consolidate these groups with African Americans to form a majority-minority district.[91]

---

[85] Reynolds v. Sims, 377 U.S. 533 (1964); Pildes, *supra* note 11, at 1519–20 (2002) (observing that every ten years, "there is an automatic constitutionally grounded trigger that requires ... updating of the law's application based on the most current social-scientific findings....").

[86] Karcher v. Daggett, 462 U.S. 725 (1983).

[87] David T. Canon, *Race, Redistricting, and Representation* 99 (1999).

[88] *Id.*

[89] *Id.* at 104.

[90] *Id.* at 102.

[91] *Id.* at 105; *Shaw I*, 509 U.S. at 634 (noting that North Carolina's population was 78% white, 20% black, 1% Native American, with the remaining 1% mostly Asian).

After the 1990 census, the state's General Assembly appointed a redistricting committee—heavily loaded with both Democrats and black legislators—to come up with a new plan.[92] This process led to legislative consideration of no fewer than twenty proposals.[93] On July 9, 1991, the General Assembly approved a plan that included one majority-black congressional district.[94] That was the First District, located in the northeastern part of the state where it was feasible to draw a reasonably compact district with an African–American majority. In drawing only a single black-majority district, the state legislature acted contrary to the wishes of civil rights groups such as the National Association for the Advancement of Colored People and the American Civil Liberties Union, which had argued for the creation of a second black district. These groups criticized the plan for serving the interests of incumbent legislators rather than black voters, arguing that in a state that was 22% black, one black congressional district out of twelve was inadequate.[95] For its part, the Republican Party advocated a plan with two majority-black districts, but one that would give Republicans the edge in seven of the remaining ten districts, effectively reversing the partisan makeup of the state's congressional delegation.[96] In making this proposal, the Republicans hoped to replicate the gains they had made in the state General Assembly during the 1980s, when the changes required by the district court's decision in another redistricting case helped the party double its legislative delegation.[97]

Because some of North Carolina's counties were covered jurisdictions under Section 5 of the Voting Rights Act, the 1991 plan could take effect only if it was precleared by either the Justice Department or the federal district court in Washington, D.C. As interpreted by the Supreme Court, Section 5's core purpose was to stop changes that would lead to "retrogression" in the position of racial minorities.[98] On December 18, 1991, the Justice Department denied preclearance of North Carolina's plan, citing the fact that it created only one black district and pointedly noting that this district was of "unusually convoluted" shape.[99] The

---

[92] Canon, *supra* note 87, at 104.

[93] Kousser, *supra* note 14, at 268.

[94] Pope v. Blue, 809 F. Supp. 392, 394 (W.D.N.C. 1992).

[95] Canon, *supra* note 87, at 105, 107.

[96] *Id.* at 106. This was known as the "Balmer Plan," named after its author, Republican state representative David Balmer.

[97] Thernstrom, *supra* note 55, at 234.

[98] Beer v. United States, 425 U.S. 130, 141 (1976).

[99] Canon, *supra* note 87, at 109.

Justice Department's objection letter further explained that "the proposed configuration of the district boundary lines in the south-central to
southeastern part of the state appear to minimize minority voting
strength given the significant minority population in this area of the
state," pointing out that there were "several plans" that would provide a
second majority-minority district, including the one that the Republicans
had supported.[100] The letter suggested that the Justice Department
would approve this plan, which both created a second minority-black
district and enhanced the prospects of Republicans' taking most of North
Carolina's congressional seats. Although some critics accused federal
officials of using the preclearance power for partisan purposes, the North
Carolina General Assembly chose to go back to the drawing board,
rather than to seek preclearance from the United States District Court
for the District of Columbia.[101]

The Justice Department's disapproval of the 1991 plan left North
Carolina's Democratic-dominated state legislature with a dilemma. It
was apparent that the Justice Department would continue to deny
preclearance unless a second majority-black district was created. One
possibility was to create a second black district in the southern part of
the state, similar to that which the state's Republicans had proposed.
From the Democratic perspective, this option was unpalatable because it
would drain black voters from incumbent Democrats' districts, thus
reducing their chances of reelection.[102]

John Merritt, an aide to Democratic Congressman Charles Rose of
North Carolina, successfully proposed an alternative solution.[103] Merritt
suggested creating a second black district, the Twelfth District, which
would stretch some 160 miles along I–85 from Charlotte in the southern
part of the state to Durham in the north. This urban district would be
composed of people with similar interests, and travel within its boundaries would be relatively easy.[104] From the Democrats' perspective, this
new plan was the best of both worlds. It would create a second majority
black district[105]—thus placating the Justice Department and civil rights
groups—without sacrificing the interests of Democratic incumbents. In

---

[100] Shaw v. Barr, 808 F. Supp. 461, 463–64 (1992) (quoting Letter from John R. Dunne,
Assistant Att'y Gen., Civil Rights Div., U.S. Dep't of Justice, to Tiare B. Smiley, Special
Deputy Att'y Gen., State of N. C. (Dec. 18, 1991)).

[101] Canon, *supra* note 87, at 110.

[102] *Id.* at 116.

[103] Kousser, *supra* note 14, at 268–69; Canon, *supra* note 87, at 110.

[104] Kousser, *supra* note 14, at 269.

[105] Under Merritt's plan, the First and the Twelfth Districts both had a voting age
population that was just over 53% black. Canon, *supra* note 87, at 113.

fact, Merritt's plan slightly improved Democratic prospects, giving them eight of the state's twelve congressional seats, with a chance of picking up a ninth.[106]

The problem with the Merritt plan was that it resulted in districts that, from an aesthetic perspective, were quite oddly configured. Most of the criticism was directed at the new Twelfth District, but some criticism was also directed at the more rural First District, which included pieces of four prior congressional districts. To create the Twelfth District, portions of the First District had been removed and other areas added, leaving the First District less compact than under the 1991 plan. The new First District had a hooked shape going southward from the Virginia border down to the southern part of the state, and then back up again in a westerly direction.[107] Predictably, Republicans who had been hoping to pick up at least one additional congressional seat from North Carolina were livid. They noted that for much of its length, the Twelfth District was no wider than I–85 and that, at one point, the district actually "changed lanes" along the highway.[108] Even some Democrats were apologetic. Speaker of the State House Daniel Blue, a moderate African–American Democrat, admitted that it was an "ugly plan."[109] The State Assembly nevertheless approved the Merritt plan on January 24, 1992, and the Department of Justice granted preclearance on February 6, 1992.[110]

The District Court Litigation

Following through on a vow made during the legislative debate, the Republicans immediately brought suit to challenge the 1992 plan. The complaint in *Pope v. Blue* was filed in the U.S. District Court for the Western District of North Carolina, on behalf of the Republican Party of North Carolina and forty-two individual voters. Plaintiffs did not make a race discrimination argument, instead asserting that the 1992 plan was an impermissible partisan gerrymander that violated the Fourteenth Amendment. By federal statute, challenges to the constitutionality of congressional districts are assigned to three-judge district court panels,[111]

---

[106] Canon, *supra* note 87, at 110. In fact, Democratic candidates ended up winning only eight of the twelve seats in 1992 because Republican incumbent Charles Taylor won in a district with a slight Democratic majority. *Id.*; *see also* Kousser, *supra* note 14, at 268 (predicting eight seats from Merritt plan).

[107] Canon, *supra* note 87, at 113.

[108] *Id.* at 110–11.

[109] Canon, *supra* note 87, at 112.

[110] Pope v. Blue, 809 F. Supp. at 394–95.

[111] 28 U.S.C. § 2284 (2007).

and on April 16, 1992, the panel dismissed the complaint. Because the Republican Party could not allege that it had been "shut out of the political process," the district court rejected plaintiffs' Fourteenth Amendment claim.[112] On October 5, 1992, the Supreme Court affirmed without opinion.[113]

Even before the district court opinion in *Pope v. Blue*, a separate group of voters had brought suit in the Eastern District of North Carolina, challenging the 1992 plan on an entirely different theory. The complaint in *Shaw v. Barr*, filed on March 12, 1992, alleged that the General Assembly's consideration of race in the redistricting process violated the Fourteenth Amendment. The plaintiffs were five voters from Durham County, all of whom had been residents of the old Second Congressional District which had been split up by the 1992 plan. Only two of the plaintiffs (Ruth O. Shaw and Melvin G. Shimm) were registered to vote in the majority-black Twelfth District at the time of the plan's adoption, and none resided in the majority-black First District.[114] The complaint named as defendants not only North Carolina state officials, but also the Attorney General of the United States William Barr and Assistant Attorney General for Civil Rights John Dunne, who allegedly had compelled the creation of a second majority-black district.

Defying the motto that the lawyer who represents himself has a fool for a client, one of the five named plaintiffs was also lead counsel. That was Robinson O. Everett, a member of the Duke Law School faculty and a self-described "loyal Democrat."[115] Everett had served as Chief Judge of the U.S. Court of Military Appeals between 1980 and 1990, but he had little experience in the area of voting rights at the time he brought the *Shaw* complaint. In explaining how his interest in redistricting developed, Everett has written that he was "incredulous" when he saw the two majority-black districts created by the 1992 plan.[116] From his perspective, the state's consideration of race in drawing legislative districts was indistinguishable from the use of race as a basis for peremptory

---

[112] 809 F. Supp. at 397.

[113] 506 U.S. 801 (1992).

[114] *Shaw II*, 517 U.S. at 904; *see also* Shaw v. Barr, 808 F. Supp. at 464 (noting that only Shaw and Shimm resided in the Twelfth District at time of plan's enactment, and that James Everett registered to vote in the Twelfth after plan's enactment). For this reason, the *Shaw II* Court concluded that only Shaw and Shimm had standing, and only with respect to the Twelfth District. 517 U.S. at 904.

[115] Robinson O. Everett, *Redistricting in North Carolina—A Personal Perspective*, 79 N.C. L. Rev. 1301, 1311 (2001).

[116] *Id.* at 1309.

strikes in court trials,[117] a practice struck down in *Batson v. Kentucky*.[118] As Everett put it: "My own motivation for initiating a court action to overturn the gerrymander was my firm belief that use of data about the racial composition of census blocks in the creation of congressional districts appeared to give governmental approval to the use of racial stereotypes and racial quotas."[119] His experience with the Armed Services led him to believe in the principle of raceblindness.[120] Everett has denied any partisan motivation for initiating the *Shaw* litigation.[121]

A three-judge district court threw out Everett's lawsuit at the pleading stage. The court announced its judgment after a hearing on the defendants' motion to dismiss on April 27, 1992, and subsequently issued an opinion explaining the reasons for its decision.[122] The opinion first addressed the argument that Justice Department officials had "coerced" the state into adopting an unconstitutional plan by denying preclearance.[123] All three judges concluded that the court lacked jurisdiction to hear these claims.[124] That authority resided exclusively in the United States District Court for the District of Columbia. Congress had vested jurisdiction in this court to prevent southern judges, unsympathetic to minority voting rights, from obstructing the Justice Department's enforcement efforts. As a result, a district court in North Carolina lacked authority to consider a challenge to the Justice Department's alleged misuse of its preclearance power.[125]

The claims against the state defendants, on the other hand, required the district court to confront Everett's constitutional arguments on the merits. These claims divided the court. Judges J. Dickson Phillips and W. Earl Britt noted that some allegations in the complaint seemed to

---

[117] *Id.*

[118] 476 U.S. 79 (1986).

[119] Everett, *supra* note 115, at 1310.

[120] *Id.* at 1310–11.

[121] *Id.* at 1311. While denying any partisan motivation, Everett has acknowledged that, had his motivation been partisan, he would have opposed the deliberate creation of majority-minority districts on the additional ground that they "mak[e] it more difficult for moderate white Democrats to be elected." *Id.*

[122] Shaw v. Barr, 808 F. Supp. 461 (E.D.N.C. 1992).

[123] *Id.* at 465.

[124] *Id.* at 467, *See also* 42 U.S.C. § 1973b(b) (vesting exclusive jurisdiction in Washington, D.C. federal district court, over actions seeking injunctive relief against federal officers pursuant to VRA).

[125] Alternatively, the majority concluded that the claim against the federal defendants should be dismissed, because the Justice Department's section 5 power is "discretionary" and therefore not subject to judicial review. Shaw v. Barr, 808 F. Supp. at 467.

suggest that *any* consideration of race during the redistricting process was unconstitutional.[126] While observing that the plaintiffs had cited several textual bases for this assertion (including the Equal Protection Clause; Fifteenth Amendment; and Article I, Section 4), the court considered equal protection to be the appropriate vehicle.[127] The majority first expressed puzzlement over the fact that the plaintiffs had not identified their race in the complaint, and specifically that they had not identified themselves as being of a different race than that of the black voters for whom the challenged congressional districts were created.[128] The majority took this omission to be "a deliberate (and humanly, if not legally, laudable) refusal to inject their own race[s] into a claim whose essence is to deplore race-consciousness in voting-rights matters," but nevertheless took judicial notice of the fact that all five plaintiffs were white.[129]

The majority concluded that the equal protection claim was foreclosed by the Supreme Court's decision in *United Jewish Organizations v. Carey*.[130] In that case, Hasidic Jewish voters asserted that their votes were diluted by the New York state legislature's deliberate creation of a majority-black district. Rejecting this claim, the *UJO* plurality declared that "the Constitution does not prevent a State subject to the Voting Rights Act from deliberately creating or preserving black majorities in particular districts in order to ensure that its reapportionment plan complies with [the Voting Rights Act]."[131] The majority went on to reject the plaintiffs' contention that the Supreme Court's later affirmative action opinions, including *City of Richmond v. J.A. Croson Co.*,[132] revealed a new commitment to raceblindness that undermined *UJO*.[133]

Chief Judge Richard Voorhees dissented from the dismissal of the equal protection claim against the state defendants. In his view, the majority's approach would "give the North Carolina legislature unbridled discretion to implement race-conscious reapportionment plans."[134] He distinguished *UJO* based on the odd shape of the two North Carolina

---

126 *Id.* at 468.

127 *Id.*

128 *Id.* at 470.

129 *Id.*

130 430 U.S. 144 (1977).

131 *Id.* at 161.

132 488 U.S. 469 (1989) (striking down race-conscious affirmative action program in public contracting).

133 Shaw v. Barr, 808 F. Supp. at 471–73 (1992).

134 *Id.* at 474 (Voorhees, C.J., dissenting).

districts. In a description later quoted by the Supreme Court, Chief Judge Voorhees asserted that the legislature had drawn a "First District map which looks like a Rorschach ink-blot test" and "a serpentine Twelfth District that slinks down the Interstate Highway 85 corridor until it gobbles in enough enclaves of black neighborhoods to satisfy a predetermined percentage of minority voters."[135] The strange shape of these districts, according to Judge Voorhees, belied any suggestion that they were drawn according to "traditional and constitutionally-espoused redistricting principles."[136] He would therefore have allowed the claims to proceed, citing in the conclusion to his opinion a *Wall Street Journal* op-ed that had labeled the North Carolina districts "political pornography."[137]

The Supreme Court Litigation

With the district court opinions nicely framing the controversy, the case moved to the Supreme Court. The procedure for review of three-judge district court decisions is different from that in other types of cases. A direct appeal may be taken to the Supreme Court without going through the courts of appeals.[138] Rather than petition for certiorari, litigants seeking review of three-judge district court orders file a jurisdictional statement, which identifies the questions that the appellants ask the court to address. The Supreme Court may respond to a jurisdictional statement by summarily affirming the district court's decision (as it did in *Pope v. Blue*), by summarily reversing, or by noting probable jurisdiction. The effect of noting probable jurisdiction is roughly equivalent to a grant of a petition of certiorari in other cases, indicating that the matter will be briefed and argued on the merits.[139]

Everett filed a jurisdictional statement on behalf of the plaintiffs on August 25, 1992. The statement identified six separate questions for review. The first broadly asked whether the state legislature had "violate[d] Article I, Section 2, and the Fourteenth and Fifteenth Amendments of the United States Constitution by creating two majority-minority congressional districts for the purpose of assuring the election of minority persons from these districts to the United States House of Representatives."[140] So stated, this question effectively encompassed all

[135] *Id.* at 476.

[136] *Id.*

[137] *Id.* at 480 (citing *Political Pornography–II*, Wall St. J., Feb. 4, 1992, at A14).

[138] 28 U.S.C. § 1253 (year).

[139] Robert L. Stern et al., *Supreme Court Practice* 491 (8th ed. 2002).

[140] Jurisdictional Statement, Shaw v. Barr *sub nom.* Shaw v. Reno (Shaw I), 509 U.S. 630 (1993) (No. 92–357), 1992 WL 12012102 (capitalization omitted).

of the constitutional arguments pressed below. Plaintiffs' second question was more narrow, asking whether the district court erred in holding that *UJO* "authorized the North Carolina Legislature to create two majority-minority congressional districts for racially conscious purposes." The third question was whether the state legislature had a "discriminatory or invidious purpose." While not defining the source of the constitutional right asserted, both of these questions implicitly addressed whether the plan violated equal protection. The remaining three questions were whether the U.S. Attorney General misinterpreted the Voting Rights Act, whether the plaintiffs had standing, and whether the appellants were entitled to sue the federal defendants.[141]

The Supreme Court's deliberations over whether to note probable jurisdiction, like its deliberations over whether to grant certiorari petitions, are not made public. The papers of the late Justice Harry Blackmun, however, shed some light on what went on behind closed doors during the Court's consideration of the first *Shaw* appeal. Included among these papers are not only the notes of Justice Blackmun and his clerks, but also memoranda circulated by the Justices regarding the case.

In late November 1992, the Court voted, apparently unanimously, to note probable jurisdiction.[142] On November 30, 1992, Justice Sandra Day O'Connor wrote a memorandum to the other Justices suggesting that the questions raised by Everett be reframed for purposes of briefing and oral argument. Her memorandum stated that the first question was unworthy of review because it asked "nothing more" than whether the plan was constitutional. She also agreed with the three judges in the court below, who had concluded that the Attorney General's implementation of the Voting Rights Act was beyond that court's jurisdiction. Justice O'Connor opined that the question of standing was also inappropriate for review, for she saw "nothing in [the district court's] decision suggesting that appellants might lack standing because of their race."

That left the two questions relating to the scope of *UJO v. Carey* and to racially discriminatory purpose. Justice O'Connor suggested an order noting probable jurisdiction which combined the questions, to ask: "Whether, under *United Jewish Organizations v. Carey*, 430 U.S. 144 (1977), a state legislature's intent to comply with the Voting Rights Act and the Attorney General's interpretation thereof precludes, in a suit brought outside the District Court for the District of Columbia, a finding that the legislature's congressional redistricting plan was adopted with invidious discriminatory intent where the legislature did not accede to

---

[141] *Id.*

[142] Preliminary Memorandum from Sherry Colb, (Oct. 20, 1992) (Shaw v. Reno (Shaw I)), No. 92–357, Box 624, Harry A. Blackmun Papers, Manuscript Division, Library of Congress, Washington, D.C. (indicating conference date of November 25, 1992).

the plan suggested by the Attorney General but instead developed its own." In explaining the need to restate the issue, Justice O'Connor remarked: "I know that this order may be unusual, but I fear that appellants are unusually needful of firm guidance on what to brief and what to ignore."[143]

Justice O'Connor's reframing of the question raised problems of its own. Her proposed order focused narrowly on the potential distinctions between *Shaw* and *UJO*. Although O'Connor asked whether race-conscious redistricting could be justified based on the need to comply with the Attorney General's interpretation of the VRA, the Attorney General technically has the power to grant or deny preclearance but not to make "suggestions." Before the order was released, Justice Antonin Scalia successfully prevailed upon Justice O'Connor to change the wording of the question. In a November 30, 1992 memo, Justice Scalia made two significant suggestions: first, that the Court's order not single out *UJO* for special consideration and, second, that the Court's consideration not be limited to cases arising outside the Washington, D.C. district courts. Justice O'Connor agreed to Justice Scalia's suggestion, reframing the question as: "Whether a state legislature's intent to comply with the Voting Rights Act and the Attorney General's interpretation thereof precludes a finding that the legislature's congressional redistricting plan was adopted with invidious discriminatory intent where the legislature did not accede to the plan suggested by the Attorney General but instead developed its own." On December 7, 1992, the Court issued an order noting probable jurisdiction and directing the parties to brief and argue this single question. So framed, the question practically answers itself. The intent to comply with the VRA, or any other federal statute, could not possibly immunize a plan from a *constitutional* challenge.[144]

What the question did accomplish was to highlight the tension between the Justice Department's interpretation of the VRA and the Supreme Court's interpretation of the Fourteenth Amendment in the *Croson* line of cases. The desire to focus on this tension explains another suggestion made by Justice Scalia and agreed to by Justice O'Connor: that the order "make clear that *all* parties (including the [United States] Attorney General) are requested to brief the reformulated question."[145]

---

[143] Memorandum from Justice O'Connor, U.S. Sup. Ct., to the Conference (Nov. 27, 1992) (Shaw v. Reno (Shaw I), No. 92–357), Box 624, Harry A. Blackmun Papers, Manuscript Division, Library of Congress, Washington, D.C.

[144] Pamela S. Karlan, *All Over the Map: The Supreme Court's Voting Rights Trilogy*, 1993 S. Ct. Rev. 245, 277 (1993) ("The answer to this question was obvious and probably could have been answered unanimously by a two-sentence per curiam.").

[145] Memorandum from Justice Scalia, U.S. Sup. Ct., to Justice O'Connor, U.S. Sup. Ct. (Nov. 30, 1992), Shaw v. Reno (Shaw I), No. 92–357, Box 624, Harry A. Blackmun Papers, Manuscript Division, Library of Congress, Washington, D.C.

Justice Scalia noted that the Justice Department's motion to affirm had not addressed the constitutionality of North Carolina's redistricting plan, apparently out of a desire to "avoid that difficult subject." Concerned that federal officials might feel that they were off the hook by virtue of the Court's decision not to grant probable jurisdiction over the claims against them, Justice Scalia requested—and the rest of the Court agreed—that "all parties" be directed to brief the reframed question. The Court's order signaled that the Justice Department's race-conscious interpretation of the VRA was in play, even if federal officials were not proper defendants.

The caption of *Shaw v. Barr* (later changed to *Shaw v. Reno* after Janet Reno became Attorney General) is therefore odd in one sense, but quite appropriate in another. It is odd that the Attorney General is the lead defendant, given the unanimous agreement that Justice Department officials were *not* appropriate defendants. It is highly appropriate, given that the propriety of the Justice Department's implementation of the VRA was at the center of the case, notwithstanding the dismissal of the federal defendants.

Everett's brief and oral argument drew on the rhetoric of raceblindness, including Justice John Harlan's famous statement in his *Plessy v. Ferguson* dissent that the "Constitution is color-blind."[146] Creating majority-minority districts in order to elect a "quota of minority persons to Congress" was, according to Everett, flatly inconsistent with this principle. Everett also emphasized the odd shape of the two majority-black districts, particularly the "snaking" Twelfth District's "bizarre" shape, which he compared to "black townships under South Africa's apartheid system."[147] Echoing Chief Judge Voorhees' dissent, Everett borrowed from a *Wall Street Journal* editorial that had condemned the plan as "political pornography."[148] At oral argument, Everett opened with the "political pornography" reference and added that "the only way to understand what took place in North Carolina is to look at the evidence thereof," namely the map of the districts challenged.[149] Everett's suggestion called to mind Justice Potter Stewart's "I know it when I see it"

---

[146] Appellants' Brief on the Merits at 18, Shaw v. Reno (Shaw I), 509 U.S. 630 (1993) (No. 92–357).

[147] *Id.* at 9, 31, 61; *see also* Oral Argument, Shaw v. Reno (Shaw I), 509 U.S. 630 (1993), 1993 WL 751836, at *8 ("Take the 12th district.... It snakes along Interstate I–85.... It snakes along. At some points it is no wider than I–85.").

[148] Appellants' Brief on the Merits, *supra* note 146, at 10 (quoting Shaw v. Barr, 808 F.Supp. at 480 (Voorhees, J., dissenting) (quoting *Political Pornography–II*, Wall St.J., Feb. 4, 1992, at A14)).

[149] Oral Argument, *supra* note 147, at *3.

test for obscenity.[150] When the Solicitor General took the position that
the VRA required majority-minority districts, Everett vigorously disagreed, asserting that "there's no compulsion, no authorization to have a
majority-minority district."[151] But when pressed, even Everett acknowledged that consideration of race might sometimes be warranted, acknowledging that "the Voting Rights Act could authorize race-conscious
corrective action" where a compact minority group is broken apart.[152]

Despite Everett's disavowal of absolute raceblindness, there can be
little doubt that the Justices recognized the potential implications for the
VRA, as it had been interpreted and implemented. Even before the
Justices voted, a memorandum to Justice Blackmun from one of his
clerks suggested that the Court's decision could sound the Act's death
knell. On April 22, 1993, the day before the conference in *Shaw v. Reno*,
this clerk reported on his conversations with other Justices' law clerks.
The clerk anticipated that there would be five votes to reverse and
remand: Chief Justice William Rehnquist, Justice O'Connor, Justice
Anthony Kennedy, Justice Scalia, and Justice Clarence Thomas. According to the clerk, the Chief Justice was especially "interested in applying
Croson's strict scrutiny analysis to race-conscious redistricting." The
clerk reported that Justice O'Connor appeared to be the swing vote, but
that she too was inclined to apply *Croson*'s reasoning to the case. Such a
holding, Justice Blackmun's clerk wrote, "would be a most unfortunate
turn of events and would go a long way toward ruling the VRA unconstitutional."[153]

This prediction of reversal proved to be correct. In fact, there were
not just five but *six* votes to reverse when the Justices met in conference
on April 23, 1993. Only the Justices attend the conferences in which
votes are taken. Justice Blackmun's notes show that, in addition to the
five Justices identified in his clerk's memorandum, Justice David Souter
also voted to reverse.[154] Only later would Justice Souter switch sides to

---

[150] *See* Conference, *The Supreme Court, Racial Politics, and the Right to Vote:* Shaw v.
Reno *and the Future of the Voting Rights Act*, 44 Am. U.L. Rev. 1, 6 (1994) (comments of
Professor Samuel Issacharoff) (noting that in both the First Amendment pornography
cases and *Shaw*, "the Court is trying to identify a constitutional doctrine of 'Don't do it to
excess in a way that is offensive,' without defining substantive underlying principles.").

[151] Oral Argument, *supra* note 147, at *53.

[152] Oral Argument, *supra* note 147, at *16.

[153] Memorandum from Bill Dodge to Justice Blackmun, U.S. Sup. Ct. (Apr. 22, 1993),
Shaw v. Reno (Shaw I), No. 92–357, Box 624, Harry A. Blackmun Papers, Manuscript
Division, Library of Congress, Washington, D.C.

[154] Justice Blackmun's Conference Notes (Apr. 23, 1993), Shaw v. Reno (Shaw I), No.
92–357, Box 624, Harry A. Blackmun Papers, Manuscript Division, Library of Congress,
Washington, D.C.

join Justices Byron White, Blackmun, and John Paul Stevens in voting
to affirm the district court's decision.[155]

The Supreme Court Opinion

Justice O'Connor wrote the majority opinion for the Court. Internal
memoranda show only a handful of changes between the initial draft
that she circulated on June 1, 1993 and the final version issued on June
28, 1993.[156] The majority opinion makes only passing reference to the
practices that had excluded blacks from democratic politics throughout
most of the twentieth century. The Court noted that "[f]or much of our
Nation's history, [the right to vote] sadly has been denied to many
because of their race," citing practices such as literacy tests, "good
character" requirements, and racial gerrymanders.[157] Justice O'Connor
devotes no attention to North Carolina's particular history of racial
exclusion, including not only measures to prevent blacks from voting but
also the almost complete absence of blacks from the state legislature
until the 1980s and the state's failure to send a single black to Congress
from 1900 until 1992. Nor does she discuss the state's history, extending
through the 1980s, of using gerrymanders to prevent the election of
candidates who would appeal to black voters.[158]

Despite her earlier suggestion that appellants were "unusually needful of firm guidance," Justice O'Connor borrowed heavily from Everett's
description of the districts, emphasizing the "bizarre shape"[159] of the two
majority-black districts drawn in 1992:

> The first of the two majority-black districts contained in the
> revised plan, District 1, is somewhat hook shaped. Centered in the
> northeast portion of the State, it moves southward until it tapers to
> a narrow band; then, with finger-like extensions, it reaches far into
> the southernmost part of the State near the South Carolina border.
> District 1 has been compared to a "Rorschach ink-blot test," and a
> "bug splattered on a windshield."

> The second majority-black district, District 12, is even more
> unusually shaped. It is approximately 160 miles long and, for much

---

[155] Memorandum from Bill Dodge to Justice Blackmun, U.S. Sup. Ct. (June 25, 1993)
(Shaw v. Reno (Shaw I), No. 92–357), Box 624, Harry A. Blackmun Papers, Manuscript
Division, Library of Congress, Washington, D.C.

[156] *Compare* Draft Opinion (June 1, 1993), Shaw v. Reno (Shaw I), No. 92–357, Box
624, Harry A. Blackmun Papers, Manuscript Division, Library of Congress, Washington,
D.C, *with* Shaw v. Reno (Shaw I), 509 U.S. 630 (1993).

[157] *Id.* at 639.

[158] *See* Kousser, *supra* note 14, at 247–59.

[159] Shaw v. Reno (Shaw I), 509 U.S. 630, 655–56 (1993).

of its length, no wider than the I–85 corridor. It winds in snakelike fashion through tobacco country, financial centers, and manufacturing areas "until it gobbles in enough enclaves of black neighborhoods." Northbound and southbound drivers on I–85 sometimes find themselves in separate districts in one county, only to "trade" districts when they enter the next county. Of the 10 counties through which District 12 passes, 5 are cut into 3 different districts; even towns are divided. At one point the district remains contiguous only because it intersects at a single point with two other districts before crossing over them. One state legislator has remarked that " '[i]f you drove down the interstate with both car doors open, you'd kill most of the people in the district.' " The district even has inspired poetry: "Ask not for whom the line is drawn; it is drawn to avoid thee."[160]

Also following Everett's brief, Justice O'Connor's analysis of the equal protection issue drew from two lines of precedent. The first was the Court's raceblindness cases, from Justice Harlan's *Plessy* dissent through the affirmative action decisions in *Bakke* and *Croson*. The Court did not hold that all race-conscious redistricting was unconstitutional. It did, however, conclude that the plaintiffs had stated a claim by alleging that North Carolina's plan was "so extremely irregular on its face that it rationally can be viewed only as an effort to segregate the races for purposes of voting, without regard for traditional districting principles and without sufficiently compelling justification."[161] The second line of precedent was that concerning racial gerrymandering, most notably *Gomillion v. Lightfoot*, in which the City of Tuskegee's city fathers had redrawn municipal boundaries to keep blacks out.[162] Again borrowing the loaded rhetoric from Everett's brief and argument, Justice O'Connor's opinion asserted that using race to draw districts "bears an uncomfortable resemblance to political apartheid."[163]

The obvious difference is that, while the *Gomillion* plan was designed to exclude African Americans, the *Shaw* plan was designed to bring them in—more specifically, to ensure that at least some blacks in North Carolina would have the opportunity to elect a congressperson of their choice. Drawing on its raceblindness cases, the Court concluded that taking account of race to *include* blacks was no less constitutionally suspect than using race to *exclude* them. Justice O'Connor's rhetoric of political apartheid failed to capture the problem that the majority

---

[160] *Id.* at 635–36 (citations omitted).

[161] *Id.* at 642.

[162] *Id.* at 644–45 (citing Gomillion v. Lightfoot, 364 U.S. 339 (1960)).

[163] *Id.* at 647.

perceived to exist with North Carolina's redistricting.[164] It was not that whites and blacks were put in separate districts by the plan, nor even that the majority-minority districts were segregated. To the contrary, the challenged Twelfth District was among the most integrated in the state, with a population of 41.8% white and 56.6% black.[165] Rather, it was the very fact of taking race into consideration that inflicted the injury. This concern is best captured by the Court's assertion that what was so "pernicious" about North Carolina's plan was the "message" it sent:

> When a district obviously is created solely to effectuate the perceived common interests of one racial group, elected officials are more likely to believe that their primary obligation is to represent only the members of that group, rather than their constituency as a whole. This is altogether antithetical to our system of representative democracy.[166]

Subsequent commentators have described *Shaw* as adopting a theory of "expressive" harm, a term that the Supreme Court embraced in its post-*Shaw* cases to capture the idea that the injuries caused by race-conscious districting stem from the "very meaning they convey."[167] Individuals whose race is taken into consideration in placing them within a district suffer harm simply by virtue of that fact, irrespective of whether their political influence has been strengthened or weakened by redistricting.

This conception of equality, more fully developed in later cases,[168] relies on an atomistic vision that defines constitutional harms in highly individualized terms. The victims are those whose race has been considered in government decisionmaking; the perpetrators are those government actors who have taken race into consideration in making decisions. From this perspective, the fundamental command of the Equal Protec-

---

[164] *See* Conference, *supra* note 150, at 65 (criticizing the *Shaw* Court's reference to apartheid on the ground that "we are not talking about total exclusion of any population, we are talking about inclusion") (comments of Loretta King).

[165] State Appellees' Brief, *cited in* Karlan, *supra* note 144, at 282 n.168.

[166] *Shaw I*, 509 U.S. at 648.

[167] Richard H. Pildes & Richard G. Niemi, *Expressive Harms, "Bizarre Districts," and Voting Rights: Evaluating Election–District Appearances after* Shaw v. Reno, 92 Mich. L. Rev. 483, 507 (1993); *see also* Bush v. Vera, 517 U.S. 952, 984 (1996) (referring to "expressive harms" as the injury in redistricting cases).

[168] *See* Miller v. Johnson, 515 U.S. 900, 911 (1995) ("At the heart of the Constitution's guarantee of equal protection lies the simple command that the Government must treat citizens 'as individuals, not "as simply components of a racial, religious, sexual or national class." ' ") (quoting Metro Broadcasting, Inc. v. FCC, 497 U.S. 547, 602 (1990) (O'Connor, J., dissenting)); United States v. Hays, 515 U.S. 737, 745 (1995) (to establish standing, plaintiffs in *Shaw* cases must show "individualized harm," which requires that they live in district challenged or provide evidence that they were subjected to a racial classification).

tion Clause is that government shall not take race into account, including the race of voters placed in districts. The atomistic vision is captured in Justice O'Connor's plurality opinion in *Croson*, which speaks of the "dream of a Nation of equal citizens in a society where race is irrelevant to personal opportunity and achievement."[169]

A competing vision of equal protection views the constitutional harm as *systemic* rather than atomistic. Instead of focusing on individual victims and perpetrators, this view emphasizes the eradication of inequalities among groups, with respect to such social goods as higher education, access to public contracts, and political power. A systemic approach places a premium on examining how historical practices have served to create material inequalities among racial groups, so as to necessitate group-based remedial action.

In the early days of VRA enforcement, neither Congress nor the Court had to choose between these two visions because both counseled in favor of dismantling barriers to African Americans' participation. After the elimination of blatantly discriminatory practices like the literacy test, however, the systemic perspective counseled in favor of race-conscious redistricting to promote minority representation, while the atomistic perspective suggested a raceblind approach. The Justice Department selected the systemic path, refusing to preclear plans without sufficient majority-minority districts, and Congress signaled approval of this vision through the 1982 amendments to the Voting Rights Act. In *Shaw I*, the Court suggested that this path is inconsistent with equal protection because righting individual wrongs is all that matters.

The Court's commitment to the atomistic theory of equal protection is epitomized by a change that Justice O'Connor made to the *Shaw v. Reno* opinion at the request of Chief Justice Rehnquist. The first two drafts of her opinion observed that: "Racial gerrymandering, even for remedial purposes, may balkanize us into competing racial factions and carry us further from the goal of a fully integrated society that the Fourteenth Amendment embodies...." An internal memorandum from the Chief Justice objected to this language, stating: "The Fourteenth Amendment prohibits discrimination; it does not require integration, and I think it is a mistake to intimate that it does even as a 'goal.' "[170] Put another way, government does wrong when it distinguishes between individuals based on race; consequently, government has no affirmative obligation to promote integration or, more broadly, substantive racial equality in politics or any other sphere. The role of the courts, under this

---

[169] 488 U.S. 469, 505–06 (1989).

[170] Memorandum from Chief Justice Rehnquist, U.S. Sup. Ct., to Justice O'Connor, U.S. Sup. Ct. (June 7, 1993), Shaw v. Reno (Shaw I), No. 92–357, Box 624, Harry A. Blackmun Papers, Manuscript Division, Library of Congress, Washington, D.C.

view, is to police "discrimination"—a term that, in context, suggests a raceblind approach.

Justice O'Connor acquiesced to the Chief's suggestion, and in the final version of the opinion, the sentence reads: "Racial gerrymandering, even for remedial purposes, may balkanize us into competing racial factions; *it threatens to carry us further from the goal of a political system in which race no longer matters*—a goal that the Fourteenth and Fifteenth Amendments embody...."[171]

Still, *Shaw I* did not represent a complete triumph for raceblindness. The majority recognized that the reapportionment process "differs from other types of government decisionmaking in that the legislature always is *aware* of race when it draws district lines."[172] Although Justice O'Connor's opinion largely embraced the atomistic view of racial equality, the Court's refusal to prohibit any consideration of race in redistricting may be seen as a concession that—given the long history of taking race into consideration to weaken blacks' influence—an absolute rule of raceblindness would have entrenched existing disparities in political power.[173]

Although *Shaw v. Reno* represents a major victory for the atomistic view of equal protection, the majority left some wiggle room for the deliberate creation of majority-minority districts. In the last paragraph of its opinion, the Court noted the Justice Department's view that the North Carolina legislature could have created a more compact (and less oddly shaped) majority-minority district in the south-central to southeastern part of the state by adopting the plan the states' Republicans had advocated. The Court did not say whether a more compact majority-black district would have offended the Equal Protection Clause. Instead, it limited its holding to a reapportionment that was "so irrational on its face that it can be understood only as an effort to segregate voters into separate voting districts because of their race," at least where the "separation lacks sufficient justification."[174] Left undetermined were two important doctrinal questions: first, how courts should go about determining the "irrational[ity]" of a district's boundaries and, second, what counts as "sufficient justification." The Court's articulation of an "analytically distinct" equal protection claim was therefore not really the end

---

[171] 509 U.S. at 657 (emphasis added).

[172] *Id.* at 646.

[173] *See* Samuel Issacharoff & Pamela S. Karlan, *Standing and Misunderstanding in Voting Rights Law*, 111 Harv. L. Rev. 2276, 2291–92 (1998) (suggesting that the Court realistically recognizes that "today's private preferences are in part the product of the government's prior impermissible actions" and therefore that "to ignore race in drawing district lines would perpetuate race-conscious voting practices").

[174] 509 U.S. at 658.

of the story of *Shaw v. Reno*, but rather the beginning of a new story—one for which the conclusion has yet to be written.

The Dissents

If a systemic vision of racial justice was largely missing from the majority opinion, this approach did not fare much better in four separate dissents by Justices White, Blackmun, Stevens, and Souter. With Justice Thurgood Marshall's departure from the Court two years before *Shaw I* was decided, the Court lost the most articulate proponent of race-conscious remedies as a response to an ongoing legacy of discrimination and segregation. In his *Croson* dissent, for example, Justice Marshall explained his disagreement with the majority's decision to strike down the City of Richmond's affirmative action program:

> It is a welcome symbol of racial progress when the former capital of the Confederacy acts forthrightly to confront the effects of racial discrimination in its midst . . .

> The essence of the majority's position is that Richmond has failed to catalog adequate findings to prove that past discrimination has impeded minorities from joining or participating fully in Richmond's construction contracting industry. I find deep irony in second guessing Richmond's judgment on this point. As much as any municipality in the United States, Richmond knows what racial discrimination is; a century of decisions by this and other federal courts has richly documented the city's disgraceful history of public and private racial discrimination.[175]

None of the four dissents in *Shaw I* evoked North Carolina's history of excluding blacks from democratic politics with comparable force. Justice White's dissent asserted that the Court glossed over the similarities to *UJO* by focusing on the district's unusual shape, although he did gesture toward a systemic vision of equal protection in urging that the Court focus on the ability of *groups* to influence the political process.[176] In a similar vein, Justice Souter noted that legislators might have to take account of racial bloc voting in order to avoid dilution of minority voting strength.[177]

None of the Justices, either those in the majority or the dissenters, did an effective job of tying the justification for race-conscious action to the virtual exclusion of African Americans from Southern electoral politics for most of the twentieth century. They largely ignored the fact that the challenged reapportionment led directly to the election of the

---

[175] *Croson*, 488 U.S. at 528–29 (Marshall, J., dissenting).

[176] *Shaw I*, 509 U.S. at 662–63.

[177] *Id.* at 680.

first blacks to Congress from North Carolina in over nine decades. Even
the Justices supportive of majority-minority districts gave short shrift to
the stark history of disfranchisement that made the VRA necessary.

Shaw's *Reverberations*

In the immediate aftermath of *Shaw I*, voting rights advocates
feared the worst. At a doctrinal level, some saw *Shaw I* as the first step
toward holding the Voting Rights Act unconstitutional, at least insofar
as it mandated that race be taken into consideration in drawing districts.
At a political level, others worried that *Shaw I* would chill redistricting
efforts and significantly decrease the number of minorities elected to
legislative office.[178] In reality, the sky did not fall: Neither of these fears
came to pass. To understand why, it is necessary to trace the cases that
followed *Shaw v. Reno*, including three additional Supreme Court opinions on North Carolina's post–1990 congressional apportionment.

Most significant in defining the legal standard for a *Shaw* claim was
the Court's decision in *Miller v. Johnson*, issued before the North
Carolina reapportionment returned to the Supreme Court.[179] In *Miller*,
the Court considered the constitutionality of a Georgia reapportionment
plan that created three majority-black congressional districts in response
to pressure from the Justice Department. As in *Shaw,* the Supreme
Court emphasized the state's responsibility to treat citizens as individuals rather than as members of a racial group.[180] While quoting the
Almanac of American Politics' description of Georgia's Eleventh District
as a "[m]onstrosity,"[181] the Court rejected the contention that a district
must be "bizarre on its face" to violate the Constitution.[182] Instead, the
proper question was whether race was the "predominant factor" moti-
vating the legislature's creation of the district. Although the shape of a
district might bear on the question, a bizarre configuration was neither
necessary nor sufficient to find that race predominated in the districting
process. Even if race was the predominant factor, the district could still
be upheld if it was narrowly tailored to serve a compelling interest.[183]

---

[178] *See* A. Leon Higginbotham, Jr. et al., Shaw v. Reno: *A Mirage of Good Intentions
with Devastating Racial Consequences*, 62 Fordham L. Rev. 1593, 1603 (1994) (raising
possibility that *Shaw* would lead to "lily white" legislative representation).

[179] 515 U.S. 900 (1995).

[180] *Id.* at 911 (quoting M. Barone & G. Ujifusa, *Alamanac of American Politics* 356
(1994)).

[181] *Id.* at 909.

[182] *Id.* at 912.

[183] *Id.* at 920.

In *Miller,* the Court found that race was the predominant factor, but avoided the question of whether compliance with Section 5 of the Voting Rights Act was a compelling interest under the Fourteenth Amendment test. Instead, the Court assumed that VRA compliance was a compelling interest, but found that the district was not narrowly tailored because Section 5 did not require the state to "maximize" the number of majority-black districts. *Miller* thus failed to resolve the conflict between the Voting Rights Act and the Fourteenth Amendment that emerged in *Shaw v. Reno.* Left unclear was exactly what it meant for race to be the predominant factor, much less how courts were supposed to probe the intentions of state legislators to determine which of the many factors taken into consideration in drawing district lines was predominant. *Miller* was even less clear in defining the VRA's requirements. While holding that Section 5 of the VRA did not require the *maximization* of majority-minority districts, it left uncertain what this section *did* require.

The other redistricting cases that made their way up to the Supreme Court in the 1990s did little to clarify either question.[184] Underlying the Court's lack of clarity on the meaning of both the Equal Protection Clause and the Voting Rights Act is a still unresolved ambivalence about the relationship between racial equality and democratic representation. The Court's uncertainty is most evident in three subsequent decisions on North Carolina's congressional redistricting. After the Supreme Court remand, the North Carolina plan returned to the three-judge district court. After a six-day trial, the court found that the plan did not violate the standard that the Supreme Court had articulated in *Shaw v. Reno.* Once again, the district court was split two-to-one on this question.[185] All three judges agreed that the plan's lines "were deliberately drawn to produce one or more districts of a certain racial composition,"[186] thus triggering strict scrutiny. Two members of the district court, Judges Phillips and Britt, nevertheless found that plan permissible on the ground that it was narrowly tailored to further the state's compelling interest in complying with Sections 2 and 5 of the Voting Rights Act.[187] As in the first *Shaw* case, Chief Judge Voorhees dissented, concluding that strict scrutiny was not satisfied.[188]

---

[184] *See, e.g., Bush v. Vera,* 517 U.S. 952 (1996) (holding three Texas congressional districts in violation of Fourteenth Amendment, without majority opinion); *United States v. Hays,* 515 U.S. 737 (1995) (voters who did not live in challenged congressional district lacked standing).

[185] Shaw v. Hunt, 861 F. Supp. 408 (E.D.N.C. 1994).

[186] *Id.* at 417.

[187] *Id.* at 475.

[188] *Id.* at 476–97 (Voorhees, C.J., dissenting).

Again, the Supreme Court reversed. In its opinion in *Shaw v. Hunt* (*Shaw II*),[189] the same five-Justice majority that had reversed the complaint's dismissal in *Shaw I* concluded that the Twelfth District violated the Fourteenth Amendment.[190] And again, four Justices dissented.[191] This time, Chief Justice Rehnquist wrote the majority opinion. The majority first found that race was the predominant factor in the drawing of the district, citing the acknowledgment in the state's preclearance submission that the legislature's "*overriding* purpose" was to comply with the Attorney General's objections by creating two majority-black districts.[192] The Court proceeded to reject the argument that the use of race in creating the Twelfth District was justified in order to comply with the Voting Rights Act. Without deciding whether VRA compliance was a "compelling" justification, the Court found that a second majority-black district was not narrowly tailored to comply with the VRA. As in *Miller*, the majority rejected the argument that Section 5 required the maximization of majority-minority districts; thus, it reasoned that the creation of the Twelfth District was not necessary. As for Section 2, the majority viewed the injury against which the VRA protects as highly individualized, emphatically rejecting the idea that the "right to an undiluted vote ... belongs to the minority as a group and not to its individual members."[193] As in *Shaw I*, the Court was more clear in defining what the VRA did *not* require than in elucidating what it did require. Nor did *Shaw II* lend much clarity to the meaning of the predominant factor test for determining whether the Fourteenth Amendment had been violated.

By the time *Shaw II* was decided on June 13, 1996, it was too late to draw new districts for that year's elections. Instead, the district court instructed the North Carolina legislature to draw a new map in time for the 1998 elections. The legislature responded with yet another plan in 1997, which divided the state's congressional seats equally between the Democratic and Republican parties, giving each a majority within six

---

[189] 517 U.S. 899 (1996).

[190] Only the Twelfth District, and not the First District, was addressed in *Shaw II*. Relying on United States v. Hays, 515 U.S. 737 (1995), the Court concluded that only plaintiffs who reside in an allegedly gerrymandered district have standing to challenge that district. Because two of the plaintiffs resided in the Twelfth District, they had standing. But none of the *Shaw* plaintiffs resided in the First District, and therefore none could challenge its creation. *Shaw II*, 517 U.S. at 904.

[191] By the time of *Shaw II*, Justices Ruth Bader Ginsburg and Stephen Breyer had replaced Justices White and Blackmun. Both Ginsburg and Breyer dissented in *Shaw II*, as their predecessors had in *Shaw I*.

[192] 517 U.S. at 906.

[193] *Id.* at 917. For a critique of the position espoused by the *Shaw v. Hunt* majority, see Heather Gerken, *Understanding the Right to an Undiluted Vote*, 114 Harv. L. Rev. 1663 (2001).

districts. This time, though, blacks did not constitute a majority of the voting-age population in either the First or the Twelfth District.[194] The new Twelfth District "pruned the ends and fattened the middle" of its predecessor.[195] It also made the majority-black First District, and other surrounding districts, more compact. The three-judge panel in *Shaw* approved the new plan and dismissed the challenge to the 1992 plan as moot.[196]

After the *Shaw II* opinion, Everett filed a new complaint in the District Court for the Eastern District of North Carolina, styled *Cromartie v. Hunt*.[197] The original complaint in this new case was on behalf of three residents of the First District, to address the Supreme Court's conclusion that only citizens of a district may bring a racial gerrymandering claim against that district. *Cromartie* was assigned to a new three-judge district court panel, consisting of two Republicans (District Judge Terrence Boyle and Chief Judge Voorhees) and one Democrat (Circuit Judge Sam Ervin III). Everett later added four Twelfth District residents as co-plaintiffs, to challenge both the First and Twelfth Districts under the 1997 plan.[198]

This time, a majority of the three-judge panel granted Everett's motion for summary judgment with respect to the Twelfth District, but denied it as to the First. Judge Boyle and Chief Judge Voorhees concluded that race was the predominant factor in the creation of the Twelfth District, but found a genuine issue of fact as to whether race was the predominant factor in the creation of the more compact First District.[199] Judge Ervin dissented, emphasizing that neither of the newly created districts was majority-black and concluding that race was not a predominant factor in the creation of either. Instead, Judge Ervin found the legislature's "predominant motives" to be the maintenance of a 6–6 division among Democratic and Republican seats and the protection of incumbents.[200]

---

[194] Under the proposed 1997 plan, 46.57% of the First District's voting-age population and 43.36% of the Twelfth District's voting-age population were black. Cromartie v. Hunt, 1998 WL 35254678 (E.D.N.C. 1998) (Ervin, J., dissenting).

[195] North Carolina Redistricting Cases: The 1990s, available at http://www.senate.leg. state.mn.us/departments/scr/redist/redsum/NCSUM.HTM (last visited March 20, 2007).

[196] Shaw v. Hunt, No. 92–202–CIV–5–BR, slip op. at 8 (E.D.N.C. Sept. 12, 1997).

[197] 34 F. Supp. 2d 1029 (E.D.N.C. 1998).

[198] Cromartie v. Hunt, 1998 WL 35254678 (E.D.N.C. 1998); *see also* Cromartie v. Hunt, 133 F. Supp. 2d 407, 409 (E.D.N.C. 2000) (describing prior proceedings).

[199] Cromartie v. Hunt, 1998 WL 35254678.

[200] *Id.* at *46.

On January 20, 1999, the Supreme Court heard argument on the constitutionality of North Carolina's congressional reapportionment for the third time in six years. And for the third time, the Court reversed the district court.[201] This time, however, the Court was unanimous in concluding that the lower court was wrong to grant plaintiffs' motion for summary judgment with respect to the Twelfth District. Justice Thomas' opinion for the Court in *Cromartie v. Hunt* noted that plaintiffs had introduced only "circumstantial evidence" in support of their claim that race was the predominant factor in the creation of this district.[202] While that evidence tended to support the inference of an "impermissible racial motive," summary judgment was inappropriate because there was evidence that the protection of incumbents and preservation of the 6–6 split between Republicans and Democrats was the legislature's principal goal. In other words, there was evidence to support the conclusion that politics, not race, was the predominant motive.[203]

On remand, the district court conducted a three-day trial, at the conclusion of which a majority concluded that the Twelfth District violated equal protection but the First District did not. Once again in the majority, Chief Judge Boyle and Judge Voorhees this time concluded that race was the predominant motive in the creation of both the First and the Twelfth Districts. However, only the First was narrowly tailored to serve a compelling government interest, that is, the interest in avoiding a violation of Section 2 of the VRA.[204] Judge Lacy Thornburg (who had replaced Judge Ervin as the third judge on the panel) dissented from the majority's holding that the Twelfth District was unconstitutional, concluding that race was not the predominant factor in the creation of either district.[205]

The matter returned to the Supreme Court for argument on November 27, 2000 and, on April 18, 2001, the Court issued its opinion in *Easley v. Cromartie*.[206] For the fourth time in eight years of litigation over North Carolina's congressional districts, the Supreme Court reversed the three-judge district court. This time, Justice O'Connor joined the four Justices who had dissented in *Shaw II*. In an opinion by Justice Stephen Breyer, the majority concluded that the Twelfth District was constitutional because politics not race had been the predominant factor

---

[201] Hunt v. Cromartie, 526 U.S. 541 (1999).

[202] *Id.* at 547.

[203] *Id.* at 549–54. The four Justices who had dissented in *Shaw II* separately concurred. *Id.* at 555–58 (Stevens, J., concurring).

[204] Cromartie v. Hunt, 133 F. Supp. 2d at 418–23.

[205] *Id.* at 427–33 (Thornburg, J., dissenting).

[206] 532 U.S. 234 (2001).

in its creation. State officials were primarily motivated by the protection of incumbents and the balancing of party power.[207]

In reaching this conclusion, the Court acknowledged that in North Carolina, race and political behavior were closely correlated. Where race and political affiliation are so correlated, plaintiffs must establish that "the legislature could have achieved its legitimate political objectives in alternative ways that are comparably consistent with traditional districting principles" *and* that "those districting alternatives would have brought about significantly greater racial balance."[208] Although the disputed issue in the case turned on findings of fact, the Court declined to defer to the district court. Instead, the Justices focused on the "demanding" burden of proof that plaintiffs face in challenging districts under *Shaw I* and its progeny.[209] Sorting through the evidence, the majority found little support for the district court's conclusion that "race not politics" was the predominant factor in the North Carolina reapportionment.

Easley not only brought the North Carolina litigation to an end, but also made it more difficult to prevail on a *Shaw* claim. By making plaintiffs show that racial considerations predominated over political ones, Justice Breyer's opinion provides a recipe for state officials seeking to avoid a *Shaw* claim: Argue that partisan interests, rather than race, are the basis for the challenged plan. So long as legislators can show political rather than racial reasons for a plan—something that is almost always possible—a redistricting plan may be defended. This indeed seems to be the lesson that lower court judges have drawn from *Easley*, and helps explain why relatively few racial gerrymandering cases have been brought in the wake of redistricting based on the 2000 census results.[210] Viewed in this light, *Easley* is a much more significant decision than its fact-intensive analysis would suggest. Like the Court's affirmative action decisions in higher education,[211] *Easley* gives the government

---

[207] *Id.* at 257.

[208] *Id.* at 255, 258.

[209] *Id.* at 241.

[210] *See* Pamela S. Karlan, *Exit Strategies in Constitutional Law: Lessons for Getting the Least Dangerous Branch Out of the Political Thicket*, 82 B.U. L. Rev. 667, 691 (2002) (noting that at least some federal judges are convinced that any district may be defended under *Easley*). Another possible explanation for the paucity of racial gerrymandering cases in the 2000s is that the Justice Department, chastened by the 1990s redistricting cases, has been less vigorous in requiring the creation of new majority-minority districts.

[211] *See* Grutter v. Bollinger, 539 U.S. 306 (2003). For a fuller account of this case, see Rachel F. Moran, *The Heirs of* Brown: *The Story of* Grutter v. Bollinger in Race Law Stories 451 (R. Moran & D. Carbado eds. 2008).

some latitude to take race into account, so long as it avoids doing so in an overly heavy-handed fashion.

What explains the Court's relaxation of the raceblindness mandate that some of *Shaw I*'s rhetoric suggested? One explanation is that such a mandate would have been unenforceable. The problem with this view is that the Court could have imposed a much more demanding standard, holding *any* consideration of race subject to strict scrutiny. Legislators could still use proxies for race to accomplish their redistricting objectives, but such a rigorous standard at least would have made it more difficult for them to do so.

An alternative explanation is that the Court either lost its nerve or came to its senses—depending on one's perspective on its voting rights jurisprudence. For Robinson Everett and others who applauded the move toward raceblindness, *Easley* must have come as a profound disappointment. For those who were worried that *Shaw* dealt a fatal blow to the Voting Rights Act, *Easley* was cause for a sigh of relief—if only a momentary one, given the recent changes on the Supreme Court. With the arrival of new Justices, the pendulum may well swing back toward a greater skepticism of race-conscious redistricting.[212]

Another possible explanation is that the Court found other ways of limiting compelled creation of majority-minority districts. The strongest case for this perspective is *Georgia v. Ashcroft*,[213] in which the Court held that a redistricting plan may comply with Section 5, even though it reduces the number of safe minority seats.[214] The Court rested its conclusion on the increase in the number of "influence districts," ones in which minorities may exert some influence on their representatives even though they cannot elect their candidate of choice. The Justices also noted that most black Representatives to Congress (including Representative John Lewis) had signed off on the plan. In the Court's view, Section 5 "gives States the flexibility to choose one theory of effective representation over the other."[215] That is, a majority-minority district is just one way to ensure access to the democratic process. For proponents

---

[212] *See* Richard H. Pildes, *The Roberts Court and the Decline of Legally Mandated Minority Representation*, 68 Ohio St. L.J. 1139, 1141 (2007) (suggesting that the Court's decision in *LULAC v. Perry*, 126 S.Ct. 2594 (2006), may presage a rollback of legal mandates for minority-majority districts).

[213] 539 U.S. 461 (2003).

[214] When Congress reauthorized the VRA in 2006, it explicitly reversed the Court's interpretation of Section 5 in *Georgia v. Ashcroft*. Fannie Lou Hamer, Rosa Parks, and Coretta Scott King Voting Rights Act Reauthorization and Amendments Act of 2006, Pub. L. 109–246, 120 Stat. 577, §§ 2(b)(6), 5 (2006), codified at 42 U.S.C. §§ 1973 note, 1973c(b) (2007).

[215] *Id.* at 482.

of greater minority representation, the problem with *Georgia v. Ashcroft* is that states can easily pay lip service to racial minorities in redrawing districts without enhancing participation.[216]

For advocates of raceblindness, on the other hand, *Ashcroft* is troubling because it presumes that race-conscious decisionmaking is justified under the VRA. Justice Kennedy reflects the concern that Georgia paid *too much attention* to race when he suggests that the redistricting plan might violate the Equal Protection Clause because race was the "predominant factor" in drawing the boundaries. As he puts it, "considerations of race that would doom a redistricting plan under the Fourteenth Amendment ... seem to be what save it under § 5 [of the VRA]."[217] Whether or not one agrees with Kennedy's position on the merits, he is correct to note the unresolved tension between the qualified raceblindness mandate of *Shaw* and the qualified race-consciousness mandate of the VRA.[218]

While the future is anything but certain, so far *Shaw* has not had the disastrous consequences for minority representation that some feared. A number of majority-minority districts were in fact dismantled as a result of *Shaw I* and its progeny. The Court ordered the redrawing of nine majority-minority congressional districts, and in eight of those districts the black population fell below 50%. But contrary to the expectations of some, all but one of the black incumbents sought reelection and everyone who ran was successful.[219] As shown in the chart below, minority representation in Congress actually held steady through the 1990s and into the next decade.[220] Minority representation in the

---

[216] As the dissent put it, the opinion threatens a "preclearance regime that defies reviewable administration." *Id.* at 496 (Souter, J., dissenting).

[217] *Id.* at 491 (Kennedy, J., concurring).

[218] This tension remains after the Roberts Court's first foray into racial redistricting in *LULAC v. Perry*, 126 S.Ct. 2594, 2663 (2006), which held that the State of Texas violated Section 2 by redrawing a congressional district in which Latinos had been poised to elect a representative of their choice. As a formal matter, the Court's opinion relies on *Gingles'* interpretation of Section 2 to protect minorities' representational interests. At the same time, the opinion draws at least in part on the *Shaw* line of cases, in emphasizing that states may not remedy a Section 2 violation through creation of a noncompact majority-minority district. *LULAC* has been read in competing ways: on one hand, as implying a stronger mandate for authentic racial representation and, on the other, as signaling skepticism of legally mandated majority-minority districts. *Compare* Guy–Uriel E. Charles, *Race, Redistricting, and Representation*, 68 Ohio St. L.J. 1185, 1190–96 (2007), *with* Pildes, *supra* note 212, at 1141.

[219] Grofman et al., *Effective Minority Districts*, *supra* note 74, at 1397–98.

[220] The information in this chart is derived from Mildred L. Amer, CRS Report for Congress, Black Members of the United States Congress: 1870-2004, at 58–59 (2004) (showing the number of blacks serving in the House of Representatives through 2005);

House gradually increased between the 1960s and 1980s and then increased significantly in the early 1990s. Although there was a slight decline in the late 1990s, the number of minority representatives has remained largely unchanged since *Shaw I* was decided in 1993. There were thirty-nine African Americans in the House of Representatives at that time. Ten years later, there were still thirty-nine African Americans in Congress.[221] Meanwhile, the number of Latinos in the House increased from twenty to twenty-five between 1993 and 2003, largely as the result of increases in the Latino voting population.[222] Looking beyond Congress, the overall number of black officials continued to increase steadily during the 1990s. If there were no dramatic increases after *Shaw I*, there were also no precipitous declines.

Minorities in United States House of Representatives

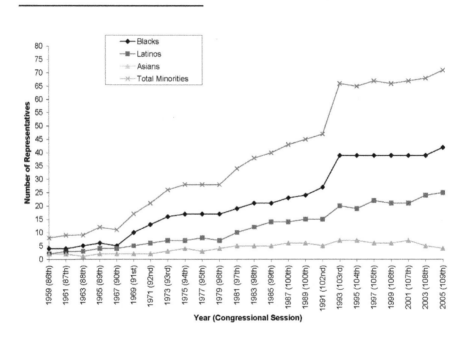

Lorraine H. Tong, CRS Report for Congress, Asian Pacific Americans in the United States Congress (2003) (showing Asian Americans serving in the House through 2005); Hispanic Americans in Congress, *available at* http://www.loc.gov/rr/hispanic/congress/chron.html (showing Latinos elected to Congress up to 2005).

[221] Amer, *supra* note 220, at 59.

[222] Hispanic Americans in Congress, www.loc.gov/rr/hispanic/congress/chron.html (showing Latinos elected to Congress up to 2005).

Why did the racial gerrymandering cases not have the impact on minority representation that some feared? At least when it comes to Congress, minority incumbents have been able to win even when running from districts that were no longer majority-minority—so long as their party was still in the majority. The main reason is not a decrease in racially polarized voting, or the incumbency advantage enjoyed by black legislators.[223] Although white crossover voting has increased,[224] the most important factor appears to be whether a black candidate runs against a white incumbent.[225] This suggests that the most important factor in promoting minority representation was the application of the VRA to dislodge white incumbents.[226] Once entrenched incumbents were removed, it was possible for minority candidates to retain those seats in at least some majority-white districts.

Conclusion

Like many stories in the area of race law, *Shaw v. Reno* does not have a tidy ending. The good news for advocates of minority representation is that, in the decade following *Shaw I*, the Court did not declare the VRA unconstitutional. Even the most ideologically conservative Justices have thus far shown little appetite for invalidating the core provisions that effected a quiet revolution in voting rights.[227] Despite the Court's limitations on the creation of majority-minority districts, African–American representation held steady and Latino representation increased throughout the 1990s and into the new century. To the extent that there really was a counterrevolution against minority voting rights, it has not prevailed. So far, the second Reconstruction has not met the same fate as the first.

The bad news for voting rights advocates is that it is too early to know for sure whether the improvements in minority representation

---

[223] Grofman et al., *Effective Minority Districts, supra* note 74, at 1400.

[224] Pildes, *supra* note 11, at 1530 (noting that "one-third of white voters regularly vote for black candidates" in southern congressional elections) (citing Grofman et al., *Effective Minority Districts, supra* note 74, at 1399–1400).

[225] Grofman et al., *Effective Minority Districts, supra* note 74, at 1400–03.

[226] *Id.* at 1423.

[227] Nevada Dept. of Human Resources v. Hibbs, 538 U.S. 721, 741 (2003) (Scalia, J., dissenting) (citing the VRA as an example of legislation that the Court has found to be within Congress' enforcement power, and contrasting the Family Medical Leave Act as an expansion beyond the legitimate scope of congressional power); *id.* at 744, 756–57 (Kennedy, J., dissenting, joined by Scalia and Thomas, JJ.) (citing VRA's literacy test ban as an appropriate exercise of congressional enforcement power); *see also* Tennessee v. Lane, 541 U.S. 509, 554, 562 (2004) (Scalia, J., dissenting) (asserting that title II of the Americans with Disabilities Act of 1990 goes beyond Congress' enforcement power, while suggesting that Congress has more "expansive" power when it comes to enforcement of guarantees against racial discrimination).

that have resulted from aggressive enforcement of the Voting Rights Act will last. To be sure, the Supreme Court has rendered the VRA neither unconstitutional nor toothless. But its teeth have been dulled, not only through the equal protection cases that followed *Shaw I* but also through the Court's interpretation of the Voting Rights Act in cases such as *Georgia v. Ashcroft.*[228] Although social science research provides encouraging evidence that some white voters are more willing to vote for minority candidates than they once were,[229] it is not clear that the increases in African American and Latino representation that occurred in the 1980s and 1990s will be sustained.

The uncertain status of *Shaw v. Reno*'s legacy is compounded by two major developments in the middle of the first decade of the twenty-first century. One is the renewal of key provisions of the Voting Rights Act that were to expire in 2007, including the preclearance requirement.[230] The constitutionality of preclearance will undoubtedly be the subject of more litigation, which is likely to wind up before the Supreme Court. The other development is the changing composition of the Court, marked by the death of Chief Justice Rehnquist and the retirement of Justice O'Connor, who was the swing vote in *Shaw* and the key voting rights cases that followed. For those seeking to soothsay, these developments further cloud a vision of the future. But if the Roberts Court remains as ambivalent in its conception of meaningful representation as was the Rehnquist Court, the legacy of *Shaw v. Reno* will remain a subject of vigorous contestation.

---

[228] 539 U.S. 461 (2003); *see also* Reno v. Bossier Parish Sch. Bd., 528 U.S. 320, 340 (2000) (holding that Section 5's "purpose" prong applies only to changes that have a *retrogressive* purpose); Reno v. Bossier Parish Sch. Dist., 520 U.S. 471 (1997) (preclearance under section 5 may not be denied simply because a change would violate Section 2 of the VRA).

[229] Keech & Sistrom, *supra* note 8, at 174.

[230] Fannie Lou Hamer, Rosa Parks, and Coretta Scott King Voting Rights Act Reauthorization and Amendments Act of 2006, Pub. L. 109–246, 120 Stat. 577.

15

Eric K. Yamamoto and Catherine Corpus
Betts

Disfiguring Civil Rights to Deny Indigenous Hawaiian Self–Determination: The Story of *Rice v. Cayetano*

Introduction

In 1965, Governor George Wallace infamously blocked a schoolhouse door at the University of Alabama to prevent the first two African–American college students from attending class there. Television images from that day are still burned in America's memory—frightened, neatly dressed black students racially taunted and physically assaulted. In the early 1960s, Wallace had run for election on a states' rights platform (and diminished federal government power), courting Alabama's conservative white vote. His anti-civil rights "segregation now, segregation forever" inaugural speech written by Ku Klux Klan branch leader Asa Carter[1] roused support for the continued harsh Jim Crow subordination of African Americans—one hundred years after the Civil War and a decade after the Supreme Court pronounced equality for blacks in *Brown v. Board of Education*.[2]

Four decades later in *Doe v. Kamehameha Schools*, 295 F. Supp. 2d 1141 (2003), George Wallace's ghost reappeared in the schoolhouse door—again in the service of white Americans, but in a different way. In

---

[1] Asa Carter, writer of George Wallace's "Segregation Now, Segregation Forever" speech, was also a founder of a Ku Klux Klan branch. See PBS, *Timeline of George Wallace's Life, available at* http://www.pbs.org/wgbh/amex/wallace/timeline/index_2.html (last visited June 11, 2006).

[2] 347 U.S. 483 (1954).

2003, against a backdrop of successful conservative attacks on civil rights gains by women, minorities, immigrants, and gays and lesbians, attorney John Goemans redeployed Wallace's image in an effort to dismantle a private school for indigenous Hawaiian children—but this time in the name of "civil rights." Goemans reportedly declared that, like George Wallace, "the trustees of Kamehameha Schools are standing in the schoolhouse door to prevent the admission of qualified children simply because they have the wrong skin color and bloodline."[3]

The Kamehameha Schools are a private institution established in 1884 by the land trust of the late Princess Bernice Pauahi Bishop. Pauahi Bishop witnessed the decimation of Hawai'i's indigenous population—from over 400,000 at the time of the first European contact in 1778 to less than 45,000 a century later.[4] Indeed, Congress described Native Hawaiians as a "dying race."[5] In the face of accelerating American military and economic control of the Hawaiian islands, with the accompanying loss of Hawaiian life and the destruction of Hawaiian culture, Pauahi Bishop dedicated her royal land holdings to create a school to educate Hawaiian children in order to ensure their physical, as well as cultural and economic, survival.[6] Pauahi Bishop's grasp of the urgency of changing circumstances proved prescient. In 1893, the United States assisted in the illegal overthrow of the sovereign Hawaiian nation. President Grover Cleveland's emissary, James Blount, later investigated the United States' role in the overthrow and found it to be a stark violation of international law. In 1897, most of the adults who survived the overthrow, a total of 27,000 Native Hawaiians led by former Queen Lili'uokalani, sent Congress a petition opposing U.S. annexation of Hawai'i.[7]

Nevertheless, with the end of Cleveland's presidency in 1896, the American military and plantation owners lobbied hard for annexation of

---

[3] Rod Antone et al., *Kamehameha Sued Over Its Admissions*, Honolulu Star–Bull., June 26, 2003, *available at* http://starbulletin.com/2003/06/26/news/story2.html.

[4] David E. Stannard, *Before the Horror: The Population of Hawai'i on the Eve of Western Contact* 3 (1989).

[5] H.R. Rep. No. 839, 66th Cong., 2d Sess. 4 (1920).

[6] Because of its "Hawaiians first" policy in admissions, all 2000 Kamehameha students were of at least part Hawaiian ancestry. Various other ethnicities were reflected widely across the student body, including Native American, Caucasian, Japanese American, Native Alaskan, Filipino American, Chinese American, and Arab American. For this essay, we use the terms "Native Hawaiian" and "Hawaiian" interchangeably to denote persons whose ancestry is traceable to the indigenous Polynesian people populating the Hawaiian islands at the time of initial Western contact in 1778.

[7] *See* NoeNoe Silva, *Kanaka Maoli Resistance to Annexation*, Vol. 1, 'Oiwi: A Native Hawaiian J., 40 (1999).

the Hawaiian islands, racializing the indigenous people as either uncivilized or childlike—in either case, in need of American control.[8] With a
military base at Pearl Harbor and a hot commodity (sugar) at stake, the
United States annexed Hawai'i in 1898. After the United States declared
sovereignty over the islands, officials confiscated all former Hawaiian
government and royal lands—two-thirds of Hawai'i's fertile territory.[9]
The beloved former queen was imprisoned for "treason"; Hawaiian
language was barred from the schools; plantations diverted water from
agrarian Hawaiian communities. More and more Hawaiians were separated from the land to which they bore a cultural, economic, and
spiritual connection.[10] American colonialism, spreading worldwide during
Pauahi Bishop's era, reached its heyday in 1898 with the United States'
territorial acquisition of the Philippines, Puerto Rico, and Guam, along
with Hawai'i.[11]

This colonial expansion, or "American westernization," hastened
the near demise of indigenous Hawaiians. Today, Hawaiians in their
homeland still suffer the worst socioeconomic outcomes of all Hawai'i's
people—the highest rates of serious illness, prison incarceration, and
homelessness, and the lowest rates of higher education attainment and
family income.[12] Indeed, in its Apology Resolution of 1993, Congress
acknowledged these facts and commanded the President to apologize for
the United States' active role in the illegal "conspiracy" to overthrow
the internationally recognized Hawaiian government and for the "devastating" impact on the Hawaiian people.[13] The Apology Resolution also
recognized that the "indigenous Hawaiian people never directly relinquished their claims to their inherent sovereignty as a people or over
their national lands to the United States."[14]

Notwithstanding this harsh colonial legacy, Hawaiians have progressed. A Hawaiian renaissance in the last quarter of the twentieth
century, rooted in cultural resurrection and political awakening, drew
upon the international human rights principle of self-determination for

---

[8] See Lilikala Kame'eleihiwa, *Native Land and Foreign Desires: Pehea La e Pono Ai?*
305 (1992).

[9] *Id.*

[10] See NoeNoe K. Silva, *Aloha Betrayed: Native Hawaiian Resistance to American
Colonialism* 3, (2004).

[11] See Kame'eleihiwa, *supra* note 8, at 305.

[12] Doe v. Kamehameha Schools/Bernice Pauahi Bishop Estate, 416 F. 3d 1025, 1041
(2005).

[13] Apology Resolution, Pub. L. No. 103–150, 107 Stat. 1510 (1993).

[14] *Id.*

indigenous peoples.[15] Along with significant supportive government programs, private Hawaiian efforts targeted housing, employment, healthcare, and, most importantly, education. The Kamehameha Schools, with a dramatically expanded endowment linked to rising land values, played an important part by sending nearly all recent graduates to college.[16]

Attorney Goemans conjured Wallace's ghost, then, not to help end or redress the longstanding subordination of Native Hawaiians in America. Instead, he appeared to deploy Wallace's white supremacist image in a twisted present-day attempt to benefit white Americans and others at the expense of Native Hawaiian children—and all in the name of civil rights. How did Kamehameha Schools' opponents distort the very idea and language of civil rights in order to characterize two hundred years of anti-black apartheid in America as the moral and legal equivalent of one private school's attempt to educate indigenous Hawaiian children and repair the continuing damage of twentieth century American colonialism? What lay behind the apparent distortion of history and twisting of the language of equality—the disfiguring of civil rights to deny indigenous Hawaiians' claim to the international human right of self-determination?

In part, the answers to the foregoing questions relate to events that occurred seven years earlier. In 1996, the very year a federal appellate court ruled in *Hopwood v. Texas* that diversity is an insufficient justification for affirmative action,[17] Goemans set the historical and rhetorical stage for his Kamehameha Schools challenge with *Rice v. Cayetano*.[18] Goemans teamed with Freddy Rice to sue the State of Hawai'i and the Office of Hawaiian Affairs (OHA), a state constitutionally-created organization dedicated to implementing land trust obligations to Hawaiians and to fostering Hawaiian cultural preservation and political participation.[19] Rice claimed that as a white American he was unconstitutionally denied the right to vote for the OHA Board of Directors based on his race.[20] Although his lawsuit formally challenged the OHA Board's Hawaiians-only voting restriction, Rice was in fact challenging much more.

---

[15] S. James Anaya, *The Native Hawaiian People and International Human Rights Law: Toward a Remedy for Past and Continuing Wrongs*, 28 Ga. L. Rev. 309, 311–20, 336–57, 359–62 (1994).

[16] In 2004, for the first time, 100% of the school's graduating class of 400 was accepted to college. Kamehameha Schools, Facts About Kamehameha Schools (2006), *available at* http://www.ksbe.edu/about/facts.php.

[17] 78 F.3d 932 (5th Cir. 1996).

[18] 528 U.S. 495 (2000).

[19] Haw. Const. art XII, §§ 5–6 (added by the Constitutional Convention of 1978 and ratified by general election on Nov. 7, 1978).

[20] Rice v. Cayetano, 941 F. Supp. 1529 (D. Haw. 1996).

Narrowly viewed, his lawsuit was designed to fire conservative enmity by characterizing programs for indigenous Hawaiians as simply "racial preferences" and to ignite a rash of new "civil rights" lawsuits to dismantle Hawaiian health care, education, housing, and cultural programs.[21] More broadly seen, the *Rice* suit initiated a fierce threshold battle over the collective memory of America's injustice in its treatment of native peoples—particularly America's taking of homelands and destruction of culture and self-governance.[22] And it highlighted the salience of that battle over collective memory to the legal struggles for redress for the continuing harms of twentieth century American imperialism.[23] This essay offers a behind-the-scenes story of that struggle and how it played out in America's high court and beyond. We begin with a discussion of Freddy Rice—who he is and what motivated him to bring suit.

Freddy Rice and OHA

Rancher Harold "Freddy" Rice's white American ancestors came to Hawai'i as Christian missionaries in the mid–1800s and built a ranching empire on formerly royal land on the Big Island of Hawai'i. Rice, a Big Island rancher and graduate of the prestigious Punahou Schools on O'ahu and New York's Cornell University, joined with Goemans to sue the OHA. Goemans grew up on the continental United States and moved to Hawai'i before statehood. In addition to representing Rice, Goemans supported eliminating all federal funding for Hawaiian programs in the state as part of his "commitment to the civil rights laws of this country and to the Constitution."[24]

Regardless of what motivated Goemans, Rice believed that he was "helping" Hawaiians, whom he saw as taking advantage of the welfare system by choosing not to work.[25] Later, Rice would praise the Supreme

---

[21] Carroll v. Nakatani, 342 F.3d 934 (9th Cir. 2003) (challenging OHA, Hawaiian Homelands and Native Hawaiian gathering and access rights); Arakaki v. Lingle, 305 F. Supp. 2d 1161 (D. Haw. 2004); Doe v. Kamehameha Sch./Bernice Pauahi Bishop Estate, 295 F. Supp. 2d 1141 (D. Haw. 2003) (challenging Kamehameha Schools admissions policy), *aff'd in part, rev'd in part*, 416 F.3d 1025 (2005), *en banc rehearing granted*, 441 F.3d 1029 (2006).

[22] *See generally* Rennard Strickland, *The Genocidal Premise in Native American Law and Policy: Exorcising Aboriginal Ghosts*, 1 J. Gender Race & Just. 325 (1998); Jo Carrillo, *The American Indian and the Problem of History*, 33 Ariz. L. Rev. 281 (1991); Robert A. Williams, Jr., *The American Indian in Western Legal Thought*, 326 (1990).

[23] *See* Ediberto Roman, *Reparations and the Colonial Dilemma: The Insurmountable Hurdles and Yet Transformative Benefits*, 13 Berkeley La Raza L.J. 369, 384–385 (2002); Pedro A. Malavet, *Puerto Rico: Cultural Nation, American Colony*, 6 Mich. J. Race & L. 1, 12, 16, 49–57 (2000).

[24] Bruce Dunford, *Attorney Launches Assault on Programs for Native Hawaiians*, Associated Press, June 22, 2002, *available at* http://www.moolelo.com/goemans.html.

[25] *See* Naomi Sodetani, *Rice on Rice: Q & A with Waimea Rancher Harold "Freddy" Rice*, Haw. Island J. Oct. 16–31, 2003, *available at* http://www.hawaiiislandjournal.com/stories/2003/10b03b.html.

Court decision in his case: "I'm proud to be part of Hawai'i's history. . . .
It was good for Hawaiians, and certainly good for the state. Got every-
body thinking. Hawaiians took advantage of being able to play the part
of victim and get entitlements based on race. They stepped over the line.
The *Rice* decision made everyone step back."[26] Whatever Rice meant by a
"step back," he did not mean an engagement with Hawai'i's colonial
history, a history within which Rice and his family are deeply implicated.

In 1848, former American lawyers working for Hawaiian King
Lunalilo orchestrated the "Mahele" (western-style land division and
allocation) that privatized Hawai'i's collective land usage system.[27] In a
short time, the Mahele allowed white ranchers and plantation owners
(many descendants of missionaries) to acquire fee title to most of
Hawai'i's non-government lands—leaving the majority of ordinary Hawaiians landless in their homeland. Forty years later, in 1887, Rice's
great-grandfather William Hyde Rice helped engineer the "Bayonet
Constitution" that stripped the Hawaiian kingdom of much of its power.[28] A secret society of mostly white businessmen, with the threat of
U.S. military assistance, forced King Kalakaua to sign a new constitution
effectively transferring key aspects of the monarch's political power.

Queen Lili'uokalani's plan to undo the Bayonet Constitution and
restore the powers of the Hawaiian government in 1893 in turn triggered
a coup led by the "Committee of Safety" (organized by the Annexation
Club, a group of American and former American businessmen) and
backed by an American warship and soldiers.[29] In 1898, despite the
illegality of the overthrow, the U.S. annexed Hawai'i—again through
apparently unlawful means. Because of strident opposition from Native
Hawaiians and their many supporters, Congress could not muster the
two-thirds majority needed to authorize the mandated "treaty of annexation" and instead passed only a simple majority Joint Resolution. On
this dubious legal foundation the colonization of Hawai'i as a United
States territory proceeded.[30]

In 1920, recognizing that landless and disenfranchised Native Hawaiians were a "dying race," Congress passed the Hawaiian Homes
Commission Act.[31] That legislation placed 200,000 acres of formerly

---

[26] *Id.*

[27] *See* Silva, *supra* note 10, at 42–43.

[28] *See* Sodetani, *supra* note 25.

[29] Silva, *supra* note 10, at 129–130.

[30] Anaya, *supra* note 15, at 311–320, 336–57, 359–62. *See also* Silva, *supra* note 10, at
146.

[31] Hawaiian Homes Commission Act, 1920, ch. 42, 42 Stat. 108 (1921) (characterizing
Hawaiians as a dying race, in part as a result of land dispossession following the

Hawaiian lands (taken upon annexation) into a "Homelands Trust" administered by the federal government for homesteads for Native Hawaiians. The Act, which defined "Native Hawaiians" as those with at least 50% Hawaiian blood quantum and a traceable bloodline to those living in Hawai'i prior to Western contact in 1778,[32] sought to restore Hawaiians' spiritual and economic ties to their homelands. The federal government, however, badly neglected its trust obligations under the Act. Officials failed to fund the operations of the homelands program and thereby scuttled any serious effort to return Hawaiians to their land. The government ultimately leased substantial acreage meant for Hawaiians to well-connected, non-Hawaiian ranchers and businessmen at nominal rents.[33]

Upon statehood in 1959, the Hawai'i legislature formed a compact with the United States. As part of that compact, the state incorporated the Hawaiian Homes Commission Act (including its definition of the term "Native Hawaiian") into the new Hawai'i Constitution.[34] The federal Admissions Act also provided that the public lands taken from the former Hawaiian nation (except for military and other valuable lands used by the federal government) would be conveyed by the federal government to the new state to be held in trust.[35] The state, as trustee, was required to administer the "ceded lands" trust, covering one-third of the state's lands, for five beneficial purposes, including the betterment of conditions for Native Hawaiians.[36] For the next twenty years, however,

---

annexation); *see also* Hearings on the Rehabilitation and Colonization of Hawaiians and Other Proposed Amendments to the Organic Act of the Territory of Hawai'i before the House Committee on the Territories, 66th Cong., 2d Sess. (1920); H.R. Rep. No. 839, 66th Cong., 2d Sess., at 2, 4 (1920) (Sen. Wise testified, "[T]he Hawaiian people are dying.... [T]he only way to save them ... is to take them back to the lands and give them the mode of living [of] their ancestors ... and in that way rehabilitate them.").

[32] *Id.* at § 201. (Definitions: "Native Hawaiian" means any descendant of not less than one-half part of the blood of the races inhabiting the Hawaiian Islands previous to 1778.)

[33] Hawai'i Advisory Committee to the United States Commission on Civil Rights, Broken Trust, The Hawaiian Homelands Program: Seventy Years of Failure of the Federal and State Governments to Protect the Civil Rights of Native Hawaiians (1991). *See also* Hawai'i Advisory Committee to the United States Commission on Civil Rights, Reconciliation at a Crossroads: The Implications of the Apology Resolution and Rice v. Cayetano for Federal and State Programs Benefiting Native Hawaiians (June 2001).

[34] *See* Hawai'i Admissions Act, Pub. L. No. 86–3, 73 Stat. 4 (1959).

[35] *Id.*

[36] Haw. Rev. Stat. § 10–2 (2005) defines "Hawaiian" as "any descendant of the aboriginal peoples inhabiting the Hawaiian Islands in 1778, and which peoples thereafter have continued to reside in Hawai'i," and "native hawaiian" as "any descendant of not less than one-half part of the races inhabiting the Hawaiian Islands previous to 1778."

like the federal government before it, the state breached its land trust obligations to Native Hawaiians, first by taking trust lands for non-trust purposes, and then by failing to use the resources on those lands to benefit Hawaiian people.[37]

With the Hawaiian Renaissance of the 1970s emerging out of the Civil Rights Movement and Native American rights movement, self-identified indigenous Hawaiians, many of part-Hawaiian blood, joined with other members of Hawai'i's multiracial population to amend the state constitution to create the OHA. In 1978, twenty-eight representatives of Hawaiian organizations created the Native Hawaiian Legislative Package, which emerged as the premier accomplishment of the State Constitutional Convention.[38] The Convention created the OHA as a semi-autonomous government agency to oversee Hawaiian affairs, and more specifically, to administer ceded lands trust resources to better the conditions of indigenous Hawaiians and to serve as a "receptacle for reparations."[39] After a rocky start, and amid sporadic controversy, the OHA contributed to improvements in day-to-day Hawaiian life through its support of Hawaiian language, education, and healthcare; the facilitation of Hawaiian self-determination on political matters; and the protection of environmental resources and sacred cultural sites.[40]

In recent years, the OHA has expanded its endowment to over 300 million dollars, with operating funds of 23 million dollars per year.[41] Rice's attempt to vote for OHA board members represented an attempt to assert non-Hawaiian control over the OHA's assets and, more importantly, to redirect the use of those assets to benefit whites and other non-Hawaiians. Perhaps because of this dramatic shift, the controversy over Rice's attempt to vote traveled all the way to the United States Supreme Court.

---

[37] *See* Eric K. Yamamoto, *Critical Race Praxis: Race Theory and Political Lawyering Practice in Post–Civil Rights America*, 95 Mich. L. Rev. 821, 896–899 (1997).

[38] Establishment of the Office of Hawaiian Affairs, *available at* http://www.oha.org/ index.php?option=com_content & task=view & id=25 & Itemid=213.

[39] Under the OHA, "Native Hawaiian" means any descendant of not less that one-half part of the races inhabiting the Hawaiian Island previous to 1778, as defined by the Hawaiian Homes Commission Act, 1920, as amended; provided that the term identically refers to the descendants of such blood quantum of such aboriginal peoples which exercised sovereignty and subsisted in the Hawaiian Islands in 1778 and which peoples thereafter continued to reside in Hawai'i.

[40] Office of Hawaiian Affairs, Strategic Plan, *available at* http://www.oha.org/cat_ content.asp?contentid=21 & catid=41.

[41] Office of Hawaiian Affairs, Annual Report 2005, available at http://www.oha.org/ index.php?option=com_weblinks & catid=96 & Itemid=188.

The Path to the Supreme Court

Rice Files Suit

In March of 1995, Freddy Rice applied to vote for the OHA Board of Directors and was denied a ballot because he was not of Hawaiian ancestry. Rice then filed a lawsuit in the United States District Court in Hawai'i, claiming that his rejection as a white person violated the Voting Rights Act of 1965 as well as the Fourteenth and Fifteenth Amendments to the U.S. Constitution. The Fifteenth Amendment provides that "[t]he right of citizens of the United States to vote shall not be denied or abridged by the United States or by any state on account of race or previous condition of servitude."[42] The Amendment was part of the post-Civil War "Reconstruction" Amendments, and it was intended to prohibit voting discrimination against newly freed African American slaves. The Fourteenth Amendment's Equal Protection Clause provides that states cannot treat people unequally on the basis of race.[43]

Although Rice framed his lawsuit narrowly, as one white man's fight against a "discriminatory" voting scheme, his lawsuit had a much broader impact. The case opened the floodgates to non-Hawaiian attacks on major programs benefiting Native Hawaiians. High-profile, staunchly conservative organizations lent support. Those organizations' names suggested a pro-civil rights stance that belied their anti-civil rights agendas: The Campaign for Color Blind America; Americans Against Discrimination and Preferences; and the New York Civil Rights Coalition (with the assistance of Abigail Thernstrom). Thernstrom, a Senior Fellow at the conservative Manhattan Institute who is known for her strident anti-affirmative action views, had previously characterized *Brown v. Board of Education*[44] as a "mess" that "barely qualified as constitutional reasoning."[45] She had also cited progressive white racial attitudes in the 1960s as the main source of progress for the Civil Rights Movement.[46] Failed Supreme Court nominee Robert Bork, writing for the Center for Equal Opportunity, a think tank devoted to eradicating color-conscious remedies, entered the *Rice* case as a "friend of the court."[47]

---

[42] U.S.C.A. Const. Amend. XV § 1.

[43] Bolling v. Sharpe, 347 U.S. 497 (1954).

[44] 347 U.S. 483 (1954).

[45] Abigail and Stephan Thernstrom, Secrecy and Dishonesty: The Supreme Court, Racial Preferences, and Higher Education, 21 Constitutional Commentary 251 (2004)

[46] Interview by David Gergen with Abigail and Stephan Thernstrom, *Newshour with Jim Lehrer: In Black and White*, (PBS television broadcast Nov. 11, 1997), *available at* http://www.pbs.org/newshour/gergen/november97/thernstrom_11-11.html.

[47] *See* Brief of Amici Curiae Center for Equal Opportunity, New York Civil Rights Coalition, Carl Cohen, and Abigail Thernstrom, in Support of Petitioner, Rice v. Cayetano, 528 U.S. 495 (2000) (No. 98-818).

Using the language of colorblindness, Bork used the lawsuit to stoke the smoldering "reverse racism" fires nationwide. He argued that the dangers of "allowing a state's cultural justifications to supersede the limitations of the Equal Protection Clause are quite evident: One need only change the state from Hawai'i to Louisiana and the year from 1999 to 1896."[48] In drawing this analogy to a Jim Crow caste system, Bork ignored the OHA's mission of uplifting Hawaiian people to rectify the long-term effects of American colonization. Instead, he likened the philosophy underlying the OHA's programs to the racism that led to pervasive segregation of African Americans in the South in the late nineteenth century.[49]

According to Bork, the OHA's Hawaiians-only voting policy merely resurrected the discredited doctrine of "separate but equal" treatment for different races. In 1895, a Louisiana law denied Homer Plessy access to the white section of a train because he was one-eighth black. In *Plessy v. Ferguson*,[50] the United States Supreme Court upheld the law because the separate train cars for whites and blacks were supposedly equal. The *Plessy* separate-but-equal doctrine allowed states to segregate blacks under often horrid and demeaning conditions while claiming that blacks were treated "equally." Stark differences in education, employment, housing, and transportation meant superior treatment of whites and across-the-board subordination of African Americans. Bork twisted this painful history of 200 years of all-encompassing, often violent white subordination of blacks into the equivalent of the OHA's programs for indigenous Hawaiians.

Rice's supporters knew the import of the lawsuit: if the OHA's programs were found to be mere "racial preferences," as Bork argued, they could not be legally funded by any state, local, or federal government. In addition, hundreds of other programs of reparation for Hawaiians would be at risk—including Hawaiian health care, housing, and job training initiatives; tuition assistance for Hawaiian college students; and possibly even private schooling through Kamehameha Schools. Indeed, Rice's challenge would later prove groundbreaking. He would become one of the first white Americans to successfully invoke the civil rights language of equality to deny indigenous peoples' self-determination.

The District Court Decision

In the federal district court, Judge David Ezra applied the Constitution's "rational basis" analysis to the OHA's voting requirement.[51] In

---

[48] *Id.* at *24.

[49] *See id.* at *11.

[50] Plessy v. Ferguson, 163 U.S. 537 (1896).

[51] Rice v. Cayetano, 963 F. Supp. 1547, 1554–55 (D. Haw. 1997).

order for a state political or economic program to survive an equal protection challenge, there must be a rational connection between the means chosen and a legitimate legislative objective. Rational basis analysis almost always results in validation of the government's action because the court usually defers to the legislative branch. In contrast, a "strict scrutiny" analysis almost always results in invalidation of the government action. Strict scrutiny is applied when the government action involves a "racial classification" and it requires that an invidious racial classification be justified by a "compelling governmental interest" and be "necessary" to further that interest. Judge Ezra chose rational basis analysis because he viewed "Hawaiian" as primarily a political rather than a racial classification.[52] He reached this conclusion by comparing Native Americans (who are deemed political rather than racial minorities in the U.S. because of their semi-sovereign status) with Native Hawaiians, Hawai'i's indigenous people.[53]

Appointed over a decade ago by a Republican president, and known for his independence, Judge Ezra acknowledged the overthrow of Hawai'i as a sovereign nation.[54] He recited the historical facts of the overthrow and the subsequent decimation of Hawaiians, as well as the dismantling of traditional Hawaiian land usage by Western economic forces.[55] He also noted numerous legislative acts by Congress and the Hawai'i state legislature benefiting Hawaiians as a group, including the federal Hawaiian Homes Commission Act (later incorporated into state law), the federal Admissions Act, and the state constitutional amendment creating the OHA. By recognizing Native Hawaiians as the indigenous people of Hawai'i whose continuing "guardian-ward" relationship with the federal government resembled the relationship between Native Americans and the federal government, Judge Ezra found the OHA's voting requirement to be rationally tied to state and congressional trust obligations to Native Hawaiians.[56] He therefore rejected Rice's Fourteenth and Fifteenth Amendment challenges.[57]

---

[52] *Id.* at 1554.

[53] *Id.* For an illuminating discussion of "preferential treatment" in Native American law, see Carole Goldberg, *American Indians and "Preferential" Treatment*, 49 UCLA L. Rev. 943 (2002). See also Carole Goldberg: *What's Race Got to Do With It?: The Story of* Morton v. Mancari, in *Race Law Stories* 237 (R. Moran & D. Carbado eds. 2008).

[54] *Rice*, 963 F. Supp. at 1550.

[55] *Id.*

[56] *Id.*

[57] According to Rice, indigenous Hawaiians never achieved federal recognition as a "Native tribe." The state, he said, was falsely equating Hawaiians with Native Americans simply to grant "special racial rights." Rejecting Rice's argument, U.S. District Judge David Ezra declared that, "[t]he State of Hawaii merely enacted a reasonable method to

The Circuit Court Decision

Rice appealed to the U.S. Circuit Court of Appeals for the Ninth Circuit, which upheld Judge Ezra's ruling in 1998. The court of appeals agreed that the OHA's voting restrictions were "not primarily racial, but legal or political"[58] and "rooted in historical concern for the Hawaiian race."[59] Although Native Hawaiians and Native Americans are different in many respects, the court reasoned, the larger congressional concern for Native Americans as indigenous peoples mirrored its concern for Native Hawaiians.[60] The Ninth Circuit therefore rejected Rice's contention that the voting restrictions denied all non-Hawaiians the right to vote on a purely racial basis. The three-judge panel unanimously observed that

> the voter qualification at issue here—albeit clearly racial on its face—does not exclude those who ever had, now have, or ever can have interest in the outcome of the special election for trustees.... Under these circumstances, to permit only Hawaiians to vote in special elections for trustees of a trust that we must presume was lawfully established for their benefit does not deny non-Hawaiians the right to vote in any meaningful sense.[61]

In response, Rice petitioned for a writ of certiorari, which allows the U.S. Supreme Court to decide if it will hear an appealing party's case. Rice's petition argued that the Ninth Circuit's ruling "provides a road map for the wholesale circumvention of the Fourteenth and Fifteenth Amendments"[62] because every racial minority group could claim a special relationship with the government and there would be no end to the discrimination against whites.[63] Rice thus asked that the Court hear his case because Hawai'i had become a supporter of racially segregated voting. Signaling the importance of the issues, the Supreme Court granted Rice's *certiorari* petition. The decision to review the case was especially significant because out of the 8,000 petitions received annually, the Court chooses to hear only about 85.[64] To understand why the

---

satisfy its obligation to utilize a portion of the proceeds from the lands for the betterment of Native Hawaiians. This is clearly consistent with and pursuant to Congress' mandate and intent." *Id.* at 1555.

[58] Rice v. Cayetano, 146 F.3d 1075, 1079 (9th Cir. 1998).

[59] *Id.* at 1080.

[60] *Id.* at 1081.

[61] *Id.*

[62] Petition for a Writ of Certiorari at *2, Rice v. Cayetano, 528 U.S. 495 (2000) (No. 98–818).

[63] *Id.*

[64] 2003 Year-End Report on the Federal Judiciary, Jan. 1, 2004, *available at* http://www.supremecourtus.gov/publicinfo/year-end/2003year/endreport.html.

Justices found *Rice* significant enough to put on the docket, the case must be seen as part of a broader movement to dismantle the legacy of the civil rights movement by eliminating color-conscious remedies.

The Supreme Court Setting For Rice: The Conservative Dismantling of Civil Rights

Sustained attacks on affirmative action, welfare, immigration, and human rights had intensified throughout the 1990s. In California, Proposition 209 banned affirmative action in all state programs, and Proposition 187 targeted undocumented immigrants by denying them access to social services.[65] Those initiatives spurred similar civil rights attacks in states throughout the country. English-only initiatives snuck onto many states' ballots.[66] Court challenges to major new civil rights legislation succeeded, invalidating key parts of the Americans with Disabilities Act[67] and the Violence Against Women Act.[68] Even as the number of hate crimes increased across the nation, conservative politicians blocked legislation to deter these acts of violence.[69] Ward Connerly, an African–American Regent of the University of California, spearheaded nation-wide attempts to end all affirmative action programs in the name of civil rights.[70]

Civil rights victories for subordinated communities came few and far between.[71] Piece by piece, a divided U.S. Supreme Court and lower federal courts dismantled civil rights. By the time the Supreme Court considered Rice's challenge in 1999, it had banned claims of institutional discrimination, invalidated federal and state affirmative action programs, limited federal court powers over school desegregation, rejected claims of

---

[65] CA. Const. Art. 1, Sec. 31.

[66] English-only initiatives appeared on state ballots in Arizona, California and Utah in the late 1990s.

[67] Board of Trustees of University of Alabama v. Garrett, 531 U.S. 356 (2001).

[68] United States v. Morrison, 529 U.S. 598 (2000).

[69] In 1991, California Governor Pete Wilson vetoed a statute passed by the legislature which would include immigrants and the homeless as protected groups under hate crime law. Later that year, he vetoed a statute protecting gays and lesbians from job discrimination, claiming that such protection would cost small businesses.

[70] As a founder of the American Civil Rights Institute and an African–American University of California Regent, Mr. Connerly urged fellow Regents to end the University's use of affirmative action. He succeeded, and later spearheaded the California Civil Rights Initiative, which abolished affirmative action in public employment, public education, or public contracting throughout California in the name of civil rights. *See* American Civil Rights Institute website, *available at* http://www.acri.org (follow "California's Prop. 209" link on left menu bar) (last visited June 11, 2006).

[71] Grutter v. Bollinger, 539 U.S. 306 (2003).

discrimination in death-penalty sentencing, scuttled state hate crimes legislation, and allowed the Boy Scouts to ban gay troop leaders.[72] Under the banner of the "New Federalism" hoisted by conservative think tanks and legal advocacy groups, the Court also limited civil rights and indigenous peoples' rights under the Eleventh Amendment (limiting the Americans with Disabilities Act and Native American sovereignty) and under the Commerce Clause (striking down part of the Violence Against Women Act). This New Federalism embraced a malleable version of states' rights with federal courts deferring to states when they limited civil rights and overruling states when they expanded civil rights protections.[73]

What, then, was really going on? In a country dedicated to the proposition that all are created equal, but with a stark history of racial and gender discrimination, civil rights progress under the law was supposed to be a hard but steady upward pull toward real equality. This often told story, however, was part truth and part illusion.

After the Civil War, as part of the First Reconstruction, America promised equality to African Americans, enabling them to make important political and economic gains. American politicians and judges, however, soon revoked that promise. The civil rights laws adopted as the Reconstruction's foundation were undermined by court rulings and massive popular and political resistance. Strict legalized segregation was enforced by violence. This became America's first broken civil rights promise. In the 1960s, after years of sustained African–American protests, the nation again committed itself to equality. Reinvigorated older civil rights laws and new ones embraced equality and affirmative action to level a grossly unequal playing field. A Second Reconstruction initiated new progress.[74]

But then, as before, came a cultural and political backlash against the gains of minorities, women, and immigrants, followed by court decisions dismantling civil rights. This attack on the Second Reconstruction pushed the United States backward by "re-segregating" America. This became the second broken civil rights promise.[75]

While the old conservatism was openly racist, sexist, nativist, homophobic, and explicitly anti-civil rights ("no blacks allowed"), the conservative "New Federalism" differed. It employed the language of "equality," "colorblindness," and "responsibility." By emphasizing "fairness to the individual" and "states' rights," the New Federalists purported to

---

[72] Eric K. Yamamoto, *Reclaiming Civil Rights in Uncivil Times*, 1 Hastings Race & Poverty L.J. 11, 16 (2003) (collecting cases).

[73] *Id.*

[74] *Id.* at 19.

[75] *Id.*

embrace civil rights. Although the New Federalism changed its language, it was and remains today the old conservatism in substance.

> By focusing tightly on fairness to the individual, it wants us to ignore the reality that decisionmakers tend to treat people as members of groups.... [I]t wants us to ignore the still existing institutional barriers to advancement in jobs, education and housing. It wants us to blind ourselves to the reality faced by hate crime victims ... [that] your identity matters. By ignoring real continuing obstacles of race, gender, sexuality and immigrant status, the new conservatism says, "any problem, limitation or failure is your fault and your fault alone." You don't need the law's intervention to help you overcome long-standing group practices and institutionalized discrimination. Moreover, if you get any government help, that help constitutes unfair "preferences" in your favor, regardless of how tilted the playing field remains.[76]

Rice's Anti–Civil Rights Advocates

In this milieu, the *Rice* case connected many seemingly unrelated individuals and groups in a complex web of conservative attorneys, think tanks, advocacy organizations, judges, and politicians. Although *Rice* started as one white rancher's attempt to vote on Hawaiian affairs, the case created a national backlash against all Native Hawaiian programs and it employed the New Federalism's disfigured civil rights language as the catalyst.

Rice's supporters before the Supreme Court read like a "who's who" of conservatives against civil rights protections for communities of color. Robert Bork supported Rice through his amicus brief. As acting Attorney General in the early 1970s, Bork carried out President Richard Nixon's order to fire Watergate Special Prosecutor Archibald Cox, who had requested Nixon's incriminating cover-up tapes—a chain of events infamously known as the "Saturday Night Massacre."[77] Bork served as Solicitor General from 1972 to 1977, and was later nominated to the Supreme Court. During the nomination hearing in 1987, the American public learned of Bork's extremist ideology, as reflected in his writings as a law professor, judge, and commentator. His popularity declined, and in an extraordinary move, the United States Senate rejected his nomination.[78]

---

[76] *Id.* at 21–22.

[77] *The Watergate Story; Watergate Chronology*, Wash. Post, *available at* http://www.washingtonpost.com/wp-srv/onpolitics/watergate/chronology.htm (last visited June 11, 2006).

[78] *Revisiting Watergate; The Watergate Story; Key Players; Robert Bork*, Wash. Post, http://www.washingtonpost. com/wp-srv/onpolitics/watergate/robert.html (last visited June 11, 2006).

Bork's amicus brief on behalf of The Center for Equal Opportunity, joined by the New York Civil Rights Coalition and Abigail Thernstrom, asserted that the OHA's voting scheme relied on an extreme racial preference that excluded "not just Caucasians from voting in elections for the Office of Hawaiian Affairs [but also turned] away citizens who are African–Americans, Japanese–Americans, Chinese–Americans, and indeed members of all racial and ethnic groups except the preferred Hawaiians."[79] Without analyzing the Hawaiian history of colonization, Bork argued that the OHA scheme represented nothing but raw racial discrimination.

Theodore "Ted" Olson was lead counsel for Rice on the Supreme Court appeal. Previously, Olson had served President Ronald Reagan as Assistant Attorney General for the Office of Legal Counsel from 1981 to 1984. In 1993, as partner with the large national firm of Gibson, Dunn, and Crutcher, Olson unsuccessfully defended the Virginia Military Institute against gender discrimination charges based on its male-only student admissions policy. In 1996, Olson defended Stacey Koon, a white police officer in Los Angeles, on appeal to the Supreme Court from his sentence for federal civil rights violations in the beating of African–American Rodney King. Also in 1996, Olson assisted the Center for Individual Rights in the *Hopwood* case, which challenged affirmative action in admissions at the University of Texas Law School.[80] *Hopwood* ultimately banned all state affirmative action in the Fifth Circuit.[81] In 2000, Olson represented George W. Bush before the Supreme Court in the Florida presidential election recount case, *Bush v. Gore*[82]—an overtly political decision by activist judges described by a highly regarded constitutional scholar as "courting anarchy."[83]

Presumably as a reward for Olson's legal representation on behalf of conservative causes, newly-elected President George W. Bush appointed Olson to the post of Solicitor General of the United States, the most prestigious position for a government lawyer. During Bush's first term, Olson argued before the Supreme Court on behalf of the American

---

[79] Brief of Amici Curiae Center for Equal Opportunity, *supra* note 47, at *7–8.

[80] Profile of a Right Wing Conspirator, The Case of Theodore Olson, World Socialist Website, available at http://www.wsws.org/articles/1999/feb1999/ols-f13.shtml (last visited January 13, 2007). *See also Divisive Ashcroft Sends Strong Message*, Feminist Daily News Wire, *available at* http://www.feminist.org/news/newsbyte/uswirestory.asp?id=5957 (last visited January 23, 2007).

[81] Hopwood v. Texas, 78 F.3d 932 (5th Cir. 1996); *see also* Rachel F. Moran, *The Heirs of* Brown: *The Story of* Grutter v. Bollinger, in *Race Law Stories* 451 (R. Moran & D. Carbado eds. 2008).

[82] 531 U.S. 98 (2000).

[83] Aviam Soifer, *Courting Anarchy*, 82 B.U. L. Rev. 699 (2002).

people. Meanwhile, Olson remained a supporter of the conservative Federalist Society, whose members are known opponents of affirmative action, the right to choose, gay and lesbian rights, and immigrant rights. Backed by this coterie of conservative advocates and armed with the New Federalism language of colorblind equality, Freddy Rice emerged as a white American intent on dismantling programs for indigenous peoples, all in the name of civil rights.

The Supreme Court Litigation

Before the Supreme Court, the OHA was represented by Hawai'i attorney Sherry Broder and law professor Jon Van Dyke. The State, supporting the OHA, was represented by Deputy Attorney General Gerard Lau and Washington, D.C. attorney John Roberts (now Chief Justice of the U.S. Supreme Court). In response to Rice's arguments, the OHA's attorneys argued that the Hawaiians-only voting limitation was permitted under the Supreme Court's line of cases allowing preferential treatment for Native American tribes because the special relationship between the federal and state governments and Hawaiians is akin to the trust relationship between Native Americans and the United States government.[84]

The Majority Opinion

The Supreme Court rejected the OHA's defense. Writing for six others (Chief Justice William Rehnquist and Justices Antonin Scalia, Clarence Thomas, Sandra Day O'Connor, Stephen Breyer, and David Souter), Justice Anthony Kennedy declared that the OHA's argument "rests on the demeaning premise that citizens of a particular race are somehow more qualified than others to vote on certain matters."[85] There is no "room under the [Fifteenth] Amendment," Kennedy said, "for the concept that the right to vote in a particular election can be allocated based on race.... All citizens regardless of race, have an interest in selecting officials who make policies on their behalf, even if those policies will affect some groups more than others."[86] The Court thus invalidated the Hawaiians-only voting limitation and opened up the OHA's electoral process to all Hawai'i residents.

The strategic power of Kennedy's majority opinion lay not in its use of legal abstractions, but rather in its selective historical account of Hawaiian "circumstances" that made the Court's judgment against the OHA seem natural and correct. As we discuss more fully later, struggles for justice are, first and foremost, active, present-day struggles over

---

[84] Rice v. Cayetano, 528 U.S. 495, 518–20 (2000).

[85] *Id.* at 523.

[86] *Id.*

collective memory. How a community frames past events and connects them to current conditions often determines the power of justice claims or opposition to them. This was certainly true in *Rice*. Was the OHA simply about conferring racial privileges, tilting an otherwise level playing field in favor of Native Hawaiians? Or was the OHA part of concerted, long-term state and federal efforts to rectify the continuing harms of U.S. colonialism, in which race, economics and politics played major roles? The Court entered the fray over these conflicting histories. Yet, the majority cast its account as neutral and uncontroversial. The Court was not interpreting history, Justice Kennedy said, but was simply "recounting" it.[87] The question is: What was the content of this recounting? And here one has to consider not only what the Supreme Court's opinion includes, but what it excludes as well. We begin with the latter.

Nowhere did Kennedy's opinion address U.S. colonialism in 1898, either in Hawai'i or contemporaneously in the Philippines, Puerto Rico, and Guam. Instead, the majority made only an oblique reference to the colonization of Hawaiians by describing "the culture and way of life of a people ... all but engulfed by a history beyond their control."[88] Nor did the majority acknowledge specifically the destruction of Hawaiian culture through the banning of Hawaiian language or the current effects of homelands dispossession, including poverty, low levels of education and health, and high levels of homelessness and incarceration. Never did the majority opinion recognize that colonial powers often used race to legitimize conquest, denigrating, in racial terms, those colonized.[89] The opinion even failed to mention whites, although their racism was central to much of Hawai'i's recorded history[90] and Rice's claim was implicitly one of reverse discrimination against whites.

In addition, the majority opinion completely ignored the present-day Hawaiian sovereignty and self-determination movement that gave birth to the OHA.[91] Perhaps most astonishing was the majority's dismissive treatment of two hugely significant facts. First, there was little mention of the extraordinary Congressional Apology Resolution of 1993 in which the United States explicitly acknowledged the bitter legacy of colonization and committed the government to future acts of reconciliation.[92] Second, there was no mention that the OHA and its voting limitation

---

[87] *Id.* at 500.

[88] *Id.* at 524.

[89] *See generally* Albert Memmi, *The Colonizer and The Colonized* (expanded ed., Beacon Press 1991) (1971).

[90] *Id.*

[91] *Id.*

[92] Apology Resolution, Pub. L. No. 103–150, 107 Stat. 1510 (1993).

were created by the overwhelming vote of Hawai'i's multiracial populace, partly to rectify the injustices of American colonialism by affording Hawai'i's indigenous peoples a measure of self-determination.[93]

What collective story, then, did the majority's opinion in *Rice* tell? Relying selectively on historical works written by two non-Hawaiians long before the contemporary Hawaiian sovereignty movement, Kennedy's decision generated a remarkable narrative reminiscent of the familiar tale of how Western culture and law, more or less naturally, "civilized" the native savage—this time in Hawai'i. The majority began by describing how the Hawaiian people found "beauty and pleasure in their island existence" but how life was not "idyllic" because there was internecine warfare among kings who "could order the death or sacrifice of any subject." Moreover, Hawaiians were "polytheistic."[94]

Kennedy's opinion characterized the nineteenth-century missionaries not as uninvited cultural invaders but as civilizers who "sought to teach Hawaiians to abandon religious beliefs and customs that were contrary to Christian teachings."[95] The majority blandly described often-greedy Western encroachment as a "story of increasing involvement of westerners in the economic and political affairs of the Kingdom."[96] The *Rice* decision characterized the 1848 Mahele, which precipitated massive foreign private land ownership, and which most Native Hawaiians regard as a disaster, simply as a "fundamental and historic division" of land after which land "ownership became concentrated."[97] The majority identified Western disease as "no doubt" the source of the "despair, disenchantment, and despondency" of the descendants of the early Hawaiian people.[98] It failed, however, to also connect despondency and despair to the loss of national sovereignty, the confiscation of homelands, and the denigration of native culture.

Perhaps for this reason, the majority overlooked the significance of the stinging 1897 protest of almost all adult Native Hawaiians, who signed petition to Congress condemning the impending U.S. annexation of Hawai'i.[99] The *Rice* majority also relied on a strikingly revisionist history of the "[t]ensions" between an "anti-Western, pro-native

---

[93] Sharon K. Hom & Eric K. Yamamoto, *Collective Memory, History, and Social Justice*, 47 UCLA L. Rev. 1747, 1773 (2000) (citing *Rice*, 528 U.S. at 534 (Stevens, J., dissenting)).

[94] *Rice*, 528 U.S. at 500.

[95] *Id.* at 501.

[96] *Id.*

[97] *Id.* at 503.

[98] *Id.* at 506.

[99] Silva, *supra* note 10, at 158–159.

bloc" and "[W]estern business interests and property owners."[100] Turning the past upside down, the majority intimated that the overthrow was justified by Queen Lili'uokalani's undemocratic actions. Her attempt to restore "monarchical control ... and limit the franchise to Hawaiian subjects" compelled pro-democracy Americans to seize control.[101] In fact, Lili'uokalani was reacting to white businessmen's imposition of the Bayonet Constitution in 1887, under which native voters were largely excluded by property voting requirements, and whites and foreigners achieved grossly disproportionate political power.[102]

Finally, Kennedy's majority opinion alluded to "Chinese, Portuguese, Japanese, and Filipino" immigrants to Hawai'i and how they faced and overcame discrimination.[103] One implicit message was that these immigrant groups had picked themselves up by their bootstraps, so why haven't the Hawaiians? A second and even more troubling message lay in the majority's willingness to equate Hawai'i's "immigrants" with communities of color while omitting white Americans from the status of immigrants. Nor did the majority mention the deep history of white racism integral to the dismantling of the Hawaiian nation.

What emerges from the Court's selective, often revisionist historical framing is a simple story of racial discrimination against Freddy Rice. Hawaiians had a rough go of it, as did immigrant groups, but the playing field now is nearly level. According to the majority's construction of Hawai'i's history, because there are no effects of U.S. colonization, "privileges" for Hawaiians are not only undemocratic, they are illegal.[104] With this sanitized history, the majority issued a stern warning to the OHA and its Hawaiian supporters: "The law itself may not become the instrument for generating the prejudice and hostility all too often directed against persons whose particular ancestry is disclosed by their ethnic characteristics and cultural traditions."[105]

Yet, to what "prejudice and hostility" was the Court referring? It was not the prejudice and hostility directed at Native Hawaiians by American businessmen and military forces as part of the overthrow and its aftermath. Instead, the majority worried about the ill will towards whites living in Hawai'i—in particular, Freddy Rice. According to this view, the OHA's Hawaiians-only voting policy made whites the misplaced

---

[100] *Rice*, 528 U.S. at 504.

[101] *Id.*

[102] Silva, *supra* note 10, at 125.

[103] *Rice*, 528 U.S. at 506.

[104] Hom & Yamamoto, *supra* note 93, at 1775; *see also Rice*, 528 U.S. at 529.

[105] *Rice*, 528 U.S. at 517.

targets of hostility and prejudice. Yet, any assessment of misdirected hostility and prejudice needs to occur in context. The majority's opinion left out key facts that defied a simple characterization of the OHA policy as reverse discrimination: the history of Westernization and colonization, the white oligarchy that completely controlled all aspects of Hawai'i's economy and social and political life for the first half of the twentieth century,[106] and the current reality that whites now comprise the largest ethnic group in Hawai'i and maintain dominant positions in business and media.

The Dissent

Recognizing the limits of the majority's analysis, Justices John Paul Stevens and Ruth Bader Ginsburg dissented. In their view, the "Court's holding today rests largely on the repetition of glittering generalities that have little, if any, application to the compelling history of the State of Hawai'i."[107] Those "glittering generalities" painted Native Hawaiians as just another immigrant group and the OHA as simply an organization steeped in racial preference. The dissent criticized the majority's inaccurate characterization of the OHA, which Stevens observed was not only created "to carry out the duties of the trust relationship between the islands' indigenous peoples and the Government of the United States."[108] It was also created by Hawai'i's multiracial populace "to compensate for past wrongs to the ancestors of these peoples" and to "help preserve the distinct, indigenous culture that existed for centuries before Cook's arrival."[109]

According to the dissent, the OHA and its Hawaiians-only programs could only be properly understood as a state response to historic injustice. Justice Stevens thus refocused the constitutional analysis of the OHA board voting restriction by relying on the "compelling history of the State of Hawai'i"[110] and the aftermath of American colonization to explain the need for restorative justice. In Stevens' view, there was "simply no invidious discrimination present in this effort to see that indigenous peoples are compensated for past wrongs, and to preserve a distinct and vibrant culture that is as much a part of this Nation's heritage as any."[111] Viewed through the lens of indigeneity, colonization,

---

[106] *See generally* Lawrence H. Fuchs, *Hawaii Pono: An Ethnic & Political History* 153 (illustrated ed., Bess Press 1997) (1961).

[107] *Rice*, 528 U.S. at 527–28 (Stevens, J. dissenting).

[108] *Id.* at 528.

[109] *Id.*

[110] *Id.*

[111] *Id.* at 529.

and redress, the OHA's Hawaiians-only board voting limitation became integral to the OHA's mission of rebuilding the Hawaiian people and resurrecting Hawaiian culture. The electoral process was simply one aspect of Hawaiian self-determination.

In this respect, the dissent noted, Native Americans and Native Hawaiians were similarly situated.

> Among the many and varied laws passed by Congress in carrying out its duty to indigenous peoples, more than 150 today expressly include native Hawaiians as part of the class of Native Americans benefited. By classifying Native Hawaiians as "Native Americans" for purposes of these statutes, Congress has made clear that native Hawaiians enjoy many of "the same rights and privileges accorded to American Indian, Alaska Native, Eskimo, and Aleut communities."[112]

Justice Stevens concluded his sharp dissent by reemphasizing the majority's falsification of history to justify its twisted legal result. It is a "painful irony indeed to conclude that native Hawaiians are not entitled to special benefits *designed to restore a measure of native self-governance* because they currently lack any vestigial native government—a possibility of which history and *the actions of this Nation have deprived them*."[113] Viewed properly, the OHA's voting limitation

> is based on the permissible assumption in this context that families with "any" ancestor who lived in Hawai'i in 1778, and whose ancestors thereafter continued to live in Hawai'i, have a claim to compensation and self-determination that others do not. For the multiracial majority of the citizens of the State of Hawai'i to recognize that deep reality is not to demean their own interests but to honor those of others.[114]

The dissent closed by highlighting the difference between indigenous peoples in America seeking to restore the loss of self-governance, land, and culture and racial groups originally from elsewhere seeking to be treated equally—a distinction totally disregarded by the majority:

> The Court today ignores the overwhelming differences between the Fifteenth Amendment case law on which it relies and the unique history of the State of Hawai'i. The former recalls an age of abject discrimination against an insular minority in the old South; the latter at long last yielded the "political consensus" the majority

---

[112] *Id.* at 533–34 (footnote omitted) (citing Native Hawaiian Healthcare Act, 42 U.S.C. § 11701 (2006)).

[113] *Id.* at 535 (emphasis added).

[114] *Id.* at 545.

claims it seeks—a consensus determined to recognize the special claim to self-determination of the indigenous peoples of Hawai'i.[115]

Lessons for Justice Advocates: The Threshold Battle over Collective Memory of Injustice and the Foundation for Redress

The majority and dissenting opinions in *Rice* reveal that the threshold battle there was not about legal niceties. Rather the first battle was over who would tell the definitive story of native peoples within America's borders. The power to shape that story would determine whether, and to what extent, historical injustice occurred, and, concomitantly, the need (if any) for rectification. Thus the stakes at the threshold in *Rice* were huge: who would tell the history of Native Hawaiians' interactions with the United States and how would injustice be framed? Would the collective memory embedded in the legal text illuminate or shroud America's history of nineteenth-and twentieth-century colonialism and the ensuing cultural, economic, and political devastation for indigenous peoples?

Our point of departure for engaging these questions is the observation that in the struggle to frame historical injustice, "[i]ndividuals, social groups, institutions, and nations filter and twist, recall and forget 'information' in reframing shameful past acts (thereby lessening responsibility) as well as in enhancing victim status (thereby increasing power)."[116] These dynamic aspects of the memory of injustice implicate political and legal moves by those seeking, as well as opposing, redress. There are six strategic dimensions for guiding, as well as assessing, this threshold struggle among competing groups working to shape (and reshape) the collective memory of injustice as the foundation for redress.[117]

First, as mentioned, justice claims (seeking reparations, compensation, an apology, or public truth-telling) begin with back-and-forth struggles over the creation of public or collective memory. Those struggles are a fight over who will tell the dominant story of injustice (or absence thereof) and how that story will be shaped.[118]

---

[115] *Id.* at 546 (citation omitted).

[116] *See* Hom & Yamamoto, *supra* note 93, at 1758. ("Collective memory not only vivifies a group's past, it also reconstructs it and thereby situates a group in relation to others in a power hierarchy" placing some above others in terms of economic and political power.)

[117] This section is drawn substantially, and at times verbatim, from Hom & Yamamoto, *supra* note 93.

[118] George Lakoff, *Don't Think of an Elephant!: Know Your Values and Frame the Debate—The Essential Guide for Progressives* (2004).

Second, group memory of injustice as the foundation for redress is not simply a recounting of "facts" about the past. Instead, it is the active, present-day reconstruction of the past. Rather than simply recalling past events, collective memory is constructed in the present and it emerges from interactions among individuals, institutions, and media. The memories are constructed through these interactions and are therefore subject to continual alteration.

Third, this constructed memory implicates politics because struggles over memory are often struggles between colliding ideologies and differing worldviews. "Remembering" what happened thus entails not only recounting "facts" but also grasping how selected experiences shape the group's story and public image. Both proponents and opponents of redress select certain events or images to shape their version of the story.[119]

Fourth, collective memories are formed and transformed through cultural mediums—news accounts, movies, music, books, sermons, and the like. Particularly for decisionmakers, "[m]emories of past events, persons, and interactions are culturally framed because they are subject to socially structured patterns of recall, they are often triggered by social stimuli and they are conveyed through communal language."[120] It is through cultural mediums that these common stories about what happened and who is responsible bear on the legitimacy of present-day justice claims and responses to demands for redress.

Fifth, when attempting to generate a collective memory to support a justice claim, it is crucial for redress proponents not to frame injustice narrowly according to existing legal norms. Prevailing legal dictates, both substantive and procedural, often tend to constrict the telling of the full story of wrongdoing and harm. Rather, larger social justice strategies should employ the legal process with dual goals in sight: to achieve the specific legal result, if possible, and, regardless of legal outcome, to contribute publicly through media attention to the generation of a compelling memory of injustice to help drive the political battle over redress.[121]

Finally, the ability to frame injustice empowers a community to more fully depict its history. In turn, the power to claim one's history, rather than have it retold by an outsider looking in, is increasingly

---

[119] *See generally* Stephanie M. Wildman, *Privilege Revealed: How Invisible Preference Undermines America* 45 (1996).

[120] Hom & Yamamoto, *supra* note 93, at 1761; *see also* Linda Hamilton Krieger, *The Content of Our Categories: A Cognitive Bias Approach to Discrimination and Equal Employment Opportunity*, 47 Stan. L. Rev. 1161, 1202 (1995).

[121] Hom & Yamamoto, *supra* note 93, at 1764.

important to community self-definition—an integral component of the human rights principle of self-determination.

In accepting *Rice* for review, the Supreme Court opened up Hawaiian history for the telling. No prior Supreme Court opinion had recited a comprehensive, up-to-date history of the state.[122] The key question, then, was what story the Court would tell, and that question was in turn informed by cultural forms of communication. Judges' interpretative choices do not occur in a vacuum.[123] Rather, as mentioned, the choice of what story to tell is determined by a sifting of the relevant from the irrelevant—a process itself affected by the decisionmaker's cultural framework. That often-evolving framework is comprised of social perceptions, beliefs, and practices that form the lens through which an individual sees and evaluates both daily happenings and society as a whole.[124]

In contemplating *Rice*, the Supreme Court faced two framing options. The Court could choose to see the Hawaiian people through a limited cultural lens as simply another racial group in America, no different from any other immigrant ethnic group and no different from white Americans. Or it could shift that framework and refocus the lens to see Hawaiians as indigenous people whose nation was illegally overthrown by the United States as part of late nineteenth-century American colonialism (with military and economic roots) in Hawai'i, the Philippines, Puerto Rico, and Guam.[125]

As discussed earlier, with the New Federalism as the backdrop, the Court's majority chose to sanitize America's history of colonialism in order to view the OHA's voting limitation as nothing more than a "special privilege" granted to Native Hawaiians. The majority "turn[ed] a blind eye to Hawaiian history (and the significance of the loss of Hawaiian nationhood)"[126] by embracing a cultural framework that ignored the profound material ramifications of "Western influence"[127] on indigenous Hawaiians.

---

[122] In *Hawaii Housing Authority v. Midkiff*, 467 U.S. 229 (1984), the Supreme Court upheld the state's mandatory lease-to-fee conversion law that deployed the state's eminent domain power to condemn private leasehold property for resale to private lessees. The Court described how the Bishop Estate (the trust funding the Kamehameha Schools) controlled large tracts of Hawai'i's lands and chose to lease rather than sell the fee to homeowners. The Court's recitation of history, however, did not directly address U.S. participation in the overthrow of the Hawaiian nation or the acquisition of Hawaiian lands.

[123] Eric K. Yamamoto, *Practically Reframing Rights: Culture, Performance and Judging*, 33 U.C. Davis L. Rev. 875 (2000).

[124] *Id.* at 881.

[125] *Id.*

[126] *Id.* at 882.

[127] Doe v. Kamehameha Sch./Bernice Pauahi Bishop Estate, 295 F. Supp. 2d 1141, 1150 (2003).

Kennedy's opinion began by announcing the Court's "more limited" role in assessing Hawai'i's history.[128] With that caveat, the majority went on to distort Hawai'i's racial experience. The majority observed that Hawai'i's many ethnic groups, although at one time facing discrimination, "succe[eded]."[129] Kennedy's rhetorical framing of "the immigrant success story" in Hawai'i set the stage for a tacit condemnation of Native Hawaiians who still required special assistance. Of course, this framework was possible only because the majority ignored the momentous difference between the harsh consequences of colonization for unwilling indigenous people and the experiences of voluntary immigration by ethnic groups seeking a better life.[130] The majority did not discuss how colonialism has operated worldwide through political and economic aggression that deploys race to justify the colonizer's control over "inferior or uncivilized" indigenous peoples, and why race therefore must be an integral part of political-economic reparatory responses to the harms of colonization.[131] Through this partial history, the majority undercut the very foundation of Hawaiian restorative justice claims.[132]

Stripped of context, Freddy Rice emerged simply as a long-time Hawai'i resident prohibited from voting by the OHA's race-based eligibility requirements. Without an explicit grounding in the roots and consequences of colonialism, the majority's decontextualized framing erased the heart of indigenous peoples' struggles in the United States and throughout the world—the loss of life and self-governance, the confiscation of homelands, the destruction of culture, and the suppression of identity. As Justice Stevens and Ginsburg's dissent highlighted, this narrow framing treated indigenous people as just another immigrant ethnic group. Once characterized in that fashion, programs to uplift indigenous people in their homeland could be recast as simply wrongheaded "racial preferences." The twenty-year, conservative New Federalism attack on civil rights bolstered this approach by transforming the dominant narrative about minorities. From this ideological perspective, despite past inequities, all racial groups were now operating on a level

---

[128] Rice v. Cayetano, 528 U.S. 495, 500 (2000) (In the "posture of this particular case, [the Court's role] is to recount events as understood by the lawmakers, thus ensuring that we accord proper appreciation to their purposes in adopting the policies and laws at issue.").

[129] *Id.* at 506.

[130] Eric K. Yamamoto, *Interracial Justice: Conflict and Reconciliation in Post–Civil Rights America* 91 (1999).

[131] Memmi, *supra* note 89.

[132] Hom & Yamamoto, *supra* note 93, at 1777.

playing field, and "preferences" for one racial minority therefore violated the civil rights of whites.

Through this narrative, Rice morphed into a person struggling for racial equality in the face of discrimination by Hawaiians. This portrait of Rice masked his position as a well-to-do white rancher whose ancestors profited from the colonization of Hawai'i. Despite these gains, he now wanted to benefit from Hawaiian land resources placed in trust to compensate Native Hawaiians for the devastation of colonization. Instead of acknowledging the predictable long-range consequences of American colonialism, the Supreme Court majority chose to re-characterize the harm to indigenous Hawaiians in social Darwinist evolutionary language, describing them as a people "all but engulfed by a history beyond their control."[133] This framing obliterated colonialism from America's collective memory and hinted that Hawaiians suffered a decline as a result of natural selection, not injustice.[134]

In generating the controlling version of collective memory, the majority opinion proffered bits and pieces of history and partial truths masked as legal truth telling—"glittering generalities" supporting a harsh "judgment at law." From one perspective, the Court's majority opinion reflected what rhetoric scholar David Breshears calls a "refusal to remember."[135] Breshears interprets the growing mainstream acceptance of colorblindness in lieu of traditional civil rights racial awareness as a convenient "forgetting" used to "assuage the feelings of guilt that plague the collective white conscience."[136] Further, by ignoring the historical context in which racism and colonialism occur, Breshears observes that it becomes easier for judges to blot out the collective memory of racism (for example, if "they" haven't made it yet, it must be "their" fault), and thereby "disqualify group-based remedies to current inequalities by denying the continuing relevance of discrimination in the past."[137] *Rice* exemplifies this refusal to remember and its power to perpetuate injustice and inequality.

Conclusion: The Aftermath of Rice v. Cayetano

As feared by many Hawaiians, the Supreme Court's ruling in *Rice* opened the floodgate to suits to end all state-supported programs for

---

[133] *Rice*, 528 U.S. at 524.

[134] *Id.* at 523.

[135] David Breshears, *One Step Forward, Two Steps Back: The Meaning of Equality and the Cultural Politics of Memory in* Regents of the University of California v. Bakke, 3 J.L. Soc'y 67, 83 (2002).

[136] *Id.* at 88.

[137] *Id.*

Hawaiians—all OHA programs, homelands housing, agriculture, health care, traditional Hawaiian land access, and gathering rights.[138] *Rice* also set the historical and rhetorical stage for the legal challenge to the private Kamehemeha Schools for Hawaiian children mentioned earlier.

On August 2, 2005, at attorney John Goeman's urging on behalf of an anonymous student believed to be white, the Ninth Circuit Court of Appeals declared the Kamehameha Schools' preference for indigenous Hawaiian children to be discriminatory. The majority held that the admissions policy violated a post-Civil War federal civil rights statute aimed at preventing the re-subordination of freed black slaves.[139] And what key case did the opinion cite for legal support, particularly for a recitation of Hawai'i's "history" that ignored the legacy of colonialism and thus demonstrated that any favorable consideration for Native Hawaiians was merely a "racial preference"?[140] None other than *Rice v. Cayetano.*

The Court of Appeals decision in *Doe v. Kamehameha*, authored by Judge Jay Bybee, a recent President George W. Bush appointee, shocked Hawai'i's multiracial populace. Many Native Hawaiians in their homeland felt that they and their right of self-determination were under attack.[141] Like Justices Stevens and Ginsburg in their dissent in *Rice*, Ninth Circuit Judge Susan Graber dissented in *Kamehameha* and observed that indigenous Hawaiians face a multitude of ills traceable to the illegal overthrow of the Hawaiian nation. In her view, congressional intent spoke to the dire need for educational programs serving Native Hawaiians.[142]

Judge Graber's dissent echoed the earlier findings of United States District Court Judge Alan Kay when he upheld the Schools' admissions policy in 2002.[143] After a full hearing on the merits, Judge Kay found no civil rights violation. He fully recounted Hawaiian history (countering the sanitized "memory" of Hawaiian injustice recited in Justice Kennedy's opinion in *Rice*) and closely examined the long-range negative consequences of growing Western influence on Hawai'i's indigenous people. With a firm grasp on what was at stake and what was actually behind the lawsuit, Judge Kay declared that it

---

[138] Carroll v. Nakatani, 188 F. Supp. 2d 1219 (2001).

[139] Doe v. Kamehameha Sch./Bernice Pauahi Bishop Estate, 416 F.3d 1025 (9th Cir. 2005).

[140] *Id.* at 1043 n.11.

[141] Shirley Garcia and Hokulei Lindsey, Opinion, *Court Ruling Based on Fundamental Flaw*, Honolulu Advertiser, Aug. 18, 2005, at 18A.

[142] Doe v. Kamehameha Sch./Bernice Pauahi Bishop Estate, *416 F.3d* at 1049.

[143] It was Judge Kay's ruling that was appealed to the Ninth Circuit.

"would be ironic indeed if a [civil rights] law triggered by a Nation's concern over centuries of racial injustice [based on slavery and its legacy] and intended to improve the lot of those [African Americans] who had 'been excluded from the American dream for so long,' " constituted the first legislative prohibition of [a] voluntary, private[144] school for native children created in light of "their unique status as the *indigenous people* of a once sovereign nation as to whom the United States has established a *trust relationship*."[145]

At a press conference shortly after the Ninth Circuit's 2005 decision reversing Judge Kay and outlawing the Kamehameha Schools' admissions policy, plaintiff's attorney Goemans again reportedly likened George Wallace-type racism to the Kamehameha Schools' admissions preference—the "Kamehameha Schools is the last example of this sort of brazen racial exclusions. You had them in the south in the '60s and '70s but the civil rights statutes ended those."[146] What gave him license, once again, to disfigure civil rights? The lessons of *Rice* point to two key contributing factors: the first is the success of the conservative New Federalism's disfiguring of civil rights language and law to legitimize the maintenance of inequality (making it seem natural or the fault of those struggling); and the second is the constricted collective memory of indigenous Hawaiian injustice given authoritative legal status by the majority in *Rice*.

Will that refusal to remember Hawaiian injustice be countered and the misuse of civil rights laws be corrected on appeal to the United States Supreme Court? More broadly, will civil and human rights for subordinated groups survive in the face of withering coordinated attacks—supported not only by conservative advocates, politicians, and think tanks, but also by newly appointed judges? How will supporters of genuine racial equality and indigenous self-determination resist? And with what strategy for reframing the collective memory of injustice and the compelling need for justice? These questions speak to the future of

---

[144] Doe v. Kamehameha Sch./Bernice Pauahi Bishop Estate, 295 F. Supp. 2d 1141, 1164–65 (2003) (citing United Steelworkers of America v. Weber, 443 U.S. 193 (1979) (quoting 110 Cong. Rec. 6552 (1964)) (remarks of Sen. Hubert Humphrey)).

[145] *Id.* at 1152.

[146] Rick Daysog, *Court Rules Against Kamehameha Admissions*, Honolulu Advertiser, Aug. 2, 2005, *available at* http://the.honoluluadvertiser.com/article/2005/Aug/02/br/br01p. html (reporting Goemans' and Grant's statements).

Native Hawaiian self-determination and to the prospects of restorative justice, or continuing injustice, in America.[147]

---

[147] On February 22, 2006, the Ninth Circuit agreed to hear *Doe v. Kamehameha* en banc (with the full appellate court presiding rather than the traditional three-judge panel) after considering the request for an unprecedented six months. 470 F.3d 827 C.A.9 (Haw. 2006) (in an 8 to 7 decision, upholding the Kamehameha Schools' admissions policy).

16

Paulette M. Caldwell

Intersectional Bias and the Courts: The Story of *Rogers v. American Airlines*

Introduction

In *Rogers v. American Airlines*,[1] a federal district court concluded that an employer could prohibit the wearing of all-braided hairstyles in the workplace without violating proscriptions against race or gender discrimination in employment under Title VII of the Civil Rights Act of 1964. Arguing that American's grooming policy discriminated against her as a woman and, specifically, as a black woman, the plaintiff chose to rely on the interactive and mutually-reinforcing impact of race and gender as well as their independent effects. However, the court chose to treat the allegations of race and gender discrimination in the alternative—as wholly separate from each other—thus, denying any interactive relationship between them. The judge denied the plaintiff's sex discrimination claim because all of American's employees in customer-contact positions, whether male or female, were prohibited from wearing all-braided hairstyles. The court also denied the race discrimination claim on the ground that the grooming policy similarly restricted members of every race and did not single out any particular group for differential treatment. The court drew a distinction between biological and cultural conceptions of race, limiting protection against discrimination to the physical manifestations of racial identity—those over which an individual has no control—and denying protection for identity-related choices of personal expression. According to the court, all-braided hairstyles were not the product of natural hair growth, but of "artifice."

---

[1] 527 F. Supp. 229 (S.D.N.Y. 1981).

Like many cases in anti-discrimination law, *Rogers* has long been criticized by legal scholars as an example of how courts unnecessarily limit the definition of discrimination and, ultimately, the reach of law. The decision permits employers to discriminate based on race, so long as they do so using factors other than immutable traits. This distinction allows employers to create myriad proxies for race—hairstyle, name, speech pattern, accent, dialect, language choice—and, without judicial review, to disprefer members of subordinated racial groups on the basis of aesthetic, cultural, and statistically associated traits.[2] What the *Rogers* decision did not say is that Congress nowhere dictated this limitation in Title VII. The court also failed to acknowledge that discriminatory intent often manifests itself in policies that do not explicitly mention race but mention instead proxies for race or racially associated traits such as hairstyles. Making matters worse, nothing in the decision requires employers to make their aesthetic choices known to employees and job applicants, with the result that affected individuals often do not even know why they have not been hired or promoted.[3] The *Rogers* picture becomes even more disturbing when it is kept in mind that the court takes no account of the dignitary and psychological interests involved in individual expressions of racial and ethnic identity[4]—expressive interests which frequently have been taken into account in defining the protections available against gender discrimination—and it does not consider the message of hostility, intimidation, and inferiority communicated by

---

[2] *See, e.g.*, Paulette M. Caldwell, *A Hair Piece: Perspectives on the Intersection of Race and Gender*, 1991 Duke L.J. 365 (1991); Devon W. Carbado & Mitu Gulati, *Working Identity*, 85 Cornell L. Rev. 1259 (2000); Mari J. Matsuda, *Voices of America: Accent, Antidiscrimination Law, and a Jurisprudence for the Last Reconstruction*, 100 Yale L.J. 1329 (1991); Angela Onwuachi–Willig & Mario L. Barnes, *By Any Other Name?: On Being "Regarded As" Black, and Why Title VII Should Apply Even If Lakisha and Jamal Are White*, 2005 Wis. L. Rev. 1283 (2005); Juan F. Perea, *Ethnicity and Prejudice: Reevaluating "National Origin" Discrimination Under Title VII*, 35 Wm. & Mary L. Rev. 805 (1994); Camille Gear Rich, *Performing Racial and Ethnic Identity: Discrimination by Proxy and the Future of Title VII*, 79 N.Y.U. L. Rev. 1134 (2004); Kenji Yoshino, *Covering*, 111 Yale L.J. 769 (2002).

[3] *See* McBride v. Lawstaf, Inc., No. 1:96–CV–0196–CC, 1996 WL 755779 (N.D. Ga. Sept. 19, 1996). McBride, an employee at the defendant temporary employment agency, objected to the agency's policy of refusing to refer for temporary employment individuals who wore all-braided hairstyles. She told Lawstaf that she thought its grooming policy served as a proxy for discrimination against blacks and that she intended to report the policy to the Equal Employment Opportunity Commission ("EEOC"), the federal agency which administers Title VII, if the practice continued. McBride was terminated, and she subsequently lost her retaliation suit against Lawstaf. The court ruled that she could not have had a reasonable, good faith belief that Lawstaf's grooming policy violated Title VII, since courts had held since the late 1970s that hairstyle and similar choices were not protected by law.

[4] Caldwell, *supra* note 2, at 390–93.

workplace rules that target the culturally specific behaviors of tradition-ally subordinated racial groups.[5]

Rogers also reflects a standard judicial response to a classic intersec-tional claim. The plaintiff argued that she suffered a form of discrimina-tion that cannot be understood by analyzing one of the enumerated bases of discrimination—race or sex—isolated from the other. Intersec-tional claims require an intersectional analysis, one which proceeds from the understanding that "[i]t is impossible to isolate any one of the components" of an interacting complex of two or more forms of discrimi-nation "or to separate the experiences that are attributable to one component from the experiences attributable to the others."[6] In a case such as *Rogers*, an intersectional analysis would necessarily examine the issue at the core of the plaintiff's complaint: that race and gender discrimination operated together to affect her as a black woman in a way that was not experienced by either white women or black men.

The logic of the intersectional critique is difficult to refute; it is supported by a substantial body of scholarship in law and across aca-demic disciplines.[7] The legal academic debate was initiated by women of color who challenged the ways in which problems arising at the intersec-tion of race and gender are marginalized in law, feminism, and anti-racist politics. This early scholarship also made clear that the intersec-tional critique extends to other forms of bias, including class and sexual orientation, to any intersectional group, and to any area of law. Subse-quent legal scholarship has developed analyses that take account of multiple systems of subordination, the ways in which they interact,[8] and the bodies of law that support them.[9]

Though issues of intersectional bias began to appear in court deci-sions shortly after the passage of Title VII, courts have been slow to accept the basic tenets of the intersectional critique and to apply a coherent intersectional analysis to cases that call for it. This chapter examines the judicial reception of intersectional analysis in three sorts of cases, all of which include race as one of two or more protected

---

[5] Martha Chamallas, *Structuralist and Cultural Domination Theories Meet Title VII: Some Contemporary Influences*, 92 Mich. L. Rev. 2370 (1994).

[6] Dorothy E. Roberts, *Punishing Drug Addicts Who Have Babies: Women of Color, Equality, and the Right of Privacy*, 104 Harv. L. Rev. 1419, 1424 (1991).

[7] *See* Adrien Katherine Wing, *Critical Race Feminism* (2d ed. 2003); Symposium, *Theorizing the Connections Among Systems of Subordination*, 71 UMKC L. Rev. 227 (2002).

[8] *See* Nancy Levit, *Introduction: Theorizing the Connections Among Systems of Subor-dination*, 71 UMKC L. Rev. 227 (2002).

[9] *See* Emma Coleman Jordan & Angela P. Harris, *Economic Justice: Race, Gender, Identity and Economics* (2005); Dorothy Roberts, *Killing the Black Body: Race, Reproduc-tion, and the Meaning of Liberty* (1997).

categories involved in the dispute. First, based primarily on a sense that, in enacting Title VII, Congress intended to provide protection against intersectional bias, the courts have recognized the right of individuals to bring intersectional claims. However, judges have yet to set forth a coherent theory of intersectional discrimination or a proof model for establishing it. Second, in employment discrimination cases involving the intersection of categories of protection, one covered by Title VII, and the other, such as age or disability, by another employment discrimination statute, courts have equivocated over the availability of intersectional protection absent a clear congressional mandate to permit cross-statutory claims. Third, in jury discrimination cases brought under the Fourteenth Amendment, the Supreme Court has thus far refused to protect against intersectional bias, though some state courts have done so under comparable state constitutional provisions.

Courts first dealt with intersectional claims involving race and gender bias brought by women of color. Accordingly, many, though not all, of the cases examined here involve the intersection of race and gender as it affects this group. For this reason, the story of *Rogers v. American Airlines* is a particularly apt way to explore the implications of intersectional claims. But as the cross-statutory employment discrimination and jury selection cases demonstrate, the intersectional critique has broad application to discrimination directed at any individual or group affected by two or more bases of subordination.

The Rogers *Case*

The Promise of Brown

One cannot fully understand the anti-discrimination approach the *Rogers* court takes without introducing the case in a broader doctrinal context. *Rogers* is part of a long line of cases that failed to realize the promise of *Brown v. Board of Education*.[10] Central to this promise are three interrelated ideas: (1) that law should be employed as a tool both to identify and to eliminate the material manifestations of, and social forces that produced, racial and other forms of inequalities; (2) that racial stigmatization is not beyond the remedial reach of the law; and (3) that the law should be concerned with discriminatory effects and/or conditions.

Within a relatively short time, this vision of law faded and the Supreme Court began increasingly to interpret anti-discrimination law by focusing less and less on the conditions of subordination, instead adopting the perspective of the individuals and entities regulated by the

---

[10] 347 U.S. 483 (1954).

anti-discrimination norm.[11] Today, courts almost exclusively search for fault in a putative perpetrator of discrimination with a view toward eliminating the improper actions of that perpetrator alone. Fault turns on whether or not, in the courts' view, of the myriad possible reasons for an alleged perpetrator's actions, the reasons articulated are race-or gender-dependent. In addition to fault, courts search for causation: even if a wrong is attributable to a particular perpetrator, is the particular act complained of one out of the complex of acts and consequences associated with discrimination which the law will address?

By 1981, when Renee Rodgers[12] challenged American Airlines' grooming policy prohibiting its public-contact employees from wearing all-braided hairstyles, the "perpetrator perspective" was clearly present in the decisions of the federal judiciary. Rodgers began working for American Airlines in 1970 as a ticket agent. Thereafter she held various positions, and for more than a year prior to her suit, she worked as an airport operations agent. Her duties involved extensive passenger contact, including greeting passengers, issuing boarding passes, and checking luggage. In September 1980, shortly after she began wearing her hair in a completely braided hairstyle, Rodgers was told by her immediate supervisor that American's grooming rules for customer-contact ground personnel precluded hairstyles "which customers might regard as extreme or inappropriate for business," including a hairstyle consisting entirely of braids.[13] If she wanted to keep her job, her supervisor advised, she would either have to unbraid her hair or conceal it under a wig.

Since the grooming policy permitted a "partially braided hairstyle" and, according to American, in order to allow her to wear her hair as she chose when off duty, Rodgers was also told that while at work she could conceal her braids by pulling her hair back into a bun and wrapping a hairpiece around it. Rodgers chose the latter option but soon experienced headaches and other discomforts because the hairpiece was cumbersome and unwieldy. Rodgers then appealed her supervisor's decision to Robert Zurlo, the manager of passenger services.

---

[11] For a full explication of the view that the Supreme Court has adopted a "perpetrator perspective" in interpreting anti-discrimination law, see Alan David Freeman, *Legitimizing Racial Discrimination Through Antidiscrimination Law: A Critical Review of Supreme Court Doctrine*, 62 Minn. L. Rev. 1049 (1978).

[12] The case is officially denominated *Rogers v. American Airlines*, but the record reveals that the correct spelling of the plaintiff's surname is "Rodgers." Complaint, Class Action, at 1, Rogers v. Am. Airlines, Inc., 527 F.Supp. 229 (S.D.N.Y.1981) (No. 81 Civ. 4474 (AS)).

[13] Memorandum of Defendants in Support of Motion to Dismiss, at 2, Rogers v. Am. Airlines, Inc., 527 F.Supp. 229 (S.D.N.Y. 1981) (No. 81 Civ. 4474 (AS))

In a letter to Zurlo, Rodgers emphasized the care and serious attention she gave to the decision to braid her hair. Apparently unaware of the absolute prohibition against all-braided hairstyles, she had evaluated a variety of braided styles in anticipation of any objections American might have. She chose a braided style which she thought "would best fulfill my needs as well as American Airlines' policies [:] ... neatness; tastefully business like; and not flambouyant [sic] nor extreme."[14] With the tacit approval of her supervisor, she braided her hair. Only later did she learn that the style did not meet the standards of the newly revised regulations. According to Rodgers' letter, the policy was not communicated to local management or passenger service personnel until September 25, 1980, approximately three weeks after she had braided her hair.[15]

Rodgers' letter also specified the precise nature of her concern about the revised grooming regulations. From her perspective the use of the word "extreme" itself connoted a position of bias against ethnically-oriented social and cultural expressions. An absolute prohibition did not allow for the possibility of a tasteful adaptation of an all-braided hairstyle to conform to the requirement of a conservative, business-like appearance. "My hairstyle is not ornate in design, nor is there any flashy ornamentation of any kind. It is very simply parted to one side and braided straight to shoulder length. In my estimation, it does reflect an overall business appearance *which just so happens to be braided*."[16]

Zurlo declined to approve the hairstyle but offered to assist Rodgers in framing a complaint against the no-braids rule to be considered by higher ups. Rather than appeal to Zurlo's superiors at American, Rodgers instituted suit. Represented by the Social Contributions Fund of the National Association for the Advancement of Colored People, Rodgers sought initially to have her suit certified as a class action, but the court agreed with American that she should be prohibited from doing so. She also argued that, apart from the discrimination inherent in the policy

---

[14] Letter from Renee Rodgers to Robert Zurlo (Sept. 27, 1980), *in* Notice of Motion at Exhibit B, Rogers v. Am. Airlines, Inc., 527 F. Supp. 229 (S.D.N.Y. 1981) (No. 81 Civ. 4474 (AS)).

[15] There is some confusion in the record over when the precise regulation prohibiting all braided hairstyles was adopted. According to Zurlo, who had first objected to Rodgers' hairstyle and initiated the sanction against it, American's grooming regulation prohibiting all-braided hairstyles had been in place for several years, at least since 1975. However, Rodgers' letter of appeal to Zurlo stated that the general regulation prohibiting "extreme" hairstyles had been amended in May 1980 as follows: "The following styles, and others that may be considered 'extreme,' are not appropriate for business-wear:.... Hairstyles consisting completely of braids." *Id. See also* Affidavit of Robert Zurlo, *in* Notice of Motion, *supra* note 14, at 3.

[16] Letter from Renee Rodgers to Robert Zurlo, *supra* note 14.

against all-braided hairstyles, American had singled her out for disparate application of its appearance regulations: white female employees in her job classification were not sanctioned for violations of appearance regulations prohibiting hairstyles such as ponytails and "shag" haircuts. The record contains photographs of several employees that Rodgers took to support her claim.[17]

Anticipating the courts' continued interpretation of employment discrimination law based on the interests of employers, American's lawyers responded to Rodgers' complaint by framing a defense squarely within the perpetrator perspective. They argued that American went out of its way to accommodate Rodgers. Nevertheless, Rodgers herself rejected all attempts at reasonableness and had instead decided to make a federal case out of a simple incident. She had been given the option to retain her hairstyle if she would just cover it up while on duty. Every manager connected with the case submitted an affidavit asserting the absence of racial intent and the desire to work the matter out in Rodgers' favor. One supervisor affirmed that he had arranged to take pictures of Rodgers so that there would be a visual record of her hairstyle to accompany any internal complaint she might file.[18]

From a victim's perspective, however, taking into account the experience of discrimination and the culture that supports it, Rodgers' conduct made a lot of sense. Despite American's emphasis on its attempts at accommodation, the company clearly understood the burden it had imposed on her. The very distinction between partially braided and all-braided hairstyles was racially coded. Why would customers object to one and not the other? Did they, like Rodgers, associate one with black women and the other with women in general, unmarked by race? The policy also was not gender-neutral, as American had asserted, because the provision that permitted partially-braided hairstyles presumably did not permit male customer-contact employees to wear portions of their hair in braids.

American's lawyers placed great emphasis on the fact that its policy was neutral: men and women alike, regardless of race, were prohibited from wearing all-braided hairstyles. In support of a motion to dismiss Rodgers' complaint, American pointed to the seven federal courts of appeal that had ruled that employer dress and grooming codes do not constitute discrimination within the meaning of Title VII, even where they impose different standards on male and female employees.[19] Ameri-

---

[17] Affidavit of James J. Meyerson, at 2–4, Rogers v. Am. Airlines, Inc., 527 F. Supp. 229 (S.D.N.Y. 1981) (No. 81 Civ. 4474 (AS)).

[18] Affidavit of Mary Jane McDermott, at 2, in Notice of Motion, Rogers v. Am. Airlines, Inc., 527 F. Supp. 229 (S.D.N.Y. 1981) (No. 81 Civ. 4474 (AS)).

[19] *See* Memorandum of Defendants in Support of Motion to Dismiss, *supra* note 13, at 12.

can noted that three of the courts had ruled further that grooming and dress requirements do not violate Title VII unless they affect an immutable characteristic or constitutionally protected interest of the employee. American's defense drew on the "sex-plus" theory of discrimination that is often used in claims involving victims of intersectional bias. This theory treats race and other covered traits as additional factors that can bolster a claim of gender discrimination.[20]

But this emphasis on neutrality helped mask the race-sex coding of American's rule. If context means anything, the circumstances under which these judicial decisions were rendered make them, if not irrelevant, certainly not dispositive of Rodgers' claim. In each of the cases cited by American, the court refused to strike down grooming regulations that prohibited *men* from wearing long hair even if no similar rule applied to women in the job classifications in question. None of the cases held that absent a concern for safety or another comparable justification, wearing long hair—a cultural practice associated with women, though not based on any immutable characteristic or constitutional interest— would support an employer's decision to dismiss or fail to hire a woman based on her long hair alone.

American argued for a broad rule that would leave wholly unprotected employees who are differentially affected by grooming and other standards as a result of the exercise of personal preferences. In truth, the interpretation of the law has been less than even-handed. Courts regularly have gone out of their way to be solicitous of the claims of women when they have not been similarly concerned about the claims of men. Grooming codes and other employment practices burdening the personal preferences of some women have been struck down, notwithstanding the fact that the practices did not limit women's access to employment nor implicate an immutable characteristic or constitutionally protected interest. These cases demonstrate that whether employer mandates are stated in neutral or non-neutral terms, judges have not articulated a consistent or coherent theory of discrimination in all cases. Instead, courts often have applied a commonsense judgment that, at least to some extent, respected women's expressive choices, even when those choices did not implicate an immutable characteristic or a fundamental right.[21] In this respect, one might think of the presence of an immutable trait or fundamental interest as creating a floor of protection, but not a ceiling or limit on further relief.

The effect on Rodgers of this disregard for the context in which courts have rendered judgments about grooming and matters of personal

---

[20] *See infra* note 45 and accompanying text.

[21] *See, e.g.,* Allen v. Lovejoy, 553 F.2d 522 (6th Cir. 1977). *See also* Carroll v. Talman Fed. Sav. and Loan Ass'n, 604 F.2d 1028 (7th Cir. 1979).

preference demonstrates that the category "woman" is often racially coded. Although the gender impact of policies frequently has been scrutinized to accord a certain solicitude toward women, the same has not been the case either for men or for claims based on race. Given the fact that the court analyzed the race and gender aspects of her claim independently of each other, Rodgers was treated the way judges have typically treated male plaintiffs claiming sex discrimination. She did not receive the solicitude that has accompanied judgments where women were thought to be affected only as women, regardless of their racial identity.

The racially coded nature of the category "woman" was further evidenced by American's insistence on the racial neutrality of its grooming code. Defense counsel masked Rodgers' race-sex claim by arguing that the policy applied equally to all races and did not affect an immutable racial characteristic or fundamental constitutional interest. The defense further contended that the law did not provide protection for the cultural associations that an individual might bring to racial identity. Most important, although American claimed it had prohibited all-braided hairstyles since at least 1975, American's counsel argued that Rodgers did not become enamored of such styles until she had seen the actress Bo Derek wear an all-braided hairstyle in the movie *10*, released in 1979.[22] In effect, American argued that even if the law did protect the cultural manifestations of racial identity, there was no clear connection between blacks and all-braided hairstyles: Bo Derek became the cultural referent, not African Americans.

Broken Promises

Not surprisingly, the federal district court's opinion tracks the perpetrator perspective that was reflected in the strategy of American's counsel. Focusing on the universal application of American's policy to men and women of all races and the de minimis review accorded by courts to grooming regulations, the court found neither race nor, alternatively, sex discrimination. To the extent that the judge gave any implicit consideration to the intersectional aspects of the plaintiff's claim, he dismissed the notion that American's policy affected Rodgers specifically as a black woman. Relying on the "sex-plus" theory of discrimination, the court concluded that even if the policy imposed different grooming standards for men and women, it would still not constitute sex discrimination unless it infringed on an immutable characteristic or fundamental right protected by the Constitution, such as the right to marry or bear children. Based on this theory, the court rejected the plaintiff's attempt to analogize all-braided hairstyles to Afro

---

[22] See Affidavit of Robert Zurlo in Notice of Motion, *supra* note 14, at 2.

or "natural" styles, which she assumed, perhaps erroneously, would necessarily be protected expressions of racial identity. Even assuming that some, if not all, "natural" hairstyles would be protected, the court distinguished "natural" or Afro from all-braided hairstyles: the former are the product of natural, biological growth, the latter are the result of "artifice."[23]

The court was unequivocal in its rejection of any attempt to include within the definition of discrimination any policy that affects the sociocultural or ethnic aspects of defined categories such as race. The judge compared the plaintiff's desire to "perform her identity" or express cultural aspects of race as a black woman to the attempts by others—whether or not they identified themselves as intersectional groups—to argue for Title VII protection, for example, in the use of languages other than English in the workplace. Relying on a decision of the Fifth Circuit denying a plaintiff the right to speak Spanish on the job except when doing so to serve the employer's needs,[24] the court rejected the plaintiff's association of all-braided hairstyles with her understanding and experience of race.[25]

These separate aspects of *Rogers* are mutually reinforcing. Whether by virtue of its limited response to intersectional claims, its narrow definition of race, or its cultural understanding of the ways of women framed only by the experiences of whites, the court imposed a view of anti-discrimination law that is unduly narrow and out of touch with the realities of the modern workforce. Appeals to neutrality and evenhandedness across categories of protection mask an underlying devotion to color- and gender-blind individualism and to an excessive concern for the interests of those regulated by the anti-discrimination norm. The court's perpetrator perspective reinforces interlocking systems of subordination by reifying the status quo.

Intersectional Claims Prior to Rogers

Employment discrimination claims based on the intersection of two bases for discrimination were not new to courts when *Rogers* was decided. Considering whether to add protection against sex discrimination to Title VII—a suggestion designed initially to defeat the passage of the law—several members of Congress discussed the effect the legislation would have on black women. One thought that the inclusion of sex as a basis for discrimination would add irrelevant issues to a statute

---

[23] *Rogers*, 527 F. Supp. at 323.

[24] Garcia v. Gloor, 618 F.2d 264 (5th Cir. 1980) (holding that a rule prohibiting employees from speaking Spanish on the job unless they are communicating with Spanish-speaking customers does not constitute national origin discrimination).

[25] *Rogers*, 527 F. Supp. at 323.

devoted primarily to the employment problems of blacks; another thought inclusion would assist all women; still another thought that failure to include the word "sex" would provide black women with a remedy that white women did not possess.[26] Ultimately the word "sex" was included, but it cannot be said with any certainty that Congress was influenced ultimately by its concern for the employment problems of women of color as a distinct subgroup protected by the statute.[27]

Against this confusing legislative background, in the early years after the passage of Title VII, courts rejected intersectional claims outright, reflecting in some cases the idea implicit in the congressional debate: that race and gender protections necessarily compete with each other. *Degraffenreid v. General Motors Assembly Division, St. Louis*[28] stands out as an example of this early thinking. In *Degraffenreid*, five black women sued General Motors alleging that the company's seniority system perpetuated the discrimination against black women that existed prior to the passage of Title VII. Before 1964, the company did not hire black women, and all of the black women in its employ at the time the suit was brought had been hired after 1970. In a seniority-based layoff following a recession, all of the black women lost their jobs.

Although the company did not hire black women prior to 1964, it did hire white women. Examining General Motors' seniority system for its effects on women, the court found no sex discrimination because the company retained white women under the layoff plan. As to the black women's race discrimination claim, the court held that they could not maintain a separate claim as blacks who were women. Instead, their claim had to be consolidated with another action alleging race discrimination against both men and women.

Responding to the plaintiffs' argument that such a consolidation would nullify their interactive claim—a claim based on the effects of race *and* sex discrimination, and not one or the other alone—the court concluded:

> The legislative history surrounding Title VII does not indicate that the goal of the statute was to create a new classification of "black women" who would have greater standing than, for example, a black male. The prospect of the creation of new classes of protected minorities, governed only by the mathematical principles of permu-

---

[26] *See* Cathy Scarborough, *Contextualize Black Women's Employment Experiences*, 98 Yale L. J. 1457, 1465–66 (1989).

[27] *See* Jefferies v. Harris County Cmty. Action Ass'n, 615 F.2d 1025 (5th Cir. 1980).

[28] 413 F. Supp. 142 (E.D. Mo. 1976), *aff'd on other grounds*, 558 F.2d 480 (8th Cir. 1977).

tation and combination, clearly raises the prospect of opening the hackneyed Pandora's box.[29]

The *Degraffenreid* court also rejected the claim on the ground that the plaintiffs were not entitled to some "super remedy" as a result of their combining causes of action under Title VII and another anti-discrimination statute.[30] The result of the court's refusal to acknowledge the existence of interactive claims was to provide protection for black women against sex discrimination only to the extent that their experiences coincided with those of white women and against race discrimination only to the extent that their experiences coincided with those of black men. Where experiences of black women were distinct, courts erroneously assumed that to grant protection would provide a benefit to one group that no other individual or group could claim.[31]

In 1980, however, a year prior to *Rogers*, in *Jefferies v. Harris County Community Action Association*, the Fifth Circuit Court of Appeals rejected *Degraffenreid* and held that black women constituted a distinct subgroup entitled to protection under Title VII.[32] Jefferies claimed she had been denied a promotion based on her race *and* her sex. The district court dismissed her complaint, basing its decision on the fact that a black man had received a promotion and the staff also included white women. The Fifth Circuit held, however, that an employer could not defend its discrimination against black women by pointing to progress with respect to the treatment of blacks or women in general. The court reasoned that Congress had included the word "or" in the statute as evidence of its intention to prohibit discrimination on any and all bases listed. Further, Congress's rejection of an amendment that would have added the word "solely" to modify the word "sex" was additional

---

[29] *Degraffenreid*, 413 F. Supp. at 145.

[30] *See id.* at 143 ("The initial issue in this lawsuit is whether or not the plaintiffs are seeking relief from racial discrimination, or sex-based discrimination. The plaintiffs allege that they are suing on behalf of black women, and that therefore this lawsuit attempts to combine two causes of action into a new special sub-category, namely, a combination of racial and sex-based discrimination.... However, they should not be allowed to combine statutory remedies to create a new 'super-remedy' which would give them relief beyond what the drafters of the relevant statutes intended. Thus, this lawsuit must be examined to see if it states a cause of action for race discrimination, sex discrimination, or alternatively either, but not a combination of both.").

[31] Several other cases involving black women's intersectional claims decided prior to *Rogers* were dismissed by the courts. *See* Caldwell, *supra* note 2, at 374–75; *see generally* Kimberlé Crenshaw, *Demarginalizing the Intersection of Race and Sex: A Black Feminist Critique of Antidiscrimination Doctrine, Feminist Theory and Antiracist Politics*, 1989 U. Chi. Legal F. 139 (1989).

[32] *Jefferies*, 615 F.2d at 1034 n.7.

proof of a legislative intent to permit application of the law to discrimination on the basis of multiple characteristics.[33]

Nothing on the face of the *Rogers* decision suggests that the court embraced the reasoning of *Degraffenreid*. Though silent about *Jefferies*, *Rogers'* reasoning does not necessarily foreclose all intersectional claims. However, the court's choice to treat the race and sex claims separately led to a *Degraffenreid* result: because the no-braids rule applied to all employees without regard to race or gender, to countenance the plaintiff's claim that the rule affected her *as a black woman* would provide her with a benefit or privilege—a super remedy—not available to other employees. Thus, *Rogers* missed the central point of *Jefferies*: women of color should not necessarily be denied relief because a challenged employment practice does not harm the men of their racial group or white women.

Intersectional Claims After Rogers

Although *Rogers* constituted a defeat for an individual plaintiff, the failure of courts to recognize intersectional claims has consequences that go well beyond the permissibility of American Airlines' grooming policy. These consequences include the regulation of other employment discrimination practices, and they also limit the ability of courts to remedy the longstanding practice of discriminatory jury selection.

Title VII and the Regulation of Racialized Sexual Harassment

Today, more than twenty-five years after *Jefferies* rejected the reasoning of *Degraffenreid*, the courts' treatment of intersectional claims remains mixed. A few courts clearly recognize that forms of discrimination are often interrelated and therefore adopt an intersectional framework when analyzing such claims. The Ninth Circuit Court of Appeals, for example, did so in 1994 in *Lam v. University of Hawaii*.[34] Lam, a Vietnamese law professor, sued the University of Hawai'i for discrimination based on race, sex, and national origin. Lam argued that the university had discriminated against her on two separate occasions when she had applied for a director's position in the school's legal studies program. She sued for discrimination in hiring in connection with her first attempt to secure employment, and claimed discrimination in hiring, plus retaliation, in connection with the second hiring process. The district court found in favor of the university with respect to both hiring searches.[35]

---

[33] *Id.* at 1032.

[34] 40 F.3d 1551 (9th Cir. 1994).

[35] Lam v. University of Hawaii, No. 89–00378 HMF, 1991 WL 490015 (D. Haw. Aug. 13, 1991).

Although the Ninth Circuit agreed with the district court regarding the second search, it disagreed regarding the first. The Court of Appeals stated that, regarding the second search, the evidence supported the lower court's finding that Lam was less qualified than the other applicants. The failure to hire her was therefore not discriminatory. With respect to the first search, the lower court concluded that no discriminatory motive could have existed because the university had considered both an Asian man and a white woman for the position. The Court of Appeals found that this conclusion was in error: the lower court appeared to be "looking for racism 'alone' and looking for sexism 'alone,' with Asian men and white women as the corresponding model victims."[36] Like the Fifth Circuit in *Jefferies*, the Ninth Circuit held that this method of analysis was misplaced in a case involving two forms of discrimination: "where two bases for discrimination exist, they cannot be neatly reduced to distinct components. Rather than aiding the decisional process, the attempt to bisect a person's identity at the intersection of race and gender often distorts or ignores the particular nature of their experiences."[37]

Despite the progress of some courts, however, intersectional claims continue to baffle most courts and practitioners,[38] and many such claims, like Rodgers', fall through the cracks of single-axis approaches to discrimination. True intersectional analyses are rare, and courts have yet to develop a coherent analytical construct for evaluating the way two forms of discrimination operate together. Some jurists, convinced by the *Rogers* court's emphasis on the universal application of American's no-braids rule, may find it hard to see the intersectional claim there. Others, seeing the claim, may nevertheless agree that grooming and appearance regulations are sufficiently peripheral to employment rights that they should remain within the zone of employer prerogative that was not intended to be invaded by anti-discrimination law. Still others may agree with the court's refusal to include cultural manifestations in the definition of race, either because they were not intended by Congress to be protected by law or because giving courts the power to define race through culture would ultimately be harmful to subordinated groups.[39]

---

[36] *Lam*, 40 F.3d at 1561.

[37] *Id.* at 1562 (citations omitted).

[38] Practitioners often are confused about what type of claim to file—race or sex—and are reluctant to rely on intersectional claims without clearer evidence that courts recognize and understand these claims. Also, prior to 1991, the plaintiff's choice of remedy made a significant difference in federal cases because Title VII did not provide compensatory or punitive damages. This type of relief was available under 42 U.S.C. § 1981, another statute that covered racial, but not gender, discrimination.

[39] *See* Richard Ford, *Racial Culture: A Critique* (2004).

However, courts also have difficulty with intersectional claims involving employment practices, such as workplace harassment, that are central to the purpose of legal regulation and which dominate employment discrimination enforcement today. This difficulty grows out of the courts' failure to understand the true nature of intersectional injury and the evidence needed to establish it. In *Hicks v. Gates Rubber Co.*,[40] for example, the Tenth Circuit Court of Appeals held that evidence of racial hostility could be combined with evidence of sexual hostility to satisfy the requirements of a cause of action for hostile environment sex discrimination, a ruling which, consistent with *Jefferies*, recognizes the possibility of intersectional bias. Hicks, a black female security guard, sued her employer for racial and sexual harassment. Company employees testified that an atmosphere existed in which racial slurs and jokes were tolerated, supervisors referred to black employees as "niggers" and "coons," and Hicks herself was referred to as "Buffalo Butt." One employee grabbed Hicks by her breasts, and when she fell over he got on top of her. The district court rejected Hicks' racial harassment claim due to insufficient evidence of inappropriate racial conduct, and it denied her sexual harassment claim, finding that the elements of quid pro quo harassment did not exist.[41] The Court of Appeals did not reverse the lower court's finding on the racial discrimination claim, but it did remand the case on the sexual discrimination claim on the ground that the district court should also have considered whether Hicks could have satisfied the elements of hostile environment sexual harassment. It instructed the district court to consider evidence of both racial and sexual hostility in evaluating this claim.

But the court of appeals never indicated why the district court should consider race, given that it had agreed that Hicks had not made out a claim for racial discrimination, nor did it indicate what weight to give to the racial incidents. Because the racial incidents did not satisfy an independent racial harassment claim, apparently the court of appeals thought that they at most could shore up the proof of severity in a sexual or intersectional race-sex harassment claim.[42] But without clearer guid-

---

[40] 833 F.2d 1406 (10th Cir. 1987).

[41] The Supreme Court has recognized two distinct causes of action for discriminatory harassment. Meritor Savings Bank FSB v. Vinson, 477 U.S. 57, 67 (1986) (holding that harassment that is not "sufficiently severe or pervasive 'to alter the conditions of [the victim's] employment and create an abusive working environment'" does not result in actionable discrimination under Title VII). Quid pro quo harassment occurs when a tangible benefit, like hiring, promotion, or compensation, is conditioned on the granting of sexual favors. Hostile environment discrimination occurs when a pervasive pattern of hostile or intimidating conduct alters an employee's work environment and the harassing conduct is directed at the employee because of a trait, like race or sex, protected by Title VII. *Id.* at 65.

[42] *See* Judy Winston, *Mirror, Mirror on the Wall: Title VII, Section 1981, and the Intersection of Race and Gender in the Civil Rights Act of 1990*, 79 Cal. L. Rev. 775, 800 (1991).

ance, the district court's finding on remand is not surprising: operating out of an either/or framing of intersectional injury, and seemingly understanding sexual harassment to be essentially about sexual desire rather than general gender or racial hostility or both, the district court found against Hicks on the sexual harassment hostile environment claim.[43] This finding was subsequently upheld by the court of appeals.[44]

Although *Hicks* allows some room to consider the impact of both race and gender, it differs in important ways from the *Jefferies* decision. *Jefferies* treats race and gender discrimination as co-contributors to interactive claims, either of which could be viewed as the main or equal causative agent with the other, but rejects the notion that the two can be readily pulled apart. *Hicks*, however, imposes a "sex-plus" theory of discrimination onto intersectional claims, one which considers the effects of an employer's actions on a subgroup only if the interests affected are based on a category covered by Title VII, like race or gender, and also touch on a fundamental interest like the right to marry or bear children.[45] Race or gender is treated as a "plus" factor in a cause of action that is essentially about either one or the other.

But the application of a "sex-plus" theory to women of color is misplaced. As victims of discrimination, they often are unsure about whether the harassment they suffer is racial or sexual in nature, or a combination of both. In fact, they are protected in their own right under Title VII and not as a subgroup either of women or of their racial or ethnic group. There is nothing "plus" about either the race or gender aspect of their identity. To capture the sense of injury, some scholars refer to the injury many women of color suffer as "race-sex harassment" or "racialized sexual harassment," with the understanding that, from the victim's perspective, attempts at disaggregation make no sense and result in a denial of justice. The difference may not seem critical to employment rights relating to grooming and dress codes, an area of regulation which courts have concluded does not affect employment rights, but the distinction is central to the regulation of race-sex harassment in the workplace.

The fact that few courts understand the racial component of behavior that they consider primarily sexual in nature reflects the way race and gender intersect in the definition and understanding of discrimination and in the politics and legal scholarship concerning it.[46] Sexual

---

[43] *Hicks*, 928 F.2d 966, 968 (10th Cir. 1991).

[44] *Id.* at 973.

[45] This is the same theory that was applied in *Rogers* to uphold American's no-braids policy against the plaintiff's claim of special application to black women. *See Rogers*, 527 F. Supp. at 229.

[46] *See* Judy Winston, *supra* note 43, at 797. *See also* Tanya Katerí Hernández, *A Critical Race Feminism Empirical Research Project: Sexual Harassment & the Internal*

harassment is typically thought of as occurring solely because of gender, unaffected by the race of the victim. When a woman of color experiences interactive workplace harassment, some courts feel compelled to divide the offending conduct into two categories, separating the racial components from those based on gender. In *Jones v. Chicago Research & Trading Group*,[47] the plaintiff sued for both racial and sexual harassment, and the court determined that she could maintain independent claims for each alleged harm. The judge then engaged in the hopeless and unworkable task of dividing up the conduct, characterizing some aspects as racial in nature, others as sexual, and leaving still others unclassified.[48] The court found the following to be evidence of racial harassment: "[F]rom the date she was hired ... she continuously faced inappropriate comments and jokes about race, was called a 'slave' by one of her supervisors, was ordered to 'fetch' drinks for others in the work place, and was referred to as 'Washington' [a reference to the former black mayor of Chicago, Harold Washington] by another supervisor.... [She was also] ignored by her co-workers."[49] As to sexual harassment, the court cited a co-worker's statements "that 'women should be barefoot and pregnant,'" and that the plaintiff and other women "were treated like servants by the men in the department during the weekly card games."[50] The court failed to classify incidents in which co-workers toasted the death of Mayor Harold Washington, and a supervisor allegedly commented, referring to the plaintiff, that "'Washington's alive and hanging on for the life of her job.'"[51] Another supervisor made rude comments about black people, and black women in particular, commenting that "it was 'disgraceful' that black women didn't shave their legs, and made jokes about the 'dress and walk' of black women."[52]

The *Jones* court ultimately granted the defendant's motion for summary judgment on the sexual harassment claim, but denied the defendant's motion on the racial discrimination claim. This either/or framing of interactive harassment works to protect women of color in a case like *Jones*, where the conduct described satisfies the elements of at

---

Complaints Black Box, 39 U.C. Davis L. Rev. 1235, 1240 n.15 (2006); Crenshaw, *supra* note (describing the separate political movements that have grown up around anti-racism and feminism).

[47] No. 88 C 8532, 1991 WL 70889 (N.D. Ill. Apr. 29, 1991).

[48] *Id.*

[49] *Id.* at 5.

[50] *Id.* at 6.

[51] *Id.* at 1.

[52] *Id.* at 2.

least one of the independent causes of action[53]—racial or sexual harassment. In other cases, the separate categorization of elements of the discriminatory conduct may result in a ruling that the plaintiff has failed to satisfy the elements of either a race or a sex discrimination claim.[54] In such cases, the courts should be required to aggregate the elements of racial and sexual harassment to determine whether or not they make out a claim of race-sex workplace harassment. *Hicks* and *Jones* could have followed this approach, consistent with the precedent in *Jefferies*, without introducing needless confusion into the proof of discrimination claims.

Even the latest developments in the management of workplace harassment claims of women of color present a mixed picture. The recent settlement of a major race-sex harassment case brought by the Equal Employment Opportunity Commission ("EEOC") against two major retailers is a significant development, but the underlying theory of the settlement and its significance for future cases is far from clear.[55] At the same time, the impact of the Supreme Court's 1998 rulings in *Burlington v. Ellerth*[56] and *Faragher v. City of Boca Raton*[57] ultimately may be disadvantageous to victims of harassment generally and could have a disparate impact on those affected by multiple forms of discrimination. The Court's rulings permit employers to invoke an employee's failure to utilize internal complaint mechanisms to resolve harassment complaints as a defense against some claims. This defense is not available where the employee's failure to report a claim internally is deemed reasonable. Sociological research demonstrates that people subject to discrimination have reason to be leery of company-controlled dispute resolution mechanisms. Human resources personnel are not inclined to

---

[53] See, for example, *Jew v. Univ. of Iowa*, 749 F. Supp. 946 (S.D. Iowa 1990), where a woman of Chinese descent sued for sexual harassment. The court described instances of racial bias directed toward her, but made clear that Jew did not sue for racial or national origin discrimination, instead relying solely on claims for quid pro quo sexual harassment. Nevertheless, the harassment she suffered grew out of stereotypical notions related to her identity not simply as a woman, but as an Asian woman. *See also* Sumi K. Cho, *Converging Stereotypes in Racialized Sexual Harassment: Where the Model Minority Meets Suzie Wong*, 1 J. Gender Race & Just. 177, 195–199 (1997).

[54] Winston, *supra* note 42, at 800.

[55] *See* Press Release, U.S. Equal Employment Opportunity Comm'n, Nine West, Jones Apparel Group to Pay $600,000 to Settle National Origin and Sex Bias Suit (May 22, 2006), *available at* http://www.eeoc.gov/press/5-22-06b.html (in which Latina employees of Nine West and Jones Apparel Group won a $600,000 settlement after being subjected to sexually harassing conduct including solicitation for sex, unwelcome sexual advances, sexually explicit jokes and comments, groping of women's bodies, and insulting comments about their Hispanic origin).

[56] 524 U.S. 742 (1998).

[57] 524 U.S. 775 (1998).

find their employers in violation of employees' legal rights,[58] and aggrieved individuals often feel re-victimized as a result of these internal processes.[59] Women of color are further affected by the fact that most human resources personnel—the people who would receive their complaints—are white.[60]

Some scholarly research examining lower court cases applying this defense suggests that the complaining party who fails to report is automatically penalized. Consistent with the perpetrator perspective of discrimination, courts are not making any inquiry into whether the failure to report was reasonable.[61] Because of the courts' uncritical approach to internal complaint processes, employers can establish a formal reporting structure to manage discrimination without requiring the structure to be effective in eradicating discrimination. Company managers may be even less likely than courts to grasp the true nature of race-sex workplace harassment. This managerialization intensifies the power of the perpetrator perspective by effectively altering the nature of discrimination claims: civil rights issues disappear and managers transform them into some other kind of problem. In this setting, the likelihood that managers will be sensitive to the nature and extent of intersectional workplace harassment is low. Also, if research demonstrating a racial disparity in reporting is correct, automatically penalizing employees who fail to report harassment internally may harm women of color disproportionately, even though the failure to report may be entirely reasonable from their perspectives.[62]

Intersectional Claims Involving Bias Covered Under Two or More Statutes

Apart from claims arising under a single statute like Title VII, some plaintiffs have attempted to bring intersectional employment discrimination claims where the prohibited bases of discrimination are covered under separate statutes. These cases present the courts with distinct theoretical and practical problems. To date, relatively few cross-statutory intersectional discrimination cases have been adjudicated, and academic research on such claims is sparse.[63] Nevertheless, the probable increase

---

[58] See Hernández, *supra* note 46, at 1257–58.

[59] See Cho, *supra* note 53, at 179 (describing this re-victimization as the "secondary injury").

[60] Hernández, *supra* note 46, at 1255–57.

[61] *Id.* at 1264–68.

[62] *Id.*

[63] See Paulette Caldwell, *Proceedings of the 1999 Annual Meeting, Association of American Law Schools Section on Employment Discrimination Law: Is There a Disconnect Between EEO Law and the Workplace?*, 3 Emp. Rts. & Emp. Pol'y J. 131, 158 (1999).

in the number of such claims in the future has attracted the attention of the EEOC, and the final report of the Glass Ceiling Commission also takes note of cross-statutory intersectional claims.[64]

The courts' response to these claims has been mixed. Several district court decisions follow *Jefferies* and *Lam* and permit suits alleging, for example, interactive gender and age, or age and disability discrimination. One decision allowed a plaintiff to proceed with a claim alleging discrimination on three distinct bases—gender, age, and disability—arising under three separate statutes.[65] However, the majority of cross-statutory claims have been rejected, consistent with the reasoning in *DeGraffenreid*: various federal employment discrimination statutes provide distinct protections for different forms of discrimination reflecting Congress' intention to treat them distinctly. These courts apparently distinguish the Fifth and Ninth Circuits' opinions in *Jefferies* and *Lam*, respectively, as decisions closing a loophole in Title VII alone.

The case for expanding the reach of intersectional theory in this area is not clear. Under Title VII, courts have ruled that intersectional analysis grows out of the intent of Congress to protect individuals from discrimination in employment on any and all bases covered by that statute. For intersectional claims involving discrimination covered by separate statutes, no such congressional intent can be found. When Congress passed employment discrimination legislation in the 1960s, it treated the separate statutes as responding to distinct social and economic problems. Though individuals affected by racial and gender discrimination are protected under Title VII, and those affected by age bias are protected by the Age Discrimination in Employment Act, the groups always overlapped, and the extent of the overlap has grown over time. Older women, racial minorities, and women of color have high participation rates in today's workforce, and the stereotypes that affected them early in life persist and may intensify as they grow older.

But courts may be particularly sensitive to the *DeGraffenreid* court's fear of opening Pandora's box when contemplating the myriad subgroups presenting claims both within and across statutory protections. The use of intersectional theory in some cross-statutory claims also can be disadvantageous to claimants. The same theories of discrimination may apply from one employment discrimination statute to another, but proof requirements often vary. The proliferation of cross-statutory claims

---

[64] Glass Ceiling Commission Report, A Solid Investment: Making Full Use of the Nation's Human Capital 18 (1995).

[65] Soggs v. American Airlines, Inc., 603 N.Y.S.2d 21 (N.Y. App. Div. 1993); *see also* Zell v. United States, 472 F. Supp. 360 (E.D. Pa. 1979) (alleging combined discrimination based on three factors—sex, age, and national origin—under two statutes).

could water down proof requirements to the level permitted in a statute most favorable to the rights of employers.[66]

Intersectional Constitutional Injury and the Problem of Jury Selection

Not all intersectional claims involve the interpretation of federal employment discrimination statutes. Some challenges arise directly under the Constitution and implicate other areas of law in which bias can infect the proceedings. In the realm of constitutional adjudication, where the Supreme Court's interpretation is all that matters, the need to consider intersectional bias in certain areas is clear, but courts have rejected requests to do so. One important example involves discrimination in jury selection, and another involves the trend toward non-unanimous verdicts in criminal cases as a way to marginalize jurors with dissenting views.

At the very least, the overrepresentation of people of color as defendants in the criminal justice system in contrast to their under-representation as judges, prosecutors, and police officers makes non-discrimination in jury selection a major civil and human rights issue.[67] The Supreme Court has outlawed race-based exclusion from jury service, has extended that protection to gender, and has developed procedures designed to eliminate discriminatory barriers to full participation. But the failure to take account of the perspectives offered by an intersectional framework contributes to limitations on the effectiveness of these reforms. Equally important, this failure impoverishes the debate over additional reform proposals whether or not they appear to be directed specifically to the problem of discrimination.

Intersectional Analysis and Peremptory Challenges

Through the exercise of peremptory or automatic challenges,[68] litigants may remove prospective jurors from service in an individual case so long as they do not do so in a racially or sexually discriminatory manner. In *Batson v. Kentucky*,[69] the Supreme Court held that a defen-

---

[66] For example, in 2005, in *Smith v. City of Jackson, Miss.*, 544 U.S. 228 (2005), the Supreme Court resolved a longstanding controversy by permitting the disparate impact theory of discrimination developed in Title VII cases to be applied to age discrimination litigation, albeit under proof requirements substantially more favorable to employers than has been the case in Title VII litigation. These reduced proof requirements in age discrimination cases may ultimately undermine Title VII standards.

[67] Shirley S. Sagawa, Batson v. Kentucky: *Will It Keep Women on the Jury?*, 3 Berkeley Women's L.J. 14, 15 (1987–1988).

[68] Peremptory challenges are exercised "without a reason stated, without inquiry, and without being subject to the court's control." Swain v. Alabama, 380 U.S. 202, 220 (1965).

[69] 476 U.S. 79 (1986).

dant in a criminal case could challenge racial discrimination under the Fourteenth Amendment's Equal Protection Clause by relying solely on the manner of jury selection in the defendant's trial. Under prior law, a defendant was required to show that the prosecutor had followed a pattern of racial discrimination against the defendant's racial group over a series of cases, a showing that was next to impossible for the defendant to make. The resulting practice before *Batson* was, therefore, not surprising: the open, routine, and systematic elimination of African Americans and other people of color from jury service.[70]

In the six years following the 1986 *Batson* decision, courts instituted significant reforms designed primarily to end the all-too-common practice of using all-white juries to try defendants from subordinated racial groups.[71] But *Batson*'s effectiveness in combating racial discrimination was immediately undermined by the Supreme Court's failure for eight years to extend the approach to the deliberate exclusion of prospective jurors on the basis of gender. Prosecutors routinely struck women of color from juries by using gender as a pretext for eliminating them on the basis of race.[72] Ultimately, in *J.E.B. v. Alabama* ex rel. *T.B.*, the Court did extend *Batson* to gender,[73] and most of the cases arguing for this extension involved women of color stricken from service in circumstances indicating that race, not gender, was the reason for their exclusion.[74]

Despite the formal jurisprudence of non-discriminatory jury selection, juries remain largely white and male.[75] In practice, the extension of *Batson* to cover gender discrimination in the use of peremptory challenges has done little to protect women of color from exclusion. The Supreme Court has since retreated substantially from the *Batson* mandate, making it easy to circumvent except in the rarest cases.[76] The

---

[70] Barbara Allen Babcock, *A Place in the Palladium: Women's Rights and Jury Service*, 61 U. Cin. L. Rev. 1139, 1144–45 (1993).

[71] *Id.* at 1141 n.7 (arguing that the *Batson* ruling actually extends to every case, criminal or civil, in every court, federal or state).

[72] Sagawa, *supra* note 67 at 36–37 (noting that women of color had been "largely invisible in the debate about the use of the peremptory challenge" and predicting that such women "will be the first to be excluded from the jury if *Batson* does not cover gender").

[73] 511 U.S. 127 (1994).

[74] *See* Sagawa, *supra* note 67, at 36–37; Babcock, *supra* note 70, at 1163.

[75] *See* Kim Taylor-Thompson, *Empty Votes in Jury Deliberations*, 113 Harv. L. Rev. 1261, 1262 n.4 (2000).

[76] See, for example, *Hernandez v. New York*, 500 U.S. 352 (1991), in which the court used peremptory strikes in the trial of a Latino defendant to rid the jury of all Spanish-speaking jurors. The government argued that the strikes were race-neutral, and the

Court has yet to address the issue of intersectional bias in jury selection, though the issue has arisen before both state and lower federal courts.[77]

Focusing on single-axis discrimination, many scholars argue that peremptory challenges should be eliminated entirely, on the grounds that they cannot be managed effectively.[78] Given this argument, the fact that courts and scholars typically do not consider the problem of intersectional bias seems beside the point. But peremptory challenges have existed in the American legal system for more than two centuries, and nothing in the Supreme Court's recent pronouncements suggests that these challenges are about to be abolished. *Batson* and its progeny make clear that the Constitution protects a defendant's "right to be tried by a jury whose members are selected pursuant to nondiscriminatory criteria,"[79] assures the individual juror's right to participation in democratic processes free from discriminatory stigma regarding the individual's fitness to serve, and protects the right of the public to be free from the racial and gender prejudice that undermines confidence in the justice system.[80]

If race and gender discrimination matter, intersectional bias must also matter. Failure to account for it is inconsistent with the values and goals of *Batson*.[81] Stereotypical ideas about members of race-gender

---

Supreme Court agreed, suggesting that a prosecutor's strikes may survive *Batson* so long as they are not expressly race-based.

[77] *See, e.g.*, United States v. Nichols, 937 F.2d 1257 (7th Cir. 1991), *cert. denied*, 502 U.S. 1080 (1992) (declining to find, pre-*J.E.B.*, that the exclusion of black women from a jury constituted a *Batson* violation); United States v. Dennis, 804 F.2d 1208 (11th Cir. 1986) (declining to recognize black males as a cognizable group for purposes of a *Batson* challenge). *See also* Jean Montoya, *"What's So Magic[al] About Black Women?" Peremptory Challenges at the Intersection of Race and Gender*, 3 Mich. J. Gender & L. 369 (1996) (exploring the need to extend the prohibition against race-based premptory challenges to claims of intersectional discrimination in jury selection).

[78] *See* Batson v. Kentucky, 476 U.S. 79, 107 (1986) (Marshall, J., concurring); Sheri Lynn Johnson, *The Language and Culture (Not to Say Race) of Peremptory Challenges*, 35 Wm. & Mary L. Rev. 21, 29–59 (1993).

[79] *Batson*, 476 U.S. at 85–86.

[80] Sagawa, *supra* note 67, at 37–38.

[81] The normative underpinnings of *Batson* also require that the protection against intentional intersectional bias be extended to men of color and at least one state court has done so. *See* State v. Gonzales, 804 P. 2d 40 (N.M. App. 1991) (holding that two Latino defendants had established a prima facie case of discriminatory exclusion of Latinos in general and Latino males in particular where prosecutor used peremptory challenges to exclude all Latino males from a jury which consisted of four Latina females, one Native American, and seven Anglos—in all, eleven women and one man.) But see *U.S. v. Dennis*, 804 F. 2d 1208 (11th Cir. 1986), decided before the extension of *Batson* to gender discrimination, in which the court declined to hold black males as a distinct group,

intersectional groups necessarily affect the use of peremptory challenges against them. These ideas do not always mimic the historic biases against women or against people of color in general. The failure to account for intersectional bias undermines the goals of non-discrimination in the jury system by depriving the defendant of a representative group of jurors, hindering full participation by all members of the community, and distorting public perceptions of fairness and inclusion.

Non-unanimous Verdicts

The need for an intersectional critique is also evident in the analysis of other equally important jury reforms, especially those threatening to undermine the progress made in ridding jury selection of discriminatory bias. Despite the limitations of *Batson*, the number of women and members of subordinated racial groups serving on juries has increased, and this increased presence has met with considerable controversy. African–American jurors and other jurors of color have been accused of disregarding the evidence presented in particular cases and introducing a color-conscious sense of justice into a system that should be colorblind. Critics argue that these race-based notions lead to wrongful acquittals and high rates of hung juries, especially in jurisdictions in which people of color represent the majority of the local population.

Following the high-profile acquittal in the O.J. Simpson criminal trial, the mainstream press exploded with accounts of a crisis in the American jury system. This crisis purportedly challenged the basic understanding on which the jury system rests: that jurors from different backgrounds—even twelve angry men—can deliberate and agree on a common truth. Commentators questioned whether jurors in particular cases could ever reach agreement across racial lines. These accounts elevated the norm of colorblindness "as the ideal for jurors and the salient feature of the justice system in the days before black jurors [and other jurors of color] injected their race-based perspective."[82] White jurors were assumed to be colorblind. Unlike commentators who argued that jurors divide increasingly along racial lines, some critics of the jury system singled out African–American women for special scrutiny.[83] In a

---

historically singled out for different treatment under the laws based on the intersection of race and gender. In *Gonzales*, avoiding an intersection theory, the court found that Latino males were protected against race <u>and</u> sex discrimination and that targeting them for exclusion amounted to discrimination on either or both grounds. *See also* Montoya, *supra* note 77, at 392–411 (describing approaches available to courts to extend protection against intersectional bias to various groups).

[82] Elissa Krauss & Martha Schulman, *The Myth of Black Juror Nullification: Racism Dressed up in Jurisprudential Clothing*, 7 Cornell J. L. & Pub. Pol'y 57, 65 (1997).

[83] See United States v. Nichols, 937 F.2d 1257, 1263 (1991), in which the defendant, whose only witness was a black woman, complained that the prosecutor excluded black

sensationalized account entitled "One Angry Woman," published in *The New Yorker* magazine, law professor Jeffrey Rosen argued that the nature of the crisis in the jury system had been mischaracterized.[84] Rather than a problem arising from racially polarized reactions to high-profile cases, the problem could be traced to a significant rise in the number of hung juries since the mid–1970s. Further, unlike the reactions to the Simpson trial, which divided largely along racial lines, hung juries were not merely an artifact of racial differences. According to Rosen, hung juries instead resulted from the presence on the jury of an irrational holdout—typically one angry black woman—who not only frustrated the will of the majority, but also thwarted the judgment of other blacks on the jury.

Relying on conversations with judges and prosecutors, as well as the words of some of the holdout jurors themselves (either told to him firsthand or reported to him by other jurors), Rosen argued that "black women contrarians"[85] have many reasons for hanging juries:

> Some of these women have had especially searing experiences with the police; some are eccentric or disengaged; some are overcome by religious beliefs; some are incapable of understanding the evidence; some refuse to send another black man to jail. Most say that they have reasonable doubts about the defendant's guilt, even when their doubts appear, to many, to be unreasonable.[86]

Rosen took great pains to assure the reader that the problem he described was not limited to poor black women with low educational attainment. He described in considerable detail a "run-of-the-mill" drug possession case in which the lone holdout was a forty-year old black woman who grew up in a stable, two-parent, working-class family, and who graduated from Mount Holyoke College and Yale Law School. The jury split, six for conviction and six for acquittal, after the first day of deliberations. By the second day, three holdouts remained. Two of them, both black men, gave in quickly, one of them indicating that he was not educated or articulate and could not hold his own in arguments with other jurors who favored conviction.[87] For Rosen, who dismissed as

women from the jury, and there was speculation that the juror who had hung the jury in the original trial had been a black woman.

[84] Jeffrey Rosen, *One Angry Woman: Why Are Hung Juries on the Rise?*, New Yorker 54 (Feb. 24 & Mar. 3, 1997).

[85] *Id.* at 55.

[86] *Id.* at 55.

[87] Class bias also played a significant role in Rosen's account of this case. When the lone black female juror held to her position in favor of acquittal, other black jurors attacked her on the basis of her class position: "You're just one of those highfalutin'

insignificant a discrepancy in the testimony of the two arresting officers, this black woman just could not get beyond her suspicion of police.[88]

Rosen not only claimed that the typical irrational holdout was a black female juror, he purportedly backed up this claim with case after case in which a lone black female juror frustrated the will of the majority. Prompted by sharp criticism of the one-sided, prosecution-oriented, anecdotal quality of his account, Rosen published a second article in which he admitted that prosecutors' impressions of the rise in hung juries since the 1970s were not borne out by statistical analysis. He also conceded his failure to include in "One Angry Woman" accounts of trials in which the holdout was a white woman or a black man.[89] This second article was published in a law review, with far more limited circulation than *The New Yorker*, and citations to the *New Yorker* piece far exceed citations to the subsequent publication, even in other law reviews.[90]

In describing the problem of irrational holdouts, Rosen did not aim to return jury selection procedures to the pre-*Batson* days of unfettered use of peremptory challenges. Instead, he argued that though such jurors were the exception rather than the rule, they were increasing in number and posed a growing dilemma for prosecutors whose most pressing problem was to eliminate unyielding jurors who would not listen to reason. These individuals were difficult to identify because they concealed their pro-defense biases during voir dire. The problem was made more difficult by *Batson* and its progeny, which, by limiting race-and gender-based peremptory challenges, lessened the discretion of prosecutors and judges to eliminate citizens who were "irrational, eccentric, or simply angry."[91] Because of this reduced discretion, Rosen continued, jurors were free to refuse to listen to, or be persuaded by, the evidence

---

liberals. We have to live with this crime, while you probably live in the suburbs. I hope he turns up at the door and terrorizes you, and robs you." The holdout juror also objected when several other black jurors referred to the defendant, who was on probation for stealing, as "low-life scum." *See id.* at 62.

[88] In addition to her concern that the police might have lied, the holdout juror had doubts about the failure of the police to dust the drugs found at the crime scene for fingerprints. There was a discrepancy in the officers' testimony concerning whether the drugs were on the defendant's person or had been thrown to the ground. The juror worried that the police had not tested for fingerprints because they planted the drugs. *See id.* at 62–63.

[89] Jeffrey Rosen, *After "One Angry Woman,"* 1998 U. Chi. Legal F. 179 (1998).

[90] A search conducted on February 15, 2007 in the Journals and Law Reviews database of Westlaw indicates that Professor Rosen's *New Yorker* article has been cited 23 times in law reviews. By contrast, his follow-up article in the *University of Chicago Legal Forum* has been cited only eight times in law reviews.

[91] Rosen, *supra* note 84, at 56.

before them. He advocated, therefore, the adoption of non-unanimous decision-making in criminal trials—cases in which ten, or even nine, members of a jury of twelve would decide the verdict.

Professor Rosen tied his recommendation for non-unanimous verdicts and his characterization of the behavior of female African–American jurors directly to the debate over jury nullification. Since prosecutors cannot tell one angry black woman from another—and, because of *Batson*, cannot be assured that they have eliminated all of them—non-unanimous verdicts were the obvious means of nullifying the nullifiers. Professor Kim Taylor–Thompson has argued that the trend toward non-unanimous verdicts in criminal cases restrains the American jury's deliberative character—its "distinctive and defining feature"—and threatens to undermine the limited progress we have made in recent decades to render jury selection less discriminatory.[92] Arguing that the debate over race-and gender-based peremptory challenges may not reflect the full extent of the problem of discriminatory exclusion, Taylor–Thompson concludes that the move to non-unanimous verdicts "threatens quietly—but effectively—to deprive individuals with diverse views who actually serve on juries from exercising any real voting power."[93]

Majority rule has the specter of fairness and gives the appearance of consonance with core democratic values, but recent jury research indicates that eliminating the requirement of unanimity reduces or eliminates deliberation. Empirical research comparing juries operating under both unanimous and majority decision rules indicates that a shift to majority rule appears to change both the quality of the jury's deliberations and the reliability of the jury's judgment. Once juries reach the majority required for a verdict, deliberation ceases immediately. The flow of information is constricted, and jurors lack any incentive to hear, respect, or vigorously challenge each other's views. Jurors operating under majority rule also express less confidence in the rightness of their decisions.[94]

Taylor–Thompson argues that majority rule presents significant constitutional and policy problems if it results in diminished participation of the very groups that we have worked so long to include. Empirical evidence on the effect of race on jury decision-making reveals that conscious and unconscious racial biases affect jury deliberations and outcomes in a number of ways. Racial stereotypes influence recall, memory, the complex decision-making process necessary to determine guilt or innocence, and perceptions of the accused's honesty and guilt.

---

[92] Taylor–Thompson, *supra* note 75, at 1316.

[93] *Id.* at 1263.

[94] *Id.* at 1272–74.

Stereotypes also affect the treatment accorded by juries to victims of color.[95] Taylor–Thompson further argues that to the extent that people of color serve on a jury, they may need to bring attention to the evidence that they alone have recalled and to push their fellow jurors to consider information that challenges stereotypic assumptions. Under majority rule, however, their power to do so is seriously curtailed.[96] For the most part, juries remain predominantly white and male. When people of color do serve, they do so most often as members of a numerical racial minority. Without full participation by jurors of color, "the criminal justice system structurally reinforces and perpetuates the racial dominance of white decisionmakers."[97]

Jury research, supported by the teachings of feminist theory, suggests that men and women bring different perspectives and decision-making behaviors to jury deliberations.[98] The behavior of male jurors tends to differ from that of female jurors in ways that mirror traditional societal roles. Jury research demonstrates that women tend to speak less often than men and to take longer to participate in the discussion. When they do speak, they are interrupted and ignored by men, which in turn leads them to speak less over time.[99] Research also indicates that a juror's own recall and confidence in the recollection of witnesses differs according to gender. Taylor–Thompson concludes that because of these gender-based perceptual and behavioral differences, majority rule generally operates as a structural impediment to the participation of women. Their contributions can be reduced to empty gestures that give the appearance of participation without its real effects. [100]

Just as majority rule can hinder the participation of non-whites and women on juries, the rule also can create unique impediments to women of color. As intersectionality critiques indicate, women of color often have experiences and insights that others of either their racial or gender group do not share. As a result, these women may be able to broaden the jury's context for evaluating evidence and rendering judgment. Because women of color will typically be a minority of the jurors selected for any panel, a majority rule necessarily can silence them by marginalizing their perspectives and rendering them irrelevant to the outcome. In addition, as Professor Rosen's works make clear, women of color are affected by a unique set of stereotypes bearing directly on their fitness to

---

[95] *Id.* at 1294–95.

[96] *Id.* at 1295.

[97] *Id.*

[98] *Id.* at 1297.

[99] *Id.* at 1299–1300.

[100] *Id.* at 1298.

serve as jurors. These stereotypes are distinct from those that apply based on either race or gender standing alone.

Professor Taylor–Thompson argues that because juries must deliver the judgment of the community, they should include the perspectives of all members of the community who emerge from the voir dire process. Considering intersectional bias is not a matter of assessing the merits of one group in comparison with another. On the contrary, the values of inclusion underlying *Batson* suggest that the diversity of values and beliefs that jurors bring from their individual and group experiences must be encouraged if we are to achieve impartiality in, and respect for, a jury's decision-making process. Women of color serving on juries under unanimous decision rules may force other jurors to engage in a dialogue that might not otherwise occur. Taylor–Thompson concludes that without such a rule, we can expect the experience outside of the jury room to recur within it: "the views of women of color will be ignored or discounted."[101]

Conclusion

Through the adoption of a perpetrator perspective of discrimination, one which views discrimination from the perspective of those regulated by anti-discrimination norms rather than that of victims of discrimination, courts have legitimized and perpetuated conditions of racial subordination. This perspective is reflected in narrow pronouncements of what counts as a violation and an equally narrow view of what should be required as remedy. This is not to say that anti-discrimination law should be interpreted exclusively from the perspective of victims of discrimination, nor is it to suggest that all of the consequences of an historic and continuing discriminatory impulse are remediable through law. Yet the near exclusive adoption of a perpetrator perspective amounts to a betrayal of the early promise of anti-discrimination law. Courts have substituted a formal anti-discrimination principle for the pre-*Brown* legally-sanctioned system of discrimination; this formalism is devoid of the aspirations for full and equal participation that flowed from *Brown*. A formalistic approach separates the fact of discrimination from the history, culture, and conditions of the society that produced and continues to produce inequality. As a consequence, discrimination is situated in what appears to be the isolated, increasingly rare wrongful acts of one party against another. Rules like the one in *Rogers*, which rely on proxies for race rather than overt racial classifications and blatant stereotyping, go largely unexamined by law.

The issues at the core of *Rogers*, and those exemplified by the other employment discrimination and jury selection cases examined here, grow

---

[101] *Id.* at 1308.

out of a mismatch between the aspirations of law, flowing from a victim's perspective, and the on-the-ground application of legal rules. Intersectional analysis is but one tool among many which reveals the failure of anti-discrimination law to draw appropriate distinctions between those consequences of discrimination that can be remedied by law and those that cannot. Law sets a low level of protection—one that often operates as hardly any protection at all. The result is that people are protected against an old, pervasive, overt, and increasingly rare regime of discrimination, while a new and often equally effective regime continues to operate beyond legal scrutiny. Plaintiffs like Renee Rodgers find their everyday stories of discrimination go unheeded because they do not fit into the rigid and unresponsive categories of an anti-discrimination law that identifies with the status quo, rather than with social justice.

Biographies of *Race & Law Stories* Contributors

Catherine Corpus Betts graduated in 2006 from the William S. Richardson School of Law, University of Hawai'i, and serves as a judicial law clerk for the Circuit Court, State of Hawai'i.

Paulette Caldwell is Professor of Law at New York University School of Law. She received both her B.S. and J.D. from Howard University. After graduating from law school, she worked for Patterson, Belknap, Webb & Tyler before transferring to The Ford Foundation, where she counseled the organization on its civil and human rights programs. Since joining the New York University School of Law faculty in 1979, Professor Caldwell has instructed courses in education law, employment discrimination law, real estate transactions, and race and legal scholarship. Professor Caldwell's research and scholarly works are focused on Critical Race Theory, employment discrimination law, education law and policy, and the intersection of race and gender. She has published articles in the Michigan Journal of Race and Law, the Duke Law Journal, and the Journal of Modern Critical Theory.

Devon W. Carbado is Academic Associate Dean and Professor of Law at University of California, Los Angeles, School of Law. Professor Carbado writes in the areas of critical race theory, employment discrimination, criminal procedure, constitutional law, and identity. He is currently studying African–American responses to the internment of Japanese Americans and working on a book on employment discrimination tentatively titled "Acting White." He was elected Professor of the Year by the UCLA School of Law Classes of 2000 and 2006, is the 2003 recipient of the Rutter Award for Excellence in Teaching, and was recently awarded the University Distinguished Teaching Award, The Eby Award for the Art of Teaching. He is a former Vice Dean of the Law School and a faculty associate of the Ralph J. Bunche Center for African American Studies. He wishes to acknowledge the valuable research assistance he received from Jacob Clark and Emily Wood. A longer

version of his chapter will appear as *Yellow by Law*, ___ Cal.L.Rev. ___
(forthcoming 2008).

Carole E. Goldberg is Distinguished Professor of Law at University of California, Los Angeles School of Law, where she directs the Joint
Degree Program in Law and American Indian Studies. She graduated
from Smith College and Stanford Law School. Prior to teaching at UCLA
School of Law, Professor Goldberg was a law clerk for U.S. District
Court Judge Robert F. Peckham for the Northern District of California.
She presently teaches courses in tribal legal systems, federal Indian law,
civil procedure, and conducts the tribal legal development clinic. She has
published work on federal Indian law and tribal law, including both the
1982 and 2005 editions of *Cohen's Handbook of Federal Indian Law*, and
co-authored the casebook, *American Indian Law: Native Nations and the
Federal System* (LexisNexis, 5th ed. 2007). Professor Goldberg is also the
Faculty Chair of UCLA School of Law's Native Nations Law and Policy
Center and a Justice of the Court of Appeals of the Hualapai Tribe.

Ian Haney López is Professor of Law at the University of California, Berkeley, where he teaches in the areas of race and constitutional
law. He received his B.A. and M.A. from Washington University, his
M.P.A. from Princeton University, and his J.D. from Harvard Law
School. He has published ground breaking books on the social, and
specifically legal, construction of race: *Racism on Trial: The Chicano
Fight for Justice* (Harvard/Belknap, 2003) documents how police violence
not only radicalized but racialized Mexican–American activists during
the late 1960s, helping to spark the development of a non-white Chicano
identity; *White by Law: The Legal Construction of Race* (NYU Press,
revised ed. 2006) details judicial efforts to interpret the "white person"
prerequisite in place in U.S. naturalization law until 1952. Haney López
also edited an anthology entitled *Race, Law and Society* (Ashgate, 2006).
His numerous articles have appeared, among other places, in the Stanford Law Review, Yale Law Journal, California Law Review, and Pennsylvania Law Review; he has published opinion pieces in the New York
Times and the Los Angeles Times; and his work has been featured in
over two dozen anthologies and encyclopedias. His current research
critiques the emergence and operation of colorblindness in U.S. constitutional law as a new racial ideology that legitimates and preserves the
racial status quo.

Kevin R. Johnson is the Mabie–Apallas Professor of Public Interest Law and Chicana/o Studies and Associate Dean of Academic Affairs
at University of California, Davis, School of Law. He graduated from
University of California, Berkeley, and Harvard Law School. Prior to
entering the academic profession, he clerked for Judge Stephen Reinhardt of the U.S. Court of Appeals for the Ninth Circuit and later
worked for Heller Ehrman White & McAuliffe. At UC Davis School of
Law, Professor Johnson has taught courses in immigration law, refugee
law, Critical Race Theory, public interest law, and Latinos and Latinas

and the Law. He has published extensively in national and international journals, on issues of civil rights, racial identity, and immigration law and policy. In 2000, Professor Johnson was nominated for the Robert F. Kennedy Book Award for his book, *How Did You Get to Be Mexican? A White/Brown Man's Search for Identity* (Temple University Press, 1999). His latest book is *Opening the Floodgates: Why America Needs to Rethink Its Borders and Immigration Laws* (NYU Press, 2007). The recipient of many awards and honors, including being named the 2007 Law Professor of the Year by the Hispanic National Bar Association, Professor Johnson is president of the board of directors of Legal Services of Northern California and serves on the board of the Mexican American Legal Defense and Educational Fund. He is a member of the American Law Institute.

Jerry Kang is Professor of Law at University of California, Los Angeles, School of Law, where he teaches civil procedure, Asian American Jurisprudence, and Communications Law & Policy. A graduate of both Harvard College (physics) and the Harvard Law School, he writes on race, communications, and their intersection. On race, he has focused on the Asian American community and on the legal implications of recent discoveries in social cognition. He is a co-author of *Race, Rights, and Reparation: The Law and the Japanese American Internment* (Aspen Law & Business, 2001). On communications, he has published interdisciplinary articles on information privacy, pervasive computing, and mass media policy. He is also the author of *Communications Law & Policy* (Foundation Press, 2d ed. 2005). At the nexus of these fields, he has published two groundbreaking articles in the Harvard Law Review about how race is constructed in cyberspace (*Cyber-Race*, 113 Harv. L. Rev. 1130 (2000)) and how FCC media policy inadvertently exacerbates implicit bias (*Trojan Horses of Race*, 118 Harv. L. Rev. 1489 (2005)). At UCLA, he was elected Professor of the Year in 1998, and received the Rutter Award for Excellence in Teaching in 2007. Much of this chapter draws heavily from two prior articles, *Denying Prejudice: Internment, Redress, and Denial*, 51 UCLA L. Rev. 933 (2004), and *Watching the Watchers: Enemy Combatants in the Internment's Shadow*, 68 Law & Contemp. Probs. 255 (2005). Research assistance was provided by Tami Kameda and Nathaniel Ross. This chapter was supported in part by the UCLA Asian American Studies Center and the UCLA School of Law.

Erika Lee is Associate Professor in the Department of History and the Asian American Studies Program at University of Minnesota. She graduated from Tufts University and the University of California, Berkeley. Professor Lee specializes in migration history, immigration policy, Asian Americans, transnationalism, and comparative ethnic studies. Her publications include: *At America's Gates: Chinese Immigration and American Exclusion, 1882–1943* (University of North Carolina Press,

2003), which won the Theodore Saloutos Prize in Immigration Studies and the History Book Award from the Association of Asian American Studies, and *Enforcing the Borders: Chinese Exclusion Along the U.S. Borders with Canada and Mexico, 1882–1924*, 89 Journal of Am. History 54 (2002).

R. A. Lenhardt is Associate Professor of Law at Fordham Law School. She graduated from Brown University, the Harvard Law School, and the Georgetown University Law Center. Before joining the Fordham faculty, she clerked for Judge Hugh H. Bownes of the U.S. Court of Appeals for the First Circuit and for Justice Stephen G. Breyer of the U.S. Supreme Court. She also served as a Skadden Fellow at the Lawyer's Committee for Civil Rights, an attorney advisor with the U.S. Department of Justice's Office of Legal Counsel, and a Counsel at Wilmer, Cutler, and Pickering, where she helped to litigate the Michigan affirmative action cases. Her scholarship focuses on issues of race and civil rights, constitutional law, and family law and civil procedure. Her work has appeared in various books and law reviews, including the *New York University Law Review*, the *California Law Review*, and the *UCLA Law Review*. She is grateful for the generosity of Fay Botham and Dara Orenstein and the research assistance provided by Larry Abraham, Juan Fernandez, Gowri Krishna, and Amy Licht.

Pedro A. Malavet is Professor of Law at University of Florida, Fredric G. Levin College of Law. He received his B.B.A. from Emory University, and his J.D. and L.L.M. from Georgetown University Law Center. Professor Malavet teaches and writes in the fields of civil procedure, comparative law, Critical Race Theory, evidence, and U.S. territorial possessions. His publications include *America's Colony: The Political and Cultural Conflict between the United States and Puerto Rico* (NYU Press, 2004); *Introduction: LatCritical Encounters With Culture, in North–South Framework*, 55 Fla. L. Rev. 1 (2003); and *Literature and Arts as Antisubordination Praxis, LatCrit Theory and Cultural Production: The Confessions of an Accidental Crit,* 33 U.C. Davis L. Rev. 1293 (2000).

Rachel F. Moran is the Robert D. and Leslie–Kay Raven Professor of Law at University of California, Berkeley, School of Law. She graduated from Stanford University and Yale Law School. After graduating from law school, Professor Moran clerked for Chief Judge Wilfred Feinberg of the U.S. Court of Appeals for the Second Circuit. At Berkeley, Professor Moran has taught courses on torts, education & the law, and a seminar entitled Cities, Stratification, & Separation. She has written extensively on questions of education and inequality. Among her publications are several on affirmative action, including *Of Doubt and Diversity: The Future of Affirmative Action in Higher Education,* 67 Ohio St. U. L. Rev. 201 (2006); *Diversity and Its Discontents: The End of Affirmative Action* *at Boalt Hall*, 88 Cal. L. Rev. 2241 (2000); and *Unrepresented*, 55 Representations 139 (1996). She is also the author of *Interracial Intimacy: The Regulation of Race and Romance*, published by the University of Chicago Press in 2001, and is co-author (with Mark Yudof, David Kirp, and Betsy Levin) of the fourth edition of *Educational Policy and the Law* (2002). In 2003, Professor Moran became director of UC Berkeley's Institute for the Study of Social Change. She is grateful for the research assistance she received from Katina Boosalis, Carol Chacon, Ming Su Chen, Sonia D. Cook, and Jenny Lam.

Reginald Oh is Professor of Law at Cleveland–Marshall College of Law. He received his B.A. from Oberlin College, his J.D. from Boston College Law School, and his L.L.M. from Georgetown University Law Center. Following law school, he clerked for the Honorable John Dooley of the Vermont Supreme Court. Professor Oh teaches courses in civil procedure, education law, and constitutional law. He writes primarily in the area of equal protection law and theory, and focuses on issues of residential and school segregation, prohibitions on interracial marriages, and affirmative action. Professor Oh has published widely in law reviews such as the Wisconsin Law Review, U.C. Davis Law Review, and American University Law Review. He wishes to acknowledge that his chapter reflects earlier work that appeared in *Re–Mapping Equal Protection Jurisprudence: A Legal Geography of Race and Affirmative Action*, 53 Am. U.L. Rev. 1305 (2004).

Michael A. Olivas is the William B. Bates Distinguished Chair in Law at the University of Houston Law Center and Director of the Institute for Higher Education Law and Governance at UH. In 1989–90, he was a Visiting Professor of Law at the University of Wisconsin, and Special Counsel to then-Chancellor Donna Shalala. In 1997, he held the Mason Ladd Distinguished Visiting Chair at the University of Iowa College of Law. He holds a B.A. (Magna Cum Laude) from the Pontifical College Josephinum, an M.A. and Ph.D. from the Ohio State University, and a J.D. from Georgetown University Law Center. He is the author or co-author of twelve books, including *The Dilemma of Access* (Howard University Press, 1979), *Latino College Students* (Teachers College Press, 1986), *Prepaid College Tuition Programs* (College Board, 1993) and *The Law and Higher Education* (3rd ed., Carolina Academic Press, 2006). His most recent books are *"Colored Men" and "Hombres Aqui,"* published by Arte Publico Press in 2006, and *Education Law Stories* (co-edited with Ronna Greff Schneider), published by Foundation Press in 2007. In 2010, Harvard University Press will publish his 13th book, on the subject of undocumented immigrant children. He has been elected to membership in the American Law Institute and the National Academy of Education, the only person to have been selected to both honor academies. He served as General Counsel to the American Association of

University Professors (AAUP) from 1994–98. He has chaired the AALS
Section on Education Law three times, and has twice chaired the Section
on Immigration Law. In 1993, he was chosen as Division J's Distinguished Scholar by the American Educational Research Association, and
in 1994, he was awarded the Research Achievement Award by the
Association for the Study of Higher Education (ASHE). ASHE also gave
him its 2000 Special Merit Award. He has been designated as a NACUA
Fellow by the National Association of College and University Attorneys.

Angela Onwuachi–Willig is Professor of Law and the Charles M.
and Marion J. Kierscht Scholar at University of Iowa College of Law.
She graduated from Grinnell College and the University of Michigan
Law School. Prior to her entering academia, she clerked for both U.S.
District Court Judge Solomon Oliver, Jr. of the Northern District of
Ohio, and Judge Karen Nelson Moore of the U.S. Court of Appeals for
the Sixth Circuit. Professor Onwuachi–Willig teaches and researches in
the areas of employment discrimination, evidence, Critical Race Theory,
family law, and feminist legal theory. Her articles have been published in
the California Law Review, Iowa Law Review, Michigan Law Review,
Minnesota Law Review, and Wisconsin Law Review. Professor Onwuachi–Willig also received the Derrick A. Bell Award from the Minority
Group Section of the Association of American Law Schools in 2006.

Thomas Ross is Professor of Law at University of Pittsburgh
School of Law. He received both his B.A. and J.D. from the University of
Virginia. Following law school, Professor Ross worked as an associate for
Cravath, Swaine & Moore and, later, for Hogan & Hartson. He is the
author of *Just Stories: How the Law Embodies Racism and Bias* (Beacon
Press, 1996) as well as numerous articles in various journals including
the Columbia Law Review, Georgetown Law Journal, and Texas Law
Review. He wishes to acknowledge that his chapter makes extensive use
of work that first appeared in *The Richmond Narratives*, 68 Tex. L.Rev.
381 (1989). Professor Ross also writes and teaches on the subject of legal
ethics. In addition to his academic work, he was instrumental in the
founding of Sarah's Place, a foundation devoted to people suffering from
neurological/psychological deficits that defy conventional categories.

Rennard Strickland is Professor Emeritus of Law at University of
Oregon School of Law. He received his B.A. from Northeastern State
College, his M.A. from University of Arkansas, and his J.D. and S.J.D.
from University of Virginia. Professor Strickland is a legal historian of
Osage and Cherokee heritage and has written extensively on the topic of
Indian law. He is the author of *Tonto's Revenge: Reflections on American
Indian Culture and Policy* (University of New Mexico Press, 1997) and
was the editor for the revisions to the *Handbook of Federal Indian Law*
(Michie–Bobbs–Merrill, 3d. ed. 1982). Professor Strickland was the dean
of University of Oregon School of Law from 1997 to 2002 and was the

original director of the Center for the Study of American Indian Law and Policy at the University of Oklahoma. He was awarded the American Bar Associate's Spirit of Excellence Award and the Society of American Law Teachers Award.

Ronald S. Sullivan Jr. is a Clinical Professor of Law at Harvard Law School and the Director of the Harvard Criminal Justice Institute. Professor Sullivan teaches and writes in the areas of criminal law, criminal procedure, legal ethics, and race theory. He also is a founding fellow of the Jamestown Project, a think tank affiliated with the Harvard Law School. He graduated from Morehouse College and the Harvard Law School, where he served as president of the Black Law Students Association. Professor Sullivan served as a staff attorney, General Counsel, and then Director of the Public Defender Service for the District of Columbia. He wishes to thank Drew Days, Eddie Glaude, Mark Jefferson, Charles Ogletree, Paul Taylor, and the participants in the Yale Law School Faculty Workshop for comments on drafts of his chapter. Professor Sullivan appreciates the research assistance provided by Andrea Armstrong, Bessie Dewar, Mary Hunter, and Jason Pielemeier.

Daniel Tokaji is Associate Professor of Law at The Ohio State University, Michael E. Moritz College of Law. He graduated from Harvard College and Yale Law School. Prior to his academic career, Professor Tokaji clerked for Judge Stephen Reinhardt of the U.S. Court of Appeals for the Ninth Circuit and was a staff attorney for the ACLU Foundation of Southern California. He specializes in election law, civil rights, federal courts, and civil procedure. His publications include *Early Returns on Election Reform: Discretion, Disenfranchisement, and the Help America Vote Act*, 73 Geo. Wash. L. Rev. 1206 (2005) and *First Amendment Equal Protection: On Discretion, Inequality, and Participation*, 101 Michigan L. Rev. 2409 (2003). In addition to his academic work, Professor Tokaji serves on the boards of the ACLU of Ohio, the Asian Pacific American Bar Association of Central Ohio, and the Conference of Asian Pacific American Law Faculty. He thanks Morgan Kousser, Rick Pildes, Mike Pitts, as well as participants in the Moritz College of Law's Faculty Workshop, the Ohio Legal Scholarship Workshop, and the Race Law Stories Conference at Fordham Law School, for their thoughtful comments on earlier drafts of his chapter. Caitlin Dowling and Mitch Witkov provided outstanding research assistance.

Eric K. Yamamoto is Professor of Law at University of Hawai'i, William S. Richardson School of Law. He graduated from University of Hawai'i and University of California, Berkeley School of Law. Before becoming a Professor of Law, Professor Yamamoto was recognized for his civil rights and racial justice work, most notably serving as coram nobis co-counsel in the reopening of Korematsu v. U.S. in 1982. At the William S. Richardson School of Law, Professor Yamamoto teaches courses in advance procedure/complex litigation, race, reparations, civil procedure, public law litigation, and culture and the law. He has published a vast number of articles, including the books, *Interracial Justice: Conflict and Reconciliation in Post–Civil Rights America* (NYU Press, 1999), and *Race, Rights, and Reparation: Law and the Japanese American Internment* (Aspen Law & Business, 2001) (with Margaret Chon, Carol L. Izumi, Jerry King, and Frank Wu). In 2005, Professor Yamamoto received the Regents Medal for Teaching Excellence from the University of Hawai'i and the Society of American Law Teachers' Award for Teaching Excellence.

†